Marketing Research

A South African Approach

Editors

J H Martins
M Loubser
H de J van Wyk

Unisa Press, Pretoria

© 1996 University of South Africa

First edition, first impression

ISBN 0 86981 941 0

Typeset by Pretoria Setters, Pretoria
Printed by CTP Book Printers, Parow
Published by Unisa Press,
PO Box 392, 0001 Pretoria

House editors: Sarie Moolman, Liz Stewart
BMR editors: Barbara Gilmour, René Nänny
Layout and cover design: Karin Maul
Graphics: Thea Venter

Contents

Authors

J A Bennett DCom
Associate Professor, Department of Business Management, Rand Afrikaans University

M Leibold DComm
Professor, Department of Strategic Management and Director of the Centre for International Business, University of Stellenbosch

A A Ligthelm DComm
Professor and Research Director of the Bureau of Market Research, University of South Africa

M Loubser DCom
Professor and Research Director of the Bureau of Market Research, University of South Africa

J H Martins DCom
Professor and Director of the Bureau of Market Research, University of South Africa

T Oosthuizen DLitt et Phil
Director 02 Communications

G Puth DPhil
Professor and Head of Department of Marketing and Communication Management, University of Pretoria

N J Smith DCom
Executive Director Programme Group: Marketing, Technikon SA

L R J van Rensburg PhD
Senior Lecturer, Department of Business Management, University of Potchefstroom

H de J van Wyk DCom
Professor and Research Director of the Bureau of Market Research, University of South Africa

T Wegner PhD
Associate Professor, Department of Statistical Sciences, University of Cape Town

Preface

The quality of marketing decisions depends to a great extent on the information available to the marketing decision maker. The function of marketing research is to provide information for this decision making. *Marketing research: a South African approach* is a comprehensive, practical and extremely accessible presentation of the field of marketing research. What you will want to learn from this book will depend in part on whether you plan to be or are in a management position in which you will use marketing research, or whether you intend to do, or are doing marketing research. Those who are or will be users of research need to learn to judge how useful research information is in helping to solve specific marketing problems, and how to evaluate the quality of the information promised by a research proposal. Those who are or will be marketing researchers need to learn how to design and conduct sound research projects at the least possible cost.

In South Africa the field of marketing research literature was pioneered by Professors P A Nel, F E Rädel and M Loubser, authors of the handbook *Researching the South African market*, which was published by the University of South Africa in 1988. Parts of *Marketing research: a South African approach* originate from *Researching the South African market* and are acknowledged as such. Whereas *Researching the South African market* was the product of researchers and lecturers at Unisa, *Marketing research: a South African approach* was compiled by four professors of the Bureau of Market Research at Unisa and seven other academics. Five of these academics are at other universities, one lectures at a technikon and another is in private practice in South Africa.

The book is in four parts. Part 1 deals with the need for marketing research, the ethical issues in marketing research, and the size, structure and state of development of the South African economy. Part 2 describes the construction of a research plan and the collection of secondary and primary data. Part 3 explains the treatment and dissemination of the data. The last part of the book, part 4, explores special areas of marketing research.

A book as comprehensive as this represents the work of many people. First there are the authors whose names appear with their chapters. The language of the manuscript was edited by Liz Stewart and Sarie Moolman of Unisa Press, assisted by Barbara Gilmour of the Bureau of Market Research. Chapters 16 and 17, the statistical section of the book, benefited from the revision by Professor J L Fresen of the Department of Statistics at Unisa. Liaison between authors, editors and publishers, secretarial work, technical editing, checking of tables, figures and proofreading were done by René Nänny assisted by Dawn Gorringe, Triny Davidson and Alet Julyan. The figures were drawn by Thea Venter of Unisa Press. The many revisions of the manuscript were typed by Luiza van Vuuren,

Madeleine Goetz and Pamela Venter. Thanks are also due to Mrs P van der Walt, Head of Unisa Press.

To avoid the continuous use of 'his or her', 'he or she' or cumbersome descriptions, the personal pronouns 'he' and 'his' will be used to denote the feminine as well as the masculine person. No discrimination regarding the sex of a interviewer/respondent/researcher is indicated.

Prof J H Martins

Part 1

Introduction to marketing research

This book is in four parts. Part 1 deals with the need for marketing research, the ethical issues in marketing research, and the size, structure and state of development of the South African economy. In chapter 1 marketing research is defined and its origin, history and role in the marketing information system are discussed. Chapter 2 describes the organisation of marketing research and the organisational environment of marketing research in South Africa. Chapter 3 focuses on ethics in marketing research and chapter 4 concludes this part with a discussion of the South African market. The market is subdivided into the consumer market and the industrial market and an overview is presented of the major segments of these two markets.

Marketing research in perspective

Chapter 1: J H Martins

(This chapter is partly based on chapter 2 'The meaning and history of marketing research' and chapter 3 'Marketing research in perspective' by F E Rädel in Nel *et al* 1988.)

1 ROLE OF MARKETING RESEARCH

The focus of the market-oriented economy is the consumer. The marketing manager performs his task in a marketing environment, harnessing a group of uncontrollable factors and a group of controllable factors to satisfy the consumer's needs and preferences (fig 1.1). The marketing manager's essential task is to combine price, product, place (distribution) and promotion – the marketing mix – so effectively that all the elements complement each other and strengthen the product's chances of competing successfully in the marketplace. His task would be much simpler if he could control all the elements that could affect consumer satisfaction and if he could predict the consumer's reaction to any

Figure 1.1 Task of marketing management

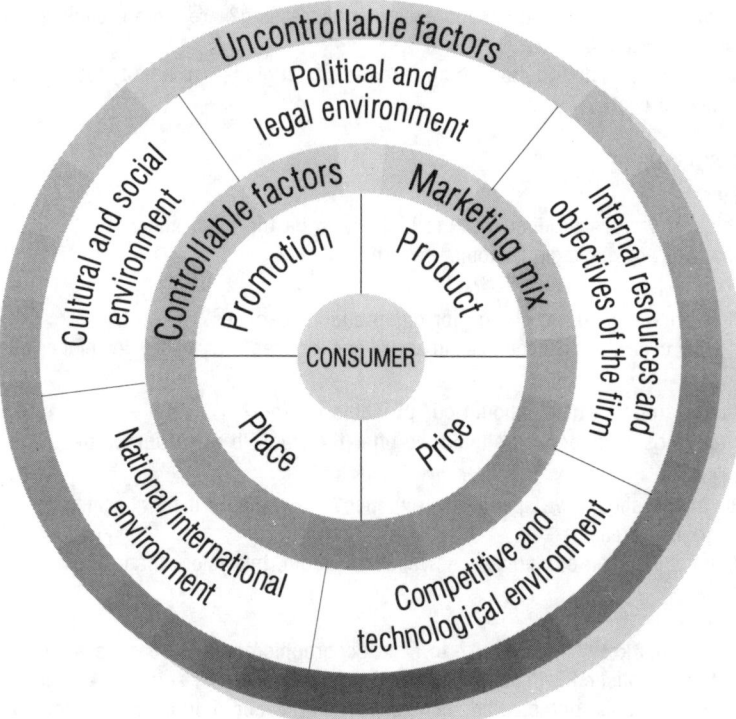

Source: Adapted from Churchill (1992:6).

contemplated change. Usually a number of factors which affect the success of the marketing effort are beyond the marketing manager's control, and the behaviour of individual consumers is largely unpredictable. Marketing research is the firm's formal communication link with the environment. It is the means by which the firm generates, transmits and interprets information from the environment about or relating to the success of the firm's marketing plans (Churchill 1992:5).

From a management point of view marketing research is vital in planning, problem solving and control. Marketing research, when used for planning, deals largely with the identification of marketing opportunities (table 1.1). The emphasis is on determining those opportunities that are viable and those that are not promising for the firm, and on providing estimates of the viable opportunities so that marketing management can better assess

Table 1.1 Kinds of questions marketing research can help answer

I   **PLANNING**
  A   What kinds of individuals and institutions buy our products? Where are they? How much do they earn? What is their turnover? How many of them are there?
  B   Are the markets for our products increasing or decreasing? Are there promising markets that we have not yet reached?
  C   Are the channels of distribution for our products changing? Are new types of marketing institutions likely to evolve?

II **PROBLEM SOLVING**
  A **Product**
    1   Which of various product designs is likely to be the most successful?
    2   What kind of packaging should we use?
  B **Price**
    1   What price should we charge for our products/services?
    2   As production costs decline, should we lower our prices or try to develop higher-quality products?
  C **Place**
    1   Where, and by whom, should our products be sold?
    2   What kinds of incentives should we offer the trade to push our products?
  D **Promotion**
    1   How much should we spend on promotion? How should it be allocated to products and to geographic areas?
    2   What combination of media — newspapers, radio, television, magazines — should we use?

III **CONTROL**
  A   What is our market share overall? In each geographic area? By each customer type?
  B   Are customers satisfied with our products? How is our record for service? Are there many returns?
  C   How does the public perceive our company? What is our reputation with the trade?

Source: Adapted from Churchill (1992:6).

the resources needed to develop them. Problem-solving marketing research focuses on the short- or long-term decisions that the firm must make regarding the elements of the marketing mix, while control-oriented marketing research helps management to isolate trouble spots and to keep abreast of current operations. The kinds of questions addressed by marketing research with regard to the planning, problem solving and control decision functions are listed in table 1.1. The ties between the marketing manager's responsibilities and the typical questions dealt with by marketing research are evident.

2 DEFINITION OF MARKETING RESEARCH

Many authors, as well as the American Marketing Association (AMA), have attempted to frame a definition of marketing research. The AMA's first definition of marketing research, published in 1960, reads: 'marketing research is the systematic gathering, recording and analysing of data about problems relating to the marketing of goods and services'.

In January 1987, after a year-long study by a special committee, the American Marketing Association published a new definition which reads as follows:

> Marketing research is the function which links the consumer, customer, and public to the marketer through information used to identify and define marketing opportunities and problems; generate, refine, and evaluate marketing actions; monitor marketing performance; and improve understanding of marketing as a process.

> Marketing research specifies the information required to address these issues; designs the method for collecting information; manages and implements the data collection process; analyzes the results; and communicates the findings and their implications.

It is doubtful that this new definition is indeed an improvement on the old one. It is far more detailed but the essence of marketing research is not described as succinctly or as clearly as in the old definition.

Even this broader definition, in our opinion, does not altogether do justice to the essential nature of marketing research. The application of marketing research is generally concerned with the solution of marketing problems, but in many marketing-oriented firms it may also involve decisions other than purely marketing decisions, such as the advisability of launching a new product. In fact, the vital question of whether to establish a new enterprise depends, in the final instance, on a thorough assessment of the market, that is on marketing research.

> **Marketing research** is the systematic and objective collection, analysis and interpretation of information for decision making on marketing problems of all kinds by recognised, scientific methods.

Marketing research relates to research on or the study of any problem in the sphere of marketing. Thus it includes research on marketing strategy and procedure, the market, product, distribution, promotion and price strategy. This definition includes the planning and interpretation of data and recognises that the information is required for decision making in marketing. Research on the market as such is termed market research.

> Like marketing research, **market research** involves the systematic, objective collection of information by recognised, scientific methods, but it is usually confined to the collection of data about the size and other characteristics of a specific market.

Marketing management seeks the answers to questions such as the following about the market: 'Who buys it?' 'What is bought?' 'Where is it bought?' 'When is it bought?' 'How is it bought?' 'Why is it bought?' The answers to these questions are supplied by market research. Market research is therefore a subdivision of marketing research.

3 FACTORS CONTRIBUTING TO THE DEVELOPMENT OF MARKETING RESEARCH

Above we referred briefly to the so-called market mechanism in a market economy and the need for a formal communication link with the environment as primary reasons for the development of marketing research. More particularly, the following factors contributed to the development of marketing research to its present stage.

3.1 Transition from a production-oriented to a marketing-oriented economy and management philosophy

Until more or less the third decade of this century the Western economy was predominantly production oriented, that is the accent was on production, both technically and managerially. Attention was focused mainly on better and more efficient production techniques, while scientific management's task was seen as the development of new methods for the effective control of the increasingly complicated production process.

Production-oriented thinking improved living standards and opened the floodgates for an unparalleled supply of goods. These goods were readily consumed until the Great Depression when, suddenly and for the first time, a worldwide, seemingly chronic oversupply was experienced. Although we know today that the Great Depression was not merely a technical problem of oversupply, it focused attention more strongly than ever before on the marketing side of an enterprise. The transition to marketing-oriented thinking had begun.

The next period of oversupply was experienced after the Second World War when former munitions factories started turning out a flood of consumer goods. By that time the gap between producer and consumer had widened so far that management needed guidance on how best to meet consumer needs. In other words, the leap from sales to marketing orientation had been made. Management realised it needed information on more than just the selling message and price of its products; it wanted reliable information on the quality, packaging and distribution of its products and on the informative function of advertising as well.

3.2 Change in the cost structure of industry

With increasing mechanisation, industries generally become more capital intensive and their fixed-costs component becomes relatively greater. A cost structure of this kind reduces adaptability to changes in demand and dictates the maintenance of a high level of production and sales. In this situation, where an industry is compelled to do everything in its power to sell its products, the best possible knowledge of unexploited market potentials is required.

3.3 Shift from price to non-price competition

The cost structure described above leaves less room for price manipulation as a means of combating competition. Moreover, price fixing by the government and quasi-monopolistic price collusion among manufacturers make for a relatively rigid price structure. Because the opportunities for price competition are severely curtailed in this situation, the emphasis shifts increasingly to non-price competition, such as advertising, product differentiation and attractive packaging. All these measures presuppose an expert knowledge of the consumer and the competition, which can be acquired only by intensive research.

3.4 Extension of roundabout production

Because of the very high degree of horizontal and vertical division of labour in the modern production structure, roundabout production has become longer and more differentiated. The stages of production, however, depend for their profitability on the market for the final product. The market for wood, for instance, along the roundabout production from forest → sawmill → paper manufacturer → printer → publisher is determined in the final instance by the demand for books, magazines and newspapers. The further a producer is removed from the final stage of consumption, the greater the risk involved in marketing his product. This risk can be reduced only by acquiring a thorough knowledge of the existing and, more especially, the future market for a particular final product.

3.5 Increase in discretionary purchasing power

Generally speaking living standards in Western countries have improved considerably. In times of rising living standards Engels' well-known law, which postulates relatively lower expenditure on essentials with rising household income, applies in principle to whole populations as well. Discretionary purchasing power, which is that part of income not spent on basic necessities, rises progressively as communities become more prosperous. This is true not only of developed, industrial countries such as the USA, but also of South Africa, as demonstrated by the income and expenditure pattern studies of the Bureau of Market Research and the Central Statistical Service. It is this discretionary purchasing power that is of particular importance to the marketing researcher.

The less essential and the more luxurious goods are considered to be, the less definite the demand for them. Put differently: the more luxurious an article, the greater the competition from other luxury goods or the more total competition becomes. A diamond ring, for instance, is in direct competition not only with other expensive rings, but also with an overseas trip or a fur coat. Competition of this kind makes it extremely difficult for individual suppliers to estimate their market share correctly. It is no coincidence therefore that marketing research originated in this sector and is still widely conducted in it today.

3.6 Increasing differentiation of supply

It is clear that greater discretionary purchasing power on the demand side can be absorbed only by a wider variety of goods and services on the supply side. Thus, in national economies where living standards are high, there is increasing differentiation of supply, as demonstrated by the multitude of new products on the market every year.

3.7 High cost of marketing

For a variety of reasons, chiefly the geographical expansion of markets and more severe competition, the share of marketing costs in the price of consumer products has increased steadily over the years. In the USA it was estimated at 58 to 60 % as far back as the fifties and is almost certainly higher now (Luck, Wales, Taylor & Rubin 1982:5). In South Africa, with its relatively long distances and generally low population density, the situation is probably very similar. Marketing research can therefore play a major part in rationalising the marketing of goods and services and controlling marketing costs.

3.8 Emergence of the professional manager

More recently in South Africa and elsewhere business management has experienced a gradual but unmistakable shift from the 'self-made man' type of owner-manager to the professional manager who is a graduate of a business school and/or the product of various management training programmes. Whereas the owner-manager tended to rely for the most part on experience and intuition, the professional manager is more amenable to scientific management methods and approaches such as marketing research.

All these trends and structural changes point in the same direction: a growing precedence of marketing over production, a stronger position of the consumer and his preferences, more severe competition and a greater complexity of the market. Put differently: by becoming less transparent, the market is presenting the marketer with new problems whose solution defies intuition and experience and requires instead supplementary scientific methods such as marketing research.

4 HISTORICAL DEVELOPMENT OF MARKETING RESEARCH

Having discussed the factors contributing to the development of marketing research in the preceding section, we now briefly review its historical development abroad and in South Africa.

Determining whether an individual enterprise actually conducts marketing research, as defined above, is just as difficult as fixing an exact date for the beginning of marketing research in a particular country or industry. The extensive networks which merchant houses such as Fugger and Rothschilds maintained in the Middle Ages and which were also used for gathering marketing information can scarcely be regarded as marketing research (Lockley 1950:733).

In the USA as early as 1879 the advertising agency Ayer & Son conducted a survey of agricultural products to determine the market for farming implements. Charles Parlin, however, is usually regarded as the pioneer of marketing research in the USA. In 1911 he established a division of commercial research at the Curtis Publishing Company which applied systematic methods of gathering marketing data for drawing up effective advertising programmes. This new activity was termed commercial research. It was not until the early twenties that the term 'marketing research' came into vogue.

The first attempt at conducting marketing research in the United Kingdom dates back to 1911 when Bowley conducted a market survey based on a sample. The first independent marketing research organisation, London Research and Information Bureau, was established in 1924 by H G Lyell, although the Unilever Company had been doing consumer research since 1920 (Bottomley 1964:3).

In Germany the father of marketing research is considered to be W Vershoven who started an institute for market observation (Institut für Wirtschaftsbeobachtung der Deutschen Fertigware) at the Economic High School (now University) of Nuremberg in 1925.

In all three countries marketing research remained sporadic until the late twenties, but it gained ground during the Great Depression and from then on was conducted on a wider front. 'One cannot say that marketing research was formed in the Depression, but it received its first nourishment then' (Bottomley 1964:5).

After the much-publicised failure of the Literary Digest Poll in the USA in 1936, the emphasis shifted from large unsophisticated samples to more refined sampling methods which were designed to obtain reliable results from relatively small samples. The advent of computers after the Second World War gave marketing research its ultimate boost, promoting both its use and the refinement of its techniques.

In South Africa the first market survey was a consumer survey conducted by J Walter Thompson for Royal Baking Powder in 1935. There were no further surveys until after the Second World War when marketing research operations started more or less simultaneously in three different quarters. In 1947 Davenport and Meyer started a company in Johannesburg called South African Research Services which collected audience data for Lourenço Marques Commercial Radio. Both partners had gained experience in listenership research in the United Kingdom before they emigrated to South Africa after the war. They were joined by W Langschmidt who played a major part in the company's listenership survey, a research area in which he would later become a leader in South Africa and overseas. In the same year Lever Brothers (South Africa) established a research unit under J Stacey to undertake surveys for the firm. At about the same time J Walter Thompson set up a consumer research unit for consumer surveys under Kent Durham.

5 MARKETING RESEARCH AND DECISION MAKING

As stated, marketing research is always intended for decision making; in other words, marketing research has merely a supportive function, and its value for a business depends on the extent to which the information it makes available is converted into decision-making and action or policy. Otherwise marketing research remains a mere academic exercise.

In a free market economy management in general, and marketing management in particular, has to make decisions in a situation fraught with many variables and uncertainties and incomplete information. Logically, of course, the more comprehensive the information (the lower the level of uncertainty) the greater the chance that management will make correct decisions. The task of marketing research therefore is to produce information that will serve as a sound base for decision making; but at the same time it is the task of management to take cognisance of the information supplied by marketing research and formulate its policy accordingly. Thus we see that marketing research and decision making are closely interdependent, though they remain two separate issues. In terms of business economics, marketing research is a *staff function* and decision making an *executive* one. Far from being a substitute for marketing policy, as is often believed, marketing research plays a supportive role. Let us take an example from the world of medicine to illustrate the relation between marketing research and decision making.

Modern medicine has a wealth of instruments and apparatus for diagnosing a health problem. A poor doctor, however, might well make a correct diagnosis but prescribe the wrong therapy; or a good doctor might dispense with complicated instruments to arrive at a correct therapy simply by relying on experience and intuition. Undoubtedly the probability of prescribing the correct therapy depends on the correct diagnosis, and this is far more likely if the doctor uses modern diagnostic instruments. Similarly in business an experienced manager can apply his intuitive powers to arrive at the correct decision without the help of scientifically collected market information, whereas a poor manager could make a wrong decision in spite of a wealth of market information. But certainly the chances of making a correct decision are considerably enhanced if relevant market information is available and is given due consideration by management.

So far we have been speaking of marketing research as a service or contribution to decision making as though decision making was a single action. The fact is that decision making is a whole sequence of actions or steps. Although decision-making theorists are not in full agreement on the number and types of steps necessary in decision making, for our purpose we distinguish the following basic steps using an example to illustrate them:

(1) Tracing and defining a problem (for example a manufacturer of photographic cameras notices a falling off in sales of a particular type of camera).

(2) Identification of some possible explanations for the decline in sales (for example decline in the quality of the camera, appearance on the market of a better camera in the same price range, deterioration of the service by the retailers handling the camera).

(3) Preliminary investigation of the various alternatives with a view to eliminating some of them (this preliminary investigation shows that the cause of the problem is the appearance of a competitive new camera on the market).

(4) Prediction of the result of possible alternative policies (the result of withdrawing the camera from production, or introducing an improved, more competitive camera).

(5) Final decision on the policy to be followed (improvement of the existing camera).

(6) Implementation of the decision (instructions for improving the camera, trademark, advertising, and so on).

Next we must know to which steps research can make a contribution. Analysis of the various steps clearly shows that research has inputs to offer in particular to steps 1, 2, 3 and 4 and that liaison between research and management, especially in regard to these steps, must be very close indeed. The following schematic representation will make things even clearer (fig 1.2).

Figure 1.2 Decision-making process and inputs of marketing research

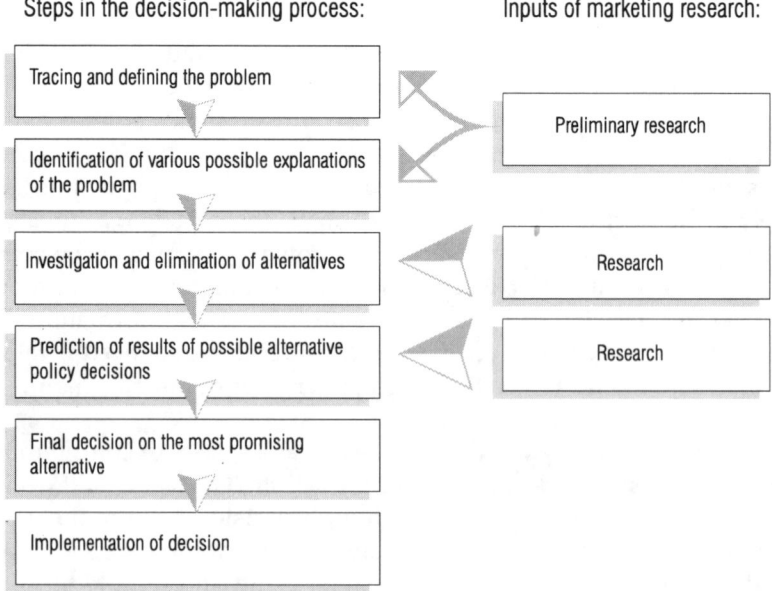

Steps in the decision-making process:

Inputs of marketing research:

Tracing and defining the problem

Identification of various possible explanations of the problem

Investigation and elimination of alternatives

Prediction of results of possible alternative policy decisions

Final decision on the most promising alternative

Implementation of decision

Preliminary research

Research

Research

6 MARKETING RESEARCH AND INFORMATION SYSTEMS

So far we have been speaking of marketing research; but in recent years the term 'marketing information systems', indicating a broader conceptual context, has come into use. The term denotes the growing body of knowledge which has become available to marketing management since the arrival and increasing use of the computer and has been systematically arranged into marketing information systems.

6.1 Marketing information systems

A **marketing information system (MIS)** can be defined as a planned combination of ways and methods for continuous gathering, filtering, analysing, storing and flow of relevant information for the purpose of marketing decision making (Kurtz 1984:154).

Marketing information systems differ according to the type of enterprise and industry. A small enterprise usually has a simple MIS and a large enterprise has an extensive one. In industries such as agriculture and mining, information systems are generally more simplistic, because of the relatively homogeneous nature of products or lower intensity of competition.

The thrust in designing an MIS is a detailed analysis of each decision maker who might use the system, in order to secure an accurate, objective assessment of each person's decision-making responsibilities, capabilities and style. According to Churchill (1992:27) several things had to be done to develop this information system. First, the decision makers affected by the planned system had to be identified. Then their information needs had to be determined, both with respect to the type of information each person needed and the form in which they could best use it. It was then necessary to specify the data that would be input to the system, how the data could be secured, how they would be stored, how the data in separate data banks would be accessed and combined, and what the report formats would look like. Only after these analyses and design steps were completed could the system be constructed, which was essentially a programming task. As the system evolved, managers at the company could access reports directly through computer terminals on their desks.

A simple MIS is illustrated in figure 1.3. Such an MIS consists of two data components: everyday or routine data and special purpose data. For a local independent retailer the routine data would include, for example, routine information from internal sources, such as cash flow, sales, stocks, debtors and creditors. From external sources information such as local population growth, competitive activities and trade association statistics would be collected regularly. The special purpose data include marketing research.

Figure 1.3 A simple marketing information system (MIS)

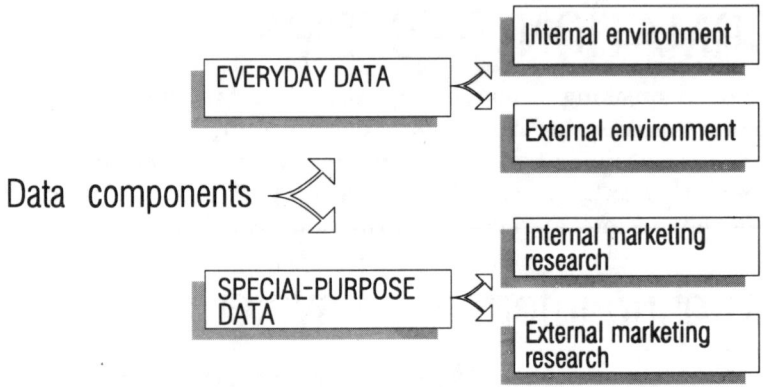

Larger enterprises which have the necessary resources usually operate an extensive MIS. Figure 1.4 indicates the major components of an extensive MIS and the interaction among its components.

Figure 1.4 An extensive marketing information system (MIS)

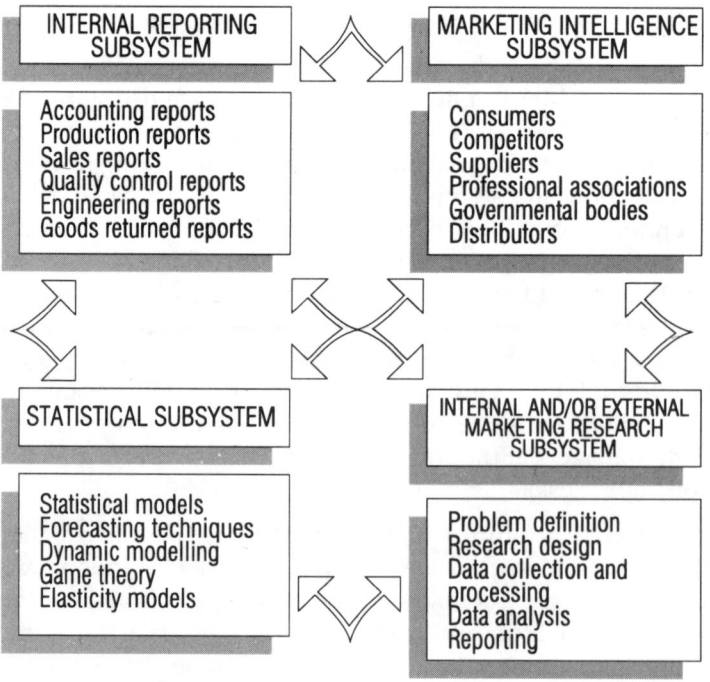

Source: Adapted from Kotler (1988:103).

According to Tull and Hawkins (1990:26) three distinct types of information are generally supplied to marketing managers through the MIS: recurrent, monitoring and requested.

Recurrent information is information that is provided on a continuous basis. Market share by region, customer awareness, prices of leading competitors, customer satisfaction and customer purchase intentions are examples of information that managers frequently receive weekly, monthly, quarterly, or annually. Recurrent information is particularly useful for indicating problems and opportunities. It can also be used to determine the effects of solutions to potential problems. For example, regular market share reports can be used to analyse the impact of price changes. Recurrent information is based on both internal and external data sources. Accounting records and sales call reports are major internal sources. Consumer surveys, consumer panels and store audits are important external sources.

Monitoring information is information derived from the regular scanning of certain sources. For example, a marketing manager may desire a summary of any articles on the competition or the industry. All relevant journals including trade association publications, government reports, and the general business press are examined as they are issued. Article summaries are prepared and distributed any time a relevant article appears.

Monitoring information comes primarily from external sources. Government reports, articles, annual reports of competitors, and public activities of competitors are common sources that are monitored. Internal sales call reports and accounting records are also subject to monitoring. Monitoring information is particularly useful for alerting firms to potential problems such as new competitors or new marketing activities by existing competitors. It can also help identify opportunities such as new product uses, new market segments and improved product features.

Requested information is developed in response to a specific request by a marketing manager. Without such a request the information would not flow to the manager and might not exist in the system. For example, a manager might request information on the size of a market not currently served by the firm along with an assessment of the intensity of competitive rivalry in the market and the level of customer satisfaction with the current brands in the market. Much of this information would not be available in the system and would have to be generated.

Only a few of the types of information available to marketing management in an MIS are illustrated in figure 1.5. This figure will also give you some idea of the difficulties experienced by designers of an MIS.

When they were first proposed, MISs were held up as an information panacea. Churchill (1992:28–30) thinks the reality often falls short of the promise. The primary reasons are as much behavioural as they are technical. People tend to resist change, and with an MIS the changes are often substantial. Also, many decision makers are reluctant to disclose to others what factors they use and how they combine these factors when making

Figure 1.5 Typical information requirements from an MIS

Organisation position	Recurrent	Monitoring	Requested
Salesperson	Regional economic data Regional market share Competitor prices/ promotions	Competitor product changes Customer acquisitions, other key changes New entrants	Customer profiles Customer needs/ satisfaction Customer attitudes
Sales manager	Product margins Cost per call per customer Share by salesperson	Regional economic changes New competitive activities Salesforce performance	Contribution per customer Salesforce effectiveness vs competitors
Brand manager	Brand share Customer satisfaction Feature preferences	Competitor activities Technology changes Government regulations	Test of new formulation Price elasticity study Brand testing
Advertising manager	Advertising awareness Media habits of target audience	Media rates Ad themes of competitors Media effectiveness studies	New commercial theme test Communications impact of competitor's advertisement
Public relations manager	Key public attitudes towards the firm Company plans to affect the public	Legislative activities Trade and popular publications News clips	Impact on buyers' attitudes of a strike by the union Impact of responses of firms of other industries to safety problems
Marketing manager	Net contribution by product line Market share by product line/market Customer satisfaction levels	New competitors Developments in related markets New product launches by competitors	Impact on related products of dropping one product line Price, income and advertising elasticities across products

Source: Adapted from Tull & Hawkins (1990:28).

a decision about a particular issue. Without such disclosure it is next to impossible to design reports that will give them the information they need in the form they need it. Even when managers are willing to disclose their decision-making calculus and information needs, there are problems.

Different managers typically emphasise different things and consequently have different data needs. There are very few report formats that are optimal for different users. Either the developers have to design 'compromise' reports that are satisfactory for a number of users, although not ideal for any single user, or they have to engage in the laborious task of programming to meet each user's needs, one at a time.

Another fundamental problem with MISs is that the systems do not lend themselves to the solution of ill-structured problems, which are the most common kind of problems managers face. Since a manager's decision making is often ad hoc and addressed to unexpected choices, standardised reporting systems lack the necessary scope and flexibility to be useful. Nor can managers, even if they are willing to, specify in advance what they want from programmers and model builders, because decision making and planning are often exploratory. As decision makers and their staffs learn more about a problem, their information needs and methods of analysis evolve. Further, decision making often involves exceptions and qualitative issues that are not easily programmed.

As these problems with MISs became more apparent, the emphasis in regularly supplied marketing intelligence changed from the production of preformatted batch reports to a *marketing decision support system (MDSS)*.

6.2 Marketing decision support systems

A **marketing decision support system** (MDSS) is an integrated system of data, statistical analysis, modelling, and display formats using computer hardware and software to provide information for the marketing decision-making process (Kinnear & Taylor 1991:158).

An MDSS should have five components: (1) data sources which form the backbone of an MDSS, (2) data management, (3) display, (4) statistical analysis, and (5) modelling. Figure 1.6 on page 18 illustrates a typical MDSS.

According to Kinnear and Taylor (1991:160) an MDSS must have the following four features:

☐ The system must be interactive. The system must provide the manager with easy-to-follow instructions and give results on the spot. The manager must control the process and must not need to wait for the results.

Figure 1.6 A typical marketing decision support system (MDSS)

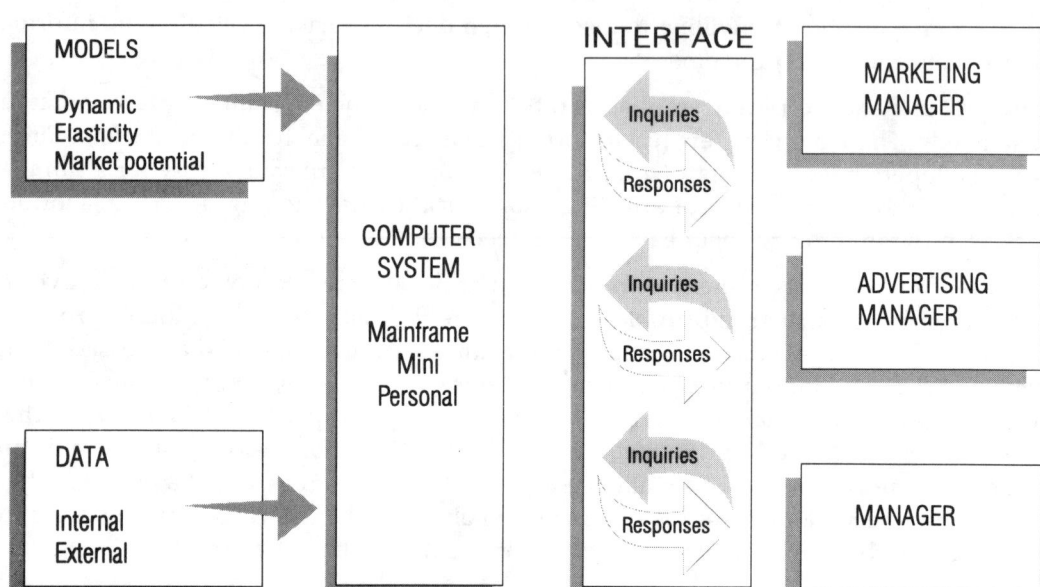

Source: Adapted from Tull & Hawkins (1990:31).

☐ The system must be flexible. The manager can sort, average, total, or otherwise manipulate the data. The manager's needs are hard to predict; a particular problem may mean looking at the data in a totally unique way.

☐ The system must be discovery oriented. The manager can search for trends, identify problems and ask new questions on the basis of information provided.

☐ The system must minimise the frustration quotient. Novice users who are not particularly computer knowledgeable should be able to work the basic system easily and eventually learn the more intricate parts of the system through continued use and experimentation.

There are a number of systems in an MDSS. The *data system* in an MDSS includes the processes used to capture and the methods used to store data from marketing, finance and manufacturing, as well as information from any number of external or internal sources.

The typical data system has modules containing customer information, general economic and demographic information, competitor information, distributors information and industry information, including market trends. One of the significant trends in the development of MDSSs is the explosion in databases that provide such information. Many of these databases can now be accessed on-line via computer.

The *model system* in an MDSS includes all the routines that allow the user to manipulate data so as to conduct the kind of analysis the individual desires. In recent years there has been an increase in the application of formal decision models to marketing situations. The credit approval and salesperson-routing models could be considered operational models. The pricing, sales territory assignment and advertising media selection models could be considered more tactical. The new product-evaluation and product-deletion models could be considered more strategic in nature.

A *dialogue system*, which is also called a language system, according to Churchill (1992:34) is the most important system in an MDSS and clearly differentiates an MDSS from an MIS. Dialogue systems permit managers, who are not programmers themselves, to explore the databases by using the system models to produce reports that satisfy their own particular information needs. The reports can be tabular or graphical, and the report formats can be specified by individual managers. The dialogue systems can be passive, which means that the analysis possibilities are presented to the decision makers for selection via menu, a few simple key strokes, a light pen, or a mouse device, or they can be active, requiring the users to state their requests in a command mode. A key feature is that managers, instead of funnelling their data requests through a team of programmers, can conduct their analyses by themselves (or through one of their assistants) at a computer terminal using the dialogue system. This allows them to target the information they want and not be overwhelmed with irrelevant data. Managers can ask a question and, on the basis of the answer, a subsequent question, and then another, and another, and so on.

Figure 1.7 illustrates the use of an MDSS in decision making and in launching a new product on the market. In the sales forecasting model hypotheses are generated and assumptions are made about product design and development, market structure, entry strategy and the firm's competitive environment. Over and above existing (secondary) data, marketing research data may be required for generating hypotheses and making assumptions. Figure 1.7 illustrates the use of the model in forecasting sales and profit, given a set of assumptions and a planned marketing strategy. It allows the manager to run sensitivity analyses on the various assumptions and to easily evaluate the profit impact of differing marketing strategies.

The explosion in databases and the emergence of MDSSs have not eliminated traditional marketing research projects for gathering marketing intelligence. The two activities are not competitive mechanisms for marketing intelligence; rather, they are complementary ones. While MDSSs provide valuable input for broad strategic decisions, allow managers to stay in tune with what is happening in their external environments, and serve as an excellent early-warning system, they sometimes do not provide enough information about what to do in specific instances. When actionable information is required to address specific marketing problems or opportunities, the research project will probably continue to play a major role.

Figure 1.7 New product sales forecast module

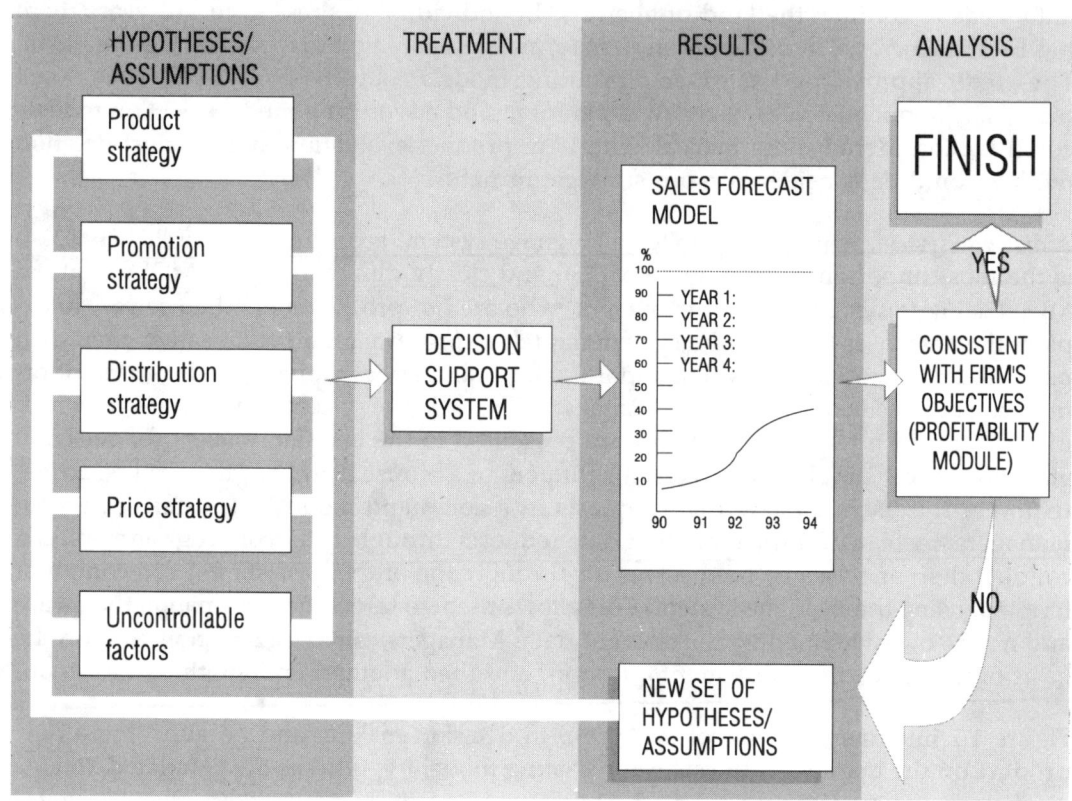

Source: Adapted from Tull & Hawkins (1990:37).

7 MARKETING RESEARCH AS A SCIENCE

Before we close our discussion of the fundamentals of marketing research, we must also be quite clear about this subject as a science and its position in the scientific system. It will help to reveal the nature of marketing research and at the same time produce criteria differentiating marketing research from other scientific disciplines which are so often confused with it. Marketing research is a relatively young science but it has already assembled a body of widely accepted terminology and methods of research. Marketing research is generally accepted as belonging to the group of social sciences which study man in a social context. In this group we distinguish as a subgroup the economic sciences, which investigate the relation between people and groups from an economic perspective. Within the economic sciences we distinguish between macro-economics or political or social economics on the one hand and micro-economics or business economics on the other. The first subgroup studies how the scarce resources of nature are used to satisfy man's needs, and the second investigates how the means of production must be used in an establishment to ensure the highest possible output. Since the business undertaking in a capitalist market economy does not produce for its own consumption but for the market, its products must be manufactured as well as marketed. Thus marketing is clearly a task or function of business economics. Because of the increasing distance between producer and consumer, seller and buyer, the task of marketing is becoming more and more important, and in the past few decades has begun to overshadow the production function. According to estimates, over 50 % of the final consumer price of products in advanced Western countries is ascribable to marketing costs. Therefore the more efficient marketing is, the greater the chance of maintaining or expanding the market share, or, in scientific terms, the more favourable the ratio of revenue to costs, of output to input, the greater the firm's profitability.

Once marketing is recognised as a function of business economics, marketing research logically becomes a function of *business economics*. It is not by chance that in the USA, the United Kingdom and Germany marketing research originated in a business context. Today, of course, we find marketing research being practised not only by business establishments but also by a variety of other organisations: consultants, advertising agencies, scientific institutes, etc. However, the primary function of these institutions is to produce information for use in policy decisions. We can therefore say that marketing research is a field of study intended to maximise the marketing efficiency of a firm or institution.

8 SUMMARY

In a market economy a businessman needs accurate data on the size and structure of the market segment in which he chooses to operate and on his position vis-à-vis his competitors. In olden times the artisan-producer had an intimate knowledge of his market, which was geographically limited. But after the Industrial Revolution mass production and the geographical extension of markets created the need for an organised systematic means of collecting market data. It was first called market research and then, after the whole marketing process was subjected to research, the wider term 'marketing research' gained general acceptance. The following factors contributed to the development of marketing research: transition from a production-oriented to a marketing-oriented economy and management philosophy, change in the cost structure of industry, shift from price to non-price competition, extension of roundabout production, increase in discretionary purchasing power, increasing differentiation of supply, high cost of marketing and the emergence of the professional manager. When precisely marketing research actually became the systematic collecting, recording and analysing of data relating to the marketing of products and services is difficult to say, since the process of transition from informal market scanning to formal marketing research was a gradual one.

Marketing research is a staff function and decision making an executive (management) function. Marketing research serves decision making and is justifiable in a business only if and in so far as it is in fact used for decision making. Research therefore supports but never replaces decision making. In an ever-changing environment where the information for decision making is incomplete, marketing research broadens the information base. Thus research and decision making are interdependent. Effective decision making is possible only when reliable information is available for this purpose and to this end effective communication between the research division and management is a prerequisite. Decision making is not a single activity but consists of a whole sequence of steps. These steps are identified and the contribution of research to these steps is analysed.

The concepts of marketing information, marketing information systems (MIS) and marketing decision support systems (MDSS) have come into use with the arrival of the computer. Both systems are geared to storing information and retrieving it for management on request. The systems differ chiefly in their degree of sophistication. Depending on the size of the enterprise, that is how many management staff members require information and the type of product or service sold, MISs can become very complicated and difficult to use. As these problems with MISs have become more apparent, the emphasis in regularly supplied intelligence has shifted from the production of preformatted batch reports to MDSSs.

As a scientific discipline, marketing research is a relatively young science but it has already assembled a body of widely accepted terminology and methods of research. There is agreement that marketing research belongs to the group of social sciences which study man in a social context. Within this group it falls under the economic sciences, which in turn comprise macro-economics (political or social management) and micro-economics (business economics). Business economics studies the use of the economic means available to an enterprise for the maximisation of output or returns in the marketplace. Considering that marketing costs often comprise more than 50 % of the final consumer price in developed Western countries, the rationalisation of marketing has become imperative for producer and consumer alike. The most important instrument to this end is marketing research. Since marketing is a function of business management, marketing research also belongs to the field of study of business economics and its objective is the maximisation of marketing efficiency.

REFERENCES

Bottomley, D T 1964. The origin of marketing research. *Commentary*, 13:3–5.
Churchill, Gilbert A (Jr) 1992. *Basic marketing research*. Second edition. Fort Worth: The Dryden Press. (The Dryden Press Series in Marketing.)
Kinnear, Thomas C & Taylor, James R 1991. *Marketing research: an applied approach*. Fourth edition. New York: McGraw-Hill. (McGraw-Hill Series in Marketing.)

Kotler, P 1988. *Marketing management: analysis, planning, implementation and control*. Englewood Cliffs, NJ: Prentice Hall.

Kurtz, D L & Boone, L E 1984. *Marketing*. New York: The Dryden Press. (The Dryden Press Series in Marketing.)

Lockley, L C 1950. Notes on the history of marketing research. *Journal of Marketing*, 14(4):733.

Luck, David J, Wales, Hugh G, Taylor, Donald A & Rubin, Ronald S 1982. *Marketing research*. Sixth edition. Englewood Cliffs, NJ: Prentice Hall.

Tull, Donald S & Hawkins, Del I 1990. *Marketing research: measurement and method: a text with cases*. Fifth edition. New York: Macmillan. (The Macmillan Series in Marketing.)

Organisation and organisational environment of marketing research

Chapter 2: H de J van Wyk

1 INTRODUCTION

The marketing function is one of the principal functions of an organisation. Unless the firm is able to dispose of its products, there is no further reason for its existence. The function of marketing research interacts with other functions in the organisation and determines the place occupied by the marketing research function in the organisation. Marketing research can be done internally by the organisation's own staff, or it can be farmed out to marketing research consultants. Because organisations do not operate or do marketing research in a vacuum, their external marketing research environment – as personified inter alia by marketing research associations – is also of importance. We shall deal with all these aspects in the sections that follow.

2 THE POSITION OF MARKETING RESEARCH IN THE ORGANISATION

Making decisions is an essential element of management, and the marketing function is one of the principal management functions that call for decision making. Management needs information in order to make decisions. Kinnear and Taylor (1991:15) believe that marketing managers rely on two information inputs: their own experience and judgement, and the more formalised information available from the marketing research system. The authors single out non-routine decision-making situations as the ones in which managers most often lack relevant information or are reluctant to place all their trust in their own judgement.

As we saw in chapter 1, section 5, marketing research is involved in four of the six stages of the decision-making process. In view of its role in marketing decisions one might well ask where the marketing research function fits into the organisational structure of the organisation. It goes without saying that the size and nature of the establishment are key considerations. Small establishments generally do not have separate marketing research divisions and may not even employ a full-time researcher. In such organisations the function of marketing research naturally devolves on the marketing department, but sometimes the person doing the organisation's marketing research reports direct to top management. Wherever the size and nature of the organisation justifies a separate marketing research division, it may fall under the marketing department or be classed as a staff function of top management. Both arrangements have advantages and disadvantages. Some argue that the marketing research division should report to the marketing department because marketing research plays a supporting role in the marketing function. Others fear this arrangement will jeopardise the independence of the marketing research division because of the pressure the head of the marketing department can bring to bear, for instance in changing or simply ignoring research results that are detrimental to his image or the image of his department. The risk of undue influence falls away when the marketing research division reports to top management, but then top management may either make poor decisions or leave the research reports to gather dust if it lacks the expertise to evaluate research results. There are other considerations as well. The organisational location of marketing research is governed by the information needs of the organisation. If these needs are chiefly technical marketing problems, it makes sense to place the research function under the marketing department. Location under top management is, however, indicated in matters of policy, such as new product development and the location of branches, which only top management can decide. Generally speaking the level of management which sets the research department's tasks should also be organisationally responsible for it.

There are various ways of dealing with these sometimes conflicting considerations in practice. Some organisations have only one marketing research division which is responsible for all research projects; others have decentralised the research responsibility by functional divisions in which decentralised sales and distribution cost analysis are conducted by the accounting department, advertising research by the advertising department and forecasting by the chief executive's department. Still others decentralise by production or sales divisions (Tull & Hawkins 1990:15).

Decentralisation obviously holds certain advantages, but sometimes its drawbacks can be serious, especially when marketing research functions are allocated to divisions which are ill equipped to handle them and whose heads see little purpose in marketing research.

Churchill (1992:13) suggests three ways of organising the marketing research function:

☐ organisation by area of application, such as product line, by brand, by market segment, or by geographic area

☐ organisation by marketing function performed, such as field sales analysis, advertising research, or product planning

☐ organisation by research technique or approach, such as sales analysis, national and/or international analysis, field interviewing, or questionnaire design.

These arrangements may lead to duplication, and the only way of avoiding it is to define the functions of the respective divisions in detail. In addition a coordinating division with clearly defined functions is required.

In conclusion we turn to marketing research practice in South Africa. Unfortunately the only recent research on the organisation of marketing research in this country refers to the manufacturing industry. A Bureau of Market Research (BMR) study in 1989 found that only 23,8 % of the establishments in the manufacturing sector undertook marketing research. This figure rose to just over 50 % for manufacturers with more than 600 employees. Of the manufacturers who did marketing research only 6,9 % had formal marketing research departments, but 20 % employed market researchers full time and nearly 60 % employed part-time research staff. Close to 57 % of the heads of marketing research departments reported to top management and fully 29 % reported to the marketing manager. Fully 75 % of the marketing managers were involved in implementing research findings. A further 20 % were informed of the progress of implementation of the research findings (Martins, Van Helden & Nel 1989:5).

3 INTERNAL AND EXTERNAL MARKETING RESEARCH

Internal marketing research is undertaken by the organisation's own staff; **external marketing research** is undertaken by consultants and agencies on behalf of the organisation.

Internal marketing research may be defined as research undertaken by the organisation's own staff; external marketing research is contracted out to consultants and agencies outside the organisation. As we have seen, the nature and size of the organisation among other things determine where the marketing research function fits into the organisational structure of the organisation. Whether an organisation should do its own marketing research or farm it out is also dependent on its nature and size, but in this instance other conditions also play a role. If research is contracted out, choices also have to be made between consultants and types of research. For instance, the organisation may select a private consultant or a research institute to do research on its behalf. Further it may commission research which will remain its exclusive property. Another option would be to take part in a syndicated research project whose results are shared by the sponsors of the project.

The choice between internal and external marketing research should be governed by cost and effectiveness. An organisation obviously needs the services of a marketing research department, or at least a person well versed in marketing research, in order to formulate marketing research goals and interpret the results of the research. Continuous research which will occupy the research staff effectively, or research which requires an intimate knowledge of the organisation's internal activities should preferably be undertaken internally. In contrast, comprehensive projects undertaken on a one-off basis should be contracted out. In organisations which do all their research internally the effectiveness of larger divisions may be impaired by a poor staff-output ratio if the staff are not kept fully occupied at all times. There is also a very real risk of 'empire building', a phenomenon which is naturally not confined to the marketing research function. It is also possible that research may be undertaken merely for the sake of doing research.

In the sections below we shall examine the advantages and disadvantages of internal and external research and we shall see that they are not quite as straightforward as one might think.

(a) Knowledge of marketing philosophy and the organisation's needs

An organisation's own staff have a more intimate knowledge of its marketing function and its needs. But very often outsiders can be a great help in formulating these needs because they have the advantage of being at a distance from the problem and are not hampered by preconceived ideas. This argument is particularly valid in cases in which the internal research staff are inexperienced.

(b) Effective control of the duration of research

Very often an internal research project is delayed indefinitely because the researcher keeps getting other urgent work to do. Also, it is not always possible to make an accurate assessment of the amount of work a project will require. In contrast, a contract for external research specifies the time period for completion of a project. A possible disadvantage is that external consultancies tend to extend the research time specified in the proposal beyond their probable requirements to make provision for unforeseen delays, or to insert escape clauses for their own protection.

(c) Cost of research

The reasoning about the effective control of the duration of research projects is applicable here too. Contracts for external research projects specify the cost of the research to the client. The consultancy or research house undertaking the research, however, has to make ample provision for unexpected expenses and for profit in its cost estimate. All things being equal a research project undertaken internally should therefore be cheaper. This does not apply in cases in which syndicated research results* can be purchased.

---

* In syndicated research two or more organisations share the costs and the results of the research. Syndicated research is discussed in chapter 6.

In 1994 the cost of employing a senior researcher (salary and indirect costs) was already in excess of R1 500 per day. By way of illustration we shall evaluate the costs of the syndicated research undertaken by the Bureau of Market Research. In 1994 it cost R4 500 to sponsor one of the BMR's research divisions and R7 500 to sponsor all seven. If an organisation saves three days of research by sponsoring one division of the BMR and five days of research by sponsoring all seven divisions, it has already reached breakeven point in terms of the cost of employing its own researcher for those days. Naturally these arguments apply to all syndicated research. However, syndicated research is typically characterised by compromise, and its results may have limited value in some instances.

To determine whether expanding the research division, farming work out, or purchasing syndicated research results would be more profitable for the organisation, management should calculate new appointees' direct and indirect costs (salaries and fringe benefits, additional office space, telephone calls, etc) before making a final decision. Furthermore, the total costs should be reduced to cost per day or per hour. When weekends, public holidays, leave and provision for sick leave are taken into account, the average worker in South Africa does not spend much more than 200 days per year actually working. As stated, the cost of employing a senior researcher in 1994 was already in excess of R1 500 per day.

(d) Knowledge of particular research methods

Except in large marketing research divisions, research staff are seldom familiar with the whole range of research methods applied in marketing research or with the latest developments in the field. External research houses should be requested to furnish proof of their expertise and experience in a particular field. As most of these houses specialise to a greater or lesser extent, management should have little difficulty in making the best possible choice.

(e) Confidentiality of the research

In theory there is less chance of a competitor gaining access to an organisation's research results when the research project is conducted internally. Yet industrial espionage is not unknown in South Africa, and there is nothing to stop an unscrupulous staff member from leaking research results to a competitor. Research results should therefore be treated as confidential even within the firm and be divulged to staff only on a 'need-to-know' basis. The risk of a competitor laying hands on external marketing research results is greater because so many more people handle the results, but as long as the marketing research consultant is a reputable one the chances are quite small.

(f) Independent and unbiased research results

There can be no doubt that external research results tend to be more independent and unbiased than internal research results because of the greater objectivity and independence of outside consultants. Internal research results may possibly be ignored or rejected as invalid because of internal politics and preconceived ideas. This does not mean that unpopular external research results will be accepted without argument, but in such instances the arguments have to be far more convincing.

(g) Handling of large research projects

Very few marketing research divisions are geared for really comprehensive projects, over and above their usual activities. A division may therefore choose to contract a project out, either wholly or in part. For instance it may contract out the survey part (if that is more convenient) and/or the processing of the results. Provided that the contract allows it, parts of the survey may also be subcontracted out by the principal. Another possibility is to divide the project into more manageable units and to contract out some or all of them.

(h) Quality of internal and external research

It is very difficult to lay down guidelines that are valid in every situation. Possibly the quality of internal research can be more easily controlled if the necessary expertise and insight are available in the firm. In some cases it may be advisable to call in an expert from outside to assess the validity of internal research results. The quality of external research can be controlled by drawing up specific tender conditions; inserting conditions in the contract; giving the client or the client's deputy permission to run certain checks; and evaluating the results scientifically. However, this does not alter the fact that unscrupulous consultants may take short-cuts. It also serves to underline the importance of engaging the services of a reputable consultant. Tenders that are appreciably lower than others are especially suspect.

What is the position in South Africa regarding internal and external marketing research? Figure 2.1 depicts the results of a survey of manufacturers undertaken in 1989 (Martins, Van Helden & Nel 1992:9):

> Looking at the figure it seems that the smaller manufacturers tend to do their own research and the bigger manufacturers tend to make use of consultants. Of all the manufacturers and non-manufacturing head offices that do marketing research, less than half (48,8 %) make use of consultants. Among the last-mentioned 39,6 % farm out their research work to consultants on a fairly continuous basis. In 54,9 % of the cases the consultants are responsible for the whole research project and in 20,3 % of the cases only for the collection of the data.

Figure 2.1 Internal and external marketing research by employment size

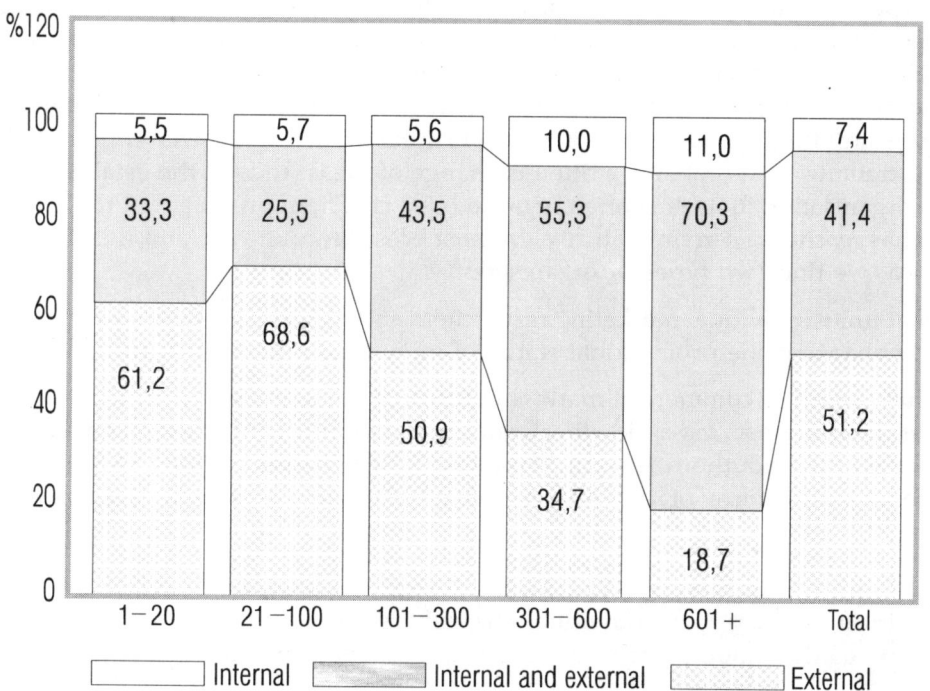

Source: Martins *et al* (1992:11).

4 THE MARKETING RESEARCH ENVIRONMENT

As we have said, the marketing research profession does not exist in isolation; it is influenced and itself exerts influence in many spheres of society. In this section we shall deal with the external marketing research environment, which is made up of marketing research associations in South Africa, international marketing research associations and other organisations in which South African marketing researchers have an interest.

4.1 Marketing research associations in South Africa

The post-pioneering phase of marketing research was marked in South Africa, as in other parts of the world, by a growing movement towards organisation of the industry. In the early years the new discipline was practised by people with such different backgrounds, levels of expertise and sense of responsibility that a situation was created in which charlatanism flourished. It was obvious to responsible practitioners that ways and means of conferring professional status on marketing research were desperately needed. Usually this is done by founding professional associations whose purpose is to ensure and enhance professional status through admission of members in accordance with given criteria, codes of conduct, training, and oral and written exchange of ideas. Indeed the establishment of such an organisation in itself is often regarded as a criterion, proving that the activity concerned has reached a certain maturity. In most Western countries, and this includes South Africa, we find two types of organisations:

☐ those that unite individual marketing researchers and aim for the most part at ensuring and enhancing the professional status of individual researchers, and

☐ those that consist of commercial marketing research companies and act as a mouthpiece for their interests vis-à-vis other institutions. In South Africa we find the first in the form of the Southern African Marketing Research Association (SAMRA) and the second in the form of the Association of Marketing Research Organisations (AMRO).

> **SAMRA** is an association of individual researchers.
> **AMRO** acts as the mouthpiece of commercial marketing research companies.

4.1.1 The Southern African Marketing Research Association (SAMRA)

4.1.1.1 Introduction

SAMRA's inaugural meeting was held in the Philadelphia Hall at Unisa in Pretoria on 10 May 1963. Seventy-four foundation members were present at this meeting. The association's task, as defined in its constitution, is to

☐ achieve professionalism in research practice, and

☐ promote the effective use of marketing research by decision makers.

Its main aims and objectives are therefore

☐ to promote and protect marketing research based on sample surveys and other techniques

☐ to promote and protect the interests of SAMRA members and of those who use the services of members of the profession and of respondents who supply information in marketing research studies

☐ to foster scientific study and research in the fields of marketing, social and communication decision making

☐ to foster research into and to improve the methods and techniques of marketing research

☐ to contribute to the improvement of the teaching of marketing research

☐ to encourage and uphold sound, honest practices, to keep marketing research practices on a high ethical plane and to assist in the maintenance of high standards in the profession.

Membership is confined to individuals, and the following categories of membership exist: founder members, honorary members, full members, associate members, affiliate members and student members. Membership criteria include both educational qualifications and experience in marketing research, and the nomination of at least two full members is required. SAMRA had 680 members in 1994. The association has its headquarters in Johannesburg, has four regional branches and is controlled by a council supported by standing and ad hoc committees. Since its inception SAMRA has tried to actualise its aims through a code of conduct and by education and training.

4.1.1.2 Code of conduct

One of the most important measures for ensuring that in practice marketing research conforms with recognised scientific and moral standards was a code of conduct drawn up as early as 1964, which was accepted and made obligatory for members. The code of conduct has been revised several times. It regulates in detail the rights and duties of the parties involved in marketing research, that is the buyer or client, the seller or practitioner, the source of information or respondent, the reader of the research report, and the general public. Members of AMRO (Association of Marketing Research Organisations) also abide by this code.

In particular the code includes stipulations on how to raise a charge of transgression of the code in a Standards Committee of the SAMRA council, how it should be considered, decided upon and how appeal against its findings is launched. The code also provides guidelines for the control of interviewing of children and the conduct of mystery shopping excursions.

In general the code's greatest value is its setting out of the requirements of recognised research procedures and the duties and rights of people concerned, thus providing a yardstick for evaluating research activities. Whereas in the early years research reports concentrated on findings, the new code of conduct prescribes more particulars on the universe, method of sampling, fieldwork and degree of reliability of the results. To the extent that these prescriptions are met, they will considerably enhance the credibility of research reports. SAMRA's requirements for report writing are outlined in chapter 18.

4.1.1.3 Training

Training is a most important instrument, if not the most important, for raising the standard of a profession. Here we are speaking of training in its broadest sense: not only through formal training programmes but also through the exchange of ideas by way of seminars, individual lectures, conferences, publications, etc.

Since its inception SAMRA has regarded training in this broad sense as one of its main tasks. During the year seminars, lectures and luncheon sessions, sometimes in association with other organisations, are arranged. The major training event is the annual convention.

In 1993, after an extensive investigation and the establishment of an education policy, SAMRA launched its one-year postgraduate diploma in marketing research.

4.1.2 Association of Marketing Research Organisations (AMRO)

Whereas SAMRA is an association of individual marketing researchers, AMRO is an organisation of commercial marketing research companies or, in the words of the statute, of 'independent companies incorporated in terms of the Companies Act and practising marketing research services; which means the regular collection and analysis of data'. The association was formally founded on 21 August 1970, and after some years of very little activity was revived in its current form in 1980. AMRO's constitution defines its mission as 'to encourage the use and quality of research'.

The major aims and objectives of AMRO are

☐ to set and ensure high quality standards for members of the organisation

☐ to work together with SAMRA and other bodies to establish professionalism in the industry

☐ to share relevant statistics among members

☐ to create a positive image in terms of standards for the organisation and to communicate the benefits of using member companies to users of research

☐ to promote education and training in marketing research, particularly for the historically disadvantaged

☐ to improve the knowledge of members of business practice and the external environment

☐ to encourage, develop and support research capacity, building at all levels amongst the historically disadvantaged.

Other activities of AMRO are the following:

☐ AMRO provides an annual bursary for the South African Marketing Research Associ-ation (SAMRA) postgraduate diploma course. AMRO also invites research users and other organisations to contribute to its bursary scheme.

☐ AMRO members have agreed to abide by a strict set of marketing research standards, which also incorporates the SAMRA code of conduct.

☐ AMRO has appointed an independent Director of Standards, who is an experienced lawyer. Any complaints about the work or conduct of an AMRO member can be sent to the AMRO Director of Standards. The Director of Standards will then investigate the complaint and provide a ruling. All costs will be borne by AMRO.

☐ AMRO has established an indemnity fund, which is held in trust by the executive of AMRO. The fund has been established to reimburse, in whole or in part, people who may suffer pecuniary loss as a result of failure of a member of AMRO to maintain the standards set by AMRO.

In the event that the AMRO Director of Standards rules in favour of a client, and the AMRO member fails to follow the recommendation of the Director of Standards, the other AMRO members will use the resources of the fund, together with their own good services, to provide the client, as far as possible, with satisfaction.

In 1994 ten companies were members of AMRO. According to an AMRO estimate the joint turnover of their ten members makes up roughly 80 % of the total turnover of all marketing research companies in South Africa.

4.2 Other organisations of importance to marketing research in South Africa

Besides the marketing research associations in South Africa which were discussed in the previous section, we are going to discuss briefly some organisations which influence mar-keting research in South Africa and may, as it were, constitute an environmental scenario of marketing research. They are the Bureau of Market Research (BMR), the Institute of Marketing Management (IMM), the South African Society of Marketers (SASM), the As-sociation of Advertising Agencies (AAA) and the South African Advertising Research Foundation (SAARF).

4.2.1 Bureau of Market Research (BMR)

Founded as a research institute of the University of South Africa in 1960, the BMR is a combined research and training institution for commercial and industrial firms, banking institutions, marketing boards, cooperatives, advertising agencies, commercial marketing research companies, government departments and the like. Membership of all divisions stood at 606 in 1994.

Projects committees select research projects and monitor their progress in eight research divisions.*

The results are published in the form of research reports. At the end of 1994 the number of published reports stood at 274. Being available to members and non-members these reports benefit the marketing community and the general public. Commissioned research (totalling 430 projects at the end of 1994) is also undertaken and with the permission of the client the results are published in full or in part. Specialised library and statistical information services are maintained and marketing, research and statistical communiqués are published occasionally. Training in marketing research is promoted through seminars, and courses in marketing research are taught on behalf on Unisa's Department of Business Management, which offers a postgraduate Diploma in Marketing Management with marketing research as a compulsory subject. The BMR further presents, in collaboration with Unisa's Department of Business Management, a Certificate Programme in Marketing and Marketing Research for students without a degree.

4.2.2 Institute of Marketing Management (IMM)

The Institute of Marketing Management is a non-profit, non-aligned professional organisation. Founded in 1949, the IMM is committed to upgrading and upholding the standard of marketing expertise in South Africa.

The mission of the IMM is to promote the importance of marketing in a free enterprise economy. Two of its main aims are to promote excellence and professionalism in the practice of marketing, and to provide and encourage education and training in all aspects of marketing.

The latter aims are achieved by the numerous diplomas and certificate courses that the IMM offers through various accredited tuition centres in southern Africa.

The most advanced of the IMM courses is the three-and-a-half year Diploma in Marketing Management, which comprises thirteen courses and emphasises marketing and marketing-related subjects.

To meet the growing need for an even higher level of marketing education, the IMM introduced the Diploma in Advanced Marketing. The admission requirements are stringent and the course is modelled along business school lines in lecture procedures, the intensity of study and the standard to be attained before the diploma is awarded. A dissertation is required to be presented on completion of the programme.

---

* See chapter 6 for a discussion of the research activities of this organisation.

The following certificate courses are offered by the IMM: Salesmanship Certificate, Sales Management Certificate, Retail Marketing Certificate, and the Certificate in Marketing Communication. The IMM also offers the IMM/AAA Diploma in Advertising Management.

The IMM's national office is situated in Johannesburg and it has regional offices in Cape Town and Durban. There are IMM branches in these cities as well as in East London, Port Elizabeth, Pietermaritzburg and Pretoria. There are IMM affiliate branches in Namibia, Botswana, Zimbabwe, Swaziland and Mauritius.

In order to upgrade the status and skills of the selling profession, the Professional Sales Association was established as a division of the IMM. This association has branches in Johannesburg, Bloemfontein and Port Elizabeth. The branches hold regular functions and workshops to which guest speakers are invited to give presentations on a variety of marketing- and sales-related topics.

The IMM is a member of the European Marketing Confederation and has a close relationship with the following overseas institutes: Hellenic Institute of Marketing, Canadian Institute of Marketing, Marketing Institute of Singapore, Australian Marketing Institute, Japan Marketing Association, Chartered Institute of Marketing (Britain), Hong Kong Institute of Marketing, Institute of Marketing and Management (India), and Cyprus Institute of Marketing.

The IMM recently increased its activities in the training arena, offering companies tailor-made courses and specific training programmes. The IMM will also evaluate and accredit companies' own training courses. The IMM is broadening its role in providing education and training to students and marketers in neighbouring countries.

4.2.3 Association of Marketers (ASOM) (previously South African Society of Marketers)

Founded in 1951 as the Society of Advertisers, this society changed its name to the South African Society of Marketers in 1977 and to the Association of Marketers in 1986. Its main aim is to represent the interests of advertisers vis-à-vis the advertising industry, the media and the government. Its change of name reflects a broader perspective of this task, namely to act as a mouthpiece of the free market system and promote the marketers' interests and their inherent right to use advertising as a marketing instrument. Membership is corporate and consists of most of the major marketing companies (158 in 1994) who are responsible for 82 % of the total expenditure on advertising in South Africa. The association has four regional branches, with headquarters in Johannesburg.

Advancement of the association's aims is assured by branch meetings, seminars and the presentation of special awards. Each year the association confers Loerie Awards for the best advertising in the print and broadcast media. The Protea Award, which is the Association of Marketers' premier award, is presented annually to an individual who has made an outstanding personal and public contribution to the furtherance of the advertising/marketing industry in South Africa.

The association introduced the first two national readership surveys in South Africa (see section 4.2.5). It founded the South African Advertising Research Foundation (SAARF) and was responsible for introducing the All Media and Products Survey (AMPS), peoplemeters for television research and radio diaries within SAARF. The association was involved in the founding of the Advertising Standards Authority and the Radio Research Advisory Committee. The association takes action wherever measures restricting advertising and marketing are envisaged. Its function is clearly expressed in its mission statement: 'To represent, protect and promote the interests of marketers to assure a market-place conducive to the principle of entrepreneurship and free enterprise without unnecessary restrictive regulation. To address, through the process of liaison or any other means, all issues which violate, oppose or threaten these principles.'

The association was instrumental in setting up marketing chairs at the universities of the Witwatersrand and Stellenbosch in order to introduce a professional marketing degree and postgraduate qualifications.

Internationally the association is affiliated to 28 similar organisations via the World Federation of Advertisers.

4.2.4 Association of Advertising Agencies (AAA)

Thirty-two advertising agencies were members of the AAA in October 1994. In general they represent the bigger agencies, as evidenced by their turnover which represents about 80 % of the total agency turnover in South Africa.

The AAA is a voluntary professional organisation of agencies which aims at

☐ representing and promoting the interests of advertising practitioners

☐ providing for training and development of the advertising industry at large

☐ representing, liaising and/or negotiating with industry-related bodies such as AMRO, the ASA, ASOM and media groups

☐ representing, liaising and/or negotiating with government and influence groups which may impact upon the advertising business

☐ considering and promoting all possible avenues to advance the advertising industry and the role of advertising in society to be developed into plans for execution.

Of special importance is the AAA School of Advertising, which provides practical training commensurate with the needs of the advertising industry and the communications business at large. It provides two diploma courses in advertising with specialisation in options such as media management, client services and copywriting, and two diploma courses in advertising art and graphic design. The AAA School offers these courses at its two campuses in Johannesburg and Cape Town. Apart from the diploma courses, part-time modular courses in strategic planning, marketing research, international advertising, publishing, etc are also offered in cooperation with other bodies.

4.2.5 South African Advertising Research Foundation (SAARF)

Reliable information on the media which carry and disseminate advertising messages is among the prerequisites for effective advertising. Although the Audit Bureau of Circulations has been publishing circulation figures of newspapers and magazines since 1947, these figures are only the first step towards effective choice of media. Even more important are reliable figures on the number of persons who read (readership data), listen to (listenership data) and view (viewership data) the various media.

In 1948 SA Research Services, an affiliate of Davenport and Meyer, undertook the first readership and radio-listenership survey, and in 1951 the SABC introduced their radio-listenership surveys. The first national readership survey (which included some product data) was only conducted in 1962, and the second in 1968 (at the instigation of the South African Society of Marketers). Eventually in 1972–73 a comprehensive readership survey was launched, which included a wide variety of product data. But there were big gaps in the information: rural blacks and coloureds were not included in the readership surveys and the radio-listenership surveys did not cover any product data.

To fill these gaps and to make comprehensive comparative and reliable media data available the South African Society of Marketers (now the Association of Marketers (ASOM)), whose members accounted for approximately 80 % of the total national advertising expenditure, initiated the establishment of SAARF in 1973 with the idea of carrying out, promoting or encouraging multimedia and multiproduct surveys and of enhancing the professional standards and methods of advertising and marketing research. SAARF was established as a company and was composed of ASOM as a foundation member, and the AAA, SABC, NPU, Cinemark and the Outdoor Advertising Association of South Africa as founder members.

These organisations and the National Association of Broadcasters are all represented on the board of directors. SAARF is financed by a levy of 0,5 % on media fees. Roughly 90 % of the funds accruing from this system go towards financing the All Media and Products Survey (AMPS), which has been in existence since 1975, two annual AMPS Radio Diary Surveys, and the AMPS Meter system to measure TV audiences. SAARF itself does not undertake AMPS; the surveys are awarded on the basis of open tender.

The AMPS family of surveys is certainly the most comprehensive and costly annual survey undertaken in South Africa today. SAARF monitors and validates the surveys and uses brochures, slides, video programmes and seminars to explain and encourage the use of the results. Besides AMPS, SAARF is involved in a variety of other studies, such as a Child Study, Product Definition Study, Age of Copy Survey, Sample Design and Response Rates, and Validation of Audience Levels for Electronic Media, which are carried out on its instructions by commercial research institutions.

SAARF's newsletter, first published in 1975, is distributed to 2 400 persons or bodies, informing them of the foundation's activities and research results. In the sphere of education SAARF is involved in various committees in conjunction with member organisations.

4.3 International associations

At international level there are many different marketing and/or marketing research associations, but only those in which South African marketing researchers take a keen interest will be mentioned here.

First, there is the American Marketing Association (AMA) with its approximately 42 000 members, 3 000 of whom are in countries outside the USA including South Africa. South African marketing researchers participate in the AMA's annual general and special conferences. The lectures and discussions that take place on these occasions are published as conference proceedings. The AMA also publishes books and nine periodicals in all, of which *Journal of Marketing, Journal of Marketing Research, Marketing Education Review, Marketing Management Magazine, Marketing News* and a periodical called *Marketing Research: A Magazine of Management and Applications* are the most important.

In 1948 the European Society for Opinion and Marketing Research (ESOMAR) was founded in Europe and, with the rapid post-war development of marketing research in Western Europe, rose to equal prominence with the AMA at international level. Indeed, South African marketing researchers tend to liaise more closely with ESOMAR than with the AMA, especially when it comes to attending the annual conferences and seminars and special group sessions. Every other year the conferences are held in conjunction with the World Association for Public Opinion Research (WAPOR). Group sessions fall into two categories: technical aspects and special subjects. Membership of ESOMAR is restricted to individuals who have the same status, so that there is only one category of membership (except for some honorary members) comprising about 2 000 members.

ESOMAR publishes the papers read at its conferences and seminars. It also issues the quarterly *Marketing and Research Today* (formerly *European Research*) and a newsletter with domestic information for members. Of particular importance is ESOMAR's code of practice drawn up in 1948, which makes ESOMAR the first professional marketing association to compile a code of this kind. In 1981 it authorised an addition to its code, the International Code of Practice for the Publication of Public Opinion Poll Results, which is obligatory for ESOMAR members. National associations value ESOMAR's codes more particularly as a source of reference for drawing up their own codes of practice. Many of the guidelines incorporated in SAMRA's code of conduct (see above) are modelled on ESOMAR's prescriptions.

5 SUMMARY

The marketing function is an integral part of an organisation, and marketing research in support of the marketing function is undertaken formally or informally in almost all organisations. The reason is that marketing research plays a strategic role in most stages of the decision-making process. It is this strategic role that raises the question of where the marketing research function fits into the organisational structure of the organisation. There are no sure answers to this question because optimum positioning is dependent on the size and nature of the organisation. Roughly 60 % of the heads of marketing research divisions in manufacturing concerns report to top management.

A variety of factors, such as the size of the organisation, the scope and nature of its marketing research projects and its level of expertise, are taken into account in deciding whether to tackle a project internally or appoint an external consultant to do the job. Each of these choices has advantages and disadvantages which vary from one project to another.

There are two major marketing research associations in South Africa: the South African Marketing Research Association (SAMRA) which represents individual researchers, and the Association of Marketing Research Organisations (AMRO), an association of marketing research companies. Other South African organisations of note are the Bureau of Market Research (BMR) at Unisa, the Institute of Marketing Management (IMM), the Association of Marketers (ASOM), the Association of Advertising Agencies (AAA) and the South African Advertising Research Foundation (SAARF). Most of the marketing researchers in South Africa also liaise with the American Marketing Association (AMA) and the European Society for Opinion and Marketing Research (ESOMAR).

REFERENCES

Churchill, Gilbert A (Jr) 1992. *Basic marketing research*. Second edition. Fort Worth: The Dryden Press. (The Dryden Press Series in Marketing.)

Kinnear, Thomas C & Taylor, James R 1991. *Marketing research: an applied approach*. Fourth edition. New York: McGraw-Hill. (McGraw-Hill Series in Marketing.)

Martins, J H, Van Helden, M J & Nel, P A 1992. *Marketing research practice in manufacturing industry in South Africa, 1989*. Unisa, Bureau of Market Research. (Research Report no 183.)

Tull, Donald S & Hawkins, Del I 1990. *Marketing research: measurement and method: a text with cases*. Fifth edition. New York: Macmillan. (The Macmillan Series in Marketing.)

Ethics in marketing research

Chapter 3: T Oosthuizen

Ethics in marketing research

1 INTRODUCTION

Any business operates within a certain set of values to which all employees should, at least theoretically, adhere. In turn every individual adheres to his own set of values. When conflict occurs between the value systems of an individual and the company he works for, or is contracted to, it creates tension. Conflict is a daily occurrence, as the goals of individuals and business vary and often cause friction. Ethics often underlie this tension, as they define the frames of reference of the various individuals involved in the research process.

Ethics are a normal part of business practice, and in marketing research are a much-disputed issue today. In fact, conflict between the interests of the consumer (for example his privacy) and big business is jeopardising the very future of marketing research.

2 WHAT ARE ETHICS IN MARKETING RESEARCH?

Ethics deal with the development of moral standards that can be applied to situations in which there can be actual or potential harm to an individual or a group (Churchill 1992:68). Kinnear and Taylor (1991:51) add that the conflict between having to do something and the fact that in such practice certain activities may be inappropriate is a question of ethics.

Choosing a research technique involves an implicit judgement about the ethics of the procedure (Churchill 1992:57). Researchers often ignore ethical problems because they are difficult and real, and growing. Many people take the view that if something is legal, it is ethical. There are many instances, however, of ethical issues conflicting with legal issues (for example abortions may be legal in some countries, yet many people have ethical objections to them). Although the practice of observing consumers who have given their consent may be legal, it may still not be ethical. Ethics are of particular concern to research practitioners because their very profession is based on the principle of consumer/public cooperation. Churchill (1992:58) further distinguishes between the researcher's awareness of an ethical dilemma and his philosophical value systems. These two factors jointly constitute the researcher's ethical framework and thus his ultimate measure of ethical behaviour.

Taylor (1975:1) defines ethics as 'inquiry into the nature and grounds of morality'. Here morality means moral judgements, standards, and rules of conduct. All parties in the research process have their own sets of judgements, standards and rules of conduct. These set the backdrop for the attitudes, beliefs and behaviour of the parties involved in the research process.

Although marketing research, as indeed all social research, is part of the scientific method, it is still constituted within the framework of a given philosophical school of thought. Meaning is created within this context.

Churchill (1992:59) distinguishes between two major philosophical foundations for ethics: deontology and teleology. Whereas deontology analyses the impact of any action on the rights of the consumer, the client and the researcher, teleology analyses the benefits realised from such action for these three parties.

3 THE PARTIES INVOLVED IN THE RESEARCH PROCESS

There are at least three, often four, sets of people involved in the research process. They are: the researcher or research supplier, who may be an outside contractor or an in-house research practitioner; the respondent, or person being surveyed in the instance of research among consumers; and the research user. In some instances intermediaries are also involved, such as advertising agencies who commission research on behalf of their clients.

In all these instances parties operate from within their own macro and micro frames of reference. These frames of reference determine the definition of the research or marketing problem, the proposed research methodology, the proposed analytical tool(s) used in the analysis of the raw data, and finally, the interpretation and presentation of the findings, looking to marketing decisions being taken. In all five of these steps, decisions will be taken dependent upon the knowledge, the experience, the frames of reference, the existing attitudes and beliefs, and the vested interests of all the parties involved.

In figure 3.1 we outline a systematic analysis of the interaction of rights and obligations as defined by Zikmund (1989:764).

In any society, certain rights and obligations are associated with a given role (that is as a researcher and as a respondent). If there are conflicting perspectives about the behaviour that is expected, ethical problems will occur. Whereas researchers believe they have a right to ask questions, respondents believe they have a right to privacy.

Figure 3.1 Interaction of rights and obligations in marketing research

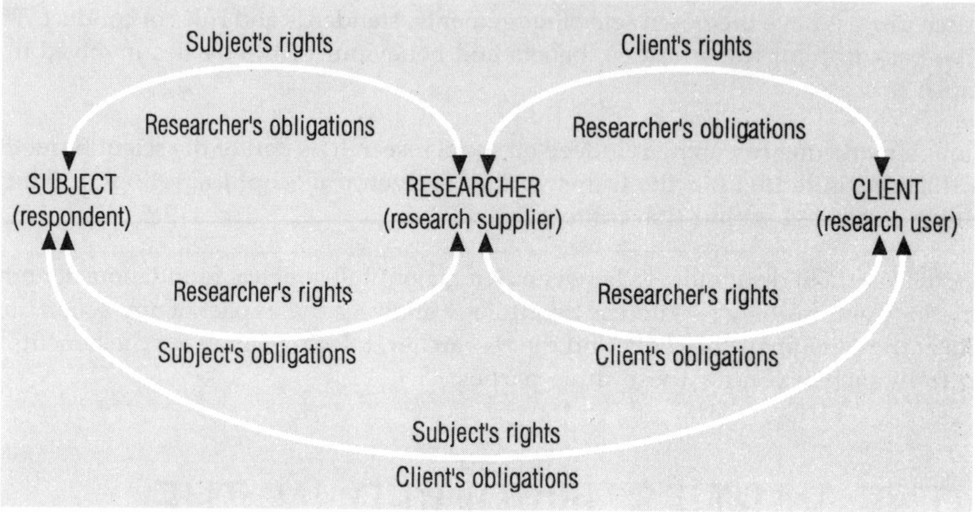

Subject's rights

Client's rights

Researcher's obligations

Researcher's obligations

SUBJECT
(respondent)

RESEARCHER
(research supplier)

CLIENT
(research user)

Researcher's rights

Researcher's rights

Subject's obligations

Client's obligations

Subject's rights

Client's obligations

Source: Adapted from Zikmund (1989:764).

3.1 The researcher or research supplier

The researcher is first and foremost a human being with his own subjective mindset and frame of reference. The degree to which he has sound theoretical research knowledge and encompassing experience will determine his competency as a practitioner and have a significant impact on the most appropriate research design to resolve a particular problem. Research design should always be customised, and once a practitioner becomes technique driven (locked into a given set of techniques or a given technique), he may lose his ability to add value as a provider of objective solutions.

Several issues are important for a research practitioner:

3.1.1 Internal validity: a question of methodology

The practitioner must ensure that the chosen research methodologies/instruments are able to measure what they set out to measure. In other words, he has to ensure that he uses the most appropriate methodology to resolve the key research questions.

3.1.2 External validity: a question of sampling

The practitioner must ensure that, within the confines of the chosen sample, the findings are representative of the universe from which the sample was drawn. External validity is a prerequisite for any research as, after all, the purpose of research is to reduce uncertainty in real-life decisions. A sample has to represent the real world as closely as possible.

3.1.3 Reliability and objectivity: a question of repeatability and transparency

Transparency of research methodology is a prerequisite for ethical research practice. Unless a researcher is clear about all the steps taken and the techniques used, methodologically and statistically, he cannot talk about objective and transparent research. Reliability of research implies that another researcher would be able to replicate the research process exactly, and that the findings should theoretically be the same within the confines of statistical variance.

3.1.4 Research as a Social Science: beauty is in the eye of the beholder

All science, by its very nature, is an interpretation of the world by a certain individual. Marketing research is part of the scientific method and permits empirical verification of the relationships between sets of variables. As a social science the interpretation of the world, and therefore the conduct of marketing research, is infinitely varied as it depends on the person conducting the research – his frame of reference, knowledge, experience and the people with whom he interacts. It is therefore impossible to assume that all researchers will approach a research or marketing problem in the same way, or interpret results in the same way; as, for example, behaviourism and phenomenology are two different, not right and wrong, ways of interpreting the world. The more holistic the scientific understanding and background of a researcher, the more he will apply a multiple-paradigm understanding of a research and marketing problem. The more a researcher becomes locked into a particular kind of research as the best or the ultimate (that is semiology, survey research), the less able he will be to holistically and objectively address a problem.

3.2 The respondent: the source of research output

Without consumers, or informants, there would be no marketing research. Therefore, much of the obligation of ethical research focuses on them. Key aspects include (SAMRA 1994) the following:

☐ All assurances given to an informant to secure cooperation in the research should be honoured.

☐ The research should be endorsed by a reputable research practitioner/supplier and an official regulatory body such as the Southern African Marketing Research Association (SAMRA).

☐ The information gained through marketing research should not be used to compile sales lists, databanks and credit ratings, or to conduct industrial espionage – in fact, anything other than legitimate marketing research.

☐ The identity of informants should not be revealed to anyone who is not directly involved with the conduct of the research project.

☐ The informant must have the right to withdraw from the interview at any time during the interview.

☐ The informants should be told when the research is about sensitive topics and be given the option of refusing to answer any of the questions.

☐ The informant should be given adequate reasons for the survey being undertaken.

☐ Informants must be told when recording equipment is being used, or when they are being observed.

3.3 The research user: the recipient of research output

The research user may be divorced from the scientific method, relatively ignorant of and indifferent towards it, and have strong views about what decision he would like to take. Sometimes the research will either support it subtly, or contradict it. Research which reflects on the research user's own performance (that is service quality research, advertising performance tracking) can become highly personalised and compromising. Then it is vital to retain the utmost objectivity in assessing the research findings dispassionately and independently before discussing the decision options available, including those supported by the research user(s). Often different users may internally support different viewpoints, and then the onus is on the research practitioner to be utterly honest, professional and objective in his methodology, analysis, interpretation and recommendations. Sometimes a roundtable discussion about the options or the research findings puts the options clearly on the table and gets all the parties involved to debate the issues, look at the research objectively and take the most appropriate course of action.

A key responsibility of a research user is to remain objective and not compromise the researcher subtly or directly. This is one of the core problem areas for researchers in companies.

3.4 The intermediaries: outside specialists with their own vested interests

Intermediaries are outside parties such as advertising agencies and management consultants. They are often involved in the research outcome, either by being affected by it directly (for example advertising pre-testing) or by having vested interests (supporting actions which may directly or indirectly affect their income). Intermediaries may or may not be research professionals themselves – often they will not be. However, as a result of their credibility networks and support within research user companies, they can have a dramatic impact on whether and how the research is used.

4 THE KINDS OF ETHICAL PROBLEMS THE RESEARCHER FACES

According to Bogart (1969:3) the researcher experiences conflict between his professional ethos (his chosen field of expertise and resultant discipline) and business achievement (advancement of his career from a specialist to a line function, should he choose or have the option to do so). His life is a progression of decisions about means and ends. If research results come into conflict with company management the researcher will be compromised and may be forced to choose between his professional integrity and his own short-term popularity and career advancement. Bogart (1969:3) outlines the researcher's problem as follows:

☐ As a professional, the researcher is preoccupied with techniques and therefore aspires to the goals of a craftsman.

☐ A professional researcher may think of himself as a scientist pursuing truth.

☐ He would like to advance his own career by enhancing the status of the research function within his organisation and ultimately even by being promoted beyond the staff function of research.

☐ As a businessman, his knowledge base equips him better than most for a broad understanding of the business.

Often this conflict involves ethics.

A survey by Hunt, Lawrence and Wilcox (1984:312) identifies the areas below as key ethical problems.

4.1 Research integrity: deliberate bias

Bias includes deliberately withholding information, falsifying figures, altering research results, misusing statistics, ignoring pertinent data, compromising the design of a research project, and misinterpreting the results of a research project with the objective of supporting a predetermined personal or corporate point of view.

4.2 Confidentiality: the difference between 'the research shows' and 'from previous research we know'

Researchers often work with highly confidential information and have to move between different functions within the same organisation without breaching confidentiality. When a research supplier works for more than one client or company, he acts, at least partly, on the knowledge he already has of a given industry. It can become very difficult to decide where to draw the line between experience gained from previous pieces of research – which by implication is what a research buyer buys – and confidential information about a category, some of which has been gained from previous proprietary research. In an advertising agency this is a particularly difficult ethical dilemma: where does 'background knowledge' stop and client confidentiality start?

4.3 Balancing the interests

Balancing the interests of self against the interests of other parties and balancing the interests of the company against the interests of other parties can be a major problem. These issues range from being forced by senior management to change research results to using the researcher as an objective specialist to 'dream up' answers to unresearched questions. Both courses of action jeopardise research integrity.

5 WAYS TO INHIBIT UNETHICAL BEHAVIOUR

The most important determinant of ethical behaviour has to be the scientific and professional foundation of the researcher and his resultant integrity – not wanting to jeopardise his status and integrity by actions which are explicitly subjective or dishonest. Beyond that, according to Hunt *et al* (1984), there are a number of outside determinants:

5.1 Codes of ethics

Each marketing research industry has a code of ethics which outlines the obligations of the various parties involved in the research process. These are always voluntary codes to which a researcher chooses to adhere. Non-adherence can lead to a researcher being penalised or, in extreme cases, expelled from a professional research body. Unfortunately, in most instances violations are difficult to identify or assess, and even gross violations will not prevent a researcher from practising and therefore embarking on more unethical behaviour. The codes therefore have no real effect beyond sanctioning by colleagues.

5.2 Top management guiding research

The leadership ethics of a research supplier or a client company determine whether unethical behaviour is condemned. If the leadership is highly ethical, unethical research practices will not be acceptable. This will aid a researcher in his ability to remain objective and truthful.

In an article Ossip (1985:11) claims from his own experience that:

> (1) good management wants objectivity and to deal with controversy; (2) the fortunes of a Marketing Research Department group are really tied in to the bottom-line performance of a total company, and not to being popular; (3) if you get agreement on your role you can get personal acceptance while promulgating unpopular results; and (4) you can gain respect and trust if you own up to mistakes, correct them, learn from them.

The very level at which research is used and debated in an organisation will be a vital determinant of ethical behaviour. The more seriously research is considered within an organisation, the more likely it is to be used and researchers will be expected to be honest brokers in taking sounder, fact-based decisions – and, by implication, the more likely that the researcher will be represented at a very senior executive level. If he finds that research is continuously being compromised, a researcher may have to leave a company to retain his integrity.

5.3 The researcher as a co-decision maker

If a researcher is made a vital component of the decision-making process, he has to retain his objective and professional integrity, while remaining an independent facilitator. Researchers cannot simply be analysts. This demands a different level of thinking, and also puts them in jeopardy – but it retains the integrity of research.

5.4 In-house researchers versus independents

Although in-house researchers and independents have their own strengths and weaknesses, it is useful to have them cooperate in critical research projects. An in-house researcher can add value because he knows the business, the marketing problem and the people intimately, can add value to the understanding of the research in organisational terms, and can aid the implementation of findings. An outside researcher can add objectivity, independence and greater specialist focus, as well as knowledge and experience gained from other research projects, in the same way that both qualitative and quantitative research have their distinctive roles in the process of research, using multiple techniques to understand a problem better. Such cooperation can aid ethical behaviour and add value to the final outcome of the research process.

5.5 Qualitative research such as in-depth interviews, projective techniques and semiology

In areas of research (that is semiology) in which no respondents are involved, or interpretations, by their very nature, are more subjective and specialist (for example in-depth interviews and projective techniques), a researcher needs to take special care not to bias or misinterpret results. Often, using an outside research company to co-interpret part of the research, or even replicate a subsection of it, can overcome this dilemma.

5.6 Multiple indicators are better than single indicators

Different research techniques provide different angles, aiding a more detailed, in-depth understanding of a problem. In fact, in a landmark article Van Leent (1965) investigated assigning a breadth, height and depth dimension to every single research problem, suggesting a multiple methodological solution to most research. By looking at a problem from multiple angles, one minimises the likelihood of bias.

6 CORE FOCUS AREAS IN THE SAMRA CODE OF CONDUCT

The SAMRA code of conduct covers the following areas:

☐ Section D: What a research report should contain.

☐ Section E: What a research user (client) can expect from a research practitioner in terms of research specifications, confidentiality, description of how the field work was done, etc.

☐ Section F: Safeguards for anonymity and confidentiality of informants/respondents.

☐ Section G: What a practitioner may expect from a brief, answering proposals, storage of records and results, publishing findings, interviewing children and testing lawful products.

☐ Section H: Confidence of the general public in market research.

☐ Section I: How complaints of an ethical nature are to be dealt with.

7 SUMMARY

Every day the researcher faces the philosophical issue of retaining his professional integrity, at the same time managing his relationships with his peers and colleagues, and his research users. This can only be done if a researcher remains knowledgeable about his chosen field of expertise, continuously reads and consults widely, and customises research solutions as a matter of course. A researcher has to respect his obligations to his respondents. When he has no respondents, as in semiology, he has to be truly aware of issues such as internal and external validity and reliability. A researcher has to report openly and objectively, against prevailing attitudes if that becomes necessary.

A research user has to respect the status and integrity of research, and leave the researcher to be the honest, non-partisan broker he is supposed to be.

The overall attitude of management and adherence to professional codes of ethics can aid the integrity of research.

REFERENCES

Akoah, I P & Riordan, E A 1989. Judgements of marketing professionals about ethical issues in marketing research: a replication and explanation. *Journal of Marketing Research*, XXVI:112–120.

Bogart, L 1969. *Current controversies in marketing research*. Chicago: Markham Publishing Company.

Churchill, Gilbert A (Jr) 1992. *Basic marketing research*. Second edition. Fort Worth: The Dryden Press. (The Dryden Series in Management.)

Dilton, W R, Madden, T J & Firtle, N H C 1990. *Marketing research in a marketing environment*. Homewood: Irwin.

Ferber, R 1974. *Handbook of marketing research*. New York: McGraw-Hill.

Ferrell, O C & Skinner, S J 1988. Ethical behaviour and bureaucratic structure in marketing research organisations. *Journal of Marketing Research*, XXV.

Hunt, S D, Lawrence, B C & Wilcox, J B 1984. Ethical problems of marketing researchers. *Journal of Marketing Research*, XXI:312.

Kinnear, Thomas C & Taylor, James R 1991. *Marketing research: an applied approach*. Fourth edition. New York: McGraw-Hill. (McGraw-Hill Series in Marketing.)

Ossip, A 1985. Ethics – everyday choices in marketing research. *Journal of Advertising Research*, 25:RC10–RC12.

SAMRA Yearbook; 1993/94, Johannesburg.

Southern African Marketing Research Association *see* SAMRA.

Van Leent, J A A 1965. *Sociale psychologie in drie dimensies*. Utrecht: Aula.

Zikmund, William G 1989. *Business research methods*. Third edition. Chicago: The Dryden Press. (The Dryden Series in Management.)

Interface between the economy and the market

Chapter 4: J H Martins

(This chapter is partly based on chapter 1 'The South African market' by F E Rädel and P A Nel in Nel *et al* 1988.)

Interface between the economy and the market

1 INTRODUCTION

It is a truism that a marketing researcher should be familiar with the market in which he operates. How else can he select and apply the appropriate research tools? Although the basic methods of marketing research are universal, irrespective of the market environment, their application and adaptation vary from country to country. This applies particularly to South Africa where certain basic methods and techniques have to be adapted to its unique population structure. For instance, the traditional grouping of Asians, blacks, coloureds and whites is not primarily colour oriented. There are cogent demographic and economic reasons as well, which will remain valid for some time to come. A general knowledge of the structure of the South African market is indispensable if the specific problems, approaches and techniques which will be discussed in this book are to be fully understood. For this reason a broad overview of the South African market and its structure will be presented.

An overall picture of a country's market generally reveals little if anything about the market of the individual firm. Nevertheless each firm is embedded in the national and international economy, and an assessment of the size of an entire market and its structure is a valuable basis for evaluating a firm's standing and performance in the general market situation.

After defining the somewhat ambiguous term 'market' we shall give an overview of the total South African market and its major segments in this chapter.

2 WHAT IS A MARKET?

As the term 'market' has more than one meaning we should be quite clear about what is meant by it in a specific context. In its oldest sense the word 'market' denotes a place where suppliers and buyers meet to exchange goods. Many such markets exist to the present day in the form of fruit and vegetable markets, fairs and fleamarkets, and market places in towns and cities.

In economic theory a market denotes a mechanism whereby supply and demand are regulated and prices are fixed. Typical of this type of market is a stock exchange, although its atmosphere and functioning – as its visitors will affirm – bear little resemblance to what is generally associated with a market. Since a market in this sense is the typical mechanism in Western countries, we refer to market economies as opposed to socialist economies where supplies and prices are controlled by planning authorities.

Finally, when we refer to a car market, a property market, and so on, we actually mean aggregate demand. Marketing research is generally concerned with *aggregate* demand. A typical research project would be to establish a pharmaceutical firm's share of the toothpaste market. If the firm's competitors are included in the brief, the research will involve both the demand and the supply side of the toothpaste market.

Generally, however, the emphasis in marketing research practice is on demand. In this chapter the term market will denote aggregate demand.

Aggregate demand can be expressed in different units of measurement. The consumer market, for instance, can be expressed in terms of the number of people or households, and the industrial market in terms of the number of establishments, persons employed, etc. As some people consume more than others and some industrial establishments produce more than others, the expression of consumption or production in monetary terms would be more precise. Also, monetary value is a common denominator which allows the measurement of items of different kinds such as food and clothing on the same scale. In marketing research heterogeneous items are usually expressed in monetary terms, except when other units are specified, such as persons per household, employees per establishment and so forth. In this chapter the South African market is expressed mainly in monetary terms.

3 SOUTH AFRICA IN THE WORLD ECONOMY

The latest *World development report* (World Bank 1994) classifies economies as low income, middle income (subdivided into lower-middle and upper-middle), or high income on the basis of their gross national product (GNP) per capita. Of the 132 countries classified in the report Mozambique is the poorest with a per capita income of US $60 in 1992. South Africa is classed as upper-middle income with a per capita income of $2 670. Eighty-eight countries have a lower GNP per capita figure than South Africa and 43 a higher. Switzerland's income per capita, $36 080, is the highest. The average for 132 countries is $4 280.

The gross domestic product (GDP) is a measure of the total output of goods and services for final use produced by the residents and non-residents of a country, regardless of the allocation to domestic and foreign claims. It is also a measure of the total demand for goods and services in a country. Table 4.1 shows that in 1992 the GDP in South Africa was $103 651 million, that is 1,8 % of the USA's GDP of $5 920 199 million. Only 27 of the 132 countries in the World Bank report have a higher GDP than South Africa.

Table 4.1 Gross domestic product of selected countries, 1992

Country	GDP US$ million	% of world total
1 United States	5 920 199	25,7
2 Japan	3 670 979	15,9
3 Germany	1 789 261	7,8
4 France	1 319 883	5,7
5 Italy	1 222 962	5,3
6 United Kingdom	903 126	3,9
7 Spain	574 844	2,5
8 China	506 075	2,2
9 Canada	493 602	2,1
10 Russian Federation	387 476	1,7
11 Brazil	360 405	1,6
12 Mexico	329 011	1,4
13 Netherlands	320 290	1,4
14 Korea Republic	296 136	1,3
15 Australia	294 760	1,3
16 Switzerland	241 406	1,0
17 Argentina	228 779	1,0
18 Sweden	220 834	1,0
19 Belgium	218 836	1,0
20 India	214 598	0,9
21 Austria	185 235	0,8
22 Indonesia	126 364	0,5
23 Denmark	123 546	0,5
24 Norway	112 906	0,5
25 Saudi Arabia	111 343	0,5
26 Thailand	110 337	0,5
27 Iran Islamic Republic	110 258	0,5
28 South Africa	103 651	0,4
29 Other 104 countries	2 563 458	11,1
Total — 132 countries	**23 060 560**	**100,0**

Source: World Bank (1994:166–167).

The South African Customs Union (comprising South Africa, Lesotho, Namibia, Botswana and Swaziland) exported an estimated 90 021 million rands' worth of merchandise and services and imported 79 542 million rands' worth of merchandise while payments for services amounted to R31 310 million in 1994 (SA Department of Finance [S a]:239–240). The four principal exports were base metals and articles of base metal (R11 853,0 million), precious or semi-precious stones and similar items (R10 213,3 million), mineral products (R7 712,4 million) and products of the chemical and allied industries (R4 756,8 million).

The four principal imports were machinery and mechanical appliances, electrical equipment, parts thereof, sound recorders and reproducers, television image and sound recorders and reproducers, and parts and accessories of such articles (R24 804,5 million); vehicles, aircraft, vessels and associated transport equipment (R11 283,6 million); products of the chemical or allied industries (R8 291,7 million); and articles of stone, plaster, cement, asbestos, mica or similar materials, ceramic products, glass and glassware (R4 884,8 million). The major export countries were Switzerland (R6 071,8 million), the United Kingdom (R5 939,4 million), the USA (R4 378,0 million), Japan (R4 158,3 million) and Germany (R3 706,6 million). South Africa imported mainly from Germany (R12 985,5 million), the USA (R12 523,5 million), the UK (R8 960,8 million) and Japan (R7 893,5 million).

4 THE SOUTH AFRICAN MARKET

A national market is composed of a *consumer market* and an *industrial market*. A consumer market represents demand for products (goods) and services for final consumption, whereas an industrial market represents demand for products and services used in the creation of further products and services. The consumer market represents expenditure on products and services by private persons and non-profit institutions. The industrial market consists of four components: the first two are gross domestic fixed investment, which is self-explanatory, and change in inventories, which denotes materials and supplies in stock for use in the production process. An increase in inventory levels in a particular period signifies either a demand for such materials and supplies or a deceleration in economic activities. In the latter situation stocks accumulate without there being a greater demand for such materials and supplies. The opposite is true for a decrease in inventory levels. The third component is the consumption expenditure of general government which includes supplies used and salaries and wages paid by government departments/agencies.

Intermediate demand, the fourth component of the industrial market, requires further explanation. In economic theory the final goal of all economic activity is consumption. In the modern economy, characterised as it is by a division of labour, products pass through a series of processes before the consumption stage is reached. The cereals on our breakfast tables are processed in factories whose raw materials are supplied by agriculture, which in turn requires machinery and implements produced by manufacturers who, in their turn, are dependent on the mining of iron and other ores. The packaging of the cereals is supplied by paper manufacturers whose raw materials come from pulp mills which depend on sawmills and, in the final instance, on forestry. In this chain, which is termed roundabout production, each link is a market for the link that precedes it. All the markets in the chain are intermediate markets.

The sum of the consumer and industrial markets is termed the *potential domestic market* for South African producers. This market includes imports which are a potential market for South African producers by way of import substitution. Without imports the potential domestic market becomes the *actual domestic market* for South African producers. As some South African goods are also produced for markets abroad, exports are added to the actual domestic market to arrive at the total actual market for South African producers. This is the size of the market that is supplied by South African producers.

The total South African market and the two broad subdivisions are presented in table 4.2. The structure of the South African market is brought out more clearly in figure 4.1. Figure 4.1 shows that the industrial market represents roughly 78 % of the total market demand and the consumer market 22 %.

In the industrial market intermediate demand represented by far the largest share (83,0 %), followed by consumption expenditure by general government (9,6 %) and gross domestic fixed investment (7,1 %).

Table 4.2 Size and composition of the South African market, 1994

Consumer market	R million
Private consumption expenditure	230 630
Industrial market	827 033
Intermediate demand	686 742
Gross domestic fixed investment	58 837
Consumption expenditure by general government	79 047
Change in inventories	2 407
Potential domestic market for South African producers	1 057 663
Less imports	76 155
Actual domestic market for South African producers	981 508
Plus exports (including re-exports)	91 013
Total market for South African producers	**1 072 521**

Source: South African Reserve Bank (1995:S–94), SA Central Statistical Service 1995.

5 SEGMENTS OF THE SOUTH AFRICAN MARKET

Having discussed the macrostructure of the South African market we now deal with its constituent parts or *segments*. A market can be divided into many different parts or segments, but here the discussion will be confined to the segments that are of particular interest to marketers and for which statistics are available. In section 4 we saw that the total market comprises the consumer market and the industrial market. In the sections that follow we shall discuss relevant segments of the consumer and industrial markets.

Figure 4.1 Structure of the potential domestic market, 1994

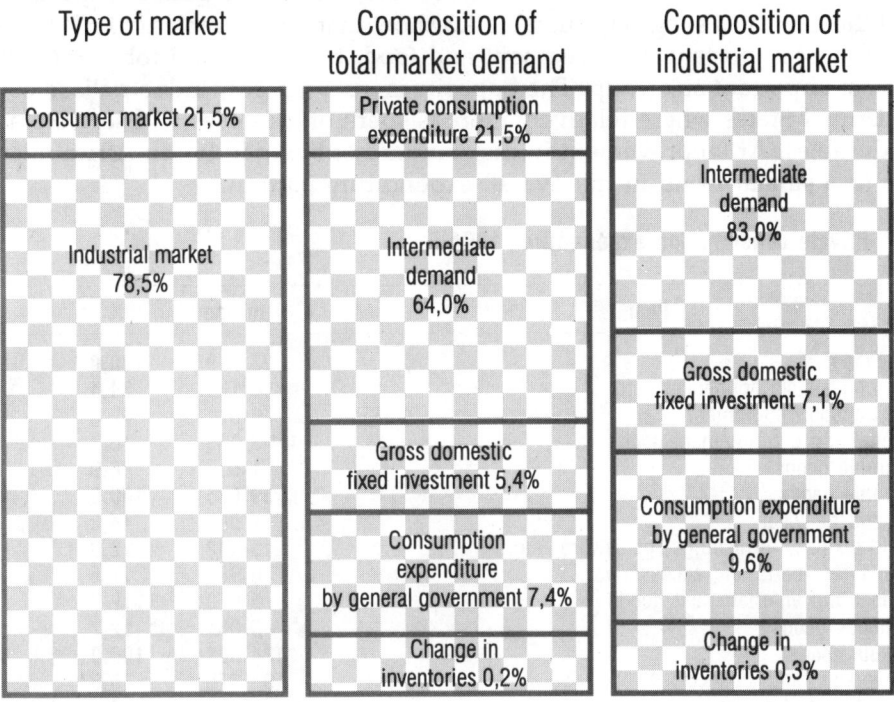

Source: SA Central Statistical Service 1995.

5.1 The consumer market

The consumer market represents *private consumption expenditure,* that is expenditure on products and services by private households and non-profit institutions. In the following sections the consumer market will be divided into segments by showing, first, the items purchased by the total population. Having done this we shall discuss the population which represents the consumer units in the consumer market. As there are marked differences in income per capita between population groups, and population merely gives us a broad indication of the consumer market, we shall turn our attention at this stage to a discussion of the personal income of the respective population groups. Lastly, the differences in the expenditure patterns of the population groups will be distinguished and household expenditure will be analysed by broad geographic area.

5.1.1 Components of private consumption expenditure

From the marketing perspective it is important to know how income is spent. In South Africa private consumption expenditure statistics are subdivided into four main groups (durables, semi-durables, non-durables and services) and 21 subgroups. The amount and shares of the main and subgroups in table 4.3 show that non-durables (48,6 %) constitute by far the most important main segment and food, beverages and tobacco (75,8 %) by far the most important subgroup. The opposite is true in highly industrialised countries like the United States where relatively more is spent on durables and services and less on non-durables. An improvement in the standard of living in South Africa might well give rise to a similar trend in the overall expenditure pattern.

Table 4.3 Private consumption expenditure, 1994

Item	R million	%	%
Durable goods	**23 529**	**100,0**	**9,2**
Furniture, household appliances, etc.	8 100	34,4	
Personal transport equipment	9 877	42,0	
Recreational and entertainment goods	3 935	16,7	
Other durable goods[1]	1 617	6,9	
Semi-durable goods	**39 835**	**100,0**	**15,5**
Clothing and footwear	17 587	44,2	
Household textiles, furnishings, glassware, etc.	5 142	12,9	
Motor car tyres, parts and accessories	6 985	17,5	
Recreational and entertainment goods	5 070	12,7	
Miscellaneous goods[2]	5 051	12,7	
Non-durable goods	**124 521**	**100,0**	**48,6**
Food, beverages and tobacco	94 370	75,8	
Household fuel and power	8 632	6,9	
Household consumer goods	5 502	4,4	
Medical and pharmaceutical products	3 461	2,8	
Petroleum products	10 337	8,3	
Recreational and entertainment goods	2 219	1,8	
Services	**68 435**	**100,0**	**26,7**
Rent[3]	18 821	27,5	
Household services, including domestic servants	4 006	5,8	
Medical services	9 640	14,1	
Transport and communication services	15 526	22,7	
Recreational, entertainment and educational services	7 648	11,2	
Miscellaneous services[4]	12 794	18,7	
Total private consumption expenditure	**256 320**	**–**	**100,0**

1 Jewellery, watches, therapeutic appliances, etc.
2 Personal goods and writing and drawing equipment and supplies.
3 Including imputed rent for owner-occupied dwellings.
4 After adjustment for net expenditure of foreigners in the domestic market.

Source: South African Reserve Bank (1995:S–97).

5.1.2 The population of South Africa

The broadest indicator of a consumer market is population and its composition and distribution. Table 4.4 shows the South African population by population group as on 7 March 1991 and projections to the year 2011. Table 4.5 sets out the annual population increments.

Table 4.4 Population of South Africa, 1991–2011

Population group		1991	1996	2001	2006	2011
Asians	No	986 600	1 054 400	1 119 200	1 173 200	1 213 800
	%	2,6	2,5	2,4	2,4	2,3
Blacks	No	28 396 700	31 964 700	35 750 000	39 497 300	42 998 900
	%	75,3	76,5	77,7	78,8	79,8
Coloureds	No	3 285 600	3 529 100	3 756 700	3 954 400	4 112 700
	%	8,7	8,4	8,2	7,9	7,6
Whites	No	5 068 300	5 242 200	5 383 400	5 480 200	5 528 800
	%	13,4	12,6	11,7	10,3	10,3
Total	**No**	**37 737 200**	**41 790 400**	**46 009 300**	**50 105 100**	**53 854 200**
	%	**100,0**	**100,0**	**100,0**	**100,0**	**100,0**

Source: Sadie 1993:4.

Table 4.5 Annual population increments, 1991–2011

Population group		1991–1996	1996–2001	2001–2006	2006–2011
Asians	No	13 000	13 000	10 800	8 100
	%	1,34	1,20	0,95	0,68
Blacks	No	713 600	757 100	749 500	700 300
	%	2,40	2,26	2,01	1,71
Coloureds	No	48 700	45 500	39 500	31 700
	%	1,44	1,26	1,03	0,79
Whites	No	34 800	28 200	19 400	9 700
	%	0,68	0,53	0,36	0,18
Total	**No**	**810 700**	**843 800**	**819 200**	**749 800**
	%	**2,06**	**1,94**	**1,72**	**1,45**

Source: Sadie (1993:5).

According to these projections the South African population will increase from 37 737 200 in 1991 to 53 854 200 in 2011, or by 16 177 000 in total. The average annual increment will rise from 810 700 in 1991 96, peak at 843 800 in 1996–2001 and then drop to 749 800 in the first decade of the twenty-first century (table 4.5). Accordingly the growth rate will decline to 1,45 % per annum at the end of the twenty-year period. Population growth rates will decline across the board, the rate of deceleration being greatest among the whites, followed in descending order of magnitude by the Asians, the coloureds and the blacks. At 0,18 % per annum the white population will be approaching the zero population growth stage by the year 2011.

The above changes in the growth rate probably herald transformations in the age structures as well. Immigration is not reflected in table 4.6 because the age composition of immigrants is vastly different from that induced in natural growth and because the figures in the table are only intended to reveal the effects of the forces of fertility and mortality.

Table 4.6 reflects the well-known ageing process accompanying declining fertility and mortality. The economically beneficial secondary stage of age transformation can be

Table 4.6 Age structures of population groups in South Africa, 1991–2011

Population group	Year	Age group				Dependency ratio
		0–14	15–64	65 +	Total	
Asians	1991	30,5	66,1	3,4	100,0	51
	1996	28,6	67,3	4,1	100,0	
	2001	26,5	68,8	4,7	100,0	45
	2006	25,1	69,3	5,6	100,0	
	2011	23,5	69,8	6,7	100,0	43
Blacks	1991	40,9	55,6	3,5	100,0	80
	1996	38,8	57,6	3,6	100,0	
	2001	36,9	59,4	3,7	100,0	68
	2006	34,9	61,1	4,0	100,0	
	2011	32,6	63,1	4,3	100,0	58
Coloureds	1991	33,4	63,2	3,4	100,0	58
	1996	31,6	64,9	3,5	100,0	
	2001	29,1	67,0	3,9	100,0	49
	2006	27,1	68,7	4,2	100,0	
	2011	25,3	70,2	4,5	100,0	42
Whites	1991	22,1	68,5	9,4	100,0	46
	1996	21,2	68,8	10,0	100,0	
	2001	19,6	69,8	10,6	100,0	43
	2006	18,7	69,5	11,8	100,0	
	2011	17,3	69,3	13,4	100,0	44

Source: Sadie (1993:6).

inferred from the increase in the relative size of the 15–64 age group – usually referred to as the economically active ages – and the reduction in the dependency ratios (the numbers aged 0–14 and 65+ per 100 aged 15–64). The white population is demographically the oldest and the blacks the youngest. All four groups are recording some degree of ageing, but up to 2011 it is only the white group which will have reached the tertiary stage where the 65+ category is growing faster than the 0–14 category is diminishing, to raise the dependency ratio.

The distribution of the population by population group and geographic area is of vital importance for marketing purposes in view of the differences between the expenditure patterns of the population groups. In table 4.7 it can be seen that in 1994 21,2 % of the population of South Africa lived in KwaZulu-Natal. More than three-quarters of the Asians (78,5 %) and 22,9 % of the blacks lived in KwaZulu-Natal. Most of the coloureds (61,0 %) lived in the Western Cape and the highest percentage of whites (41,2 %) lived in Gauteng.

Table 4.7 Distribution of total population by group and province, 1994

Province	Asians '000	Asians %	Blacks '000	Blacks %	Coloureds '000	Coloureds %	Whites '000	Whites %	Total '000	Total %
Western Cape	30	2,9	632	2,1	2 101	61,0	872	16,8	3 635	9,0
Northern Cape	2	0,2	237	0,8	389	11,3	121	2,3	749	1,9
Eastern Cape	15	1,4	5 678	18,5	433	12,6	377	7,3	6 503	16,1
Free State	1	0,1	2 325	7,6	73	2,1	368	7,1	2 767	6,9
KwaZulu-Natal	809	78,5	7 024	22,9	107	3,1	612	11,8	8 552	21,2
Mpumalanga	11	1,1	2 589	8,4	16	0,5	296	5,7	2 912	7,2
Northern Province	4	0,4	4 863	15,8	6	0,2	140	2,7	5 013	12,4
Gauteng	151	14,6	4 302	14,0	279	8,1	2 132	41,2	6 864	17,0
North-West	8	0,8	3 039	9,9	38	1,1	264	5,1	3 349	8,3
Total	**1 031**	**100,0**	**30 689**	**100,0**	**3 442**	**100,0**	**5 182**	**100,0**	**40 344**	**100,0**

Source: Martins *et al* (1994:24).

5.1.3 Personal income of the population

The composition and distribution of the population is a very vague indicator of consumer demand, especially in South Africa where there are wide variations in the income per capita in the four population groups. A more accurate indicator is the composition of personal income and disposable personal income (that is personal income less direct taxes) by population group.

Personal income in South Africa totalled roughly R340 billion in 1994. This sum includes the income of people in the informal sector and income in the form of goods and services (such as food and free housing for farm workers). Of the total, R44,3 billion (13,0 %) will be paid to the state, chiefly in the form of income tax, leaving the South African population with just over R295 billion to spend on goods and services or to save. This sum of R295 billion is termed the personal disposable income of South Africa.

Table 4.8 sets out the share of each population group in total personal disposable income in the respective provinces in 1994. It is worth noting that black people commanded over 50 % of the total personal disposable income in five of the nine provinces, namely the Northern Province (70,9 %), North-West (58,3 %), Mpumalanga (55,4 %), Eastern Cape (52,4 %) and Free State (50,7 %). Whites commanded over 50 % of personal income in four provinces: Gauteng (58,7 %), Western Cape (54,4 %), Eastern Cape (53,4 %) and Northern Cape (50,5 %). Coloureds were relatively important in the Western Cape (35,5 %) and Northern Cape (26,3 %) and the Asians' sphere of importance was restricted to KwaZulu-Natal (17,1 %).

Table 4.8 Personal disposable income by population group and province, 1994

Province	Asians		Blacks		Coloureds		Whites		Total	
	R million	%	R million	%	R million	%	R million	%	R million	%
Western Cape	358,0	0,8	4 178,0	9,3	16 007,0	35,5	24 486,6	54,4	45 029,6	100,0
Northern Cape	22,0	0,4	1 263,6	22,8	1 459,0	26,3	27 991,1	50,5	5 543,7	100,0
Eastern Cape	289,0	1,2	12 321,8	52,4	2 584,0	11,0	8 319,0	53,4	23 513,8	100,0
Free State	20,0	0,1	9 486,1	50,7	440,2	2,4	8 782,2	46,9	18 728,5	100,0
KwaZulu-Natal	7 694,0	17,1	19 493,3	43,4	1 362,0	3,0	16 395,4	36,5	44 944,7	100,0
Mpumalanga	179,0	1,1	9 178,6	55,4	227,0	1,4	6 978,7	42,1	16 563,3	100,0
Northern Province	82,0	0,8	7 503,2	70,9	63,0	0,6	2 939,1	27,8	10 587,3	100,0
Gauteng	2 795,0	2,4	40 851,5	35,5	3 908,8	3,4	67 664,4	58,7	115 219,7	100,0
North-West	116,0	0,8	8 852,4	58,3	289,0	1,9	5 922,8	39,0	15 180,2	100,0
South Africa	**11 555,0**	**3,9**	**113 128,5**	**38,3**	**26 340,0**	**8,9**	**144 287,3**	**48,9**	**295 310,8**	**100,0**

Source: Martins *et al* (1994:34.)

5.1.4 Expenditure patterns of the population groups

Whites were responsible for 53,5 % of the total expenditure of R279,1 billion in 1993 (fig 4.2). However, when it comes to expenditure on main expenditure items (table 4.9), blacks were responsible for 92,5 % of the total expenditure on fuel and light. They also contributed 84,3 % of the R4,7 billion spent on support of relatives and 79,5 % of the R911,0 million spent on dry-cleaning and laundry in 1993. Expenditure by black people exceeded that of the other three population groups on alcoholic beverages (58,4 %), washing materials, plastic bags, insecticides and disinfectants (56,8 %), clothing, footwear and accessories (55,7 %), cigarettes and tobacco (55,5 %) and food (50,6 %). Whites were responsible for over half of the total expenditure on servants (87,2 %), holidays (84,5 %), income tax (80,4 %), recreation, entertainment and sport (73,6 %), insurance and funds (72,6 %), housing and electricity (69,1 %), transport (66,2 %), medical and dental expenses (65,9 %), miscellaneous items (61,6 %), reading-matter and stationery (53,2 %) and education (51,5 %).

Table 4.9 Market shares of the respective population groups in household expenditure in South Africa by main expenditure group, 1993

Main expenditure group	Asians	Blacks	Coloureds	Whites	Total
	%	%	%	%	%
Total expenditure	3,9	34,9	7,7	53,5	100,0
Food	4,5	50,6	10,1	34,8	100,0
Clothing, footwear and accessories	3,6	55,7	7,2	33,5	100,0
Housing and electricity	4,3	18,4	8,2	69,1	100,0
Fuel and light	0,3	92,5	2,3	4,9	100,0
Transport	3,7	23,9	6,9	66,2	100,0
Medical and dental	4,4	22,5	7,2	65,9	100,0
Education	4,8	37,9	5,8	51,5	100,0
Insurance and funds	4,2	17,1	6,1	72,6	100,0
Recreation, entertainment and sport	3,8	13,1	9,5	73,6	100,0
Furniture and household equipment	3,9	43,1	6,1	46,9	100,0
Alcoholic beverages	3,1	58,4	5,8	32,7	100,0
Cigarettes and tobacco	4,4	55,5	13,2	26,9	100,0
Washing materials, plastic bags, insecticides and disinfectants	4,4	56,8	10,9	27,9	100,0
Dry-cleaning and laundry	0,9	79,5	2,0	17,6	100,0
Personal care	4,2	40,0	11,1	44,7	100,0
Communication	6,8	31,4	13,9	47,9	100,0
Reading-matter and stationery	4,8	33,2	8,8	53,2	100,0
Servants	3,0	6,2	3,6	87,2	100,0
Support of relatives	0,7	84,3	3,1	11,9	100,0
Holidays	2,5	10,6	2,4	84,5	100,0
Income tax	3,6	11,2	4,8	80,4	100,0
Miscellaneous items	1,5	30,2	6,7	61,6	100,0
Unspecified items	9,6	36,7	6,8	46,9	100,0

Source: Martins (1994:5).

Figure 4.2 Household expenditure in South Africa by population group, 1993

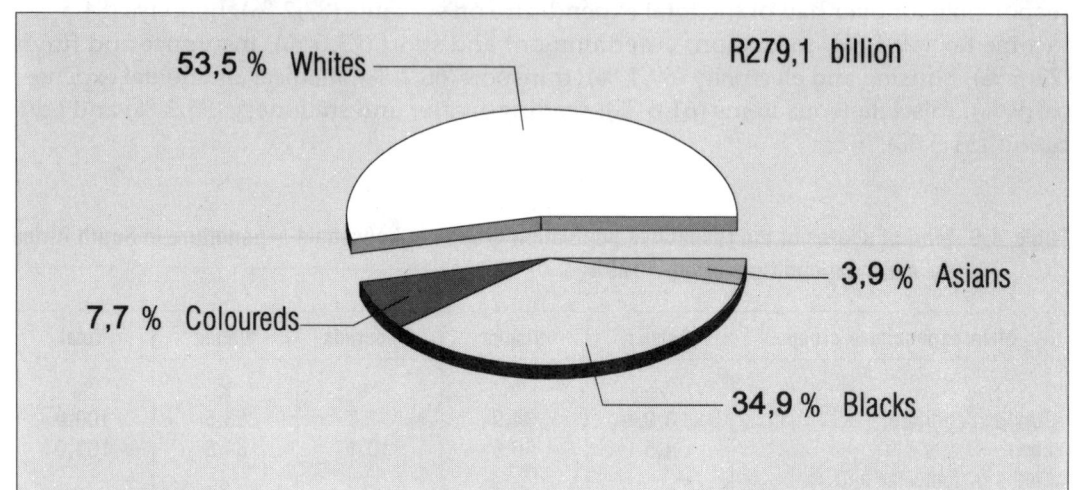

Source: Martins (1994:4).

There are marked differences in the expenditure patterns of the four population groups (table 4.10). In 1993 whites spent more on housing and electricity (18,9 % of their total expenditure) than on food (14,7 %) and income tax (14,9 %). In the other three population groups food was far and away the most important item in the household budget. It made up 33,0 % of the black household budget and 29,9 % and 25,8 % of the coloured and Asian budgets respectively. This is not surprising in the light of Engels' law which postulates that relative expenditure on food decreases with rising income. Relatively speaking blacks spent quite large sums on clothing, footwear and accessories (9,7 %).

Marketers are also interested in the geographical distribution of household expenditure. Figure 4.3 (page 70) depicts the estimated household expenditure figures (excluding income tax) for 1994 by province. Gauteng leads with a share of 35,7 % (R102,7 billion of the total of R287,8 billion) followed by KwaZulu-Natal with 14,9 %. The Northern Cape has the smallest share (2,1 %).

5.2 The industrial market

We have seen that the components of the industrial market are intermediate demand, consumption expenditure by general government, gross fixed investment and change in inventories. Intermediate demand is presented by sector in the input-output tables. In view of the comprehensive nature of the tables and because they are dealt with in chapter 20, further discussion of intermediate demand is not required here. Fully 60 %

Table 4.10 Percentage distribution of household expenditure in South Africa by main expenditure and population group, 1993

Item	Asians	Blacks	Coloureds	Whites	Total
Food	25,8	33,0	29,9	14,7	27,7
Clothing, footwear and accessories	5,6	9,7	5,6	3,8	6,1
Housing and electricity	16,0	7,7	15,7	18,9	14,7
Fuel and light	0,1	3,0	0,3	0,1	1,1
Transport	8,7	6,3	7,4	11,3	9,2
Medical and dental	4,6	2,7	3,9	5,1	4,1
Education	1,8	1,6	1,1	1,4	1,5
Insurance and funds	7,8	3,6	5,9	10,0	7,4
Recreation, entertainment and sport	1,4	0,6	1,8	2,0	1,5
Furniture and household equipment	3,7	4,6	3,0	3,3	3,7
Alcoholic beverages	2,8	5,9	2,7	2,2	3,5
Cigarettes and tobacco	2,5	3,6	3,9	1,1	2,3
Washing materials, plastic bags, insecticides and disinfectants	1,5	2,2	1,9	0,7	1,3
Dry-cleaning and laundry	0,1	0,7	0,1	0,1	0,3
Personal care	2,6	2,8	3,5	2,0	2,4
Communication	2,7	1,4	2,8	0,5	0,5
Reading-matter and stationery	0,6	0,5	0,6	0,5	0,5
Servants	0,7	0,2	0,4	1,6	1,0
Support of relatives	0,3	4,1	0,7	0,4	1,7
Holidays	0,6	0,3	0,3	1,5	0,9
Income tax	9,0	3,2	6,2	14,9	9,9
Miscellaneous items	0,9	2,2	2,2	2,9	2,6
Unspecified items	0,2	0,1	0,1	0,1	0,1
Total expenditure	**100,0**	**100,0**	**100,0**	**100,0**	**100,0**

Source: Martins (1994:49).

of consumption expenditure by general government is made up of salaries and wages. Here, too, we shall avoid further discussion for lack of information on the rest of the expenditure items. In sections 5.2.1 and 5.2.2 we shall analyse the composition of the gross domestic product (GDP) and of gross domestic fixed investment. Change in inventories represents such a minor share in the domestic market that it may safely be ignored in this discussion.

Figure 4.3 Household expenditure in South Africa by province, 1994

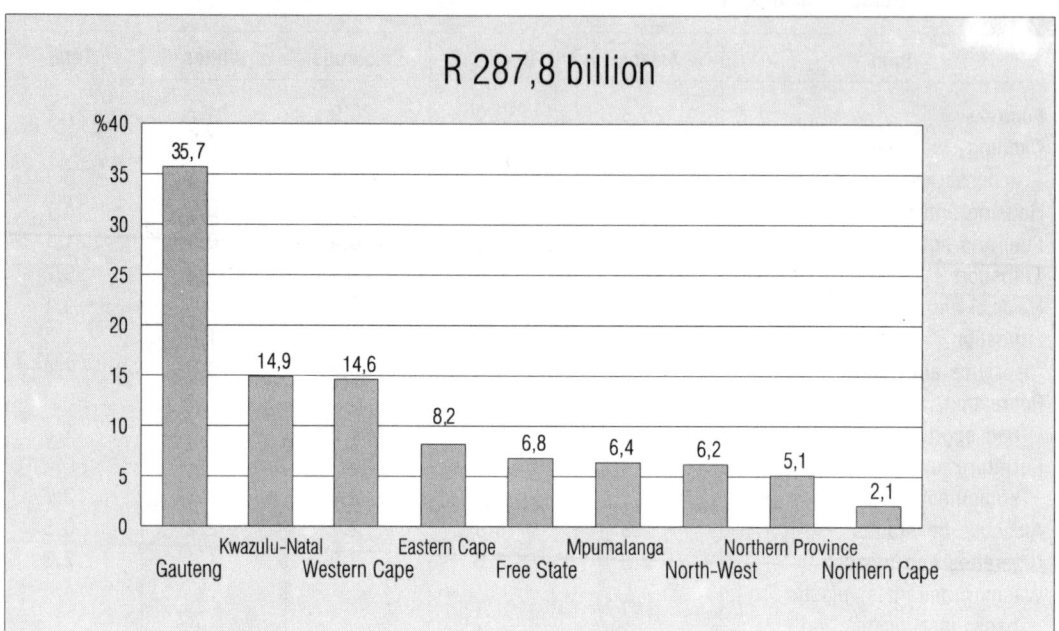

Source: Martins *et al* (1994:43).

5.2.1 Gross domestic product

The shares of the sectors of production in South Africa's gross domestic product in 1994 are set out in table 4.11. In that year the GDP totalled R382 561 million. The largest share was that of manufacturing (R89 765 million or 23,4 %), followed by finance, insurance, real estate and business services (16,6 %) and wholesale and retail trade, catering and accommodation (16,1 %).

Changes in the relative importance of the sectors are reflected in their growth rates over time (table 4.12) and their percentage shares in the GDP over time (table 4.13). The figures in these two tables are seasonally adjusted, that is average figures are calculated for three consecutive years instead of working with figures for single years. This procedure is recommended especially for calculations involving agriculture on account of the impact of climatic conditions on production in this sector.

Table 4.11 Composition of the GDP at current prices, 1994

Sector	R million	%
Agriculture, forestry and fishing	17 930	4,7
Mining and quarrying	33 168	8,7
Manufacturing	89 765	23,4
Electricity, gas and water	15 751	4,1
Construction (contractors)	12 265	3,2
Wholesale and retail trade, catering and accommodation	61 648	16,1
Transport, storage and communication	28 976	7,6
Finance, insurance, real estate and business services	63 411	16,6
Community, social and personal services	7 573	2,0
Less Imputed financial service charges	− 14 559	− 3,8
General government	58 678	15,3
Other producers	7 955	2,1
GDP at factor cost	382 561	100,0

Source: South African Reserve Bank (1995:S–92).

Table 4.12 Annual growth in the shares of sectors of production in the GDP, 1962–1994

Sector	1962–64 to 1972–74	1972–74 to 1982–84	1982–84 to 1992–94	1962–64 to 1992–94
	%	%	%	%
Agricultural, forestry and fishing	2,6	0,7	2,1	1,8
Mining and quarrying	0,8	0,0	− 0,5	0,1
Manufacturing	7,8	3,5	− 0,6	3,5
Electricity, gas and water	7,4	6,4	3,4	5,7
Construction (contractors)	10,7	− 0,1	− 2,4	2,6
Wholesale and retail trade, catering and accommodation	7,3	3,2	0,4	3,6
Transport, storage and accommodation	6,6	3,9	1,5	4,0
Finance, insurance, real estate and business services	5,7	3,5	1,9	3,7
Community, social and personal services	3,6	4,8	2,4	3,6
General government	4,4	3,9	2,3	3,5
Other producers	2,4	2,7	2,1	2,4
Total GDP at constant prices	**5,3**	**2,8**	**0,7**	**2,9**

Source: South African Reserve Bank (1994:B–8–10), (1995:S–92).

Between the three-year periods 1962–64 and 1992–94 the rate of growth was highest in electricity, gas and water (5,7 % per annum) and lowest in mining and quarrying (0,1 % per annum) (table 4.12). The growth rate in construction declined from a high of 10,7 % per annum between 1962–64 and 1972–74 to −2,4 % per annum between 1982–84 and 1992–94. Among the sectors with poor performance figures between 1982–84 and 1992–94 are manufacturing and mining and quarrying with negative growth rates of 0,6 % and 0,5 % per annum respectively. Between 1962–64 and 1992–94 the percentage share of mining and quarrying in the GDP dropped from 22,8 % to 9,9 % (table 4.13). Manufacturing with the second largest share (20,5 %) in the GDP in 1962–64 rose sharply as one might expect in a developing country to 27,6 % in 1982–84, only to fall to 24,2 % in 1992–94. In 1992 the share of manufacturing in the GDP of developed countries stood at 42 % in Japan, 39 % in Germany, 36 % in Austria and 32 % in Sweden (World Bank 1994:167).

Table 4.13 Percentage contribution of sectors of production to the GDP, 1962–1994

Sector	1962–64	1972–74	1982–84	1992–94
	%	%	%	%
Agricultural, forestry and fishing	6,5	5,0	4,1	4,7
Mining and quarrying	22,8	14,8	11,2	9,9
Manufacturing	20,5	25,9	27,6	24,2
Electricity, gas and water	2,1	2,6	3,6	4,8
Construction (contractors)	3,4	5,5	4,2	3,0
Wholesale and retail trade, catering and accommodation	12,3	14,9	15,4	14,9
Transport, storage and communication	5,8	6,5	7,2	7,8
Finance, insurance, real estate and business services	12,3	12,8	13,6	15,3
Community, social and personal services	1,6	1,4	1,6	1,9
Less: Imputed financial service charges	− 2,3	− 2,7	− 3,0	− 3,4
General government	12,4	11,3	12,5	14,6
Other producers	2,6	2,0	2,0	2,3
Total	**100,0**	**100,0**	**100,0**	**100,0**

Source: South African Reserve Bank (1994:B–8–10), (1995:S–92).

5.2.2 Gross domestic fixed investment

Gross domestic fixed investment is made up of expenditure on residential buildings, non-residential buildings, construction works, transport equipment, and machinery and equipment. Table 4.14 shows that in 1994 machinery and equipment (41,2 %) was by far the most important component of gross fixed investment, followed by transport equipment (17,0 %) and construction works (15,9 %). Private business enterprises were responsible for most of the expenditure on each of the items except construction works whose main investor was public authorities.

Table 4.14 Gross domestic fixed investment by type of asset and organisation, 1994

| Type of asset | Type of organisation | | | | | | | |
| | Public authorities | | Public corporations | | Private business | | Total | |
	R million	%	R million	%	R million	%	R million	%
Residential buildings	937	9,7	36	0,4	6 841	13,8	7 814	11,5
Non-residential	1 274	13,2	384	4,3	5 331	10,8	6 989	10,2
Construction works	6 941	72,0	813	9,1	3 078	6,2	10 832	15,9
Transport equipment	75	0,8	823	9,3	10 657	21,5	11 555	17,0
Machinery and other equipment	418	4,3	6 843	76,9	20 787	41,9	28 048	41,2
Transfer costs	–	0,0	–	0,0	2 863	5,8	2 863	4,2
Total	**9 645**	**100,0**	**8 899**	**100,0**	**49 557**	**100,0**	**68 101**	**100,0**

Source: South African Reserve Bank (1995:S–104).

The contribution of the various sectors to gross domestic fixed investment in 1994 is presented in table 4.15. Manufacturing was the largest investor – R17,2 billion or 25,3 % of total fixed investment – with finance, insurance, real estate and business services in second place (R17,0 billion or 24,9 %). Community, social and personal services, which include the central and provincial governments and local authorities, occupied third place with a gross fixed investment of R8,6 billion. The contribution by type of organisation (table 4.15) shows that private business enterprises contributed 72,8 %, public authorities 14,1 % and public corporations 13,1 % of the total investment of R68,1 billion in 1994.

Table 4.15 Share of the respective sectors in gross domestic fixed investment, 1994

Sector	R million	%	%
Agriculture, forestry and fishing	2 503	3,7	—
Mining and quarrying	6 142	9,0	—
Manufacturing	17 204	25,3	100,0
Private business enterprises	17 067		99,2
Other	137		0,8
Electricity, gas and water	5 979	8,8	—
Construction (contractors)	752	1,1	—
Wholesale and retail trade (catering and accommodation)	4 540	6,7	—
Transport, storage and communication	5 466	8,0	100,0
Transnet	1 011		18,5
Other	4 455		81,5
Finance, insurance, real estate (and business services)	16 962	24,9	100,0
Private residential buildings	6 374		36,6
Other	10 588		62,4
Community, social and personal services	8 553	12,5	100,0
Central government	3 397		39,7
Provincial governments	863		10,0
Local authorities	3 467		40,5
Other	826		9,7
Total fixed investment	**68 101**	**100,0**	
By type of organisation			
Public authorities	9 645	14,1	—
Public corporations	8 899	13,1	—
Private business enterprises	49 557	72,8	—

Source: South African Reserve Bank (1995:S–100).

6 SUMMARY

It is a truism that a marketing researcher should be familiar with the market in which he operates. This applies particularly to South Africa where certain basic methods and techniques have to be adapted to its unique population structure. Each firm is embedded in the national and international economies. An assessment of the size of an entire market and its structure is a valuable basis for evaluating a firm's standing and performance in the general market situation.

With the lifting of sanctions against South Africa the international market will become more important. South Africa is classified by the World Bank as an upper-middle-income country and only 27 of the 132 countries have a higher GDP than South Africa.

The national market consists of two major components: the consumer market and industrial market. The former comprises private consumption expenditure and the latter intermediate demand, gross domestic fixed investment, change in inventories and consumption expenditure by the general government.

REFERENCES

Martins, J H 1994. *Household expenditure in South Africa by area, population group and product, 1993.* Pretoria: Unisa, Bureau of Market Research. (Research Report no 205.)

Martins, J H, Ligthelm, A A, Loubser, M & Van Wyk, H de J 1994. *Socio-economic profile of the nine provinces in South Africa, 1994.* Pretoria: Unisa, Bureau of Market Research. (Research Report no 207.)

Sadie, J L 1993. *A projection of the South African population, 1991–2011.* Pretoria: Unisa, Bureau of Market Research. (Research Report no 196.)

South Africa. Central Statistical Service 1995. *Input-output tables, 1993: estimates according to the Ras method.* Pretoria. *(In press.)*

South Africa. Department of Finance, Customs and Excise [s a]. *Monthly abstract of trade statistics: foreign trade statistics of the common customs area of Botswana, Lesotho, South Africa and Swaziland released by the Commissioner for Customs and Excise of the Republic of South Africa.* January–October 1994 [s l:s n].

South African Reserve Bank 1994. *South Africa's national accounts 1946–1993: supplement to the South African Reserve Bank Quarterly Bulletin June 1994* [s l].

South African Reserve Bank 1995. *Quarterly Bulletin.* March 1995, no 195. Pretoria.

World Bank 1994. *World development report: infrastructure for development.* New York: Oxford University Press.

Part 2

The research process and methodology

The next two parts deal with the research process. This part describes the construction of a research plan and the collection of secondary and primary data. The next part explains the treatment and dissemination of the data. Chapter 5 outlines the various steps in the research process and preparation of the research plan. Chapter 6 deals with the role of secondary data in marketing research and the different types of secondary data. The various methods of collecting primary data are reviewed in chapters 7 to 10. Chapter 11 explains questionnaire design and chapter 12 is concerned with the selection, training and control of interviewers. Sampling, one of the most important steps in marketing research, is discussed in chapter 13. The researcher is prepared for errors that may occur in the course of a survey by the discussion of survey errors in chapter 14.

The research process and the research plan

Chapter 5: G Puth

The research process and the research plan

1 INTRODUCTION

Every marketing research problem is in some way unique and will invariably require careful and appropriate planning and execution. There are, however, a number of elements, or steps, which are common to most marketing research processes. As the word 'process' implies, marketing research involves a series of steps or phases which cannot be viewed in isolation, but which should be seen and dealt with as an integrated whole. This integrated evolvement of steps which are followed when planning and executing a research project is known as the research process.

From a practical point of view, the research process is certainly one of the most important aspects in the study and practice of marketing research. The purpose of this chapter is to provide an overview of the different steps in the marketing process. In addition some guidelines will be given for the practical logistics involved in the planning and execution of a marketing research project.

2 STEPS IN THE MARKETING RESEARCH PROCESS

Many different steps and permutations of steps are distinguished in various sources of marketing research literature. For instance, Nel, Rädel and Loubser (1988:89) propose a classification and use terminology that have been established over time at the Bureau of Market Research (BMR). Different practitioners and research institutions may have different frameworks that they have developed and found useful in their particular contexts. Although this section of the present chapter reflects and represents a combination and synthesis of the different sources referred to in the bibliography at the end of the chapter, it should be stated that the framework provided by Emory and Cooper (1995), which is depicted in figure 5.1, was found to be particularly useful and that extensive use has been made of this source. In addition a number of other steps identified by various other authors have been included in order to provide a comprehensive overview of the research process. Naturally all the steps are not applicable in all types of research.

Figure 5.1 A model of the research process

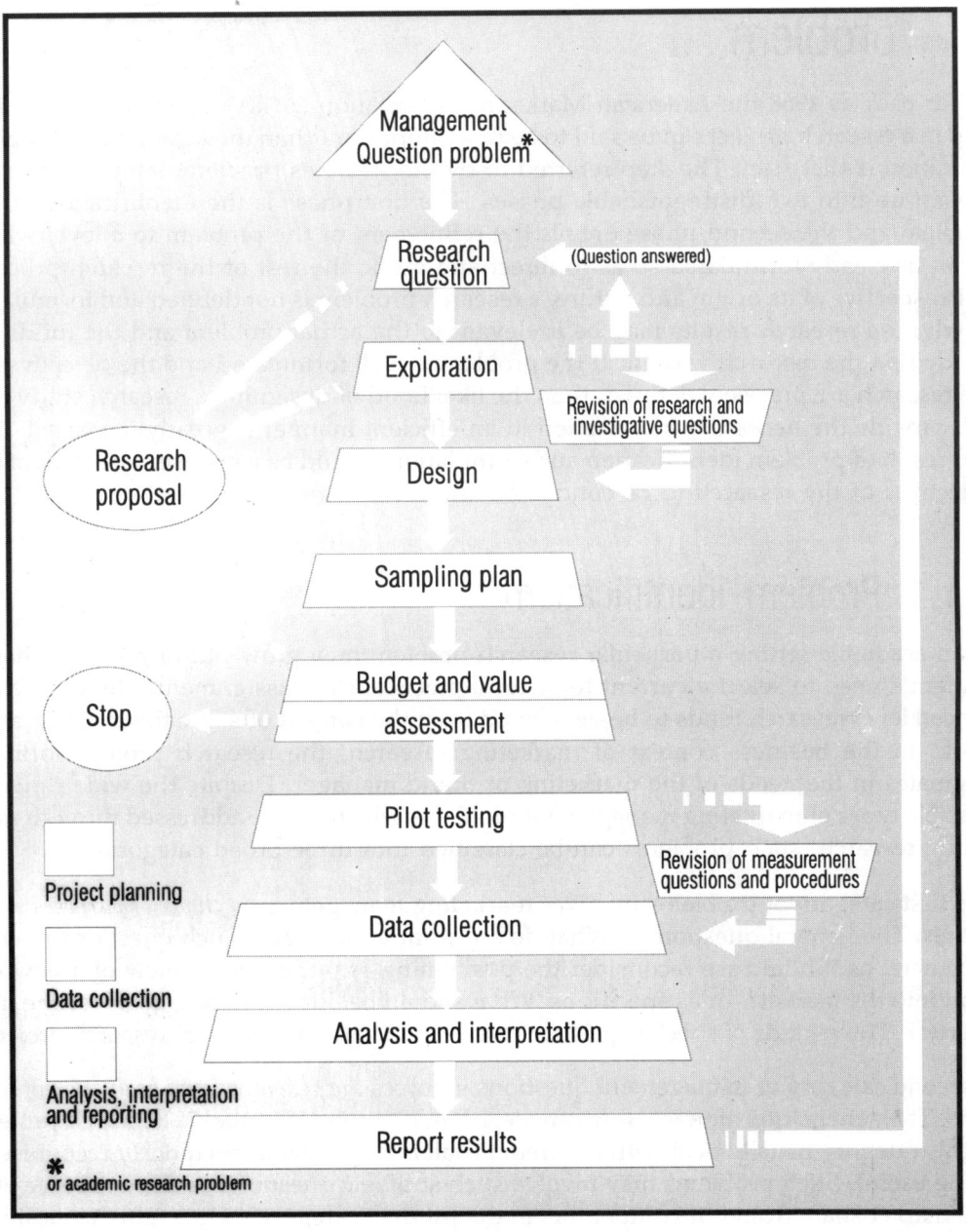

Source: Adapted from Emory & Cooper 1995.

2.1 Step 1: Identifying and formulating the problem

As far back as 1968 the American Marketing Association (AMA) concluded that if any step in a research project can be said to be more important than the others, then problem definition is that step. The step referred to by the AMA as problem definition may be broken up into two distinguishable phases. The first phase is the identification of the problem and the second phase entails the refinement of the problem to a level where it can be clearly formulated so as to direct and guide the rest of the research process. If, irrespective of its origin and nature, a research problem is not defined and formulated clearly, the research results may be irrelevant to the actual problem and the funds expended on the research wasted. If the problem is well formulated and the objectives of the research are precisely defined, then the likelihood of designing a research study that will provide the necessary information in an efficient manner is greatly increased. The end result of problem identification and formulation should be a precise statement of the objectives of the research to be conducted and a set of research questions.

2.1.1 Problem identification

In an academic setting a particular research problem may grow out of no more than a student's need to select a current topic for a practical class assignment. On a more advanced level research tends to be developed from the context of some theoretical framework. In the business context of marketing research, the research project normally originates in the needs of the marketing or brand manager. Despite the wide range of possible types of marketing management problems which can be addressed through marketing research, such problems can be classified into three broad categories.

The first category of problems involves marketing management's *choice of purposes or objectives*. The general question is 'What do we want to achieve?' Such questions may be as general as 'Should we reconsider the positioning of our brand in view of a new entrant into the market?' or as specific as 'What should be our marketing goals for the next quarter?' These kinds of specific questions can lead to various studies or research projects.

A second category of management questions involves *the generation and evaluation of solutions*. The general question is 'How can we achieve the ends we seek?' Research projects in this category usually deal with concrete problems that managers quickly recognise as being useful. Such problems may involve such strategic questions as 'How can we gain 5 % market share from our competitors in the product category?' On a more tactical level, the questions may be as specific as 'Which of three proposed advertising platforms would be the most effective way of gaining a competitive edge in the market?'

A final category of management problems concerns the *trouble shooting* or control situation. The problem usually involves monitoring or diagnosing various ways in which a company or a marketing division appears to be failing to achieve its established goals. This group includes such questions as 'Why do we fail to gain market share despite considerable increases in advertising spending?'

No matter how the management problem is formulated, there are various research directions that can be taken. It is the joint responsibility of the researcher and the manager to choose the most appropriate and productive approach. From the researcher's point of view, it should never be assumed that management is aware of the exact nature of its problems or that their instructions to the researcher or research institution are necessarily a valid description of the real problem. More often than not the research need may appear to management in the guise of symptoms rather than real, underlying problems.

2.1.2 Problem formulation

Having clearly identified the management problem or research need, the next phase of step 1 is to formulate or describe the problem in such a way as to provide direction and guidance to the remaining steps in the research process. A useful way to approach the research process is to state the basic problem that prompts the research. From this, other questions can be developed by progressively breaking down the original question into more specific ones. Emory and Cooper (1995) refer to this as a four-tier question hierarchy:

☐ The process begins at the most general level with the management question. *The management question represents a decision that a manager must make and is the problem prompting the research.* Since the definition of the management problem sets the research task, it follows that a poorly defined management problem or question will misdirect research efforts.

☐ Once the management problem has been identified and described, it needs to be translated into a general research question. *A research question is the single question or hypothesis that best states the objective of the research study.* Although there may be times when there is more than one question, more often than not it is just a single, predominant question. An appropriate research project will be one that would provide the manager with the desired information to answer the research question.

☐ Once the general research question has been selected, the question hierarchy moves to a more specific level, that of investigative questions. *Investigative questions are those that the researcher must answer in order to satisfactorily answer the general research question.* The purpose is to take the more general research question and to break it up into more specific questions about data that need to be gathered. This process can continue down through several levels of progressively more specific questions. These are all questions which a researcher must ask and be able to answer in order to develop the research direction. The investigative questions also form the basis for generating research hypotheses. Generally speaking there can be many assumptions or hypotheses for a particular management or research problem.

☐ The final level of the question hierarchy entails formulating measurement questions. *Measurement questions are those questions which respondents must answer if the researcher is to gather the needed information to provide answers to the management problem.*

The way in which the research is structured sets the direction of the project. Using the question hierarchy as four sequential stages moving from the general to the specific is a good way to do this.

2.2 Step 2: Deciding what kind of data are required

After the identification, formulation and refinement of the research problem, the researcher should have a relatively clear idea of the nature of the data required to answer the research questions and to solve the management problem. The data relating to the research objectives may be facts, levels of awareness, opinions, attitudes, preferences, motives or behaviour, each of which will be briefly discussed.

2.2.1 Facts

Facts are data which are clearly defined and measured. Examples are expenditure on a product in monetary terms or physical units, the number of people of a certain demographic description residing in a certain area, or the number of vehicles per capita in a certain section of the population.

2.2.2 Levels of awareness

Awareness refers to what respondents do or do not know about some object or phenomenon. Information on awareness can relate to products (for instance cellular telephones) where the researcher wishes to establish whether and to what extent the respondent is aware of the product, its features, brand, price, manufacturer, place of manufacture, sales outlet, etc. Information on awareness is particularly important in advertising research in which the researcher wants to find out whether and to what extent the respondent is aware of an advertisement (either by recognition or by aided or spontaneous recall), the theory being that the greater the awareness the more effective the advertisement and the greater the probability that the respondent will buy the advertised product.

2.2.3 Opinions and attitudes

While awareness is relatively neutral in relation to the various products or phenomena, opinions or attitudes contain a certain element of judgement. Opinions or attitudes are a person's ideas, convictions or likes/dislikes regarding a certain object or phenomenon. While some authors use both concepts interchangeably, others differentiate between the two. Despite these various approaches and differences in definition, generally speaking it can be said that if a person's attitude towards a product is positive, he will be more inclined to buy it than when his attitude is negative. Attitudes may therefore be said to be the forerunners of preferences and behaviour. In our example in the previous section, the researcher may want to establish opinions on or attitudes to various types and brands of cellular telephones.

2.2.4 Preferences

Preferences are closely related to opinions or attitudes. In our example we may wish to know which brand of cellular telephone the various respondents prefer. Such questions obviously have to be formulated differently from those probing opinions or attitudes and will probably have to contain some ranking procedure.

2.2.5 Motives

Motives, or predispositions, are the reasons that people act as they do. More specifically, motives can be defined as the factors that energise, activate, move, direct or channel behaviour towards goals. Reliable information on motives for decision making on marketing strategies is as valuable as it is difficult to obtain. In some cases it may be possible to get information on motives by asking respondents direct questions, for instance about the reasons (price, availability, technical specifications, etc) that they prefer a certain brand of cellular telephone. But there are many cases in which the respondent himself is unaware of his real motives or is reluctant to reveal them, for instance motives for consuming alcohol or using certain personal toiletries. In such cases more subtle qualitative research methods may be required.

2.2.6 Behaviour

Behaviour is the manner in which people behave in the marketplace. In a way it can be seen as the final result of attitudes, preferences and motivation. Behaviour finds expression in a variety of dimensions contained in such questions as what, how, how much/often, where, when, in what situation. It is interesting to note that all of these questions are factual questions, but in their totality they reflect a certain pattern of behaviour.

2.3 Step 3: Exploring secondary data sources

Every research project is a search for information on some topic. By tapping all of the relevant sources researchers can be more confident of the quality and appropriateness of their information. Often there is a wealth of information and data on the research problem already collected by others, in which case it may not be cost effective or necessary to conduct a whole new research project in order to answer the research question. In many instances existing secondary data may be sufficiently relevant and comprehensive to answer at least a certain part of the overarching research question.

An exploration typically begins with a search of published data. In the case of marketing research such information can often be found inside the company or with the company's current advertising agency. All research commissioned by the company, even through an advertising agency or external research institution, remains the property of the company and should be made available and accessible to any subsequent researchers. In addition researchers may be able to seek out well-informed people on the topic or problem area. Whatever the sources of secondary data may be, it is essential to explore all possibilities before proceeding with the remaining steps of the research process.

The sources, interpretation and uses of secondary data will be fully discussed in the next chapter.

2.4 Step 4: Revising and fine-tuning the research question

Although the term 'fine-tuning' may seem somewhat odd in the context of marketing research, it describes an image that most researchers will recognise and understand. Fine-tuning the research question is precisely what the researcher needs to do after the exploration of secondary data sources. This is the stage at which a clearer picture of the problem starts to emerge and where the project begins to crystallise in one of two ways:

☐ It is apparent that the question has been answered and the research process has been completed.

☐ The original question has been modified in some way by the gathered information. The research question may not be drastically different, but it will probably have evolved in some way. In most instances such a refined question will provide a better focus and move the research forward with greater clarity than the original question.

To effectively complete the fine-tuning of the original question, a number of other problem-related activities should be considered during this step of the research process:

- ☐ Examine whether the concepts and constructs to be used in the investigation have been satisfactorily defined. Have operational definitions been employed where appropriate?

- ☐ Review the investigative questions with a view to breaking them down into more specific levels of questions.

- ☐ If hypotheses are used, they must be relevant to the refined research problem.

- ☐ Determine what evidence needs to be collected to answer the various questions and hypotheses.

- ☐ Set the limitations of the investigation by stating what is part of the problem and what is not. In this way it will be ensured that the study remains focused on the primary objective of the research.

2.5 Step 5: Designing the research study

The research design provides the blueprint for reaching the objectives of the research and answering the questions originating from the management problem. Various aspects of research design will be dealt with in considerable depth in subsequent chapters, and the discussion here in the context of the research process is only a brief summary.

Selecting an appropriate research design is often complicated by the availability of a large variety of methods, techniques, procedures, and ever-more-sophisticated computer programming and technology. In the first instance the researcher may be able to select a secondary data study, a case study, survey research, an experiment or a simulation. In the case of survey research a decision must be made on whether to use postal questionnaires, telephone interviews, personal interviews or observation. Should all relevant data be collected at one time, or at specified intervals? What should the structure of the questionnaire entail? What format of question wording will be most appropriate? Should the questions be scaled or open-ended? How will reliability and validity best be achieved? These questions represent only a few of the decisions the researcher needs to make about the research design.

2.6 Step 6: Determining the sample

The next step in the research process is to identify the target population and determine the sample characteristics. The researcher has to determine how many people should be interviewed and who they will be. If the population consists of events rather than people, it should be determined how many there will be. The sample frame may consist of records or documents of some kind. The most important criterion, however, is that the researcher should ensure that the sample will be totally representative of the population relevant to the solving of the management problem and the ensuing research questions.

If, for instance, information is required about preferences for photographic cameras, consumers may be interviewed, or camera dealers may be a quicker, cheaper source of the same information. If the expenditure of households in Soweto is being researched, the universe is the sum total of all the households in Soweto. All the households may then be interviewed, in which case a census is taken, or only a number of households, which is termed a sample. In marketing research practice the use of samples is usually the rule rather than the exception. The specific techniques of sampling will be discussed in greater detail in chapter 13.

2.7 Step 7: Allocating funds and resources

Depending on the nature and scope of a specific study, marketing research can be costly, and without appropriate budgetary planning the research effort may have to be terminated for a lack of resources. A research budget may require significant planning and documentation in grant or contract research, or may require less attention when the research is in-house investigations or projects funded out of the researcher's own resources.

General thinking about research expenditure often singles out data collection as the most costly activity in the research process. Although data collection does require substantial resources, it may not always be as big a part of the budget as clients or researchers would expect. Employee salaries, training and travel, and other miscellaneous expenses are incurred during data collection, but this phase of the project often takes no more than a third of the research budget. The geographic scope and number of respondents naturally affect the cost, but much of the cost is relatively independent of the extent and size of the data-gathering exercise. A suggested guide may be that project planning, data collection and analysis, interpretation and reporting each have a share more or less equal in the budget.

2.8 Step 8: Writing and presenting the research proposal

The research proposal is typically developed and refined concurrently with the exploring and planning phases of the project. The proposal would thus incorporate the decisions and choices the researcher has made in the preliminary stages of the research. The primary purpose and benefit of the research proposal is that it assures that all parties understand the project's purpose and the proposed methods of research. In most instances time limits and budgets are spelled out and justified, and various responsibilities and obligations clarified. Should the client's circumstances or knowledge levels require it, there may be substantial detail and explanation of proposed techniques.

Every proposal should contain two basic sections, namely the problem statement and a statement of what will be done and how it will be done. In a brief research proposal the problem statement may entail not more than a paragraph setting out the situation and stating the specific task that the researcher is going to undertake. In marketing research most problem statements will probably detail and describe the particular problem management is facing, and generally point out the nature of the research that will be undertaken. With regard to the statement of what will be done, the nature and breadth of such a statement will once again be determined by the characteristics of the particular research problem. Sometimes the description of the proposed operational steps is rather brief, while in other cases it is much more detailed and may include specific measurement instruments that will be used, time and cost budgets, sampling plans, and many other details. In its varied forms the research proposal can include any number of the following elements: executive summary; problem statement; research objectives; literature review; importance and benefits of the study; research design; data analysis; nature and form of results; qualification of researchers; budget; time schedule; facilities and special resources; project management; bibliography; appendices.

In essence, however, the research proposal is a roadmap which clearly indicates the location from which the journey begins, the destination to be reached, and the method of getting there.

2.9 Step 9: Conducting a pilot test

The primary purposes of a pilot test are to detect weaknesses in design and instrumentation and to provide a sound base for determining and refining the sample. During the pilot test, subjects are drawn from the target population and the procedures and protocols of the research project are simulated. The pilot test should simulate the proposed research project in all respects. If the study will entail a mail survey, the pilot questionnaire should also be mailed. This should apply to any of the possible research techniques. The number of elements in a pilot test would depend on the research methodology and the characteristics of the target population. However, elements need not be statistically selected. In very small populations or special applications, care should be taken not to exhaust the supply of respondents or sensitise them to the purpose of the study. Therefore this risk should be calculated and evaluated in view of the possible improvements that can be attained by conducting the pilot study.

2.10 Step 10: Collecting primary data

The data-gathering process may vary from a relatively simple observation at one specific location to an extensive survey of large corporations in different parts of the world. The method that is selected will largely determine the way in which the data are collected.

Different data-collection methods such as questionnaires, standardised tests, observation forms, laboratory notes, and transcribed recordings of focus group discussions will all have different implications for data collection. Each of the methods of data collection has its own, unique advantages and disadvantages, qualifying it rather than one of the other techniques for the collection of certain types of data. Although in certain circumstances a combination of methods can be considered, it is often not done for reasons of cost and the researcher invariably has to decide on the method that will yield the most satisfactory range of reliable data as cost-effectively and as quickly as possible.

To ensure consistency across respondents and to identify and isolate omissions and spoilt responses, data need to be edited quite rigorously. In the case of survey methods editing is essential to reduce recording errors, to improve legibility, and to identify and filter unclear and inappropriate responses. Editing provides data in a form which can be analysed and interpreted. The various aspects and contexts of data collection are covered in greater detail in chapters 6 to 14 of this book.

2.11 Step 11: Analysing and interpreting the data

After the data have been collected, captured and edited, the information still needs to be analysed and interpreted in terms of the original management problem and the proposed research objectives. Data analysis in essence involves reducing the accumulated data to a manageable size to allow summarising, comparing, synthesising and applying statistical techniques with a view to eventually interpreting the results in relation to the research problem. The process of interpretation is primarily one of logical thinking coupled with the ability to draw logical conclusions. In practical terms, conclusions are logical if they do not infer more from the findings than is justified. The specific nature and requirements of data analysis and interpretation will be covered in more detail in chapters 15 to 18 of this book.

2.12 Step 12: Reporting the results

Preparing the research report and conveying the research findings and recommendations to the client represent the final step in the research process. The ultimate objective is to enable the client to make an informed and scientifically verified decision to solve the original problem that prompted the undertaking of research in the first place. The style and organisation of the research report will once again vary according to the specific circumstances and the nature of the preceding research project. Factors that may influence the report are the target audience, the occasion, and the purpose of the research. In marketing research, communication of the research results will normally involve both a written report and a personal presentation of the findings and recommendations. Marketing research reports should in most instances be prepared and executed from the client's perspective. This means that the researcher should accurately assess the manager's needs throughout the research process and incorporate this point of view into the final product. In practice it is not so much the research results per se as how they are presented that motivates management to use them. The items to be included in a research report are essentially the same as those identified in the discussion of the research proposal. The proposal should in fact be a relatively accurate preview of the research report. The research report is covered in more detail in chapter 18.

3 THE RESEARCH PLAN: MANAGING THE RESEARCH PROJECT

The research plan is a blueprint for the implementation and management of a given research project. Nel *et al* (1988) liken it to the building plan for a house, or a roadmap for arriving at a set destination. The latter analogy is particularly relevant, because in the research process the researcher should never lose sight of the 'destination', namely the research objectives. In the preceding section the various steps in the research process were identified and described. In the research plan the researcher is required to implement the steps and all the underlying and accompanying logistical decisions in the most cost- and time-effective way without compromising on any of the scientific and methodological standards expected in the process.

Development of a research plan is a critical step in conducting research. Occasionally it may even become apparent in formulating a plan that the proposed study is not feasible in its present form. This decision is best made before expending considerable time and energy on a study that cannot be adequately executed. While very few research plans are executed exactly as planned, the existence of a plan permits the researcher to assess the overall impact of any changes on the study as a whole.

However, even before considering the various elements of the research plan, it is essential to realise the importance of the relationship between the main partners in the research endeavour.

3.1 The client–researcher relationship

In commissioned research probably one of the most important aspects of the management of a research project is the relationship between the client and the researcher. In internal research there should be a close relationship between the research department and management. Although strictly speaking this is not a specific component of the research plan, these relationships can, and do in fact, influence every other facet of the research project.

Both clients and researchers have important obligations in making a research project successful. The obligation of clients is to specify their problems and provide researchers with adequate background information relating to those problems. In most instances the process is facilitated when managers state their problems in terms of the decisions they have to make rather than to specify the information they think they will need. If this is done, the client and the researcher can jointly determine the kinds of information needed.

Naturally researchers also have obligations. They are expected to develop a creative research that will provide answers to important management questions. Not only are researchers expected to provide data analysed in terms of the particular problem, but they should also point out the implications that flow from the results. In the process conflict may arise between what the client wants and what the researcher can provide. Normally the client wants certainty and simple, explicit recommendations, while the researcher often can offer only probabilities and tentative interpretations. This conflict is inherent in their respective roles and there is no simple solution to it. However, a workable balance can usually be found if each person is sensitive to the demands and restrictions imposed on the other.

3.2 Critical decisions in the research plan

In dealing with the research process in section 2 above it would have become clear that not only are there various steps in the process, but there are alternatives in each step. In managing and implementing the research plan the researcher has to choose the most suitable alternative for achieving the research goals. Decisions have to be made about the research design and method of data collection, the sample size, the sampling method, the method of data processing, and the format of the research report. By implication the researcher should be fully familiar with the various alternative methods, and their advantages and shortcomings. It should be clear, however, that there is no single best standard plan, and in some cases different plans may be equally effective from both the methodological and the economic perspective, just as different roads may lead to the same destination.

3.3 The time schedule

After the research plan has been drafted the researcher needs to determine how long its implementation will take and so form an idea of whether the results will be in time for the decision. It does not often happen that a researcher has as long as he pleases to conduct a study, and if the decision has to be made long before the results will be available, there is little point in proceeding with the research. On the positive side, however, the existence of deadlines typically necessitates careful budgeting of time. Basically the time schedule includes a list of the major activities or phases of a proposed study and a corresponding expected completion time for each activity.

There are various ways in which to approach a research time schedule. Two of the most frequently used methods are the Gantt chart and the critical path method (CPM).

Developed by H L Gantt, one of the pioneers of management, the Gantt chart is useful in planning and controlling non-repetitive activities such as research studies. To construct a Gantt chart, the tasks to be completed are listed vertically on the left-hand side of the chart and the time to be covered by the entire project horizontally on the top of the chart. An example of a Gantt chart, which allows the researcher to easily visualise the entire project and identify concurrent activities, can be seen in figure 5.2.

Figure 5.2 Time schedule for a research plan up to questionnaire completion

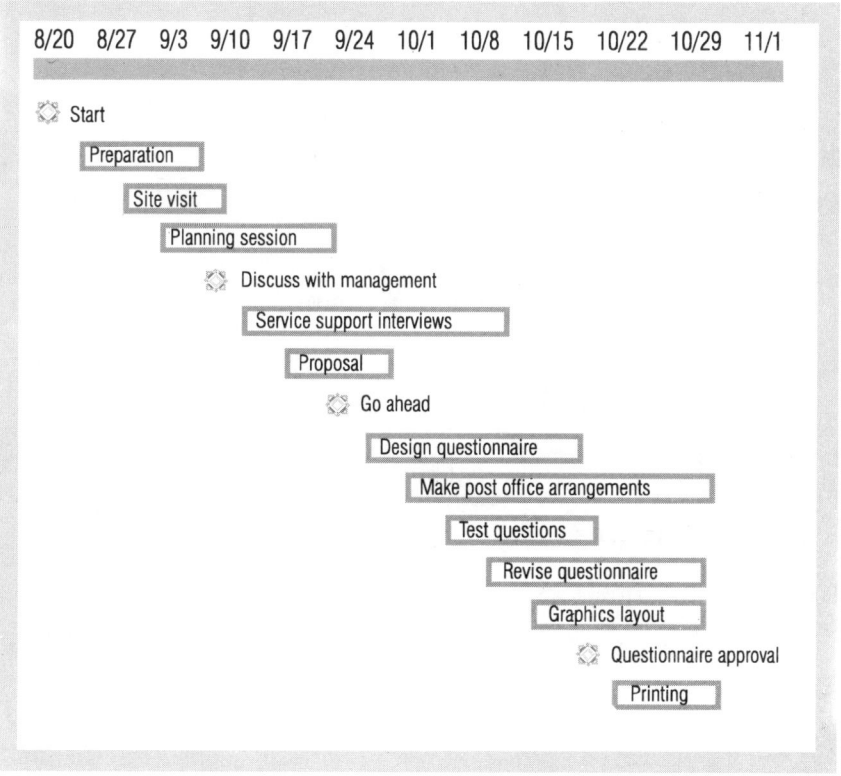

Source: Adapted from Emory & Cooper (1995).

In a CPM chart, as depicted in figure 5.3, the nodes represent the major milestones and the arrows suggest the work needed to get to the milestone. More than one arrow pointing to a node indicates that all those tasks have to be completed before the milestone can be reached. Usually a number is placed beside the arrow to indicate the number of days or weeks required for that task to be completed.

The entire pathway from the beginning to the end is called the critical path. Software programs designed for project management, which will simplify scheduling, are freely available for use on personal computers.

Figure 5.3 Time schedule for a research plan (critical path method)

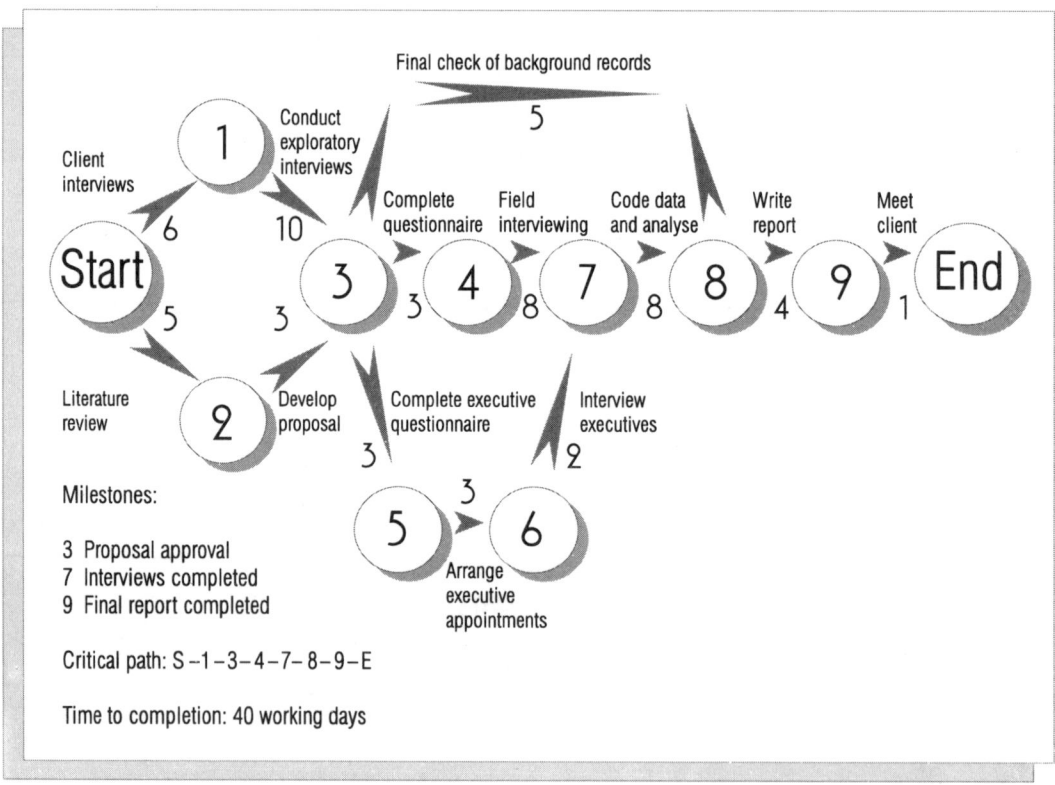

3.4 The research budget

Marketing research takes place in an extremely cost-conscious environment, with the result that costs usually feature prominently in management's decision on whether to proceed with the research. Cost estimates should therefore be as accurate as possible, and their preparation will be greatly enhanced by a time schedule as discussed in the previous section. The budget usually distinguishes between direct and indirect costs.

The direct costs consist of all items directly related to the project, such as preparation and planning, sampling and interviewing, editing, coding, capturing and processing of data, tabulation and data analysis, and writing and presenting the report. Indirect costs usually include office rental and other overheads.

In the end, however, the budget should be presented in the format required by the client or sponsor of the research. Typically a budget should be no more than one or two pages, and in many instances a standard form can be used. An example of a typical research budget can be seen in figure 5.4 on page 96.

3.5 Evaluating a research plan

Evaluation of a research plan can involve both informal and formal procedures. The formal method is usually employed in cases in which competitive plans or proposals for a particular research project are considered. Although the formal method has some variations, in essence it entails that criteria are established before the research plan is received. These criteria are given weights or points and the plan is evaluated against a checklist compiled in this way. Points are scored for each category reflecting the client's assessment of how well the plan meets the category's established criteria. In the end the category scores are added to provide a cumulative total, and the plan with the highest number of points will win the contract.

Non-competitive and small-scale projects are more suited to informal evaluation. With informal evaluation, the project needs and the related criteria are well understood but not necessarily well documented. In contrast to the formal method, no quantified points system is used and the criteria are not ranked or weighted. The process is more qualitative and impressionistic in nature.

3.6 The research proposal

The research proposal, which has been discussed as one of the steps in the research process above, is in fact the written and documented research plan. In other words, it contains all the particulars necessary for a decision by the client on whether the research plan should be implemented. Thus all the requirements set out in the above discussion of the research

Figure 5.4 A typical research budget

	R
1 *Planning*	
Head of Research Department (1 day)	2 000
2 *Questionnaire*	
(a) Design: Senior researcher (2 days)	3 000
(b) Typing (1 day)	552
(c) Pre-testing (20 cases)	
− Remuneration of interviewers	1 200
− Researcher (2 days)	2 064
(d) Printing costs (1 200 questionnaires of 12 pages each)	2 000
3 *Sample*	
Drawing of sample: Researcher (1 day)	1 032
Part-time clerks (3 days)	492
Listing of addresses: Part-time clerk (1 day)	164
4 *Interviewing*	
(a) *Pretoria*	
Recruiting of interviewers: Researcher (1 day)	1 032
Briefing and supervision: Researcher (15 days)	15 480
Travelling costs: 500 km at R1,00 per km	500
Remuneration of interviewers: 500 cases at R60	30 000
Control visits: 50 cases at R30,00	1 500
(b) *Durban*	
Recruiting of interviewers: Researcher (1 day)	1 032
Briefing and supervision: Researcher (3 days)	3 096
Travelling costs: Air travel	1 000
Motoring	928
Allowances: 3 days at R300,00	900
Revisit: Researcher (1 day)	1 032
Travelling costs: Air travel	1 000
Motoring	344
Allowances	300
Remuneration of supervisors	4 000
Remuneration of interviewers: 500 cases at R60	30 000
Control visits: 50 cases at R30	1 500
5 *Processing of data*	
Checking of fieldwork and remuneration of interviewers:	
Part-time clerk (10 days)	1 640
Programming	8 000
Checking of questionnaires:	
Part-time clerk (30 days)	4 920
Coding: Part-time clerk (180 days)	29 520
Data capturing	4 000
Computer costs	6 000
6 *Writing of report*	
Senior researcher (20 days)	30 000
7 Typing of report (10 days)	5 520
8 Editing of report (3 days)	2 160
9 Critical evaluation of report by committee of senior researchers	4 800
10 Printing and binding of report	1 200
11 Overheads (10 % of above items)	20 391
12 Unallocated time (10 % of salaries)	11 340
13 **Total** (1 000 questionnaires)	**235 639**
AVERAGE COST PER QUESTIONNAIRE: R235,64	

Source: Adapted from Nel *et al* (1988:108–109).

proposal also pertain to it here as the explication of the research plan. It should be noted, however, that the proposal is not the last step in the research plan but a critical decision-point in the middle of the process when it is determined whether to start implementing the actual operationalisation of the research process. Once the proposal is accepted, it becomes the guiding framework for the actual execution of the research project. As such, there should in most instances be a close resemblance between the proposal and the final research report, which should be reporting on each of the completed steps envisaged in the research proposal.

4 SUMMARY

This chapter entails an outline and discussion of the research process and the research plan. The research process can be roughly divided into a conceptualisation phase constituted by steps 1 to 5 of the research process and an operationalisation phase involving steps 6 to 12. Although the research process and the research plan may seem to be two separate entities, they can in fact not be divorced. Rather, the research plan represents a systematically ordered and documented written record of the conceptualisation phase of the research process which should, if approved by the client, serve as a guide for the operationalisation of the research project.

REFERENCES

American Marketing Association 1968. *Problem definition*. Chicago. (Marketing Research Technique Series no 2.)

Boyd, H W, Westfall, R & Stasch, S F 1989. *Marketing research: text and cases*. Seventh edition. Homewood, Ill: Irwin.

Churchill, Gilbert A (Jr) 1992. *Basic marketing research*. Second edition. Fort Worth: The Dryden Press. (The Dryden Press Series in Marketing.)

Dillon, W R, Madden, T J & Firtle, N H 1994. *Marketing research in a marketing environment*. Third edition. Boston: Irwin.

Emory, C W & Cooper, D R 1995. *Business research methods*. Fifth edition. Homewood, Ill: Irwin.

Gay, L P & Diehl, P L 1992. *Research methods for business and management*. New York: Macmillan.

Mouton, J & Marais, H C 1985. *Metodologie van die geesteswetenskappe: basiese begrippe*. Pretoria: RGN.

Nel, P A, Rädel, F E & Loubser, M 1988. *Researching the South African market*. Pretoria: University of South Africa. (Manualia Didactica 3.)

Secondary data: sources, interpretation and uses

Chapter 6: H de J van Wyk

1 INTRODUCTION

Information is the very foundation of marketing research. Without information or data it is not possible to make analyses, draw conclusions or put forward recommendations. There are two main sources of data: primary and secondary. Subsources are also distinguished, as illustrated below:

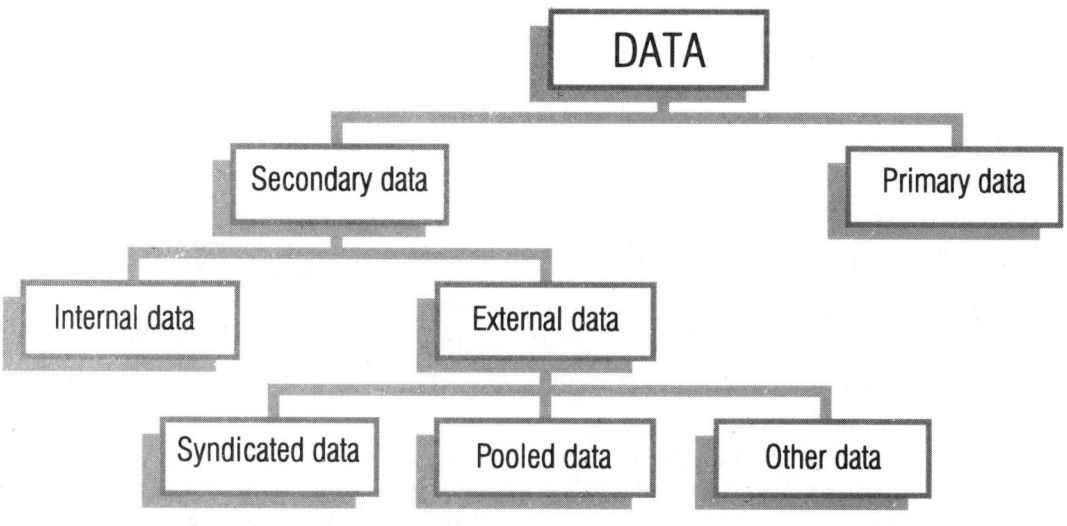

Secondary data are defined as existing data which can be used in solving the problem under study. **Primary data** are original data collected specifically for solving the problem in hand.

Secondary data will be discussed in this chapter and primary data in the chapters that follow. Secondary data are subdivided into internal secondary data, that is information generated by the establishment itself as a spin-off from its business transactions, and external secondary data, that is information acquired from sources outside the establishment. External secondary data in turn can be subdivided into syndicated data, that is information gathered by external organisations to which the establishment is required to subscribe, pooled data and other secondary data. We shall discuss each type of secondary data after we have briefly examined the role of secondary data in the marketing research process.

2 THE ROLE OF SECONDARY DATA IN THE RESEARCH PROCESS

Secondary data play a vital role in the research process. Because secondary data by definition are existing data, such data have the advantage of being readily available, whereas there is an inevitable delay before the results of primary surveys become available. In addition secondary data are generally much cheaper than primary data.

A researcher who initiates a project should make an inventory of the secondary information available in order to establish whether there is existing data that will meet the needs of the project before he even examines the possibility of doing a primary survey. He should also evaluate existing data in terms of suitability and quality (see section 3.2.3).

Secondary data are most useful in the spheres of formulating the decision problem, suggesting methods and types of data for meeting information needs, and serving as a source of comparative data for the interpretation and evaluation of primary data (Kinnear & Taylor 1991:182). Nel, Rädel and Loubser (1988:122) add two other major uses. The first of these is to monitor the external environment of the establishment. (This involves inter alia the events in the macro-economy, technological developments affecting the establishment, and the actions of competitors.) The second use is to serve as a base for final decision making.

In some problem situations all the required data are available from secondary sources. Sometimes lack of time or funds precludes launching a primary survey and final decisions have to be made on the strength of data from secondary sources alone.

3 TYPES OF SECONDARY DATA

3.1 Internal secondary data

> **Internal secondary data** are data generated by an organisation in the course of its business activities.

Internal secondary information is surely one of the most usable types of secondary data used in marketing research. Internal data are contained in the records of the establishment and only have to be adapted and arranged in the required format. Nonetheless it is very often one of the most neglected, especially in establishments which are not market oriented. Crimp (1990:18) states: 'Whether or not the operating records are kept in such a way that they can be used to allocate marketing costs to specific branded products, and to help monitor marketing performance, indicates whether the company is truly focused on the market.' Also, it is not uncommon for a researcher to experience lack of cooperation and even active opposition when he asks for the cooperation of colleagues outside his department. Sales staff, for instance, may be reluctant to complete invoices in full when additional information is required to identify the type of customer. The same goes for data processing, such as allocating codes to the towns where customers live, by staff who are not at all interested or fail to see the value of allocating correct codes. The researcher should educate his colleagues in this respect with the support of top management. The introduction of various measures will facilitate his task, especially among sales staff. Tull and Hawkins (1990:82) suggest the following:

(1) a clear, concise statement, repeated frequently, of the type of information desired; (2) a systematic, simple process of reporting the information; (3) financial and other rewards for reporting information; and (4) concrete examples of the actual use of the data.

Churchill (1992:189) emphasises the importance of integrating the data in the establishment's marketing information system (MIS) or marketing decision support system (MDSS), adding that this type of information typically forms the basis of a firm's marketing intelligence system. Cluttering the system with unnecessary information should, however, be avoided.

The integration of internal data begins with an examination of source documents which contain promising data. Once a document's potential has been established the next step is to consider how the data should be adapted if necessary.

As a practical example we look at an information system developed by a car manufacturer, which is based mainly on invoices. This manufacturer markets his cars through roughly 200 dealer agencies in South Africa. Each of these dealers was given a computer which is linked to the manufacturer's computer by telephone on condition that certain information is keyed into the network.

The manufacturer's source document is the invoice issued to the dealer (there is a separate invoice for each vehicle). This invoice shows inter alia the dealer's name, address and number, date, vehicle model code (each model has a unique code which also indicates whether the vehicle is manual or automatic), body colour code, upholstery colour code, codes for optional extras fitted at the factory (for example air-conditioning, radio), and the vehicle's unique code. However, the manufacturer also markets direct to major customers such as the state and car-hire companies. Such customers in turn have their own unique numbers with codes, inter alia, for type of customer. The agency is expected to adapt its invoices to enter the following information: unique vehicle code (read off from the manufacturer's invoice); whether an individual, a partnership, company or other type of organisation is purchasing the vehicle; whether the organisation is a fleet-owner of this type of vehicle; the suburb and town/city where owner lives/organisation is head-quartered; the age of the owner (if applicable – sourced from identity document); population group of individual purchasers (only symbols A, B, C, W appear on the invoice); whether the vehicle is on hire-purchase or bought for cash; details of trade-in vehicle; and optional extras added at customer's request. This information is keyed direct into the network but only the manufacturer has access to it. He refers to it for the compilation of reports containing unique information for each dealer. Thus each dealer is able to compare his performance nationally and regionally over a particular period with the performance of other dealers. (Individual dealers are not identified in the reports because dealers may also be competing with one another.)

The manufacturer has the advantage of being able to ascertain inter alia the average length of time particular models/colours remain on the dealer's floor, the age and other particulars of the buyers of specific models, and popular optional extras among buyers. He is also able to calculate the rate of repeat purchases and monitor brand switching between his and other makes of vehicle.

Initially the system caused various problems. For instance, dealers used to receive lists of codes with vehicle/model names which they keyed in to identify trade-in vehicles. However, it was found that dealers had given the wrong codes (this problem was mentioned earlier). Now the full particulars of the trade-in are keyed in from the invoice. The same holds for the suburb and town/city. Some of this information is forwarded to the National Association of Automobile Manufacturers of South Africa (NAAMSA) for the motor vehicle sales pool.

Other important source documents for internal secondary research are prior internal reports. Churchill (1992:189) thinks they are often overlooked, but prior marketing research studies on related topics typically form the basis of a firm's marketing information system.

Planning for the integration of internal information should consider compatible format, bearing in mind the usual format of external data, especially the coding systems that are in general use. The classification of business customers, for instance by the Standard Industrial Classification (SIC) subgroup, has various advantages. A comparison of customers classified according to this system with the total number of establishments in a specific subgroup will reveal the degree of market penetration achieved by the establishment, and potential customers can be identified. (See chapter 18 for a more detailed discussion.) A further requirement for the integration of internal information concerns the regional classification of the data, which should also be compatible with the classifications used by institutions like the Central Statistical Service (CSS). The estimation of regional market penetration, for instance, will be much easier if this requirement is met. We shall examine this aspect in greater detail in chapter 21.

3.2 External secondary data

> **External secondary data** are existing data which are obtained from sources outside the organisation.

Almost without exception external, like internal, secondary data are much cheaper than primary information. External secondary data are obtained free of charge, from subsidised sources (for example government publications), or the costs are shared with a number of other users. A further advantage is that the information, by definition being existing information, is available for use without delay.

3.2.1 Types of external secondary data

Although the distinction is not watertight, three principal types of external secondary data are distinguished: syndicated data, pooled data, and data from other sources. We shall discuss each of these three types in the sections that follow.

3.2.1.1 Syndicated data

> **Syndicated data** are data which are standardised on behalf of a group of clients, that is a syndicate, by a marketing research organisation.

Briefly, an organisation places a research product on the market and offers it to various potential clients. Members of a syndicate sometimes also have a say in such aspects of the research as the survey method and coverage. A fairly recent example of syndicated research took the form of a series of surveys on the use of banking services. The research consultant's clients were a number of banks. Each paid a fraction of what it would have cost to undertake or commission the surveys as individual banks, but they also shared the results and therefore failed to gain a competitive advantage.

As we have said, the distinction between various types of research is not watertight. There are those who argue that for the most part syndicated research entails primary research. However, syndicated data are classified as secondary data in this book for the following reasons: syndicated data are not collected to solve a specific problem; the cost of secondary data is a fraction of what it would cost an individual client; the data are collected on behalf of clients and offered for sale; the client spends little or no time on the planning and execution of the research; and in some instances the client has no say in the contents, scope and format of the data which are offered on a take it or leave it basis.

Syndicated sources should not be confused with omnibus surveys. In an omnibus survey several clients buy space in a primary survey questionnaire. Thus the cost of the survey is spread among a number of clients but the results of an individual client's part of the survey remain the client's exclusive property. Only when several clients have access to the results of a specific category of questions in an omnibus survey can the results be labelled syndicated data.

The incidence of syndicated sources in South Africa will be discussed in section 3.2.5.4.

3.2.1.2 Pooled data

> **Pooled data** are standardised data which a number of interested organisations of equal status voluntarily submit to an independent, impartial organisation for processing and redistribution to the participating parties.

The principle in pooled data is that the participating parties benefit equally by pooling the information. When all the organisations in a specific sector of the economy participate in the pooling system, information may be released quite freely but possibly in less detail than to the participating parties.

In South Africa, for example, the collection of motor vehicle sales statistics is administered by NAAMSA. Because all the motor manufacturers in the country participate and detailed statistics are collected, individual manufacturers are able to calculate their own and their competitors' market shares. Information pooling systems do not necessarily divulge individual participants' statistics. Most pools confine themselves to the calculation of total figures which allow participating institutions to estimate their own market shares but not their competitors'. However, the participants in a pool tend to withhold their figures for fear of placing themselves at a disadvantage if one of their number withdraws from the pool, and then the whole system collapses. Also, a participant may deliberately submit erroneous figures to gain the advantage over other participants. For this reason most pool administrators will accept only audited figures.

Pooled data are classified as external secondary data for much the same reasons as syndicated data: the information is not collected to solve a specific problem, and costs to participants are relatively low. However, in this type of data collection the participants always have a great deal of say in the sort of information that is collected and the format in which it is released.

3.2.1.3 External data other than syndicated and pooled data

Most organisations regard external data other than syndicated and pooled data as the most important of all the types of external secondary data. In terms of variety and volume there is a great deal of it, and in most instances it is readily available. Much of this type of external secondary data is published by government and semi-government institutions as part of their functions. For instance, government departments publish annual reports containing information which the department is required to gather in any case in the course of its supervisory and other functions. The Central Statistical Service (CSS) is another example which we shall discuss more fully later and which is responsible for collecting all the statistics required by the authorities for policy formulation and evaluation and by other organisations for planning purposes. Generally the price of these reports merely covers printing costs because the collection and processing costs are recovered from state funds. Sometimes these are the only feasible sources of information. Certain categories of corporate information such as turnover figures are regarded as so confidential by some firms that they are only divulged to the CSS* and then only because it is a statutory requirement. The sources of this type of information will be discussed in greater detail in section 3.2.5.

3.2.2 Application of external secondary data to the problem in hand

The researcher is seldom fortunate enough to find external secondary data that meet his every requirement. Very often it is not available in the required format, or its format and method of collection and scope are a compromise designed to satisfy a large number of interested parties. Tull and Hawkins (1990:79) mention four common problems which reduce the relevance of data that would otherwise be useful.

We shall discuss these problems below and put forward suggestions for lessening their impact. Indeed one of the trademarks of a good researcher is the skilful application of less than ideal data in the course of his work. The constraints of cost and time associated with primary data collection and the absence of more appropriate secondary data may well leave the researcher no other alternative. He should, however, never lose sight of the fact that less than ideal information can be extremely misleading.

☐ Different units of measurement. Sales data may, for example, be available only in rand values whereas information on the number of physical units sold is required. Here the researcher may decide to calculate an average price per unit. By dividing the total rand value of sales by the average unit price he arrives at the number of physical units sold.

---

* The CSS is required by law to release information in a form that will not allow individual organisations to be identified.

☐ It may be necessary to use surrogate data because the required information is not available. A researcher who needs to know how many office workers there are in a particular area may find that the only relevant figures available are for total office floor space. He now has to make an assumption about the average floor space occupied by one worker. To estimate the number of workers, he divides total floor space by average floor space per worker.

☐ The definition of classes may vary greatly. For instance, a researcher may want to know the number of children in the 6–11 age group, but the population census only gives this information for age groups 5–9 and 10–14. His only alternative in this situation is to proceed from the assumption that the number of children in each age group is evenly distributed over the individual ages. Thus he will add together four-fifths of the number of children in the 5–9 age group (there are five individual ages in that age group and of these, four fall into the researcher's group) and two-fifths of the 10–14 age group. This method should yield fairly accurate results, provided the birth-rate remains constant.

☐ Time. Relevant information may well be available but not for the required time period. In South Africa sectoral censuses in manufacturing, for example, are taken at intervals of three to five years and there is quite a long delay before the results are published. The regional results of the 1988 Census of Manufacturing were not available until 1994 because the collection of census data is a very lengthy process indeed. Obviously there may have been major structural changes in manufacturing in the interim. A researcher using outdated figures should make doubly sure that his calculations do not produce misleading results. It is possible to adjust figures by making use of more recent indicators. In the past the Workmen's Compensation Commissioner used to publish recent figures regarding employees and compensation in selected categories of economic activity by district. The information was not complete but it served as an indicator of change, assuming that the degree of incompleteness remained constant from year to year.

3.2.3 Evaluation of the quality of external secondary data

Because in most instances the researcher has no control over the collection and compilation of external secondary data (unlike internal secondary data and primary data), the evaluation of the accuracy of such data is an essential step in the research process. Kinnear and Taylor (1991:183) distinguish three criteria for evaluating the accuracy of secondary data: source, purpose of the publication, and evidence concerning quality.

☐ *Source:* There are original (or primary) sources of secondary data and acquired (or secondary) sources. As the terms indicate, an original source originated the data, while an acquired source is a source which procured the data from an original source. An example of an acquired source in South Africa would be *South African statistics*, a publication compiled annually by the CSS from census reports and other sources of statistics.

Although it is quite a lengthy publication it obviously contains very much less detail than the original sources and almost no regional data. Some of these acquired sources present an excellent general picture of the available statistics and therefore an indication of sources of more detailed information. Generally speaking it is, however, advisable to consult original sources, for several reasons. First, the source references and explanatory notes in the original source are more detailed than in the acquired source. The explanatory notes in particular are of interest to the researcher because they generally describe the survey method (census survey or sample and in the latter instance the type of sample), the universe (for example only people older than a certain age, or the entire population) and coverage (for example the whole country), the rate of response and so forth. These details are of the greatest importance to a researcher who wishes to use the information in his own work. Information procured from acquired sources should also be scrutinised for errors in transcription and for omissions of key aspects such as footnotes and other textual comments.

☐ *Purpose of the publication:* Kinnear and Taylor (1990:184) quote Nemmers and Myers (1966:43) in this context:

> Sources published to promote sales, to advance the interests of an industrial or commercial or other group, to present the cause of a political party, or to carry on any sort of propaganda, are suspect. Data published anonymously, or by an organisation which is on the defensive, or under conditions which suggest a controversy, or in a form which reveals a strained attempt at 'frankness', or to controvert inferences from other data, are generally suspect.

In addition the researcher should evaluate the status of the publication. Family magazines for the popular market are seldom reliable sources of reference. At best such sources point the researcher in the general direction of the information.

☐ *Evidence concerning the quality of the data:* First and foremost the researcher should assure himself of the scientific credentials of the publication. Does it specify the method of data collection, coverage, limitations and the like? Is the technical editing of a high standard? Does the appearance of the publication as a whole inspire confidence, or are the overly lavish paper and printing style perhaps designed to mislead? Does a profusion of printing, language and numbering errors suggest a generally sloppiness which probably extends to the computations as well? Last, the researcher should examine the tables and figures for consistency, check totals, etc. Other points to consider are whether the contents of the publication are arranged in logical sequence and the recommendations are well reasoned and well presented. (See chapter 18 for the requirements of a good report.)

3.2.4 Tracing external secondary data

As we have said, a researcher should find out whether existing secondary data are available before instituting a primary survey. The question is how to set about tracing relevant information. Briefly there are two ways: the researcher can look for the information himself, or he can obtain the services of an organisation which specialises in tracing sources of secondary information.

A researcher undertaking the search for sources of secondary information himself may begin with the reference section in a library. Some acquired sources have an advantage in that they provide an overview of the kind of statistics that are available. One such publication is *South African statistics*, which is published annually by the CSS. The CSS also runs an information tracing service, but it only covers data collected by the CSS. Many other institutions collect a wide variety of statistics, other than those assembled by the CSS, which are not covered in the umbrella publications or information service run by the CSS. The researcher should therefore also consult specialist publications for secondary sources of information. One of these is published by the Bureau of Market Research (BMR) under the title of *A guide to statistical sources in the Republic of South Africa*. Updated periodically it contains approximately 6 000 research topics (mostly products) listed alphabetically in the first part of the book with the titles of publications which contain information on the topic printed opposite. The second part of the book lists all the publications referred to in the first part with the following details: publisher, date of latest edition with frequency of publication if known, number of pages and short description of the contents. Unpublished sources are not listed as a rule, nor are acquired sources unless they also contain statistics that are not given in any original source.

Another BMR report which also serves as a source reference is entitled *A guide to associations, employee/employer organisations, industrial councils, co-operatives and agricultural boards in the RSA*. It is updated periodically and consists of two parts: a functional classification of associations and an alphabetical index. Most of the associations listed in the guide are of interest to the businessman. Purely social and sports bodies are excluded. Each listing contains the following details (if available): full name and acronym, street and postal addresses, telephone and fax numbers, official title of contact person, size of membership, details about publications and/or statistics, research facilities and availability of membership lists to non-members. There are over 2 600 listings in the guide. Lastly the BMR has also published *A guide to directories, year books and buyer's guides in the Republic of South Africa*.

Instead of instituting an information search himself a researcher may engage the services of an organisation specialising in the tracing of secondary sources. Tull and Hawkins (1990:85) believe it is sometimes more effective to have an information broker than to conduct an external search for resources in-house.

3.2.5 Sources of external secondary data

As we saw in the previous section, researching sources of information is a difficult task. The discussion that follows is not intended to cover all the major sources of data in the country; it is merely a brief overview of some of them.

The focus here will be on sources of statistical data. Researchers in need of non-statistical data are advised to consult their local general or specialised libraries.

The following principal sources of statistical information will be distinguished: government institutions, parastatals, universities, commercial marketing research consultants, banks, and miscellaneous organisations.

3.2.5.1 Government institutions

In this section we shall confine ourselves to government institutions in South Africa. However, for all practical purposes the other members of the Southern African Customs Union – Botswana, Lesotho, Swaziland and Namibia, or the so-called BLSN countries – are part of the South African market as well. In all these countries there are government institutions, mostly central government departments, which release statistical information.

In South Africa government institutions may be divided into two groups: the Central Statistical Service (CSS) whose mission it is to collect and release statistics to consumers in the public and private sectors, and other government departments which generate statistics in the course of their activities. The CSS gathers information with the aid of questionnaires which respondents, irrespective of whether they are institutions or individuals, are required by law to complete. These questionnaires collect the basic information published in census reports, including censuses of the population, and virtually every sector of the economy. The census reports contain national and regional statistics on such aspects as the number of establishments, number of employees and financial statistics by sector. In practice it takes several years to collect and process all the information. Less cumbersome sample surveys are also conducted to gather data which are published in statistical news releases. The sample survey data are more recent though less detailed than the census data. Besides collecting information on its own behalf, the CSS is also a repository of information from other sources, mostly government departments. The CSS, for example, systematises and publishes information on treasury receipts and payments by category and government department. In addition the CSS is responsible for the National Accounts of South Africa, including the gross domestic product (GDP), which is a common measure of economic growth.

Statistics are also generated and published by other state institutions such as central and provincial government departments. Their statistics are usually published in their annual reports, although there are departments such as the Department of Agriculture which publish statistical reports in their own right. Very often government institutions which engage in economic, physical and sociological planning also publish statistics. Local authorities do a great deal of planning in the course of their duties. Through their planning departments they generate statistics which are of interest to the researcher but difficult to come by unless they are published. Local authorities whose internal statistics are systematised have the potential to become major sources of statistical information for their own use and for the use of the researcher. (For a discussion of internal secondary data, see section 3.1.)

3.2.5.2 Parastatals

We shall confine ourselves to the discussion of only two parastatals, the Human Sciences Research Council (HSRC) and the CSIR. The HSRC conducts research in the sphere of human sciences and maintains registers such as the Register of Graduates. The CSIR specialises in the natural sciences and generates mostly technical and techno-economic statistics. The CSIR is doing research in the following fields: building technology, earth/marine atmospheric science and technology, energy technology, food science and technology, forest science and technology, manufacturing and aeronautical systems technology, materials science and technology, microelectronics and communications technology, road and forest technology, technology for developing communities, and water technology.

3.2.5.3 University institutes

Along with teaching and community services, research is part of the mission of a university. Research is carried out by individual lecturers (or informal groups of lecturers) and by formal research institutes. In this section we shall confine our discussion to formal research institutes undertaking socio-economic research, and which responded to the request for information about their activities.

(a) Bureau of Market Research (BMR), University of South Africa

Since its inception in 1960 the BMR has done a great deal of socio-economic research (see chapter 2, section 4.2.1). Currently the BMR's basic research activities are organised into nine research divisions. Organisations join one or more of these divisions. A projects committee elected by the members of a division supervises its research activities by rating, approving and supervising the execution of projects. In reality this type of research is syndicated research in the sense that standardised research results are supplied to organisations that pay membership fees. The BMR undertakes basic research in the fields described below.

(i) Household income and expenditure

The BMR's income, expenditure and demographic data from surveys conducted over more than 30 years are coupled with secondary data in a comprehensive data base for the calculation of

☐ average income and expenditure figures by household size, income group and geographical area

☐ total household expenditure in South Africa on 500+ products and services by population group and geographical area

☐ income elasticities of demand for products and services.

(ii) Personal income and personal disposable income

The BMR first calculated personal income figures for 1960 and continues to calculate personal income, personal disposable income and income per capita at regular intervals. Besides the national figures, regional figures are also calculated by district at five-year intervals. The district figures are combined by region as required.

(iii) General market potential indices for consumer goods

From time to time indices are compiled from personal disposable income, population and retail sales figures by district.

(iv) Economic growth areas

Roughly 100 magisterial districts with better than average absolute and relative growth potentials are selected from time to time. Recent and projected employment, personal disposable income and population figures are calculated for them by population group. Combined share and growth indices are also compiled. In addition focus studies of areas with exceptional growth potential are also undertaken. Statistical series which serve as growth indicators are published twice a year in the *Growth areas monitor*.

(v) Demographic research

Projections are prepared of the South African population and labour force by population and age group. Post-censal estimates of the population are also prepared by population group and district. Internal migration patterns are studied. Special fields of interest are the validation of population figures and population estimation in 'open' areas.

(vi) Retail sales forecasts

Retail sales are predicted annually by product group.

(vii) Business environment studies

At least once a year executives of the top 100 manufacturers are canvassed for their views on the expected business environment in the year ahead. Topics include the inflation rate and economic growth rate, the political situation, level of unrest and strike action.

(viii) BMR registers

These registers list the names and addresses of more than 140 000 institutions/establishments in the major sectors of the economy in South Africa. Each listing includes size indicators such as number of employees and electricity consumption, SIC code* and district code. Selections are specified by users. The information is transferred to diskettes, gummed labels, index cards, tapes, floppies and stiffies.

The following registers are maintained:

☐ Associations and trade unions

☐ Business services (legal, accounting, data processing, architecture, quantity and land surveyors, advertising, market researchers)

☐ Commercial farmers

☐ Construction

☐ Exporters/importers

☐ Financial institutions

☐ Hotels (registered hotels and off-sales)

☐ Manufacturing

☐ Mines

☐ Trade (wholesalers and retailers except motor trade).

(ix) Behavioural and communications research

Psychological, motivation and media research studies include reports on the advertising and marketing environment, aspects of the marketing environment in developing countries, factors in advertising effectiveness, advertising testing, aspirations, value systems and consumer expectations (with special reference to young consumers) and status products lifestyles and facilities of the newly emerging middle class.

---

* The Standard Industrial Classification (SIC) codes designate type of economic activity of an establishment. For a full description of the system see chapter 19.

(x) Living level studies

Primary data are collected for the calculation of Minimum and Supplementary Living Levels which are widely used by organisations as a guideline for fixing wage levels and granting wage increases. The figures are calculated for 26 areas throughout South Africa. MLLs and SLLs are calculated for different household sizes and types of residence.

Besides the basic research described above, the BMR is also involved in other research and related activities. Research is undertaken on behalf of clients, information pooling systems are maintained and secondary information services include consultation, and library and statistical broker services to members. The Statistical Clearing House comprises all the major statistical reports published in South Africa. The BMR has access to the CSS database.

(b) Bureau for Economic Research (BER), University of Stellenbosch

The Bureau for Economic Research (BER) monitors the national and international economy. The bureau also regularly produces forecasts of macro-economic trends from two econometric models and a host of business surveys. Data are collected (in the surveys) from manufacturers, retailers, wholesalers, motor traders, architects, surveyors, building contractors and sub-contractors, and consumers. The first business surveys were conducted in 1954 and the first consumer surveys in 1975. The BER's econometric work has come into prominence since 1980.

(c) Bureau for Statistical and Survey Methodology (Statomet), University of Pretoria

Statomet was established in 1992 to advise on all aspects of research design and management, improve the quality of research and provide training in research methodology.

Although Statomet is part of the Department of Statistics of the University of Pretoria, its activities are multidisciplinary. It is active in the following fields of research: marketing, consumer products, surveys, organisations, demography, biostatistics, econometrics, psychometrics, sociometrics, biometrics, ecclesiometrics, insurance, strategic positioning of offices and centres.

(d) Bureau of Financial Analysis (BFA), University of Pretoria

The BFA undertakes research projects in four fields of research on a contractual basis:

□ inter-firm comparative studies (of industries, professions and services)

□ analysis of financial statements of listed companies, calculation of ratios and electronic dissemination of processed data via the BFA-NET system

□ financial research projects for financial and industrial companies, and

□ diverse regular short-term statistical surveys.

The BFA maintains databanks on a variety of industries, professions and services.

(e) Centre for Development Support, University of the Orange Free State

The Centre for Development Support has two main foci: maintaining and extending a computerised empirical database of development information on the Free State for use in analysis, planning, monitoring and evaluation of development, and providing capacity building and training in public and private sector management of development. In addition it renders ad hoc development services on request to a variety of players in the development field. The centre operates mainly in the economic field but can mobilise inputs from a wide range of capacities and information sources in the whole development field.

(f) Institute for Futures Research (IFR), University of Stellenbosch

Established in 1974, the IFR is a research institution which specialises in future studies as a support service for strategic corporate management.

The philosophy of the institute is that organisations can create the future they desire by clearly visualising what they want and achieve it by understanding positive factors and obstacles on the path to success. Innovative leadership and the cooperation of all stakeholders are prerequisites for creating the desired future. An essential part of the process is a shared understanding of the patterns of change in the broader South African context.

To help decision makers, the IFR organises meetings, workshops and courses on current political and economic developments and other themes of importance to South African organisations. The following are publications of the IFR:

- ☐ *Business Futures* is a comprehensive handbook of over 800 pages on trends and forecasts in the economic, technological, social, political and natural/physical environments with emphasis on the South African context.

- ☐ *Strategy Insights* is the IFR's monthly monitor series which interprets current issues within the longer-term context. These publications deal with political, labour, economic and business issues.

- ☐ *The Business Futures Bulletin*, published quarterly, is an analysis of a specially selected practical long-term issue of specific relevance to South African business.

- ☐ *SCAN* is a monthly environmental scanning publication of extracts from periodicals and reports of possible strategic importance to associates.

- ☐ *Friday at Noon* is a weekly one-page newsletter on strategic relevant current affairs which is distributed electronically on Fridays.

(g) Institute for Planning Research (IPR), University of Port Elizabeth

The Institute for Planning Research has done a wide variety of surveys in Port Elizabeth, the Eastern Cape region and nationally. They include analyses of the retail structure, the manufacturing sector, land use, shopping patterns, location factors and population distributions. Besides doing economic studies, the IPR also publishes data biannually on the Household Subsistence Level of the low-income and low-middle-income groups in 27 urban centres throughout South Africa.

(h) Institute for Social and Economic Research (ISER), University of Grahamstown

The institute is involved in a wide range of socio-economic research studies with a strong Eastern Cape bias, which include rotating credit associations (stokfels) in informal settlements, community-based organisations, and population mobility and settlement patterns.

(i) Institute of South African Studies (ISAS), National University of Lesotho

ISAS is a centre for promoting, planning and coordinating interdisciplinary, policy-related and development-oriented research. Projects with socio-economic components examine grassroots marketing strategies. The following two projects are of interest: the Participating Environmental Action Programme of Rural Women in Lesotho examines the role of edible wild vegetables in the lives of Basotho, and the Innovative Rural Action Learning Areas (IRALA) project examines, among other aspects, the marketing strategies of successful farmers.

(j) The Breakwater Monitor (BWM), University of Cape Town

The absence of reliable and integrated human resource information at a national level and by economic sector led to the establishment of a national human resource database at the UCT Graduate School of Business. The Breakwater Monitor (BWM) project is managed in collaboration with more than 100 major South African organisations representing over one million employees in the formal sector. The following strategic objectives are pursued:

- [ ] to inform strategic human resource management of development challenges, including affirmative action
- [ ] to monitor trends and practices in human resource management and development
- [ ] to establish meaningful measures of human resource information for benchmarking purposes
- [ ] to provide forums for information sharing and debate.

Data are collected in four categories:

- [ ] permanent staff strength by level, race and gender (stock and flow data – recruitment, promotion and termination patterns by level, race and gender)

☐ training and development

☐ education

☐ remuneration.

3.2.5.4 Commercial syndicated research

In the section that follows we shall turn our attention to the commercial research consultants who responded to the request for information about their activities. They are arranged in alphabetical order with short descriptions of their research activities. This might be regarded as syndicated research.

(a) Decision Surveys International (DSI) (formerly IMS South Africa)

The following regular surveys are undertaken by DSI:

☐ *Pharmaceutical Market South Africa – Retail:* Monthly data from 14 wholesalers and 160 pharmacies.

☐ *Pharmaceutical Market South Africa – Institutional:* Quarterly survey of provincial hospitals.

☐ *National Disease and Therapeutic Index:* Semi-annual survey of 375 general practitioners and specialists.

☐ *Medical Promotion Index:* Quarterly survey of 150 general practitioners.

☐ Besides the regular services mentioned above, DSI provides on-line access to these services through a database known as SANDS (SA National Database System).

(b) Douglas Parker Associates

Douglas Parker Associates is a firm of business development consultants who specialise in the assessment and evaluation of commercial business ventures and market potentials, including concept testing, feasibility studies and forecasting in marketing, retailing and property development. A further speciality is the integration of census-based geodemographic data with consumer motivation and attitudinal and behavioural data.

The company maintains an extensive database on population demographics, lifestyle patterns and consumer market potential.

(c) Market Research Africa (MRA)

The MRA provides the following syndicated data series:

☐ *Adindex:* The MRA Adindex (advertising expenditure index) covers advertising expenditure in newspapers, magazines, and on radio and TV. Cinema and outdoor advertising are also covered.

☐ *Black, coloured and Indian household studies:* These studies provide insight into the standard of living, behaviour and attitudes of urban and rural blacks, and urban coloureds and Indians.

☐ *Financial tracking and Adexpose:* This is an annual study of the effectiveness of financial institutions in relation to consumer needs. There is also a separate study on hire-purchase.

☐ *Money Monitor:* This is a quantitative consumer survey of the financial status and behaviour of urban adults.

☐ *Omnibus studies:* The questionnaires for these studies contain questions for various clients, and clients only pay for those questions related to their product or area of concern. The studies are designed to address questions to the general public, that is males and females 16 years and older. (The results of omnibus surveys are classed as syndicated data only in so far as certain categories of results are shared by more than one organisation – see section 3.2.)

(d) Market Support Associates (Pty) Ltd (MSA)

MSA specialises in black consumer trends research and in communications and advertising research projects.

(e) Marketing Surveys and Statistical Analysis (MSSA)

Marketing Surveys and Statistical Analysis focuses on marketing research and exploratory analysis using multivariate statistical techniques. Other areas of survey research are educational research, building research, basic marketing research and strategic marketing research, using a variety of mapping techniques.

(f) Markinor

Markinor has specialised research divisions covering the following areas: personal and household products, automotive and durable products, financial services, retail, research business, information technology and agriculture, qualitative research, sociopolitical research, public sector research, media research, liquor and health care. The company offers two syndicated omnibus surveys with fieldwork nine times a year.

Markinor has a portfolio of over 20 research products covering advertising, brand equity, corporate image, staff studies, customer service, new product development, sociopolitical opinions, market segmentation, public sector research, psychographics and qualitative research.

(g) Neville Berkowitz and Associates

This firm produces *The Property Economist Opportunity Report* infrequently. This publication contains information on the current and likely future state of the property industry in South Africa.

(h) Nielsen South Africa (formerly IBIS)

Nielsen South Africa has three business units:

- ☐ Nielsen provides a continuing measurement of food, grocery, confectionery, toiletry and liquor markets which is derived from a combination of store audits, electronic input and a panel of households. This division also provides a range of software which enables manufacturers and retailers to optimise their resource utilisation and market knowledge insights.

- ☐ Nielsen Media provides continuing measurement of advertising expenditure and provides information on readership and listenership.

- ☐ Market Research Africa provides traditional large-scale and ad hoc consumer research (see section (c) above).

(i) PE Corporate Services

This firm provides professional management consulting, training and research services and undertakes national and industry level salary surveys.

(j) Research Surveys (Pty) Ltd

This firm developed the conversion model, which segments users of brands or products based on commitment and non-users of brands or products based on availability.

(k) Rode & Associates (formerly Real Estate Surveys)

The results of Rode & Associates' ongoing property market research surveys are regularly published in the following publications:

- ☐ *Rode's Report on the SA Property Market ('The Rode Report')*. Published quarterly, it covers commercial, industrial and residential rental levels and capitalisation rates by property type, grade, node/township, building costs, building activity.

- ☐ *Rode's New Office Developments ('Rode's NOD')* is a quarterly summary of new office developments and refurbishments in the main metropolitan areas.

- ☐ *Rode's Retail Report on South Africa ('Rode's Retail Report')*, which contains retail property information covering shop rentals, operating expenses, and escalation rates for about 100 shopping centres and 120 street-front micro-locations, is published quarterly.

- ☐ *Rode's SA Property Trends* is published twice a year. It comprises five-year forecasts of office and industrial rentals, capitalisation rates, building costs, house prices, flat rentals, the property cycle, gross domestic fixed investment in residential and non-residential buildings, and forecasts for property unit trusts.

3.2.5.5 Banks

Given the key role banks play in the South African economy, many of them generate and compile statistics.

(a) South African Reserve Bank (SARB)

The *Quarterly Bulletin* published by the Economics Department of the SARB contains statistics on national accounts,* the balance of payments, exchange rate, capital market, etc. Occasional publications deal with special topics such as the national accounts or balance of payments.

(b) Development Bank of Southern Africa (DBSA)

In the nature of its activities the DBSA requires a great deal of information for decision making. Besides demographic series and gross geographic product figures for individual districts, the DBSA has assembled a sizeable body of knowledge about the former black states. The information has been published in a wide range of reports.

(c) Other banks

Virtually all of the banks in South Africa have economics departments which publish information that is of interest to their clients, such as analyses and forecasts of economic trends. Absa Bank, for instance, publishes house prices in different areas of the country, and Nedcor collects and publishes news about major capital projects.

3.2.5.6 Miscellaneous organisations

Several other organisations in the country also generate information. At one time agricultural marketing control boards were major sources of statistics on the production and consumption of their products. These sources gradually declined in importance because several of the marketing boards were disbanded and the control functions of others were severely curtailed. The remaining boards are still useful sources of information.

Some trade and production associations gather information from their members and other institutions and disseminate it to their members. Non-members generally do not have access to such information or have only limited access to non-detailed statistics. Motor vehicle sales figures, for example, are collected and disseminated by NAAMSA. The South African Advertising Research Foundation (SAARF) publishes the results of the All Media and Products Survey (AMPS) which is conducted among private households of all population groups in all areas of South Africa. The reports contain audience data on all

---

* Some of the national accounts statistics in the *Quarterly Bulletin* are acquired from sources obtained from the CSS (see chapter 6, section 3.2).

types of electronic and printed media, consumption figures for selected products, and incidence data on durables and motor vehicles. SAARF is also involved in a client study, product definition study, age of copy survey, sample design and response rates, and validation of audience levels for electronic media. In addition SAARF has developed the AMPS Living Standards Measure (LSM) which classifies households by living standard, using a battery of variables.

The Africa Institute of South Africa generates information on countries in South Africa and is a major source of reference for the expansion of trading activities in Africa. Finally the reports published by the United Nations and World Bank contain comprehensive international statistics.

4 SUMMARY

Secondary statistics clearly play a key role in the marketing research process. The use of secondary statistics very often expedites the process and saves money. Secondary information should, however, be evaluated before use in terms of its accuracy and relevance.

REFERENCES

Churchill, Gilbert A (Jr) 1992. *Basic marketing research*. Second edition. Fort Worth: The Dryden Press. (The Dryden Press Series in Marketing.)

Crimp, Margaret 1990. *The marketing research process*. Third edition. New York: Prentice Hall.

Kinnear, Thomas C & Taylor, James R 1991. *Marketing research: an applied approach*. Fourth edition. New York: McGraw-Hill. (McGraw-Hill Series in Marketing.)

Nel, P A, Rädel, F E & Loubser, M 1988. *Researching the South African market*. Pretoria: University of South Africa. (Manualia Didactica no 3.)

Tull, Donald S & Hawkins, Del I 1990. *Marketing research: measurement and method: a text with cases*. New York: Macmillan. (The Macmillan Series in Marketing.)

Primary research: verbal communication

Chapter 7: J A Bennett

Primary research: verbal communication

1 INTRODUCTION

In the previous chapter we highlighted the collection of secondary data, including the evaluation and sources of secondary data. This chapter is the first of three which deal with the collection of primary research data. As we have noted earlier, primary research involves the collection of problem-specific data to solve a research problem. Once the researcher realises that primary research has to be undertaken, he must decide on an appropriate data-collection method. The researcher has four options: data can be collected through verbal communication, written communication, observation and experimentation.

> **Verbal communication** refers to the collection of primary research data by questioning the respondents to obtain their responses.

It can take the form of personal interviews at the respondents' homes or at shopping malls, telephone interviews, depth interviews, or focus group discussions. Personal and telephone interviews are normally quantitative in nature, while depth interviews and focus groups are qualitative in nature.

Data collected through *written communication* requires respondents to write down their responses to the researchers' questions. The mail survey, where the respondent completes the questionnaire in the privacy of his office or home, and mail panels are examples of data collected through written communication.

With *observation* the researcher studies humans and other phenomena, most often without their knowledge or cooperation. Relevant facts, actions and behaviours are noted, and the researcher uses them to draw appropriate conclusions. Observation can take many forms: it can be undertaken by a person studying other people; it can be done with the aid of mechanical devices such as scanners and cameras; or it can be carried out by researchers going through the garbage of households to establish their consumption patterns.

Experimentation is used to determine cause and effect relationships between independent and dependent variables. By controlling independent variables, the researcher can determine their effect on dependent variables. Experiments can be carried out in the field or in controlled environments, also known as laboratories.

In this chapter the focus is on the collection of primary data through verbal communication. All the examples refer to consumer research, although most of the techniques discussed can also be applied in industrial research. Since chapter 19 deals extensively with industrial research, we shall focus mainly on consumer research here.

Figure 7.1 provides a schematic presentation of the different primary data-collection methods referred to in the preceding paragraphs. From the figure it can be seen that verbal communication can be broken down into two major types: quantitative and qualitative research methods. This distinction is followed in this chapter.

Figure 7.1 Primary data-collection methods

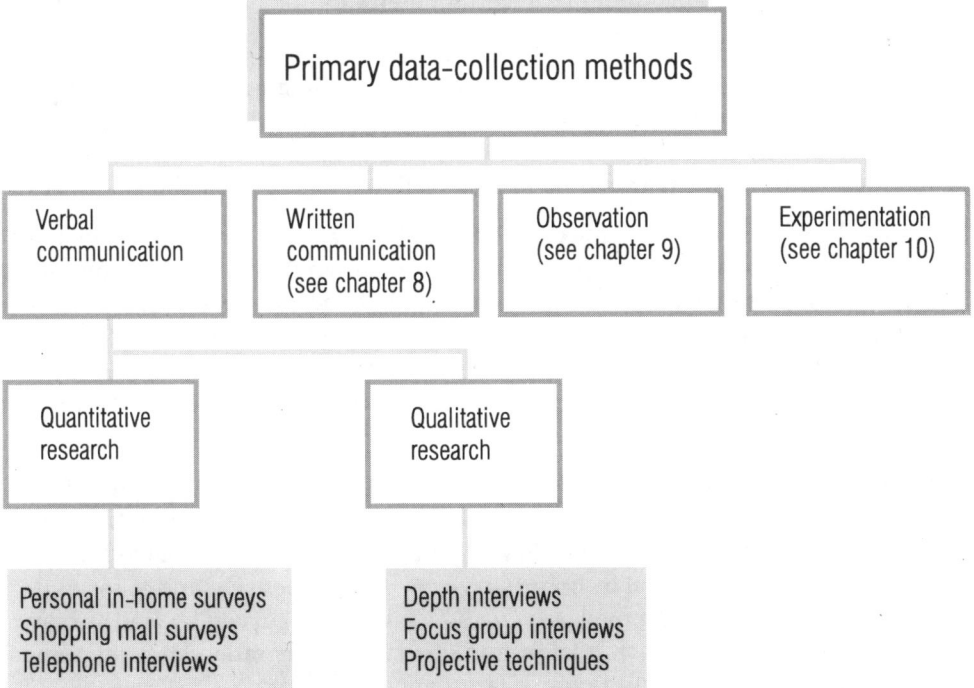

2 CHOICE OF A DATA-COLLECTION METHOD

In essence the choice of an appropriate data-collection method is dependent on the accuracy of the information which will be obtained by a particular method, the cost involved and the time factor. The ability to make a correct decision depends on a thorough knowledge of the various methods of data collection and the inherent strengths and weaknesses of each. These methods will be discussed in subsequent chapters. Factors that should be considered include the volume, variety, objectivity and reliability of data required as well as the cost and duration of the study.

(a) *Volume and variety of data required:* Although there are limits to the volume and variety of data that can be collected by means of marketing research, some methods lend themselves to the collection of a greater volume and wider variety of data. Generally it may be said that a greater volume and wider variety of data can be collected by verbal and written communication methods than by observation and experimentation. Verbal communication for quantitative research allows a greater volume and wider variety of information to be collected by personal in-home surveys than by shopping mall surveys and telephone interviews. The inclusion of visual aids such as photographs in interviews limits their use to certain methods such as personal in-home surveys and shopping mall surveys.

(b) *Objectivity and reliability of data required:* Objectivity of data means that the method of data collection should be free from personal prejudice on the part of the researcher or the interviewer. Reliability of data means that similar results would be provided by independent but comparable measures of the same object, trait or construct.

The most objective method of collecting data is observation by mechanical instruments and laboratory experiments. The most reliable data would be obtained by repeating the observation, using the same instrument and laboratory experiment. In verbal and written communication and in human observation there is the risk of subjectivity which may lead to bias in the results. People are simply not able to be completely objective and this is why it is essential to impress the need to beware of bias on the researcher and the interviewer.

(c) *Cost and duration of the study:* Every study should be carried out at the lowest possible cost but with due consideration of the objectivity and reliability of the data. The time required for decision making by management is very often a decisive factor in the choice of method. A personal in-home survey is more expensive and takes more time to complete than a shopping mall survey and a telephone survey. A mail survey takes longer to complete than a personal in-home survey but is much cheaper, especially when the survey is conducted over a large geographic area.

Interviewing is usually faster and cheaper than research by observation and experiment. Interviewers have more control over their data-collecting activities than observers who have to wait until something happens before they can record it. Further, experiments are usually conducted over a long period. Of the quantitative verbal methods discussed in this chapter, telephone interviews produce data most rapidly, followed by personal interviews. Self-completion methods such as the mail survey generally take longest to yield results. However, the duration of the data-collection process is determined primarily by the number and geographical distribution of the personal interviews to be conducted, the number of postal follow-up mailings necessary for mail surveys, and the time coverage in diary studies.

The cost of personal interviews with individuals or private households in comparable studies is normally four times the cost of telephone interviews and eight to nine times that of a mail survey. In the industrial market the cost of personal interviews is generally higher than in the consumer market.

The cost of an individual depth interview is usually 18 times that of a structured single-call interview with a private individual. The collection of data through panels is also considerably more expensive than through structured single-call interviews. The cost of a focus group discussion by a group consisting of eight members is about 2,5 times that of an individual depth interview. The cost of collecting data through observation methods is also usually higher than for structured single-call interviews, while experiments are appreciably more expensive than observation methods.

Besides the direct cost of collecting the data, the total research costs should also be considered. It is, for example, far cheaper to process data collected from structured single-call interviews than to process data obtained from qualitative methods such as depth interviews and focus group discussions.

3 QUANTITATIVE RESEARCH

Quantitative research generally involves the collection of primary data from large numbers of individuals, frequently with the intention of projecting the results to a wider population.

The aim is to generalise about a specific population, based on the results of a representative sample of that population. With qualitative research the aim is not to generalise about any population, but rather to obtain greater clarity on a vague research problem.

3.1 Personal interviews

Personal interviews, also referred to as face-to-face interviews, involve asking questions to a sample of respondents. It is the interviewer's task to contact the respondents, ask the questions and record the answers. Respondents would be expected to answer the questions as they are put to them. The interview can take place in the respondent's home or at shopping malls. Although these methods have much in common, they exhibit unique characteristics and application possibilities, and therefore warrant separate discussions.

3.1.1 Personal in-home surveys

Over the last decade or so there has been a marked decline in the use of in-home surveys (Dillon, Madden & Firtle 1994:157). This can be attributed largely to the high cost of in-home surveys and the increasing difficulty of gaining access to residences. This tendency is also prevalent in South Africa, especially in metropolitan areas where access to flats or residences can be obtained only through an electronic card, or where intercom systems allow residents to screen visitors. In certain residential areas researchers may perceive it as unsafe to conduct interviews after dark.

(a) Complexity and versatility

In-house surveys are normally conducted between 08:00 and 21:00 at the respondents' homes. Because the interviewer and respondent meet face to face, the interviewer can demonstrate products or show advertisements to the respondent and obtain his reactions. It is also possible for the interviewer to explain instructions or questions to the respondent, as long as he does not lead the respondent to a specific answer. Furthermore, the method is very flexible, allowing the interviewer the opportunity to probe for deeper feelings or meaning. In terms of the depth and detail of data that can be secured, the personal interview is far superior to the telephone or mail survey (Cooper & Emory 1995:271).

The in-home personal survey allows the collection of large volumes of data on just about any subject, such as demographic characteristics, attitudes, opinions, awareness, knowledge, intentions and motivations underlying the individual's actions.

(b) Quality of the data

The quality of the data obtained can be enhanced because the interviewer can clarify instructions and questions and can make observations about the house, furniture, clothes or car of the respondent, allowing him to verify some of the respondents' responses. Where applicable, interviewers can also ask to observe a brand in the kitchen cupboard to verify the respondents' response.

The face-to-face nature of the interview can help to reduce the anxiety of the respondent, thereby increasing the response rate and decreasing the potential for measurement error. Researchers must be aware, however, that interaction between the interviewer and the respondent may lead to bias. Respondents may be reluctant to answer sensitive or embarrassing questions, or they may provide socially acceptable answers instead. The interviewer's tone of voice, body language or other intentional or unintentional cues might also influence the respondent's responses. Interviewer cheating also occurs, that is, interviewers complete whole or parts of questionnaires themselves. This occurs because interviewers mainly work independently with limited supervision.

(c) Quantity of data obtained

The in-home survey is far superior with regard to the volume of data that can be collected, mainly because of its personal nature and the rather limited effort expected from respondents. Interviews of up to one hour have been undertaken without great difficulty, although this is exceptional.

(d) Response rate

The response rate refers to the percentage of designated respondents whose cooperation has been secured for the survey. The Council of American Survey Research Organizations (Churchill 1991:617) suggests the response rate should be calculated as follows:

<u>Number of completed interviews with responding units</u>
Number of eligible responding units in the sample

The response rate for personal in-home surveys can be as high as 65–85 % (Boyd, Westfall & Stasch 1989:239). Response rates can be improved by call-backs, that is when interviewers are expected to return to an address for a second or even third time if they found no-one at home during their first call. Market Research Africa (MRA), for example, insists on two call-backs, which should be on different evenings of the week at different times, if possible. It is also recommended that the interviewer vary the call-back time by day or by week. It should be kept in mind, however, that call-backs are expensive and add to the cost of the survey.

Controlled entry, not-at-homes, refusals and high crime occurrences are the most frequently cited reasons for poor response rates in personal interviews (Boyd *et al* 1989:239 and Dillon *et al* 1994:159). In an effort to address the first three obstacles, researchers can send an advance letter to prospective respondents to inform them about the imminent survey, or to telephone respondents to make an appointment. Obviously the latter approach can be employed only when the researcher has the telephone number of the prospective respondent, which is not always the case.

(e) Control of the sample

In theory all consumers can be reached by in-house personal surveys. The researcher can specify the exact household to be interviewed, the number of call-backs that should be made, the conditions under which the survey must be conducted, etc. In practice this is not so easy to achieve, mainly because of not-at-homes, refusals, reluctance of interviewers to venture into areas with high crime rates or the absence of a complete address list of the universe from which a representative sample can be drawn. With many South Africans living in informal settlements this is a serious problem. Even when an address list is available to the researcher, it is very often difficult to locate the household since few of the streets in certain areas have signs indicating the street name. Unless the interviewer is familiar with the area, it is almost impossible to find the designated household.

(f) Cost

In-house interviews are the most costly data-collection method. Not only are they very labour intensive, but the travel time and expense involved add to the cost incurred, especially when interviewers have to return for a second or even a third time. When respondents are scattered geographically, the cost can be even higher. In an effort to control the interviewing cost, interviewers can telephone the respondent in advance to schedule an interview, or self-administered questionnaires can be used. In the case of the latter method a questionnaire would be left at the respondent's home, to be completed whenever the person is available and free to do so. The interviewer would then collect the completed questionnaire at a later stage (Cooper & Emory 1995:279).

(g) Time

The in-house survey typically takes longer than both telephone and mail surveys. After the questionnaire has been compiled, field workers have to be recruited and/or trained. The fieldwork has to be planned and fieldwork schedules have to be worked out. Collection, verification and processing of data follow, and only then can the results be made available.

(h) Application

In-house personal interviews are applicable when products, advertisements, etc have to be demonstrated to respondents; when large quantities of data have to be collected; when flexibility is required; when there is a low incidence of telephone ownership; when respondents cannot be reached by telephone; or when respondents are illiterate or have a low level of education.

3.1.2 Shopping mall surveys

The shopping mall survey, also known as a mall intercept, is a variation of the personal interview. It involves recruiting shoppers in a shopping mall, qualifying them and conducting the interview at the researcher's interviewing facilities in the mall. To qualify a respondent, he might be asked a few screening or filter questions, such as whether he has used a particular product in the past few weeks, or where he lives. Only if the responses match the desired respondent profile would such a person be invited to participate in the rest of the survey. Respondents who do not comply with the desired profile would be thanked for their cooperation and the interview would be terminated.

Intercept surveys are not limited to shopping malls. They are used increasingly at other locations, depending on the movements of the relevant population (Hawkins & Tull 1994:132–134). Variations include in-store intercepts, airport intercepts, roadside intercepts, hotel intercepts and attraction intercepts. The latter are often employed by the tourism industry when the researcher is dealing with a migrating population.

(a) Complexity and versatility

The shopping mall survey is even more flexible than the in-house personal survey. The researcher may demonstrate products or bring any material into the test facility. Products or other materials may be permanently exhibited, doing away with the time required to set up or unpack products or other material, as is the case with in-house surveys. The researcher also has full control over the interviewing environment, such as lighting, noise and furniture, allowing them to easily observe or interact with respondents. This is not the case in the in-house survey.

(b) Quality of the data

As with the in-house survey, the opportunity of face-to-face contact with the respondent tends to reduce respondent anxiety and thereby help to reduce the potential for measurement error. Interviewer bias may occur but, because of closer supervision, it is possible to reduce this. The opportunity for interviewer cheating is greatly reduced in the mall survey, since it lends itself to closer supervision. As with in-house surveys, sensitive or embarrassing questions may yield more socially acceptable responses rather than true responses.

Because of the unnatural testing environment, mall surveys may produce biased responses from the respondents being interviewed under these conditions. 'Mall burnout', or the repeated interviewing of the same people in shopping malls, may reduce the quality of the data (Dillon *et al* 1994:161).

(c) Quantity of data obtained

Shoppers in a shopping mall generally tend to be in a hurry, which limits the interviewing time. On average, surveys are kept fairly short, so less data can be collected.

(d) Response rate

Response rates for mall surveys is in the order of 80 %, but refusals tend to be in the order of 10–30 %, which is much higher than in-house surveys (Dillon *et al* 1994:161). Fortunately it is much quicker to find a substitute, which is far more difficult in the case of the in-house survey.

(e) Control of the sample

One of the most critical drawbacks of the mall survey is the lack of sample control. Boyd *et al* (1989:238) claim that respondents in a mall intercept survey tend to be much younger, more likely to have children younger that 18, more affluent, and spend more time shopping than the average. In an effort to address this problem, sampling of respondents takes place at different times of the day, on different days of the week, and at different places in the shopping centre. However, in some instances, such as in a durable goods survey, the researcher might deliberately seek a sample that is more affluent.

When interviewers are allowed to select respondents, there is clearly an opportunity for bias. Interviewers tend to select people who look fairly accessible. In a survey in which the author was involved, one of the male interviewers selected only the more attractive young ladies to interview! Close supervision is required to avoid such practices.

(f) Cost

Mall surveys are less expensive than in-house surveys. First it is possible to employ fewer interviewers, therefore fewer interviewers have to be trained for the survey. Second, travel expenses, a major part of the in-house survey budget, are limited because the interviews take place at a central location, and because there are no call-backs involved (Cooper & Emory 1995:271). Third, it is far easier to find a substitute for a refusal.

(g) Time

The mall survey can be conducted far more quickly than the in-house survey, mainly because of the speed of data collection from a single location. The data are verified and processed on the spot as each interview is completed.

(h) Application

This method of data collection is especially useful when respondents have to see, handle or consume a product before they can provide meaningful data about it (Malhotra 1993:192). It is therefore most useful for concept testing, product testing, package testing, copy testing, etc. The speed of data collection makes it ideal for surveys when results are needed quickly, although the telephone method would still be superior if speed were the only criterion. When the researcher is only collecting data from respondents in a specific consumer stratum, the mall intercept survey would be the obvious choice.

3.2 Telephone interviews

In telephone surveys the respondents are phoned, usually at home, and interviews are conducted with them. The telephone survey has become increasingly popular in recent years, but it is not without its problems. This section, like those above, provides more information on this method of data collection.

(a) Complexity and versatility

As in the personal interview, interviewers are required to conduct the telephone interview. This allows for the use of complex interviewing procedures such as skip patterns, probes, and refer-backs. In terms of versatility, the method has some limitations, however. Products or items cannot be shown to the respondent; the use of certain measurement scales such as the constant-sum scale poses problems; the use of lengthy interviews is problematic; and unstructured questionnaires or questions that require long and elaborate answers impose limits on the versatility of this method. The use of rating scales can be facilitated by asking the respondents to look at the dialling numbers of their telephone. This procedure provides them with a visual image of the scale and makes it easier to answer the questions.

(b) Quality of the data

When interviewers conduct telephone surveys from a centralised location, there is usually close supervision of the data-collection process and the data that are collected under these circumstances improve in quality. However, in some instances when the interviewers are allowed to conduct interviews from home, this advantage is neutralised. Check-backs, generally in the order of 15 %, are designed to ensure high data quality.

Telephone interviewing is very challenging because the interviewer is wholly dependent on his voice. Cooper and Emory (1995:281) found there was less rapport with respondents in telephone interviews than in personal interviews. The respondents tend to answer open-ended questions as briefly as possible and are reluctant to provide personal information to interviewers. On the positive side, it is possible to collect information about activities such as watching television and listening to the radio while they are happening (Boyd *et al* 1989:225–226).

(c) Quantity of data collected

Telephone interviews are generally short, mostly between 10 and 20 minutes, although longer interviews have been recorded (Cooper & Emory 1995:281). This time limit obviously reduces the quantity of data that can be collected.

(d) Response rate

The response rate in a telephone survey is in the order of 60–80 % because a ringing telephone is seldom ignored when there is someone at home. Also, call-backs are easy and cheap to make. As a general rule three call-backs are recommended, two of which should be outside office hours.

Conversely it is much easier for the respondent to terminate a telephone interview because there is no face-to-face contact. Telemarketing practices also contribute to the termination of interviews by respondents. In-house technology is set to complicate data-collection procedures in the future. One of these innovations is the telephone answering machine. In a pioneering study Tuckel and Feinberg (as quoted by Cooper & Emory 1995:282) report a higher contact rate for households with telephone answering machines than without. They also found that households with answering machines were more likely to participate in the survey; that the machines were used more often over weekends; and that their use was more commonplace in urban than in rural areas.

(e) Control of the sample

Poor sample control remains one of the most critical drawbacks of the telephone survey. First, there are many households which do not have a telephone, especially in South Africa. Subscription generally varies among income groups, household composition, education levels and employment status (Dillon *et al* 1994:150 and Cooper & Emory 1995:280). Currently it is estimated that only 1 in every 3,06 households in South Africa has a telephone. The 1994 AMPS statistics show that ownership varies greatly according to ethnic group (blacks = 14,7 %; Asians = 78,8 %; coloureds = 50,7 % and whites = 86,6 %), and also according to geographical location, degree of urbanisation and income. Second, the researcher has to contend with unlisted telephone numbers and outdated telephone directories. This problem can be overcome through Random Digit Dialling (RDD), which involves the generation of telephone numbers with the aid of a computer. The number of digits and the appropriate number ranges are specified. This method will solve the problem of unlisted numbers, but will also include the telephone numbers of businesses, which should be eliminated from the sample.

Another technique for addressing the problem of unlisted numbers is termed the 'directory assisted sampling design'. In this method a telephone number is selected in some way or other from a telephone directory and a number, say 1, is added to or subtracted from it to give unlisted numbers a chance of being selected as well. If, say, 967 2310 is selected, 967 2311 is taken if the method of adding 1 is applied. Generally the number that is added or subtracted varies between 1 and 9.

This method may still not give all telephone subscribers an equal chance of being selected because new series of numbers might have been introduced after the publication of the directories. Such telephone subscribers will still have no chance of being selected. In addition, quite a number of unproductive calls will have to be made because the numbers selected might include those of businesses or other institutions.

Once the telephone has been answered, the researcher still has to decide whom to interview. If an adult answers the phone and is questioned, the proportion of females and older respondents will exceed their proportion in the population (Boyd *et al* 1989:232). This problem can be resolved by listing all the adults in the household and randomly selecting one. If that person is not available, three call-backs should be made in an effort to contact him or her.

(f) Cost

The telephone method is very attractive because of its moderate cost. It is more expensive than the mail survey, but the data-collection cost of telephone surveys is lower than that of personal interviews. This saving arises mainly from the reduced travel costs and administrative savings from training interviewers and supervision.

In the USA researchers can utilise the WATS (Wide Area Telephone Service) system, which allows them to phone nationwide at a reduced cost. In South Africa, for want of a similar service, national surveys are undertaken from various centres, often requiring trunk calls, which are more expensive. Even so, it is estimated that the cost of the telephone survey is not more than 60 % of that of the personal interview.

(g) Time

The telephone interview is by far the quickest data-collection method. Call-backs can be made throughout, adding very little cost or wasted time. By employing a technique termed Computer-Assisted Telephone Interviewing (CATI) in which interviewers read the questions from an on-screen questionnaire and respond by entering the number which corresponds with the respondent's answer, the results can be made available almost instantaneously. National surveys can be completed in a few days at most. Some local research agencies have developed their own computer support systems for telephone interviews, while others indicate that the traditional pencil-and-paper method is still preferred.

(h) Application

Telephone interviews are used when data are required very quickly, when the information to be collected is of a more factual nature, when respondents are geographically widely dispersed, and in national surveys. They are not applicable when products or items have to be demonstrated to the respondents.

The data-collection methods discussed up to this point are generally quantitative in nature, that is they are used to collect data from large numbers of respondents (or samples) in order to be able to generalise about the characteristics of the specified population. To do this, the researcher uses a structured questionnaire which ensures uniform phrasing of the questions.

4 QUALITATIVE RESEARCH

In the following sections we turn our attention to qualitative research methods in which the purpose is not to generalise about the specified population, but to uncover new ideas from or hidden feelings of respondents. This can best be achieved by unstructured interviews in which respondents can talk freely without too much leading from the interviewer. There are three basic methods of accomplishing this: depth interviews, focus group interviews and projective techniques.

4.1 Depth interviews

Interviews conducted on a one-on-one basis to collect qualitative data from respondents are called **depth interviews**.

The interviewer does not use a fixed set of questions, although an interviewing outline may be followed. There is ample opportunity to create questions or probe to ensure the best possible set of data. The specific content of each of the depth interviews conducted will therefore vary.

In particular, the depth interview is useful in the following circumstances:

☐ when the issue under investigation is embarrassing, stressful or of a confidential nature

☐ when a detailed analysis needs to be conducted of rather complex situations such as attitudes, beliefs and feelings

☐ when peer pressure may cause some respondents to conform to societal norms when in reality they would not

☐ when the interviewer needs a progressive set of images, such as a buying decision with regard to overseas holidays

☐ in complex situations when the aim is to explore rather than measure (Webb 1992:122).

With interviews lasting from 30 to 60+ minutes it is sometimes difficult to obtain the cooperation of respondents. Also, in larger studies the use of multiple interviewers to conclude the study within a realistic time period may introduce response variances induced partly by interviewers with different approaches.

Depth interviewing requires the services of skilled interviewers. Because they are few in number and are highly paid, and depth interviews take a long time to complete, skilled interviewers are fairly expensive. The researcher therefore works mainly with small samples, which limits his ability to generalise about the population. This, as we have noted above, is rarely the aim of depth interviewing.

On the positive side, however, it can be said that depth interviews

☐ provide a richness and depth of data which cannot be matched by most of the other forms of data collection

☐ allow the opportunity to ascribe a response to a single individual

☐ allow the interviewer to develop close rapport and a high degree of trust with the respondent, which may encourage a freer flow of conversation and more valid results

☐ overcome overt peer pressure to conform to societal or other norms (Webb 1992:124).

When conducting the interview, the interviewer may employ three techniques: laddering, hidden-issue questioning and symbolic analysis.

(a) Laddering

This technique involves having respondents identify attributes that differentiate brands from each other. The interviewer attempts to find out why a specific attribute is important or meaningful by in-depth probing of the reasons provided by the respondent. In this way the researcher links (or ladders) the attributes (A), consequences (C) and values (V) of consumers, which can be very helpful in developing advertising messages.

If, for example, the researcher wants to develop an advertising campaign to improve the image of an airline, the interviewers will ask respondents to list the most important attributes of an airline. Next they find out why they are important to the respondent and what benefits they provide. Durgee, as quoted by Malhotra (1993:171), indicates that managers preferred advanced seat reservation, wide-body aircraft, and first-class seating which provided greater physical comfort. These attributes enabled them to get more work done during the flight and enhanced their sense of accomplishment and self-esteem. Ideally the advertising campaign should therefore concentrate on bolstering the self-esteem of managers.

(b) Hidden-issue questioning

The aim of this technique is to assess the respondents' feelings about sensitive issues, or personal sore spots rather than socially shared values. Respondents are therefore asked about fantasies, work lives and social lives to identify hidden-life issues (Malhotra 1993:171).

(c) Symbolic analysis

To learn what something is, the researcher may ask the respondent to say what it is not and then analyse his reply. Beer, for example, may be described as the opposite of fine wine (sophisticated, glamorous, upscale, expensive, subtle, and consumed primarily with good food). Beer can therefore be regarded as unsophisticated, common, inexpensive, straightforward, and inappropriate with good food (Hawkins & Tull 1994:307).

When conducting depth interviews, interviewers must

- [ ] realise that respondents may perceive the experience as very frightening and unnerving
- [ ] initially establish rapport with the respondent, for example by manipulating aspects such as tone of voice, dress, body language and facial expressions
- [ ] work to maintain rapport with the respondent throughout the interview
- [ ] explain to the respondent in the beginning the boundaries that circumscribe the interview situation
- [ ] reassure the respondent that all his answers will be treated in the strictest confidence
- [ ] move from the general to the specific, and from topic to topic, in a logical manner (Webb 1992:123–124).

Interviewers should possess the following skills to be effective in their tasks:

- [ ] intellectual ability/common sense
- [ ] imagination/logic
- [ ] conceptual ability/an eye for detail
- [ ] detachedness/involvement
- [ ] neutral self-projection/instant empathy
- [ ] non-stereotypical thinking/capacity to spot the typical
- [ ] expertise with words/good listener
- [ ] literary flair/ability to summarise concisely
- [ ] analytical thinking/tolerance of disorder (The Market Research Society, as quoted in Webb 1992:124).

Interviewers, even experienced ones, should guard against what is termed interviewer burnout. It is often impossible to complete more than four or five hour-long interviews in one day without sacrificing quality. With every completed interview it becomes more difficult to concentrate on what the respondent is saying and to ask appropriate questions to probe for real meaning. Even after the interviews have been completed the researcher should guard against stimulus overload – everything that has been said must be analysed thoroughly (Hawkins & Tull 1994:309).

4.2 Focus group interviews

A focus group interview – or simply focus group – is conducted by trained moderators who are responsible for directing the discussion. Between 8 and 12 respondents gather in a central research facility to discuss a research topic. In this section we discuss the main features of and issues to consider when conducting focus groups.*

(a) Recruiting and screening

Researchers recruiting participants for a focus group must specify who is eligible for inclusion and who is not. In the absence of such guidance, recruitment personnel may recruit the most accessible people. If, for example, the researcher wants to conduct a focus group with young BMW owners, he should specify the age brackets, for example between 30 and 40 years of age. When for some reason or other it is impossible to observe whether someone is eligible for inclusion in a focus group, the researcher may have to ask the prospective participant a series of screening questions to assess eligibility. Such questionnaires are generally not as elaborate as those used in the typical survey and may consist of as few as two or three questions.

Ideally, unless the aim is to interview non-users of the product, the researcher should recruit people who have had experience with the product to be discussed. Such people can make a valuable contribution to the discussion. However, researchers should avoid recruiting the same persons more than once a year because such people tend to regard themselves as experts, and the more they take part in such discussions, the more their opinions, views and reactions will vary from those of other people in the population.

Once a person has indicated his willingness to participate in the focus group discussion, an appointment is made. The date, time, venue and other details are supplied to the prospective respondent. Because not all recruits honour their agreement with the recruitment officer, it is customary to recruit 10–15 % more people than required for the focus group. Should most or all of them arrive, the researcher should exclude the excess, compensate them, and dismiss them, rather than include too many people in the session. Experience with university students shows that fewer than one in every three actually arrives for the discussion.

(b) Group composition and number of groups

A focus group should be as homogeneous as possible in terms of demographic and socio-economic characteristics to ensure increased levels of spontaneity and participation. If, for example, a group of married women consists of employed and unemployed mothers, there may be vast differences in experiences, problems, frustrations and so on. In contrast a group consisting only of working mothers would share many experiences and perspectives. In the first group, the psychological distance between the respondents may be too great, whereas the makeup of the second group would be very beneficial to group dynamics. It follows therefore that the researcher would have to schedule separate groups for separate customer segments.

---

* Unless stated otherwise, this section is based mainly on Alreck, P L & Settle, R B 1995, *The survey research handbook*, Chicago: Irwin:393–407.

Strangers, it is believed, feel less inhibited in focus group discussions and so express their attitudes and behaviour more freely (Boyd *et al* 1989:104). Steps should therefore be taken to ensure that individuals who partake in focus group discussions do not know each other.

But how many focus groups should the researcher have? There is no absolute answer to this question. As a rule of thumb the researcher should continue to have more groups if every new group still generates sufficient new information. This point may be reached after the second or third interview, or only after the tenth. Because the phrase 'sufficient new information' lends itself to subjective interpretation, it is hard to provide an exact indication.

(c) The role of the moderator

The moderator plays a crucial role in the focus group discussion. Ideally he should let the group carry on the conversation by itself. Interventions are deemed necessary only to introduce a new topic if it does not come up spontaneously or to bring the discussion back on track if participants have strayed into irrelevant areas. Moderators should exercise just enough authority to direct and control the flow of conversation without affecting its content.

Ideally, moderators should blend in with the group. If the group consists of teenagers, the moderator should be fairly young himself. The reason for this is clear, as Alreck and Settle (1995:402) explain: 'People are vastly more comfortable and at ease, and are thus more candid and open, with people who are similar to themselves than with those who are quite different.'

It is the responsibility of the moderator to elicit inputs from all participants throughout the discussion. Participants who are shy or quiet should therefore be encouraged to share their views with the group. The moderator can do this direct by asking all participants (including the shy ones) for their opinions on a particular topic, or more subtly by making eye contact with them or leaning towards them. In contrast, domineering personalities must be kept in check, for example by withdrawing eye contact with them while they talk, by leaning away from them, or by getting up from the chair and taking a position behind them. In the latter situation they find it difficult to look over their shoulder while talking to the moderator, and will talk less as the discussion progresses. It is important, however, to allow everyone to talk within the first five minutes, otherwise the anxiety of those excluded will increase, often to a point where they will withdraw from the group (Webb 1992:116–118).

Chase, as quoted by Malhotra (1993:163), lists the following key attributes of focus group moderators:

☐ *They must mix kindness with firmness:* The moderator must combine a disciplined detachment with understanding empathy in order to generate the required interaction.

☐ *Permissiveness:* The moderator must be permissive yet alert to signs that the cordiality or purpose of the discussion is disintegrating.

☐ *Involvement:* The moderator must encourage and stimulate intense personal involvement.

☐ *Incomplete understanding:* Participants must be encouraged to be more specific about generalised comments by exhibiting incomplete understanding.

☐ *Encouragement:* Unresponsive members must be encouraged to participate.

☐ *Flexibility:* The moderator must be willing and able to deviate from the agenda, yet stay true to the purpose of the discussion.

☐ *Sensitivity:* The moderator must be sensitive enough to guide the group discussion at an intellectual and an emotional level.

As regards procedure, the moderator first has to establish rapport with the participants; then state the rules of the discussion; next formulate objectives; then spend most of the time probing the participants to provoke intense discussion in the relevant areas; and conclude by attempting to summarise the group's response to determine the extent of agreement (Malhotra 1993:165).

(d) The facilities

Focus group interviews can be held in specially constructed facilities, in hotels, at conference centres, at universities, etc. Specially constructed facilities will have a one-way mirror through which clients or researchers may observe the proceedings without disturbing the participants. Since virtually all discussions are recorded, these rooms will have built-in microphones and some will have video cameras. Microphones and cameras should be hidden to avoid constantly reminding participants of their presence.

It is recommended that the room where the interview is conducted be made as informal and comfortable as possible to facilitate free expression and physiological comfort.

At purpose-built facilities, a reception area, small waiting room, bathrooms, administrative offices and equipment storage rooms may border the discussion room, but they are not prerequisites.

(e) Focus group agenda

Because of their exploratory and dynamic nature, focus groups are typically not conducted with a questionnaire. The moderator would rather compile a series of loosely and broadly framed questions for discussion, also referred to as a focus group agenda. On this agenda, the moderator would have all the topics to be covered during the discussion. Once the topics for the agenda have been established, it is necessary to prioritise them. Three levels of information can be specified:

☐ essential information

☐ important information

☐ supportive information.

The moderator avoids introducing topics in a question-and-answer format as with personal or telephone interviews, but phrases them in the form of trigger questions designed to elicit various opinions and stimulate a conversation about some issue. It should also be stressed that all views are acceptable, and the aim is not necessarily to achieve consensus within the group. This will help to prevent domineering personalities from influencing other participants unduly.

(f) Advantages and limitations

Like any other technique, the focus group interview has definite advantages and limitations. Malhotra (1993:167–168) has condensed the advantages to the ten Ss and the limitations to the five Ms. They are shown in table 7.1 on the next page.

(g) Application

Focus group discussions can be used very effectively to help marketers understand consumers' perceptions, preferences and behaviour concerning a product category; they can obtain impressions of new product concepts; they can generate new ideas about older products; they can be used as a source of creative concepts and copy material for advertisements; they can secure price impressions; and they can be used to obtain consumer reaction to specific marketing programmes (Malhotra 1993:168).

4.3 Focus groups or depth interviews?

Both depth interviews and focus groups can be employed to collect qualitative data. But which one should be used? The answer depends on a variety of factors. Table 7.2 provides some guidelines in this regard.

From table 7.2 on page 141 it is clear that the focus group and the depth interview each have their merits and, depending on the situation, one might be better than the other. The researcher should bear this in mind when selecting a data-collection method.

4.4 Projective techniques

When respondents are reluctant or unable to provide information about their attitudes or beliefs, the researcher can employ projective techniques. Respondents are asked to respond to a range of vague or incomplete stimuli and, depending on their response, the researcher can draw certain conclusions about their attitudes, emotions, motives,

Table 7.1 Advantages and limitations of focus groups

Advantages	Disadvantages
Synergism: A group of people will produce a wider range of information, insight and ideas than individual responses secured separately.	*Misuse:* Focus groups can be misused and abused when the results are considered to be conclusive rather than exploratory.
Snowballing: One participant's remark may trigger a chain reaction from other participants.	*Misjudge:* Results may very easily be misjudged. Focus groups are particularly susceptible to client and researcher bias.
Stimulation: After only a brief introductory period do participants want to express their ideas and expose their feelings as the general level of excitement over the topic increases in the group.	*Moderation:* Focus groups are difficult to moderate. Good interviewers are scarce and costly, but the results depend heavily on their ability.
Security: Participants feel comfortable and secure because their feelings are similar to those of other group members.	*Messy:* Their unstructured nature makes coding, analysis and interpretation very difficult. Data tend to be very messy.
Spontaneity: Participants are not asked to answer specific questions, which increases the spontaneity and should therefore provide an accurate idea of their views.	*Misrepresentation:* Results are not representative, and cannot be projected for the whole population. Results should not form the sole basis for decision making.
Serendipity: Original ideas are more likely to arise out of a group than an individual interview.	
Specialisation: Because many participants are involved at the same time, this justifies the use of a highly trained and expensive moderator.	
Scientific scrutiny: The group interview allows close scrutiny of the data-collection process, with observers following the discussion, and recording of the session for later analysis.	
Structure: The process is flexible in the topics covered and in the depth at which they can be explored.	
Speed: Data collection is relatively fast since many individuals are interviewed at the same time.	

Source: Adapted from Malhotra (1993:167–168).

Table 7.2 Focus groups vs depth interviews

Factor	Focus group	Depth interview
Value of interaction	Use when interactions of participants will spark new thought	Use when interactions are limited or appear to be non-productive
Sensitivity of subject matter	Use when subject matter is not too sensitive for participants to withhold information or to temper remarks	When subject matter is so sensitive that few respondents would speak openly in a group setting
Cost and timing	Use when time is crucial and the need to economise is present	Use when time is not crucial and budget permits the high cost of interviewing and reporting
Depth of information per respondent	Assumes that most respondents can say all they know in 8–12 minutes	Allows greater depth per individual. Used when subject matter is complex and participants very knowledgeable
Logistics	A number of participants can be assembled in one location	Respondents are geographically dispersed and travel costs prohibit respondents from travelling to a central location

Source: Adapted from Dillon *et al* (1994:125).

values and beliefs. The more vague or ambiguous the stimuli, the more one must reveal of oneself to complete the stimuli. Hawkins and Tull (1994:313) are of the opinion that marketing researchers have used these methods out of context and tend to expect more from them than they were designed to provide. When used in its proper context, however, the projective technique can provide valuable marketing information.

4.4.1 Word association

With word association a number of words are read aloud to the respondent. Some of the words are neutral and included only to conceal the purpose of the study. Words are read one by one to the respondent and he has to mention the first word that comes to mind. The assumption is that such responses are likely to contain the respondent's true feelings. To ensure that the respondent provides the first word that comes to mind, responses are timed. Those that are provided too slowly can then be discarded since it is assumed that the respondent rationalised about such words.

When respondents are asked to provide only one word per stimulus, it is known as *free word association*. Respondents may, however, also be asked to provide more responses, typically three or four, per stimulus word. This is called *successive word association*. Another version of this technique, used primarily in advertising research, is the *benefit chain*. According to this technique, respondents are asked to name all the benefits that a product or service provides. For every benefit mentioned the respondent is asked to provide two more benefits from this benefit, two more benefits, and so on. This continues until the respondent can mention no more benefits. The benefits generated in this way are used in product positioning and advertising (Hawkins & Tull 1994:314).

Word association tests are fairly easy to develop, but to interpret them demands some skill and experience. The most common approach in interpretation is to analyse a word's frequency of mention and the time lapse before a response is given, and also to note the number of respondents who fail to respond after a reasonable period of time (Churchill 1991:323).

Table 7.3 (page 143) presents examples of projective techniques which may be used to assess the holiday needs and preferences of respondents.

4.4.2 Sentence completion

In sentence completion the interviewer reads a number of uncompleted sentences to the respondent, who is requested to complete them with the first word or words that come to mind, or anything that makes sense. Responses are analysed to uncover the respondent's feelings toward the subject or product. Because the respondent is not asked to associate himself with the response, conscious and subconscious defences are relaxed,

Table 7.3 Projective techniques to assess holiday needs

Word association	What word comes to mind first when I mention the following: ☐ hotel ☐ bank teller ☐ entertainment ☐ bicycle ☐ word processor ☐ holiday, etc.
Sentence completion	When I go on holiday, I like to … My idea of an ideal holiday is … What I like most about a sea holiday is … People who go on holiday are …
Story completion Joan and Steve went to the Seychelles for their last summer holiday. Their plane arrived on the Monday morning and after they booked into the hotel they sat down for a drink in the local ladies' bar. While enjoying their drinks, they discussed what they planned to do in the next week.	What did they say?
Third-person role play	When your colleague planned his last holiday, what possible destinations would he have considered?
Cartoon completion	

providing more revealing answers from respondents. This method is less disguised than word association, since respondents can often detect the topic under investigation.

4.4.3 Story completion

With story completion the interviewer sketches a mental picture and the respondent is asked to complete the story. Enough information is provided to focus the respondent's attention on the subject under investigation. Table 7.3 provides an example of story completion. Enough information is provided to direct respondents in a particular direction, in this case what Joan and Steve are likely to do while on holiday in the Seychelles.

4.4.4 Third-person role play

With this technique respondents are asked to project attitudes onto someone vague, or a third person. This person is often a neighbour, a colleague or the average man in the street. Respondents may, for example, be asked to discuss the fears and expectations of most of their neighbours with regard to the new political dispensation in South Africa. Once again it is believed that the respondent would report his own fears and expectations. Because respondents are asked to respond on the behaviour of their neighbours, they would be less inclined to provide more socially acceptable, and often inaccurate answers.

A useful variation of this technique is to provide respondents with a list of features or characteristics of a person or item and ask them to describe the individual's possessions, purchases, activities or other characteristics of interest. When instant coffee was first introduced in the 1950s, many housewives refused to use the product. Contrary to taste tests, they claimed that it did not taste good. The researchers then compiled two shopping lists: one with instant coffee on the list and another with ground coffee. Respondents were then asked to describe the personality and character of the woman who would purchase the items on the shopping list.

The woman with the ground coffee on her shopping list was described as more or less average, while the one with the instant coffee was described as lazier, more spendthrift, and not a good cook. According to the researchers, these responses were more revealing about the woman's attitudes to instant coffee than the 'I don't like the taste' response generated by means of more direct questioning (Haire as reported by Hawkins & Tull 1994:317).

4.4.5 Cartoon completion

When respondents are shown a cartoon with two characters and asked to respond to it, this is referred to as cartoon completion. Table 7.3 illustrates this technique with an appropriate example. The comments of one of the characters in the cartoon would be shown, with the other bubble left blank. Respondents are then asked to complete the blank bubble to show the response of the other character. The words in the first bubble serve to define the issue at hand.

To allow respondents to provide even freer responses, one of the bubbles can indicate the unspoken thoughts of one of the characters. This would allow respondents to air ideas that might be considered too sensitive, even in a cartoon setting.

4.4.6 Limitations of projective techniques

Projective techniques, however useful in practice, suffer from a number of limitations. First they are very expensive, mainly because they require highly trained interviewers and interpreters to evaluate them. Second, because of the high costs, they rely on small sample sizes, which increase the possibility of sampling error. Third, researchers often rely on non-probability selection, paving the way for selection error. Because projective techniques typically demand long interviewing times and respondents are often asked to engage in behaviour which is strange to them, many people simply refuse to take part in them. This may contribute to non-response error, a fourth possible limitation. In the fifth place, researchers must deal with measurement error. Because all of the techniques except word association are of an open-ended nature, the opportunity for interpretation bias, or for the interpreter to misinterpret a vague and contradictory story, is apparent (Hawkins & Tull 1994:318–320).

5 SUMMARY

When the researcher cannot solve a marketing problem with the aid of secondary data, he has to resort to the collection of primary data. This can take many forms: verbal communication, written communication, and observation and experimentation. This chapter explores the collection of problem-specific data with the aid of verbal communication. The choice of an appropriate data-collection method is essentially dependent on the accuracy of the information which will be obtained by a particular method, the cost involved and the time factor. Generally, verbal communication can be classified into two main categories: quantitative methods and qualitative methods. Quantitative methods include in-house surveys, shopping mall surveys and telephone surveys. Here the aim is to generalise about the population from which the sample is taken. Qualitative methods include depth interviews and focus group discussions, and there is no attempt to generalise about the population.

Although there has been a marked decline in the use of in-house surveys, they are still used when products, advertisements, etc have to be demonstrated, when large quantities of data have to be collected, when a certain degree of flexibility is required, when there is a low incidence of telephone ownership, or when respondents cannot be reached by telephone.

Shopping mall surveys also involve face-to-face interviewing at a central location, thereby greatly reducing the time and cost of fieldwork. Because a sample of respondents in a shopping mall survey would not reflect the population very accurately, the method must be considered carefully before selecting it.

In terms of cost and timing, telephone surveys are by far the best of the three methods discussed in this chapter. Data can be collected very cheaply and extremely fast. The length of the interview is generally limited to about 10–15 minutes and more factual questions are generally preferred.

The choice of a specific method will depend on a number of factors: the complexity of the data that need to be collected and the versatility required to collect it; the quality and quantity of the desired data; the likely and desired response rate; the degree to which sampling needs to be controlled; the cost; and the time frame available for the collection of the data.

When the purpose is not to generalise about the specified population but to uncover new ideas from or the hidden feelings of the respondents, unstructured interviews can be employed. Respondents can talk freely without too much leading from the interviewer. Depth interviews involve interviewing one person at a time, while focus group interviewing involves simultaneous interviewing of 6–12 respondents in a group setting. With both techniques the interviewer (moderator in the case of focus groups) needs to be thoroughly trained and experienced. Collected data are difficult to process, requiring highly skilled researchers. When considering which method to use, the researcher must consider a variety of factors: the value of interaction between participants; the sensitivity of the subject matter; the cost and timing; the depth of information desired per participant; and the logistics involved in setting up the interview or focus group.

When respondents are reluctant or unable to provide information about their attitudes or beliefs, the researcher can employ projective techniques. Respondents are asked to respond to a range of vague or incomplete stimuli and, depending on their response, the researcher can draw certain conclusions about their attitudes, emotions, motives, values and beliefs. Five techniques were covered in this chapter: word association, sentence completion, story completion, third-person role play and cartoon completion. Although these methods have proved to be very useful in practice, they should not be used out of context. Due regard must be had to the specific limitations of these techniques to avoid mistakes.

REFERENCES

Aaker, David & Day, George 1990. *Marketing research*. Fourth edition. New York: Wiley.

Alreck, P L & Settle, R B 1995. *The survey research handbook*. Chicago: Irwin.

Boyd, H W, Westfall, R & Stasch, S F 1989. *Marketing research: text and cases*. Seventh edition. Homewood, Ill: Irwin.

Churchill, Gilbert A (Jr) 1991. *Marketing research: methodological foundations*. Fifth edition. Chicago: The Dryden Press. (The Dryden Press International Edition.)

Cooper, D R & Emory, D R 1995. *Business research methods*. Fifth edition. Chicago: Irwin.

Dillon, W R, Madden, T J & Firtle, N H 1993. *Essentials of marketing research*. Homewood, Ill: Irwin.

Dillon, W R, Madden, T J & Firtle, N H 1994. *Marketing research in a marketing environment*. Third edition. Burr Ridge, Ill: Irwin.

Hawkins, D I & Tull, D S 1994. *Essentials of marketing research*. New York: Macmillan. (The Macmillan Series in Marketing.)

Malhotra, N K 1993. *Marketing research: an applied orientation*. Englewood Cliffs, NJ: Prentice Hall.

Webb, J R 1992. *Understanding and designing marketing research*. London: Academic Press.

Primary research: written communication

Chapter 8: N J Smith and J H Martins

1 INTRODUCTION

Once the management problem has been reformulated as a research problem, the researcher's first task is to trace all the relevant internal and external secondary data and decide whether there is sufficient secondary information to solve the research problem. If not, the researcher's next step is to decide on the method of primary research. His decision will be guided by the volume, variety, objectivity, reliability and cost of the data required, including when the data are required. The various methods of collecting primary data are set out in figure 8.1. (There are more details about written communication because this chapter deals with written communication.)

Figure 8.1 Primary data-collection methods

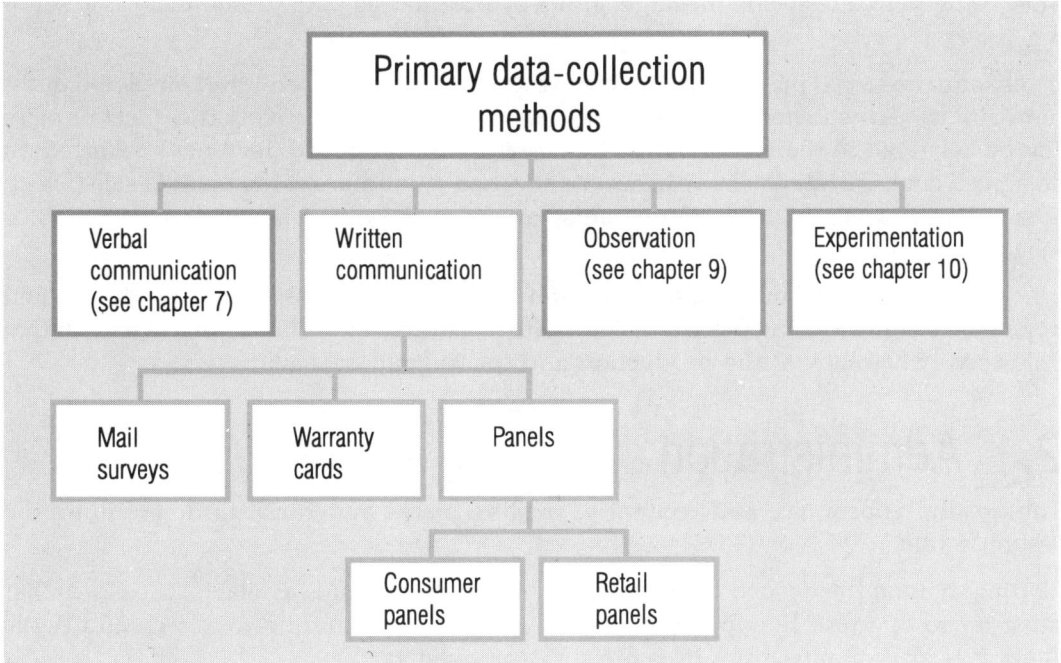

In written communication the questionnaire is completed by the respondent, the research-er, or the researcher's employee (fieldworker), for the most part without conducting a personal interview, as discussed in chapter 7. The questionnaire may be completed in the traditional manner with a pen or pencil or with an electronic device such as a scanner or light pen.

The rest of the chapter will be devoted to the discussion of mail surveys, warranty cards and panels.

2 MAIL SURVEYS

> In a **mail survey** the researcher sends a structured questionnaire to a group of respon-dents who complete it in their own time and return it to the research unit.

In this type of survey, communication is restricted to the questionnaire and the covering letter. There is no interviewer to explain points that are not clear. This means that the questionnaire must be worded in such a way that all respondents in the target popula-tion will interpret and understand it in the same way.

Since an error in the wording of a question cannot be rectified afterwards, each question must be rigorously tested on the target group before finalising the questionnaire and send-ing it off.

Questionnaires are typically sent direct to respondents by post, and the completed ques-tionnaire is also returned by post to the research unit. Alternatively the questionnaire can be delivered to the respondents' homes and the completed document collected on an agreed date. Questionnaires can also be attached to products at the point of sale (which is standard practice with warranty cards) or they can be circulated in newspapers or magazines.

Since the mail survey makes use of a self-administered questionnaire, the design and appearance of the mailing piece as a whole are of cardinal importance. In the section that follows we shall look at the production and 'packaging' of mailing pieces.

2.1 Administration of mailing pieces

The quality, appearance and content of mailing pieces are crucial in determining the response rate.

Bearing in mind the desired response rate, as well as the funds available, the researcher must try to optimise the quality of the mailing piece. According to Alreck and Settle (1985:194–204) 'quality' comprises certain components:

☐ *Paper:* The quality of the paper used influences the general impression the recipients have of the research project. A general rule is that standard size paper that is not too thin should be used. Textured paper should be used only when an impression of top quality is to be created. Matching envelopes should be used. Envelopes which have a special shape should be avoided since they cost too much.

☐ *Colour:* Since colour can have different meanings for different people, bright and un-usual colours should not be used. White paper is acceptable to most people, as is the use of black ink. Corporate letterheads and envelopes can be used for the covering letter and the return of the completed questionnaire.

☐ *Printing:* Printing should be of high quality, using ordinary typefaces. When more than one page is used for the questionnaire, the pages should be firmly attached to one another so that they do not separate. A general rule is that the mailing piece should not appear too bulky and look like hard work.

☐ *Layout:* The more reader-friendly the layout, the higher the response rate will be. A reader-friendly layout is clear, pleasing to the eye, and engages the reader's interest. The layout of the questionnaire should be simple, clear and uncluttered. The general impression should be one of straightforward simplicity.

☐ *Dispatch and mailing lists:* Although most people have some experience of dispatching mail, they do not usually send out thousands of items at a time. This is where a mail dispatch organisation can be useful. Mailing lists can be purchased from firms which specialise in the compilation of such lists. In South Africa such lists are available from inter alia the Bureau of Market Research. Other organisations, such as newspaper and magazine publishers, have lists of their subscribers.

2.2 Components of a mailing piece

In a typical survey, a mailing piece consists of the following components: dispatch enve-lope, covering letter, questionnaire, return envelope and sometimes an offer or some other incentive to respond.

The mailing piece must be an integrated package with all the components linked together. The researcher must bear in mind that a change in one component will have an effect on the impact of the other components.

2.2.1 The dispatch envelope

The dispatch envelope should be a standard business envelope. It should bear the name and address of the respondent, the return address and a stamp. The name and address can be typed or printed with a laser printer on the envelope or questionnaire to show through a window at the front. Self-adhesive address labels can also be used. The Post Office sets rules and regulations about the size and shapes of postal articles.

All envelopes must bear a return address which will allow the Post Office to return the articles it was unable to deliver.

The type and value of postage stamps can affect the response rate. The response rate is highest when ordinary postage stamps are used and lowest when a bulk post permit is utilised.

Bulk post in South Africa is faster than ordinary mail but slower than fastmail. Fastmail costs almost twice as much as ordinary mail while bulk mail is approximately 7 % cheaper than ordinary mail.

2.2.2 The covering letter

The covering letter gives respondents information about the survey. Since there is no personal contact, it must explain the project clearly and arouse respondents' interest in participating.

The covering letter must therefore

☐ motivate respondents to cooperate by describing the project

☐ state why the respondents have been selected

☐ emphasise the benefits to respondents of completing the questionnaire.

Questions about the research project that the covering letter must answer include the following: what the research is about, who wants to know the answers, why they want to know, why the respondent has been selected, why this research is important, will answering the questionnaire be difficult, how long will it take, will it cost the respondent anything, will the respondent be identified, how the information will be used, how the respondent could benefit by participating, by when must the questionnaire be completed.

With the above in mind, we can now look at the various examples of appeals to respondents focused upon in the covering letter.

Three types of appeal are usually exploited:

☐ *Social utility:* The covering letter focuses on the advantages or benefits to the individual, the group of respondents or society as a whole.

☐ *Assistance and support:* Respondents are asked to assist the research firm in completing a useful study. The value of respondents' support and cooperation to the success of the project is emphasised.

☐ *Egoistic:* The importance of the individual respondent's contribution is stressed.

Needless to say, a combination of any of these appeals can be used.

The type of appeal is not the only factor which affects the rate of response. Besides appearance, quality and the subjects of the questionnaire, the type of post and type of research organisation also play a part. Section 2.4 deals with factors affecting mail survey response rates. Table 8.1 shows response rates, speed of response and items omitted in mail surveys using different appeals by type of research organisation.

Table 8.1 Response rates, speed of response and items omitted in mail surveys using different appeals by type of research organisation

Appeal	Rate of response (%)		Average number of items omitted per questionnaire		Average speed of response in days	
	University	Commercial enterprise	University	Commercial enterprise	University	Commercial enterprise
Social utility	47,2	38,8	3,02	5,62	7,31	6,19
Assisting the research organisation	44,8	36,8	6,03	7,72	6,65	7,24
Egoistic	35,6	46,8	7,00	6,86	7,73	7,76
Combined	41,4	39,2	5,72	7,01	7,83	7,56
Average	42,3	40,4	5,34	6,80	7,35	7,21

Source: Houston & Nevin (1978:334–339) in Nel *et al* (1988:192).

In terms of response rates this research shows that the most effective appeal that can be used in the covering letter depends on the type of organisation doing the research. For the university the social utility approach was the most effective, while the response rate was poorest when the egoistic appeal was used. Yet the latter was the most successful for the commercial enterprise. The average response for the university was also somewhat higher than for the commercial enterprise.

As to the effect of the various appeals on quality in terms of items omitted, the table shows that the social utility appeal in both the university and the commercial enterprise resulted in the lowest average number of items omitted. Furthermore the average number of item omissions is lower in the university survey than in the commercial enterprise.

On average, social utility appeal also seemed to result in the quickest return of completed questionnaires. Although the results show that the questionnaires were mostly returned more quickly to the commercial enterprise than to the university, the difference was not statistically significant. However, Peterson (Nel *et al* 1988:192) found that the speed of returning the questionnaires was greater when a university did a survey than when a commercial enterprise did.

In a study undertaken by a research organisation among businessmen and academics, Childers, Pride and Fenel (Nel *et al* 1988:192) found that the egoistic and help-the-sponsor appeals yielded higher response rates than the social utility appeal. Moreover, the use of different appeals had no effect on the quality of responses. In another research project Kerin and Harvey (Nel *et al* 1988:193) found that the help-the-sponsor appeal produced a higher response rate than the egoistic appeal.

The apparently contrasting results show that the appeal most likely to produce the best results is dependent on the type of population involved, the nature and general importance of the study, the type of research body/sponsor and the way the covering letter is formulated. As for the research body/sponsor, the better known and more respected they are, the higher the chances of a good response rate (Nel *et al* 1988:92–94).

While the questions in the questionnaire may be phrased fairly informally, the covering letter should be more formal. Although a covering letter can be too formal, readers expect a certain degree of formality from a business letter. These expectations should be complied with.

2.2.3 The questionnaire

On receiving the mailing piece, respondents usually read the covering letter first. They then glance quickly at the questionnaire. The easier the answers to the questions seem to them, the better their response rate. A well-constructed and well-administered questionnaire will generally yield higher response rates.

Since the questionnaire is the core component of the research, it is essential that each facet of the document be critically examined before being finalised for dispatch. The whole questionnaire must form a cohesive, integrated package and stand out as one document.

The questionnaire must set out clearly defined tasks. The entire answering procedure should be broken down into short, simple sub-tasks, and a special effort made to keep the sequence of questions logical and straightforward. We shall discuss questionnaire design in greater detail in chapter 11.

2.2.4 The reply envelope

The reply envelope is used to return the completed questionnaire to the research organisation.

It is not merely a matter of common courtesy to enclose a reply envelope in the mailing piece: research has shown that the response rate is substantially lower when a pre-paid reply envelope is not enclosed (Nel *et al* 1988:195).

As we have seen, the use of ordinary postage stamps encourages recipients to respond. This also applies to the use of postage stamps on reply envelopes. The typical respondent sees the stamp as something that has cost money and therefore feels virtually compelled to return the questionnaire. However, affixing stamps to reply envelopes may be a costly practice in surveys with a poor rate of response.

2.2.5 Incentive to respond

The response rate of mail surveys is usually fairly low. This means that large samples have to be drawn to ensure that enough completed questionnaires are returned for processing. Errors arising from non-response, such as information from questionnaires being only provided by respondents with the same views, can have serious limitations on the research results. Special efforts, such as use of incentives, have to be made to increase response rates. Examples of incentives that can be used to raise the response rate are discussed below.

(a) Advance notice

Respondents are given advance notice that questionnaires will be sent to them. This can be done by letter, postcard, telephone or through the media. Advance notice is regarded as a fairly effective method of raising response rates. For example, Parsons and Metford (Nel et al 1988:189) found that advance notice increases the response rate and also ensures the quick return of questionnaires. According to Nel et al (1988:190) advance notice by telephone calls is the most effective way of raising the response rate.

(b) Rewards and incentives

These are other techniques for increasing the response to mail surveys. Rewards and incentives may consist of books, pens and pencils, cash, postage stamps, cards, product prizes, and so forth. Research shows that incentives or rewards consistently raise the response rate. Kanuk and Berenson (Nel et al 1988:190) found that on average the response rate can be raised by 24 % if the right incentives are used. These researchers also found that the incentives or rewards should actually be sent with the questionnaire and not merely promised.

The advantage offered by incentives/rewards is that they stimulate the respondents' interest, putting them in a positive frame of mind. For instance, on opening a mailing piece a bright, shiny coin immediately draws the recipient's interest.

Not all incentives or rewards have the same incentive value, so we shall briefly discuss some criteria for evaluating various incentives.

☐ The incentive gift should not be too expensive. If thousands of questionnaires are sent out, an expensive gift can raise the cost of the survey unduly.

☐ The gift should not be linked directly to the subject of the questionnaire. The gift should not affect the recipients' responses to the questions.

☐ The incentive should be unique: the respondent should regard the gift as special but not necessarily expensive.

☐ The gift should be sufficiently valuable to underscore the importance of the survey.

☐ Gifts that respondents could not buy for themselves are more effective.

☐ Although cash does not conform with most of these criteria, it is widely used as an incentive by research firms. Prepaid monetary incentives cause substantial increases in response rates. The trouble with cash is that once it is spent there is nothing to remind recipients to complete the questionnaire.

Although it is best to use a combination of methods to improve the response rate, the research organisation should make every effort to strike a balance between the response rate and survey costs.

2.3 Timing of dispatch

It is very important to schedule the dispatch of mailing pieces so that respondents can complete the questionnaire within a reasonable time on the assumption that sample elements will be at home or at the office (depending on the target population). Therefore it is not a good idea to send out mailing pieces during holidays. Also, at certain times during the year post offices are busier than usual, resulting in hold-ups and delays. Needless to say, these peak times must be avoided.

It is often important that surveys be conducted and finalised within a given period. Dispatch should be planned so that the questionnaires reach the respondents early enough for them to complete the questionnaires properly and return them by the proposed return date. Care should be taken to note events that could distort responses, for example trying to measure the inclination to take up farming while the country is in the grip of a severe drought.

Cut-off date

Although most questionnaires are returned within three to four weeks, a final cut-off date must be decided upon. The cut-off date can be determined by checking the volume of questionnaires being returned. Initially large quantities will pour in, becoming progressively smaller. At some stage, having received x number of questionnaires, it could be decided that the analysis of the survey results should commence within x number of days and this will become the cut-off date.

2.4 The response rate

The low response rate often obtained in mail surveys is a major disadvantage of this type of research. That is why it is particularly important for the response rate to be monitored so that, if required, steps can be taken in good time to raise the rate to a satisfactory level. Many factors have an influence on the response rate. Table 8.2 gives a summary of factors affecting mail survey response rates. The table distinguishes between factors over which the researcher has no or limited control and factors over which the researcher has full control. In South Africa the effect of these factors may not be the same as indicated in the table.

Table 8.2 Summary of factors affecting mail survey response rates

Factor	Effect
No/limited control	
Respondents' interest in topic	Strong
Questionnaire length	Weak
Identity of survey sponsor	Moderate
Full control	
Advance notice	Moderate
Type of return postage	Moderate
Monetary incentives	Strong
Non-monetary gifts	Moderate
Promised monetary incentives	Weak
Physical characteristics	Weak
Degree of personalisation	Weak
Anonymity and/or confidentiality	Weak
Type of appeal	Weak
Lottery	Weak
Return deadlines	None
Follow-up contacts	Strong

Source: Adapted from Tull & Hawkins (1990:166).

We discussed the effect of most of these factors on the completion of the questionnaire in the previous sections. The three factors with the strongest effect on the response rate are the respondents' interest in the research topic, monetary incentives, and follow-up contacts.

The initial response rate to a mail survey is strongly influenced by the respondent's *interest* in the subject matter of the survey. Interest levels can be the cause of a serious non-response bias in the survey results. Tull and Hawkins (1993:162) illustrate this as follows:

> Consider a firm that is evaluating the potential for introducing a new tennis elbow remedy. A survey is conducted to determine incidence and severity of the problem among the general population. Those individuals most interested in tennis elbow, and thus most likely to respond to the survey, are probably currently suffering from the problem or have recently suffered from it. Therefore, initial returns are likely to overstate the incidence of the problem. This could easily lead the firm to the wrong conclusion concerning the size of the market.

Most mail surveys show a fairly similar response pattern. However, the speed of response and even the final percentage of responses can vary widely. If the histories of surveys similar to the one in hand are available, the same trends can be expected. If such information is not available, the researcher must decide how the response rate is to be estimated. Although various statistical techniques are available, for the sake of simplicity extrapolation is used.

For instance, the researcher can draw up a small test sample of the target market and send the research documents to these respondents. Their curve of response (comprising volume and time) can then be used to estimate, by extrapolation, the response rate and time requirements for the final survey.

Although not as accurate as the above methods, the response in the first few weeks of a mail survey can be used to estimate the final response.

☐ *Remailing:* It may be necessary to remind recipients to respond. This is referred to as remailing. A postcard reminder could be sent or even another questionnaire if it appears likely that the recipient has lost the original questionnaire. This can be followed by a second mailing to increase response rates. The introduction of a deadline date for the return of the questionnaires is recommended at this stage.

☐ *Response bias:* The researcher should try to determine whether the results from non-respondents would have differed significantly from those received from respondents. This can be done by drawing a sample of non-respondents of the mail survey and doing telephone or personal face-to-face interviews with them. If the pattern of results obtained from respondents would probably not be materially affected by the results (should they have been received) from non-respondents, there is no further point in trying to get completed questionnaires from the non-respondents.

☐ *Treatment of incomplete questionnaires:* Characteristics can be assumed to apply to respondents where these have been omitted in completing the questionnaire. For example, a respondent has certain demographic characteristics but has failed to state his or her income in the questionnaire. The income of another respondent with the same demographic characteristics is then assumed to apply to the first respondent. In the same way other characteristics and features that have been omitted can be added.

2.5 The accuracy of data

The accuracy and reliability of data collected by mail surveys are affected by the composition of the sample, sample loss, reporting errors due to respondents giving incorrect answers on the questionnaire, and the completion of questionnaires by the wrong person.

☐ *Sample composition and loss:* A major problem in mail surveys is that mailing lists (names and addresses of respondents) are not necessarily complete and up to date. This results in questionnaires being returned undelivered or sent to respondents who do not form part of the target population. In a study among private households Petersen and Kerin (Nel *et al* 1988:186) found that 8 % of the questionnaires had been completed by people other than the addressee.

However, the biggest problem is a low response rate. The response rate depends on the type of data being collected, the level of interest in the subject covered, the population being researched and the techniques applied. Section 2.4 dealt with response rates. Usually sample losses are higher than permissible in mail surveys, and the problem of non-response, and therefore of unrepresentative samples, limits the overall effectiveness of mail surveys.

☐ *Reporting errors*: Reporting errors in mail surveys may be due to respondents' incorrect answers. These may be premeditated to mislead the researcher or be due to lack of knowledge or misunderstanding of the questions. Mail questionnaires are completed in the respondents' own time, which allows them to consult other people and records. In the collection of factual information this is an advantage. However, in the collection of opinion data the respondents have time to consult other people and so their opinions may no longer be truly their own.

The greatest problem in reporting errors in mail surveys is item omission, that is the tendency of respondents not to answer all the questions. Such non-answering of questions not only makes processing difficult but also causes reporting bias in that the answers of those who have not answered all the questions would in most cases differ from those who have.

☐ *Completion of the questionnaire by the wrong person:* Another problem in mail surveys is that the researcher has no way of ensuring that the right person completes the questionnaire. This problem can be of major importance in industrial marketing research when the designated person (such as the executive manager) passes the questionnaire to a junior (secretary).

2.6 Mailing costs

The cost of mailing varies with the nature of the questionnaire, the sample size and the number of reminders sent out (table 8.3). The cost consideration in selecting a survey method must include the cost of initial contacts, the cost of any call-backs, the remailings, and all aspects designed to increase the response rate.

These, of course, are in addition to the normal costs of designing, developing and testing the questionnaire and other mailing items.

Table 8.3 Data-collection costs in the USA per completed questionnaire for selected methods of communication

Method of communication	Cost range		
	High $	Low $	Typical $
Mail	15	4	8
Telephone	25	6	12
Personal: shopping centre	40	8	15
Personal: home	100	25	40
Per focus group (5–12 people)	3 000	1 000	1 800

Source: Boyd, Westfall & Stasch (1989).

Table 8.3 shows that mail surveys are the lowest-cost type of survey. This applies particularly to comprehensive surveys carried out over large geographical areas. In South Africa the cost of telephone surveys compares favourably with mail surveys and, depending on the length of the questionnaire and the geographical area covered, telephone surveys may even be cheaper than mail surveys.

2.7 Advantages and disadvantages of mail surveys

2.7.1 Advantages

☐ *Costs:* Unit costs are relatively low. Usually there are no costs for travelling and subsistence, etc. Costs are limited mainly to design and development, printing, postage and remailings.

☐ *Homogeneous stimulus:* Since the questionnaire is the only channel of communication between respondents and the researcher, the type of stimulus the respondents receive is identical. Individual variations can be ascribed only to the individual respondent, not to the questionnaire.

☐ *Geographical coverage:* Mail surveys are particularly useful when the geographical area covered by the research is extensive.

☐ *Processing:* Since mail surveys are usually fully structured, most of the information is already categorised and little time is required to process it on computer.

2.7.2 Disadvantages

☐ *Non-representative:* Regardless of how well the sample has been designed, a high non-response rate can introduce bias in the data.

☐ *Impersonal:* There is no personal contact between research and respondent. The questionnaire is anonymous and impersonal.

☐ *Confined to literates:* To be able to complete a questionnaire the respondent must have a basic comprehension, reading and writing proficiency. The problem in South Africa at present is that this proficiency is far from universal.

☐ *Negativism towards questionnaires:* Since the public is subjected to a constant barrage of opinion polls and surveys, many of them are not interested in participating in research. Without personal contact this may lead to non-response or little or no commitment to complete the questionnaire properly.

☐ *Absence of control:* There is no control over who completes the questionnaire or whether the answers given are true.

☐ *Mailing lists:* Up-to-date and complete mailing lists are seldom available.

3 WARRANTY CARDS

Warranty cards typically accompany durable consumer goods such as CD players, radios and stoves, and also serve as a means of data collection of buyers' names, addresses, age, gender and profession. By analysing this kind of information the researcher gets demographic and geographic data on buyers. For their part buyers complete warranty cards in order to validate the undertaking as to the quality of the goods sold, liability for repairs, etc.

4 PANELS

A **panel** consists of a sample of respondents who have agreed to provide information at specified intervals over an extended period.

Panels are maintained by marketing research organisations, and panel members are usually compensated for their participation by payment of television licences or cable connecting fees on their behalf, gifts, coupons, information or cash. Panels are used mostly to provide quantified information either on market characteristics (market measurement panels) or on the use of the media (media panels). Panel members' behaviour rather than their attitudes is measured since there are problems involved in questioning respondents on repeated occasions about their attitudes towards products. The members of media panels are expected to keep a record of their purchases and reading and viewing habits. Peoplemeters, which automatically record whether the television set is switched on or off and the channel to which it is tuned, can be installed. Other information gathered by peoplemeters is discussed in chapter 24. Kent (1993:151) distinguishes two main kinds of market measurement panels: consumer and retail panels.

4.1 Consumer panels

Consumer panels are representative samples of individuals or households whose purchase and use of defined groups of product is recorded either continuously or at regular intervals, usually over a considerable period of time (Kent 1993:155).

A fixed sample of respondents which is measured repeatedly over time with respect to the same variables is called a true panel; the variables in an omnibus panel change from measurement to measurement. Generally the two are combined and panel members are repeatedly questioned about the same products or services, with a limited number of questions on other products and services being asked only once. Limits are placed on the number of additional products and services to retain the cooperation of the respondents.

The principles of sample design for selecting panellists are similar to those for single-call surveys conducted by personal in-home interviews, as discussed in the previous chapter. Sampling is explained in chapter 13. Recruiting panel members tends to be more difficult than securing participation in single-call surveys since respondents are asked to do rather more than in a one-off survey.

Once the panel has been recruited it needs to be maintained at a consistent level of representativeness. New panel members have to be recruited continuously, for two reasons. The first is that panel members tend to drop out because they are moving away, their circumstances have changed due to marriage, divorce, etc, or simply because they are tired of serving on the panel. Unsatisfactory panellists may also be asked to leave the panel. The second reason is the ageing of the panel over time. For the sake of representativeness the age structure of the panel members should mirror that of the population, and for this reason the composition of the panel is changed from time to time.

Panel data are captured mainly by using one of the three instruments: diaries, question-naires and electronic devices.

4.1.1 Diaries

According to Kent (1993:85) questionnaire design is a topic which is treated at great length in all texts on marketing research as opposed to diary design, which is rarely mentioned. Although problems of design typically associated with questionnaires apply equally in the construction of diaries, there are sufficiently distinct characteristics to require separate treatment. Diary purchase panellists record their purchases on or between specific dates or even by time of day. They are also expected to record repeat purchases during the whole period relevant to the diary. Diaries have to be kept up to date – new brands or brand variants may need to be added and others deleted if manufacturers have dropped them from their range.

In considering the overall layout and design of diaries it is necessary to bear in mind the potential sources of error in diary-keeping (Kent 1993:89):

☐ The diary-keeper forgets to enter purchases in the diary. Instead of making entries as they go along, many respondents will try to remember after a couple of days or even at the end of the week before sending the diary off.

☐ The record-keeper makes an entry, but makes a mistake in the details through faulty memory or erroneous recording.

☐ The diary is deliberately falsified either by omission of purchases or by the inclusion of imaginary purchases.

☐ The diary-keeper is unaware of purchases made by other members of the household.

Three types of diaries are distinguished:

☐ the *journal diary* in which purchases are entered in order of purchase, but which shows neither product categories nor data on outlets, though it has a checklist of products and services at the front

☐ *outlet diaries* in which expenditure is recorded in order of purchase by type of store or service

☐ *product diaries* which are arranged by product group and do not request data by type of outlet.

Figure 8.2 (page 164) gives an example of a page from a product diary.

In continuous research a new diary may be issued to members of a panel every week or two weeks. Or panel members may only be asked to complete a diary for two weeks every six months. Thus panellists have a rest between periods of diary-filling.

Figure 8.2 Example of a page from a product diary

Soap powder	Date bought	Brand name	Hand wash Tick (✓)		Automatic Tick (✓)		Package size	No of packs bought	Price paid per pack		Name of outlet
			Ordi-nary	Micro	Ordi-nary	Micro			R	c	
Liquid soap											

4.1.2 Questionnaires

Questionnaires can be used in consumer mail panels or in-home audits. In a consumer mail panel, members are asked to give details of expenditure and usage of a selected group of products and services by returning their mail questionnaires. Their opinion about different things can also be solicited in this manner. From time to time a product may be sent to members to try out.

The home audit method implies that panel members are visited at regular intervals, say week-ly, to carry out a visual inspection of stocks of groceries and other household items by checking cupboards, pantries, fridges and so on, and enter all items purchased since the previous week on a questionnaire. In addition the research organisation provides panel members with a special receptacle for empty cartons, wrappers, etc. Items consumed during the week are recorded from packaging or labels that are retained. The costs of undertaking home audits are clearly high and this method is now seldom used in marketing research.

4.1.3 Electronic recording devices

New technology has made it possible to transform consumer data-collection techniques. Now panel members can be equipped with computer terminals and laser scanners to read the barcodes on packs after each shopping trip. All the panellists need do is run the scanner or light pen over the barcode as they unpack their shopping. The barcode instantly records the country of origin, the manufacturer and the product (see chapter 9, section 7.3.2). If a panel member has a telephone the information is transferred daily to the research organisation's computer. Otherwise it is taken from the panel member's mini computer from time to time. Panels of this kind are expensive to establish, but over the long term, like peoplemeters in television research (see chapter 24), they are important options when the volume, variety, objectivity, reliability and time of collecting the data are taken into account.

4.2 Retail panels

> **Retail panels** are representative samples (or, in some cases, the complete universe) of retail outlets whose acquisition, pricing, stocking and display of a defined group of products are recorded either continuously or at regular intervals (Kent 1993:155).

According to Kent (1993:155) retail panels are used largely to provide estimates of over-the-counter sales of products (brand-by-brand and brand variant). This information is sometimes available directly from the use of electronic data-capture techniques; otherwise retail audits have to be undertaken. This involves physically counting the stocks in the panel shops at the beginning and at the end of the audit period. Even where electronic data are available it is often still necessary to undertake retail audits in order to determine prices, shelf space and position allocated to brands, quantities held in storerooms, and in-store promotions.

Where universe data are not available it is necessary to take a sample of shops from which to make estimates. It is virtually impossible to select a representative number of stores as panel members because there is a limited number of stores, unlike individuals and households. However, turnover is the key indicator in the sampling process and in raising the data collected to the universe, and turnover is treated as a highly confidential matter.

4.3 Consumer panels versus retail panels

Both consumer panels and retail panels generate estimates of sales volumes, values and market shares on a brand-by-brand and brand variant basis. According to Kent (1993:156) such information helps companies to

☐ evaluate company strengths and weaknesses in the marketplace

☐ diagnose market opportunities and competitor threats

☐ set realistic long-term objectives

☐ develop plans to achieve these objectives

☐ monitor the impact of trends in the market.

Beyond this, consumer panels and retail panels suit different purposes. Consumer panels are able to track consumer behaviour in, say, terms of purchase frequency and brand loyalty. Retail panels track events in the distribution system up to the point where the consumer makes a purchase without supplying personal details about the consumer. This information is matched with the consumers' demographic and other characteristics.

5 SUMMARY

Primary data collection by written communication can be done by mail surveys, warranty cards and panels. In a *mail survey* the researcher sends a structured questionnaire to a group of respondents who complete it in their own time and return it to the research unit. The quality, appearance and content of mailing pieces are crucial in determining the response rate; therefore the production of the mailing pieces is of special importance. A typical mailing piece consists of a dispatch envelope, covering letter, questionnaire, return envelope and sometimes an offer or other incentive to respond. The dispatch of mailing pieces should be scheduled so that respondents can complete the questionnaire within a reasonable time. Response rates in mail surveys are usually low. Many factors affect the response rate. The researcher has limited control over some of these factors and full control over others. The three factors with the most impact on response rates are respondents' interest in the research topic, monetary incentives and follow-up contacts. It may be necessary to remind recipients to respond by sending them a second questionnaire. The researcher should try to quantify the differences in the characteristics of respondents and non-respondents in a mail survey by conducting telephone and/or face-to-face interviews with non-respondents. Significant differences between them will cause a bias in the survey results. Questionnaires with missing answers may be completed by the researcher, provided that the answers are based on sound assumptions.

The accuracy and reliability of data collected by mail surveys are affected by the composition of the sample, sample loss, reporting errors and the completion of the questionnaire by the wrong person.

The cost of mailing varies with the nature of the questionnaire, the sample size and the number of reminders sent out. Mail surveys compare favourably with other types of surveys in terms of cost. The advantages of mail surveys are relatively low costs, homogeneous stimulus, wide geographical coverage and easier processing of questionnaire data. The disadvantages are that they can be non-representative, impersonal and confined to literates. They are also subject to negativism towards questionnaires, lack of control and incomplete sample frames.

Warranty cards also serve as a means of data collection. Information that can be gathered includes names, addresses, age, gender, profession and level of education.

A *panel* consists of a sample of respondents who have agreed to provide information at specified intervals over an extended period. Panels are used mostly to provide quantified information either of market characteristics (market measurement panels) or of the use of media (media panels). The main types of market measurement panels are consumer and retail panels.

Consumer panels are representative samples of individuals or households whose purchases and use of defined groups of products are recorded either continuously or at regular intervals. Data capturing from panellists is achieved by diaries, questionnaires or electronic instruments. Journal, outlet and product diaries are distinguished.

Retail panels are representative samples, or in some cases the complete universe, of retail outlets, whose acquisition, pricing, stocking and display of defined groups of products are recorded continuously or at regular intervals. This information is sometimes available direct through the use of electronic data-capturing techniques; otherwise retail audits have to be undertaken.

REFERENCES

Alreck, P L & Settle, R B 1985. *The survey research handbook*. Homewood, Ill: Irwin.

Boyd, H W (Jr), Westfall, R & Stasch, S F 1989. *Marketing research: text and cases*. Seventh edition. Boston: Irwin.

Kent, Raymond A 1993. *Marketing research in action*. London: Routledge.

Nel, P A, Rädel, F E & Loubser M 1988. *Researching the South African market*. Pretoria: University of South Africa. (Manualia Didactica 3.)

Tull, Donald S & Hawkins, Del I 1990. *Marketing research: measurement and method: a text with cases*. Fifth edition. New York: Macmillan. (The Macmillan Series in Marketing.)

Primary research: observation

Chapter 9: L R J van Rensburg

Primary research: observation

1 INTRODUCTION

Observation is a daily occurrence. We constantly observe what other people are doing and what is happening around us and in this way gather information about the environment. Observation is a means of taking note of events. However, the purpose of observation may vary. Some people do little more than observe and take note. A person watching a weather report, for instance, may merely note that rain is predicted for the next few days; other than that the weather report holds no further interest except perhaps that a drop in temperature will be most welcome. Another person, perhaps a farmer, who watches the same report will take note that in a few days he can start ploughing and planting and get on with the business of farming.

Observation may be casual, but it may also be planned to access information for a specific purpose. Very often firms opt for observation of popular response to a new advertisement rather than questioning people direct.

Like all the other methods of data collection, observation requires a scientific approach. Certain conditions, however, must be met before observation is applied in marketing research.

> The **observation method** of collecting primary data on human behaviour relies on observation by humans or recording devices and the relevant facts, actions, or behaviours are recorded.

In this chapter we shall deal with the various reasons for using observation techniques. We shall also describe the various types and methods of observation and conclude with an overview of the use of observation as a research method.

2 CONDITIONS FOR THE USE OF OBSERVATION

Tull and Hawkins (1990:416–417) set three minimum conditions for the use of observation in applied marketing research.

☐ *The data must be accessible to observation:* Observation is not an appropriate technique for researching motivations, attitudes and the like. The reason is that motives and attitudes are shaped and measured from within.

☐ *The behaviour must be repetitive, frequent, or otherwise predictable:* Because the behaviour is repetitive, it is possible to make inferences about it. A situation in which the behaviour of people at a point-of-purchase display of a new product is observed is repetitive in nature. Observation is not limited to the behaviour of just one person. The behaviour of 100 people can be observed and certain trends can be observed in their behaviour.

☐ *An event must cover a reasonably short timespan:* It is not feasible, for example, to observe the entire decision-making process in a family who are buying a new car. The cost of the exercise and the time it will take exceed the value of the observation. Observation is better suited to the collection of data over a relatively short time such as a few days.

3 REASONS FOR PREFERRING OBSERVATIONAL DATA

This discussion is not intended to prove that the observation method of research is more important than the other methods. The mere fact that information is suited to measurement by observation does not mean that the observation method must be applied. But in certain situations where observation is the only means of accessing the data, observation techniques become obligatory. Observation is the only technique that can be used in measuring the food and toy preferences of children who cannot yet talk. In certain situations people or employees are reluctant to answer questions in interviews. The information may then be collected by observation, for instance by monitoring competitors' prices, despite the fact that the competitors were unwilling to supply the prices voluntarily. Consumers are often reluctant to answer questions about their consumption of so-called negative products such as alcoholic beverages. Observation can sometimes produce the data on consumption of such products.

In a research situation, such as counting traffic into and out of a store or on the pavement, it is much cheaper to apply observation techniques than any others. Here mechanical devices would be a more accurate and reliable means of counting people.

Sampling for observational techniques presents unique problems and is more difficult than sampling for other research methods. To return to our point-of-purchase display, it would not be practical to draw a sample and then follow the sample units to see whether they purchase the product. Instead, a sample should be drawn from a number of stores where the product is on display and the behaviour of consumers at those stores should be observed. Or the researcher may decide to draw samples of times of the day, week, month or year and make a count of all the traffic into and out of the store at the specified time.

4 TYPES AND METHODS OF OBSERVATION

A study of the literature reveals only two basic types of observation, but each of them encompasses several methods. The methods are the same for both types of observation. The various methods and techniques are represented graphically in figure 9.1 and are discussed individually in the sections that follow.

As can be seen in figure 9.1, observation can take place by human or mechanical means, and each of these two main types of observation is made up of various methods. These methods are not mutually exclusive, and in certain situations they are combined. The selection of one of the eight methods does not conclude the decision-making process because the researcher still has to decide how he will apply the method.

Figure 9.1 Types and methods of observation

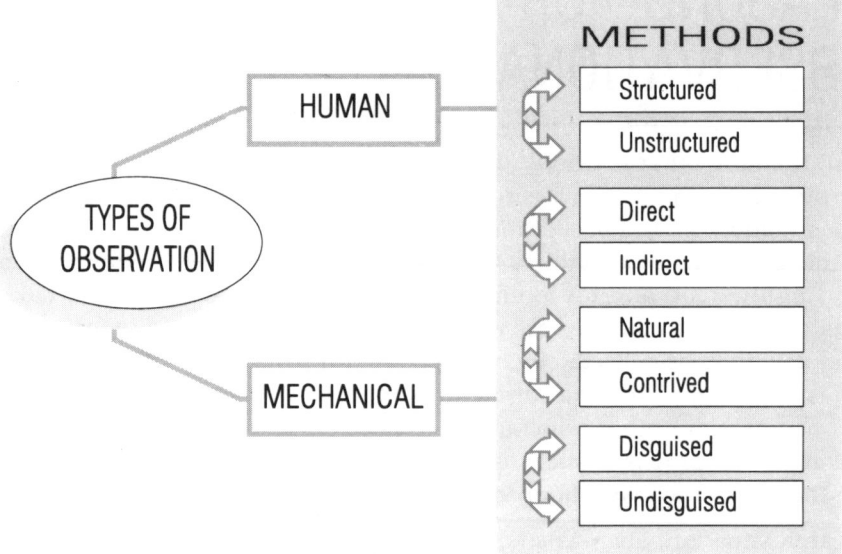

Source: Adapted from Churchill (1992:254).

4.1 Structured observation

In structured observation the observer knows beforehand precisely which aspects of a situation are to be observed and which criteria will apply. These decisions are made before the process begins. Measurement by structured observation may be human or recorded.

The observer may decide to make use of a form specifying all the behaviours to be observed. Devices are also used in structured research, for instance to monitor the eye movements of a person in response to advertisements in a magazine. The term 'structured research' applies to all observation which specifies beforehand the aspects of behaviour to be observed, irrespective of the use of devices.

4.2 Unstructured observation

Unstructured observation encompasses all measurement by observation that is not specified in advance. There is a great deal of latitude in the aspects of the situation to be observed or recorded. Again we return to our observer at the point-of-sale exhibit: in unstructured observation he or she would observe and record the behaviour of the shoppers which seemed to be of interest and then decide afterwards whether the observations were of any use. Or the observer would install a video camera at the exhibit to record all aspects of the shoppers' behaviour and study the recording afterwards for aspects of interest.

4.3 Direct observation

Direct observation is the most common type of observation. It takes place while the customer is displaying a particular type of behaviour, and the observation may be human or mechanical, etc in nature.

4.4 Indirect observation

Certain types of behaviour do not lend themselves to direct observation and indirect observation is used. A case in point is past behaviour. In this situation it is the result or effect of the behaviour rather than the behaviour itself that is observed.

The examination of archives is an example of indirect observation. Another example involves physical traces of past behaviour, such as empty cartons and packaging. Analysis of the household waste from various communities, for instance, will reveal their purchasing and consumption patterns. The pantry audit also makes use of physical traces by examining the pantries of respondents with their permission for traces of pre-specified items. An audit merely indicates that the products have been purchased, not that they have been consumed. Examining household waste tells the researcher that the product has indeed been purchased and consumed.

Indirect observation is applied in garages, for example by noting the setting of radios in cars brought in for service or as trade-ins. A researcher who gathers sufficient data over a period is able to advise advertisers on the best stations for their advertisements.

4.5 Natural observation

In natural observation the subject is observed in its natural setting or its daily or usual surroundings. An observer, with or without a camera, who counts the number of persons entering and leaving the bank every day is observing a natural phenomenon. In other words, nothing is done to encourage or discourage the flow of people, on the assumption that the people visiting the bank regard it as natural behaviour on their part.

In other situations the behaviour which the researcher wishes to observe does not readily occur in natural surroundings. A contrived environment is created for measurement by observation in such cases.

4.6 Contrived observation

In contrived observation the objects are observed in a specially contrived or controlled environment. A group of people, for example, may be assembled in a room with several television sets. Each person is shown a number of commercials and his or her comments and behaviour are noted. This method of research has yielded a great deal of data on the factual aspects of commercials. Such data would not be so readily measured by natural observation.

Contrived observation facilitates the process of data collection. There is no delay in waiting for a specific event to occur; it can be made to happen. Many observations can be made in a relatively short period and in most cases they are more accurate. Contrived observation is one of the methods which encourages the use of mechanical devices.

4.7 Disguised observation

In this type of observation the person being observed is not aware of it. The method is applied for the very reason that many people tend to behave differently when they know they are being watched. A bank clerk who helps new clients open accounts will behave differently if it becomes apparent that the 'client' is there to observe his or her behaviour. The method has two disadvantages. First, it is not always possible to remain effectively disguised and, second, it is not always possible to secure certain background data which might have been supplied by a person who knew that his or her behaviour was being observed.

4.8 Undisguised observation

In undisguised observation the people who are being observed know that they are being watched. A device attached to a television set to record the viewing habits of the household is also an example of undisguised observation. It should be borne in mind, however, that people may not behave naturally when they are aware of a human observer. They are more likely to behave naturally when their behaviour is being recorded by a mechanical device.

We have already mentioned one type of observation that is readily made by a mechanical device. In the sections that follow we shall deal briefly with a few of the devices in current use.

5 DEVICES USED IN OBSERVATION

There are several devices for measurement by observation. The researcher's choice of device will depend on the purpose of the observation. If a physical response is to be measured directly, the process is termed physiological measurement and then the researcher applies the devices discussed below.

5.1 Brain-wave analysis

The human brain emits brain waves which can be monitored. These waves are a measure of the respondent's interest in a stimulus with which he is confronted (Tull & Hawkins 1990:425). The respondent's head and certain parts of his body are wired to a machine which registers brain waves as the person is exposed to stimuli. Thus the respondent's brain waves reflect his level of interest in an advertisement, a new product or a package. By carefully controlling the various components of the advertisement or package shown to the respondent, the researcher is able to measure the interest in the components of the stimulus. The principal advantage of brain-wave analysis is that it teaches marketers more about the best ways of communicating with consumers. The greatest drawback of the method is the artificial environment in which it is conducted, usually a laboratory where the respondent is exposed to the advertisement or package. Brain-wave analysis, however, is seldom used, because it is so controversial.

5.2 The oculometer (eye camera)

Eye movements are tracked with the aid of an eye camera or oculometer which is mounted on the respondent's head in such a way that it follows the movements of the eyes. Or it may take the shape of a large pair of spectacles worn by the respondent, which performs the same functions as the camera. The third option involves merely sitting in a chair at a desk and paging through a magazine while an eye-tracking device sends an undetectable beam of filtered light into the respondent's eyes. This beam reflects off the respondent's eyes and the reflected beam represents the focal point of the respondent's eyes. In this way the researcher determines what is being viewed.

The oculometer is intended to reveal the effectiveness of advertisements, packages and point-of-sale exhibits. The camera follows the respondent's eye movements while he is reading, say, an advertisement. It allows the researcher to determine the parts of the advertisement that draw the respondent's attention first, how long the respondent spends looking at a specific part of the advertisement, and whether the respondent scrutinises the whole advertisement. Eye tracking is a fairly common method of observation in some countries.

5.3 The tachistoscope

The tachistoscope is an observational device which allows the researcher to time the respondent's perception and interpretation of a visual stimulus, say an advertisement. It is not an observational device in the true sense of the word because it is used merely to expose the stimulus for a few seconds. After exposure of the stimulus the respondent is asked to tell the researcher how much he remembers of the advertisement. The respondent's ability to recall certain aspects of the advertisement is evident from systematic varying of the exposure. This device merely flashes the advertisement.

5.4 Response latency

Response latency denotes the time a respondent takes to respond to a question and is directly related to the respondent's degree of uncertainty about the answer. The method is helpful in determining the strength of a respondent's preference for a brand. The longer the respondent takes to choose between alternative brands, the more difficult the choice and the smaller the preference for one brand rather than another.

Measurement of response latency is by voice-operated relay which triggers an electronic stopwatch. When the interviewer reaches the end of a question, he presses a pedal which sets the stopwatch to zero and activates an electronic mechanism to listen for the voice of the interviewer. The moment the interviewer reaches the end of the question, the stopwatch is activated automatically, and the moment the respondent begins to reply, the stopwatch stops automatically. A digital readout system records the response latency which the interviewer enters on a special form.

There are several advantages to this system (Churchill 1992:299). First the researcher obtains an accurate measurement of response latency without the respondent's knowledge. Second, the measurement occurs automatically, which takes some of the pressure off the researcher and takes no extra time to administer.

5.5 Voice pitch analysis

Voice pitch analysis monitors changes in the relative frequency of the human voice that accompany emotional arousal. In normal circumstances the human voice has a baseline frequency. Deviations from this baseline indicate response to stimuli. Such stimuli may take the form of questions a respondent is asked about, say, a new product, package or advertisement. The pitch of the respondent's voice is taken as a measure of his feelings about the product, etc. The deviations can be assessed by special computer equipment. The degree of deviation from the baseline is a measure of the respondent's reaction to the stimuli. The greater the deviation, the greater the emotional intensity of the respondent's reaction is said to be.

Voice pitch analysis has two advantages over other physiological methods of observation. The first is that it measures both the intensity of the response and the direction of feeling: the respondents are questioned about their feelings while their voice pitch is measured mechanically. Second, the technique allows the researcher and respondent to converse naturally, without having the respondent attached to mechanical equipment. The respondent feels more at ease and the process is less time consuming.

5.6 The galvanometer

Dillon, Madden and Firtle (1990:169) define a galvanometer as an instrument which determines excitement levels by measuring the level of electrical activity in a person's skin. Electrodes are attached to the respondent's palms or forearm and the respondent is exposed to advertisements, new packages or new products. The galvanometer responds to changes in the electrical resistance of the skin associated with the minute degree of sweating that follows emotional arousal. It is a handy device for revealing excitement levels induced by various advertisements.

5.7 The peoplemeter

The peoplemeter is a device used to measure when a television is on, to what channel it is tuned, and who in the household is watching it.

Peoplemeters are installed in the homes of television owners to make up panels of viewers. Ideally the peoplemeter should automatically record the use of television sets and video cassette recorders, while one or more of the family members register the viewing pattern of individuals on the peoplemeter. The use of peoplemeters is discussed in detail in chapter 24 under television media research.

5.8 The optical scanner

The optical scanner is an observational device commonly used in supermarkets. This is the device which automated the checkout process. It also allows management to monitor product sales in terms of number and brand. The device reads the barcodes printed on packaging. We shall return to the use of barcodes later in this chapter.

5.9 Traffic counters

Traffic counters are suitable for counting internal and external traffic. External traffic means vehicles in particular. Internal traffic relates more particularly to pedestrians entering and leaving a store or shopping centre.

Outdoor advertising is widely used today. Hoardings should be positioned where they will be seen by the largest possible number of people. Such positions are identified by making use of traffic counters in densely populated areas where they keep count of the passing traffic (Lamb, Hair & McDaniel 1994:246). The device is also helpful in determining the best locations for convenience stores which require a strong flow of traffic to be profitable. In all of these situations a count of external traffic is helpful in selecting locations for hoardings or for businesses.

It is advisable to ascertain beforehand whether the flow of pedestrian traffic warrants opening a store in a shopping centre. Internal traffic in a centre can be counted in several ways. For example, a researcher may position a person at each entrance to the centre with instructions to count everyone entering the building. A drawback of this method is that the person doing the count may be distracted and lose count. Or the researcher may install turnstiles at each entrance to the centre and attach traffic counters to them. A third option is electronic eyes at entrances, which register incoming traffic. Internal traffic counts at specific store premises are also helpful in establishing shopping trends at a specific store. The devices mentioned above are suitable for installation at the door of the store to count incoming traffic and identify the busiest days, weeks and months of the year. The information is incorporated in the marketing programme in accordance with shopping trends at the store.

6 HUMAN OBSERVATION

As we have said, there are various ways in which a human observer can gather data. The question is what part the observer will play in the process of observation. There are several possibilities, just as there are several devices to choose from in mechanical observation.

6.1 Participatory observation

Participatory observation has long been in use as a research method, inter alia in ethnology, sociology and criminology, the sciences concerned with the customs of various cultures or the criminal patterns of behaviour of specific groups. In participatory observation the researcher becomes part of the group being researched. The non-participating observer tries to distance himself from the object of observation. Because this is not always possible, there are different degrees of participatory observation. Generally the degree of participation in the group's activities is related to the duration of the research. The longer the research takes, the greater the degree of participation is likely to be. Through participatory observation the researcher discovers the meanings which his subjects attach to activities in their worlds and tries to describe and understand them.

Participatory observation takes various forms (Schurink 1988:81), in which the observer assumes four different guises. First there is the role of *full participant*. In this situation the researcher takes part in and tries to guide the direction taken by a group's activities. The role is not a common one because it can be counter-productive. To manipulate the group's activities the researcher has to be familiar to the group, and such familiarity may elicit a negative response. The researcher circumvents this possibility by keeping his identity secret when he joins the group, but in doing so he sacrifices the opportunity to manipulate the group's activities. Second, the researcher assumes the guise of *participant-as-observer* who not only observes but also participates in the activities. The researcher does not reveal that the group is being observed but he has access to relevant behaviour because he participates without manipulating. Third, in the role of *observer-as-participant* the researcher keeps his contact with the group to a minimum. This role is the least satisfactory, however, because the researcher is not really part of the group. Lastly there is the role of *complete observer* in which the researcher has no contact with and is not part of the group in any way.

Marketers also make use of participatory observation. A wholesaler, for instance, who has to choose between various retailers can engage the services of mystery shoppers to observe the quality of service of the retailers. In most of the observation techniques discussed in this chapter the observer assumes one of the four roles described above. In the USA there are research consultants who specialise in participatory observation.

6.2 Non-participatory observation

Researchers make use of one-way mirrors and video cameras to observe respondents without their knowledge. In such situations the researcher is purely an observer and nothing more. Lamb *et al* (1994:248) reveal that Fisher-Price, the famous toymakers, frequently make use of these devices as a research aid. Small children, who are their target market, are brought in groups to the Fisher-Price laboratory where they spend twelve sessions playing with toys of different makes. In the laboratory the children are allowed to play with the toys without interference in a natural way. Researchers observe the children through a one-way mirror, comparing the children's reactions to, say, Fisher-Price toys and other makes of toys. The authors mention Fisher-Price's problems with designing a toy lawnmower. A designer who observed the children through the one-way mirror noticed that the children were fascinated with soap bubbles. He promptly designed a toy mower which blew soap bubbles while it was being pushed. Millions of these toy lawnmowers were sold.

Another possibility is inconspicuous human observation, for instance at a traffic light or stop sign where a researcher sits and counts the passing traffic. The observer is visible but his visibility does not affect the respondents.

7 OBJECTS OF OBSERVATION

From the above it is evident that various objects can be the focus of observation. We have already discussed how these objects can be observed. In the sections that follow we shall turn our attention to the different objects of observation.

7.1 Observation of people

People must surely be the most common objects of observation. The focus of attention, however, is not so much the people themselves but their actions and behaviour. Marketers are particularly interested in the observation of two groups of people. The consumer is without doubt the most important object of observation, followed by corporate employees. The movement of consumers in a store, how often they look at a certain product, their reaction to certain packages and the brand they choose – all of these aspects of consumer behaviour are observed. Employees are observed primarily to determine the standard of their service, but also to rate their skills and abilities.

As we have said, people and mechanical devices are used to observe other people, as in participatory observation, and in measurement involving voice pitch, response latency, brain waves, the tachistoscope, eye camera, galvanometer and one-way mirror and video camera.

7.2 Observation of physical traces

In this context the object of research is not the person: it is the result of the person's behaviour. This type of observation is known as *indirect observation*. How it is accomplished is discussed above. You may now ask why it should be necessary to provide physical evidence of the object of observation.

Very often situations arise where people are reluctant to participate when they know they are being subjected to direct observation. Human nature being what it is, people tend to present themselves in a different light when they are being monitored by something or someone. Some people are merely unwilling to participate. This type of attitude is not uncommon in the context of data collection by questionnaire. In such cases the researcher has to find an alternative, and this alternative is to make the results of human behaviour the object of research. Valuable buying habits and usage data are collected in this way to serve as decision-making data for management.

7.3 Observation of records and inventories

In this section we shall confine ourselves to a discussion of only two aspects: store audits and automated store checkouts.

7.3.1 Store audits

Store audits take place when data on purchases and beginning and ending inventory are collected from a sample panel of retailers (Nel, Rädel & Loubser 1988:209). The retail stores selected are visited at regular intervals and inventories are taken of the products concerned. The store also supplies the invoices of products purchased since the last visit. Sales of the products concerned are calculated in this manner. The calculations are similar to the calculations in the store's income statement:

Initial stock + Purchases in the given period − Final stock = Sales in the given period

Provided that the sample of retailers is representative of all the retailers in the country, inferences from the data can be raised to the universe. Typical inferences would relate to market potential and brand share. Projects which focus on consumer behaviour and buying habits yield information only about the market potential of consumers and tell us nothing about institutional purchasers. Store audits also reflect the purchases of government and institutional users at outlets of this kind. Thus the data present a total picture of the potential. A further advantage is that a large number of consumers are covered in a limited survey. A disadvantage of this method is that it does not reflect the demographic diversity of a country such as South Africa (Nel *et al* 1988:209).

7.3.2 Automated store checkouts

We referred to automated store checkouts very briefly in a previous section. Here, too, inventory is the object of observation. McCarthy and Perreault (1993:159) see automated store checkouts as a major breakthrough in marketing research, especially in the sphere of observation. This system has replaced traditional cash registers. It operates with the aid of scanners connected to the cash registers and to the store's inventory system.

The operation of automated checkouts is dependent on the allocation of a code consisting of a certain number of bars to each product the store has in stock. The process is termed barcoding. When a consumer arrives at the cash register with his or her products, each product in turn is drawn across the path of the scanner which registers the code, price and type of product. The store's cash registers are all linked to a central computer which registers the same information. Thus the sales records are available for any specific product at any time of the day, week, month or year.

As we have said, the operation of the technique is dependent on the printing of bar codes on products and on the introduction of scanners in the store. The scanning system was introduced in South Africa with the assistance of the South African Numbering Association (SAANA) which was founded in 1982 (Marx & Van der Walt 1993:254).

The code printed on the packaging of the product consists of parallel bars of varying width. The structure of the code is predetermined. Numbers are usually printed below the bars. The standard number in use in Europe, Japan, Australia, New Zealand and South Africa comprises 13 digits which refer to the manufacturer and product specifications, as follows:

- ☐ The first three digits (prefix) identify the digit bank administered by the National Numbering Association. For SAANA these digits are 600.
- ☐ The next four digits are the ones allocated to the member by SAANA.
- ☐ The next five digits are the ones allocated to the product by the manufacturer in order to identify the product.
- ☐ The final digit, a check digit, calculated over the preceding 12 digits ensures the correct composition of the code.

Besides offering the manufacturer, dealer and consumer several advantages which enhance its attraction as an observation technique, the barcode system has the added advantage of improving and facilitating administration.

8 OBSERVATION IN PERSPECTIVE

As a method of collecting primary information, observation is a very useful tool in marketing research. On its own, however, it may not be satisfactory in every situation. The method is designed merely to throw light on human behaviour or the results of past behaviour. It does not explain human behaviour; nor does it provide data on the process of decision making which determines human behaviour. It focuses strongly on the 'what' rather than on the 'how' and 'why' of human actions. This is not to say that observation is worthless as a method of data collection; it means that inferences drawn from observation data should not be regarded as superior to all others.

9 SUMMARY

There are three conditions for the use of observation in applied marketing research: the object of the research has to be accessible; it has to be repetitive, frequent or otherwise predictable; and the event should cover a relatively short timespan. Observation can be used in combination with other methods of primary data collection. In certain situations involving, say, small children, observation may be satisfactory on its own. Observation may be accomplished by people, devices, or both. Eight methods of observation and nine observational devices are distinguished. Observation of a group by a person who becomes part of the group is termed participatory observation; in non-participatory observation the researcher observes from a distance. The objects of observation may be people, physical traces, and records and inventories. Records and inventories are observed through store audits and automated store checkouts.

REFERENCES

Churchill Gilbert A (Jr) 1992. *Basic marketing research*. Second edition. Fort Worth: The Dryden Press. (The Dryden Press Series in Marketing.)

Crimp, Margaret 1990. *The marketing research process*. Third edition. New York: Prentice Hall.

Dillon, W R, Madden, T J & Firtle, N H 1990. *Marketing research in a marketing environment*. Homewood, Ill: Irwin.

Lamb, C W, Hair, J F & McDaniel, C 1994. *Principles of marketing*. Cincinnati, Ohio: South-Western.

Marx, S & Van der Walt, A 1993. *Marketing management*. Cape Town: Juta.

McCarthy, E & Perreault, W D 1993. *Basic marketing*. Homewood, Ill: Irwin.

Moutinho, L & Evans, M 1992. *Applied marketing research*. Woking, England: Addison-Wesley.

Nel, P A, Rädel, F E & Loubser, M 1988. *Researching the South African market*. Pretoria: University of South Africa. (Manualia Didactica 3.)

Schurink, W J 1988. Deelnemende waarneming. In *Inleiding tot kwalitatiewe metodes*. Pretoria: Raad vir Geesteswetenskaplike Navorsing.

Tull, Donald S & Hawkins, Del I 1990. *Marketing research: measurement and method: a text with cases*. Fifth edition. New York: Macmillan. (The Macmillan Series in Marketing.)

Primary research: experimentation

Chapter 10: J H Martins

Primary research: experimentation

1 INTRODUCTION

In the previous three chapters we discussed the collection of primary data by verbal and written communication and observation methods. Primary information is also collected by means of experimental methods which are designed to test cause-and-effect relationships. Descriptive research is fine for testing hypotheses, but it is not as effective as causal designs for testing cause-and-effect relationships.

Marketing research textbooks written 25 years ago contained little or no mention of the use of experimental and quasi-experimental procedures in marketing research. This accurately reflected the practice of the day. Since then these procedures have gained substantially in use and are now considered viable alternatives to other types of studies. According to Kinnear and Taylor (1991:286) there are four reasons why this trend continues:

☐ Experimentation works. Meaningful marketing results are generated by the procedures.

☐ The costs of making wrong causal inferences in marketing are increasing.

☐ Educational levels are rising, with an associated increase in the understanding of these procedures.

☐ The capabilities of computerised analysis procedures have eliminated the tedium of hand analysis of results.

Experimental research helps the marketing manager make certain causal statements about the effects of his actions, such as: 'The new advertising campaign we developed has resulted in a 10 % increase in sales', or 'Redesigning the soap powder package so that it is more bulky and less likely to tip over has improved consumer attitudes toward the product and resulted in an increase of 5 % in sales', or 'The new sales training programme has resulted in lower sales turnover', or 'A 5 % increase in the price of the product had no significant effect on the amount of products sold'. However, the fundamental question that should be asked in the presence of all causal statements is: 'Are there some other possible factors that could have caused the changes you observed?'

2 CONCEPT OF CAUSALITY

A distinction should be made between the so-called commonsense concept and the scientific concept of causality. In non-technical language, the so-called commonsense statement that one thing (x) is the cause of another thing (y) suggests that there is a single cause of an event. Here the effect always follows the cause and is referred to as deterministic causation. In science we recognise that an event has a number of determining conditions or causes which act together to make the effect probable. This is called *probabilistic causation.*

Marketing research proceeds from a scientific point of view. First, it accepts that there is more than one cause (x) which led to effect (y). Second, it holds that x does not make the occurrence of y certain; it just makes it more likely. Finally, the scientific notion holds that we can never prove that x really is a cause of y; we can only infer a causal relationship. We must always live with the possibility that we have not identified the true causal relationship.

3 CONDITIONS FOR CAUSALITY

Kinnear and Taylor (1991:266) distinguish three conditions for making causal inferences: concomitant variation, time order of occurrence of variables, and elimination of other causal factors.

Concomitant variation is the extent to which a cause (x) and an effect (y) occur together in the way predicted by the hypothesis under consideration. For instance, a marketer may hypothesise that there is a definite relation between sales and the quality of the dealer – where we have effective dealers we have good market penetration and where we have ineffective dealers we have unsatisfactory market penetration. Now if x is to be considered a cause of y, we should expect to find the following: in those territories where our effective dealers are located we should have satisfactory market shares, while in those territories where our ineffective dealers are located we should have unsatisfactory market shares. However, if we find that in a large number of territories with effective dealers we also have unsatisfactory market shares, we must conclude that our hypothesis is faulty.

Perfect evidence of concomitant variation would be provided, of course, if all effective dealers were located in territories with satisfactory market shares and all ineffective dealers in territories with unsatisfactory market shares. The 'pure' case will rarely be found in practice, as other causal factors will produce some deviation from a one-to-one relationship between x and y. Some effective dealers, for example, may be located in territories where sentiments are negative and hence sales are very low. An ineffective dealer may have no nearby competition in a territory and thus have an excellent market share despite a reputation for poor service.

Suppose that when we analysed the relationship between x and y we found evidence of concomitant variation. What can we say? All we can say is that the association makes the hypothesis more likely; it does not prove it. We are always inferring, rather than proving, that a causal relationship exists. Similarly, the lack of an association between x and y cannot be taken as conclusive evidence that there is no causal relationship between them.

The *time order of occurrence of variables* is another type of evidence of causal relationship between two variables. The general statement of this very intuitive concept is that one event cannot cause another if it occurs after the other event. The causing event must occur either before or simultaneously with the effect.

There is one complication in this seemingly straightforward concept, namely that it is possible for two events to be both a cause and an effect of each other. In our example, effective dealers may cause increases in sales, and increased sales may cause effective dealers. Thus, the relationship between dealers and sales could be that of alternately 'feeding' on each other.

The elimination of other possible causal factors is the elimination of possible explanations other than the one being studied. This may mean physically holding other factors constant, or it may mean adjusting the results to remove the effects of factors that do vary. Churchill (1992:143) explains this by means of the following example. Take the situation of the divisional manager of a chain of supermarkets investigating the effects of end-of-aisle displays on orange sales. Suppose that the manager found that per-store sales of oranges had increased during the past week and that a number of stores were using end-of-aisle displays for oranges. To conclude that the end displays were indeed the factor responsible for the sales increase, the manager would need to eliminate other possible variables such as price, size of store, and orange type and quality. This might involve looking at orange sales for stores of approximately the same size, checking to see if prices were the same in stores which had an increase in sales and stores with no increase, and checking to determine whether the type and quality of oranges were consistent with the previous week's.

4 EXPERIMENTATION

4.1 Definition and concepts

The fundamental research tool used to help identify causal relationships is the experiment.

> **Experimentation** involves the manipulation of one or more variables by the experimenter in such a way that its effect on one or more other variables can be measured (Tull & Hawkins 1990:183).

The variables that are being manipulated are called the *independent variables* and the variables that will reflect the impact of the manipulation are called the *dependent variables*. *Treatments* are the alternatives or portions of the independent variables that are manipulated and whose effects are measured. The *test units* are the entities to whom the treatments are presented and whose response to the treatments is measured. The *extraneous variables* are all the variables other than the treatments that affect the response of the test units to the treatments. An *experimental design* involves the specification on treatments that are to be manipulated, test units to be used, dependent variables to be measured, and procedures for dealing with extraneous variables (Kinnear & Taylor 1991:270).

These concepts can be illustrated in a simple example. A manufacturer of yogurt is considering changing his container. The experimental design prescribes that research should be done by test marketing (section 6). A number of stores are selected and the yogurt container is changed. Sales figures will give an indication of the effect of the change. In this example the concepts are as follows:

☐ independent variable: yogurt container

☐ treatment: change in yogurt container

☐ test units: selected stores

☐ dependent variable: yogurt sales figures

☐ extraneous variables: actions of competitors (price and advertising of rival products).

Experimental designs may be categorised into two broad groups: *basic designs,* which consider the impact of only one independent variable at a time, and *statistical designs,* which allow the evaluation of the effect of more than one. Before specific designs can be described, it is necessary to introduce the symbols that are used in their descriptions. No standard symbols exist. Some symbols used by Tull and Hawkins (1991:192) will be used in this chapter:

MB = *pre-measurement:* a measurement made on the dependent variable before the introduction or manipulation of the independent variable

MA = *post-measurement:* a measurement made on the dependent variable after or during the introduction or manipulation of the independent variable

M = *measurement:* a measurement made on a variable without being subjected to treatment

T = *treatment:* the actual introduction or manipulation of the independent variable

R = designation that the group is selected randomly.

Any symbol that is to the right of another symbol indicates that the activity represented occurred *after* the one to its left.

4.2 Validity in experimentation

Validity is the term applied to measuring instruments which show the extent to which differences in scores on the measurement reflect true differences among individuals, groups, or situations in the characteristic that it seeks to measure, or reflect true differences in the same individual, group, or situation from one occasion to another, rather than constant or random errors. Kinnear and Taylor (1991:270) distinguish two concepts of validity relevant in experimentation: internal validity and external validity.

Internal validity is the basic minimum that must be present in an experiment before any conclusion about treatment effects can be made. It is concerned with the question of whether the observed effects on the test units could have been caused by variables other than the treatment. Without internal validity, the experiment is confounded.

External validity is concerned with the 'generalisability' of experimental results. To what populations, geographic areas, treatment variables and measurement variables can the measured effects be projected?

4.3 Types of errors affecting experimental results

Tull and Hawkins (1991:185–190) and Kinnear and Taylor (1991:271–273) distinguish the following possible types of errors which could affect the validity of the results of the experiment.

4.3.1 Pre-measurement error

Pre-measurement effects occur whenever the taking of a measurement has a direct effect on performance in a subsequent measurement. The test unit's attitude towards a product or service changes in pre-measurement error, because he was questioned about the product or service. This questioning then aroused curiosity which caused the product or service to be used and not, say, an advertising campaign which ran two weeks before the questioning of the test unit. Pre-measurement is a major concern if the respondents realise they are being measured.

4.3.2 Interaction error

Interaction error occurs when a pre-measure changes the respondents' sensitivity or responsiveness to the independent variable(s). This sensitising effect is particularly important in studies involving attitudes, brand awareness and opinions.

A group of individuals may be given a questionnaire containing several attitude scales concerned with a particular brand. These individuals are then likely to be particularly interested in, or sensitive to, advertisements and other activities involving this brand. Thus an increase, decrease, or change in, say, advertising is more likely to be noticed and reacted to by these individuals than by a group who did not receive the initial questionnaire. This heightened sensitivity will often increase the effect of whatever change was made in the marketing variable and will be reflected in the post-measurement.

It is important to note how interaction differs from direct pre-measurement effects. In the example of direct pre-measurement effects, the individual involved was not exposed to the independent variable. All of the change was caused by the initial measurement itself. In contrast, interaction does not require any direct effects from the initial measurement. It simply means that the independent variable is more likely to be noticed and reacted to than it would be without the initial measurement. Thus pre-measurement error occurs when the pre-measurement, by itself, causes a change in the dependent variable. Interaction error occurs when the pre-measurement and the independent variable have a unique, joint effect on the dependent variable. This distinction is important, as experimental designs that will control direct pre-measurement effects will not necessarily control interaction effects.

4.3.3 History

History refers to the occurrence of specific events which are external to the experiment but which take place at the same time as the experiment. These events may affect the dependent variable. The condition can thus be formulated as follows:

$MB + T + H = MA$

where MB = pre-measurement of sales
MA = post-measurement of sales
T = treatment or introduction of an advertising campaign
H = history effect (for example improvement of general economic conditions)

The difference MA − MB is the measurement of the treatment effect. However, the new advertising campaign is not the only possible explanation of a positive difference between MB and MA; an improvement in general economic conditions between MB and MA is as plausible a hypothesis for explaining the observed increase in sales as the new advertising campaign. The greater the length of time between observations, the greater the chance of history confounding an experiment of this type. What we need is a procedure to control the effects of history.

4.3.4 Maturation

Maturation is similar to history except that it is concerned with changes in the experimental units themselves that occur with the passage of time. Examples would include getting older, growing hungrier and becoming more tired. Clearly people change over time. However, so do stores, geographic regions and organisations. The longer the time between MB and MA the greater the chance of maturation effects.

4.3.5 Instrumentation

Instrumentation refers to changes in the measuring instrument over time. These changes are most likely to occur when the measurement involves humans, either as observers or interviewers. Thus during a pre-measurement interviewers may be highly interested in the research and may take great care in explaining instructions and recording observations. By the time the post-measurements are taken, the interviewers may have lost most or all of their interest and involvement, and their explanations may be less thorough and their recording less precise. Alternatively interviewers or observers may become more skilled with practice and perform better during the post-measure.

4.3.6 Selection bias

Selection bias refers to the assigning of test units to treatment groups in such a way that the groups differ on the dependent variable prior to the presentation of the treatments. If test units self-select their own groups or are assigned to groups on the basis of researcher judgement, the possibility of selection bias exists. Test units should be randomly assigned to treatment groups.

4.3.7 Mortality

Mortality refers to the differential loss (refusal or inability to continue in the experiment) of respondents from the various groups. By a differential loss we mean that some groups lose respondents who are different from those lost by other groups. If the experiment involves only one group, mortality error occurs when the respondents who remain in the study differ in responsiveness to the independent variable from those who withdraw.

4.3.8 Reactive error

A reactive error occurs when the artificiality of the experimental situation or the behaviour of the experimenter causes effects that emphasise, dampen, or alter any effects caused by the treatment variable. The reason for this is that human subjects do not respond passively to experimental situations. Rather, for some subjects at least, the experiment takes on aspects of a problem-solving experience in which the subject tries to discover the experimental hypothesis and then produce the anticipated behaviour.

A reactive error cannot be controlled for by the experimental design. Rather, it must be controlled for by the structure of the experimental situation.

4.3.9 Measurement timing

Errors of measurement timing occur when pre- or post-measurements are made at an inappropriate time to indicate the effect of the experimental treatment. We sometimes assume that the effect of any independent variable is both immediate and permanent. Thus experiments occasionally manipulate independent variable(s) (price or advertising, for example), take an immediate measure of the dependent variable (sales), and then move on to the next problem. The danger in such an approach is that the immediate impact of the independent variable may be different from its long-range effect.

4.3.10 Surrogate situation

Surrogate situation errors occur when the environment, the population(s) sampled, and/or the treatments administered are different from those that will be encountered in the actual situation. A radio advertising copy test in which recall is measured after listening while driving an automobile simulator is clearly a surrogate for having the radio on while driving and may lead to substantial predictive errors of the effectiveness of radio advertising directed toward drivers.

4.3.11 Statistical regression

Statistical regression effects occur where test units have been selected for exposure to the treatment on the basis of an extreme average position with the passage of time.

4.4 Pre-experimental designs

Kinnear and Taylor (1991:273) describe the following three designs as pre-experimental designs because inherent weaknesses in the designs make internal validity very questionable.

4.4.1 After-only design

The after-only design or one-shot case study involves manipulating the independent variable and following this with a post-measurement. This is presented symbolically as:

T MA

Note that the symbol R, which means randomly selected, does not appear in the design, so there was no random assignment of test units to the treatment group. The test units were self-selected or arbitrarily selected by the experimenter.

An example of this design might be as follows. An advertising campaign is launched and a measure of sales is taken some time after the campaign has been completed. The impossibility of drawing meaningful conclusions from such a design should be apparent. The level of MA is the result of many uncontrolled factors, and it cannot be deemed to be good or bad in the absence of a pre-treatment observation of sales performance. Thus history, maturation, selection and mortality problems all serve to render this design internally invalid.

4.4.2 Before-after design

The before-after or one-group pre-test–post-test design is like the after-only design except that it also involves a pre-measurement:

$$MB + T = MA$$

Here, for example, we have added a pre-test measurement of sales performance to the after-only design. If we then took the difference between MA and MB as our measure of experimental effect, would we have a valid measure of the effect of the advertising campaign? Clearly, a number of extraneous variables could explain the difference MA − MB, rendering this design useless for reaching conclusive answers.

4.4.3 Before-after with limited control design

Kinnear and Taylor (1991:274) call this a static-group comparison. The static-group comparison design uses two treatment groups: one which has been exposed to the treatment and one which has not. Both groups are observed only after the treatment has been presented, and test units are not randomly assigned to the groups. Symbolically this design is:

Experimental group: T　MA
Control group:　　　M

Group 2 is called a control group because it has not received the treatment and so may serve as the baseline for comparison. The comparison of MA with M gives the TE (treatment effect). In marketing we often define the control group treatment as the current level of marketing activity. This design would then be presented symbolically as:

Experimental group: T　MA
Control group: B　　M

where B is the baseline marketing programme with which we wish to compare T. For example, in trying out a new sales training programme on some salespersons, the sales manager would not be likely to drop all sales training for the other salespersons. The manager is interested in comparing one programme with another, so the old programme is the control group treatment.

The overwhelming source of invalidity in this design is selection. Test units have not been randomly assigned to treatment groups; therefore the groups may differ on the dependent variable prior to the presentation of the treatment. The experimental result MA − M could clearly be attributed to this pre-test difference caused by selection procedures. Differential test unit mortality is also possible because of the nature of the treatment. More experimental-group test units may have withdrawn because of the offensive nature of the new sales training programme, for example.

4.5 True experimental designs

A true experimental design is one in which the researcher is able to eliminate extraneous variables as competitive hypotheses to the treatment (Kinnear & Taylor 1991:275).

4.5.1 Before-after with control design

The before-after with control design (also called the pre-test–post-test control groups design) involves the addition of a control group whereby test units are randomly assigned to the treatment and control groups. This design is presented symbolically as:

$$\text{Experimental group: R} \quad MB + T = MA$$
$$\text{Control group: R} \quad M_1 \quad M_2$$

The addition of the control groups allows for the control of all potential sources of experimental error except mortality and interaction. Again the control group could have a baseline treatment applied to it. The random assignment of test units to the treatment groups eliminates selection bias as a potential confounding variable.

The premise here is that all extraneous variables operate equally on both the experimental and control groups. The only difference between the groups is the presentation of the treatment to the experimental group. Therefore the difference $MA - MB$ is the sum of the treatment effect plus the effects of the extraneous variables, whereas the difference $M_2 - M_1$ is the sum of the extraneous variables only. The equation $(MA - MB) - (M_2 - M_1) = TE$ gives the true treatment effect (TE).

The experimenter does not care which extraneous variables are operative so long as they operate equally on all treatment and control groups. Even with a control group design, the experiment is confounded if an extraneous variable operates differentially among treatment and control groups. The assumption must be that they operate equally. Direct pre-measurement effects are controlled. Both groups receive the pre-measurement and any changes caused by this should influence both post-measures equally. History, maturation and instrumentation should also affect both treatment and control groups equally.

The before-after with control group design is subject to interaction effects. Suppose a researcher is interested in the effect on attitudes of a single direct-mail advertisement. A group of respondents is selected and a pre-measurement administered to all of them. Half of the respondents then receive the direct-mail advertisement (treatment group) and half receive nothing (control group). One week after the advertisement is delivered, both groups of respondents are remeasured.

Any direct effect, that is learning or attitude change caused by the pre-measurement, should affect both groups equally. However, if the pre-measure serves to increase the respondent's interest or curiosity in the brand, the treatment and the control group may be affected differently. Those respondents in the treatment group will receive a direct-mail advertisement from the firm that they may read simply because of the interest generated by the pre-measurement.

The effect of the pre-measurement (increased interest) interacts with the independent variable (advertisement) to influence the post-measurement (change of attitude). The control group may also experience increased interest because of the pre-measure. However, because the control group will not be exposed to the advertising, the increased interest will dissipate without influencing the post-measurement of attitudes. The overall result of this is that any conclusions about the effects of the advertising campaign may be generalised only to individuals who have taken the pre-measurement.

4.5.2 Simulated before-after design

The simulated before-after design was developed primarily to control for pre-measurement and interaction errors in experiments dealing with attitudes and knowledge of human subjects. The design controls for these two errors by using separate groups for the pre- and post-measurements are:

Control group: R   MB
Experimental group: R   T   MA

As in the before-after design, the measure of interest is the difference between MA and MB. Because different individuals receive the pre- and post-measurements, there can be no pre-measurement or interaction effects. This design is common in advertising research. A prerequisite is that sampling has to be done properly and the two samples should be large enough to be similar in terms of their initial attitude. However, the problems associated with the standard before-after design, particularly history, remain.

4.5.3 After-only with control

The pre-measurements in the before-after with control group design introduce the possibility of uncontrolled interaction effects. In addition, pre-measurements generally cost money and may increase the artificiality of the overall situation. They are necessary whenever there is a reasonable probability that the treatment and control groups are not initially equivalent on the dependent variables. If it is likely that the groups are initially equal on the variable of interest, then there is no reason to go to the expense of a pre-measurement. Instead, an after-only with control design (post-test-only control group design) can be used:

$$\text{Experimental group: R T MA}$$
$$\text{Control group: R   M}$$

This design explicitly controls for everything that the before-after with control design does except selection error. That is, even if random assignment is used, it is possible for the two groups to be initially unequal on the variable of interest. However, this design does eliminate the possibility of interaction. It is appropriate whenever selection error is not likely to be a problem, such as when large random samples are used. It is uniquely appropriate when selection error is not a problem but interaction is (Tull & Hawkins 1991:195).

4.5.4 Solomon four-group design

This is a combination of the before-after with control and the after-only with control designs. The Solomon four-group design, often called the four-group six-study design, consists of four groups (two treatment and two control) and six measurements (two pre-measurements and four post-measurements). An examination of the following design shows that the overall design consists of a before-after with control experiment and an after-only with control experiment run simultaneously:

$$\text{Experimental group 1: R MB + T = MA}_1$$
$$\text{Control group 1: R M}_1 \qquad \text{M}_2$$
$$\text{Experimental group 2: R} \qquad \text{T MA}_2$$
$$\text{Control group 2: R} \qquad \text{M}_3$$

The design explicitly controls for all sources of experimental error except measurement timing, surrogate situation and *reactive error*, which are not subject to control by designs. No single method T analysis makes use of all six measurements simultaneously. However, direct estimates of the effect of interaction and selection, as well as other experimental errors, can be made by various between-group analyses:

$$\text{Experimental group 1: } MA_1 - MB = TE + EXT + IT \qquad 1$$

$$\text{Control group 1: } M_2 - M_1 = \quad EXT \qquad 2$$

$$\text{Experimental group 2: } MA_2 - MB = TE + EXT \qquad 3$$

$$MA_2 - M_1 = TE + EXT \qquad 4$$

$$\text{Control group 2: } M_3 - MB = \quad EXT \qquad 5$$

$$M_3 - M_1 = \quad EXT \qquad 6$$

where EXT = extraneous variables

IT = interactive testing effect

Equations 3 and 4 are usually averaged to give

$$MA_2 - \frac{(MB + M_1)}{2} = TE + EXT \qquad\qquad 7$$

and equations 5 and 6 are averaged to give

$$M_3 - \frac{(MB + M_1)}{2} = EXT \qquad\qquad 8$$

The experimental treatment effect is then obtained by subtracting equation 8 from 7:

$$(T + EXT) - EXT = TE \qquad 9$$

This design also gives us a direct measurement of the effect of extraneous variables, EXT, and allows us to calculate the interactive testing effect IT. IT is obtained by subtracting equation 7 from equation 1:

$$(TE + EXT + IT) - (TE + EXT) = IT \qquad 10$$

4.6 Quasi-experimentation

In designing a true experiment, the researcher often creates artificial environments in order to have control over independent and extraneous variables. As a result, serious questions are raised about the external validity of the experimental findings. One response to this problem has been the development and use of quasi-experimental designs.

According to Kinnear and Taylor (1991:278) a quasi-experimental design is one in which the researcher has control over data-collection procedures (that is the 'when' and 'to whom' of measurement) but lacks complete control over the scheduling of the treatments (that is the 'when' and 'to whom' of exposure) and also lacks the ability to randomise test units' exposure to treatments.

With loss of control of test unit assignments and treatment manipulations, the possibility of obtaining confounded results is great, the researcher must then be aware of what specific variables are not controlled. An attempt must be made to incorporate the possible effects of these uncontrolled variables into the interpretation of the findings. We now turn to an examination of selected quasi-experimental designs.

4.6.1 Time-series experiment

A *time-series experiment* is an extended 'before-after' experiment. In 'real-life' market tests it is common practice to take a number of observations before and after introduction of the new product, pack, price or advertising. The interval between observations is related to the rate at which the product is purchased by consumers and the data are often derived from consumer panels. The repeat buying rate is an important factor in brand-share prediction (Crimp 1990:148). A time-series experiment may be presented symbolically as:

$$(MB_1 \ MB_2 \ MB_3 \ MB_4) + T = (MA_1 \ MA_2 \ MA_3 \ MA_4)$$

The essence of this design is the undertaking of a periodic measurement of the dependent variables for some test units. The treatment is then introduced, or occurs naturally, and the periodic measurements are continued on the same test units in order to monitor the effects of the treatment. With 'going' brands it is common practice to predict what would happen if the experimental treatment were not introduced on the basis of the trend data collected 'before'. The effect of the experimental treatment, say a pack change, is then measured by comparing the actual 'after' observations with the 'after' predictions.

This design conforms to our definition of a quasi-experiment. The researcher does have control over when measurements are taken and on whom they are taken. However, there is no randomisation of the test units to treatments and the timing of treatment presentation, as well as exactly which test units are exposed to the treatment, may not be within the researcher's control. A common example of this type of design in marketing involves the use of consumer purchase panels. These panels provide periodic measures on their purchase activity.

A marketer may undertake a change in package (the T) and examine the panel data to look for the effect. Here the marketer has control over the timing of the change but cannot be sure when the panel members were exposed to the change, or even whether they were exposed at all. Also, other consumers outside the panel would be exposed to the change. Attempting to make causal inferences from this type of situation is common in marketing. This design is of course very similar to the pre-experimental one-group pre-test–post-test design, MB x MA. Does the time-series design not suffer from all the same problems? The answer is no. Because we have taken many pre-test and post-test measurements, this provides more control over extraneous variables. Kinnear and Taylor (1991:279) illustrate this increase in control by examining some possible results of this type of design (fig 10.1). Assume that T represents a change in advertising campaign, and MB_1 and MA_1 represent the market share of the product in question. The following conclusions about the advertising campaign seem reasonable:

☐ In situation A, the campaign has had both a short-run and a long-run positive effect.

☐ In situation B, the campaign has had a short-run positive effect.

☐ In situation C, the campaign may have had a longer-term effect. Since the reaction was delayed for a period, we cannot be as sure as we were in A and B.

☐ In situations D, E, and F, the changes that occur after T are consistent with the pattern prior to T. Therefore, we cannot infer that the advertising campaign had an effect.

Figure 10.1 Some possible results of a time-series experiment

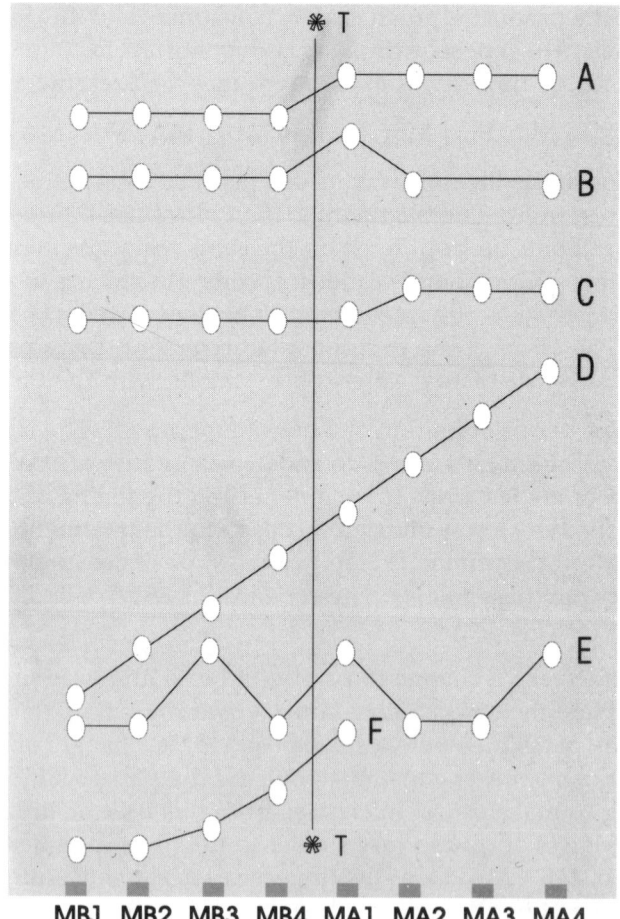

Source: Adapted from Kinnear & Taylor (1991:280).

Note that the one-group pre-test–post-test design would have measured only MB_4 and MA_1. With these measures only, we could easily infer an effect of the campaign $MA_1 - MB_4$ in situations D, E, and F; we could also miss the effect in C and the nature of the effects in A and B.

The multiple observations in this design also provide additional control of extraneous variables. For example, the maturation effect on $MA_1 - MB_4$ can be ruled out as a cause, because this effect would also show up in other observations. It would not affect the MB_4 to MA_1 period alone. By similar reasoning, pre-measurement, interaction, instrumentation and statistical regression effects can be ruled out. If we then randomly or with good judgement select our test units and take strong measures to prevent test unit mortality (panel members dropping out), we can at least partially rule out the effects of selection bias and test unit mortality.

The fundamental weakness of this design is the experimenter's inability to control history. But all is not lost; the experimenter could maintain a careful log of all possible relevant external happenings that could have an effect. If this process failed to turn up any unusual competitive activity, economic changes and so on, the experimenter might reasonably conclude that the treatment has had an effect.

The other weakness of this design is the possibility of an interactive testing effect from the repeated measurements being made on test units. For example, panel members may become 'expert' shoppers, thus making generalisations to other populations more difficult. This design is used a great deal and it can provide meaningful information if used carefully.

4.6.2 Multiple time-series design

In some studies utilising the time-series design it may be possible to find another group of test units to act as a control group. For example, an advertiser may try out a new campaign in a few cities only. Panel members in these cities would constitute the experimental group while members from other cities would constitute a control group. In symbols this design is:

$$\text{Experimental group: } (MB_1 \ MB_2 \ MB_3) + T = (MA_1 \ MA_2 \ MA_3)$$
$$\text{Control group: } M_1 \ M_2 \ M_3 \ M_4 \ M_5 \ M_6$$

If the researcher is very careful in selecting the control group, this design can add more certainty to the interpretation of the treatment effect than is obtainable with the straight time-series experiment. This is so because the treatment effect is tested both in its own group and against the control group. The main problem with this design lies in the possibility of an interactive effect in the experimental group.

4.6.3 Equivalent time-sample design

An alternative to finding a control group is to use the experimental group itself as its own control. In symbols this design might be

$$MB_1 + T_1 = MA_1 \; Y \; (MB_2 \; MB_3 \; MB_4) + T_2 = MA_2 \; M_1 \; Y \; M_2$$

where T is the experimental treatment and Y is the absence of the treatment. Here the treatment is presented twice (T_1 and T_2), measurements are taken repeatedly (eight times), and periods of treatment absence are spaced between (Y). This design is best utilised when the effect of the treatment is transient or reversible. An example of its use would be the testing of the effect of in-store conditions such as store layout on total purchases per customer. Here we could use a single store whose customers make up the test units and utilise equivalent sets of days or weeks with and without the change in layout over a period of many months.

The biggest problem with this design is the possibility of the interactive testing effect occurring. It is basically a reactive design because of all the measurements taken, and therefore it is best used where the repeated measurements are non-reactive. In situations like the store example we are able to measure per-customer sales without sensitising customers to the treatment. If we did repeated interviewing of customers about store layout, sensitisation would no doubt be a problem.

4.6.4 Non-equivalent control group design

In this design the experimental group and the control group are both given pre-test and post-test measurements, but the two groups do not have pre-experimental test unit selection equivalence. Symbolically this design is:

$$\text{Experimental group: } MB + T = MA$$
$$\text{Control group: } \quad M_1 \qquad M_1$$

This is a quasi-experimental design because the groups were not created by the random assignment of test units from a single population. However, the existence of even a non-equivalent control group improves the ability of the researcher to interpret results in comparison with the one-group pre-test–post-test design discussed previously. In this design the researcher has control over who is exposed to the treatment. Clearly the more similar the experimental and control groups are in composition and the closer the pre-test measurements, the more useful the control group becomes. If these criteria are met, this design can effectively control the effects of history, maturation, pre-measurement, instrumentation, selection and test unit mortality. Regression may provide one major source of problems in this design, that is if either group has been selected on the basis of extreme scores. In such cases some of the differences in pre-test and post-test measures may result from regression effects. Care must be taken to avoid this problem. The possibility of an interactive testing effect is also present in this design.

4.7 Control of invalidity

Table 10.1 summarises the potential errors that may affect each design. A plus sign (+) indicates that the design controls for this type of error; a minus sign (−) indicates that it is vulnerable to it; a question mark (?) indicates a possible source of concern; and zero (0) indicates that the error is independent of the type of design. Remember that potential errors are not the same as actual errors.

Table 10.1 Experimental designs and potential errors

Experimental design \ Potential error	Pre-mea-sure-ment	Inter-action	His-tory	Matu-ration	Instru-men-tation	Selec-tion bias	Mor-tality	Statis-tical re-gres-sion	Mea-sure-ment timing	Surro-gate situa-tion	Reac-tive
Pre-experimental designs											
After-only	+	+	−	−	+	−	−	0	0	0	0
Before-after	−	−	−	−	−	+	−	?	0	0	0
Before-after with limited control	+	+	+	?	+	−	−	+	0	0	0
True experimental designs											
Before-after with control	+	−	+	+	+	+	−	+	0	0	0
Simulated before-after	+	+	−	−	−	−	+	+	0	0	0
After-only with control	2	2	2	2	2	1	1	2	0	0	0
Solomon four-group	+	+	+	+	+	+	+	+	0	0	0
Quasi-experimental designs											
Time-series experiment	+	+	−	+	?	+	+	+	0	0	0
Multiple time-series design	+	+	+	+	+	+	+	+	0	0	0
Equivalent time-sample design	+	+	+	+	+	+	+	+	0	0	0
Non-equivalent control group design	+	+	+	+	+	+	+	+	0	0	0

Source: Adapted from Kinnear & Taylor (1991:197).

4.8 Statistical designs

The object of this section is to describe procedures that allow us to determine if a measured effect is greater than that due to sampling error. Statistical designs are actually a means of structuring a series of basic experiments to allow statistical control and analysis of extraneous variables. The detailed statistical calculations for these designs will not be explained here. The calculation methods are discussed in the chapters on significance testing (chapter 16) and multivariate analysis (chapter 17).

4.8.1 Completely randomised design

Completely randomised designs (CRD) are based on the assumptions that the experimental groups are initially similar on the dependent variable and that the members of these groups will react to the independent variable in a similar manner. This independent variable need only be a nominal scale, so that it may have many categories. Each category of the nominal independent variable is a treatment. As an example, suppose that the independent variable of interest is 'type of promotion programme' and has three categories:

☐ no sales promotion

☐ direct mail advertising

☐ in-store promotional activity.

In CRD the experimental treatments are assigned to test units on a completely random basis without any regard for external factors. If sales were our dependent variable we would compare the average sales level of each of the three treatment groups to see which treatment was best.

4.8.2 Randomised block design

Randomised block designs (RBD) are appropriate for situations in which the researchers suspect that there is one major external variable that might influence the results. Of course, one must be able to identify or measure this variable before one can utilise an RBD. In an RBD the experimental units are blocked, that is grouped or stratified, on the basis of the extraneous or blocking variable. What we would like to do is 'block out' the extraneous effect. By ensuring that the various experimental and control groups are matched as closely as possible on the extraneous variable, we are assured that it affects all groups more or less equally. If we want to compare types of promotional campaigns we divide the shops into categories of the same type (supermarkets, hypermarkets, etc) and turnover (large, medium and small).

The fundamental reason for doing blocking is to allow the researcher to obtain a measure of sample error smaller than that which would result from a completely randomised design. This occurs because some of the variation in the dependent variable is assigned to the blocking factor, leaving a smaller sample error.

The parallel between blocking in experimentation as discussed in this section and stratification in sampling (see chapter 13) should be apparent. In both situations we form subgroups so that the variable of interest is more homogeneous within the group than it would be across all groups. The result of this process is a smaller measure of sample error.

The number of variables used to create a blocking factor can be extended beyond two. The problem is that the number of blocks required in the blocking factor increases as a multiplicative function of the number of categories in the external variables used. The other problem with blocking by using more than one external variable is that the researcher can measure only the overall effect of the blocking factor. The separate effects of the variables defining the blocking factor cannot be isolated. A possible partial solution to this problem is the Latin square design (Kinnear & Taylor 1991:289).

4.8.3 Latin square design

According to Tull and Hawkins (1991:200) Latin square designs allow the researcher to control statistically for two non-interacting extraneous variables in addition to the independent variable. This control is achieved by a blocking technique similar to that described in the previous section on randomised block designs.

This design requires that each extraneous or blocking variable be divided into an equal number of blocks or levels, such as supermarkets, hypermarkets and discount stores. The independent variable must be divided into the same number of levels, such as high price, medium price and low price. A Latin square design is shown in the form of a table with the rows representing the blocks on one extraneous variable and the columns representing the blocks on the other. The levels of the independent variable are then assigned to the cells in the table so that each level appears once, and only once, in each row and each column.

Latin square designs are described on the basis of the number of blocks on the extraneous variables. A design with three blocks is called a 3 x 3 Latin square, four blocks is a 4 x 4 Latin square, and so forth.

4.8.4 Factorial design

Factorial designs are used to measure the effect of two or more independent variables at various levels. They are particularly useful when there is some reason to believe that interaction might occur. Interaction occurs when the simultaneous effect of two or more variables is different from the sum of their effects taken one at a time (Tull & Hawkins 1991:203). For example, an individual's favourite colour might be grey and his favourite dessert might be ice cream. However, it does not follow that he would prefer grey ice cream.

In depicting a factorial design in a table, each level of one variable can represent a row and each level of another variable can represent a column. Factorial designs require a cell for every possible combination of treatment variables. Statistically an analysis of variance can determine the effect on each variable separately and the interaction between the two.

5 TYPES OF EXPERIMENT

There are two types of environments in which an experiment may be conducted, namely a laboratory environment and a field environment. Table 10.2 shows a comparison of laboratory and field environment experiments. A carefully controlled experiment conducted in a laboratory environment yields results which are unambiguous. The experiment has high internal validity. A consequence of the artificial nature of a laboratory is the loss of generalisability to more realistic situations. The experiment lacks external validity. The field experiment or market test is conducted in the real-life context, an actual market situation, and has external validity. Field experiments provide little control over extraneous variables and therefore have a lower internal validity. According to Crimp (1990:153) field experiments may well have been distorted by market influences or local happenings so that they are ambiguous and difficult to interpret. The more that is known about the forces at work in the market from descriptive work, the easier it is to control them or to allow for them when drawing conclusions.

Laboratory experiments are less expensive than field experiments. They are smaller in size, shorter in duration, and more tightly defined geographically, which means they are much easier to administer.

Field experiments are used mainly for trying out products or marketing mix variables in the marketplace. Inevitably this makes them more expensive than laboratory experiments since products need to be made, packaged, priced, possibly even promoted, in their final form (Kent 1993:145). The simpler nature of laboratory experiments means that they require less time to execute.

Table 10.2 Laboratory versus field experiments

Aspects	Laboratory environment	Field environment
Validity	High internal validity Low external validity	Low internal validity High external validity
Cost	Less expensive	More expensive
Time	Less time consuming — on the spot assessment	Longer time — normal use
Design	Comparative or monadic	Monadic
Treatment	Usually atomistic	Usually holistic
Place	Hall, mobile van and/or test centres	In-home placement and/or store
Subjects	Expert panel, ad hoc sample(s) and/or test panel	Ad hoc sample(s) and/or test panel
Objects	Mainly for product testing, package testing and advertising effectiveness	Mainly for trying out products and marketing-mix variables

Laboratory experiments may be monadic or comparative. In a monadic design the respondent experiences only one test product. In a comparative test the respondent is given more than one product to try. The products may be given simultaneously or in sequence. While comparison sharpens perception, it is more unrealistic. Respondents do not usually compare products directly on the same occasion.

Usually treatments in laboratory experiments are atomistic. Only one variable is being manipulated at a time. In field experiments a holistic approach is more often followed where more than one variable (for example price, packaging and promotion) is being manipulated.

The three main research environments in which laboratory experiments may be conducted are hall, van and test centres. What actually takes place in a hall, van or test centre is often only a survey in which respondents are asked questions and their responses noted. Although they are usually called tests, they are experiments only if there are before and after measures and, ideally, if there are control groups. Kent (1993:144) describes the three main research environments for laboratory experiments.

In *hall tests* people are recruited off the street or shopping centre in the vicinity of the hall or room that has been hired by the research company. The purpose is to show products, packages or advertisements to people selected by quota sampling in order to measure their reaction. Selection is often restricted to users of the product being tested. Where hall tests are used for product testing the products are generally new or modified, and the aim is to obtain a measure of acceptance, preference or attitude. The tests are often blind, that is in plain packaging with no brand name, and comparative. Not all products, of course, are suitable for hall tests. For instance, toiletries would be more suited to field experiments (home placements tests). However, hall tests are popular for food and drink. Samples tend to be quite large (maybe 500 or so) and spread over several venues, probably in different parts of the country. They may be subject to various forms of experimental design such as randomised block or Latin square.

Van tests are similar to hall tests, but recruitment is to a mobile van that can be taken to many different venues. Van tests have the advantage that all the equipment needed for testing does not have to be set up in every location. However, space may be too restricted for some types of test.

Test centres may be used in preference to vans or halls where the product for testing is too large, expensive or complicated to be taken to the consumer. An example is the car clinic, which is a product test on vehicles held in a test centre. Respondents are invited to evaluate one or more individual aspects of car design such as exterior styling, roominess or interior layout.

Field experiments are done in in-home placements and by means of store tests. *In-home placement tests* give selected consumers the product to try at home and report back. The consumer may be telephoned, visited or sent a questionnaire after an agreed period of time. Consumer panels are often used for experimentation. Demographic and product-use characteristics of panel members are recorded, and experimental and control groups with the required characteristics for the particular tests are then selected. Test products are distributed to panel members who complete questionnaires on the reactions to the products received. There is the danger, of course, that panel members learn from their testing experience and cease to be typical consumers. Panels are discussed in more detail in chapter 8.

Store tests try out packaging or point-of-sale promotions in selected retail outlets. There will need to be a cross-section of types of outlet located in different regions of the country. Ideally there will be control stores matched against those trying the test product.

6 TEST MARKETING

According to Churchill (1992:146) experiments in marketing were rare before 1960, but their growth since then has been steady. One of the most significant growth areas has been in market testing, or test marketing.

> **Test marketing** is a controlled experiment carried out in one or more limited, but carefully selected, parts of a market area to predict and explore the consequences of one or more marketing actions for new or modified product introductions, or to estimate the payoffs and costs of changes in the marketing mix for existing products (Kent 1993:146).

The basic purpose of test marketing is to test the product itself in real market situations. These tests are usually for inexpensive frequently purchased consumer products and not for industrial products, especially big capital items. Segal and Johar (1992:21–23) are of the opinion that test marketing also allows the company to test its entire marketing programme for the product – its positioning strategy, advertising, distribution, pricing, branding and packaging, and budget levels. The company may also use test marketing to learn how consumers and dealers will react to handling, using and repurchasing the product. Test marketing results can also be used to make better sales and profit forecasts. Therefore good test marketing can provide a wealth of information about the potential success of the product and marketing programme. Because the majority of new products fail, test marketing can provide a necessary safeguard against product failures through the evaluation of marketing plans prior to implementation. The failure rate is set as high as 80 % of all new products (Van der Schyf 1995:18).

6.1 Stages in test marketing

Kent (1993:146–147) distinguishes five stages in test marketing.

6.1.1 Planning

This includes defining clearly the problem or problems to which the test marketing is addressed and the measures that will be used to evaluate the outcome. It also means deciding on the type(s) of test(s) and where the test is to be conducted. In selecting test areas it will be necessary to pay attention to

- the demographic structure of the area – is it a miniature replica of the national market?

- the industrial and occupational structure – the area should not be too dependent on one type of industry

- the structure of retailing and distribution – similar distribution channels to the rest of the national market

- the availability and use of media, especially local newspapers that could be used for advertising – the area should be relatively self-contained as far as media are concerned.

6.1.2 Pre-test measurement

Once the test areas have been selected it is necessary to take pre-measurements (MB) of the variables to be used to evaluate outcomes. Post-measurements (MA) of these variables will be used to evaluate the results of the test. Sometimes sufficient base data may be already available but sometimes it may be necessary to conduct primary research. Pre-tests may also be carried out in areas that are to be used as 'controls', that is areas not subject to the experimental stimulus.

6.1.3 Test

This involves the manipulation (T) of one or more variables by the researcher. It can be the launch of a new or modified product along with the change in the marketing mix itself (for example a new pricing policy). The duration of the test has to be long enough to allow the situation to stabilise after the new experimental conditions have been imposed.

6.1.4 Post-test measurement

Post-measurements (MA) are taken of the key dependent variables and compared with the pre-measurements (MB) derived in the pre-test.

6.1.5 Evaluation

Account needs to be taken of the factors that may have influenced the results and some prediction made of what is likely to happen in a national launch. This is not a simple matter of extrapolation of the results in the test area to the whole country. It means taking account of any special circumstances in the test area, including actions of competitors, that may not hold for the country as a whole. Types of errors affecting experimental results are discussed in section 4.3 of this chapter.

6.2 Types of market tests

Tull and Hawkins (1990:228–241) distinguish four basic types of market tests, namely standard, controlled, electronic and simulated tests.

6.2.1 Standard market tests

A standard market test is one in which a small sample of market areas is selected and the product is sold through regular distribution channels, using one or more combinations of product, price, and promotional levels.

The selections of test market areas are based on the following criteria:

☐ They should be large enough to produce meaningful data.

☐ The areas should have typical media available and be relatively self-contained as far as media are concerned.

☐ The test market areas should be a replica of the national market – they should be demographically similar to the larger market.

☐ The areas should be a self-contained trading area to avoid transshipments over its borders.

☐ The areas should be representative with respect to competition.

☐ The areas should be normal in the consumption pattern of a given product.

6.2.2 Controlled-store and minimarket tests

In a controlled-store test a few outlets in several areas are utilised. Typically media advertising cannot be used in a controlled-store test because of the limited distribution of the product. A minimarket test involves enough outlets to represent a high percentage of all the commodity sales volume in a relatively small community. If this area is self-contained as far as media are concerned, a treatment in advertising can be applied.

In a standard market test the product is distributed to the stores through the firm's regular distribution channels. In controlled-store and minimarket tests a market research firm handles all the warehousing, distribution, pricing, shelving and stocking. The advantages of these tests over standard test marketing are the following:

☐ It is virtually impossible for competitors to estimate the test results since the research company is the only source of sales data.

☐ The tests are less visible to competitors.

☐ Test results are obtained faster since ordinary distribution channels are not used.

☐ The tests are less expensive.

The drawbacks of this approach are as follows:

☐ The limited nature of these tests makes any projection of the results very difficult.

☐ These tests do not allow an estimate of the support the trade will give a product because distribution during the tests was artificial.

☐ It is difficult to duplicate planned national advertising programmes during the test.

6.2.3 Electronic test markets

Electronic test markets operate like minimarket tests. The research firm collects scanner-based sales from the selected outlets on an ongoing basis. This information can be linked to a scanner-based household panel in the same area. This household's television viewing patterns are monitored electronically. Thus the household's viewing patterns, scanner-based sales and the panel's purchasing patterns are linked. In addition the research firm has the capability of sending differing commercials or differing frequencies of commercials to various households in the panel.

6.2.4 Simulated test markets

Churchill (1992:152) describes a simulated test market as a study in which interviews are conducted to determine consumer ratings of products, and the consumers are then given the opportunity to purchase the product in a simulated environment. After a predetermined use period, researchers conduct follow-up telephone interviews with the participants to assess their reactions to the product and their repeat-purchase intentions.

7 SUMMARY

The concept of causality suggests that in a single-cause event one thing is the cause of another thing. There are three conditions under which we can make causal inferences.

A concomitant variation is the extent to which a cause and an effect occur together in the way predicted by the hypothesis under consideration. The time order of occurrence of variables states that one event cannot cause another if it occurs after the other event. The elimination of other possible causal factors is the elimination of possible explanations other than the one being studied.

Experimentation, which is the fundamental research tool to help identify causal relationships, involves the manipulation of one or more independent variables in such a way that its effect on one or more dependent variables can be measured. Treatments are the alternatives or portion of the independent variables that are manipulated and whose effects are measured. An experimental design involves the specification on treatments, test units to be used, dependent variables to be measured and procedures dealing with extraneous variables. Basic designs consider the impact of only one dependent variable while statistical designs allow the evaluation of more than one.

Internal validity in experimentation is the basic minimum that must be present in an experiment before any conclusion about treatment effects can be made and external validity is concerned with the generalisation of experimental results. Eleven types of errors can affect experimental results. They are pre-measurement, interaction, history, maturation, instrumentation, selection bias, mortality, reactive error, measurement timing, surrogate situation and statistical regression.

Three pre-experimental designs are distinguished. They are after-only, before-after and before-after with limited control. The true experimental designs are before-after with control, simulated before-after, after-only with control and Solomon four-groups. Time-series, multiple time-series, equivalent time-sample and non-equivalent control groups designs are quasi-experiments.

Statistical designs are a means of structuring a series of basic experiments to allow statistical control and analysis of extraneous variables. Four statistical designs are distinguished. They are completely randomised, randomised block, Latin square and factorial designs.

Experiments may be conducted in a laboratory environment and a field environment. In addition to the place of experiment a comparison of laboratory and field experiments also shows differences in validity, cost, duration, design, method of treatment, subjects used in the experiment and the objects being studied.

The main field for the use of experimental methods in marketing research is test marketing. Test marketing is used to test the product itself but also allows the company to test its entire marketing programme for the product. The five stages in test marketing are planning, pre-test, main tests, post-test and evaluation. The types of market test to choose from are standard market tests, controlled-store and minimarket tests, electronic test markets and simulated test markets.

REFERENCES

Churchill, Gilbert A (Jr) 1992. *Basic marketing research*. Second edition. Fort Worth: The Dryden Press. (The Dryden Press Series in Marketing.)

Crimp, Margaret 1990. *The marketing research process*. Third edition. New York: Prentice Hall.

Kent, Raymond A 1993. *Marketing research in action*. London: Routledge.

Kinnear, Thomas C & Taylor, James R 1991. *Marketing research: an applied approach*. Fourth edition. New York: McGraw-Hill. (McGraw-Hill Series in Marketing.)

Segal, Madhav N & Johar, J S 1992. On improving the effectiveness of test marketing decisions. *European Journal of Marketing*, 26(4):21–33.

Tull, Donald S & Hawkins, Del I 1990. *Marketing research: measurement and method: a text with cases*. New York: Macmillan. (The Macmillan Series in Marketing.)

Van der Schyf, Tony 1995. Why do 8 out of 10 new products fail? *Professional Management Review*, 2 (March):18.

Questionnaire design

Chapter 11: M Loubser

1 INTRODUCTION

Questionnaires come in many shapes and sizes, depending on the information required, the target group and the survey method. Because the questionnaire determines the type of information the research will generate, the researcher must establish three parameters before a questionnaire can be developed (Barker & Blankenship 1975:235). The first is to state the problem which initiated the research and so to determine the information needed to solve it. The second is to define the population to be surveyed, that is who has the information. And the third is to choose the best means of collecting the required information. For instance, a researcher compiling a questionnaire for a mail survey will be guided mainly by his respondents' level of literacy and involvement in the subject, whereas in a telephone survey his main considerations will be to restrict both the number of alternatives set for respondents and the length of the questionnaire.

The more versatile face-to-face interview method lends itself to the use of visual material for obtaining information from the illiterate, explaining the purpose of the survey more clearly, observing meaningful gestures on the part of the respondent and tracing the correct respondent without having all particulars about him beforehand.

Questions as well as responses can be *completely structured, partly structured or completely unstructured*. Unstructured questions are used in depth interviews and focus group discussions. In a depth interview the respondent's experience, attitude or whatever is under study. It is a discussion between a highly trained interviewer (usually the researcher himself or a psychologist) and the respondent. The interviewer asks any question or makes any comment that will encourage the respondent to furnish information on his conscious or unconscious behaviour. The sort of questions asked and their scope are governed by the respondent's answers. Except perhaps for a few notes on particular points the interviewer works without a structured questionnaire.

In focus group discussions the moderator starts off with a question to get the conversation moving. This first question may be structured or not. If the results obtained from various focus group discussion sessions are to be compared, the introduction to the discussion must be comparable and therefore structured. After the introduction each individual is exposed to the ideas of the others and submits his ideas for the consideration of the group. The moderator can ask any question or can make any comment that he feels would encourage and direct the flow of comments. Except perhaps for his introductory remarks, the first question and notes on a few points to which he will keep returning during the discussion, the moderator likewise does not make use of a structured questionnaire.

Questionnaires with structured questions and structured or unstructured responses are most commonly used in marketing research and will be dealt with in this chapter.

Broadly all questionnaires are designed to achieve three related goals. According to Cox (1979:24) these are:

☐ to maximise the relevance and accuracy of the data collected
☐ to maximise the participation and cooperation of target respondents
☐ to facilitate the collection and analysis of the data.

In this chapter we shall discuss the following five aspects:

☐ question content and phrasing
☐ question sequence
☐ question/response format
☐ physical characteristics
☐ pre-testing of the questionnaire.

2 QUESTION CONTENT AND PHRASING

The following aspects of question content and phrasing have to be considered:

☐ The questions must be kept as *concise* as possible. The fewer the words, the more evident the core of the question.

☐ If the answer required has to be definitive, the question must be *definitive*. When, for example, a manufacturer is planning a small rise in price and wants to discover its effect on the buyer of his product, he must mention the actual amount. The words 'slight rise' may mean different things to different respondents. They might mean a rise of 1 % to one, 5 % to another and 10 % to a third. Words such as 'occasionally', 'sometimes' and 'often' also mean different things to different people and should be avoided.

☐ In surveys conducted among all levels of the population the questions should be *worded* in such a way that even the less sophisticated and less educated understand them.

☐ Questions must be *simple*. A question with 'and' and 'or' may consist of two questions with only one expected answer. For example, in asking: 'Do you like rugby and cricket' the researcher wants to know whether the respondent likes both rugby and cricket, but the respondent who enjoys rugby very much, but not cricket, may simply answer: 'Yes'.

☐ Avoid *leading* questions. A leading question is one that prompts a desired answer. For example, 'It is well known that most people want lead-free fuel in motor cars made compulsory. How do you feel about it?' or, 'Why do you think that lead-free fuel in South Africa should be made compulsory?'. The answers to both these questions may possibly be influenced by information evident in the questions.

☐ Ask yourself whether the respondent has the *relevant information* or is able to answer the question. Respondents have been known to try to answer questions even when they have no opinions on a subject. The prestige or personal factor may be so strong that rather than admit ignorance of a subject, many respondents prefer to guess. In test surveys on non-existent products, persons and imaginary facts, as many as 70 % of the respondents have been found to express opinions (Elliott & Christopher 1973:93).

☐ Questions that may *embarrass* the respondent must be *avoided* as far as possible. In such questions it is advisable to use a third-party approach to the problem by citing a hypothetical situation with imaginary characters or to apply the *randomised response technique* if possible. The randomised response technique consists of three elements:

– a sensitive question which will yield the required information by eliciting a 'yes' or a 'no' answer

– a neutral question which will yield a known percentage of respondents answering 'yes' and 'no'

– a random means whereby a specific respondent selects the question he will answer.

If, for instance, our goal is to ascertain the percentage of respondents who have smoked dagga, we would ask the following questions:

(a) Sensitive question: 'Have you ever smoked dagga?'

YES	NO

(b) Neutral question: 'Were you born during the first half of the calendar year?'

YES	NO

Applying the randomised response technique we say to the respondent, 'I will now ask you to answer question (a) or (b) but I will not know afterwards which of the two questions you have answered. You can make sure of that by turning your back on me and tossing this coin which is marked 'a' on one side and 'b' on the other. After you have tossed the coin, look at the letter on top of the coin and answer the question with the same letter.' Say we obtain 200 'yes' answers out of a sample of 500.

As flipping the coin gives questions (a) and (b) equal chances of being answered we can accept that about 250 answered question (a) and about 250 answered question (b). Of the approximately 250 who answered question (b) about 125 (50 %) should have been born in the first half of the year, in other words they should have said 'yes' to question (b). If we subtract 125 from 200 we get 75. That is the estimated number out of 250 who said 'yes' to question (a). That is 30 %.

☐ Keep the questionnaire as *short* as possible. Even if the respondent's interest can be held for as long as 70 or 80 minutes, restrict the interview to 20 or 30 minutes if possible.

☐ Try to *avoid questions which necessitate reference* to files, numerical processing and other forms of additional work for the respondent. Unless a respondent is being paid for the interview the researcher cannot expect a tremendous volume of work from him.

☐ Make provision for *all possible answers*. Items included in a structured questionnaire may not cover all possibilities, the respondent may be uncertain or genuinely ignorant, or the question may not be applicable to the respondent. Provision should therefore be made for 'other (specify)', 'uncertain', 'don't know' and 'not applicable'.

☐ Help the respondent to remember *without suggesting answers*. People soon forget, and a respondent may find difficulty in saying what he was doing at 09h00 the day before yesterday. However, by reminding him that the day before yesterday was Monday and asking him at what time he arrived at the office that day, the interviewer may help him to remember walking into his office and what he did immediately afterwards.

☐ Help the respondent to express himself by including *probe questions* in the question-naire. (See chapter 12.)

☐ Avoid *prestige-loaded* questions. Writing of this, Oppenheim (1966:62) says:

> Some people will claim that they read more than they do, bathe more often than is strictly true, and fill more pipes from an ounce of tobacco than would seem likely. They claim that they buy new tyres for their car when in fact they buy retreads; they deny reading certain Sunday newspapers of dubious repute; the shirts that they buy are expensive; they would seem to brush their teeth with great frequency and to visit museums almost every week!

He admits that there is no simple solution to this problem, but he mentions the possibility of starting off with a filter question* and wording it so that a low-prestige answer is equally possible. For example, instead of asking: 'Have you read any of the following magazines within the last seven days?' the interviewer might first ask: 'Have you had time to read any magazines at all within the past seven days?'

---

* A filter question is a question that is asked to determine whether the question(s) that follow are applicable. For example, if we want to determine which brand of cigarettes are smoked most by respondents, we may ask the following two questions:
(a) 'Do you smoke?' Yes/No
(b) If 'yes', 'Which brand of cigarettes do you smoke?'
The first is a filter question. If the answer to it is 'no', the second question is not asked.

This list of pointers is by no means exhaustive and doubtless many others will occur to the experienced researcher.

The actual wording and phrasing of questions is one of the most difficult aspects of questionnaire design. Questions are survey specific, which means that some of the researcher's considerations may change from one survey to another. A further problem is that wording and phrasing are not quantifiable or empirically testable aspects of the survey. To a large extent the researcher has to rely on intuition, asking himself whether he has struck on the right way of wording and is framing the question in the context of the questionnaire and the information required (D'Alton 1970:101).

An understanding of the issues involved is essential if the question is to be framed successfully without oversimplifying or omitting certain aspects. The researcher has to proceed from the theoretical to the practical and express the issue in terms of 'who?', 'why?', 'when?', 'where?' and 'how?'. When he uses abstract concepts such as 'government' or 'freedom', he needs to define them for the respondent and the interviewer. And, as stated, he should refrain from using research jargon and should suit the vocabulary of the questionnaire to his respondents.

Besides not being mathematically testable in exclusion from the survey, the question itself is influenced by grammar, word choice, length and punctuation and by its position in the questionnaire. In the final instance the question stands or falls by whether it elicits the information required in the survey, and it is here that pre-testing the questionnaire plays a key role (Loubser & Gilmour 1991:4).

3 QUESTION SEQUENCE

Structured questions have the advantage that a good interviewer will read the questions aloud in their exact wording and sequence in the questionnaire. Thus all the respondents are asked the same questions in exactly the same order. By arranging the questions logically and observing other sequencing rules the researcher enhances the standard of the interviewing, helps the interviewer and induces a logical and harmonious flow of thought in the questionnaire.

The following points must receive thorough consideration:

☐ The first question should be *simple and interesting*, its main intention being to put the respondent at ease and motivate him to react to the succeeding questions without suspicion. This question may not even be analysed.

☐ Be sure to indicate *which respondents* have to answer *which questions*. Group the questions to be answered by a particular group of respondents.

☐ Ensure a *logical sequence of questions*. As far as possible use the funnel approach* by going from the general to the particular. A change of subject may disturb the logical flow of the interview unless there are links between subjects. Disturbance of the flow of the interview as a result of change of subject is a particular problem in omnibus surveys.**

☐ *Position sensitive questions* or questions on embarrassing subjects as *near to the end* of the questionnaire as possible. By that time relations between interviewer and respondent should be at their most cordial and the chances of receiving the best answers to them are also optimal. And should these questions cause the respondent to refuse further cooperation most of the other information will have already been gathered.

☐ Questions requiring *classification information*, such as those on age, income and marital status, may also be sensitive and should also be as near as possible to the *end* of the questionnaire. The respondent should be given sound reasons for answering these questions. Oppenheim (1966:58) suggests the following wording: 'Now, to help us to classify your answers statistically, may I ask you a few questions about yourself and your family?'

☐ Ensure that the structured answers to a question *do not provide respondents with answers* to questions lower down in the questionnaire. This will not apply where consistency is checked and the respondent is expected to give the same answer.

☐ Particularly in questionnaires designed for *opinion surveys* it may be worthwhile to consider the following sequence of questions, suggested long ago by the famous Gallup (1947:201) and still valid:

  (i) questions to ascertain the extent of the respondent's previous thinking, if any, on the subject

  (ii) open-ended questions to derive the respondent's general feelings on the subject

  (iii) questions, often multiple choice, aimed at eliciting specific information

  (iv) questions aimed at discovering the reason(s) for the views given in answers to (iii) above

  (v) questions to determine how strongly held those views are.

4 QUESTION/RESPONSE FORMAT

As mentioned earlier, structured questions with structured or unstructured responses are most commonly used in marketing research. In this section we shall discuss the structured question/structured response format before moving on to the structured question/unstructured response format.

---

 * If you want to know how much respondents spent on (a) all consumer products, (b) food, (c) meat products and (d) mutton, ask their expenditure in that sequence.
** In an omnibus survey, data are collected for various firms or bodies and so cover a variety of subjects, services, products, etc.

4.1 Structured questions with structured responses

In a structured question with structured responses the respondent is given various possible answers and has to choose one or more. In this type of question/response provision should be made for 'other (specify)'. Structured questions include

- ☐ dichotomous questions
- ☐ multiple-choice questions with single answers
- ☐ multiple-choice questions with multiple answers
- ☐ checklists
- ☐ rankings
- ☐ grids
- ☐ scaled questions.

4.1.1 Dichotomous questions

The dichotomous question is a question which offers only two fixed alternative answers to choose from, for example Yes/No, Male/Female, Agree/Disagree.

4.1.2 Multiple-choice questions with single answers

The multiple choice or multichotomous question is also a fixed-alternative question but it offers more than two fixed-alternative answers. Response is restricted to one of the given alternatives. For example:

How old are you?

(Please tick)

Under 20	
20–29	
30–39	
40 and over	

This type of question is used when information is classifiable into fairly fixed categories, or when the respondent's thoughts are deliberately channelled in a certain direction.

4.1.3 Multiple-choice questions with multiple answers

This type of question allows for more than one response. For example:

Which of the following brands of cigarettes have you ever smoked?

(Please tick)

Ransom Select

Peter Stuyvesant

Rembrandt van Rijn

Lexington

4.1.4 Checklists

A checklist typically lists a product's or a person's attributes which the respondent is required to rate in terms of given criteria that have to be rated in accordance with their importance or applicability. Usually a checklist is completed with the aid of a prompt card. A prompt card is a card which lists the possible answers to a question. For example:

The interviewer hands the respondent a prompt card bearing the name of the following brands of cigarettes: Peter Stuyvesant, Rembrandt van Rijn, Ransom Select and Lexington. He then asks:

Which of the brands of cigarettes listed on this card do you think –

(a) are liked by women?
(b) are mainly for older people?
(c) are imported?
(d) are mild?
(e) are strong?

The questionnaire (checklist) on which the interviewer is to mark the respondent's answers will be constructed to look like this:

Properties	Brands				
	Peter Stuyvesant	Rembrand van Rijn	Ransom Select	Lexington	None of them
Liked by women					
For older people					
Imported					
Mild					
Strong					

Notice that the questionnaire lists the category 'none of them', but the prompt card does not.

4.1.5 Rankings

In the rank order method the respondent is asked to rank a set of items in terms of a given criterion. For example, the interviewer gives the respondent a list and says: 'Here is a list of motorcar characteristics that motorists have mentioned to us. Please rank them in what you consider their order of importance, marking the most important as 1, etc.'

Respondents may be inclined to rate characteristics near the top of the list higher than those lower down. To obviate this each characteristic may be shown on a separate card. Macfarlane Smith (1972:77) suggests limiting the number of characteristics to six, whereas Oppenheim (1966:98) suggests a maximum of ten. If the respondent is required to rate a large number of characteristics he may be asked to divide the cards for rating the characteristics into three groups, say, very important, important, and less important, and then to rank each group.

4.1.6 Grids

A grid is a simple and straightforward means of collecting information quickly and analysing it in various ways. For example:

The respondent is handed a prompt card which bears the names of various food items and asked:

Which of the following types of food did you eat yesterday at each meal?

Meals	Bread	Mutton	Bacon	Pork	Beef	Eggs	Fish	Cheese	Chicken	Rice	Potatoes
Breakfast											
Dinner											
Supper											
Other											

The overall frequency tabulation will immediately show which foods were eaten at each meal and whether a specific kind of food was eaten at one or more meals. In this way the researcher can explore the use of particular items without the respondent knowing which they are. Here, for example, we may be interested in the respondent's eating habits only in so far as eggs are concerned.

4.1.7 Scaled questions

In this type of question the respondent is required to mark a point on a scale. It has the advantage that the response is recorded on the right of the page and a number of aspects are listed on the left, as in the following example:

Please rate Unisa in respect of the criteria listed below by ticking the appropriate square in the table:

Criteria	(1) Excellent	(2) Good	(3) Fair	(4) Poor	(5) Very poor	(6) Don't know
1 Academic standards						
2 Student orientation						
3 Facilities						
4 Lecturers						
5 Administration						
6 Top management						
7 Quality of students						
8 Friendliness						
9 Efficiency						
10 Attractive campus						
11 Helpfulness						
12 Innovation						
13 Research orientation						
14 Interpersonal relations						
15 Management style						
16 Future orientation						
17 Communication						

Verbal scales may have three, five (as in the previous example) or seven points and may be printed together or separately on prompt cards. All of them should make provision for 'don't know'.

Belson (1986:228) and Quinn and Belson (1969:50) studied the effect of reversing the order of presentation of verbal ratings. When for example 'very poor' was presented at the top of the list of verbal ratings on the prompt card there was a negative shift in the distribution of ratings. They recommend that one order of presentation of verbal ratings should be maintained throughout when brands are being compared. If an absolute rating is required, then both the traditional and the reversed order scales should be used in rotation.

Rating scales can also be non-verbal, frequently bounded at each end by two bipolar adjectives or phrases.

The following types of rating scales are most commonly used in marketing research:

☐ graphic rating scale
☐ semantic differential scale
☐ Stapel scale
☐ Likert scale
☐ Thurstone scale.

(a) Graphic rating scale

The respondent is required to indicate his response on a continuum which covers the whole range of possible ratings.

Restaurant X is:

Very expensive	Very inexpensive

A graphic scale makes use of a horizontal or vertical continuum which is sometimes marked off into divisions with numbers. It may be non-comparative, as above, or comparative when a similar question is asked about restaurant Y.

(b) Semantic differential scale

The semantic differential scale is easy and quick to administer and is very widely used in marketing research surveys. The respondent rates the object in terms of a number of rating scales bounded at each end by one of two bipolar adjectives or phrases. For example:

BEER X

Healthy	— — — — — — — — — — — — — — — — — — — —	Unhealthy
Expensive	— — — — — — — — — — — — — — — — — — — —	Inexpensive
Tasty	— — — — — — — — — — — — — — — — — — — —	Tasteless
Easily obtainable	— — — — — — — — — — — — — — — — — — — —	Unobtainable
Low quality	— — — — — — — — — — — — — — — — — — — —	High quality

Usually the semantic scale has seven points. 'Neither-nor' is the central point with 'somewhat' on either side, the next two spaces 'very' and the outside spaces 'extremely'.

The semantic differential scale is typically used in comparisons of the characteristics of two or more brands or items or attitudes towards them. The result is a profile analysis which may look like this:

BEER X AND BEER Y

Healthy $-------------x--y------------$ Unhealthy
Expensive $-----------x------y---------$ Inexpensive
Tasty $----------x--y----------$ Tasteless
Easily obtainable $---------x---y-----------$ Unobtainable
Low quality $-----------y--x---------$ High quality

The great advantage Brand X has over Brand Y is its relatively high quality, whereas Brand Y has the advantage of being relatively inexpensive.

This scale is very easy to administer. A large number of products or brands can be tested for a large number of properties in a comparatively short interview. The researcher should guard against putting all the good extremes on the right and the poor extremes on the left. Respondents are forced to think when the extremes are interchanged.

In collaboration with R E Thomas and P A Spence of the Marketing Department of the University of Lancaster, Macfarlane Smith (1972:81) evolved a wheel scale known as the Lancaster wheel which facilitates the use of the semantic differential scale.

The wheel scale is illustrated in figure 11.1 on the next page.

Each brand or item is rated on a separate wheel. By using both sides of a card, provision can be made for up to 72 rating scales on one card for one brand or item. Macfarlane Smith (1972:83) reported that respondents found the wheel interesting and soon completed the ratings without any fatigue. A respondent may begin with any spoke of the wheel, which ensures a random start. Because it is not easy to see more than one scale at a time, the respondent's concentration on a particular scale during the rating process is improved.

(c) Stapel scale

The Stapel scale differs from the semantic differential scale in that the adjective pair is replaced by a single adjective or phrase. It usually has 10 scale positions instead of 7. If we want to find out how helpful a firm's employees are, we need not find adjectives for extremely helpful and extremely unhelpful as we should if we were using the semantic differential scale. The response format is shown on the next page:

Response format:

ABC STORE

+5	+5	+5
+4	+4	+4
+3	+3	+3
+2	+2	+2
+1	+1	+1
Helpful employees	Low prices	Limited selection
−1	−1	−1
−2	−2	−2
−3	−3	−3
−4	−4	−4
−5	−5	−5

Figure 11.1 The Lancaster wheel

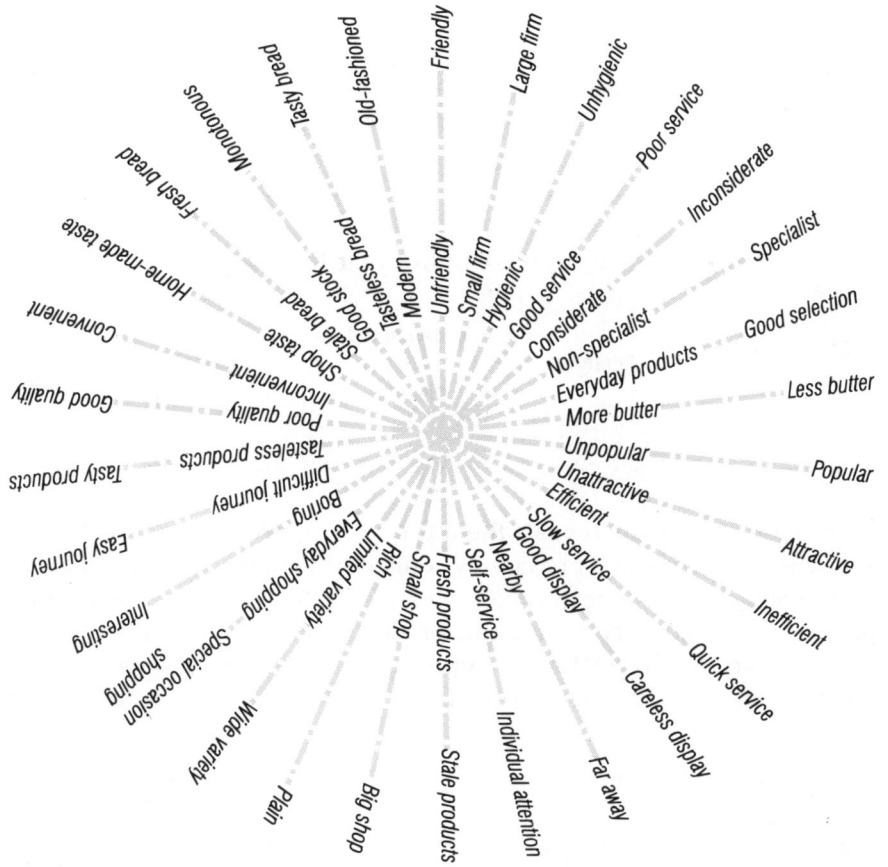

(d) Likert scale

Likert developed a verbal scale which requires a respondent to indicate a degree of agreement or disagreement with each of a series of statements related to the attitude object. For example:

(1) Consumer demand will be better in the coming year than last year.

Strongly agree	Agree	Neither agree nor disagree	Disagree	Strongly disagree

(2) The rate of inflation will be higher in the coming year than last year.

Strongly agree	Agree	Neither agree nor disagree	Disagree	Strongly disagree

(3) Interest rates will be lower in the coming year than last year.

Strongly agree	Agree	Neither agree nor disagree	Disagree	Strongly disagree

The sum of these statements reveals the attitude to or perception of a given subject or institution. The statements must be closely connected with the subject and approximately half of them should be positive and half negative. If, for example, we want the respondent's opinion on the country's economic prospects for the coming year, we would use positive statements such as the first example above and negative statements such as the second. The scores are summed after the negatives have been reversed to obtain a total score.

(e) Thurstone scale

The Thurstone scale requires merely agreement or disagreement with a number of statements which may vary from very positive to very negative. Each of these statements is allocated points in accordance with a previous study on the extent of their negativity or positivity. (Oppenheim 1966:125 explains the compilation and use of the Thurstone scale in detail.)

The respondent is ignorant of the number of points assigned to each statement. If he agrees with a particular statement he is allocated a mark equal to the mark for the statement. If his attitude to the matter is highly positive he will agree with only highly positive statements and will disagree with all others; if he has a very negative attitude he will agree with only the negative statements and will disagree with all others. Because the values assigned to the negative statements are relatively low and those assigned to the positive statements relatively high, the total score of the positively inclined respondent is high in comparison with that of the negatively inclined respondent.

4.2 Structured questions with unstructured responses

A structured question with an unstructured or open response allows the respondent to give his own answer in his own way. Open or free-response questions have several advantages:

☐ They are ideal in situations where all possible answers to a given question are not known.

☐ The researcher can usually deduce the reason for a particular response.

☐ They compel the respondent to think. (Respondents are sometimes accused of giving the first answer that occurs to them, without considering the alternatives, but they often consider their first answer to be the most important.)

☐ They may be the only ones to use when the number of possible responses is very great.

The disadvantages of open-ended questions are:

☐ They elicit much irrelevant information.

☐ They lengthen the interview.

☐ They make coding and processing more difficult.

☐ Responses are sometimes invalidated by the interviewer in his efforts to probe for relevant information.

There are various types of open questions:

(a) *Straight questions*

Example: In what part of Pretoria do you live?
Answer: Sunnyside

(b) *Straight questions with probing*

Example: Why do you prefer to live in Sunnyside?
Answer: It is very central

PROBE: What other reasons do you have?
Answer: Flat rents are relatively low

(c) *Sequence-of-mention questions*

Example: Can you give me the names of three brands of cigarettes?
Answer: 1 ....
         2 ....
         3 ....

(d) *Word association questions*

The interviewer says a word and the respondent mentions the first word that comes to mind.

Interviewer: 'Petrol'
Respondent: 'Power'

(e) *Sentence completion questions*

The respondent is required to finish a sentence started by the interviewer.

Interviewer: 'Cheese tastes best with ...'
Respondent: 'Bread and butter'

5 PHYSICAL CHARACTERISTICS OF THE QUESTIONNAIRE

The *appearance and layout* of the questionnaire are of particular concern in mail surveys and indeed in any other surveys where the questionnaire is completed by the respondent. The questionnaire should not create the impression of being overly long but its layout should allow *sufficient space* for recording the information required. Once the response to a question has been recorded, there should be no doubt about the next question to be answered by the respondent.

In some questionnaires *branching instructions* are inserted which direct the respondent to the next question he is required to answer. This technique is illustrated in figure 11.2. Here the first question is a filter question which eliminates non-users of cheese at the start, whereas users of cheddar and Gouda cheese answer only selected questions. Figure 11.2 also illustrates the funnel technique by starting with a general question on the use of cheese, proceeding to specific types of cheese and then to the packaging of cheese.

The questionnaire should present a *neat appearance*. The use of inferior paper, for example, might give the respondent the impression that the information required is of little importance and is not worthy of his time and trouble. In telephone and personal interview questionnaires it is customary to use as many computer codes as possible in order to save processing time, but in questionnaires for self-completion by the respondent computer codes should be inserted in such a way that there is no possibility of confusing the respondent.

Figure 11.2

1	Do you use cheese?	Yes	Go to question 2
		No	Stop
2	Do you use cheddar cheese?	Yes	Go to question 3
		No	Go to question 5
3	Are you satisfied with the packaging of cheddar cheese?	Yes	Go to question 5
		No	Go to question 4
4	Do you have any suggestions for improving the packaging of cheddar cheese?		Go to question 5

....

....

5	Do you use Gouda cheese?	Yes	Go to question 6
		No	Stop
6	Are you satisfied with the packaging of Gouda cheese?	Yes	Stop
		No	Go to question 7
7.	Do you have any suggestions for improving the packaging of Gouda cheese?		

....

....

6 PRE-TESTING

Pre-testing is essential if the researcher is to be satisfied that the questionnaire he has designed will perform its various functions in the interview situation: the data collected will be as relevant and accurate as possible, the target respondents will participate and cooperate as fully as possible, and the collection and analysis of the data will proceed as smoothly as possible.

Writing about the necessity for trying out a questionnaire beforehand and also for tabulating the answers to questionnaires, Churchill (1992:357) says:

> The researcher who avoids a questionnaire pretest and tabulation of replies is either naïve or a fool. The pretest is the most inexpensive insurance the researcher can buy to assure the success of the questionnaire and the research project.

Obviously aspects that have been tested successfully in previous questionnaires need not be retested. However, when the questionnaire's layout, the sequence of questions, the words, the branching instructions and the degree of difficulty of the questions are new, everything must be tested. The pre-test must be administered among respondents who correspond to those among whom the survey is to be carried out. Great care must be taken that all strata of the target population are represented in terms of intellectual ability, training, knowledge of the subject and attitude to it.

The test interviews should be conducted by a number of very experienced interviewers, a number of interviewers with some experience and one or two inexperienced interviewers. The experienced interviewers may be better able than the others to observe the respondent's reaction, and the inexperienced interviewer may be better able to point out problems the interviewer may have with the questionnaire. The interviewers with some experience will in turn be able to give a good idea of what the response rate and the average time taken by the interviewer will be. The researcher himself should be actively involved in the testing and reviewing of the questionnaire.

In dealing with large-scale attitude measurement the researcher must provide for the debriefing of respondents. After the interview respondents are asked for their reasons for giving certain answers to questions. Sometimes protocol analyses are also used where respondents are asked to think aloud when they are answering questions.

The procedure for the pre-investigation must be as nearly as possible *the same* as that envisaged for the actual investigation; a postal questionnaire being tried out by post, and a face-to-face interview questionnaire in a series of interviews. Telephone or postal questionnaires can also be tested in face-to-face interviews. An interviewer can observe whether respondents really remember the data asked, whether some questions seem confusing, and whether some respondents show hesitation in answering certain questions.

It is important to tabulate the results obtained in a pre-test. In this way the researcher can ascertain how the final tables will look and whether the information is really that needed to resolve the problem.

So far we have proceeded from the point of view that the designer of the questionnaire has carte blanche. However, the design process may start with a questionnaire drafted by the client, or the client may submit questions for inclusion in the questionnaire, or clients commissioning a multi-client or omnibus survey may all submit a certain number of questions for inclusion in the questionnaire. In such instances the researcher will probably suggest any adjustments he deems necessary and submit them to the client for approval. Or at some stage, possibly just before the pre-test, he may submit the draft questionnaire to the client for comment and then make any changes agreed upon by both parties. A copy of the final questionnaire may also be submitted to the client as a matter of courtesy. There are no hard and fast rules, however, and in most instances these matters are specified in the proposal for the study.

7 SUMMARY

Questionnaires come in many shapes and sizes, depending on the information required, the target group and the survey method. Broadly, however, all questionnaires are designed to achieve three related goals: to maximise the relevance and accuracy of the data collected; to secure the participation and cooperation of target respondents; and to facilitate the collection and analysis of the data.

Questionnaires with structured questions and structured or unstructured responses are most commonly used in marketing research and are dealt with in this chapter. The following five aspects are discussed: question content and phrasing, question sequence, question/response format, physical characteristics of the questionnaire and pre-testing of the questionnaire.

As far as question content and phrasing is concerned, questions should be kept as simple and concise as possible, the answers required have to be definitive, language should be suited to the target group, and leading questions should be avoided. Respondents must be able to answer the questions. Questions involving the respondent's prestige or ego and necessitating additional work for the respondent should be avoided as far as possible. Probes and other methods of helping the respondent to remember should not suggest answers. Provision should be made for all possible answers and the questionnaire should be as short as possible.

In considering question sequence the researcher should make the questions simple and interesting; group together the questions to be answered by a specific group of respondents; use the funnel approach where possible; ensure that the structured answers to a question do not provide respondents with answers to questions later on in the questionnaire; and insert sensitive questions as near as possible to the end of the questionnaire.

Structured questions with structured or unstructured responses are discussed. Structured questions with structured responses include dichotomous questions, multiple choice questions with single or multiple answers, checklists, rankings, grids and scaled questions. In scaled questions the ratings may be verbal or non-verbal. A variety of scaled questions are distinguished, such as the graphic rating scale, semantic differential scale, Stapel scale, Likert scale and Thurstone scale. Examples of structured questions with unstructured responses are: straight questions with or without probing, sequence-of-mention, word association and sentence completion questions.

In mail surveys the appearance and layout of the questionnaire are of especial importance. An impression of quality should be created and there should be sufficient space for recording the answers. Pre-coding should be avoided if there is a possibility of confusing the respondent. The use of filter questions and branching instructions is recommended.

A new questionnaire's layout, wording, sequence of questions and branching instructions should be tested by running a pre-test among respondents who are similar to those among whom the survey is to be carried out. The same survey method is applied in the pre-test as in the actual survey.

REFERENCES

Barker, R F & Blankenship, A B 1975. The manager's guide to survey questionnaire evaluation. *Journal of the Market Research Society*, 17(4):233–241.

Belson, William A 1986. *Validity in survey research: with special reference to the techniques of intensive interviewing and progressive modification for testing and constructing difficult or sensitive measures for use in survey research*. Aldershot, England: Gower.

Churchill, Gilbert A (Jr) 1992. *Basic marketing research*. Second edition. Fort Worth: Dryden Press. (The Dryden Press Series in Marketing.)

Cox, E P 1979. *Marketing research: information for decision making*. New York: Harper & Row.

D'Alton, Steve 1970. Questionnaire design and suggestibility of the respondent. *Australian Journal of Marketing Research*, 3(2), September:96–101.

Elliott, Ken & Christopher, Martin 1973. *Research methods in marketing*. London: Holt, Rinehart & Winston. (HRW London, Management Books.)

Gallup, R 1947. (Qualitative measurement of public opinion: the quintamensional plan of questionnaire design.) American Institute of Public Opinion:201.

Loubser, Marius & Gilmour, Barbara 1991. Questionnaire design. *Research for Marketing*, 18(2):4–15.

Macfarlane Smith, Joan 1972. *Interviewing in market and social research*. London: Routledge & Kegan Paul.

Oppenheim, A N 1966. *Questionnaire design and attitude measurement*. London: Heinemann. (Heinemann Books on Sociology.)

Quinn, Susan B & Belson, William A 1969. *The effect of reversing the order of presentation of verbal rating scales in survey interviewing*. London: The Survey Research Centre, London School of Economics and Political Science.

Selection, training and control of interviewers

Chapter 12: M Loubser

Selection, training and control of interviewers

1 INTRODUCTION

The role of interviewing in marketing research is the collection of primary data by the administration of the questionnaire, the asking of questions and the recording of answers. There are various means of collecting primary data, but personal interviewing offers distinct advantages. In a face-to-face interview the interviewer can gain a deeper understanding of the validity of the response from the facial expression of the respondent, explanations are better and easier because the interviewer can make use of charts, diagrams and the like, he can hold the respondent's interest for longer, and responses are more accurate because the respondent has time to think or consult documents (Hague & Jackson 1987:120–121). But these advantages are contingent on the satisfactory performance to the interviewer.

Like the questionnaire the interviewer is a very important link in the survey chain, but he is often the weakest link mainly because the researcher may not have the time and/or expertise to select suitable interviewers, train them properly for their task and check their work. These three aspects will be discussed in this chapter.

2 SELECTION OF INTERVIEWERS

After a thorough study of the various tests that have been used to predict interviewing ability, Joan Macfarlane Smith concludes that:

> It is clear that if objective tests could be made available for predicting interviewing ability, it would be a considerable step forward. Research projects have been carried out with this purpose in mind, but as yet no completely objective tests have been found, which can predict successfully (Macfarlane Smith 1972:29).

From her own experience and that of other researchers such as Adler, Wilcock and Hyman, to whom she often refers, Macfarlane Smith thinks that for the best chance of being efficient a fieldworker should:

□ Be a woman. Men available for part-time interviewing are seldom representative of the respondents to be interviewed. They are usually unemployed, or are students, teachers or pensioners. Women are usually more conscientious, patient, and more willing to go out in all kinds of weather. Men sometimes have difficulty in questioning women living alone and are more often regarded by respondents as potential salesmen.

□ Be between 25 and 45 years old. Women under 25 sometimes have problems interviewing older women, especially when certain personal information is needed. Women over 45 who have not worked since they were married may possibly have difficulty in understanding and implementing instructions in the various interview situations, and they often lack the physical stamina required for interviewing.

□ Be fairly free from household ties. On the whole widows and divorcees seem to make the best interviewers.

□ Be emotionally stable, with a tendency to introversion. An extrovert is sometimes inclined to be oversocial.

□ Not be extremist.

□ Have had an education between average and above-average levels, with possibly some training in informal interviewing.

□ Be adaptable and patient, with the ability to appear classless.

□ Have a working background of personal contact, but not in selling.

□ Be honest, reliable, conscientious and in good health.

□ Find interviewing enjoyable, otherwise all her good qualities are of little value.

Although the characteristics we have just mentioned are excellent guidelines for recruiting suitable interviewers, the survey population and the subject of the survey are equally important in this context. If the survey population is black men living in hostels, the first priority is to recruit black people rather than any other population group. Also, if the subject calls for communication of sensitive information, black men may be preferable to black women.

A good way of recruiting interviewers is to advertise for people with most of the above qualities. Applicants being interviewed for the job must be fully informed of the type of interviewing they will have to do and of their remuneration for it. They could be given four or five simple questionnaires with written instructions on how to complete them. Then they can be asked to hold test interviews with people who are strangers to them. If applicants are not paid to carry out these test interviews, it can serve as a filter to eliminate applicants interested only in the money aspect. Recruits who have fared best in test interviewing can then be summoned for a standard personal interview in which their personal qualities can be observed. Macfarlane Smith (1972:37) found a strong positive correlation between the quality of test interviews carried out by applicants and the quality of the fieldwork they subsequently produced.

3 TRAINING OF INTERVIEWERS

In training a national part-time field force in Britain, Macfarlane Smith (1972:39) found a three-stage training programme very satisfactory. An interviewer selected for this programme was supplied with an interviewing training manual, had to attend training classes and was given training in the field. These three phases will also be distinguished in the discussion that follows but the emphasis on specific aspects will be considerably different from Macfarlane Smith's.

In practice the procedure described in the sections below will not always be followed in its entirety, because it may be too expensive and too time consuming. However, we must discuss it in full so that researchers who do not implement it fully can form some idea of the possible errors caused by partial implementation.

3.1 Interviewers' training manual

When a manual or handbook has been prepared for the interviewers of an organisation, many of the procedures and principles that are common to all surveys can be explained in some detail. A manual of this kind is an excellent tool for training new interviewers and refreshing the memories of more experienced ones.

The contents of this manual depend on the purpose for which interviewers are being trained. If they are to be used for various future surveys the manual must contain a detailed discussion of the following:

☐ a general background to sample surveys: the reasons for making them, the types of questions asked, the types of surveys, possible types of sampling methods used, social grading, and so on

☐ preparation and readiness for the interview

☐ appearance and approach

☐ asking questions

☐ probing

☐ recording of answers

☐ closing the interview.

3.1.1 General background to sample surveys

Since the general background to sample surveys is discussed in chapter 13 in this book, we intend to confine ourselves here to the following aspects only in so far as they affect the interviewer:

☐ the concept of representativeness
☐ the selection of the element to be interviewed
☐ social grading.

3.1.1.1 The concept of representativeness

Interviewers who fully understand the concept of representativeness will also see why cheating and failure on their part to follow the selection instructions will impair the reliability of the collected information and may also render decisions based on it fatal to the firm concerned.

Potential respondents often refer interviewers to a third party for answers to their questions on the pretext that the latter knows more about the subject or has more time to answer questions. In this situation the interviewer must explain that the potential respondent forms part of a representative sample, and the third party does not. If the researcher is trying to discover what percentage of the community has heard of a certain brand of soap it is obviously wrong to question only those who have heard of it.

3.1.1.2 Selecting/finding the elements to be interviewed

Different procedures for selecting the elements to be interviewed are followed in probability and non-probability samples.

(a) Probability samples

In one-stage probability samples the elements to be interviewed are selected beforehand. The interviewers are expected to do everything in their power to interview these elements and, if they fail to make contact, to adhere strictly to the instructions for the selection of substitute elements.

Interviewers who are sent to interview a specific member of a household should be given a precise definition of the particular household member: main breadwinner, head of household, housewife, boarder, lodger. When interviewers are only given an address where one member of a household has to be interviewed, the selection procedure should be explained and selection grids should be provided for that purpose. Interviewers who fail to find respondents at home the first time they call should make at least two further calls at different times.

In space specially provided in the questionnaire the interviewer should record the date of the interview, its duration and the extent of the respondent's cooperation.

(b) Non-probability samples

In non-probability samples the interviewer selects the respondent according to specific quota controls, which should be fully understood. These controls are sometimes parallel and sometimes interlocked (see chapter 13).

The handling of contact questions and filter questions is extremely important. If a respondent has the slightest suspicion that denying that he uses a product will put an end to the interview, he will be inclined to do so if this is not true.

Interviewers should be distributed throughout the study area and not be confined to densely populated areas. Respondents living in their own or hired houses or flats may have different characteristics. If housewives have to be interviewed, interviews should be conducted at home unless otherwise stated, and in the evenings or during weekends, so that people who work are included. To avoid mutual influence, only one person should be interviewed at a specific address or in a firm. Houses should not be avoided because of their appearance.

The following people must not be interviewed: those whom the interviewer knows personally or has interviewed previously, or whose job is in any way connected with the subject being studied. Since people who live near each other tend to be homogeneous, a next-door neighbour or a near neighbour should not be interviewed. When children have to be interviewed the interviewer must first have the parents' consent.

3.1.1.3 Social grading

Often respondents have to be graded into socio-economic status groups. In normal random sampling surveys it is advisable to include questions on occupation, income and education level. When the interviewer returns to the office, the respondents can be graded accordingly. In quota sampling these status groups often serve as one of the controls. Interviewers may be given only a vague description of these groups, and are then left to do the grading themselves by noting aspects such as housing conditions and the respondent himself. This leaves room for the interviewer to select respondents who do not strictly conform to the requirements of certain control groups. Social grading should always be clearly defined in terms of particulars such as occupation, training and income. If the questionnaire includes specific questions on these particulars, the interviewer's social grading can easily be checked in the office.

3.1.2 Preparation and readiness for the interview

Before going into the field the interviewers must

☐ study the project instructions carefully

☐ carry out a 'dummy' interview to familiarise themselves with the questionnaire

☐ make sure they have all they need: the questionnaire, prompt cards, letter of introduction, possible newspaper cuttings, photographs, reports on the findings of previous similar surveys, etc.

3.1.3 Appearance and approach

Personal interaction between interviewer and respondent begins when the respondent opens the door. The respondent immediately wants to know who the interviewer is and the object of the visit. After a friendly greeting the interviewer must *show* the respondent the *letter of introduction* and/or card. The letter should contain the interviewer's name, the name of the firm he represents and, briefly, the purpose of his visit. While the respondent is looking at the letter the interviewer can go on explaining. Most respondents merely glance at the letter but listen to the interviewer, at the same time forming their own impression of him. Since the respondent should never be made to feel that his visitor belongs to a class different from his own, the interviewer should try to *appear classless* by avoiding all 'betraying' externals such as expensive clothing and an affected way of speaking. He must enter the house as soon as possible, and so be in a better position to convince the respondent of the value and importance of his cooperation.

In no circumstances should the respondent be given an opportunity to refuse the interview. He can, for example, easily say 'No' if the interviewer begins by saying: 'May I come in?' A better opening would be: 'I'd like to come in and ask you one or two questions.' If the respondent hesitates at all he must immediately be told that any information he gives will *be treated as confidential*.

At this stage the respondent may want to know how long the interview will last. The interviewer must *tell* him the *average time taken* for such an interview. He must never say, for example, that an interview will last only 5 minutes when he knows it will last 15 minutes. After 10 minutes the respondent will begin to doubt the genuineness of his visitor's initial explanations and may even refuse to continue the interview. And interviewees must certainly never be given any idea that the length of the interview will depend on whether they use a certain product, for then they may say they do not use it, even if they do.

Although it is often impossible to *interview the respondent on his own*, the interviewer should make every effort to achieve this. This is especially important in surveys of attitudes, opinions, knowledge and awareness and where impossible, the interviewer should explain to the others in the room that for the time being he is interested only in the respondent's attitudes and opinions, but that the others may voice their own ideas and opinions after the interview. In situations where factual data are needed it may sometimes be preferable, in fact even necessary, to allow others to put in a word.

A respondent may have many reasons for hesitating to cooperate, the most common being *suspicion, lack of interest* or *incivility*, but his behaviour soon makes the reason evident to the interviewer. If, for example, the respondent suspects that the interviewer is really a salesperson, the interviewer can easily dispel suspicion by saying outright that he is not, and can even go on to say how a salesperson who purports to be an interviewer makes a researcher's work much more difficult. Or the respondent may feel that he knows too little of the subject to be discussed and is afraid of appearing stupid. To this the interviewer may reply that in general people not interested in a particular subject know little about it, but that the extent to which the respondent is informed on the subject is important for this study. However, he must make sure that the respondent realises that the interviewee's answers are not tabulated separately and his name is never mentioned.

When an interviewer finds a respondent has no interest in a particular subject, he should try to show that the findings of the study are important for the community and, if possible, for the respondent himself.

As a last resort the interviewer can try to win the respondent's sympathy by saying, for example: 'The research manager will never believe that I did my best to persuade you to cooperate.'

3.1.4 Asking questions

A number of important general rules should be observed to ensure reliable and valid results from the questions asked:

☐ The exact wording of the questions in the questionnaire must be used. The interviewer should practise reading questions beforehand, using a neutral tone and reading at the rate of two words a second. In recording the respondent's answers the interviewer should show no sign of emotion.

☐ All the relevant questions in the questionnaire must be asked. For example, when asked about his attitude to the policy of a certain political party the respondent may suggest that since he supports it wholeheartedly, the interviewer may take it for granted that his answers will be 'yes' to all its aspects. The interviewer must explain that his instructions are to read every question aloud and obtain an answer to each one.

In answering a particular question the respondent may incidentally provide an answer to a subsequent question in the questionnaire. If the interviewer has any doubt whether the respondent has reacted fully, he must ask the question again with an introductory statement: 'In your answer to question 4 you provide an answer to my next question here. However, I'll ask it again in case you have anything further to add.'

☐ The questions are printed in a particular sequence for a special purpose, and the sequence must therefore be strictly adhered to. By asking question 2, say, before question 1, the interviewer may provide the respondent with information that may affect his answer to question 1.

For example:

Question 1: What advertisements did you see on television yesterday?

Question 2: This card lists ten advertisements shown in the past week on television. Which of them did you see?

If the questions are asked in this order the respondent may remember three advertisements out of a possible ten. But if question 2 is asked first, when he is asked question 1 he will probably remember five or six of the possible ten.

☐ If a respondent gives a 'don't know' answer to a question the interviewer must always make sure that it is a genuine 'don't know' and not a 'lazy' one.

Note the following question: 'Do you think that next year the country will be economically better off or worse off than this year, or do you think its economic position will be the same as this year?' If the respondent says: 'I hope it will be better off', the interviewer may reply: 'We all hope it will be better off; but do you think that next year the country will be economically better off or worse off than this year, or do you think its economic position will be the same as this year?' If the respondent says: 'I don't know', a *probe* such as: 'I want to know what you think' may elicit an answer. If the respondent sticks to his 'don't know', the interviewer should exert no further pressure, otherwise the respondent may give any answer he thinks may put an end to the subject. Remember that a genuine 'don't know' is as important as any other information provided by the respondent and must be accepted as such by the interviewer.

3.1.5 Probing

A probe is anything done or said by the interviewer to get the respondent to add to or explain something he has said, or to bring his attention back to the subject when he has strayed from it. The best probes the interviewer can use are the expectant pause, neutral comments and repetition of the respondent's reply.

☐ *The expectant pause:* A respondent often begins to answer a question and then hesitates. By remaining silent and looking at the respondent expectantly or nodding his head the interviewer may be doing all that is necessary to make the respondent continue.

☐ *Neutral comments:* Neutral comments assure the respondent that the interviewer is listening to and understanding what he says, and encourages him to talk. Examples are: 'U-huh', 'Yes', 'OK', 'I see', 'Anything else?', 'Any others?', 'Could you tell me more?'

☐ *Repetition of the respondent's reply:* By repeating the respondent's words while recording them the interviewer gives the respondent a chance to listen to his own words and to supplement them.

☐ *Repetition of the question:* This is always useful when the respondent avoids a question, gives a meaningless answer, begins a meaningful answer and then strays from the point, or simply says he does not know.

3.1.6 Recording answers

Answers to open-ended questions must be fully recorded. To obviate forgetting part of the information, the interviewer must record during the interview. If the respondent talks too quickly the interviewer can repeat his words aloud as he records them.

This will let the respondent know that he is talking too fast and will at the same time retain interest, for hearing what he has just said will stimulate his thinking.

Another important point to remember is that the interviewer should record all his own probes, thus enabling the researcher to ascertain why the respondent has answered in any particular way. For quick and easy recording the interviewer should try to sit at a table, or take a hardcover folder with him. The use of standard abbreviations is another way of speeding up recordings.

3.1.7 Closing the interview

As soon as the interview is over the interviewer briefly reports on it in the space usually left for this in the questionnaire by noting down such aspects as the respondent's attitude to the interview, all circumstances and events that may have affected the interview (such as interruptions, speech, language or hearing defects), and possible surmises on responses to certain questions.

Completed questionnaires must be edited by the interviewer as soon as possible after the interview to make sure that the writing is legible, all questions have been answered and all necessary explanations given.

3.2 Training classes

In most surveys interviewers are required to attend two training classes. As preparation for the first training class the interviewer should receive the following a week or more before the date of the class:

☐ the interviewers' training manual with specific references to the sections that require special attention in the particular survey, and

☐ the questionnaire, specific interviewers' instructions not covered in the manual, charts, etc.

At the first training class the researcher explains the background, purpose and importance of the survey and then discusses the questionnaire. This is an ideal opportunity to clarify any ambiguities in specific questions. Interviewing techniques are discussed and demonstrated. For instance, an experienced interviewer may be asked to conduct an interview with a respondent and write down the responses. The trainees also record the responses and then the experienced interviewer's and the trainee's entries are compared and discussed. Videotapes may be used to illustrate common interviewers' errors. At the end of the first session interviewers are requested to conduct one or two interviews before attending the second session. Such questionnaires are very thoroughly checked during the second session before interviewers are sent into the field.

3.3 Field training

Interviewers who are being trained to conduct a large number of interviews should preferably be accompanied by the supervisor during the initial interviews. The supervisor may even conduct the first interview while the interviewer looks on. Subsequent interviews are conducted by the interviewer and the supervisor assumes the role of observer. They discuss the interviews afterwards and in this way make quite sure that the interviewer is equal to his task.

4 CONTROL OF INTERVIEWERS

The regular checking of interviewers' work by calling back on respondents is of the utmost importance. When the same interviewers are used repeatedly and they know their work is checked regularly, they are less tempted to cheat. New interviewers are put right before falling into habits such as not checking whether they have all the answers before leaving the respondent.

Checks must be made very soon after the original interview because respondents not only forget what they said at the original interview, but also change their minds and opinions.

4.1 Postal checks

It is common practice to send reply-paid postcards or letters to respondents enquiring whether interviews have been conducted with them. Very often a few of the questions from the original questionnaire are included. Usually not many respondents react to this mail check and those who do are not regarded as representative of the respondents originally selected. Hauck (1969:117) found that households with whom interviews had been conducted were five times more likely to respond to a postal check than those with whom interviews had not been conducted.

If, therefore, out of a sample of 1 000 only 90 % (900) are interviewed and 10 % (100) are not, and 50 % (450) of the 900 interviewed respond to a postal check, only about 10 % (10) of the 100 not interviewed may be expected to respond. Therefore of the total of 460 who do respond, 450 or 98 % will confirm that they have been interviewed. The results of a postal check can therefore be misleading.

In the USA, Grey and Harris (1951) found that older, better educated and white respondents tend to have a higher response rate to postal checks. Consequently it would also be misleading to regard the response to postal checks as representative of various socio-economic groups.

4.2 Personal and telephone call-back checks

The best method of checking on interviewers is to call on respondents personally soon after the original interview. Personal call-back checks are, however, expensive.

Telephone call-back checks can also be made soon after the original interview but this method has the disadvantage that not all respondents have telephones.

4.3 Editing checks

All questionnaires must be edited and, where necessary, referred back to interviewers for missing information. A comparison of the questionnaires of individual interviewers reveals whether there are specific patterns in the work of a certain interviewer. Such patterns tend to occur more particularly in the answers to open questions.

4.4 Computer checks

In most surveys it does cost a little extra to ask for a computer analysis of the data collected by individual interviewers, but then the researcher can see at once whether the results obtained from specific interviewers differ from the rest and seek reasons for the differences. For instance, respondents with higher qualifications and/or purchasing power may live in specific areas and differ from other respondents in the characteristics being studied. Similarly the information obtained by interviewers working in relatively well-to-do or poor socio-economic areas may differ quite considerably from the information obtained by other interviewers. A further possibility is that the results of an interviewer who interviews only ten respondents may, for example, be quite different from the rest purely as a result of sample variations. If no explanation can be found for one interviewer's work differing from the rest, further checks should be made such as personal, postal and telephone call-back checks.

Researchers such as King and Trotman (1973:255–280) have calculated the averages of different characteristics being studied in various surveys, noting the number of standard deviations from interviewer averages. An average for specific interviewers further than 2,57 standard deviations from the survey average, for instance, is symptomatic of interviewers' errors. If the households living in the area where such interviewers work are not very different from the universe in the characteristics being studied, the chances are as low as 1 % that sample variations are responsible for this result. Possibly the researcher and the supervisor know that wealthy consumers live in the area and expect a big standard deviation. If not, they would be well advised to conduct personal call-back checks.

5 SUMMARY

The facts collected by inferior interviewers may be more misleading in making decisions than the lack of facts. Special care should therefore be taken in the selection, training and supervision of interviewers.

Several guidelines have been formulated for the selection of interviewers in terms of their demographic, socio-economic and personality characteristics but the target group and the subject of the survey are just as important.

Three training phases are suggested: the preparation of an interviewers' manual, attendance at training classes and training in the field. When a manual or handbook has been prepared for the interviewers of an organisation, many of the procedures and principles that are common to all surveys can be explained in some detail. Manuals of this kind are excellent tools for training new interviewers and refreshing the memories of more experienced ones. The manual, the questionnaire and specific interviewers' instructions should be given to interviewers at least a week before their first training class.

At the first training class the background, aim and importance of the particular survey are explained, the questionnaire is discussed and interviewing techniques are demonstrated. Interviewers are instructed to conduct at least two interviews before attending the second training class. At this session the test-interviews are discussed and the interviewer's ability to conduct a successful interview is assessed. When interviewers are being trained to conduct a large number of interviews, it is worth the effort and cost of sending a supervisor to attend the first few interviews which are being conducted by a new interviewer.

It is important to check the work of each interviewer. The methods chiefly used for this purpose are personal and telephone call-back checks, editing checks and computer checks.

REFERENCES

Grey, P G & Harris, A 1951. *Some notes on postal checks*. London: HM Government. (Social Survey Papers Methodological Series no 44.)

Hague, Paul N & Jackson, Peter 1987. *Do your own market research*. London: Kogan Page.

Hauck, M 1969. Is survey postcard verification effective? *Public Opinion Quarterly*, 23:177–120.

King, R C & Trotman, P M 1973. Experience of a computer system for the quality control of interviewers. *Seminar on fieldwork, sampling and questionnaire design, Amsterdam, 24–27 October 1973*. Amsterdam: ESOMAR.

Macfarlane Smith, Joan 1972. *Interviewing in market and social research*. London: Routledge & Kegan Paul.

Sampling

Chapter 13: M Loubser

Sampling

1 INTRODUCTION

Suppose we are asked by our employer to determine the average amount spent on textbooks in 1995 by students at the University of South Africa. We are given the names and addresses of approximately 125 000 students. We would really like to contact all of them (take a census). If they would all cooperate and could remember exactly how much they had spent on textbooks, we could find out precisely how much this was. But to contact all of them would be an extremely expensive and time-consuming procedure.

Obviously the cost of a survey should be kept as low as possible. It is often equally important that a survey should not last long, for information which was not available until after the decision had been made has no value for the decision concerned. Further, some information soon becomes out of date, and outdated information, however accurate, may prove more or less valueless in a rapidly changing market situation.

Besides its high cost and the relatively long time it takes, a census survey has two other drawbacks. First, its results may possibly be less accurate than those of a sample survey, even allowing for the sample error (which is discussed later). This happens when the non-sample error of a census survey is bigger than the combined non-sample and sample errors of a sample survey. One way of restricting the non-sample error is to use well-trained and well-qualified interviewers and to exercise strict control over them. However, in a census survey the large number of adequately qualified interviewers needed is often difficult to find; added to this, the work of a large group of interviewers is more difficult to control than a small group.

Nor can a census be used when the researcher applies pre- and post-testing, for instance to determine the effectiveness of an advertisement. Respondents who are interviewed about an advertisement before it appears remember it and may be on the lookout for it. Their viewpoint will therefore be different from that of respondents who are unacquainted with it. This means that the same respondents may not be interviewed in both the pre- and the post-testing stage.

2 SOME BASIC CONCEPTS

Our introductory discussion shows that it is not feasible to contact all 125 000 students to obtain the information we need, namely the average expenditure on textbooks in 1995, and so we must decide which students to question. First, however, we must define some basic concepts.

2.1 Element

An element is the unit about which we need information. This element must be clearly defined, for it is the basis of the analysis. For example, will the element be a student who registered at Unisa in 1995, or a student who merely wrote the examinations? In our example it is a student registered at Unisa in 1995. In marketing research, elements are usually individuals or households, but may also be merchants, manufacturers, companies or products.

2.2 Sample unit

A sample unit is the unit available for selection at some stage of the sampling process. In our example the element and the sample unit are the same. We have a list for drawing the elements in the first stage. However, suppose we wish to study smokers, and all we have are addresses of private households. This means that we must first select households (primary sample units) and then, when we visit the household, we must select the smoker (final sample unit). In the first stage of selection the element is not identifiable, but in the final stage the unit and the element are the same.

The sampling process may entail a number of stages. We may, for example, be interested in studying smokers in metropolitan areas and so draw a sample in the following stages:

☐ metropolitan areas (primary sample units)

☐ residential blocks (secondary sample units)

☐ dwelling units (tertiary sample units)

☐ smokers (final sample units or elements).

2.3 Population (universe)

A population or universe is the aggregate of all the elements, which means that in our example it is all Unisa students registered in 1995. A population must be defined in terms of elements, sample units, time and size. In our example these are specified as follows:

Element: registered Unisa student

Sample unit: registered Unisa student

Time: 1995

Size: South Africa

2.4 Survey population

The survey population is the aggregate of elements from which the sample is drawn. In practice we seldom find complete lists or records of all of the elements, so that the sample has to be drawn from lists that do not always contain all of the elements. And it is this population whose elements are contained in the sample frame being studied. We must therefore always notice the possible differences between the survey population and the population or universe. *Survey population = population – missing elements.*

2.5 Sample frame

A sample frame is a record of all the sample units available for selection at a given stage in the sampling process. A frame may be a register of industries or merchants, a telephone directory or even a map.

Each stage in a sampling process requires its own frame. In the example above we need a list or record of primary sample units (metropolitan areas), secondary sample units (residential blocks), tertiary sample units (dwelling units in blocks) and final sample units (smokers in houses).

A reliable sample frame meets several requirements:

☐ It represents all the elements of the population.

☐ There is no duplication of elements.

☐ It is free from foreign elements.

The treatment of a sample frame which do not meet these requirements is discussed in chapter 14, section 3.2.

3 STEPS IN SAMPLING

The following five steps are evident in sampling:

Step 1 – Defining the population

Step 2 – Identifying the sample frame

Step 3 – Selecting the sampling method

Step 4 – Determining the sample size

Step 5 – Selecting the sample elements

If our problem is to determine the average spending by Unisa students on textbooks in 1995, we have completed the first two steps: the population has been defined (all registered

Unisa students in 1995) and a sample frame has been identified (a list of the names and addresses of all students registered at Unisa in 1995). We can now turn our attention to the third step in sampling: selection of a sampling method.

Sampling methods differ from one another in several respects, one of which is the selection of sample elements. In our discussion of sampling methods we shall therefore also refer to the selection of sample elements in certain instances, even though this step is the last one in the sampling process.

4 SAMPLING METHODS

Sampling methods may be divided into two broad categories: probability and non-probability sampling. A *probability sample* is one in which every element has a known non-zero probability of being selected. It is unnecessary for all elements to have an equal chance of being selected; but each element must have a chance and that chance must be known so that the sampling results can be applied to the universe. *Non-probability samples* rely on the judgement of the researcher and are only as representative as the researcher's luck and skill permit. In non-probability sampling there is no way of estimating the probability that any element will be included in the sample, and therefore there is no method of finding out whether the sample is representative of the population.

4.1 Non-probability sampling

The following are the three types of non-probability sampling usually distinguished:

☐ convenience sampling

☐ quota sampling

☐ judgement sampling.

4.1.1 Convenience sampling

As the name implies, respondents are selected on the basis of convenience or availability. One example of this is when viewers of a television programme are asked to phone in and give their opinions of a controversial question. Such respondents are 'self-selected'. They may be more interested in the question, they may have more time at their disposal, their personalities may be different from the rest of the population, and their opinions may differ radically from them. The preferences, attitudes and interests of people approached in the street may likewise differ from others. Despite this weakness, however, the convenience sample is a useful tool in the exploratory phase of a research project, a phase in which ideas and insights are more important than scientific objectivity.

4.1.2 Quota sampling

In a quota sample the researcher takes explicit steps to obtain a sample similar to the population in some pre-specified characteristics. For example, if 20 % of the target group fall into the A income group, he provides for 20 % of the sample to fall into the A income group; and if 10 % of the target group fall into the age group 64+ he provides for 10 % of the sample to fall into this age group.

Some quotas are 'parallel' (table 13.1) and others are 'interlocking' (table 13.2). In parallel quotas a specific element has to comply with only one characteristic. As indicated in table 13.1 we need 100 elements who have to comply with the characteristic 16–24 years old. These 100 elements can be of any income group. It can also be seen in table 13.1 that we need 100 elements who have to comply with the characteristic R1 000 and under. These 100 elements can be of any age group. If the elements have to comply with the quota controls as indicated in table 13.1, we can start off by interviewing anybody aged 16 years and older. When we reach a quota of a specific cell, say the 100 of the age group 16–24 years, we are restricted to other age groups to fill the other cells (for example the 200 of the R3 000+ cell). Just before the end we may find that we need, for example, five elements over 64 years old with an income of R3 000+. These five elements therefore have to comply with two characteristics.

Table 13.1 Example of parallel quota sample

Age groups	Income groups				Total
	R1 000 and under	R1 001 to R2 000	R2 001 to R3 000	R3 000+	
16–24					100
25–34					200
35–44					400
45–64					200
64+					100
Total	100	200	500	200	1 000

In interlocking quotas a specific element has to comply with two or more characteristics, as in table 13.2. In table 13.2 we have four income groups and five age groups, giving 20 cells in total (5 x 4). If we bring in another characteristic, such as area, and provide for five areas, the number of interlocked cells increases by the factor 5 from 20 to 100. The interviewer would find it difficult to fill the quota assigned to many of these 100 cells.

Table 13.2 Example of interlocking quota sample

Age groups	Income groups				Total
	R1 000 and under	R1 001 to R2 000	R2 001 to R3 000	R3 000 +	
16–24	12	18	50	20	100
25–34	20	22	100	58	200
35–44	35	132	200	33	400
45–64	20	18	100	62	200
64 +	13	10	50	27	100
Total	100	200	500	200	1 000

Controls used in quota samples

☐ must be available and should be recent

☐ should be easy for the interviewer to use for classification

☐ should be closely related to the variables being measured in the study

☐ should be kept to a reasonable number so as not to produce too many cells.

The reliability of information based on quota samples is usually questioned on the following three grounds:

(1) the interviewer's natural inclination to obtain the information with the least possible trouble

(2) the impossibility of building in controls for all relevant variable

(3) the impossibility of verifying whether a quota sample is representative.

With reference to (1) above we confine ourselves to one or two comments. Interviewers are inclined to question people who are easily accessible, such as friends or sales personnel with time at their disposal while they are waiting for customers. And they prefer to interview people who are friendly.

Controls for all relevant variables cannot possibly be built into a sample in which variables may include a consumer's preference for a given brand, which is based on his income, age, ethnic group, home language, living environment, sex, profession, sector of employment and many other things.

Quota samples are usually 'validated' after they are taken. The process of validation involves a comparison of the sample and the population according to characteristics which are not used as control variables. If the sample differs significantly from the population in any of these characteristics, this indicates potential bias in the selection procedure. If the sample and population distribution are similar for each of these characteristics, it is still possible for the sample to be vastly different from the population in some characteristics which have not been explicitly compared.

In spite of their serious disadvantages, quota samples have certain advantages over probability sampling: firstly they are cheaper than probability sampling and secondly they can be more quickly implemented.

4.1.3 Judgement sampling

A judgement sample is one in which the researcher attempts to draw a representative sample of the population by using judgemental selection procedure. The amount of error present in a judgement sample depends upon the degree of expertise of the person making the selection. Where a new product has to be tried out in three or four towns, anyone who knows both the product and South African conditions would select a more representative set of towns than could be chosen by random selection. Further, where multiple-stage sampling is used and the first stage consists in the selection of ten or fewer towns, an expert on South African conditions is better able to select a representative set of towns than could be selected at random. However, as the sample size increases, judgement selection becomes less reliable than random sample selection. When searching for ideas and insights, the researcher is not sampling a cross-section of opinion but those who can offer some perspective on the research question. Thus researchers might wish to conduct a small pilot study, using judgement samples prior to the formal research. Judgement samples can also be quite adequate for pre-testing questionnaires.

4.1.4 Non-probability sample size

There are no statistical formulae for prior calculation of the size of a non-probability sample. The researcher relies on experience to help him determine the size of a sample that will be representative of the universe. Very often the number of respondents interviewed will depend on whether a pattern has emerged. The researcher may also allow himself to be guided by the sample size he would require if he were drawing a probability sample. Further determinants of sample size are often the time and funds available for doing the research.

4.2 Probability sampling

We have already pointed out that probability samples differ from non-probability samples in one very important respect, namely that in a probability sample the sample error for a given sample size can be calculated statistically. Before turning to a discussion of the calculation of the sample error we shall first deal with the various probability sampling methods.

4.2.1 Probability sampling methods

The following five types of probability sampling may be distinguished:

- ☐ simple random sampling
- ☐ systematic sampling
- ☐ stratified sampling
- ☐ cluster sampling
- ☐ multi-stage sampling.

4.2.1.1 Simple random sampling

Simple random sampling is unique in that all elements in the population have a *known equal chance* of being included in the sample. If balls of the same size are put into a container and ten are taken out, the procedure is simple random sampling.

Let us go back to the problem set at the beginning of this chapter. Suppose we decide to draw a simple random sample of x students, how would we set to work? To throw all the names into a container and draw x names from it would be a tremendous task.

In practice the drawing of simple random samples is facilitated by the use of tables with random numbers. Table 13.3 on the next page is an example of a table with seven-digit random numbers. These numbers are applied to draw a simple random sample from a list of names of 125 000 students.

First the students' names have been numbered from 1 to 125 000. We begin at any place in the random table, say the second row in the third column. Because our 125 000 population is a six-digit number we use the first six digits; and the first six digits in the column are 356686. Since this number is greater than 125 000 we ignore it and go to the third row in column 3, where the first six digits are 038195. This is the number of the first

Table 13.3 List of random numbers

1890902	6342074	2370660	2993716	4135643
3558091	4945913	3566865	9952923	6237682
9515874	2646130	0381956	6039194	9823162
6226789	6838022	7307580	3013172	8667288
3230033	5357768	5658586	8533760	1750603
8870395	4188133	4517913	1566387	6564748
1666580	2677528	1018109	8922213	5949860
0810197	2646547	5375815	0382345	2216851
3820572	8594300	8661394	2335243	5108139
8783566	3228385	5196070	0250305	7067194
2635548	8259106	9668827	4613167	4133933
7669279	3752432	1217803	2349117	2803441
5325133	0022136	1002352	3812246	3209945
0194315	6306028	2599676	4450032	3765256
9160765	9425035	5690333	4507286	9078888
5537100	0309136	1021354	7948874	0405940
2953747	5905364	7613969	9857016	1727032
6802232	1265187	1216062	9246075	5418952
2046456	2031171	9043430	6980134	8191743
3623589	1094349	3994256	5738327	3618801
6564823	1613842	3901767	3872373	2315250
1069805	3694684	0185565	2913157	3896496
8794380	7190678	1510563	9437715	1764239
5918161	2764413	9080342	8062972	9912879
5137278	7503298	0090797	1318174	4445308
6863152	7347976	6344183	2402243	7588360
4804486	7262913	7239386	7572002	4624715
3684265	1781705	1954284	8297282	4419968
7549827	3630721	0511683	3790225	9694454
1716459	4249516	7476807	0681341	9974863
9022504	4827220	1719509	7034291	6356528
1331398	1835066	3773000	2139706	4337260
2544226	4268371	6716906	3522188	5187275
4064472	6278445	4818794	5534816	6996231
7356887	0956503	5957706	0577467	5269053
4250713	3942434	3254752	6306171	7556797
5015819	4698599	1211512	8763126	2984902
7070852	4947836	3695226	3987549	8813857

sample element. By moving further down in the column we select numbers 730758, 565858 and 451791 which we ignore as they are greater than 125 000. The next number, 101810, is our second sample element. After reaching the end of the table we may continue anywhere, say at the top of column 3, but using the last six digits – 370660, 566865, etc. We may even use a combination of two columns, for example the last three figures of column 3 and the first three figures of column 2. The use of computer programs can save a great deal of time.

4.2.1.2 Systematic sampling

Systematic sampling* produces much the same result as simple random sampling, but is far easier to apply. If, for example, we want to draw a sample of 500 from the population of 125 000, the population is divided by the sample (500) to find n (250). We must now draw an element from the first 250 and then every 250th element. The element from the first 250 is drawn by using random numbers. The choice of the first element of the sample automatically determines the whole sample.

Another variation of the systematic sample is the choice of a sample of, say, 100 from a telephone directory with 50 pages. We can decide on the ninth name in the first column of each page and the twelfth name from the foot of the third column on each page.

When the population has been arranged and a systematic sample drawn which includes each nth element, the results will be more or less as representative as a simple random sample of the same population. If, for example, the population has been arranged from young to old, and age is connected with what is being studied, systematic sampling ensures a measure of stratification and prevents the inclusion in the sample of a disproportionate number of young or old people. If, however, there are periodic variations in the list, especially if these variations are equal to n or multiples of n, the sample may be very unrepresentative. Thus if days are selected for a study of traffic flow, and n is equal to 7 or 14, the same day of the week will be selected repeatedly.

4.2.1.3 Stratified sampling

A stratified sample is a probability sample which differs in two respects from the simple random or systematic sample. First the population is divided into segments or strata and then the drawing is done in every stratum exactly as in simple random or systematic sampling. Second a stratified sample may also be drawn disproportionately; in other words, 1 % of the elements of stratum A may be drawn and 2 % of the elements of stratum B. The requirement for a probability sample, namely that all elements must have a known

---

* Systematic sampling differs from simple random sampling in one important respect: in systematic sampling the number of possible selections is limited to n whereas in simple random sampling the number of possible selections is far greater.

chance of being drawn, still holds, but in a disproportionate probability sample this chance is not equal for all elements. However, the chance must be equal for the elements in a certain stratum. Thus the chance can be 1 % for the elements in stratum A, and 2 % for the elements in stratum B.

Stratified random sampling is used when the population is heterogeneous in the qualities being investigated, and can be divided into more homogeneous groups (strata) with reference to these qualities. For example, if we want to find out the average amount spent by Pretoria households on durable consumer goods, dividing Pretoria's residential areas into high-, middle- and low-income groups would be a meaningful stratification, since income is closely related to the amount spent on durable consumer goods.

Division of the sample into more homogeneous strata enhances the precision or reduces the sample error in two ways. First, it makes certain that the various elements are included in the sample in their correct proportions. Thus when 30 % of the population live in the higher-income areas it ensures that 30 % of the sample is drawn from these areas (proportionate stratified sample). In a simple random sample this percentage is subject to random forces, and the percentage will therefore seldom be exactly 30 %. Second, variability of the qualities being investigated decreases within the various strata: if we can succeed in dividing the population into strata whose elements are exactly the same there will be no sample error. Let us take a simple example. Suppose we begin by classifying a population of 900 elements as follows:

Stratum A with low values   300

Stratum B with middle values   300

Stratum C with high values   300

Next we distribute our sample of 90 proportionately over these three strata, namely stratum A 30, stratum B 30 and stratum C 30, and undertake the survey. Say we find that each of the elements in stratum A has a value of R10, stratum B of R20, and stratum C of R30. The variances of all three strata are therefore zero, as are the stratum standard errors. The population mean can therefore be determined precisely. Further, if we know beforehand that the elements in the strata are perfectly homogeneous, we can be content with a sample of 3, one from each stratum. In the above example there is a variability between strata but this variability did not enter into the calculation of the standard error of estimate.

An important point is that stratification is worthless unless we succeed in classifying the population into strata that are more homogeneous in the quality being investigated than the population as a whole. If, for instance, we want to establish the average height of a population and we stratify by language group, and language group is not related to height, the stratification is worthless.

4.2.1.4 Cluster sampling

If, say, we draw a simple or stratified random sample of 300 households in Pretoria, the addresses would be spread over the whole of the city. Ten of them would probably be in Lynnwood, but Lynnwood extends over such a large area that an interviewer would have to travel many kilometres just to make one call on each of the cases in Lynnwood. Even then the interviewer would have no assurance that the elements at those addresses would be at home when he called the first time. Second and even third calls might be necessary. Cluster sampling saves costs and time. By applying the cluster method we can draw a simple or stratified random sample of, say, 30 households and then interview nine further households in the immediate vicinity of each of the 30 addresses, instructing the interviewer to call at a specific address, then at the three closest addresses to the right, the three to the left and the three directly opposite.

The interviewer can do this far more easily than calling at ten addresses in different parts of Lynnwood, thus saving both time and costs. However, in keeping with the saying that birds of a feather flock together, the well-to-do are inclined to live in the well-to-do neighbourhoods. Any language or culture group tries to live near its schools and churches. In new areas we find mainly young people, and in older areas mainly old people.

It is therefore possible that the address drawn in Lynnwood is situated in the elite part of the suburb where most of the well-to-do live. But the address may also be close to the Afrikaans primary school in an area with relatively many young Afrikaans-speaking couples whose children are still at primary school. This group may be different from the representative inhabitant of Lynnwood in that their income is lower, they are younger, a larger percentage are Afrikaans-speaking and there are relatively more young children in their households. Therefore there may be considerable differences between them and the inhabitants of Lynnwood in general in the aspects under study.

If certain socio-economic groups are inclined to live close together, a number of cases spread over the whole area are more representative than a number of cases drawn in one vicinity. The extent to which elements spread over an entire area are more representative of the area than the elements from one vicinity is dependent on the strength of the tendency for socio-economic groups in the area to live close together.

In the calculation of sample error the averages of the clusters are regarded as the elements of the sample. Thus a sample comprising, say, 30 clusters has only 30 elements because only 30 independent selections have been made. In section 4.2.2.1 (d) we shall discuss the effects of variability within and between clusters.

4.2.1.5 Two- and multi-stage sampling

In section 2 we saw that a sample may have more than one stage. For example, if we want to draw a sample of 4 000 households in metropolitan areas in South Africa, we first draw metropolitan areas (the first stage), then residential areas (second stage), then residential blocks (third stage) and then the elements, say smokers (final stage). With two- or multi-stage sampling we may face either or both of two problems. The sample units of a specific stage, for example metropolitan areas, are not the same size and, secondly, they may not be identifiable in advance, for example the smokers in a specific house. Methods of dealing with these problems will be discussed in section 5.

4.2.2 Sample size and sample error

We started this chapter with a research problem, that of determining the average amount spent on textbooks by 125 000 Unisa students in 1995. It was immediately clear that it would be too costly and time consuming to contact all of the students and that we would have to undertake a sample survey. Suppose that our employer agrees on a sample survey under the following conditions: we must be able to state with 95 % confidence that our sample statistic will not differ from the population statistic by more than R100. This means that if we obtain a sample statistic of R2 000, we should be 95 % confident that the population statistic will be somewhere between R1 900 and R2 100.

From what we have learned of various sampling methods so far, we know that we can only consider a probability sampling method because we have to calculate the sample error statistically. In this section we shall explain how to do this. This explanation is rooted in an understanding of the central limit theorem and the normal distribution.

(a) Central limit theorem

This theorem states that, regardless of the shape of the population distribution, the various arithmetic means $(\bar{x})$* of a large number of random samples, each composed of the same number of elements from the same population, will distribute themselves around the population mean (μ) in a *normal curve* (see figure 13.1) described as the distribution of sampling means. The arithmetic mean of all possible samples is equal to the population mean.

(b) Normal distribution

The normal distribution is a symmetrical, continuous, bell-shaped distribution or curve (see figure 13.1). It is called a two-parameter distribution because the probability function can be specified completely by two parameters μ and σ. If μ (the population mean) and σ (the standard deviation) are known, everything about the probability distribution is known. The normal distribution is symmetrical around its mean μ. The percentage of the area lying between the mean value (μ) and any number of standard deviations is the same for all normal curves. For example, 38,30 % of the area under the normal curve is

---

* Statistical symbols are explained in table A-5 in the appendix.

Figure 13.1 Sampling distribution of the sample means

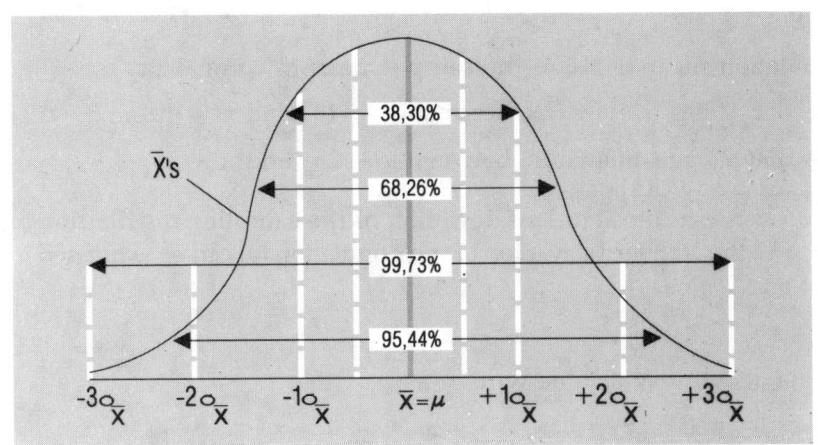

between the mean value and plus or minus 0,5 standard deviations, 68,26 % of the area is between the mean value and plus or minus 1,0 standard deviations, 95,44 % of the area is between the mean value and plus or minus 2 standard deviations, etc.*

If we draw several thousand samples, each with size n, from a universe of, say, 125 000 Unisa students and calculate the average amount spent on textbooks by the students in each of these samples, we should have several thousand 'sample means'. According to the central limit theorem the average of these several thousand sample means would be exactly equal to the population mean. We can therefore calculate the population mean simply by calculating the average of these sample means. The central limit theorem further states that the sample means will distribute themselves around the population mean in a normal curve. According to figure 13.1, the central limit theorem states, for example, that 68,3 % of these sample averages will lie within a range of $-1\sigma_{\bar{x}}$ and $+\sigma_{\bar{x}}$ of the population average; or that 95,4 % will lie within a range of $-2\sigma_{\bar{x}}$ and $+2\sigma_{\bar{x}}$ of the population mean. We can therefore say that if we draw only one sample with size n there is a 68,3 % possibility that we have drawn one of the samples whose mean falls within the range of $-1\sigma_{\bar{x}}$ and $+1\sigma_{\bar{x}}$. And there is a 95,4 % possibility that we have drawn one of the samples in the range of $-2\sigma_{\bar{x}}$ and $+2\sigma_{\bar{x}}$ of the population mean.

This shows that we can make probability statements on the range of possible values assumed by a sample mean. This range, which can be calculated if we can get a value for the standard deviation of the sample distribution ($\sigma_{\bar{x}}$), is known as the confidence interval. The probability of a sample mean falling within the confidence interval is known as the confidence coefficient or level. The confidence intervals for various confidence

---

* The percentages of the area between the mean value and any number of standard deviations are given in table A-1 in the appendix.

coefficients can be read from figure 13.1 or table A-1* in the appendix.

For example:

If the population mean is μ and the sample mean, $\bar{x}$, probability is:

(a) 68,3 % that $\bar{x}$ lies somewhere between $\mu - 1\sigma_{\bar{x}}$ and $\mu + 1\sigma_{\bar{x}}$ and

(b) 95,4 % that $\bar{x}$ lies somewhere between $\mu - 2\sigma_{\bar{x}}$ and $\mu + 2\sigma_{\bar{x}}$

The relation between the standard deviation of the sampling distribution ($\sigma_{\bar{x}}$), the sample size (n) and the standard deviation of the population (σ) can be expressed in the formula

$$\sigma_{\bar{x}} = \frac{\sigma}{\sqrt{n}}$$

The formula above may also be written as:

$$\sqrt{n} = \frac{\sigma}{\sigma_{\bar{x}}} \text{ or } n = \frac{\sigma^2}{\sigma_{\bar{x}}^2}$$

As can be seen in the formula, the sample size is determined by the size of the standard deviation of the population (σ) and the size of the standard deviation of the distribution of the sample means ($\sigma_{\bar{x}}$). The standard deviation of the population is constant. Therefore if we are able to establish or estimate it, the size of the sample required will be determined by the size of the standard deviation of the distribution of sample means (also termed sample error).

The sample error in turn is determined by the allowable error and the confidence interval required. Suppose we estimate that Unisa students spend R2 000 on average on textbooks, and we wish to state at a 95 % level of confidence that our sample average will vary by R100 at most (allowable error) from the population average. Our allowable sample error (not to be confused with the allowable error) is calculated by the formula:

$$\sigma_{\bar{x}} = \frac{E}{Z}$$

where E = allowable error (in our example above it is R100)

　　　　Z = number of standard deviation units in the normal distribution that will yield the desired level of confidence (as indicated in table A-1, it is 1,96 at a 95 % confidence level).

$$\sigma_{\bar{x}} = \frac{R100}{1,96}$$
$$= R51,00$$

* The number of standard deviations from the mean is given as Z-values in table A-1. Suppose we want to find the percentage of the total area of the normal curve between the mean and 1 standard deviation in table A-1. Next to Z = 1,000 we find the figure 0,3413. That is the portion of one half of the normal curve that lies between the mean and 1 standard deviation. The portion of both halves will therefore be 0,3413 × 2 = 2 = 0,6826 or 68,26 %.

Using the formula

$$n = \frac{\sigma^2}{\sigma_{\bar{x}}^2}$$

the required sample size can be calculated next, provided we are able to estimate the standard deviation of the population. Suppose we estimate it at R1 200, then the sample size required is

$$n = \frac{(1\ 200)^2}{(51)^2}$$

$$= 553$$

The formula for calculating the allowable sample error and the sample size can be combined as

$$\sigma_{\bar{x}} = \frac{E}{Z}$$

and

$$\sigma_{\bar{x}}^2 = \frac{E^2}{Z^2}$$

or

$$n = \frac{\sigma^2}{\sigma_{\bar{x}}^2}$$

$$n = \frac{\sigma^2 Z^2}{E^2} \text{ (substituting } \sigma_{\bar{x}}^2 \text{ by } \frac{E^2}{Z^2})$$

$$n = \frac{1\ 200^2\ (1,96)^2}{100^2}$$

$$= 553$$

(c) Determination of the standard deviation of the population

As we have seen in the previous section we need a probability sample of 553 students to be able to state with 95 % confidence that our sample statistic will not differ from our population statistic by more than R100. In this calculation we assumed that the standard deviation of the population (σ) is R1 200. An approximate value of the standard deviation of the population is obtained as follows:

(i) The standard deviations of previous similar studies may give us some indication of the standard deviation. Ten years ago a similar study may have been undertaken. Suppose the standard deviation then was R400. If we estimate that spending since that time has increased by 200 %, but can find no reason for change in the spending distribution, the standard deviation should be about R1 200.

(ii) A pilot survey could also be used to get some indication of the standard deviation.

(iii) Or an estimate could be made from finding the difference between the least and the greatest amount spent by a student. This difference ought to be equal to approximately 6 standard deviations, 3 standard deviations below and 3 above the mean.

The estimate of the standard deviation should not be too low because if it is lower than the actual standard deviation the sample will also be too small to assure the required precision.

Estimates based on sample surveys are always subject to sample variations and so is the standard deviation estimated from sample survey data. If, for example, we found in a previous sample survey that average expenditure was X and we want to be able to state at a 95 % level of confidence that the population mean μ does not deviate by more than 5 %, it would be safer to assume that the standard deviation of the sample is subject to the same degree of variation as average expenditure. Thus it may also deviate by 5 % at the 95 % level of confidence from the standard deviation of the population. Therefore the probability is 95 % that the standard deviation of the population will be between 1 140 and 1 260 (1 200 ± 5 %), or the probability is 5 % that it will not lie between 1 140 and 1 260. In other words the probability is 2,5 % that it will be below 1 140 and 2,5 % that it will lie above 1 260. Therefore we may state at a 97,5 % level of confidence that the standard deviation will be 1 260 at most. If it is 1 260, our required sample is 610.

4.2.2.1 Sample size of an infinite population

In this section we shall discuss the sample size of infinite populations. The proportion any sample represents of an infinite population is so small that it may be ignored. In the next section we shall see that when the sample is less than 8 % of the population it makes very little difference whether the population is infinite or finite in size. In marketing research samples it very seldom represents more than 8 % of the population. In determining sample size the fact that all populations are finite may therefore be ignored most of the time.

(a) Sample size of a simple random sample when estimating population mean

In section 4.2.2(b) we arrived at the following formula for determining the sample size:

$$n = \frac{\sigma^2 Z^2}{E^2}$$

This is the formula for calculating the size of a simple random sample when estimating the population mean. The allowable error (E) and the standard deviation (σ) can also be expressed as their respective percentages of the actual population mean (μ). Then the applicable formula is:

$$n = \frac{Z^2(\sigma \text{ as a percentage of population mean})^2}{(E \text{ as a percentage of population mean})^2}$$

$$= \frac{Z^2(\frac{\sigma}{M} \times 100)^2}{(\frac{E}{M} \times 100)^2}$$

If we want to be 95 % certain that our sample mean is within 10 % of the actual population mean, and we estimate the standard deviation of the population at 60 % of the population mean, we can find n by using this formula:

$$n = \frac{1,96^2(60)^2}{(5)^2}$$

$$= 553$$

Say we find, after preparing a cost estimate on the basis of this sample size, that our employer is not prepared to pay so much for the survey. Yet he wishes to continue the survey and to follow the original approach. The only alternative is to revise the employer's required degree of precision by raising the allowable error of, say, R100 to R150 and/or lowering the confidence level of 95 % to, say, 90 %.

If we raise the allowable error of R100 to R150 the required sample size will be

$$\frac{1\ 200^2 \times 1,96^2}{150^2} = 246$$

It is less than half the size of the original sample.

If we lower the confidence level of 95 % to 90 % the required sample size will be

$$\frac{1\ 200^2 \times 1,64^2}{100^2} = 387$$

If we raise the allowable error of R100 to R150 and lower the confidence level of 95 % to 90 %, the required sample size will be

$$\frac{1\ 200^2 \times 1,64^2}{150^2} = 172.$$

(b) Sample size of a stratified sample when estimating population mean

When estimating population mean we can use the following formula to arrive at the stratified sample size:

$$n = \frac{Z^2}{E^2} \Sigma W_i \sigma_i^2$$

where Z^2 and E^2 represent the same as in previous formulae, and W_i is the weight of stratum i, and σ_i is the standard deviation of stratum i.

In the previous example the standard deviation for the population was set at R1 200. We now assume two strata of respectively 70 % and 30 % of the population and standard deviations of R1 000 and R800, still keeping the allowable error at R100. Substituting the appropriate values we get

$$n = \frac{(1,96)^2}{100^2} [(0,7)(1\ 000)^2 + (0,3)(800)^2]$$

$$= \frac{3,84}{10\ 000} [(0,7)(1\ 000\ 000) + (0,3)(640\ 000)]$$

$$= 3,84 \left(\frac{700\ 000 + 192\ 000}{10\ 000}\right)$$

$$= 3,84\ (89,20)$$

$$= 343$$

The sample sizes for each stratum are determined as

$$n_1 = W_1 n = 0,7 \times 343 = 240$$
$$n_2 = W_2 n = 0,3 \times 343 = 103$$

As you will remember, the required sample in the unstratified sample was 553, which is far greater than in the stratified sample. The reason for the drastic fall is the expected smaller standard deviations of the strata. If these standard deviations were kept at R120, a sample size of 553 would still be needed.

(c) *Optimum allocation of a disproportionate stratified sample*

In the previous example we had two strata representing 70 % and 30 % of the population respectively, with standard deviations of R1 000 and R800. We can now use the following formula to calculate the optimum allocation of the sample to these two strata:

$$nA = \frac{nNA\sigma_A}{NA\sigma_A + NB\sigma_B + \ldots}$$

where nA = optimum sample size to take from stratum A

$\quad n$ = total sample size

$\quad NA$ = proportion of population in stratum A

$\quad \sigma_A$ = standard deviation of stratum A

$\quad NB$ = proportion of population in stratum B

$\quad \sigma_B$ = standard deviation of stratum B

$$nA = \frac{343(0,7)(1\ 000)}{(0,7 \times 1\ 000) + (0,3 \times 800)}$$

$$= 255$$

$$nB = \frac{343(0,3)(800)}{940}$$

$$= 88$$

(d) Sample size of a cluster random sample when estimating the population mean (cluster sampling)

Cluster sampling almost always produces larger sampling errors than other probability samples of the same size. The reason is that fewer independent selections are being made. For example, if we select 10 clusters of 5 each we do only 10 independent selections. We can think of a cluster sample as a simple random sample whose elements consist of the means of the clusters. Take the following example:

We draw the following four clusters, each consisting of four elements:

$$
\begin{array}{lccccccc}
 & & & & & & & Means \\
\text{Cluster 1:} & 5 & 6 & 5 & 17 & = & 8,25 \\
\text{Cluster 2:} & 9 & 2 & 6 & 12 & = & 7,25 \\
\text{Cluster 3:} & 12 & 13 & 13 & 15 & = & 13,50 \\
\text{Cluster 4:} & 8 & 7 & 11 & 18 & = & 11,00 \\
\end{array}
$$

Considering the means as the elements of a simple random sample, the variance, standard deviation and standard error are calculated as follows:

$$
\text{variance } (v) = \frac{\displaystyle\sum_{i=1}^{n} (x_i - \bar{x})^2}{n - 1}
$$

$$
= \frac{(8,25 - 10)^2 + (7,25 - 10)^2 + (13,50 - 10)^2 + (11,00 - 10)^2}{3}
$$

$$
= 7,96
$$

$$
\text{standard deviation } (\sigma) = \sqrt{v} = 2,82
$$

$$
\text{standard error } (\sigma_{\bar{x}}) = \frac{\sigma}{\sqrt{n}} = \frac{2,82}{\sqrt{4}} = 1,4
$$

If we assume that all 16 observations were made independently and are therefore elements of a simple random sample, we arrive at a standard error of 1,2 which is not much smaller than the 1,4 of the cluster sample. If we exchange the 2 in cluster no 2 for the 15 in cluster no 3, we obtain cluster means of 8,25, 10,50, 10,15 and 11,00 and a cluster standard error of 1,2, which is the same as the simple random sample.

(e) Sample size when estimating population proportion

Except that here we are dealing with a percentage, determination of the sample size is very much the same as determination of the sample mean. The formula is:

$$
n = \frac{Z^2 P(1 - P)}{E^2}
$$

where n = the required sample size

    Z = number of standard deviation units in the normal distribution that will produce the desired level of confidence

    P = estimated proportion of the population who possess the characteristic of interest

    E = allowable error

Suppose we want to determine the sample size required to estimate the percentage of Unisa students who use imported books, and want to be able to say with 95 % confidence that the sample statistic will not differ from the population statistic by more than 4 %. We estimated that at least 70 % of the students use imported books.

$$n = \frac{(1,96)^2(0,7)(0,3)}{(,04)^2}$$

$$= 504,2$$

To make sure we reach a confidence coefficient of 95 %, we raise 504,2 to 505.

If we have no idea beforehand of what percentage of the population has the characteristic of interest, we must be conservative and take it as 50 %. The sample size is in proportion to the product P(1–P), which is greatest when P = 0,5. See what happens when we substitute 0,5 for 0,7 in the previous example:

$$n = \frac{(1,96)^2 \, (0,5) \, (0,5)}{(,04)^2}$$

$$= 600,3$$

    $\therefore$ the sample size increases by 20 %.

4.2.2.2 Sample size when estimating mean of a finite population

The following formula can be used to calculate the sample size when estimating the population mean of a finite population:

$$n = \frac{\sigma^2}{\dfrac{E^2}{Z^2} + \dfrac{\sigma^2}{N}}$$

where N is the population size.

If we set the value of N at 1 000 and keep the other values and requirements the same as our example in section 4.2.2.1 (a), we get a sample size of 356, so that the sample represents about 36 % of the population. However, if we fix the population at 1 000 000, the sample size remains 553, as previously calculated by the formula for an infinite population. The sample now represents 0,06 % of the population.

These examples show clearly that only when the population is relatively small does it affect the size of the sample. If we calculate the sample size by the first formula and find that it represents less than 8 % of the population we can be satisfied with the sample size so obtained. A sample seldom represents as much as 8 % of the population, and therefore the formula for an infinite population is the one normally used.

5 SELECTION OF SAMPLE ELEMENTS

In section 4.1 we discussed the selection of the elements of non-probability samples. In convenience sampling respondents are selected on the basis of convenience or availability and in quota sampling according to some pre-specified characteristics. In judgement sampling the researcher uses his own judgement as to which units and elements he considers representative of the study population.

The use of random numbers in selecting a simple random sample or subsamples of a stratified sample is explained in section 4.2 and the selection of the first and nth units in systematic sampling is discussed.

In section 4.2.1.5 we saw that two problems frequently arise in two- and multi-stage sampling: the population units of a specific stage are not the same size, and the units of a specific stage are not only not the same size but are also not identified in advance.

(a) The population units of a specific stage are not of the same size and can be identified in advance

Suppose we want to determine the average commission earned by salespeople in a manufacturing establishment. Let us take the following simple example: there are ten ten firms with a total sales personnel of 960 and we want to interview ten salespeople at each of four firms.

Thus in the first stage we have to select four firms and in the second stage ten salespeople from each of these firms. Table 13.4 on page 272 shows the ten firms with the number of sales personnel in each, and the cumulative totals of the sales personnel of all ten firms.

Say that from a table with three-digit random numbers the four numbers selected were 139, 952, 661 and 370.

All selected numbers from 1 to 200 indicate the inclusion of firm A, from 201 to 360 firm B, from 361 to 500 firm C, etc. Thus 139 indicates the inclusion of firm A, 952 of firm J, 661 of firm E and 370 of firm C.

The ten salespeople in each of the firms A, C, E and J can now be drawn by obtaining lists of names from the firms and using random numbers, as explained in section 3.1.

Table 13.4 Sales personnel employed by ten firms

Firms	Sales personnel	Cumulative totals of sales personnel
A	200	200
B	160	360
C	130	500
D	120	620
E	100	720
F	80	800
G	60	860
H	50	910
I	30	940
J	20	960

A firm's probability of being included is equal to the ratio of its sales personnel to the sales personnel of all the firms. This means that the probability that firm A will be included is 200/960 and firm J 20/960. Therefore big firms have a high probability and small firms a low probability of being included. However, these probabilities are reversed when the ten salespeople are drawn in the second stage in each of the selected firms, so that a salesperson in firm A has a 10/200 probability of being drawn, and one in firm J a 10/20 probability. The total probability for individual salespeople of firms A and J being drawn is the same, namely 1/24. In firm A it is 200/960 × 10/200 × 4, and in firm J it is 20/960 × 10/20 × 4.

(b) The population units of a specific stage are not of the same size and cannot be identified in advance

In the above example we know the number of salespeople employed by each manufacturer, but let us assume we do not know the number of sales personnel for each manufacturer beforehand. We only know that the ten manufacturers employ about 1 000 salespeople in total. We still want to approach only four of the ten manufacturers and a total of 40 salespeople. We can now select the four manufacturers at random. If we succeed in selecting a complete random sample, the four manufacturers should employ a total of about 400 salespeople.* To select 40 salespeople we have to select 10 % of the salespeople of each of the selected manufacturers on a random basis.

---

* In our example it is highly unlikely that we will select a completely random sample because our universe of 10 and sample of 4 are too small. However, if we select a sample of, say, 200 from a universe of 1 000, we can expect to select a random sample, except when a few manufacturers employ a large proportion of the total sales personnel.

If in the final stage, for one reason or another, we want to interview only one element living at a particular address, we must give the element we do interview a weight equal to the total number of elements living at that address. In practice there is often an error in two- or multi-stage sampling in that in the first phase the sample units are all given the same probability of being selected as in the example above but in the second phase they are not. For example, in a survey among smokers, the smokers' addresses are not available and so addresses of households are drawn in the first phase. Now, when the interviewer goes to the relevant address, he has to draw only one smoker even if there are two or more smokers living at that address.

In this situation weighting must be applied or the sample becomes unrepresentative, because smokers in a household where there is only one smoker have twice as much chance of being drawn as smokers in households where there are two smokers.

Suppose that in a survey of smokers the sample is drawn from addresses of residences. In all of these residences the household consists of a husband and a wife. Suppose that all the men but only half of the women smoke. In 100 households there are therefore 100 male smokers as opposed to 50 female smokers. In other words, 66,7 % of the smokers are male and 33,3 % are female. If we draw a perfect random sample of 100 and where more than one smoker is found, select only one on a random basis, we may find the following situation: 50 households where only the husband smokes (in other words, where the husband will be interviewed) and 50 households where the husband and the wife smoke (in other words where 25 men and 25 women will be interviewed). We have therefore covered 75 males and 25 females in our survey. Men are therefore overrepresented and women underrepresented. By assigning a weight of 1 where there is only one smoker and a weight of 2 where there are two smokers the situation can be corrected. Then the one-smoker households will have a weight of 50, as opposed to a weight of 100 (50 × 2) for two-smoker households. Thus the total weight for male smokers will be 100 (50 + 50) and for female smokers 50, which is 66,7 % as opposed to 33,3 % – the same as the population.

The element to be interviewed can be selected merely by finding out the dates of birth of the elements and then interviewing the one whose birthday is the earliest in the year. In most studies an individual born in January, say, in no way differs from one born in July. But if, for example, they are asked whether annual bonuses should be paid at the end of the employee's birthday month or in the middle of the year, the respondent born before June will be inclined to vote for the employee's birthday month and those born after June will vote for June.

However, use of the Kish selection box technique ensures that a respondent can be selected randomly in all circumstances. Table 13.5 illustrates this.

Table 13.5 Kish selection box

Name of potential respondent	Last digits of questionnaire numbers									
	0	1	2	3	4	5	6	7	8	9
(1) Dave	1	1	1	1	1	1	1	1	1	1
(2) Jack	1	2	1	2	1	2	1	2	1	2
(3) Jean	1	2	3	1	2	3	1	2	3	1
(4) John	2	3	4	1	2	3	4	1	2	3
(5) ...	4	5	1	2	3	4	5	1	2	3

In the left of the selection box provision is made for the first names of possible respondents, and in the top right for all possible last digits of questionnaires.

Suppose there are four possible respondents (smokers) in a household and the number of the questionnaire is 128. The potential respondents are then listed alphabetically as, say,

(1) Dave
(2) Jack
(3) Jean
(4) John

The last digit of the questionnaire number is 8. Now a vertical line is drawn from digit 8 downward and a horizontal line starting from the last name is drawn to the right. Number 2 in the selection grid is the coordinate of the two lines and the number of the person to be interviewed. In our example this is Jack.

6 SUMMARY

Sample surveys save time and costs in marketing research. Despite being subject to sample variations, the data gathered in sample surveys are frequently more accurate than census data because the relatively smaller number of interviewers required in sample surveys can be thoroughly trained and supervised.

The following five steps are distinguished in sampling: defining the population, identifying the sample frame, selecting the sampling method, determining the sample size, and selecting the sample elements. Sampling methods can be divided into two broad categories: probability and non-probability samples. A probability sample is one in which every element has a known non-zero probability of being selected. Non-probability samples rely on the judgement of the researcher and are only as representative as the researcher's luck and skill permit. In non-probability sampling there is no way of estimating the probability that any element will be included in the sample, and therefore there is no method of finding out whether the sample is representative of the population.

Three types of non-probability sampling are distinguished: convenience sampling, quota sampling, and judgement sampling. In convenience sampling, as the name implies, respondents are selected on the basis of convenience or availability. In a quota sample the researcher takes explicit steps to obtain a sample similar to the population in some pre-specified characteristics. A judgement sample is one in which the researcher attempts to draw a representative sample of the population by using judgemental selection procedure.

There are five types of probability sampling: simple random sampling, systematic sampling, stratified sampling, cluster sampling, and multi-stage sampling. Simple random sampling is unique in that all elements in the population have a known equal chance of being included in the sample. Systematic sampling produces much the same result as does simple random sampling, but is far easier to apply. A stratified sample is a probability sample which differs in two respects from the simple random or systematic sample. First the population is divided into segments or strata and then the drawing is done in every stratum exactly as in simple random or systematic sampling. By applying the cluster method we can draw a simple or stratified random sample of, say, 30 households and then interview nine further households in the immediate vicinity of each of the 30 addresses.

The sample size is determined by the size of the standard deviation of the population (σ) and the size of the standard deviation of the distribution of the sample means ($\sigma_{\bar{x}}$). The standard deviation of the population is constant. Therefore if we are able to establish or estimate it, the size of the sample required will be determined by the size of the standard deviation of the distribution of sample means (also termed sample error).

The sample error in turn is determined by the allowable error and the confidence interval required.

REFERENCE

Luck, David J, Wales, Hugh G, Taylor, Donald A & Rubin, Ronald S 1982. *Marketing research*. Sixth edition. Englewood Cliffs, NJ: Prentice Hall.

Survey errors

Chapter 14: M Loubser

1 INTRODUCTION

Reference has been made in previous chapters to the errors that slip in during the collection of primary data (chapters 7, 8, 9 and 10); the design of the questionnaire (chapter 11); the selection, training and control of interviewers (chapter 12); and sampling (chapter 13). These and other errors fall into three basic types: errors of definition, estimation and explanation (see figure 14.1 on page 278). In this chapter we shall deal with survey errors and the ways in which the researcher can keep them to a minimum.

2 ERRORS OF DEFINITION

As we have said in chapter 5 it is important to begin with a precise definition of the problem, and then determine the associated variables. If we assume that the decline in the sales of a given product are due to our product, price or distribution policy and ignore our advertising policy, which is at the root of the trouble, we are in danger of undertaking a comprehensive investigation without getting any nearer to the solution to our problem. What is needed is an exploratory investigation to ensure that the problem has been correctly defined.

3 ERRORS OF ESTIMATION

Under 'errors of estimation' Cox (1979:57) includes

☐ measurement errors

☐ frame errors

☐ non-response errors

☐ selection errors

☐ sampling errors.

Figure 14.1 Survey errors

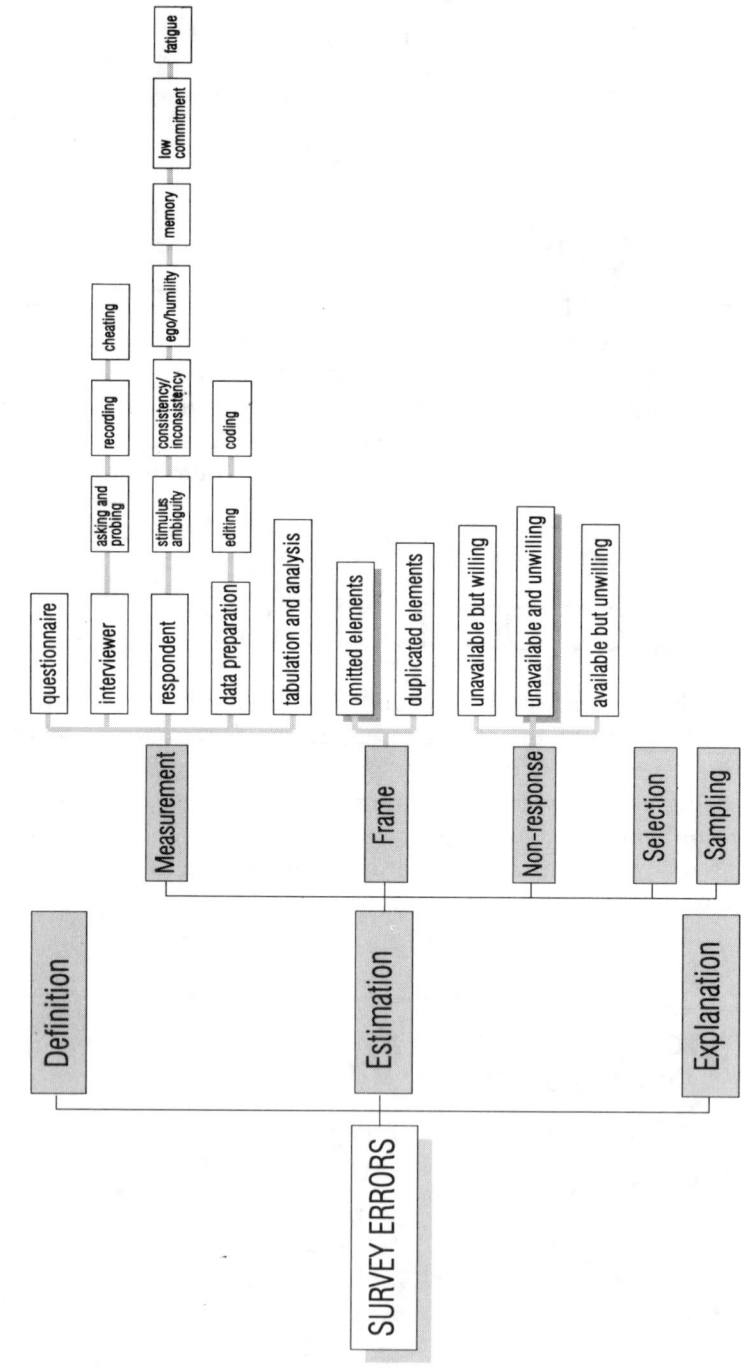

3.1 Measurement errors

Measurement errors originate in poorly designed questionnaires, the reluctance or inability of the interviewer to elicit the required information from the respondent, and the reluctance and inability of the respondent to provide it. As we have already discussed the requirements for designing questionnaires in chapter 11 we shall turn our attention here to the last two types of measurement errors.

3.1.1 Interviewer errors

Proper attention to selection and training may restrict interviewers' errors but cannot wholly eliminate them. Churchill (1992:563) points out three types of error caused by the interviewer's behaviour:

☐ errors in asking questions and in probing when additional information is required

☐ errors in recording the answer

☐ errors because of cheating.

Errors in asking questions consist mainly of reading errors, speech variations and feedbacks to the respondents, such as suggesting answers, using leading probes and changing the wording of questions (Bradburn 1979:29). These errors can be limited by proper interviewer training.

Guest and Nuckols (1950:336–352) found that of all *errors made in recording responses*, 45 % to 56 % were clerical errors, such as omitting questions, writing down answers incorrectly and deviating from the sample plan. Further, interviewers are inclined to hear what they want to hear. As Trull (1964:89–94) says:

> The interviewer must be aware of his/her own particular filters that tend to impede, if not prevent, clear and relatively undistorted reception of information. It is possible to hear at the rate of 110 to 140 words per minute over sustained periods. The thinking or thought projection rate is approximately seven times this figure. The result is surplus thinking time over listening time. The manner in which this surplus thinking time over listening time is utilized varies, of course, with the individual. However, it is at this point that the interviewer tends to project his ideas into the interview process, thereby filtering out the interviewee's responses.

Since an interviewer's obvious attributes, such as race, sex and age, may possibly influence the response, as far as possible these attributes should be the same as those of the respondent. In working with South Africa's heterogeneous population groups with their significant cultural differences, a researcher cannot afford to ignore the possible influence of the interviewer, as a member of a given population group, on the response of the interviewee. If the respondent and the interviewer belong to different population groups this single factor can cause such bias in the results as to make them of little or no value.

The interviewer may deliberately *cheat* by fabricating data so that his task is over and done with. In a study by the American Jewish Committee (Hyman 1954:26) 15 interviewers each interviewed four 'planted' respondents, who had undertaken to assume the role of very difficult people. All 15 interviewers cheated either by not asking the questions but recording answers to them, or by recording responses without having obtained any answer from the respondent.

To restrict their errors in general, and cheating in particular, interviewers must know that their work is being controlled. The most common methods of control are to contact respondents afterwards by telephone or post, or personally, to edit the interviewer's work and to carry out computer checks.

Churchill (1992:566) maintains that follow-up by post or telephone is a good way of tracing flagrant cheating, but not so effective for tracing more subtle methods of cheating. He lists some forms of 'subtle cheating':

☐ The interviewer asks only the key questions and later fills in the remaining information.

☐ The interviewer interviews respondents in groups rather than separately as instructed.

☐ The interviewer interviews the 'wrong' respondent because the designated respondent is inaccessible or difficult to contact.

☐ The interviewer employs one contact for information for two separate studies and thereby introduces contamination through respondent fatigue.

In research done by Hauck (1969:117–120) on the effectiveness of postcard verification a thank-you letter with reply-paid postcards was sent to 587 respondents who had been interviewed in a survey and to 580 persons who had not been interviewed in the survey. The postcards were returned by 49,1 % of those interviewed in the survey but by only 9,5 % of those not interviewed. Of those who had been interviewed and responded, 97,9 % confirmed that they had been interviewed, and the remaining 2,1 % confirmed – after they had been contacted by telephone – that they had been interviewed and could even remember some of their answers. Evidently they had either forgotten the interview, or another member of the family, who had known nothing of the interview, had answered the postcard. Of the persons not interviewed 85,5 % said that they had not been interviewed and the rest said that they had been interviewed.

The findings of this study suggest that the postal method of verification is not a very sound method of interviewer control. As in most mail surveys, a large percentage of the respondents do not react, and those who do may be only those that have been interviewed. The personal call-back check is usually undertaken by a supervisor who has worked in an area other than where the control takes place. The supervisor's first duty is to take with him the questionnaire which was completed initially (or a copy of it) so that any divergence can be traced immediately after the interview. This enables a supervisor to ascertain immediately whether a given interviewer's work is suspect. If it is, he should check a fairly large percentage of the interviewer's work. Between 10 % and 20 % of the respondents questioned in the initial questionnaire are usually re-interviewed. Callback checks must take place as soon as possible after the initial questioning, especially where respondents are asked for their opinions, for these so easily change.

Further, at the editing stage the individual interviewer's questionnaires can be checked to find out whether the necessary filter questions have been asked, whether the initial instructions have been strictly adhered to, and whether there are any patterned responses from individual interviewers.

Computer checks are often carried out on interviewers, the results obtained by each interviewer being compared with those obtained by the other interviewers.

3.1.2 Respondent errors

The following six types of error resulting from the respondent's reluctance or inability to provide true answers can be distinguished:

☐ stimulus ambiguity

☐ consistency/inconsistency error

☐ ego/humility error

☐ memory error

☐ low commitment

☐ fatigue.

3.1.2.1 Stimulus ambiguity

The accuracy of a respondent's reporting may be affected by motivation appeals. For example, in an income and expenditure pattern survey among consumers, respondents may be motivated in various ways to cooperate. They may be told, for example, that the information is needed for production and marketing planning. Thus, from the motivation perspective, they would have no reason for over- or under-reporting income or expenditure. Suppose, on the other hand, that to motivate respondents the researcher explains that the information is needed to determine consumers' needs with a view to finding out whether their incomes are sufficient for their needs. This may well result in over-reporting, because consumers may think that the more they over-report their expenses the more wages are likely to increase. From the interviewer's point of view, the respondent's cooperation will probably be easier to win by the latter motivation, which would make respondents feel more involved, than by the former.

3.1.2.2 Consistent/inconsistent error

A respondent who wants to represent himself as a certain type of person or consumer may consistently give answers he thinks are expected of this type of person or consumer. Therefore having expressed the opinion in answer to a previous question that smoking is the major cause of heart disease and that he intends to remain healthy, the respondent then feels obliged to say that he does not smoke, though in fact he is a moderate smoker. (Besides illustrating a consistency error, this answer shows how the sequence of questions in a questionnaire can influence respondents' answers.) Inconsistency is sometimes deliberately indulged in by a respondent for the sake of making himself seem 'interesting'. For example, the respondent is aware of the danger of smoking, but does nothing to prevent his children from smoking. In that way he tries to convey to the interviewer that he does not interfere with what other people do, not even his children.

3.1.2.3 Ego/humility error

A study by Martins (1982:5) revealed that the ego/humility error was probably the greatest single respondent error in expenditure surveys. The ego/humility error occurs as systematic under-reporting in some product groups and in others as systematic over-reporting. Table 14.1 is compiled from figures in BMR report no 98:11. The information in column 2 of table 14.1 was obtained from secondary sources and can therefore be considered fairly accurate. Under- and over-reporting of expenditure by households may be put forward as the main reasons for the differences between columns 1 and 2. With alcoholic beverages, under-reporting amounts to 213,2 %, which may be ascribed to the negative status associated with high alcohol consumption. Over-reporting on personal care amounts to 21,6 %, which may be ascribed to the positive status associated with personal care consumption.

To prevent the humility error in reporting, the BMR asked respondents in an evaluation study how much, in their opinion, the average household spent on alcoholic drinks. On the grounds of the information thus obtained under-reporting amounted to only 25,7 %.

Respondents report their spending on deodorants as higher than it really is because people who do not use deodorants are associated with lack of education. Respondents over-report their spending on newspapers because they want to represent themselves as keeping abreast of the news.

One way of restricting the ego error is for the researcher to begin with questions which give respondents a chance to report abnormally high spending and then to set a question

Table 14.1 A comparison of market potentials calculated from income and expenditure survey data and secondary data (all population groups)

Expenditure item	Expenditure data (1) R'000	Secondary data (2) R'000	Difference (Column 1 − Column 2)	
			Amount R'000	Percentage of column 1 %
Alcoholic beverages				
Malt, beer	**116 618**	**345 489**	− 228 871	− 196,3
Sorghum beer	36 672	88 276	− 51 604	− 140,7
Brandy	70 138	194 185	− 124 047	− 176,9
Gin	11 229	28 370	− 17 141	− 152,6
Cane spirits	15 944	84 723	− 68 779	− 431,4
Whisky	30 905	67 241	− 36 336	− 117,6
Vodka	6 843	36 108	− 29 265	− 427,7
Wine	52 342	232 367	− 180 025	− 343,9
Other	5 909	8 670	− 2 761	− 46,7
Total	**346 600**	**1 085 429**	− 738 829	− 213,2
Personal care				
Shampoos	16 811	11 915	4 896	29,1
Deodorants	25 079	11 009	14 070	56,1
Other	114 986	100 123	14 863	12,9
Total	**156 876**	**123 047**	33 829	21,6
Newspapers and magazines				
Newspapers	67 518	54 001	13 517	20,0
Magazines	21 106	20 314	792	3,8
Total	**88 624**	**74 315**	14 309	16,1

to which an honest answer may be expected. The interviewer, for example, may begin by asking: 'Which of the following newspapers have you bought in the past month?' Next he asks: 'Which of the following newspapers, if any, did you buy yesterday?'

3.1.2.4 Memory errors

A respondent may have completely forgotten about buying a certain article; or he may remember buying it but have forgotten when he bought it. If he is asked whether and how often he bought such an article during the past year, he may easily over-report or under-report: the former because he is mistakenly including purchases outside the period under discussion, and the latter because he is omitting purchases bought in this period. He may have bought a refrigerator fourteen months ago but mistakenly report it as having been bought during the past year. (This phenomenon of shifting spending in an earlier period to a more recent one is known as *forward telescoping. Backward telescoping* is the shifting of recent spending to an earlier period.) The refrigerator may have been bought eleven months ago but the respondent is under the impression that he bought it thirteen months ago, and so does not report it as a purchase made during the past year. A BMR study (Martins 1982:111) showed that when low-income consumers were asked about spending on refrigerators and freezers in a given year, forward telescoping was a big problem. Of 33 purchases reported 17 had been made outside the year under review. There was no backward telescoping. Among high-income consumers telescoping is comparatively rare, and forward and backward telescoping tend to cancel each other.

3.1.2.5 Low commitment

In this situation the respondent has little or no interest in the investigation, seeing it as a waste of valuable time. However, not wanting to be rude to the interviewer, he tries to end the interview as soon as possible by taking no time to think out his answers.

3.1.2.6 Fatigue

In a long drawn-out interview exhaustion of the respondent is a serious problem. To the questions lower down in the questionnaire he often answers that he does not know; or he may reply 'no' instead of 'yes', hoping to shorten the interview.

3.1.3 Calculation errors

The procedure followed to limit errors in data preparation, tabulation and analysis is discussed in chapter 15.

3.2 Frame errors

A sample frame should contain all elements of the population being studied; but a perfect sample frame is seldom available, and defects in it may be caused by one or more of the following:

☐ some elements have been omitted

☐ some have been duplicated

☐ foreign elements.

3.2.1 All elements have not been included in the frame

Incompleteness is the most general defect in sample frames. Suppose, for example, we intend to investigate furniture buying and for lack of anything better use the telephone directory as a sample frame. But the directory contains only 90 % of the furniture consumers. Although only 10 % are missing from the directory, these may be the very people who have recently bought new houses and are engaged in furnishing them. Thus there is a systematic difference between the consumers constituting the frame and those not included in it. When the elements which are not represented in the sample frame are evenly distributed over the population they can be traced during the interviewing. For example, when the interviewer calls at a certain address, he can ascertain whether the house on, say, the right has a telephone, and if not, the residents of the house concerned can be interviewed.

3.2.2 Duplicated elements in the sample frame

Suppose we are investigating farmers' attitudes to farming cooperatives. A preliminary investigation shows that 99 % of all farmers are members of some cooperative, and so we use cooperative member lists. However, some farmers are members of more than one cooperative and therefore have a bigger chance of being drawn in the sample. We can assume that farmers who belong to more than one cooperative have larger farming operations and/or are more dependent on cooperatives, and therefore may have a more positive attitude towards them than farmers who belong to only one cooperative. If it has not been possible to eliminate duplication from the sample frame before the time, it is often possible to do so after the survey. For example, in his survey the researcher may obtain information from farmers on how many cooperatives they belong to. He can then include at random only one of every two farmers who belong to two cooperatives, one of every three who belong to three cooperatives, etc. Otherwise weighting can be applied, for example by assigning a weight of 1 to farmers who belong to only one cooperative and weights of a half, one-third and a quarter to farmers belonging to two, three and four cooperatives.

3.2.3 Foreign elements

Foreign elements are part of the sample frame but not the population under study. Suppose that in a survey of smokers the sample is drawn from a list of residential addresses. The designated addresses are bound to include quite a few where all the residents are non-smokers. These addresses are the so-called foreign elements which are ignored in the survey. Foreign elements, unlike duplicated and missing elements, do not affect the representativeness of the sample, because it is inflated in the pre-sampling stage by the estimated percentage of foreign elements in the sample frame. This procedure for assuring the required number of study elements in the sample does increase the cost of the survey.

3.3 Non-response errors

The following four response/non-response population strata are distinguished:

☐ available and willing (response)

☐ unavailable but willing (not-at-homes) – non-response

☐ unavailable and unwilling (refusals) – non-response

☐ available but unwilling (refusals) – non-response.

The first stratum consists of the respondents. If we manage to reach all the elements in a survey and secure their cooperation as respondents, there is only one stratum, 'available and willing', and no response error. That would be an ideal situation. But in practice we are limited by cost and time constraints, because we cannot keep going back to the same address indefinitely and, although the more effort we put in to reduce the refusal rate the lower it will be, there will always be refusals and not-at-homes.

The reasons for non-response are many and varied. The reasons for the genuine not-at-homes (the second stratum mentioned above) and the increase in their numbers are obvious: more and more women work and are therefore less often at home. And as a result of the increase in their buying power, consumers are able to spend their leisure time more pleasantly than by staying at home.

Measures for reducing the number of not-at-homes in a survey include doing as much as possible of the *interviewing in the evenings* when there is a better chance of finding people at home. Although it is costly to revisit the same address again and again, it is absolutely essential to undertake *two further visits apart from the first one*. The interviewer will also increase his chances of contacting not-at-homes if he *schedules call-backs for different evenings and different times of the evening* and, if possible, *arranges an appointment* with the element *by telephone* before making his final call-back.

The third stratum, 'unavailable and unwilling', consists of elements who seem to be not at home but are in fact refusals. People who see the interviewer arrive do not answer his knock at the door, this being a simpler way of avoiding the interview than a face-to-face refusal to the interviewer. The reasons that these people refuse to cooperate are the same as those of the fourth stratum, 'available but unwilling'. Wiseman and Schafer (1977:8–9) convened 16 non-respondents in a previous personal interview survey for a 90-minute group discussion, and identified reasons such as:

☐ *Encroachment on privacy*: Many questions are set on socio-economic and demographic aspects for which respondents see no need. Nor do respondents see the need to discuss their private affairs with others.

☐ *Respondents doubt the genuineness of the interviews:* Interviewers are regarded as salespeople who begin by asking a few questions as introduction to the sales talk that will eventually follow. Even if the interviewer is obviously making no attempt to sell anything, he is sometimes suspected of determining sales prospects for later follow-ups, or even of obtaining information to plan a burglary of the house.

☐ *The respondent regards the information as worthless* because

– interviewers go through the questionnaire too quickly, not giving the respondent time to consider his answers

– interviewers do not write down what respondents say

– interviewers cheat by misrepresenting the characteristics of respondents to meet quotas

– alternatives in multiple-choice questions are not applicable.

☐ The interviewer misleads the respondent by telling him the interview will take less time than it actually does.

☐ Questionnaires are long and boring.

☐ A respondent begins to feel uncomfortable after answering 'no' or 'I don't know' to several questions.

For these reasons non-response (not-at-homes and refusals) is becoming an ever-increasing problem. According to Reinhold (1975:5) home interview surveys have become more expensive and more difficult. One of the researchers he cites is Mervin Field, head of the Field Research Corporation in California: 'Twenty years ago we could figure on getting 85 % with reasonable effort. Now we're hard pressed to get 60 %' (Reinhold 1975:6). With such a low response rate one can hardly talk of a response that is representative of the population. Those who do respond represent an overly large proportion of housewives or mothers with small children, who are easily accessible. Family units of this kind are in the process of becoming ever less typical of the community.

Researchers sometimes compare certain socio-economic attributes of respondents and the population obtained from census data. When they find no significant differences, they assume that the variables being studied will show no significant differences either. One of Lagay's findings (1970:615–618) was that considerable differences were possible in the variables being studied, even though the socio-economic attributes of the respondents and non-respondents corresponded. For example, in a survey on pollution, those who fear it most may welcome the opportunity to express their adverse feelings and may therefore tend to respond better than others, although their socio-economic attributes may be the same as those of non-respondents.

Politz and Simmons (1954:42–53) suggest the following procedure to combat the not-at-home problem. Suppose interviews are held in the evening, and the interviewer's calls are scheduled at random within the interviewing period. Each respondent is asked to say on which of the five previous evenings (excluding Sundays) he was at home at that time. For all five evenings at home he is assigned 1(6/6), for four evenings a weight of 6/5, and for none of the previous evenings at home a weight of 6/1. He is therefore weighted in inverse proportion to the probability of his being at home. Where not-at-homes constitute a serious problem, the not-at-home bias is considerably reduced by this method. Note, however, that there may be people who are never at home at that time in the evening, which means that they will not be represented in the survey. Also, the sample must be enlarged for loss of reliability. If, say, those at home only one evening a week constitute 6 % of the population, we can expect only 1 % of the respondents at home on the evening of the interview to be respondents who are at home one evening a week. By weighting these respondents six times as much as respondents at home every evening the ratio is corrected. But in a sample of 500, for example, there will be only 5 (1 %) of these observations instead of 30 (6 %) in a sample where call-backs are continued until all not-at-homes have been traced. This small number (5) may be very unrepresentative of the segment concerned.

Researchers sometimes try to determine whether lateness of response has any connection with, for example, consumers' attitude to a particular brand or the amount spent on a particular product, especially in mail surveys. Elliot and Christopher (1973:93) refer to a study by Hendricks in which he calculated the number of trees per farm on the basis of a postal survey. Thirteen per cent of the farmers responded to the first mailing, showing the average number of trees per farm as 456; after the second the total response rate was 26,0 %, showing an average of 408 trees per farm; and after the third the total response was 39,4 %, with an average of 385 trees per farm. In this survey it seemed that the smaller the farming operation the later the farmer responded. Therefore Hendricks represented the results up to the end of each mailing graphically with the logarithms of the average number of trees per farm along the y-axis and the logarithms of the cumulative percentage response along the x-axis. A one-hundred-per-cent response has the logarithm 2. After a freehand drawing he read off the logarithm of the average number of trees per farm on the y-axis at 2 on the x-axis as the logarithm 2,54, which gave the number of trees per farm as 344. This was about 4,6 % higher than the real number, which was known to be 329.

In this survey the 39,4 % of farmers who responded to the three mailings were not representative of all farmers in the average number of trees per farm. Their average was 385 trees per farm compared with the average of all farmers of 329 trees per farm, an error of 17 %. However, by noticing a relation between lateness of reply and number of trees per farm, he succeeded in decreasing the error to only 4,6 %.

Just as Hendricks found a correlation between lateness of response and average number of trees per farm, there may be a correlation between positiveness of attitude and the effort to find consumers at home or persuade them to cooperate. If a correlation of this kind can be found, estimates for non-response can be made by a method similar to that used by Hendricks.

In conclusion it may be stated that the absence of differences in socio-economic attributes of respondents and the population obtained from census data is no guarantee of the non-existence of differences in the variables being studied. Weighting and other methods of adjustment can be of great help in dealing with the non-response problem. However, *there can be no substitute for reducing the non-response rate to an absolute minimum by repeated revisiting*.

3.4 Selection errors

Selection errors occur when all elements in the universe do not have the same chance of being selected. They may occur in all non-probability samples and in probability samples drawn from a poor frame (see chapter 13).

3.5 Sample errors

Sample errors arise when only a fraction of the population is studied. This error is discussed fully in chapter 13.

4 ERRORS OF EXPLANATION

Cox (1979:65) holds that errors of explanation exist when a researcher makes an inappropriate inference about a cause-effect relationship. Suppose a manufacturer marketing mainly to private consumers in South Africa expects the average real household income to rise by 30 % in the next 10 years, and so wants to ascertain what effect this rise in average income will have on sales of his product X. A countrywide survey reveals that consumption of product X has a very high correlation with average household income. On the grounds of these findings the manufacturer spends a considerable sum on expanding his capacity. But when real income rises as expected, the market for product X merely expands at the same rate as the population.

Our manufacturer therefore takes another look at the information collected in the countrywide survey and notices that in his analyses the researcher has ignored the influence of household composition and size. Higher-income households are bigger and in general contain more adults than lower-income households. This, and not their higher income, is why they spend more on product X than lower-income households. When the questionnaires of households with more or less the same composition and size were classified by income group, no difference was found between the amount spent on product X by lower and higher income groups.

5 SUMMARY

Three basic types of error are distinguished in research projects: errors of definition, estimation and explanation.

It is important to begin with a precise definition of the problem, and then to determine which variables are associated with it. Errors of estimation include measurement errors, frame errors, non-response errors, selection errors and sampling errors.

Measurement errors originate in poorly designed questionnaires; the reluctance or inability of the interviewer to elicit the necessary information from the respondent; and the reluctance and inability of the respondent to provide it. A sample frame should contain all elements of the population being studied; but a perfect sample frame is seldom available, and defects may be caused by the omission or the duplication of some elements, or both. Non-response (not-at-homes and refusals) is becoming an ever-increasing problem. Measures for reducing the number of not-at-homes in a survey include doing as much as possible of the interviewing in the evenings when there is a better chance of finding people at home. Although it is costly to visit the same address again and again, it is absolutely essential to undertake two further visits apart from the first one. The chances of contacting not-at-homes will be greater if the interviewer schedules call-backs for different evenings and different times of the evening and, if possible, arranges an appointment by telephone before making his final call-back. Selection errors arise when all elements in the universe do not have the same chance of being selected. They occur in all non-probability samples and in probability samples drawn from a poor frame. Sample errors arise when only a fraction of the population is studied.

Errors of explanation occur when a researcher makes an inappropriate inference about cause-effect relationship.

RFEFERENCES

Boyd, H W, Westfall, R & Stash, S F 1985. *Marketing research*. Sixth edition. Homewood Ill: Irwin.

Bradburn, N M & Sudman, S 1979. *Improving interviewing methods and questionnaire design*. San Francisco: Jossey-Bass.

Church, J A 1983. *Marketing research*. Chicago: Dryden Press.

Churchill, Gilbert A (Jr) 1992. *Basic marketing research*. Second edition. Fort Worth: The Dryden Press. (The Dryden Press Series in Marketing.)

Cox, E P 1979. *Marketing research: information for decision making.* New York: Harper & Row.

Elliot, K & Christopher, M 1973. *Research methods in marketing.* London: Holt, Rinehart & Winston.

Guest, L A & Nuckols, R 1950. A laboratory experiment in recording in public opinion interviewing. *International Journal of Opinion and Attitude Research*, 4:336–352.

Hauck, M 1969. Is survey postcard verification effective? *Public Opinion Quarterly*, XXIII:117–120.

Hyman, H H 1954. *Interviewing in social research.* Chicago: University of Chicago Press.

Lagay, B W 1969–70. Assessing bias: a comparison of two methods. *Public Opinion Quarterly*, Winter: 615–618.

Luck, David J, Wales, Hugh G, Taylor, Donald A & Rubin, Ronald S 1987. *Marketing research.* Seventh edition. Englewood Cliffs, NJ: Prentice Hall.

Martins, J H 1982. *Validation of household survey methodology.* Pretoria: Bureau of Market Research. (Research Report no 98.)

Politz, A & Simmons W R 1954. A plan to account for 'not-at-homes' by combining weighting and callbacks. *Journal of Marketing*, July:42–53.

Reinhold, R 1975. Survey-takers face closed door policy. *Sunday Plain Dealer*, Section 4, 9 November:5.

Trull, S G 1964. Strategies of effective interviewing. *Harvard Business Review*, Jan-Feb:89–94.

Wiseman, F & Schafer, M 1977. If respondents won't respond, ask non-respondents why. *Marketing News*, XI:5:8–9.

Part 3

Data analysis and presentation

In this part of the book data processing, analysis and presentation are discussed. It consists of four chapters. The first of these, chapter 15, deals with editing and coding, which are the two primary steps in data preparation. The chapter also introduces the discussion of data capturing and data analysis by explaining the principles of simple and cross-tabulation. As decision making implies a choice between alternatives, reliable information about alternatives is a prerequisite for effective decision making. The reliability of such information is determined by significance testing, which is the topic of discussion in chapter 16. Chapter 17 explains the more advanced data-processing methods which encompass multivariate analysis. The interpretation of research results and report writing are the subjects of chapter 18.

Data analysis: processing and basic analysis

Chapter 15: J H Martins

(This chapter is partly based on chapter 16 'Data analysis – processing and basic analysis' by F E Rädel in Nel *et al* 1988.)

1 INTRODUCTION

In the preceding chapters we dealt with the various methods of data collection. A mass of raw data is without meaning, however, and tells the researcher nothing until it is processed to extract meaningful data. To be meaningful such data must be relevant to the research objective(s). Data analysis is obviously an important part of the whole research process. For this reason four chapters of this book are devoted to its discussion.

The first step in analysing the data in completed questionnaires is known as data preparation and involves three operations: editing, coding, and data capturing. Next, by a process of summation or reduction the researcher tabulates the data, thus rendering it easier to manage and interpret.

2 DATA PREPARATION

Figure 15.1 presents an overview of the traditional sequence of functions to be performed in data preparation, capturing and storing. In practice, editing and coding are very often done simultaneously or even by the same person. But they are two different operations and will therefore be discussed separately here. Data preparation is often regarded as a fairly boring administrative task but its importance can hardly be overemphasised because the quality of the analytical results is dependent on the correctness of the raw data.

2.1 Editing

Editing entails a thorough and critical examination of a completed questionnaire in terms of compliance with the criteria for collecting meaningful data and in order to deal with questionnaires not duly completed.

Figure 15.1 Classic data-processing flow

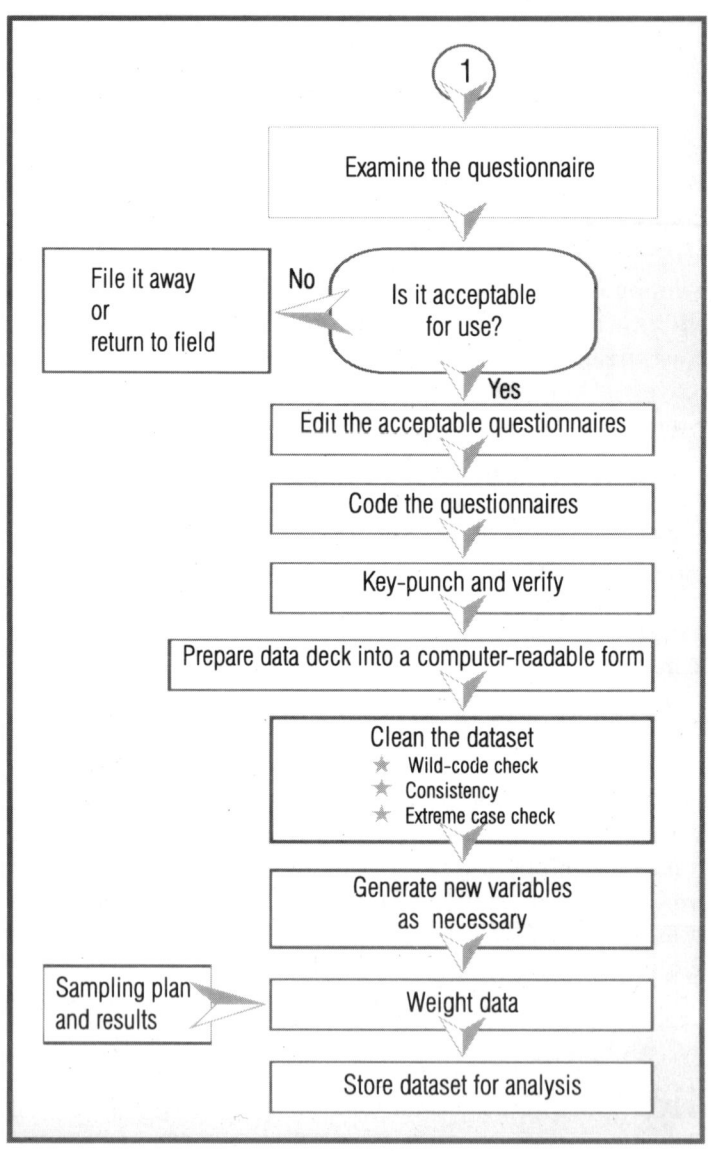

Source: Adapted from Kinnear & Taylor (1991:526).

2.1.1 The editing process

Questionnaires that have been completed by field staff are generally edited in two phases – field editing and central editing. Each questionnaire is scrutinised or edited before the responses are processed to see whether the data recorded in the questionnaire are acceptable for use and, if so, to prepare the data for coding and capturing. This is done by comparison with the following criteria:

☐ *Adherence to sample requirements:* Questionnaires should be discarded if they obviously fall outside the sample parameters. For instance, in a survey of marketing research practices in manufacturing industry in South Africa, all the completed questionnaires which had clearly been filled in by commercial and not by manufacturing firms were discarded.

☐ *Relevance:* A respondent who fills in expenditure on liquid detergent under the heading of expenditure on beauty soap has clearly misunderstood the question.

☐ *Completeness:* Completeness implies that all the sections, pages and questions have been filled in. Respondents skip questions for many reasons, the most important being that they overlook them, or deliberately leave a blank space because they are reluctant to furnish the information.

☐ *Legibility:* The seemingly obvious requirement that answers should be legible – especially those to open-ended questions – is frequently ignored under pressure of time during an interview.

☐ *Comprehensibility:* A written answer may be legible but incomprehensible. Abbreviations familiar only to the interviewer or respondent should be avoided.

☐ *Consistency:* Inconsistent answers are fairly common in primary data collection. A respondent who enters 'zero' under household expenditure on beauty soap and then circles beauty soap 'A' as the most frequently used in the household is supplying inconsistent answers. If the answer to the first question was positive and no figure was given for the second (or vice versa) the answers were clearly inconsistent.

☐ *Uniformity:* The same units of measurement should be used throughout in recording the answers to specific questions. If, for instance, the mass and sizes of food packs are not clearly defined in a consumer survey and respondents fill in '5 packets of breakfast cereal' or '6 bottles of cold drinks', the units may not be uniform, thus rendering the responses useless.

☐ *Accuracy:* Inaccuracies in the data that follow a common pattern of responses in the questionnaires of a particular interviewer point to bias or cheating on the part of the interviewer.

2.1.2 Treatment of unsatisfactory questionnaires

What does the researcher do if the questionnaires do not comply with the requirements set out above? The following options are open:

☐ *Review the quality of questionnaires and interviewers:* As a first step the researcher should critically review the quality of the questionnaire and the interviewers (in face-to-face interview surveys). Very often incomplete and incorrect responses are the result of poor questionnaire design, insufficient pre-testing of the questionnaire and/or sloppy interviewing. If such defects are detected early enough during the interviewing, the questionnaire can be improved and/or interviewers can be rebriefed or replaced. If the interviewing has been completed and the percentage of unsatisfactory responses is very high, the only solution is to stop and begin afresh, but in most instances the constraints of time and money deprive the researcher of this option.

☐ *Go back to the interviewer or respondent:* This is the best way of correcting unsatisfactory questionnaires and is quite practical while interviewing is still under way. After that it may be very expensive or impossible, or the respondent may not recollect the required information. Another practical way is to clear up problems over the telephone. In the survey of market research practices mentioned above the respondents had to fill in their names and telephone numbers on the questionnaire, which also contained the researcher's name and telephone number. Either party was therefore able to contact the other, and some problems were indeed solved in this manner.

☐ *Have questionnaires completed or corrected by the editor:* It is quite legitimate for an editor to fill in a missing answer, provided it can be inferred from other answers. If, for instance, a respondent does not answer a question on whether he owns a refrigerator but fills in the name of a particular make in another question, he obviously owns a refrigerator. The same applies to obviously incorrect answers. Again we turn for our example to the survey of marketing research practices in which respondents were asked to state their expenditure on marketing research personnel and in another question to state the number of full-time and part-time research and administrative staff in their employ. Wherever their expenditure figures were obviously unrealistic in terms of staff employed (inquiry having revealed that the staff figures were correct) the figures were adjusted on the basis of an estimated average for a similar staff structure. How far an editor should go in completing and correcting the responses is impossible to say in general terms. An editor who goes too far may introduce bias. His experience and integrity will set the limit in each case. He should fill in his own or corrected answers in a different colour, however, to distinguish them from original responses.

☐ *Discard unsatisfactory parts of the questionnaire:* If a questionnaire is incomplete or incorrect in parts, the researcher may discard unsatisfactory sections and retain those with valuable and reliable information. By implication this course of action complicates tabulation in the sense that the number of respondents will vary from one question to another but the problem can be overcome by indicating the number or percentage of respondents answering each question in the relevant table. The omission of certain items, however, may seriously impair the representativeness of the results.

☐ *Discard unsatisfactory questionnaires:* It is advisable to discard a questionnaire in total if its percentage of incomplete or incorrect responses is so high as to render the whole document suspect. In surveys with a very high percentage of discarded questionnaires the sample loss may be so high that the results are no longer representative.

2.1.3 Field versus central editing

In face-to-face interview surveys editing is usually done in two stages: in the field (field editing) and in-house or office editing (central editing).

Field editing by the field supervisor is aimed at rectifying the most glaring errors and omissions while the interviewing is still in progress. Obviously the sooner the field editing is done after completion of the questionnaire, the more time there is for central editing.

Central editing is a more thorough scrutiny of the questionnaires at the researcher's head office and should ideally be done by the researcher himself. In practice he is generally not able to perform this time-consuming task all by himself but should edit at least a satisfactory sample of questionnaires so as to prepare a written set of instructions for the editor(s). In large surveys it is best to assign specific questions rather than batches of questionnaires to individual editors, for uniformity and consistency of editing.

2.2 Coding

Coding is a technical process whereby codes are assigned to the respondents' answers preparatory to their tabulation.

Before tackling the process of data collection the researcher draws up dummy tables to help decide on the data he requires and how it should be used. Dummy tables are also useful in coding. For instance, the marital status of respondents is coded as follows:

Marital status	Code
Married	1
Divorced	2
Widowed	3
Never married	4

In coding, the first step is to refer to the categories which should have been determined during the construction of the dummy tables, for the classification of responses. There are notably three formal requirements for determining categories:

☐ *Categories should be of the 'right' size:* If monthly household income is expected to range from R0 to R10 000, 200 classes of R50 would obviously be too many and two categories of R5 000 would be too few. In the first example too many details might cause the researcher to lose sight of major findings and the number of cases in each category might be too small to yield representative results. Too few categories, on the other hand, might not reveal all the hidden information. A middle course should be sought. In practice it is preferable to start with too many categories rather than too few because categories may readily be combined at a later stage if necessary.

☐ *Categories must be mutually exclusive:* Each answer must clearly fall into one category and one category only. Income categories of R0–400, R400–800, R800–1 200, etc are unacceptable because incomes of exactly R400, R800, R1 200, etc fall into either of two categories. Correct categories would be R0–399, R400–799, R800–1 199, etc.

☐ *Categories must be exhaustive:* Besides the specified responses a classification should make provision for all possible answers, such as 'don't know', 'no answer', and 'other'. If the percentage of 'other' answers is very high, there may be too few specified alternatives in the questionnaire and further details may therefore be left undisclosed.

Usually the coding of closed questions is a simple process because it was built in during the construction of the questionnaire. Responses comprising numerical data such as the age or income of the respondent may be fed unchanged into the computer, or they may first be classified into age and income groups that are identified by codes. Nominal data* always require coding, and the coding of open-ended questions can be very difficult because responses usually take the form of words or even a few sentences. The editor's task is to reduce the words or sentences to their essential meaning, distinguish the various categories of meaning and then classify the responses accordingly. The interpretation of such responses is in a way subjective and should preferably be left to the researcher. If this is not possible, the researcher should at least classify a sample of responses and on this basis prepare a coding frame for the use of the editor/coder. Borderline cases should always be decided by the researcher himself.

---

* See chapter 16 for a discussion of nominal data.

Codes are assigned to the various answers before the questionnaire is filled in (pre-coding) or after the questionnaire has been filled in (post-coding).

Pre-coding calls for prior definition of all possible alternative responses to a particular question: for instance, all brands of coffee must be listed if the survey is about the consumption of different brands of coffee. As it is difficult to anticipate all possible answers, provision is usually made for an open alternative: 'other (specify…)'.

In *post-coding* the codes are entered by the coder after completion and editing of the questionnaire. For this the researcher designs and prepares a coding frame, specifying the codes for the various responses after coding a sample of the questionnaires himself. Obviously pre-coding greatly facilitates the coding procedure and is used wherever possible.

3 DATA CAPTURING AND STORING

3.1 Data capturing

> **Data capturing** is the transfer of data from acceptable data-collection instruments/questionnaires into the computer.

Kinnear and Taylor (1991:536) enumerate six alternative ways of data capturing: traditional, edge coding, direct punching, mark-sensed entry, respondent mark-sensed entry and direct computer entry.

The *traditional* method consists in transferring the codes to coding sheets from which key-punching and verifying of a data deck is done.

Edge coding, as the term implies, consists in recording the codes on the edges of the questionnaire in the spaces provided instead of recording them on coding sheets. The punching (keying-in) and verifying is done from the edge-coded questionnaires.

Direct punching is done by the key-punchers direct from the questionnaire. Questionnaires made up of closed-ended questions that are wholly pre-coded are needed for this process.

When a *mark-sensed entry system* is used, it is possible to eliminate the manual key-punching and verifying of the data by having coders use special mark-sensed coding sheets to record the data codes. These sheets are read into the computer by an optical scanner. The computer then stores the data on a disk file. Here the coder does not write the code number but fills in appropriate spaces on the mark-sensed sheets with a special pencil.

In the *respondent mark-sensed entry method* the respondents are asked to indicate their responses by filling in mark-sensed sheets. Both coding and key-punching are thus eliminated in the flow. For this technique to work properly the respondents must have the proper pencil and must understand exactly how to record their responses on the sheets.

Direct computer entry is used most often in telephone interviewing, but it is becoming increasingly popular in face-to-face and disk-based mail interviews. The respondent receives the questionnaire on a disk. He completes it on the same disk and returns it to the interviewer. The interviewer sits in front of the computer monitor and displays the questions one at a time. Pre-coded answers are also displayed on the monitor. The respondent indicates a response, and the interviewer types this response directly into a computer file. Thus editing, coding, key-punching, and verifying of written questionnaires are eliminated. The data are ready for instant cleaning and analysis. Also, the computer will take the correct branching and skip patterns in the questionnaire based on a respondent's answers and inform the interviewer if an illegal code is entered. The consistency of answers can also be checked instantly, and tabulations of results to questions are available immediately. Results may even be tabulated prior to the completion of the interviewing to allow for response monitoring and preliminary conclusions to be noted.

3.2 Clearing the dataset

After key-punching and verifying, the data deck is presented to the computer in such a way that data analysis computer programs can make use of it. Most of the programs that a researcher is likely to use are contained within a package of programs. The discussion of such programs falls beyond the scope of this book. We now have a dataset structured as a computer datafile, but we still have to attempt to clear the dataset of possible coding and data-capturing errors. Kinnear and Taylor (1991:534 and 535) mention three types of checks that can be run, namely a wild-code check, a consistency check, and an extreme-case check.

☐ *Wild-code check:* The first items to be removed from the dataset are so-called 'wild codes', that is codes that are not defined in the codebook for a particular variable. For example, the variable 'marital status' may have four legitimate codes. A number 5 or greater for this variable would be a wild code, probably the result of an error in coding or punching. This check can be done by having the computer list the numbers of responses in each category of each variable, which will tell us whether a wild code exists.

☐ *Consistency check:* The next step is to check the consistency of responses within each case. During the editing task we did a preliminary consistency check, but the one performed by the computer can be much more complete. For example, we might check to see that those who have a mortgage also own a house.

☐ *Extreme-case check:* An extreme case is defined as a response to a variable that is well out of the ordinary. For example, in an income and expenditure survey among households the computer can be commanded to identify all the questionnaire numbers where income exceeds expenditure and where expenditure exceeds income by a specified percentage. This is another way of identifying possible coding or punching errors.

3.3 Generating new variables

Once the originally coded dataset has been cleared, new variables are added that will be used later in analysis. These new variables are placed in the dataset for each case and assigned a variable number. There are a number of circumstances which might generate new variables. Kinnear and Taylor (1991:535) list four:

☐ We may want to add data not collected in the interview. For example, we may want to add census information about the area in which a respondent lives.

☐ We may want to divide an interval variable such as income into categories, or combine the categories of some variables to give a variable with fewer categories.

☐ We may want to form a variable to be defined by combinations of other variables. For example, the variable 'stage of family life cycle' is formed using age, marital status, presence of children, and so on.

☐ We may want to create and index to represent a number of variables. For example, we may simply add a set of scaled measures about a product to form an index related to interest in the product. More complex indices are also possible.

3.4 Weighting

> **Weighting** is a process whereby numerical coefficients (weights or weighting factors) are assigned to each of the elements in a set in order to provide them with a desired degree of importance relative to one another.

It may be necessary to weight information collected from a disproportionate sample and in summations of sample data pertaining to different strata. For example, a disproportionate sample of 5 % small, 25 % medium, 50 % large and 100 % major iron and steel manufacturers was drawn (table 15.1).

The results of each group must be raised to the universe by multiplying all the survey results of the subsample by its weighting factor. The weighting factor (column (d) in table 15.1) is calculated by dividing the number of enterprises in the stratum (column (a)) by the number of enterprises in the subsample (column (c)). After multiplication the results of the various groups are added together.

Table 15.1 Weighting factor applied in a disproportionate sample

Size of enterprise	Universe (a)	Sample as a percentage of the universe (b)	Sample (a) × (b) / 100 (c)	Weighting factor (a) ÷ (b) (d)
Small (1–50 employees)	3 197	5,0	160	20,0
Medium (51–150 employees)	833	25,0	208	4,0
Large (151–500 employees)	433	50,0	217	2,0
Major (500+ employees)	171	100,0	171	1,0
Total	4 634	16,3	756	

3.5 Storing

We now have a dataset completely ready for analysis. It is generally stored on disk file or tape.

4 TABULATION AND BASIC ANALYSIS

After the raw data have undergone the various stages of preparation they are ready for tabulation.

> **Tabulation** is the counting of the number of cases which fall into the various categories.

Basically, there are three methods of tabulation: manual, mechanical and electronic (computer).

Manual tabulation is a very simple operation whereby responses are entered in various categories on tally sheets, either after the various code numbers or directly after various categories, thus eliminating codes. For instance, the data on the members of twenty households are processed as follows:

Categories	Number of persons	
male adults	ﬀﬀﬀ ﬀﬀﬀ ﬀﬀﬀ ﬀﬀﬀ ﬀﬀﬀ	= 25
female adults	ﬀﬀﬀ ﬀﬀﬀ ﬀﬀﬀ ﬀﬀﬀ |||	= 23
male children	ﬀﬀﬀ ﬀﬀﬀ ﬀﬀﬀ ||	= 17
female children	ﬀﬀﬀ ﬀﬀﬀ ﬀﬀﬀ		= 16

Manual tabulation is still used in small samples with relatively few variables because it requires less preparation and is quicker and cheaper than computer processing. *Mechanical processing* with sorter/counter devices is outdated and will not be discussed. Today *electronic processing* is the most common. Once the data have been captured on computer disks or tapes, computer programs instruct the computer how to process the data. These programs are either written by a programmer for a specific purpose or are purchased as application packages. There are important reasons that the programmer should work with the researcher on the layout for the processing of the data. Indeed the programmer should be consulted as early as the construction and design phase of the questionnaire.

The researcher's aim in tabulating the data is to find out

☐ how the data are distributed

☐ what is typical in the data

☐ how much the data vary

☐ whether there is any significant relation between different sets of data.

This is achieved by the following techniques:

☐ by grouping the data and listing the groups as one-way frequency distributions in absolute or relative percentages/figures

☐ by reducing the data to means or averages or – in statistical terms – to measures of central tendency

☐ by applying measures of dispersion or variability

☐ by cross-tabulation.

All these techniques imply or are dependent upon the grouping or tabulation of the data in one way or another. Groupings can be one-way frequency distributions, measures of central tendency, measures of dispersion and/or cross-tabulations. When constructing a table certain guidelines should be adhered to as set out in chapter 18, section 3.5.2.

4.1 One-way frequency distributions

The spread of data over the various categories one-way or univariate is called a **frequency distribution**.

Table 15.2 reduces 1 626 responses to 10 categories and illustrates the distribution of the data, showing whether the distribution is an even one or has concentrations in one or more of the categories of electrification.

Table 15.2 Number of sawmills by degree of electrification (kilowatt (kW) per 100 m² floor space)

Electrification (kW per 100 m²)	Number of sawmills
0,0–2,0	51
2,1–4,0	124
4,1–6,0	676
6,1–8,0	227
8,1–10,0	301
10,1–12,0	80
12,1–14,0	136
14,1–16,0	15
16,1–18,0	9
18,1–20,0	7
	Total 1 626

There is a clear concentration in the 4,1–6,0 category. The pattern of distribution is even clearer when it is represented graphically as a distribution curve, or frequency polygon, as illustrated in figure 15.2. Compared with a normal distribution curve whose maximum is exactly in the middle and whose left and right slopes are symmetrical, our polygon has a clear inclination to the left (left asymmetrical).

Asymmetrical curves may also lean to the right but economic variables such as income, car ownership, etc, tend to follow a left asymmetrical pattern.

Distribution curves may be flat, show one or more points of concentration, or have regular or irregular patterns. All these characteristics are of analytical value. An irregular pattern, for instance, may be symptomatic of too little raw data from an inadequate sample; and a flattish curve indicating an even distribution tells the researcher that it would be meaningless or even misleading to express a series of data by any average because an average implies something typical.

A curve showing more than one point of concentration (in our example there is one in the 4,1–6,0 category and two lesser concentrations in the 8,1–10,0 and 12,1–14,0 categories) may be symptomatic of the presence of several groupings of elements. In other words, there may be not one but three typical sizes: small, medium and big. To test this hypothesis we divide the sawmills into three size groups according to total floor space (which is available in the sample data): small (0–3 000 m²), medium (3 001–15 000 m²) and big (15 001 m² +) and in this way arrive at the frequency distributions illustrated in table 15.3 (page 308). (Ignore the percentage columns for the time being.) If the distributions in table 15.3 are expressed graphically (see figure 15.3 on page 308) it becomes even clearer that there are three typical sizes of sawmills and that it would not have been correct to treat the series of data as homogeneous.

Figure 15.2 Frequency polygon of number of sawmills by degree of electrification (kW per 100 m²)

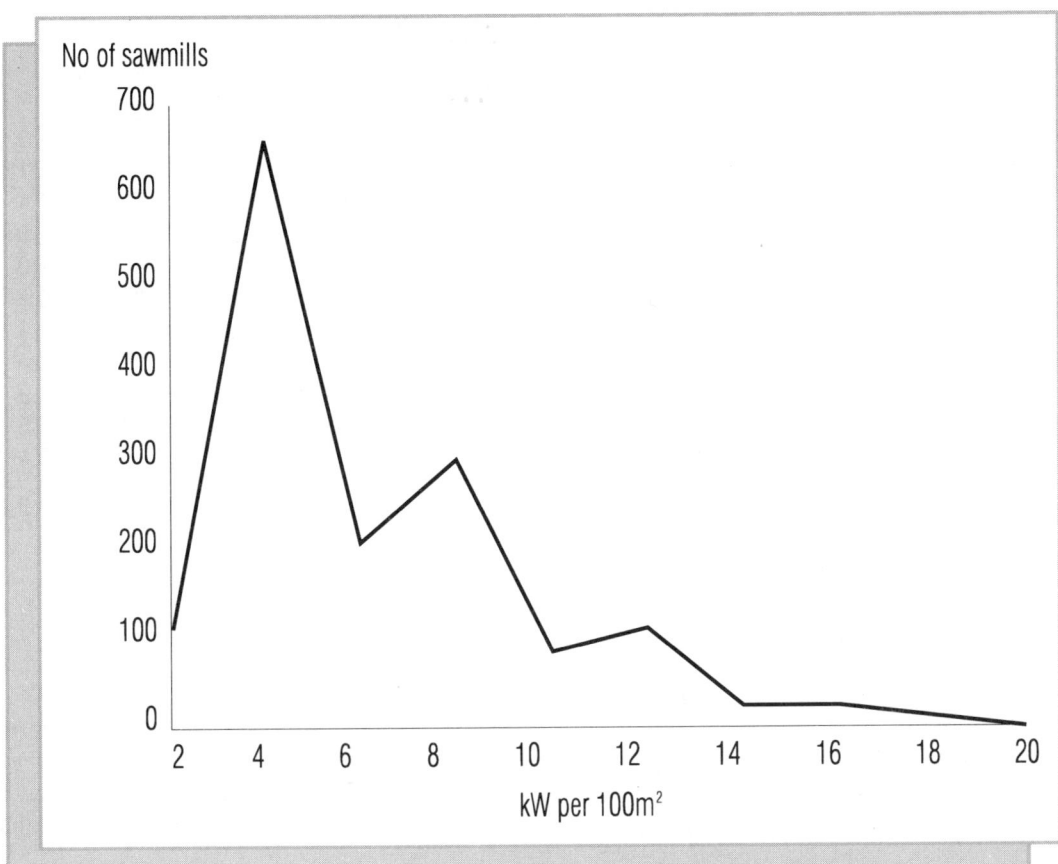

Both the table and the figure clearly indicate a relation between the size of the sawmill and its degree of electrification. If we had been satisfied with the frequency distribution in table 15.3 and figure 15.3 we would not have arrived at this conclusion or have gained a better understanding of the original data.

4.2 Percentages

A **percentage** is the proportion or rate per hundred parts.

Percentages are widely used in marketing research because the relative importance of figures is revealed more clearly by this simple tool than by the original data. In table 15.3,

Table 15.3 Number of sawmills by size group and degree of electrification

Electrification (kW per 100 m²)	Mills							
	Small		Medium		Big		Total	
	No	%	No	%	No	%	No	%
0,0–2,0	51	6,0	0	0,0	0	0,0	51	3,1
2,1–4,0	117	13,7	7	1,2	0	0,0	124	7,6
4,1–6,0	594	69,6	82	15,0	0	0,0	676	41,6
6,1–8,0	78	9,1	142	26,1	7	3,1	227	14,0
8,1–10,0	10	1,2	280	51,4	11	4,8	301	18,5
10,1–12,0	3	0,4	27	4,9	50	22,0	80	4,9
12,1–14,0	0	0,0	7	1,3	129	56,8	136	8,4
14,1–16,0	0	0,0	1	0,1	14	6,2	15	0,9
16,1–18,0	0	0,0	0	0,0	9	4,0	9	0,6
18,1–20,0	0	0,0	0	0,0	7	3,1	7	0,4
Total	**853**	**100,0**	**546**	**100,0**	**227**	**100,0**	**1 626**	**100,0**

Figure 15.3 Frequency polygon derived from table 15.3

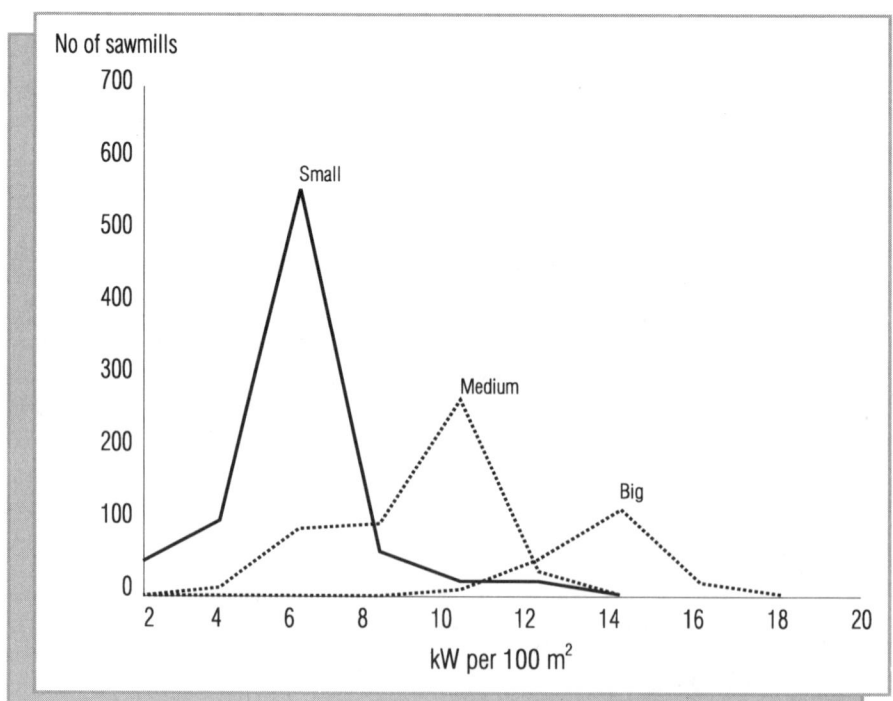

for instance, it is far easier to see from the frequency distribution patterns in the percentage column that over half of the mills in all three size groups are concentrated in one category and that the concentration is comparatively greater among the small mills. Table 15.3 further illustrates the usefulness of percentages. A researcher comparing the three types of retailers in table 15.4 will not gain a clear picture of their distribution from the number of establishments, but by expressing these numbers as percentages he renders them comparable and is able to draw the following conclusions:

☐ There is a higher degree of concentration among general dealers and chemists than among bottle stores, which have a more even spread.

☐ General dealers predominate in the lowest turnover category, chemists in the second lowest and bottle stores in the higher categories.

☐ Using the percentage distribution of the totals as a bench mark, the researcher can say that the typical size of general dealers is smaller than the overall typical size, that of chemists is broadly the same and that of bottle stores is bigger.

In relative terms general dealers are therefore typically small establishments, chemists are of medium size and there is no typical size for bottle stores. Bottle stores, however, tend to be bigger in size.

Table 15.4 Retail establishments by turnover

Annual turnover (R'000)	Type of retail establishment							
	General dealers		Chemists		Bottle stores		Total	
	Number	%	Number	%	Number	%	Number	%
0–99,9	5 823	72,8	681	31,1	408	17,1	6 912	54,9
100–199,9	1 238	15,5	884	40,4	597	25,0	2 719	21,8
200–299,9	410	5,1	383	17,5	420	17,5	1 213	9,6
300–399,9	188	2,3	132	6,0	335	14,0	655	5,2
400–499,9	101	1,3	53	2,4	212	8,9	366	2,9
500–749,9	110	1,4	43	2,0	250	10,5	403	3,2
750 +	127	1,6	14	0,6	165	7,0	306	2,4
Total	7 997	100,0	2 190	100,0	2 387	100,0	12 574	100,0

The process of drawing conclusions is very often facilitated by grouping the data into bigger categories. In our example the figures in table 15.4 can be grouped into three turnover categories: small retailers (R0–99 999), medium-size retailers (R100 000–299 999) and big retailers (R300 000 and over), as in table 15.5.

Table 15.5 Retail establishments by turnover categories

Size of establishments	General dealers		Chemists		Bottle stores	
	Number	**%**	**Number**	**%**	**Number**	**%**
Small	5 823	72,8	681	31,1	408	17,1
Medium	1 648	20,6	1 267	57,8	1 017	42,6
Big	526	6,6	242	11,1	962	40,3
Total	**7 997**	**100,0**	**2 190**	**100,0**	**2 387**	**100,0**

Being a simple but useful measure of relative relations, percentages are widely used in marketing research. Percentages, however, conceal the statistical basis and may create an impression of accuracy which may not be warranted by the small numbers in the original data. For this reason percentages and numbers should always be presented together, as in the tables above.

4.3 Measures of central tendency

Simple tabulations and frequency distributions reduce a mass of raw data to a few figures. In the extreme case of data reduction a whole series of data is reduced to a single figure, the average. In marketing research such averages or measures of central tendency are most common in comparisons, for instance between the average incomes of population groups. Averages also indicate something typical, say the typical height of Standard 10 pupils.

Although there are other measures of central tendency in statistical theory, only three types (the arithmetic average or mean, the mode and the median) are normally used in marketing research. These measures can be illustrated by the data in table 15.6.

> The **mean** is the sum of all the values of the series, divided by the number of values. The **median** is the middle value of the series after all the values have been ordered in sequence. The **mode** is the most frequently occurring value in an ordered series of data.

The mean is the sum of all the values (46) divided by the number of the values (11), that is 4,2. The information in table 15.6 ordered in sequence is 1, 2, 3, 3, 3, 4, 4, 5, 6, 7, 8. The median is 4 because it lies exactly in the middle. For an even number of observations the median would be the value halfway between the two central values (the total of the two values divided by 2). In our example the digit 3 occurs most frequently. Therefore the mode is 3. There is an interesting statistical relation between these three measures

Table 15.6 Number of tractors owned by construction firms

Firm	Number of tractors
A	8
B	1
C	3
D	2
E	4
F	3
G	4
H	6
I	5
J	3
K	7
Number　11	**Total**　46

of central tendency, which is of analytical value. All three measures are exactly the same in a perfectly symmetrical frequency distribution (normal distribution curve or polygon). The opposite is not necessarily true – if the measures are the same the distribution is not always normal. In a left asymmetrical distribution (polygon) the mean is always higher than the median, and in a right asymmetrical distribution (polygon) these positions are reversed. Figure 15.4 (page 312) is an example of a polygon derived from the figures in table 15.6. There is one firm (vertical axis) with one tractor (horizontal axis) and one with two, one with five, one with six, one with seven and one with eight tractors. There are also two firms with four tractors and three with three tractors.

Being clearly left asymmetrical, the polygon's mean is the highest value (4,2), the mode the lowest (3,0) and the median (4,0) falls between the two. As most economic variables have a left asymmetrical distribution pattern, the mean tends to be on the high side and the mode on the low side. Again, this simple argument proves the importance of frequency analysis for marketing research. If a distribution is relatively normal the researcher may use any of the measures of central tendency, but the more asymmetrical the curve the more important is the choice of the most appropriate central value.

The most appropriate central value depends on what the value is meant to express and the pattern of the frequency distribution. If the frequency distribution has an uneven or erratic pattern, any central value is a poor measure of a series. A central value, after all, represents something typical. The following are a few general hints on the selection of the most appropriate central value.

The *mean*, which is fairly easy to calculate, is a useful tool for determining the centre of gravity of the series or comparing different samples of the same population because it

Figure 15.4 Number of tractors owned by construction firms (see table 15.6)

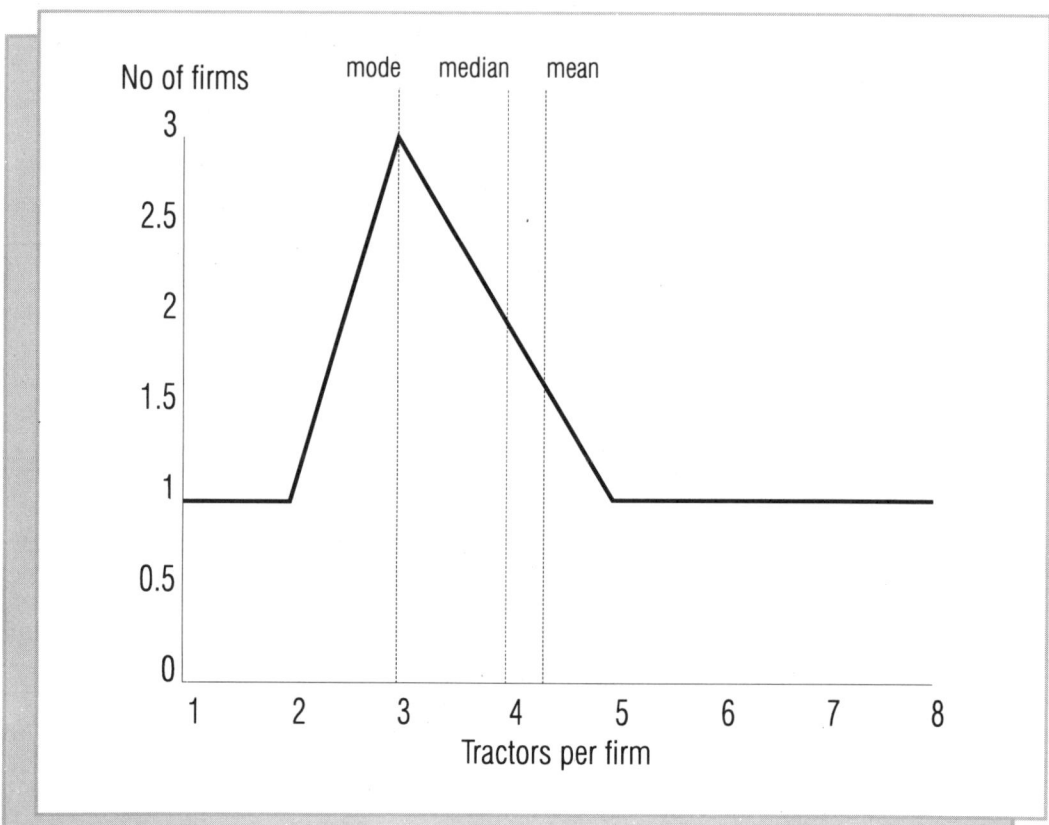

usually varies less from sample to sample than the other central values. It is also suitable for estimating a total for a population when the mean and the number of the population are known. For instance, average income per person multiplied by the population equals the total income of the population. By implication a mean is calculated for a complete series with finite extreme values. A series with an extreme value, which is common in marketing research tabulations, would therefore present difficulties. Means are generally very sensitive to extreme values.

The *median* is used when the researcher is pressed for time, when the mean is difficult to calculate, distributions are markedly skewed, or an extreme end value is quite out of proportion.

The *mode* is appropriate for establishing the most typical value of a series. A bicycle manufacturer, for instance, would establish the most typical height of children and adults before designing bicycles for these two markets.

4.4 Measures of dispersion

Applied judiciously, a central value is a useful tool for establishing the general character of a series but it is not specific enough. The mean of 4,2 tractors for 11 firms (see table 15.6) could also have been derived from five firms with the following number of tractors:

Firm	Number of tractors
V	1
W	2
X	3
Y	5
Z	10
	21 ÷ 5 = 4,2

Here the spread between the number of tractors is 1–10 instead of 1–8 as in table 15.6.

A more specific characterisation of a series is attained by calculating both the central value and the dispersion or variability around the central value (table 15.7 on page 314). The simplest measure of dispersion (or variability) is the range. It is expressed by the lowest and highest values (say, 1–10) or by the difference between them (say, 9). But the range

> The **range** is the difference between the lowest and highest value of a series.

takes only the extreme values into account, ignoring the dispersion of the values between them. The measure of dispersion that takes all the values and their relation to the central value into account is termed the variance.

> The **variance** is the mean of the squared deviations of the values from the mean.

The variance is calculated by the formula:

$$V = \Sigma \frac{(x-\mu)^{2}*}{n}$$

Where V = variance
      x = values of observations
      μ = mean of observations
      n = number of observations

The calculation of the variance of the salaries of five salesmen is illustrated on the next page, applying the formula above.

---

* Statistical symbols are explained in table A-5 in the appendix.

$$\mu = 253$$
$$\Sigma (x\text{-}\mu)^2 = 27\ 480$$
$$V = \frac{27\ 480}{5} = 5\ 496$$

The deviations are squared to cancel the effect of the signs (+ or −). Squaring has the further effect of weighting observations which are distant from the mean more heavily than those closer to the mean. Because the variance has the disadvantage of representing a squared value as opposed to the ordinary value of the mean with which it is compared, the standard deviation (σ) is a more appropriate measure of dispersion.

Table 15.7 Variance of salaries of five salesmen

Salesman	Salary (R) per week	$(x - \mu)$	$(x - \mu)^2$
A	200	− 53	2 809
B	215	− 38	1 444
C	220	− 33	1 089
D	230	− 23	529
E	400	+147	21 609
Total	**1 265**	**0**	**27 480**

The **standard deviation** is the square root of the variance.

The standard deviation is calculated by the formula:

$$\sigma = \frac{\sqrt{\Sigma(x - \mu)^2}}{n} \text{ or } \sigma = \sqrt{V}$$

The standard deviation (σ) of the salaries of the five salesmen in our example above is therefore:

$$\sigma = \sqrt{5\ 496} = 74{,}14$$

In a comparison of the dispersion of two series it is wrong to compare the two standard deviations without taking the value of the mean into account and expressing the standard deviation as a percentage of the mean.

The **coefficient of variation** is the standard deviation expressed as a percentage of the mean.

The coefficient of variation in the above example with a standard deviation of 74,14 and a mean of 253 is therefore

$$\frac{74,14}{253} \times 100 = 29,3\%$$

The appropriate value of dispersion is dependent on the degree of accuracy required. The range is very simple and quick to determine but merely gives a general indication of the spread of a series. The standard deviation is appropriate when the greatest measure of accuracy is required. The coefficient of variation is used in comparisons of dispersions of two or more series or for an indication of the relative size of deviations from the mean.

4.5 Cross-tabulation

Univariate tabulations are obviously a useful and simple means of reducing a mass of data to less data and deriving frequency distributions and measures of central tendency and dispersion. But in practice marketing researchers in most cases have to deal with more than one variable. They also have to establish the existence and extent of the relation between these variables. Here cross-tabulation is the simplest way.

A **cross-tabulation** comprises bivariate observations, each cell containing those observations which correspond both to the appropriate column heading and the appropriate side heading.

A cross-tabulation normally involves two variables (hence the terms two-dimensional, bivariate or contingency tables) or even more than two variables, as we shall see later. A simple example of a bivariate cross-tabulation of income and car ownership is presented in table 15.8.

Table 15.8 Cross-tabulation of family income and car ownership

Income category	Cars per family											
	0		1		2 and more			Total		
	No	%		No	%		No	%		No	%	
Low income	55	69	(71)	24	30	(31)	1	1	(1)	80	100	(29)
Middle income	20	22	(26)	30	33	(39)	40	45	(32)	90	100	(32)
High income	2	2	(3)	23	21	(30)	85	77	(67)	110	100	(39)
Total	77	28	(100)	77	28	(100)	126	44	(100)	280	100	(100)

Cross-tabulation is in fact a combination of two frequency distributions: a vertical one (income categories) and a horizontal one (car ownership categories). The relations between the absolute figures emerge even more clearly from a comparison of the percentages in the horizontal distribution: in the lower income groups 69 % have no cars and only 1 % have two or more cars, while in the high income group the reverse obtains.

A relation therefore exists between income and car ownership. By expressing the original data vertically (percentages in brackets) we arrive at similar conclusions: in the low income group there is a very high percentage of no-car owners (71 %) and a very low percentage of two-or-more-car owners (1 %) and in the high income group the opposite is true (the vertical and horizontal percentages of the totals can be ignored in this context).

Obviously cross-tabulations yield meaningful information only when there are logical grounds for assuming the existence of a relation. A cross-tabulation between car ownership and the owners' hair colour would be senseless. In our example logic tells us that income is the independent or causal factor and car ownership the dependent or effect factor. In cross-tabulation the independent factor is usually tabulated vertically and the dependent factor horizontally.

On the assumption that car ownership is determined not only by income but also by place of residence, a third variable is introduced, as illustrated in table 15.9.

Table 15.9 reveals the following (we again ignore the percentages of the totals):

☐ In the low-income group the overwhelming majority of those who own one car live in suburbs and only one suburban family in this group owns two or more cars.

☐ In the middle-income group the pattern is almost reversed for one-car ownership and two-car+ ownership.

☐ In the high-income group suburban and city centre families are represented almost equally in both car ownership categories, suggesting that place of residence is less important in high-income than in less well-to-do families.

Thus a three-dimensional table reveals more information than a two-dimensional one but has more breakdowns and more cells (in our examples the number of cells rises from 9 to 18 as 'No' in table 15.8 has split into 'Suburb' and 'City centre' in table 15.9). The number of cases per cell, however, may be reduced to levels that may not yield statistically valid conclusions, as can be seen in our example. The researcher must therefore be quite clear about the type and details of cross-tabulation required before deciding on the sample size. Theoretically it is possible to introduce even more variables in cross-tabulations, but the consequences mentioned above are aggravated. What is more, the tables become increasingly bigger and more complicated, making them practically impossible to read and interpret. In marketing research practice cross-tabulation is usually limited to two variables and three-dimensional tables are the exception.

Table 15.9 Three-dimensional cross-tabulation of income, place of residence and car ownership

Income category	Place of residence	Number of cars per family											
		0			1			2+			Total		
		Sub-urb	City centre	Sub-total	Sub-urb	City centre	Sub-total	Sub-urb	City centre	Sub-total	Sub-urb	City centre	Sub-total
Low income	No	10	45	55	20	4	24	1	—	1	31	49	80
	%	(18)	(82)	(100)	(83)	(17)	(100)	(100)	—	(100)	(39)	(61)	(100)
Middle income	No	10	10	20	20	10	30	10	30	40	40	50	90
	%	(50)	(50)	(100)	(67)	(33)	(100)	(25)	(75)	(100)	(44)	(56)	(100)
High income	No	—	2	2	12	11	23	44	1	85	56	54	110
	%	—	(100)	(100)	(52)	(48)	(100)	(52)	(48)	(100)	(53)	(47)	(100)
Total	No	20	57	77	52	25	77	55	71	126	129	151	280

Cross-tabulation is undoubtedly the most common technique for analysing relations between two or three variables, and practical market research studies generally go no further than that. But cross-tabulation only reveals whether a relation exists; it does not quantify the degree of the relation. For this the researcher applies a more sophisticated technique known as correlation analysis. Correlation analysis is the measurement of the degree of relation between variables. The statistical method of measuring the relation requires an analysis of two or more series to determine the extent to which they move together. The deviation of such numerical relation is termed regression analysis. If the research goal is to reveal the relation between a specific dependent variable and a number of continuous or dichotomous independent variables, multiple regression analysis is applied.

5 SUMMARY

The principal aim of data analysis is to extract all the relevant data which are hidden in the mass of collected raw information. Before analysis proper can commence the data have to be prepared by three operations: editing, coding, and data capturing. Editing comprises the scrutiny of questionnaires for a number of criteria: adherence to sample requirements, relevance, completeness, legibility, comprehensibility, consistency and uniformity. The next step in data preparation is coding.

Coding is the process whereby data are categorised and identified by assigning a code. Codes can be assigned to the various answers before the questionnaire is filled in (pre-coding) or afterwards (post-coding). The coding procedure is governed by the way in which the data are subsequently processed, that is whether tabulation is manual, mechanical or electronic (by computer).

Data capturing, that is key-punching and verifying, can be done from coding sheets or edge-coded questionnaires or by means of direct punching, mark-sensed entries, respondent mark-sensed entries or direct computer entries. The dataset is then cleared by wild-code, consistency and extreme-case checks. Once the dataset has been cleared new variables can be added. If disproportionate samples were used the data are weighted before being stored for analysis.

After data preparation has been completed, the masses of raw data are grouped together to facilitate interpretation. Groupings can be one-way or univariate frequency distributions, measures of central tendency, measures of dispersion, and/or cross-tabulations. Cross-tabulation is generally confined to two and, in exceptional cases, to three variables. Cross-tabulation of more than three variables is theoretically possible but impractical, for a variety of reasons.

REFERENCES

Churchill, Gilbert A (Jr) 1992. *Basic marketing research*. Second edition. Fort Worth: The Dryden Press. (The Dryden Press Series in Marketing.)

Kinnear, Thomas & Taylor, James 1991. *Marketing research: an applied approach*. Fourth edition. New York: McGraw-Hill. (McGraw-Hill Series in Marketing.)

Data analysis: significance testing

Chapter 16: M Loubser

Data analysis: significance testing

1 INTRODUCTION

To a large extent decision making is a choice between alternatives. Reliable information about alternatives is needed if the right decision is to be made. For instance, management of a certain bank may consider establishing a branch of the bank in a certain area provided the inhabitants of the area save at least R1 000 on average a year. Because a census is too costly and time consuming, management opts for a sample survey. But sample surveys are subject to sample variations. If, for instance, a sample survey reveals that the sample elements save an average of R1 100 a year, at what level of confidence may it be stated that the inhabitants save at least R1 000 a year? If the confidence coefficient is 90 % and management requires a coefficient of 95 % the sample statistics are invalid.

Occasionally we have to make before and after measurements on the same elements. A typical example is a comparison of sales by a number of shops before and after a sales promotion campaign. Is the difference we observe between the before sales and the after sales significant?

In another situation it may seem to management that a certain remuneration package for sales personnel gives better results than another. However, the difference in the results of the sales packages may be ascribed to variations in the abilities of sales personnel.

Answering these kinds of questions is the goal of the statistical techniques described in this chapter. We shall concern ourselves first with the steps in significance testing and then discuss a number of significance tests.

2 STEPS IN SIGNIFICANCE TESTING

There are six basic steps to be followed in significance testing. They are:

(1) Formulate the null hypothesis.

(2) Select the appropriate statistical test.

(3) Decide on a particular significance level.

(4) Determine the critical value of the test statistic.

(5) Determine the observed value of the test statistic.

(6) Compare the observed value with the critical value.

These six steps will be briefly discussed in the sections that follow.

2.1 Formulating the null hypothesis

Typically the null hypothesis is a *sceptical, negative statement which has to be proved wrong by the researcher*. The basis for statistical testing is that the null hypothesis is accepted until proof to the contrary becomes overwhelming. *A hypothesis can be directional or non-directional*. A directional hypothesis is a statement that one quantity is greater or less than another. For instance, Afrikaans-speakers spend more on meat than English-speakers. This hypothesis can be rejected by a result in just one direction – a sample of English-speakers who spend far more on meat than a sample of Afrikaans-speakers. This is known as a one-tailed test.

A non-directional hypothesis is a statement that one quantity is equal to another. For instance, English-speakers and Afrikaans-speakers spend the same on meat. A hypothesis of this kind can be rejected on the grounds of a result in either direction – a sample of Afrikaans-speakers who spend far more on meat than a sample of English-speakers, or a sample of English-speakers who spend far more on meat than a sample of Afrikaans-speakers. This is known as a two-tailed test.

2.2 Selecting the appropriate statistical test

Figure 16.1 contains a flow diagram for choosing a test to explain observed differences. The diagram shows that the nature of the data, the number of samples and the relationship of the samples are the main considerations in the selection of an appropriate statistical test.

Statistics can be divided into two main groups: *non-parametric* and *parametric statistics*. Nominal and ordinal data are non-parametric, while interval and ratio data may be treated as parametric.

Nominal data consist of numbers assigned to individuals, groups or phenomena. The purpose of these numbers is merely to identify categories. The numbers themselves have no mathematical value; they might just as well be signs or letters. If for purposes of grouping we assign the number 1 to females and the number 2 to males, it does not mean that males are ranked higher or lower than females.

Ordinal data indicate 'less than' or 'greater than'. A person may rank blue higher than green. If he then assigns the number 1 to blue and the number 2 to green, he explains

Figure 16.1 Flow diagram for choosing a test to explain observed differences

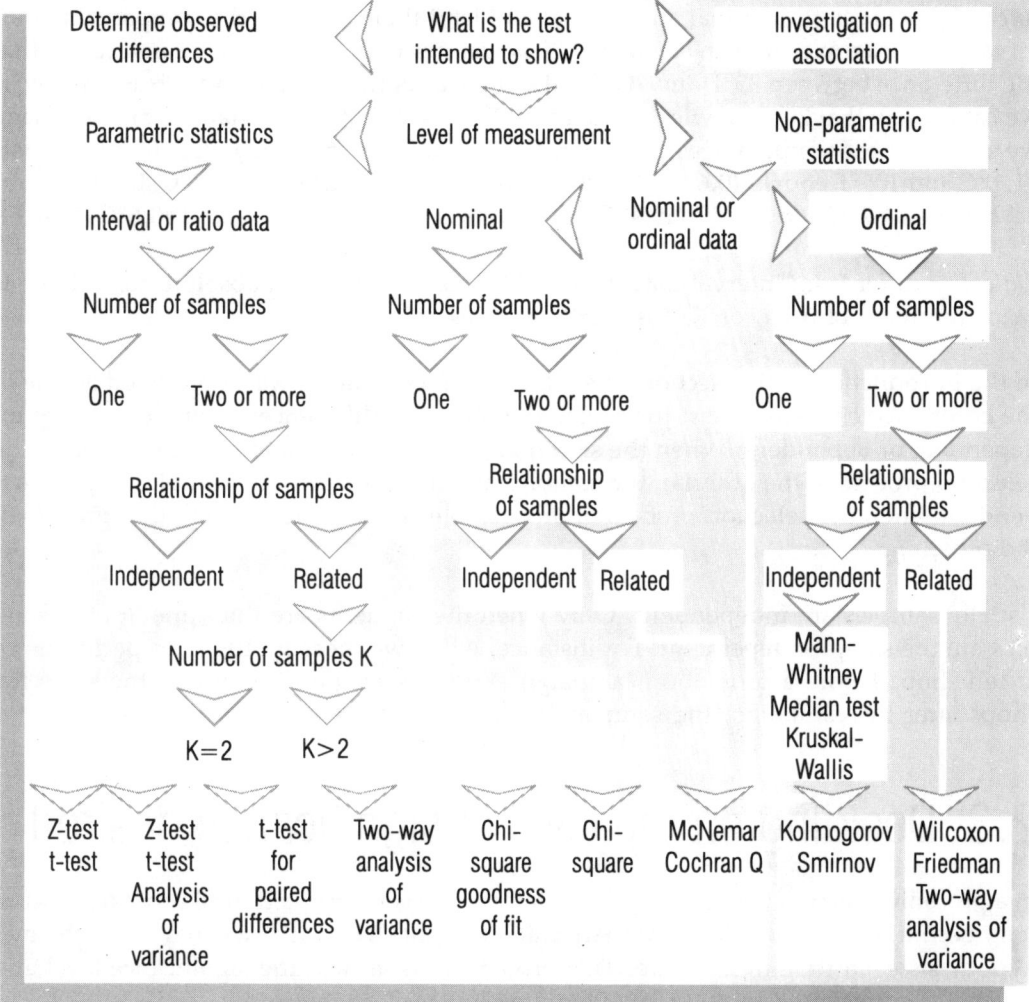

Source: Adapted from Luck *et al* (1982:375).

by this action that he prefers blue to green – therefore 1 is 'better' than 2. If John, Peter and Jack come first, second and third respectively in their class we know that John fared better than Peter and Jack and that Jack fared worst of all, but so far we know nothing of their actual performance. All three may have earned distinctions or all of them may have failed. John may have attained 90 %, Peter 39 % and Jack 38 %. We therefore do not have any information about the distance between any two of them.

Interval data are both nominal and ordinal and lend themselves to the comparison of intervals. For example, we can say that 70°F is warmer than 35°F and we can also say that the difference between 35°F and 70°F is the same as between 70°F and 105°F. However, we cannot say that 70°F is twice as hot as 35°F. To see that such a claim cannot be made we convert these temperatures to centigrade. We find that 35°F equals 1,7°C, 70°F equals 21,1°C and 105°F equals 40,6°C. 21,1°C is more than twice as hot as 1,7°C, but the interval between 1,7°C and 21,1°C (19,4°C) is the same as between 21,2°C and 40,6°C (19,4°F).

Ratio data differ from interval data in that they measure from an absolute zero: 10 kg is twice the mass of 5 kg, or R10 is worth 10 times R1.

In the introduction to this section, the relationship of samples was mentioned as one of the criteria for choosing a test for explaining observed differences. Samples may be independent or dependent. When the selection process of one sample is not related to the selection process of the other(s), the samples are independent. The samples become dependent when the selection process of one sample is related to the selection process of the other(s).

Usually samples are independent. Only when the elements are the same in both samples are the samples dependent. For instance, when we measure the sales performance of ten shops before a promotion campaign and the sales performance of the same ten shops after the campaign, the samples are dependent.

2.3 Deciding on the level of significance desired

In a preceding section we said that the null hypothesis is accepted until proof to the contrary becomes overwhelming. But there still is a slight chance that we may reject the null hypothesis even though it is true. This probability is termed the significance level and is usually represented by the Greek letter alpha (α). It is referred to as a Type I error. There is also a Type II error (accepting a false hypothesis). We shall only concern ourselves with the first type of error.

The desired level of significance most often used in practice is 0,05. This means there is only a 5 % or a 1 in 20 chance that your conclusion in rejecting the hypothesis was a mistake. By subtracting the significant level from 1,00 the confidence level is obtained. The smaller the significant level, the higher the confidence level will be that you made the correct decision.

2.4 Determining the critical value of the test statistic

The critical value is the value the test statistic would have to exceed for the null hypothesis to be rejected. This value is read off from statistical tables.* If the desired level of significance is relatively small, say 0,01, the critical value will also be relatively large.

2.5 Determining the observed value of the test statistic

The following are examples of observed values of the test statistic:

- ☐ a sample mean
- ☐ a sample proportion
- ☐ the difference between two sample means
- ☐ the difference between two sample proportions
- ☐ the calculated chi-square statistic
- ☐ the calculated F-ratio (for analysis of variance).

2.6 Comparing the observed value of the test statistic with the critical value

If the observed value of the test statistic exceeds the critical value, the null hypothesis is rejected. If not, the null hypothesis must be accepted.

3 VARIOUS STATISTICAL TESTS

As indicated in figure 16.1 the nature of the data is vital in selecting a statistical test. Techniques for lower levels of measurement (nominal and ordinal data) may be applied to higher levels (interval and ratio data), but not the other way round.

In this section we shall first discuss techniques that are appropriate for higher levels of measurement and thereafter techniques applicable to lower levels of measurement.

---

* See tables A-1 to A-4 in the appendix for statistical tables and chapter 13, section 4.2.2, for an example of their use.

Although all the available techniques will not be covered, those discussed here will meet the most general needs of marketing researchers.

3.1 Tests requiring interval or ratio data

3.1.1 Z- and t-tests

> The **Z-test** allows researchers to compare the mean generated from a sample with a mean hypothesised to exist in the population, and to decide whether the sample mean allows them to conclude that the hypothesised population mean is true.

> The **t-test** is appropriately used in hypothesis testing about means for all sample sizes when the population standard deviation (o) is unknown.

If the measurement scales are at least interval, the data are parametric, one or two groups are involved and the observations are independent, Z- and t-tests can be applied to measure differences among data.

If the population standard deviation (σ) is known, the Z-test is always appropriate. In practice the population standard deviation is seldom known. If it is not known, the Z-test is appropriate when the sample size is at least 30. If not, the t-test is appropriate.

3.1.1.1 Test of one sample mean: n > 30

To illustrate this test: A financial institution is considering launching a promotion campaign to attract the savings of households living in Cape Town. The campaign will only be launched if households living in Cape Town save more than R500 on average per month. The probability that households save an average of R500 or less per month may not be more than 0,05. In a random sample of 200 households it is found that households living in Cape Town save R550 on average per month. The sample has a standard deviation of R900 and consequently an estimated sample error ($\sigma_{\bar{x}}$) of R63,65. The formula is:

$$\sigma_{\bar{x}} = \frac{\sigma}{\sqrt{n}} = \frac{900}{\sqrt{200}}$$

Test

(a) Formulate the null hypothesis. The null hypothesis is that households save R500 or less per year. It is written formally as:

$$H_0: \mu \leq R500$$

(b) The following level of significance is selected:

α = 0,05 thus Z = 1,64 (see table A-1 and figure 16.2)

(c) Observed value of test statistic:

$\bar{x}$ (sample mean) = R550

Determine the critical value of the test statistic. Suppose the population average is R500. If we draw a large number of samples of, say, 200 each from the population, the results of such samples will lie round the population average in the shape of a normal curve, as illustrated in figure 16.2 (central limit theorem).

Figure 16.2 The normal curve

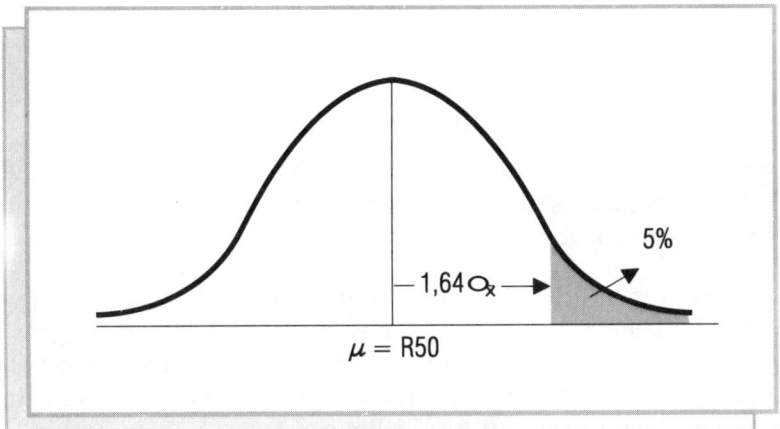

One half of the sample averages will lie to the left of the centre of the normal curve and the other half to the right. The averages of only 5 % of these samples will be equal to or higher than R(500 + 1,64 $\sigma_{\bar{x}}$), that is R604,4. The probability is 0,05 (5 %) that the sample we have drawn will be one of those with an average value of R604,4 or higher. Figure 16.2 shows that if the population average is R500, there is a 0,5 (50 %) probability that the sample value is R500 or more, and a 0,05 (5 %) probability that the sample value is R604,4 or more. Our sample value (R550) lies between R500 and R604,4. The probability that a sample value such as ours can be obtained is therefore smaller than 0,5 (50 %) but greater than 0,05 (5 %). Therefore, R(500 + 1,64 $\sigma_{\bar{x}}$) or R604,4, the critical value, is higher than the observed value of R550 and the null hypothesis cannot be rejected.

3.1.1.2 Test of one sample mean: n < 30

If our sample is smaller than 30, say 20, we cannot refer to the normal curve. Therefore we cannot use the Z-tables to determine the area under the normal curve in terms of standard errors. A unique student's distribution is used for each sample size in such cases. The appropriate t-distribution is determined by the degrees of freedom (df).

> **Degrees of freedom** equal the number of independent observations on the varia-bles of interest minus the number of statistics calculated.

For a test of a single mean the degrees of freedom are one less than the sample size (n − 1). If our sample size in the preceding example was 20, the standard error will be

$$\frac{900}{\sqrt{20}} = 201,3$$

The t-value is 1,729 in a one-tailed distribution on 0,05 level of significance (see table A-2).* The critical value will therefore be 500 + 1,729 (201,3) or R848,0.

3.1.1.3 Test of proportions: one sample

In testing a proportion the procedure is the same as it is in testing a mean, the only differ-ence being that the estimated standard error of the proportion $(\hat{\sigma}_p)$ is substituted for the estimated standard error of the mean $(\hat{\sigma}_{\bar{x}})$.

Suppose the financial institution in our preceding example is considering establishing a building society for clients. Before this step is taken, however, management wants to be very sure (0,05 level of significance) that 50 % or more of the households put their savings in building societies. According to the sample survey 58 % have savings accounts at building societies. The procedure is as follows:

(1) Specify the null hypothesis:

H_0: p < 0,50

(2) Level of significance required:

$\alpha = 0,05$ thus Z = 1,64

(3) Calculate the standard error:

$$\sigma_p = \sqrt{\frac{p(1 - p)}{n}} = \sqrt{\frac{0,5(1 - 0,5)}{200}} = 0,035$$

---

* Table A-2 presents the values for a two-tailed distribution. The level of significance for one-tailed distribution is multiplied by 2 to give 0,05 x 2 = 0,10.

(4) Calculate the critical value:
Critical value = 0,50 + 1,64(,035) = 0,557

(5) Since the observed value (0,58) is larger than the critical value, the null hypothesis is rejected.

3.1.1.4 Comparing two sample means or proportions

Very often the information gathered in sample surveys is designed to reveal whether there are differences between two or more areas in selected characteristics of elements in the areas, or whether changes over time have occurred in a particular area in selected characteristics of elements in that area. In such cases the null hypothesis is expressed as H_0: $P_1 = P_2$ (proportions) or $\mu_1 = \mu_2$ (means). The population means (proportions) are equal for the two groups. We shall discuss the comparison of two sample proportions before turning our attention to the comparison of two sample means in the sections that follow.

(a) Comparing two sample proportions – two-tailed test

This statistical test is best explained with the aid of a practical example. Let us take the following example: in sample surveys in 1985 the Bureau of Market Research (BMR) found that 169 out of 426 multiple households in Soweto owned refrigerators as against 134 out of 396 multiple households in Umlazi. We want to know whether the difference between the results is significant on the 0,05 level.

The problem can be summarised as follows:

P_1 = 169/426 = ,397 and n_1 = 426

P_2 = 134/396 = ,338 and n_2 = 396

(1) *Formulate the null hypothesis.* Our null hypothesis is that the proportions are equal for both populations, that is $P_1 = P_2$, where P_1 and P_2 are the population proportions, corresponding to populations 1 and 2 respectively.

(2) *Select the level of significance required.* The 0,05 level of significance is selected. Therefore 95 % (47,5 % on the right and 47,5 % on the left) of the area under the normal curve must be included, (that is 1,96 standard errors according to table A-1).

(3) *Determine the critical value of the test statistic.* The critical value or values can be determined after calculating the standard deviation of the difference between two sample proportions.

Where

$\bar{P}$ is the weighted average proportion of the two samples owning refrigerators. It is equal to 0,369. It is calculated as follows:

$P_1 = ,397 \ (169/426)$

$P_2 = ,338 \ (134/396)$

$\bar{P} = ,369 \ (169 + 134)/(426 + 396)$

Now that we have the estimated $\bar{P}$, the standard error of the difference between the two proportions can be calculated as follows:

$$\hat{\sigma}(P_1 - P_2) = \sqrt{\bar{P}(1 - \bar{P})(\frac{1}{n_1} + \frac{1}{n_2})}$$

$\therefore \hat{\sigma}(P_1 - P_2) = 0,0337$

The formula for calculating the critical value is:

Critical value $= 0 \pm Z \ \hat{\sigma}(P_1 - P_2)$

$\qquad\qquad 0 \pm (1,96)(0,0337)$

$\qquad\qquad 0 \pm 0,066$

If the population proportions are the same and we undertake a large number of studies with the same sample sizes as those above, the difference between the two percentages will not exceed 0,066 or 6,6 % in 95 % of the studies.

(4) *Determine the observed value of the test statistic.* The difference between the sample proportions $(P_1 - P_2)$ is the test statistic ,059 (,397 − ,338).

(5) *Compare the observed value with the critical value.* In the study in our example the percentage of households with refrigerators in Soweto was 0,059 or 5,9 % higher than the percentage in Umlazi. Put differently, the percentage of households with refrigerators in Umlazi was 0,059 or 5,9 % lower than the percentage in Soweto. Therefore the observed value is lower than the critical value (6,6 %) at a 95 % confidence level and the null hypothesis of equal proportions cannot be rejected on the 0,05 level of significance. The probability is more than 5 % that the null hypothesis may have been correct.

We can also determine a Z-value and a corresponding level of significance where the critical value is equal to the observed value:

$Z \times 0,0337 = 0,059$

$$\therefore Z = \frac{0,059}{0,0337}$$

$$= 1,75$$

In table A-1 0,9198 is the level of confidence for a Z-value of 1,75 and the level of significance is 0,0802.

(b) Comparing two sample proportions – one-tailed test

In the preceding example our main concern was whether we could state on a 95 % level of confidence that there was a difference between the proportion of households with refrigerators in Soweto and in Umlazi. We were not interested in which of the two percentages was higher. That was a two-tailed test. But we could have tested to see whether the percentage for Soweto was higher than the percentage for Umlazi. The hypothesis in this test would be that the percentage of refrigerator ownership in Soweto is equal to or lower than it is in Umlazi.

$H_0 : P_1 - P_2 \leq 0$

The procedure is the same as in the preceding example except that here only one tail of the normal curve is of interest.

Therefore the critical value is

$0 + Z \hat{\sigma}(P_1 - P_2)$

$0 + 1{,}64(0{,}0337)$

$0 + 0{,}055$

Here the null hypothesis is rejected and it can be stated that the percentage of households with refrigerators is higher in Soweto than in Umlazi.

We can also determine a Z-value and a corresponding level of significance where the critical value is equal to the observed value:

$Z(0{,}0337) = 0{,}059$

$$Z = \frac{0{,}059}{0{,}0337}$$

$$= 1{,}75$$

In table A-1 only 0,0401 or 4,01 % of the area under the normal curve in one tail is further than 1,75 σ from the centre. Whereas the preceding hypothesis could only be rejected on the 0,0802 level of significance, this hypothesis can be rejected on the 0,0401 level of significance.

(c) Comparing sample means

In calculations of significant levels for two sample proportions the Z-value of the normal distribution is an integral part of the formula for the critical value. We stated in our discussions of sample sizes in chapter 13 that when a large number of samples are drawn from the same population the sample means lie round the population mean in the shape of a normal distribution. Such samples, however, must be bigger than 30. The Z-value of the normal curve also forms part of the formula for determining the critical value in comparisons of two sample means but when samples are smaller than 30 the normal curve is not applicable and a t-value is used instead of a Z-value. In the next section we shall discuss the comparison of two sample means where the sample is bigger than 30.

(d) Comparing two sample means where samples are bigger than 30

In the following example we compare two sample means. Sample surveys among multiple households in Johannesburg and Pretoria show that a sample of 426 in Johannesburg earned R9 624 per month on average with a standard deviation of R7 451 as against a sample of 295 in Pretoria earning R9 359 on average with a standard deviation of R6 550. We want to know whether the difference between these results is significant on the 0,05 level. The problem can be summarised as follows:

$\bar{x}_1$ = R9 624, $\hat{\sigma}_1$ = R7 451, n_1 = 426

$\bar{x}_2$ = R9 359, $\hat{\sigma}_2$ = R6 550, n_2 = 295

Formulate the null hypothesis:

$\mu_1 = \mu_2$, where μ_1 and μ_2 are the respective population means

Select the desired level of significance:

0,05 level as specified.

Observed level of test statistic:

R9 624 – R9 359 or R265

Critical values for test statistic

First we determine the standard error of the difference between the two samples.

$$\hat{\sigma}(\bar{x}_1 - \bar{x}_2) = \sqrt{\frac{\hat{\sigma}_1^2}{n_1} + \frac{\hat{\sigma}_2^2}{n_2}}$$

$$= \sqrt{\frac{7451^2}{426} + \frac{6550^2}{295}}$$

$$= 525$$

The critical value is calculated by the following formula:

Critical value = $0 \pm Z\hat{\sigma}_{(\bar{x}_1 - \bar{x}_2)}$

$$0 \pm 1,96 \, (525)$$

$$0 \pm 1\,029$$

The critical values –R1 029 and +R1 029 represent the biggest differences that can occur by chance in 95 % of all possible samples of the particular sizes drawn from the two populations.

By changing the Z-value in the formula above to 2,58 we calculate the biggest differences that can occur by chance in 99 % of all possible samples of the particular sizes drawn from the two populations. They are $-$R1 355 and $+$R1 355.

Comparing the observed and critical values

The observed value of R265 falls within the two critical values, -R1 029 and +R1 029. Therefore we have to accept the null hypothesis of equal incomes on the 0,05 level of significance. Had the income in Johannesburg for instance been R1 000 or about 10 % higher or lower than the income in Pretoria, the null hypothesis of two equal incomes on the 0,05 level of significance would still be acceptable.

(e) *Comparing the sample means of small samples*

Suppose we find in sample surveys of multiple households in Johannesburg and Cape Town that samples of 25 in each area have an average income of R9 624 in Johannesburg and R6 751 in Cape Town. We further estimate the standard deviations of the two populations based on the samples at R7 451 for Johannesburg and R4 549 for Cape Town. We want to know whether there is a significant difference between the two incomes on the 0,05 level. The problem is summarised as follows:

$\bar{x}_1$ = R9 624, $\hat{\sigma}_1$ = R7 451, n_1 = 25

$\bar{x}_2$ = R6 751, $\hat{\sigma}_2$ = R4 549, n_2 = 25

The null hypothesis is that the two population averages are the same, in other words, $\mu_1 = \mu_2$. The observed value is R9 624 $-$ R6 751 or R2 873.

The difference between the procedures for small and large samples lies in the determination of the critical value. In this case the estimated standard deviation of the difference between two sample averages is calculated by the formula:

$$\hat{\sigma}_{(\bar{x}_1 - \bar{x}_2)} = \sqrt{\frac{(n_1 - 1)\hat{\sigma}_1^2 + (n_2 - 1)\hat{\sigma}_2^2}{n_1 + n_2 - 2}\left(\frac{1}{n_1} + \frac{1}{n_2}\right)}$$

$$= \sqrt{\frac{(24)55517401 + (24)20693401}{48}\left(\frac{1}{25} + \frac{1}{25}\right)}$$

$$= \text{R1 746}$$

Next we multiply the value of the standard deviation of the difference between two sample means by the t-value which corresponds to the 95 % area of the t-distribution.

In table A-2 we find the t-value in the column with a tail area of 0,05 and the row which corresponds with ($n_1 + n_2 - 2$) or 48 degrees of freedom. It is 2,01, which is very close to the Z-value of 1,96 used in large samples. In this example the use of a t-value instead of a Z-value makes very little difference. If, however, each sample consisted of at least

30 elements, the Z-value would have been used. Therefore these samples of 25 elements per sample very nearly qualified for the use of the Z-value.

The critical value

$$= 0 \pm t\hat{\sigma}_{(\bar{x}_1 - \hat{\sigma}_2)}$$

$$= 0 \pm 2{,}01(1\ 746)$$

$$= 0 \pm \text{R3 } 509$$

The observed value of R2 873 lies within the limits of the critical values of $-$R3 509 and $+$R3 509. The null hypothesis that the population means are the same is therefore accepted. Had the surveys shown that household income in Johannesburg is approximately 50 % higher than in Cape Town, rejection of the null hypothesis of two equal means would not have been possible on the 0,05 level of confidence.

3.1.1.5 Difference between two means: paired comparisons

Occasionally one has to make before and after measurements on the same elements. A typical example is a comparison of sales by a number of shops before and after a sales campaign. The test is to decide whether there is a significant difference between the means of two sets of data: set b_i, the measurement taken before, and set a_i, the measurement taken after.

The appropriate procedure is to use the t-test for related samples, or t_r.

Suppose a study is conducted on the effect of a promotion campaign on the sales of product A. The following sales from 10 randomly selected shops were recorded for the month before and after the campaign:

Shop no	Sales (R'000)	
	Before	After
1	7	8
2	4	5
3	8	12
4	12	11
5	5	8
6	3	4
7	13	13
8	2	2
9	6	5
10	10	13

Has the campaign had a positive effect on sales?

(1) Adopt the null hypothesis that the before-sales results are the same as the after-sales results or higher.

(2) Adopt a significance level, for example 0,05.

(3) Calculation: Rather than focusing on the differences in the means between the two groups, we need to analyse the differences between each individual pair of observations.

(a) Calculate a variable (d_i) which is the difference in sales between group 1 (before) and group 2 (after) for the ith stores:

$$
\begin{aligned}
d_1 &= 7 - 8 = -1 & d_6 &= 3 - 4 = -1 \\
d_2 &= 4 - 5 = -1 & d_7 &= 13 - 13 = 0 \\
d_3 &= 8 - 12 = -4 & d_8 &= 2 - 2 = 0 \\
d_4 &= 12 - 11 = 1 & d_9 &= 6 - 5 = 1 \\
d_5 &= 5 - 8 = -3 & d_{10} &= 10 - 13 = -3
\end{aligned}
$$

(b) Estimated mean difference:

$$(\bar{d}) = \frac{1}{n} \sum_{i=1}^{n} d_i = -1,1$$

(c) Estimated standard deviation of the difference is:

$$\hat{\sigma}_d = \sqrt{\sum_{i=1}^{} \frac{(d_i - \bar{d})^2}{n - 1}}$$

$$= 1,73$$

(d) Estimated standard error of the difference:

$$\hat{\sigma}_{\bar{d}} = \frac{\hat{\sigma}_d}{\sqrt{n}} = 0,55$$

(e) Critical value $= D = t_\alpha \hat{\sigma}_{\bar{d}}$

D = difference expected under the null hypothesis, which is zero in this example.

In our example there are $n - 1 = 9$ degrees of freedom. In table A-2 the t-value for $\alpha = 0,05$ is found to be 1,833.

Therefore the critical value is:

$0 + 1,833 (0,55) = 1,01$

Since our sample value of 1,10 is more than our critical value of 1,01, we reject the null hypothesis at the 5 % level of significance that there is no difference between before and after sales.

3.1.2 Analysis of variance

The analysis of variance makes it possible to compare two* or more sample means. How this is done is explained in the following example:

Our company wants to establish whether the results of three remuneration packages for sales staff differ from one another at a 0,05 level of significance. The three packages are salary only, salary plus commission, and commission only. After 30 salesmen have been randomly grouped, 10 are offered a salary only, 10 are offered a salary plus commission and a further 10 receive commission only. Table 16.1 shows the sales results of these salesmen over a period of three months.

Table 16.1 Units sold over three months by type of remuneration of salesmen

Salesmen	Salary only	Commission only	Salary plus commission
1	105	120	115
2	128	157	191
3	150	180	158
4	160	172	170
5	130	155	165
6	128	160	182
7	104	122	152
8	77	133	131
9	90	105	112
10	100	115	123
	$\bar{x}_1 = 117,2$	$\bar{x}_2 = 141,9$	$\bar{x}_3 = 149,9$

If we relied exclusively on our own intuitive logic in evaluating the performance of these salesmen, the first thing we would notice would be the differences between the average performances of the three groups of salesmen. The 149,9 units sold by salesmen on salary and commission is nearly 30 % higher than the 117,2 units sold by salesmen working for salaries only.

Judging by this relatively big variation between the three groups (columns in the table) there does seem to be a difference between them. What prevents us from stating fairly confidently that a difference does exist is that there are big variations within the groups (columns). For instance, the salesmen on salary sold only 117,2 units on average. But their individual performances vary from as low as 77 units to as high as 160. The 160 units exceed the performances of six salesmen on commission only and the performances

---

* As explained earlier, Z- and t-tests can also be applied in comparisons of two sample means.

of six salesmen on salary plus commission. Therefore our intuitive logic tells us that the greater the variation between the columns (groups) and the smaller the variation in the columns, the more confident we can be that differences do exist between the columns or groups. So we have to find two criteria: one measuring variations between columns, and one measuring variations within columns. Once we have established the between and within column variations and divide the between column variations by the within column variations we arrive at a figure indicating the level of confidence at which we are able to state that variations exist between the columns. The higher this figure, the greater our confidence will be.

(a) Measuring between column variations

The between column variation is measured by calculating the mean squares between groups (MST). The formula is:

$$\text{MST} = \frac{(\text{No of rows})[\text{sum of } \{\bar{x} \text{ each column} - \text{grand mean }\}^2]}{\text{Number of groups} - 1}$$

The details that are needed to calculate MST can be obtained from table 16.1:

Number of rows   = 10

Column means   = 117,2; 141,9; 149,9

Grand mean $= \dfrac{117,2 + 141,9 + 149,9}{3}$

        $= 136,3$

Number of groups $= 3$

MST is calculated as follows:

$$\frac{(10)[(117,2 - 136,3)^2 + (141,9 - 136,3)^2 + (149,9 - 136,3)^2]}{2}$$

$$\text{MST} = \frac{10(365 + 31 + 185)}{2}$$

     $= 2\ 905$

(b) Measuring within column variation

The variation within the groups is measured as *the mean sum of squares within groups* or mean square error (MSE).

$$\text{MSE} = \frac{\text{sum of squares within groups}}{\text{degrees of freedom}} = \frac{\text{SSE}}{\text{df}}$$

$$
\begin{aligned}
\text{SSE} = {} & (117{,}2 - 105)^2 + (117{,}2 - 128)^2 + (117{,}2 - 150)^2 + \\
& (117{,}2 - 160)^2 + (117{,}2 - 130)^2 + (117{,}2 - 128)^2 + \\
& (117{,}2 - 104)^2 + (117{,}2 - 77)^2 + (117{,}2 - 90)^2 + \\
& (117{,}2 - 100)^2 + (141{,}9 - 120)^2 + (141{,}9 - 157)^2 + \\
& (141{,}9 - 180)^2 + (141{,}9 - 172)^2 + (141{,}9 - 155)^2 + \\
& (141{,}9 - 160)^2 + (141{,}9 - 122)^2 + (141{,}9 - 133)^2 + \\
& (141{,}9 - 105)^2 + (141{,}9 - 155)^2 + (149{,}9 - 115)^2 + \\
& (149{,}9 - 191)^2 + (149{,}9 - 158)^2 + (149{,}9 - 170)^2 + \\
& (149{,}9 - 165)^2 + (149{,}9 - 182)^2 + (149{,}9 - 152)^2 + \\
& (149{,}9 - 131)^2 + (149{,}9 - 112)^2 + (149{,}9 - 123)^2 \\
= {} & 19\ 561
\end{aligned}
$$

$$
\begin{aligned}
\text{df} = {} & \text{sum of the sample sizes for all groups minus the number of groups} \\
= {} & 30 - 3 \\
= {} & 27
\end{aligned}
$$

$$\frac{\text{SSE}}{\text{df}} = \frac{19\ 561}{27} = 724$$

(c) Observed value of F

By dividing our between column variations (MST) criterion by our criterion of within column variations (MSE) we arrive at the observed value of F:

$$
\begin{aligned}
\text{F} &= \frac{2\ 905}{724} \\
&= 4{,}01
\end{aligned}
$$

(d) Determining the critical value of F-ratio

The critical value is obtained from the F-distribution table in table A-4 and is dependent on

☐ the degrees of freedom for the numerator (MST) and the denominator (MSE), and

☐ the level of significance we desire.

The degrees of freedom for MST are 2 in our example (the number of groups minus one). The degrees of freedom for MSE in our example are 27 (total number of units in all the samples minus the number of samples).

Using a level of significance of 0,05 we find that the critical value for F with 2 and 27 degrees of freedom is 3,35.

Since our observed value of 4,01 is more than the critical value of 3,35, we reject the null hypothesis of no differences between the groups.

3.2 Tests requiring ordinal data

3.2.1 The Mann-Whitney test (U-test)

The Mann-Whitney test is a non-parametric alternative to the t-test for two independent samples.

Suppose two groups of 12 salesmen are randomly selected. Group A undergoes sales training while group B receives no training. The sales performance of the two groups is as follows after two months:

Units sold

Group A: 56, 58, 60, 65, 70, 77, 77, 80, 81, 84, 85, 89
  (mean = 73,50)

Group B: 62, 64, 75, 76, 82, 86, 87, 88, 92, 96, 98, 100
  (mean = 83,83)

The means of the two samples are 73,50 and 83,83. We wish to decide whether the difference between the means is significant on the 0,05 level. The two samples are arranged jointly as if they were one sample, in order of increasing number of units sold. The ranks for each group are then summed as illustrated below:

Row scores		Combined ranks	
A	**B**	**A**	**B**
56	62	1	4
58	64	2	5
60	75	3	8
65	76	6	9
70	82	7	14
77	86	10	17
77	87	11	18
80	88	12	19
81	92	13	21
84	96	15	22
85	98	16	23
89	100	20	24
		116	184
		(R1)	(R2)

A statistic called U is computed.

$$U = \frac{n_1 n_2 + n_1(n_1 + 1)}{2} - R_1$$

OR

$$\frac{n_1 n_2 + n_2(n_2 + 1)}{2} - R_2$$

where n_1 and n_2 = sample size groups 1 and 2 respectively

R_1, R_2 = sum of ranks assigned to groups 1 and 2 respectively

$$U = (12)(12) + \frac{12(12 + 1)}{2} - 116 = 160$$

The test statistic is given by the formula

$$Z = \frac{U - \frac{n_1 n_2}{2}}{\sqrt{\frac{(n_1)(n_2)(n_1 + n_2 + 1)}{12}}}$$

$$= \frac{106 - 72}{\sqrt{\frac{(12)(12)(12 + 12 + 1)}{12}}}$$

$$= \frac{34}{17,32}$$

$$= 1,963$$

The Z-value for a 0,05 level of significance is 1,960. Since the test statistic exceeds the Z-value for a 0,05 level of significance, we reject the null hypothesis of equal means.

3.2.2 The Kruskal-Wallis one-way analysis of variance by ranks

The need to analyse ordinal data obtained from three or more independent samples arises most often when we wish to determine the acceptability of a brand among different age, language, residential or income groups. The following is one such example:

We wish to establish whether there is a difference in the rating of the taste of a certain brand of cigarette by different age groups. A taste test is conducted among three samples aged under 25, 25 to 50, and over 50. Each sample consists of 200 respondents. Each respondent is requested to rate the taste on a 1 (terrible) to 10 (excellent) scale.

The procedure is as follows:

(1) Rank order the scores from all 600 respondents together. Suppose there were 10 respondents who assigned the taste a rating of 1. The rank order of these 10 is from 1 to 10, a total of 55 and an average of 5,5. Therefore each of the 10 will be assigned an average rank of 5,5. If a further 20 respondents assigned the taste a rating of 2, their rank orders are from 11 to 30, that is 20,5 on average.

(2) Sum the scores of the ranks of each group. The total rank score from 1 to 600 is 180 300. Suppose it is distributed among the three groups as follows:

R1 (under 25 years) = 55 800 R2 (25 to 50 years) = 60 100 R3 (over 50 years) = 64 400

(3) Calculate H as

$$H = \frac{12}{N(N + 1)} \sum_{j=1}^{k} \frac{R_j^2}{n_j} - 3(N + 1)$$

n_j = size of sample j

N = total number of observations in all samples

R_j = sum of ranks in the jth sample

$$H = \frac{12}{600(600 + 1)} \left[\frac{(55\ 800)^2}{200} + \frac{(60\ 100)^2}{200} + \frac{(64\ 400)^2}{200} \right] - 3(600 + 1)$$

(4) The probability associated with a value of 6,15 is obtained from table A-3 (x^2-distribution) with k − 1 (3 − 1 = 2) degrees of freedom. The probability is less than 0,05 that there is no difference in the rating of the quality of the test of the brand of cigarettes.

3.2.3 The Friedman analysis

The Friedman analysis is appropriate for determining whether respondents prefer certain brands, colours, shapes, tastes, etc, to others. The following is an example:

Three possible brands are shown to a sample of 200 respondents who are requested to rate each brand on a scale from 1 (terrible) to 10 (excellent). An example of the ratings of five of the respondents is illustrated below:

Respondents	Brands		
	A	B	C
1	6	4	7
2	1	4	6
3	8	2	1
4	3	3	6
5	4	4	7

Assign ranks to the scores in each row from 1 to k (number of columns), with 1 representing the smallest score, and sum the ranks for each column. This is illustrated below:

Respondents	Brands		
	A	B	C
1	2	1	3
2	1	2	3
3	3	2	1
4	1	1,5	3
5	1	1,5	3
.	.	.	.
.	.	.	.
200	2	1	3
R	**430**	**410**	**360**

A value of χ_r^2 is calculated by the formula

$$\chi_r^2 = \frac{12}{Nk(k + 1)} \sum_{j=1}^{k} (R_j^2) - 3N(k + 1)$$

where N = sample size (number of rows)
      k = number of columns

$$\chi_r^2 = \frac{12}{200(3)(4)}[(430)^2 + (410)^2 + (360)^2] - 3(200)(4)$$

$$= \frac{12}{2\,400} (482\,600) - 2\,400$$

$$= 2\,413 - 2\,400$$

$$= 13$$

In table A-3 we see that with two degrees of freedom the value of χ_r^2 at a level of significance of 0,01 is 9,21. The null hypothesis of equally acceptable brands is therefore rejected.

3.3 Tests requiring nominal data

3.3.1 The chi-square test

The chi-square test applies to nominal data and is concerned with whether the differences between an observed set of frequencies and a theoretically expected set of frequencies are significant. This test will be demonstrated in the following three examples:

☐ a test of distributions by categories of a single sample

☐ a test for the independence of two nominal variables

☐ comparing sample proportions.

3.3.1.1 A test of distributions by categories of a single sample

A sample survey of 600 respondents yielded the following preferences for four brands of toothpaste:

$$
\begin{array}{l}
A = 155 \\
B = 140 \\
C = 135 \\
D = \underline{170} \\
600
\end{array}
$$

Is there a significant difference?
The null hypothesis is: there is no difference.

The chi-square (x^2) test requires the following steps:

(1) Determine the number that would be in each category if the null hypothesis were correct (E_i):

$$
\begin{array}{l}
A = 150 \\
B = 150 \\
C = 150 \\
D = \underline{150} \\
600
\end{array}
$$

(2) Calculate x^2 as follows:

$$
x^2 = \sum_{i=1}^{k} \frac{(O_i - E_i)^2}{E_i}
$$

O_i = observed number in *i*th category

E_i = expected number in *i*th category

k = number of categories

In our example we get:

$$
x^2 = \frac{(155 - 150)^2}{150} + \frac{(140 - 150)^2}{150} + \frac{(135 - 150)^2}{150} + \frac{(170 - 150)^2}{150}
$$

$$
= 5
$$

(3) The probability associated with this value is read off from table A-3 with $k - 1$ (three) degrees of freedom. On the 0,10 level of significance the value is 6,25. The observed value is therefore lower than the critical value and the hypothesis of no difference cannot be rejected on the 0,10 level of significance.

3.3.1.2 A test for the independence of two nominal variables

Let us assume that we have collected data on age versus brand of cigarette smoked. We want to determine whether there is a relation between an individual's age and the brand of cigarette smoked. The data are shown in table 16.2.

Table 16.2 Distribution of brand of cigarettes smoked by age group

Age group	Brand			Total
	A	B	C	
Under 20	15	20	25	60
21–40	30	30	30	90
41–60	40	25	25	90
Over 60	30	20	10	60
Total	**115**	**95**	**90**	**300**

Our next step is to construct a similar table of data on the assumption that there is no relation between age and brand of cigarette smoked.* The row and column totals will be the same as in the table of observed data.

Steps

(1) *Identify the null hypothesis*

Our null hypothesis for this analysis is: there is no relation between a person's age and the brand of cigarette he smokes.

(2) *Construct a table of theoretical frequencies*

Table 16.3 Distribution of brand of cigarettes smoked by age group (theoretical frequencies)

Age group	Brand			Total
	A	B	C	
Under 20	23,0	19,0	18,0	60
21–40	34,5	28,5	27,0	90
41–60	34,5	28,5	27,0	90
Over 60	23,0	19,0	18,0	60
Total	**115,0**	**95,0**	**90,0**	**300**

---

* The percentage distribution of the brands smoked is the same for all age groups.

(3) *Determine the calculated value of the chi-square statistic*

This statistic is calculated by using the following terms:

$$\chi^2 = \sum_{i=1}^{r} \sum_{j=1}^{k} \frac{(O_{ij} - E_{ij})^2}{E_{ij}}$$

$$\frac{(15 - 23,0)^2}{23,0} + \frac{(30 - 34,5)^2}{34,5} + \frac{(40 - 34,5)^2}{34,5} + \frac{(30 - 23,0)^2}{23,0} +$$

$$\frac{(20 - 19,0)^2}{19,0} + \frac{(30 - 28,5)^2}{28,5} + \frac{(25 - 28,5)^2}{28,5} + \frac{(20 - 19,0)^2}{19,0} +$$

$$\frac{(25 - 18,0)^2}{18,0} + \frac{(30 - 27,0)^2}{27,0} + \frac{(25 - 27,0)^2}{27,0} + \frac{(10 - 18,0)^2}{18,0}$$

$$= 13,46$$

(4) *Determine the critical value for the chi-square statistic*

The critical value is obtained from the chi-square distribution table (table A-3). First, we have to determine the number of degrees of freedom (df). For chi-square tests of this type df = (number of rows − 1) × (number of columns − 1) where the number of rows and columns refers to the table we are using. In this case df will be (3 − 1) × (4 − 1) or 6. Assuming that we want to test the hypothesis at the 0,05 level, the critical value is 12,60 for six degrees of freedom.

(5) *Compare the calculated chi-square with the critical value*

Since the calculated value (13,46) exceeds the critical value (12,60) we can reject the hypothesis of no relation between a person's age and the brand of cigarette he smokes.

In applying the chi-square technique it is important that each cell in the theoretical table should have a frequency of at least 5. If not, the data should be rearranged.

3.3.1.3 Comparing two or more sample proportions

In section 3.1.1.4 we demonstrated the use of Z-values from the normal distribution for determining the level of significance in comparisons of two sample proportions. The chi-square technique can be used to test the difference between two and more proportions. To illustrate the application of the chi-square technique, let us assume that the following information was collected on brand X of cigarettes smoked in four regions:

Table 16.4 Smokers and non-smokers of brand X by area (observed frequencies)

Area	Smoke brand X	Smoke other brand	Total
Area A	48	47	95
Area B	35	70	105
Area C	40	70	110
Area D	42	48	90
Total	**165**	**235**	**400**

Formulate the null hypothesis: There is no difference between areas in the percentage of smokers who prefer brand X:

$$P_1 = P_2 = P_3$$

Construct a hypothesised table in which there are no variations between areas in smoking of brand X.

Table 16.5 Smokers and non-smokers of brand X by area (theoretical frequencies)

Area	Smoke brand X	Smoke other brand	Total
Area A	39	56	95
Area B	43	62	105
Area C	46	64	110
Area D	37	53	90
Total	**165**	**235**	**400**

In the hypothesised table the row and the column totals are the same as in the table with the observed values. In the table with the observed values it can be seen that 165 of the 400 smokers smoke brand X, that is 41,25 %. In the hypothesised table the number of smokers of brand X is calculated as 41,25 % of the number of smokers in each area.

Calculate the chi-square statistic

Whether or not the null hypothesis can be rejected will depend on the degree of the variations between the observed values and the hypothesised values. A measure of the discrepancy between the two is obtained by calculating the χ^2 statistic as follows:

$$\chi^2 = \sum_{i=1}^{r} \sum_{j=1}^{k} \frac{(O_{ij} - E_{ij})^2}{E_{ij}}$$

$$= \frac{(48 - 39)^2}{39} + \frac{(35 - 43)^2}{43} + \frac{(40 - 46)^2}{46} + \frac{(42 - 37)^2}{37} +$$

$$\frac{(47 - 56)^2}{56} + \frac{(70 - 62)^2}{62} + \frac{(70 - 64)^2}{64} + \frac{(48 - 53)^2}{53}$$

$$= 8,54$$

The number of degrees of freedom is:

(number of rows − 1) × (number of columns − 1) or (2 − 1) × (4 − 1) = 3

For the 0,05 level of significance, the critical value will be 7,81. As the calculated value (8,54) exceeds this, the null hypothesis that the population proportions smoking brand X are the same for all areas can be rejected. There would be a chance of just less than 5 in 100 that the population proportions are the same.

3.3.2 The McNemar test

The McNemar test is a test of distributions by categories of two related samples. It is a common form of testing advertising effectiveness.

Suppose a manufacturer of brand A coffee conducts a sample survey among 500 respondents. The respondents are requested to select one of the four brands of coffee. Brand A is preferred by 100 respondents while the other 400 respondents prefer one of the other brands. After the manufacturer has advertised his product on television for a month the same 500 respondents are interviewed again. In the second survey 80 of the 100 who chose brand A in the first survey chose brand A again and a further 40 who chose a different brand in the first survey also chose brand A. Was the advertisement effective in inducing consumers to select brand A?

The procedure for determining this probability is:

(1) Place the observations in a 2 × 2 contingency table:

		After advertisement	
		Chose other	Chose brand A
Before advertisement	Chose brand A	206(A)	80(B)
	Chose other	360(C)	40(D)

(2) Calculate χ^2-value:

$$= \frac{(|A - D| - 1)^2}{A + D}$$

$$= \frac{(|20 - 40| - 1)^2}{60}$$

$$= 6{,}02$$

(3) Determine the probability by consulting table A-3.
The degrees of freedom $= (2 - 1)(2 - 1) = 1$. There is a less than 2,5 % probability that the results would have occurred by chance. The null hypothesis of no change can be rejected on the 0,02 level of significance.

4 SUMMARY

There are six basic steps in significance testing: formulating the null hypothesis, selecting the appropriate statistical test, deciding on a particular significance level, calculating the test statistic, determining the critical value of the test statistic, and comparing the observed value with the critical value.

Typically the null hypothesis is a negative, sceptical statement which has to be proved wrong by the researcher. The basis for statistical testing is that the null hypothesis is accepted until proof to the contrary becomes overwhelming. The nature of the data, the number of samples and the relationship of the samples are the main considerations in the selection of an appropriate statistical test. The desired level of significance most often used in practice is 0,05. This means there is only a 5 % or a 1 in 20 chance that rejection of the hypothesis was a mistake. If the observed value of the test statistic exceeds the critical value, the null hypothesis is rejected. If not, the null hypothesis must be accepted.

The Mann-Whitney test, the Kruskal-Wallis one-way analysis of variance by rank, and the Friedman analysis are typical tests requiring ordinal data. For testing nominal data the chi-square test is the most popular. Of the tests requiring interval or ratio data Z- and t-tests and analysis of variance are most often used.

Multivariate statistical techniques

Chapter 17: T A Wegner

Multivariate statistical techniques

1 INTRODUCTION

Most statistical analysis of marketing data takes place on one measure (or variable), or at most on two measures simultaneously. A frequency distribution is a typical univariate statistical technique, while simple linear regression and chi-square applied to a cross-tabulation are two typical bivariate statistical techniques. Such *univariate* and *bivariate* statistical analyses do provide valuable marketing information. However, there are a number of marketing issues which can benefit significantly from additional insights gained through the statistical analysis of more than two measures simultaneously. Such techniques are called *multivariate* statistical methods.

The primary purpose of these techniques is to identify relationships or uncover patterns of associations among multiple variables collectively which are not obvious from the simpler bivariate techniques. They afford managers or researchers the opportunity of gaining greater insight into relationships and patterns on several marketing measures simultaneously and therefore generate a more holistic picture of the marketing issues under study.

A marketer is not required to learn the technical complexities of these multivariate techniques, but does need to understand the purpose, interpretation, uses and limitations of each multivariate statistical technique. This allows a user to select the technique most suited to the objectives of a study. In addition, an overview permits a marketer to appreciate the additional information which such techniques can generate. Since each technique also has specific data requirements, an understanding of these requirements will avoid the inappropriate application of a technique with resulting meaningless output.

This chapter will give an overview of a selection of commonly used multivariate statistical methods which are of value in a marketing context. It should also assist marketing managers who commission marketing research which presents multivariate findings to appreciate the value of such information. The emphasis of this chapter will be on explaining the purpose of each multivariate technique, the interpretation of its outputs, and its possible uses and limitations.

2 CLASSIFICATION OF TECHNIQUES

There is no single classification of multivariate techniques. However, one useful classification of these techniques is to *group* them as broadly structural or functional. The class of *structural techniques* looks for underlying patterns within the datasets of multiple varia-bles to simplify the interpretations from such data. These methods are solely descriptive in nature. *Functional techniques* on the other hand look for statistical relationships between sets of variables to be used for prediction purposes. While this broad distinction is use-ful, a particular method could be classified as belonging to both groups, depending on the purpose for which it is used. An understanding of their modus operandi is therefore useful in determining how a particular method will be used.

3 THE DATA REQUIREMENTS FOR MULTIVARIATE TECHNIQUES

To apply multivariate techniques, data are required on a large number of measures relating to a particular study. The underlying assumptions of each technique determine the type of data that can be validly analysed by the technique. A potential user of multivariate techniques should therefore be aware of a particular technique's data requirements prior to conducting the study. A few techniques have been developed to further analyse associations between categorical variables (of consumers and products/brands) as represented by cross-tabulations and thus require only nominally scaled data. The tech-niques of *correspondence analysis* and *loglinear modelling* fall into this category. Another (small) set of multivariate techniques requires only the ranking of alternatives (that is or-dinal data*) as input data to evaluate consumer perceptions of product characteristics. These refer to the techniques of *multidimensional scaling* (*MDS*) and *conjoint analysis*. Fi-nally, there is a wider set of techniques, such as *factor analysis*, *discriminant analysis*, *cluster analysis* and *multiple regression analysis*, which identify and interpret relationships between essentially quantitative measures. For these techniques, at least, interval scaled data are required. Since rating scales (interval data type*) comprise a large proportion of market-ing response data (that is attitudinal rating scales), such data are readily applicable to these techniques. It should be noted, however, that these quantitative-based techniques can, with certain modifications to their assumptions and methods of analysis, accommo-date limited categorical (nominal and ordinal scaled) variables.

If the use of a particular multivariate technique is envisaged in a study, the data-collection instruments should be appropriately designed to ensure the availability of data of the correct type and in the correct format.

The following sections will review a selection of commonly used multivariate techniques with emphasis on current (or potential) marketing applications.

---

* See chapter 16 for a detailed discussion of nominal, ordinal, ratio and interval data.

4 MULTIPLE LINEAR REGRESSION AND CORRELATION ANALYSIS

If there is a relationship between two ratio-scaled random variables, for example sales and advertising expenditure, it can be quantified and measured using simple linear regression and correlation analysis. Since advertising expenditure is assumed to influence sales, it is known as the predictor variable, while sales is the response variable. However, usually more than one predictor variable influences the outcome of a particular phenomenon. In marketing, for example, the demand for a product (the response variable) may be related not only to its price, but promotional efforts such as sales force size, advertising expenditure, exposure and possibly even certain consumer demographic and socio-economic factors. When a number of predictor variables influence the outcome of a single ratio-scaled response variable, *multiple linear regression analysis* can be used to formalise the relationship.

Multiple linear regression analysis is possibly the most widely used multivariate technique in practice. Two well-known application areas are econometrics (analysing economic trends) and forecasting sales volumes. Studies have also been reported which use regression analysis to define market segments of customers, using demographics, lifestyles and psychographic measures as potential predictors.

4.1 The data requirements

The data for the response variable should be *ratio scaled*. Illustrations of ratio-scaled measures include sales (in units or rand), processing time, volume, distance and age. The data for the predictor variables, on the other hand, may be either categorical (for example gender, qualification or seniority) or continuous (quantitative) (for example age, income, duration, weight or price). The sampling units (such as products, consumers, companies) from which data on the response and predictor variables are captured are assumed to have been randomly selected.

4.2 The rationale of multiple linear regression

Multiple linear regression analysis is used to quantify the influence of two or more predictor variables (generally identified as X_1, X_2, X_3,.... X_p) on a single response variable (identified as Y). This formalised relationship can then be used to estimate values of the single response measure (Y) based on known values of the potential predictor measures. It can therefore be classified as a *functional* technique.

Additionally, the regression model can provide further insights into the identified relationship: it can identify the relative importance of each predictor variable in predicting the response variable; it can establish the overall strength of the relationship (from multiple correlation measures) and consequently provide insight into the overall usefulness of the regression model for estimation purposes; it can establish whether a linear structure is the most appropriate form of the relationship between the predictor variables and response variable; and finally it can highlight the omission of potentially useful predictor measures.

4.3 Structure and interpretation of a multiple linear regression model

A multiple regression model is fitted to the observed data using the *method of least squares* principle. This principle requires that the fitted regression equation should minimise the sum of the squared deviation between the actual Y observations and their estimated Y values based on the linear regression model.

The mathematical model produced by multiple regression analysis is a linear equation consisting of the set of predictor variables as follows:

Expected $Y = b_o + b_1 X_1 + b_2 X_2 + b_3 X_3 + \dots + b_p X_p$

The regression coefficients (b_1, b_2, b_3, etc) are weights which measure the relative importance of each predictor variable in the prediction of the response variable Y. Coefficient values which are relatively close to zero indicate that the associated predictor variable is of little value in explaining the behaviour of the response variable. The converse applies to coefficients whose values are relatively large. Classical hypothesis testing methods (such as the t-test and partial F-tests) are used to establish the statistical significance of each predictor variable. These hypothesis tests can establish not only which predictor variables are useful predictors of the response variable Y, but also their relative importance. Instead of manually performing these tests on each predictor variable in turn, most statistical software packages offer the facility of stepwise regression modelling. Stepwise regression systematically determines the most significant combination of predictor variables by testing each variable for significance prior to including it in the final significant regression model.

To obtain estimates of the response variable Y, a set of values for the significant predictor variables are substituted into the regression model. The usefulness of the regression model as a reliable estimator or predictor of the response variable Y can be gauged by the closeness of the estimated Y values to the actual Y values for the same set of predictor variable values. A statistical measure, known as the coefficient of multiple determination, R^2, gauges the overall usefulness of the predictor variables in estimating or predicting the response variable. R^2 values close to one indicate a highly useful model, while R^2 values close to zero mean that the identified predictor variables are weakly related to the response variable Y.

Multiple regression models (linear and some non-linear forms) can be produced by almost every available statistical package. These include mainframe packages such as BMDP, SAS and Genstat, and microcomputer software packages (most in a Windows environment) such as SPSS, Statgraphics, Statistica, Systat and MINITAB. Even spreadsheets such as Lotus and Quattro Pro have limited multiple regression capabilities.

4.4 An illustrative example: demand for motor vehicles

The marketing department of a motor vehicle manufacturer is investigating factors that could influence the national demand for motor vehicles (Y − in thousands of units). Four potential predictor variables are identified as prime interest rates (X_1), the business confidence index (X_2), gross national product (GNP) (in billions of Rand)(X_3), and the retail fuel price (cents per litre) (X_4).

Based on a sample of 65 sets of quarterly observations taken over a 17-year period, the following multiple linear regression model was derived (partial output shown from BMDP 1R package):

Expected $Y = 18,45 − 6,345X_1 + 1,2X_2 + 13,44X_3 − 3,55X_4$ That is expected demand = $18,45 − 6,345 \star$ prime interest rate + $1,2 \star$ business confidence index + $13,44 \star$ GNP − $3,55 \star$ retail fuel price

$R^2 = 0,604$ (coefficient of multiple determination)

Two of the four predictor variables, namely the business confidence index (X_2) and gross national product (GNP) (X_3), directly influence the demand for motor vehicles, while prime interest rates (X_1) and retail fuel price (X_4) have an inverse impact, as noted from the signs of their respective regression coefficients. This is consistent with intuition. To determine the set of significant predictors only, each regression coefficient is tested against a hypothesis that its value is actually zero. If the hypothesis is accepted, the associated predictor variable has no predictive validity. In this example, only the b_2 coefficient is found to be non-significant, implying that only the business confidence index is not a meaningful predictor of motor vehicle demand.

Each coefficient also indicates the marginal change in the value of the response variable for a unit change in the corresponding predictor variable. Thus if prime interest rates rise by one percentage point and the values of all other variables are held constant, then the demand for motor vehicles is expected to decline by 6,345 (that is 6 345) units in the given quarter. Similarly, a R1 billion rise in GNP in a given quarter is expected to increase the demand for motor vehicles by 13,44 (that is 13 440) units.

An estimate of motor vehicle demand in a given quarter for given levels of gross national product (GNP) (X_3), prime interest rates (X_1) and retail fuel price (X_4) can be made by substituting their values into the multiple regression model. To illustrate: the demand for motor vehicles for a given quarter is expected to be 39 190 units (that is 39,19 units measured in 1 000s) when the prime interest rate is 16 %; GNP is assumed to be R54 billion; and the retail fuel price is 170c per litre.

The multiple coefficient of determination, R^2, which establishes the overall usefulness of the regression model as a predictor of the response variable, is 0,604 (that is 60,4%). Since its maximum value is one, 0,604 indicates a relatively strong multiple relationship between the three significant predictor variables and the response variable, demand for motor vehicles. An analyst can have confidence in any prediction of demand for motor vehicles per quarter found from this model.

4.5 Concluding comments

There are certain cautionary issues to note. The first concerns the *required dataset size*. To obtain reliable and stable regression coefficients, the dataset should be approximately five times the number of predictor variables used in the estimation procedure. Thus a model with four predictor variables should have roughly 20 sets of observations on all variables.

Secondly, the majority of regression models constructed assume a *linear relationship* between the response and predictor variables. This may not always be true. A non-linear regression model may be a more appropriate expression of the relationship between these variables. An analysis on the nature of the relationship between the response and predictor variables should be conducted prior to the construction of a multiple regression model to ensure the most appropriate form of the model is developed.

Provided that the basic assumptions of regression analysis are reasonably met, the method is robust and capable of adequately modelling a wide spectrum of applications which require the estimation or prediction of a ratio-scaled variable based on a number of potential predictor measures.

5 DISCRIMINANT ANALYSIS

Discriminant analysis is a classification technique. Its primary task is to identify group membership of objects, which could be consumers, companies, shares or products, etc. It performs this task by identifying certain discriminating criteria which distinguish objects from the various groups. The objects within each group will have similar profiles, but will differ significantly from the profiles of objects in other groups. The groups are identified merely by labels. For example, consumer groups based on usage may be classified as heavy, moderate or light users of a product; potential store locations could be identified as high or low sales potential sites; clients applying for credit may be assigned a good or a bad credit rating; companies can be rated as progressive or conservative in their corporate image; consumers may be classified as early-adopters or late-adopters of new products.

The *discriminating criteria* are any characteristics which distinguish objects belonging to one group from objects belonging to other groups. For example, which consumer characteristics (demographic, psychographic measures, etc) distinguish heavy, medium and light users of a particular product from each other? Which performance criteria distinguish successful companies from unsuccessful companies? Which personal attributes and/or product characteristics allow us to identify consumers who prefer one product brand to other brands?

The business application which 'launched' this technique made use of discriminant analysis to identify performance measures which distinguished between failed and successful companies. This model was then used to identify companies at risk. In management practice, this technique is used extensively in the financial services sector for credit rating purposes. The technique first identifies the criteria which distinguish between good and bad credit risk customers and then applies these criteria to new applicants to establish their individual credit worthiness. The task of identifying these measures and establishing their relative importance as discriminating variables is performed by discriminant analysis. In terms of our broad classification of multivariate techniques then, discriminant analysis is a functional technique because of its classification (group assignment) role.

5.1 The data requirements

Observational data from samples of respondents (or objects) on two sets of variables, similar to regression analysis, are needed to perform discriminant analysis. The first variable set defines the predictor measures which are the potential discriminating criteria, while the second variable set consists of a single response measure only.

The response variable is the group classification variable and serves only to identify the group membership of each of the sampled objects. It is therefore only a categorical variable. To illustrate, applicants in a loan application study would be identified as potential defaulters and potential non-defaulters; in a segmentation study based on usage, potential customers could be classified as light, moderate or heavy users. Thus in discriminant analysis the response variable is only a qualitative (non-numeric or categorical) measure which is described by nominal or ordinal scaled data. Group membership of each sampled object (or individual) is indicated by a coded value.

The sets of discriminant variables are the potential predictors of group membership. These variables are object characteristics (attributes) which are used to distinguish between groups. The data type of the object attributes is similar to regression variables, namely that it can be any combination of categorical or quantitative measures. Examples of categorical discriminant variables include gender, marital status, qualifications and economic sector, while quantitative variables include all variables where the data are numeric, such as age, income, family size and number of employees.

The input data for a discriminant model require sets of observations on each attribute for each of the a priori groups. Thus input data must be available for objects belonging to each group for the analysis to proceed.

The data structure is summarised as follows:

Grouping variable (response variable)	Discriminant variables (predictor variables)
Y	$X_1, X_2, X_3, X_4, ..., X_p$
Group membership	Potential predictors
Categorical data type only	Categorical and quantitative data type is permissible

5.2 The rationale of discriminant analysis

Discriminant analysis performs two functions. First, it identifies the characteristics which best distinguish between members belonging to different groups and second, it applies these significant discriminant criteria to new objects (consumers, companies, products etc) to identify their most likely group membership. A number of statistical tests can also be performed on the discriminant model to establish its overall usefulness as a classification technique. Some of these features will be highlighted below.

Discriminant analysis begins with an examination of objects belonging to known groups. The methodology identifies a set of criteria (predictor variables) which can be used to assign a respondent (or object) to one of these groups so that the chance of misclassification is as small as possible. The predictor variables are selected from a set of potential predictors according to their ability to discriminate between members of the different groups. Statistically, the significant attributes are identified by computing a mean value of an attribute within each group and comparing these attribute means across the different groups. A significant discriminant attribute is one which exhibits large mean differences between groups, while insignificant discriminators show small between-group mean differences.

The discriminant model which results from this process of comparing between-group mean differences for statistical significance is similar in structure to a linear regression model. It has the following linear form:

$$Z = b_1X_1 + b_2X_2 + b_3X_3 + \ldots + b_pX_p$$

where Z = the discriminant (group classification) score

b_i = discriminant weights (each b_i measures the importance of the ith discriminant variable)

X_i = discriminant variables

The b_i values measure the relative importance of each predictor variable as a useful discriminator of objects between the different groups. Appropriate significance tests can be performed on each coefficient to establish whether it can meaningfully discriminate between objects from the different groups. Like multiple regression analysis, a stepwise approach can be adopted to select only the significant discriminant variables. The final discriminant function will consist only of the statistically significant discriminant criteria.

As part of this process of identifying significant discriminant criteria, discriminant analysis can also be used to confirm whether the a priori groups are genuinely distinct from each other. This is achieved statistically by testing whether mean profiles differ significantly between the a priori groups.

Once computed and tested for significance, the discriminant model is used to formulate a decision rule for classifying new respondents (or objects) on the basis of this new object's values of the significant discriminant variables. These values define the profile of the new object. The new object is assigned to the group whose profile is closest to its own profile. Statistically, an average Z-score (called a centroid) for each a priori group is computed and compared against the Z-score for a new object. The new object is assigned to the group in which the difference between its Z-score and the group centroid (that is average Z-score) is a minimum.

Figure 17.1 visually illustrates the concept of discriminant analysis between only two groups using two potential predictor variables (X_1 and X_2). Group 1 represents accountants who did not start their own practice within five years of qualifying, and group 2 consists of accountants who started their own practice within five years of qualifying.

Each of the 32 chartered accountants was measured on two potential discriminant variables, X_1 (initiative rating) and X_2 (academic performance). The nature of discriminant analysis is clearly evident from the scatterplot. Two distinct groupings appear to exist.

Furthermore, the scatterplot provides a measure of the profile of each group. By inspection, group 1 accountants are characterised by low values of X_1 and high values of X_2. Alternatively, group 2 accountants appear to be identified by higher values of X_1 and lower values of X_2. A group profile can be found for each group by averaging separately the X_1 and X_2 values within each of the two groups. These average (or centroid) values are shown by ★ for group 1 and # for group 2.

The discriminant function is represented by a line formed statistically from the maximal separation of the two group centroids as shown in figure 17.1. The projection of each

Figure 17.1 Scatterplot of response values for two groups on two discriminant criteria

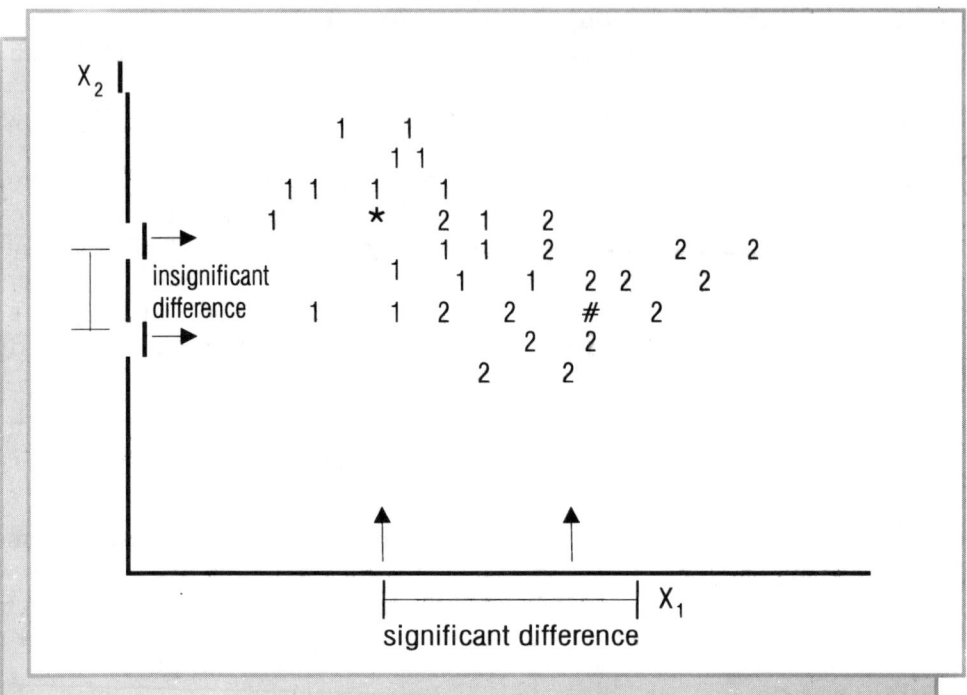

group's centroid onto this discriminant line indicates the most likely discriminant score for objects belonging to each group. The critical Z-score provides a decision rule for classifying objects into each group.

A primary task of discriminant analysis is to identify the significant discriminators. By inspection, the X_1 means (comparison of distance between ★ and # on the horizontal axis) are further apart than the X_2 means when ★ and # are compared on the vertical axis. This indicates that X_1 is a potentially better discriminating variable than X_2.

As part of the usefulness of the potential discriminators, discriminant analysis also examines whether distinct groupings exist. Statistically, the difference between the two group centroids – as represented by the average Z-scores – is tested for significance.

5.3 An illustrative example: industrial product market segmentation

A company which manufactures and markets an industrial product wishes to identify only those companies in the market that are likely to buy its product in place of a competitor's. Market research was conducted on 21 potential clients: 9 indicated they would definitely buy this product in preference to the competitive product, and 12 indicated that they would remain with the competitor. Four potential predictor variables were identified and data gathered on each of these four variables for each of the 21 company samples in the study. The four potential discriminant criteria were: (X_1) the potential customer's perception of the product's *quality* (as measured by a rating value); (X_2) the potential customer's perception of the supplier's *service maintenance* capability (also measured by a rating value); (X_3) the potential customer's *credit rating* ; and (X_4) the *economic sector* of the potential customer (1 = mining versus 0 = non-mining).

The discriminant analysis was performed by the BMDP 7M statistical package using a stepwise approach. The final discriminant function and selected output are provided below. The significant discriminant function is:

$$Z = -1{,}76049 + 0{,}44800\ X_2 - 0{,}35194\ X_4$$

Group (buyer) centroid = 1,27407
Group (non-buyer) centroid = $-0{,}95555$
F-value = 14,32 (probability value < 0,0005)

Of the four potential predictors, only two, namely X_2 (service maintenance capability rating) and X_4 (economic sector), were statistically significant in discriminating between the buyer and the non-buyer groups.

The buyer group mean (centroid) value is 1,27407 and is found by substituting all buyer attribute values on X_2 and X_4 into the discriminant function and averaging the Z-scores. For the non-buyer group, its centroid value is $-0{,}95555$. To determine if buyers can be discriminated from non-buyers based on the potential discriminators of service maintenance ratings and economic sector only, the group centroids are compared for statistical significance. The computed F-value of 14,32 (with probability value < 0,0005) indicates that the two groups have statistically distinct profiles in the two discriminant criteria. In terms of this discriminant function, a buyer is more likely to be an industrial company which rates the supplier of this product highly on service maintenance (X_2), and from the non-mining economic sector (X_4), while a non-buyer is likely to be a mining company with a low rating for this supplier's service maintenance capabilities.

The discriminant function and the group centroids can now be used to classify new companies in terms of their likelihood to be buyers or non-buyers of this company's products. A Z-score for a new company is derived by substituting the potential customer's rating value for the supplier's service maintenance capability (X_2) and the economic sector of the potential customer (X_4) into the discriminant function and comparing the distance to each group centroid.

To facilitate this process, a decision rule for assigning new respondents (cases) to each of the two groups is developed. A critical Z-score, which is a weighted average of the two group centroids, is computed and used as follows:

'Assign a new company to the buyer group if its Z-score is more than the critical Z-score, otherwise assign it to the non-buyer group.'

Each new potential industrial customer of this product can now be evaluated and classified using this single discriminant function. In this illustration, the critical Z-score is found to be zero (that is $[9 \star (1,27407) + 12 \star (-0,95555)]/21 = 0$). Hence potential industrial consumers of this product will tend to have positive Z-scores while non-buyers will have negative Z-scores. Assume that a potential customer has rated this supplier 4 out of 10 (10 = best) on service maintenance capability and operates in the mining sector. This potential customer's discriminant Z-score would be $-0,32043$ [$Z = -1,76049 + 0,44800(4) - 0,35194(1)$] resulting in the respondent being classified by the discriminant model as a likely non-buyer. Alternatively, a potential customer with the same rating value on X_2 (namely 4), but operating in the non-mining sector, would have a Z-score of 0,03151 and will consequently be classified as a likely buyer.

The discriminating ability of the discriminant model can be obtained by computing a classification table. This table is a cross-tabulation of the model's own classification of the sample objects compared to each object's actual known group membership. A 'good' discriminant model correctly identifies each object's actual group membership. Table 17.1 shows the results for this illustration.

Table 17.1 Classification table: industrial product market segmentation study

Group	Per cent	Number of cases	Classified into group
	Correct	Buy	Not buy
Buy	77,8	7	2
Not buy	83,3	2	10
Total	81,0	9	12

It is seen from the output that the discriminant model consisting of X_2 and X_4 is able to classify 81 % of the 21 respondents correctly according to their a priori grouping. In each group, two respondents are incorrectly classified. Ideally, 100 % correct classification is desired but is seldom, if ever, achieved. The 81 % correct classification achieved in this model can be considered 'reasonably good'.

5.4 Concluding comments

Although discriminant analysis is most often illustrated with only two classification groups, the concepts are readily extended to more than two groups. In a manpower planning study within an organisation, a three-group discriminant model may involve, for example, the classification of each employee in terms of not promotable, promotable in the future, and immediately promotable. The personnel manager would like to determine a decision rule whereby an employee whose performance is being reviewed can be classified into one of these three promotable categories. A selection of demographic (age, qualifications, performance measures, experience, etc) and possible psychographic measures may be used to classify employees into one of these three promotion categories. As a further illustration, consider an employee search study. A personnel manager wishes to group applicants into three categories before interviewing them. The grouping variable, Y, is referred to as 'Success Rating'. Each applicant is coded as '1' = low, '2' = medium, or '3' = high chance of success. Potential discriminant variables may be age, highest qualifications, an interpersonal skills rating, and a measure of job-related experience.

The technique to be discussed in the next section, namely cluster analysis, is also a classification technique. Discriminant analysis and cluster analysis have the same objective, which is to set up homogeneous groupings of objects. These two techniques differ substantially in their methodology, however, and in the way the results are used in practice.

6 CLUSTER ANALYSIS

Cluster analysis, like discriminant analysis, is a classification technique. However, unlike discriminant analysis, where the group classifications are known in advance, cluster analysis assumes unknown group membership of objects and proceeds to separate the objects (consumers, companies, products, etc) into distinct groupings, each with its own identity.

A key element in any marketing strategy is market segmentation. A market segment is a grouping of consumers who share common purchasing behaviour characteristics. The difficulty facing marketers, however, is identification of these homogeneous market segments. Cluster analysis is one approach which can assist marketers in this task. Through cluster analysis, marketers can identify both the size and characteristics of distinct groupings of consumers who exhibit similar purchasing behaviour. Each cluster will have a distinct profile, while the size of each cluster will depend upon the number of objects sharing similar profiles. Using cluster analysis, marketers can determine viable market segments.

6.1 The data requirements

The objects to be clustered should be described by a number of variables (or attributes). For example, a consumer could be described by various demographic, socio-economic and psychographic measures as well as certain product-specific measures such as usage levels and brand preference ratings. These descriptive measures, however, must be of quantitative data types (that is, at least interval scaled), because cluster analysis uses these attribute values to produce euclidean distance or similarity (correlation) measures between objects. Such measures are valid only for numerical data. The resultant distance or similarity (correlation) matrix computed between all pairs of objects from the attribute values is the primary input data necessary for clustering to proceed.

6.2 The rationale of cluster analysis

Cluster analysis is essentially a mathematical procedure which systematically forms clusters of objects using a measure of proximity as the primary clustering criterion. There are a number of approaches which cluster objects in distinct, homogeneous groups, but the principle remains the same for each approach. Each approach begins by considering each object as a separate cluster. Thereafter, each approach repeatedly examines and modifies the original distance (or correlation) matrix to form clusters of objects having similar profiles. The clustering process takes place iteratively by successively linking objects which are in close proximity, distance-wise or correlation-wise, to each other, into larger subgroups to form clusters. The most common linkage rule links nearest-neighbour objects or subgroups. This iterative process continues until all the objects have been merged into a single large cluster. At each stage of the iterative process a revised distance (or correlation) matrix is computed, using the averaged attribute values of clustered objects to determine new distances (or correlations) between objects or subclusters which have not yet merged.

Cluster analysis is merely an algorithmic process which continues until no further clustering can take place. Consequently, the identification of distinct clusters is left to the discretion of the researcher. This step is performed by the analyst, using judgement guided by rules of thumb. Unlike regression and discriminant analysis, there are no statistical tests of significance to determine when the clustering process should terminate. To assist with this task, however, the clustering technique produces a tree diagram – called a *dendrogram* – which indicates the distance between the merging of successive objects. Objects which group together at short distances are more similar in profile than objects which merge at greater distances. Large distances between merges tend to indicate dissimilarities between the objects and/or subgroups being merged by the algorithm. These objects would then belong to separate clusters.

Once separate clusters have been identified by the researcher (after examining the dendrogram), each cluster needs to be profiled. Again this process is subjective. A profile for each distinct cluster can be compiled by examining the attribute values of the objects within each cluster. Patterns of attribute values will emerge for each cluster and are used as the basis for profiling each cluster.

6.3 An illustrative example: images of financial institutions

Twelve financial institutions were assessed by a panel of financial experts on five attributes to identify perceived similarities and differences between these organisations. The five attributes were service quality (X_1), product range (X_2), client accessibility (X_3), perceived financial strength (X_4) and management investment expertise (X_5). Each attribute was rated collectively by the panel for each institution on a 1 to 10 scale, with 1 being very poor and 10 being excellent. Their rating responses are shown in table 17.2, and the distance matrix derived from these responses and measuring perceived 'distances' between the financial institutions appears in table 17.3 (note: only a portion of the full 12 × 12 matrix is shown).

Table 17.2 Rating responses on the five attributes

Financial institution	Attribute rating responses				
	X_1	X_2	X_3	X_4	X_5
1	7	2	8	3	5
2	6	6	9	7	7
3	5	4	4	1	4
4	5	4	8	6	5
5	9	4	8	4	5
6	8	4	7	4	5
7	5	6	5	2	4
8	7	8	8	8	5
9	6	4	4	3	3
10	8	2	7	3	8
11	6	5	5	7	6
12	6	9	6	8	6

Table 17.3 Distance matrix between financial institutions (only the first seven rows/columns)

	Financial institutions							
	1	2	3	4	5	6	7	...
1	0,00	3,06	3,13	2,18	1,84	1,40	3,10	...
2		0,00	4,56	2,04	3,18	2,87	3,88	...
3			0,00	3,18	4,08	3,21	1,18	...
4				0,00	3,15	2,50	2,68	...
5					0,00	0,96	3,79	...
6						0,00	2,94	...
7							0,00	...

The BMDP 2M statistical package was used to generate the dendrogram (given in figure 17.2) from the initial 12 × 12 distance matrix computed from the five attribute rating scales.

Figure 17.2 Dendrogram of financial institutions

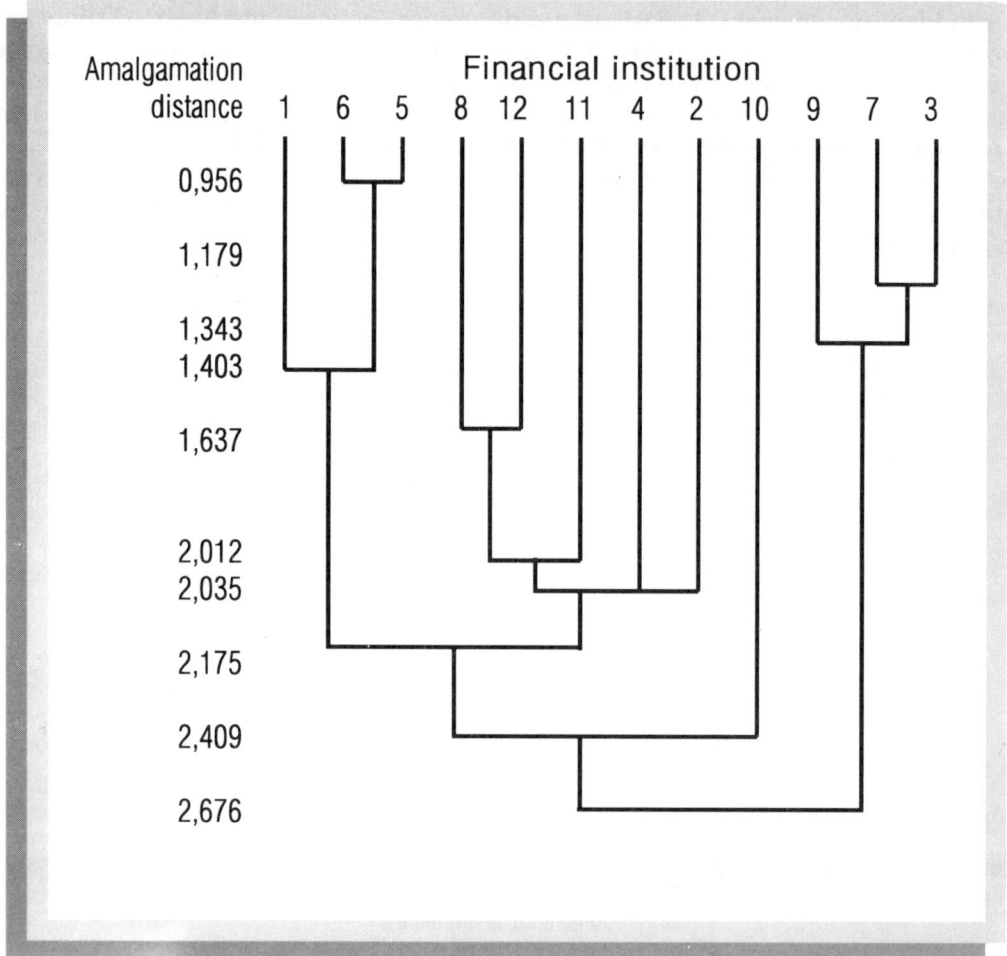

If two organisations have identical attribute ratings across all five attributes, their 'distance' measure will be zero. Conversely, the more dissimilar the attribute ratings are between the organisations, the greater is the 'distance' measure between them. In this illustration, organisations 5 and 6 have the most similar profiles as seen both from their original dataset (see table 17.2) and by noting the smallest distance measure between them in the distance matrix (as highlighted in table 17.3). Consequently these two organisations are the first to merge at a 'distance' of 0,956 to create the nucleus of the first cluster

– cluster 1. Organisations 3 and 7 also have reasonably similar profiles, but these are different from organisations 5 and 6. These two organisations merge at a 'distance' of 1,179 to create the nucleus of a second cluster (cluster 2). At the next iteration of the clustering process, organisation 9 is found to be reasonably similar in its response profile to cluster 2. It therefore merges with this group at a distance of 1,343. Organisation 1 next merges with cluster 1 at a distance of 1,403. Both clusters 1 and 2 now consist of three members each. Moderately similar profiles are now found to exist between organisations 8 and 12, which therefore merge at a distance of 1,637. This third cluster (cluster 3) also acquires organisation 11 at a distance of 2,012. At the distance of 2,035, a fourth cluster (cluster 4) is formed between organisations 2 and 4, which then merges immediately (at the same distance of 2,035) with cluster 3 to form a new larger cluster (cluster 3/4). The merging process continues iteratively to successively merge clusters 1 and 3/4 (cluster 1/3/4) which finally merge with cluster 2 to form a single cluster of all financial institutions at a distance of 2,676. It should be noted that organisation 10 is seen as an 'outlier' in that it shares virtually no common characteristics with any of the existing clusters.

From an interpretation viewpoint, the analyst must decide at what distance it is reasonable to terminate the clustering process conceptually to produce homogeneous clusters. This decision is facilitated by looking at the incremental differences in distances between groupings. Large incremental distances indicate that the merging objects are essentially dissimilar and do not belong together in a homogeneous group. In this illustration, we note a large incremental merging distance between clusters 1 and 3/4, and between clusters 2 and 3/4. It is therefore reasonable to conclude that distinct groupings exist between clusters 1, 2 and 3/4. Clusters 1 and 2 are relatively homogeneous, as noted by their shorter clustering distances. Cluster 3/4, on the other hand, is a 'loose coalition' of financial institutions with some, but not too many, similarities between them. The resulting clusters can be summarised as follows:

Cluster 1:   organisations 1, 5 and 6
Cluster 2:   organisations 3, 7 and 9
Cluster 3/4:   organisations 2, 4, 8, 11 and 12
Organisation 10 is not associated with any of the existing clusters.

The description of each cluster is guided by the profile of the companies as given in each company's data response profile to the five attributes.

Cluster 1: The profiles from the three organisations indicate strength in attributes 1 and 3, and only moderate ratings on attributes 2, 4 and 5. This cluster is characterised by good service quality and client accessibility.

Cluster 2: These financial institutions are rated only moderately to poorly on all five attributes.

Cluster 3/4: This is a relatively non-homogeneous clustering of financial institutions. The general characteristic of these organisations is their moderate-to-good performance across all five attributes, particularly in the area of client accessibility and perceived financial strength.

Financial institution 10 – the outlier – is the only financial institution to rate highly on attributes 1 (service quality), 3 (client accessibility) and 5 (management investment expertise) and poorly on product range and perceived financial strength.

6.4 Concluding comments

☐ While distance measures are more commonly computed using numerically scaled measures, there are procedures for finding distance measures between objects from categorical response data. If the data values are categorical, the similarity measures are based on *matching-type* measures, that is the extent to which attribute profiles are similar between objects. However, it is not possible to include both measurement-type data variables (that is categorical and numeric) in the same distance matrix calculation.

☐ A cautionary note: cluster analysis is an algorithmic procedure relying upon sets of rules to perform the aggregation process. There are different rules for computing *similarity measures* and for *merging* objects into clusters and these often lead to very different groupings. The validity of the various rules must be carefully assessed to ensure meaningful and accurate results.

☐ Interpretation and profiling of clusters become increasingly complex as the dataset increases both in terms of the number of objects to cluster and the number of attributes used to cluster these objects. Thus if cluster analysis is to be used, only *a few significant attributes* should be selected to form the basis of clustering. Meaningful and useful homogeneous clusters are unlikely to emerge from clustering procedures involving a large number of attributes.

☐ Data for cluster analysis should always be *standardised* to avoid attributes measured on different scales from distorting the distance measures between them.

7 FACTOR ANALYSIS

When a large number of attitudinal measures have been gathered in a market study, the collective interpretation of their findings may be difficult when all the variables are considered together. For example, a questionnaire which examines the buying behaviour of consumers for wine requests attitudinal responses to 45 semantic differential statements. A concise and cohesive interpretation of buying behaviour for wine is unlikely to emerge when each statement is analysed separately using summary descriptive measures. This battery of statement responses, however, may be concealing some underlying constructs which, if identified, would simplify the task of interpretation.

Factor analysis is an approach which examines the associations among a large set of original measures and aims at reducing them to a smaller subset of explanatory factors for easier interpretation. Hence it is often referred to as a *data reduction-interpretive* technique. Unlike regression and discriminant analyses, which are functional (or predictive) techniques, factor analysis is a structural multivariate approach aimed at identifying underlying structures (or dimensions) within a large set of observable measures. Consequently no response variable is being estimated. Instead, the emphasis is on examining the collective associations across variables for explanatory constructs.

Factor analysis is used in any management situation where underlying (non-observable) dimensions (constructs) must be identified among a large set of observable measures. The observable measures are generally respondent perceptions, expectations or preferences which describe certain personality and behaviour traits which are not directly observable. Factor analysis may also be used in a hypothesis-testing role to confirm the use of various measurable attributes to represent underlying (unobservable) dimensions. The interpretation of the dimensions uncovered from a factor analysis study is determined by the descriptions of the original variables.

7.1 The data requirements

Since factor analysis examines associations between variables, a *correlation matrix* between all pairwise measures is required as input data. To construct a correlation matrix, data on each variable must be at least interval scaled. This means that rating scale measures which are commonly used in marketing studies to capture consumer perceptions, expectations or preferences are suitable for factor analysis.

7.2 The rationale of factor analysis

Variables that are highly correlated with each other, as identified from the correlation matrix, are grouped together under a single factor. Each distinct grouping of highly correlated original variables represents a separate factor.

The identification (or extraction) of factors is performed by a method called principal components analysis. This approach identifies the number of unique factors and the significant variables associated with each. Each factor that is extracted describes a separate dimension (or construct) embedded within the large set of variables. In statistical terms, each factor explains a certain percentage of the total variation between the original variables. The principal components process can extract as many factors as there are original variables. However, not all of these factors can explain a significant percentage of total variation within the original set of variables. The significance of a factor is determined by its *eigenvalue*, which is generated by principal components analysis for each factor. A rule of thumb is applied to each eigenvalue (that is it must exceed 1) to decide how many significant factors can meaningfully be used to describe the underlying dimensionality of the original set of variables. Thus in practice only a few significant factors (whose eigenvalues exceed 1) are selected and used to interpret the original set of variables.

A factor can be seen as a new 'generic' variable used to represent a subset of the original variables which are highly correlated with it. Mathematically, each factor is a linear combination of the original variables, X_1, X_2, X_3, ..., X_p. The coefficients of the linear combination are a measure of the correlation between each variable and the given factor. To visualise this process, factors can be viewed geometrically as axes surrounded by vector coordinates representing the original set of variables. Variables that lie close to a given axis (or factor) are highly correlated with that factor and are used to describe this unique factor dimension. Refer to the illustration in figure 17.3 which shows 15 variables being described by essentially two factors.

Figure 17.3 Variables described by two factors

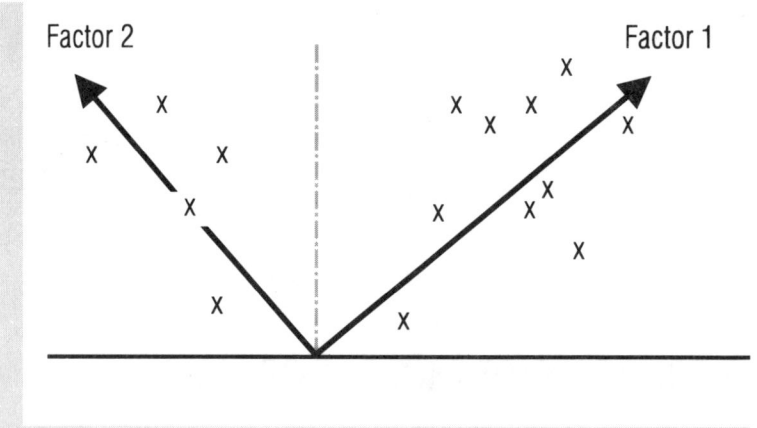

Generally, further mathematical manipulation of the initial set of factors takes place. This process is called *factor rotations* and is used to refine the associations between factors and variables. The ultimate interpretation from factor analysis is derived from the closeness of the original variables to rotated factors.

To assist with the process of interpreting factors, the principal components method also computes measures called *factor loadings*. A factor loading is a correlation measure $(-1 \leq r \leq +1)$ between a variable and a factor. A high factor loading (that is values close to ± 1) indicates a close association between a variable and a factor, while a low factor loading (that is values close to 0) indicates virtually no associations between a variable and a factor. This allows a user to identify which variables are 'explained' by a given factor. By examining the nature of the variables which 'load heavily' on a given factor, the factor can be labelled.

7.3 An illustrative example: meal preparation attitudes

A recent market study investigated the attitudes and behaviour of women towards meal preparation. Two hundred female respondents were asked to rate their opinions on 11 statements on a 1 to 8 semantic differential measurement scale. The statements were:

X_1 = 'I enjoy experimenting with new recipes.'
X_2 = 'I prefer eating at restaurants with friends.'
X_3 = 'Vitamin supplements are necessary.'
X_4 = 'I prefer to cook traditional meals.'
X_5 = 'I do not eat too much red meat regularly.'
X_6 = 'I like entertaining guests with my meals.'
X_7 = 'I find cooking a chore.'
X_8 = 'I only consume low fat milk products.'
X_9 = 'I watch my calorie/cholesterol intake.'
X_{10} = 'Fruit must form part of one's daily diet.'
X_{11} = 'I insist on one cooked meal per day.'

A *correlation matrix* was initially computed and used as input into factor analysis. While the correlation matrix indicates the association between the variables, a meaningful collective interpretation based directly on an inspection of the 11 × 11 matrix is generally very difficult. The identification of underlying dimensions would be equally difficult to establish, hence the need for factor analysis.

The factor analysis for this study was performed using the BMDP 4M statistical package. Table 17.4 on page 372 shows selected output from this analysis.

Five distinct factors were identified among the original 11 variables. However, only the first three are used to describe the original variables as these three factors account for almost 92 % of all explained variation. The rule of thumb applied selects only factors with eigenvalues greater than 1.

The variables which are associated with each of the three extracted factors are identified from the rotated factor loadings for each variable under each factor (as seen in table 17.4). Factor 1 has identified variables 3,5,8,9,10 and 11 as being closely associated with each other and consequently with the factor. Any factor loadings greater than 0,5 imply a significant association between a variable and a factor.

Table 17.4 Selected factor analysis output from BMDP 4M

(i) The extracted factors

Factor	Eigenvalue (explained variation)	Percentage of explained variation
1	4,987	45,34
2	2,827	25,69
3	2,283	20,75
4	0,728	6,63
5	0,175	1,59
		100,00

(ii) Rotated factor loadings

Variables	Factor 1 (45,34 %)	Factor 2 (25,69 %)	Factor 3 (20,75 %)
X_1	0,430	0,878	0,132
X_2	0,403	−0,307	0,841
X_3	0,824	0,013	−0,202
X_4	0,213	0,871	0,243
X_5	0,899	−0,255	0,064
X_6	0,239	−0,090	0,964
X_7	0,270	0,836	−0,379
X_8	0,955	0,223	−0,037
X_9	0,814	−0,449	−0,368
X_{10}	0,756	0,421	−0,442
X_{11}	0,911	0,050	0,222

For factor 2, the closely aligned variables are variables 1,4 and 7, while factor 3 has variables 2 and 6 highly loaded onto it.

The final stage of factor analysis is naming the resultant factors to describe the original variable set in terms of a reduced set of factors. This is a matter of judgement, guided strongly by the nature of the subset of variables which load heavily onto each factor.

In this illustration, variables 3, 5, 8 ,9 ,10 and 11 strongly suggest that factor 1 has uncovered a construct of 'health-consciousness' in meal preparation, while factor 2 appears to describe a dimension of 'preferred cooking habits' present in the original variable responses. Factor 3's interpretation can clearly be labelled 'socialising with food'.

As a final comment, it should be noted that while factor analysis is a useful analytical tool to examine underlying structures within large datasets, the final interpretation of its results rests with the analyst. Labelling factors may not always be so clearcut as would appear from the above illustration. Describing a particular factor (construct) may even be contentious, depending on the nature of the research.

8 PERCEPTUAL MAPPING TECHNIQUES

The following two techniques, namely multidimensional scaling and correspondence analysis, are classified as *perceptual mapping techniques*. A perceptual map is a graphical display, generally in two-dimensions, of respondents' perceptions of differences and similarities between objects (such as products/brands or companies) and their attributes. By examining the relative position of objects and attributes as visual displays, the task of the analyst in interpreting the way in which respondents (consumers) compare objects (such as products, services or companies) and their attributes becomes easier. Each perceptual mapping technique translates the subjective rankings or ratings of objects, and in some cases their attributes as well, into coordinates which are then plotted as points in two-dimensional space. The interpretation of each perceptual map depends upon the purpose of the study, the type of data collected and the mathematical approach used to position the points on the graph. While each technique has a different way of interpreting the associations between objects and attributes, the general idea is that the proximity of points to each other in the graph is an indication of association between the objects and, where appropriate, their attributes.

8.1 Multidimensional scaling

When consumers compare different objects, such as product brands, services, personalities, clients or companies, it is assumed that they base their evaluations on certain underlying constructs (or dimensions) which are not made explicit – either they are unwilling, or, more likely, unable to identify these constructs. Multidimensional scaling (MDS) is a perceptual mapping technique which assumes that underlying constructs do exist and therefore attempts to uncover the main constructs used by respondents in the comparative evaluation of objects. MDS is a widely used technique in marketing to deduce the primary criteria used by respondents to compare product brands, services or companies and also to identify product brand-attribute associations. It has even been used to identify issues (constructs) differentiating political candidates.

8.1.1 The data requirements

MDS requires data representing measures of similarity or dissimilarity between objects as perceived by the respondents. Three forms of data collection can be used. Firstly, such data can be gathered by asking respondents to rank all pairs of objects (ordinal-scaled data) from most similar to least similar without reference to specific criteria. Secondly, respondents can be asked to rate all pairs of objects (interval-scaled data) in terms of similarity on a 10-point rating scale. Finally, for product brand-attribute association studies, objects can be compared using attribute rating scales. Subjective distance measures between objects are derived by comparing the ratings across objects. If the ratings are similar over all the attributes, the distance will be small and visa versa. Any of these three approaches can be used to produce a similarity matrix which shows the rank order between all pairs of objects as illustrated in figure 17.4 (rank = 1: most similar; rank = 6: most dissimilar). Thus MDS requires no more than *ordinal-scaled data* (rank order responses).

Figure 17.4 Similarity matrix between four brands of petrol

Showing rank order responses

Brand	A	B	C	D
A	—	4	6	1
B		—	2	3
C			—	5
D				—

To illustrate: there are a total of six pairwise brand comparisons between the four brands of petrol. This respondent perceives brands A and D to be most similar (rank = 1), while brands A and C are perceived to be the least similar (rank = 6). As seen from the data, the rankings do not identify the underlying constructs used to differentiate between the different brands. This is now the task of MDS.

8.1.2 The rationale of multidimensional scaling

To generate the perceptual map, the technique adopted by MDS is to find a graphical display of objects which best retains the rank order relationship between the objects as defined by the similarity matrix. This implies that objects which are perceived by respondents to be similar (that is low rank values) are mapped close together and those which are perceived as being dissimilar (that is high rank values) are positioned far apart in the graphical plot.

The extent to which the original rank order distances between objects are accurately represented by the two-dimensional display is measured by a *goodness-of-fit* statistic called a *measure of stress*. The closer this stress value is to zero, the more accurately the map displays the perceived relationship between the objects as indicated by their pairwise rank orderings. High stress values, on the other hand, indicate a poor representation of the relationships between objects. Consequently, extreme caution must be exercised by the researcher not to interpret these findings too literally in these cases.

A mathematical algorithm is used to define the 'best' display. It is an interactive procedure, which begins by choosing an initial display according to some guidelines, which is tested for 'goodness-of-fit' against the original pairwise rank orders between the objects. It then applies certain error-reducing criteria to revise the display to produce a better 'goodness-of-fit' measure. It continues this iterative algorithm until certain termination criteria are met.

Once the 'final' perceptual map with the lowest possible stress level is produced and displayed, it becomes possible to focus attention on the underlying constructs which motivated the respondents' perceptions of the similarities and differences between the objects. The axes of the perceptual map are considered to represent the two primary dimensions used by respondents to differentiate between objects. Each axis represents an underlying dimension. By examining the proximity of objects *vis-à-vis* each axis, a researcher can infer these underlying constructs. To assist with the 'naming of the axes', which is subjective, a researcher could possibly refer to additional information – gathered outside the MDS study – about the attributes which characterise the objects.

Thus, while the MDS approach offers easy data collection because of the relative ease with which respondents can compare objects, it leaves the interpretation of the two key dimensions (the two axes) to the researcher's judgement. This is potentially a drawback because of the numerous possible interpretations that decision makers could ascribe to the dimensions (that is the process of 'naming the dimensions').

8.1.3 An illustrative example: rating banking institutions

Consumers were asked to compare and contrast their perceptions of nine banking institutions. The similarity matrix was derived from data collected on each banking institution based on four attribute-rating scales. These attributes refer to financial stability, product offerings, convenience and competitiveness. To illustrate, rating scale data would have been gathered by asking a respondent to consider each pair of banking institutions (36 pairwise comparisons) and indicate how similar/dissimilar they perceive them to be, using a 10-point rating scale (1 = totally similar; 10 = totally dissimilar) on each of the four attributes. The MDS method combines the attribute rating scores across all attributes for each pair of banks and then produces a pairwise rank order of all financial institutions.

Without presenting the original similarity data, the resultant perceptual map is displayed in figure 17.5 on page 376.

The stress level of 0,165 is relatively low, hence it can be assumed that the perceptual map is a reasonably accurate display of the actual perceived relationship between the banking institutions. This implies that two dimensions adequately characterise the similarities and differences between the banking institutions. The task now becomes one of identifying these two significant dimensions (or constructs).

Figure 17.5 Perceptual map of banking institutions

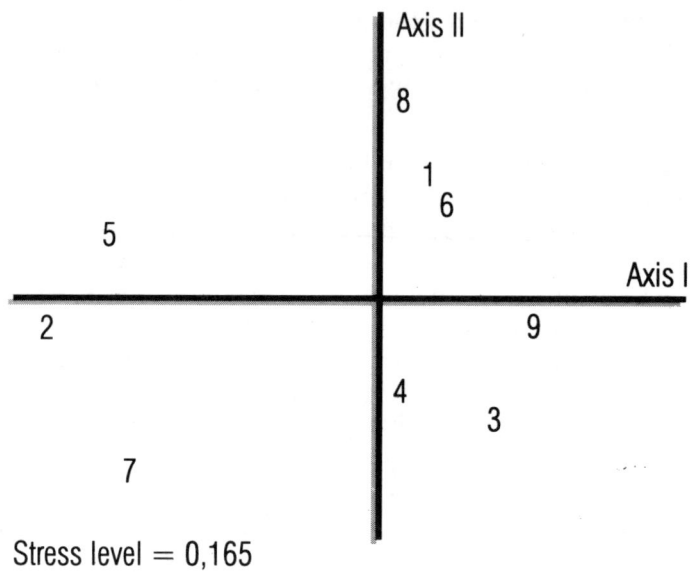

Stress level = 0,165

When evaluating a particular perceptual map, we need to examine the proximity of objects to each other (that is the interpoint distances between objects) and isolate the factors (or constructs) which appear to group or separate the objects. Thus the importance of the configuration produced by MDS lies in the relative positions of the objects being considered.

To identify the first underlying dimension, each financial institution is projected onto the horizontal axis (that is axis I). Banks 1, 3, 6 and 9 appear at the right end of the axis, while banks 2, 5 and 7 are grouped together at the left side of the axis. The researcher needs to explain these perceived separate groupings (that is naming the construct) and can be aided by referring to the semantic differential average rating scores (which were used to generate the similarity matrix). Inspection of these average rating scores indicates that banks 1, 3, 6 and 9 rated low to average on convenience, while banks 2, 5 and 7 had higher convenience rating scores. The underlying construct could therefore be identified as a convenience dimension used to evaluate financial institutions. Similarly, a projection of all banking institutions onto the vertical axis (axis II) results in banks 1, 6, 5 and 8 representing a separate grouping from banks 3, 4 and 7. Again, with reference to the average rating scores, it will be found that banks 1, 6, 5 and 8 are perceived as offering only a limited range of financial services, while banks 3, 4 and 7 are perceived to offer a wide range of financial services. Thus the second construct used by consumers to evaluate the financial institutions may be identified as a product-offering dimension. The remaining two attributes, namely financial stability and competitiveness, were unable to significantly distinguish between the banks along the two axes.

8.1.4 Concluding comments

Two final comments are appropriate:

☐ If more than two dimensions (constructs or axes) more accurately distinguish between the objects (shown by a lower stress level measure), a two-dimensional map will not be an accurate representation of the similarities and differences between the objects. However, the researcher needs to trade off ease of interpretation which results when fewer dimensions are used against greater accuracy of representation which improves with added dimensions. Generally, two-dimensional perceptual maps have been found to give acceptable interpretations. However, the stress level measure must be carefully monitored.

☐ A distinction must be made between perceptions data and preference data in the construction of the similarity data. The interpretation must be consistent with the nature of the data collected.

8.2 Correspondence analysis

As indicated, correspondence analysis, like multidimensional scaling, is a perceptual mapping technique. Whereas MDS seeks to identify the underlying constructs used by respondents to distinguish between objects, correspondence analysis looks for associations between objects and the attributes which describe the objects. The graphical display of associations between objects and attributes is of great value to marketers in identifying which product attributes consumers associate with different products or brands.

Every market researcher, almost without exception, is familiar with the chi-square statistic and its use in analysing contingency tables (or cross-tabulations) for statistical associations between two qualitative (categorical) variables. To illustrate, if gender (with male and female as categories) is statistically associated with margarine brands (with Blossom, Floro, Choice, Rama as categories), then we may, for example, conclude that there is a greater preference for Floro by women, while men are indifferent to the margarine brands. Likely statistical associations, such as these, are more readily identified when displayed as a two-dimensional graph which can be produced by correspondence analysis.

The technique was developed in France and popularised by Michael Greenacre (of Unisa) (1978) and is now widely used in marketing research studies to highlight either associations or independence between qualitative measures.

8.2.1 The data requirements

Any multi-way cross-tabulated data can be displayed graphically using correspondence analysis. This means that the input data for a correspondence analysis is any multi-way contingency table. Thus only categorical responses, as reflected in nominal-scaled data, such as responses to yes/no questions or brand-attribute selection responses, are required to develop a perceptual map using correspondence analysis.

8.2.2 The rationale of correspondence analysis

The correspondence method transforms each cell frequency in a contingency table into a graphical coordinate. Each coordinate therefore represents a category level of a cross-tabulated variable. This transformation is performed by computing distance measures based on chi-square between observed and expected cell frequencies. Since expected cell frequencies represent a scenario of 'no association', a large distance measure will indicate that there is a statistical association between category levels of two cross-tabulated variables. The resulting coordinates computed by correspondence analysis will be located well away from the origin of the two axes. If there is a minimal difference between an observed cell frequency and its expected frequency, the distance measure will be small and the resulting coordinate plotted will lie close to the origin of the two axes. This would imply a situation of no statistical association between the two levels of the measures. Thus, when we interpret a correspondence analysis map, we must examine the distance of each coordinate relative to the origin. Coordinates near to the origin imply no statistical association between the two given levels, while coordinates far from the origin imply a statistical association between the two given levels.

To display multi-way contingency table data accurately, a perceptual map should generally reflect more than two dimensions (or axes). Since the graphical display for a correspondence map is only two-dimensional, some accuracy is sacrificed. To find out how representative the two-dimensional display is of the original data relationship, a measure of *explained variation* (called *eigenvalue* or *inertia*) is computed for each of the two axes. The percentage of variation explained by each axis indicates the extent to which the axis accurately reflects the relationship between the variable categories. The higher the percentage of explained variation, the more accurately an axis portrays the relationship between the various variable categories. The converse holds for a low percentage of explained variation measure. If the two axes together, in a two-dimensional plot, account for close to one hundred per cent of explained variation, then the cross-tabulated data are accurately portrayed in two dimensions only. Because the original data are reduced from multidimensional space to only a two-dimensional space, correspondence analysis is also seen as a data-reduction technique to simplify the interpretation of multi-way data.

8.2.3 Interpretation of a correspondence perceptual map

To interpret a correspondence map appropriately, the coordinates must be projected onto each axis in turn and examined in relation to the origin. Category levels which are in close proximity to each other and far from the origin are strongly associated, while those close to the origin tend to be statistically independent of each other.

The primary advantage of correspondence analysis is the visual impact of associations between categories of variables. There are two drawbacks of note. Firstly, a two-dimensional display may not be the most appropriate form of representation of the original data. While a higher dimensional representation would be more suitable, as judged from the explained variations per axis, it impairs interpretability. Secondly, unlike MDS, interpoint distances cannot be used as measures of proximity of categories to each other because the distances computed are relative only to the origin. Correspondence analysis is purely a descriptive technique which is best suited in an *exploratory data analysis* role.

8.2.4 An illustrative example: choice of hotel accommodation

The following contingency table (table 17.5) shows the responses by 360 travellers interviewed to the question: Which hotel do you usually use when travelling?

Table 17.5 Cross-tabulation of responses on hotel choice

Hotel	Gender		Age		
	Male	Female	Under 30	30–45	Over 45
City Lodge	14	65	38	29	8
Holiday Inn	55	46	18	39	45
Southern Sun	49	67	50	30	36
Other	31	33	34	21	12

Chi-square = 26,7   Chi-square = 41,17
(p < 0,001)   (p < 0,001)

By way of comparison, two chi-square values indicate that there are significant associations between hotel choice and gender on the one hand and hotel choice and the age of the 360 respondents on the other.

The statistical output was generated by BMDP CA and selected results are presented in table 17.6 on the next page.

Table 17.6 Selected results from BMDP CA for hotel choice

Total inertia = 0,95

Axis	Eigenvalue	Percentage of inertia	Cumulative per cent
1	0,077	81,1%	81,1%
2	0,014	14,6%	95,7%
3	0,004	4,3%	100,0%
	0,095		

Perceptual plot:

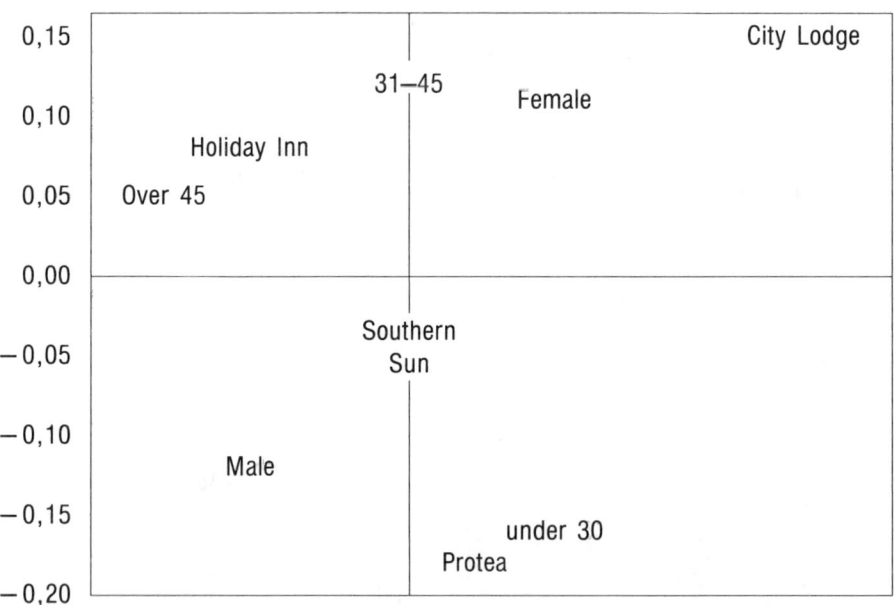

To examine the suitability of a two-dimensional display to reflect the associations between the row and column variables accurately, the *eigenvalues* and corresponding *percentage of inertia* for each axis are considered. In this illustration, the horizontal axis explains over 80 % (81,1 %) of the total variation in the data, while the second axis (vertical) accounts for only 15 % of total variability. This indicates that two dimensions are adequate to reflect the association between the variables (that is together they account for almost 96 % of all explained variation), and the associations between hotel choice on the one hand and gender and age on the other are well explained with reference to the first (horizontal) axis alone by virtue of its large percentage of inertia (namely 81 %). Individually this axis can provide the most relevant interpretation of likely associations.

If all coordinates (hotels and consumer demographics) are projected onto the first (horizontal) axis, which accounts for 81 % of the accuracy of the representation, there is a strong preference for the Holiday Inn hotel among males and travellers over 45 years of age. City Lodge in particular – and Protea hotels to a lesser extent – is preferred by females and persons under 30 years of age. People between 31 and 45 years of age appear indifferent (no association) in their choice of hotel. Southern Sun hotels appear to have no specific age/gender association. The second axis accounts for only 15 % of the accuracy of the representation and it is therefore not advisable to place too much emphasis on the associations identified along this axis.

8.2.5 Concluding comments

☐ Multi-way tables, where three or more categorical variables are analysed simultaneously, can also be represented graphically in two-dimensional space. There is a greater likelihood that the true association between the levels of all these variables will not be captured in two-dimensional space alone – resulting in a lower total inertia value for the first two axes. In these instances, these graphical displays, and the conclusions about likely associations, must be interpreted with greater care.

☐ It is worth repeating that it would be misleading and erroneous to interpret interpoint distances between coordinates in a correspondence map as measures of proximity between objects and attributes. These proximity distance measures have no meaning and cannot be used to infer associations.

9 LOGLINEAR MODELLING

One of the most commonly applied summary tools in marketing research is the cross-tabulation of responses between two categorical random variables. The chi-square statistic is then used to establish whether there is an association between the two qualitative random variables, such as job grade and academic qualifications. A limitation of the chi-square statistic, however, is its inability to test for associations and interactions between multiple categorical variables simultaneously. It is therefore suitable for two-way cross-classification analysis only. A multi-way contingency table reflects possible multiple interactions between the various variables which need to be identified and isolated. Performing multiple two-way interaction tests (using the chi-square statistic) is too simplistic and is unlikely to produce meaningful insights because of the potential complexities of the relationships. A more comprehensive and systematic approach to uncover the nature of the associations between multiple categorical random variables is needed. This task is performed by loglinear analysis.

9.1 The data requirements

Loglinear models analyse multi-way contingency tables for multiple associations. Thus the primary data requirement of the technique is cross-tabulated frequency count data. Such data are derived from nominal/ordinal scaled response variables.

9.2 The rationale of loglinear modelling

Loglinear modelling analyses multi-way contingency tables to identify significant associations between a number of categorical random variables simultaneously.

To identify these significant interaction effects, the technique first develops a linear model, similar to a multiple linear regression model, which is designed to re-construct (predict) the actual observed frequency of each cell in the multi-way contingency table. The predictor variables used in this loglinear model are the various qualitative random variables (called the *main effects*) (as described by their marginal frequencies) and their interactions between the levels of the various variables (termed the *interaction effects*). The response variable is the observed cell frequency of the multi-way table. In a three-variable cross-tabulation, for example, there is a potential three-way interaction and numerous possible two-way interactions between the variables. The loglinear model of this three-way table would look as follows:

$$\log f_{ijk} = b_1X_1 + b_2X_2 + b_3X_3 \qquad \text{(main effects)}$$
$$+ b_{12}X_{12} + b_{13}X_{13} + b_{23}X_{23} \qquad \text{(two-way interactions)}$$
$$+ b_{123}X_{123} \qquad \text{(three-way interaction)}$$

where the b values are *weight* coefficients (similar to regression modelling).

The loglinear methodology initially develops the full (or saturated) loglinear model which consists of all main effects and every possible interaction effect. This saturated model completely explains the observed frequencies in every cell of the multi-way table. Ideally, however, a researcher would like to explain the observed patterns in the multi-way contingency table in terms of the smallest number of interactions – for easier interpretation. Thus a testing and selection process of significant interactions takes place on the saturated loglinear model only to identify and remove from the model any insignificant interaction effects.

The methodology identifies significant associations between the categorical variables (as described by the loglinear model) in a manner similar to ANOVA (F-tests) as applied to regression coefficients. While ANOVA requires ratio-scaled data, loglinear modelling uses only frequency count data which are the cell values of a multi-way contingency table.

Once the saturated loglinear model has been developed, an ANOVA-type testing procedure (using a likelihood ratio chi-square statistic) is applied to each of the variables to establish which main effects and interaction effects are statistically significant. (This is similar to the stepwise procedure in multiple regression analysis.) The significant factors (main effects and/or interaction effects) are represented in a reduced loglinear model and are the only measures used to describe the relationships and influences between the various qualitative random variables.

The ability of a reduced loglinear model to explain the patterns of observed frequencies in the multi-way contingency table can be examined through a goodness-of-fit statistic (which is another likelihood ratio chi-square measure). If the observed frequencies do not differ significantly from the expected frequencies constructed from the subset of significant interaction terms only in the reduced loglinear model, then the reduced model adequately describes the structures (relationships between variables) in the multi-way table.

It should be noted that our primary interest centres only on the significant interaction effects rather than on the main effects. It is essentially the interaction between the levels of the categorical variables which is being sought to explain any associations between the variable responses.

9.3 An illustrative example: a car preference study

Consider a market study which identified car preferences between men and women for a medium-sized car. Additionally, respondents were also grouped according to their income. The three qualitative random variables are gender (male, female), income category (above R2 000 per month, below R2 000 per month) and make of car most preferred (Toyota Corolla, VW Golf). The three-way contingency table is presented below in table 17.7.

Table 17.7 A three-way contingency table for car preference

Gender	Car preferred			
	Toyota Corolla		VW Golf	
	Income group (R)		Income group (R)	
	<2 000	>2 000	<2 000	>2 000
Male	17	31	10	21
Female	25	12	19	10

The analysis was performed using the loglinear modelling option in SPSS for Windows.

To determine the final form of the loglinear model, a series of likelihood ratio chi-square tests is performed to identify the significant levels of interactions. In this example there is one possible three-way interaction (that is between gender, income and car type preferred – identified by K = 3) and three two-way interactions (that is gender versus income, gender versus car preferred, and income versus car preferred – identified by K = 2). The significance of main effects is also tested (identified by K = 1).

The following output is given:

Table 17.8 Tests that K-way effects are zero

K	Likelihood ratio chi-square	Probability value
1	5,561	0,1350
2	15,899	0,0012
3	0,005	0,9419

The table shows that there is no significant three-way interaction effect between gender, income and car type most preferred (probability value > 0,05 for K = 3). However, there is clear evidence of significant two-way (pairwise) interactions between some (or maybe all) of the three categorical variables (probability value < 0,05 for K = 2). The main effects (K = 1) are not meaningful in our study of interactions and are therefore not considered further.

We now need to explore the nature of the two-way interactions further since they are the only significant interactions in our study. Before the individual pairwise interactions are examined for significance, we can establish the overall value of the loglinear model consisting only of all three pairwise interactions (excluding the insignificant three-way interaction).

The goodness-of-fit of the loglinear model consisting only of all three pairwise interactions is identified from a likelihood ratio chi-square value and its associated probability value. For this reduced model, the likelihood ratio chi-square value is 0,00533 with a probability value of 0,942. This indicates that the loglinear model consisting only of the three pairwise interactions (that is gender versus income, gender versus car preferred, and income versus car preferred) reproduces the original contingency table reasonably well. Since the probability value exceeds 0,05 by a wide margin, there is a close similarity between the actual observed contingency table and the one generated by the loglinear model consisting of only the three two-way interaction effects.

Each two-way interaction term is now examined for significance. Table 17.9 shows the results.

Table 17.9 Significance tests for each two-way interaction effect

Interaction	Likelihood ratio chi-square	Probability value
Gender versus income	0,420	0,5170
Gender versus car preferred	15,555	0,0001
Income versus car preferred	0,109	0,7410

The only statistically significant interaction is between gender and car preferred (probability value of 0,0001 is less than 0,05). The other two interaction effects are not statistically significant and can consequently be removed from the previous loglinear model to produce a revised loglinear model consisting only of the single two-way interaction effect between gender and car type most preferred.

The final reduced loglinear model which now consists only of one significant interaction term (that is gender versus car preferred) has a goodness-of-fit value of 0,44167 and an associated probability value of 0,932 (which is greater than 0,05). Again, this goodness-of-fit measure indicates that the original contingency table frequencies can be adequately described by the loglinear model consisting only of the gender versus car preferred interaction.

Overall, we can now draw conclusions about the significant associations among our three categorical random variables. Our analysis has found that car type most preferred is dependent upon the gender of the respondent only and is independent of the income level of respondents. To identify the direction of the influence between gender and car type most preferred, the percentages for a simple two-way table between gender and car type most preferred can be inspected. Refer to table 17.10 below.

Table 17.10 Two-way contingency table between gender and car

Gender	Type most preferred		
	Toyota Corolla	VW Golf	Total
Male	27 (34 %)	52 (66 %)	79
Female	44 (67 %)	22 (33 %)	66
Total	71	74	145

This table clearly shows that more men prefer VW Golf than women. Women, on the other hand, are more partial to Toyota Corollas.

In conclusion, loglinear modelling is a useful tool for identifying the significant multiway interactions between the several categorical variables simultaneously. This permits a researcher to focus attention only on those categorical variables between which there are significant associations and eliminate the spurious associations. The insight into associations between several categorical variables gained from the use of the loglinear modelling approach far exceeds that provided by the chi-square statistic operating only on two-way contingency tables.

10 CONJOINT ANALYSIS

Marketers strive to produce products that satisfy consumer needs as closely as possible. This requires that a product should possess as many consumer-desirable attributes as possible. Conjoint analysis is a technique which can assist a marketer to identify the most desirable attributes sought in a product or service by a customer at various price levels. It is based on the assumption that consumers perceive products as consisting of a number of attributes, each offering a measure of worth/value/utility. Conjoint analysis identifies the relative worth of each of the attributes making up a product in order to find the product offering the most desirable combination of attributes (that is the greatest utility) at an acceptable price. By examining the relative utilities of attributes generated through conjoint analysis, marketers can produce new products/services or modify existing products/services which offer consumers the greatest utility for the least amount of money. As such, conjoint analysis is specifically targeted at the development or modification process of products or services.

It should be noted that both conjoint analysis and multidimensional scaling (MDS – discussed in section 8.1) are techniques aimed at identifying and quantifying consumer perceptions of products. The two approaches, however, differ in the way they identify and assign values of relative importance to product attributes from stated consumer preferences. MDS requires the researcher to infer what attributes (dimensions) were used by respondents who traded off the products, while conjoint analysis assumes all significant product attributes are known in advance (a priori) and then attempts to assign numerical values of relative importance to these pre-defined product attributes.

10.1 The data requirements and data-collection procedure

Since the conjoint method assumes that consumers view products as consisting of bundles of attributes, respondents are required to trade off sets of hypothetical products each described by a different attribute mix (called a product bundle). To define a product bundle, each predefined attribute must be described by levels which generally rank from 'worst' to 'best'. Product bundles are then constructed by combining different levels from each of the predefined attributes. By asking respondents to rank (or sometimes rate) a selection of product bundles, consumer preference data are generated for a conjoint analysis. Thus the data required are ordinal-scaled (ranking scores) and the ranking process is relatively straightforward for respondents.

Ideally respondents should be requested to rank all possible product bundles constructed from combinations of attribute levels. However, this *full factorial design* data-collection approach can be cumbersome if the number of possible product bundles is large. To illustrate, if four attributes each had three levels, then respondents would need to rank 81 separate product bundles. Such a task is unlikely to produce reliable rankings. By using a statistically valid *fractional factorial design* data-collection approach, the number of product bundles that a respondent needs to rank is greatly reduced. In the illustration of four attributes at three levels, this fractional factorial design approach would require respondents to rank a subset of only nine (instead of 81) product bundles.

10.2 The rationale of conjoint analysis

Initially, a user of conjoint analysis must identify all the important attributes which characterise a product/service. In-depth interview and focus groups may be necessary at this stage. In conjoint terms, the attributes are called *factors*. Thereafter, *levels* within factors (attributes) must be identified. Levels are alternative options for a factor. For example, if print quality is a factor in choosing a printer, then draft mode, near letter quality print mode or lithoprint mode would represent this factor's levels. These levels generally have a rank order from 'worst' to 'best'.

These different factor levels are combined across factors into *bundles* which make up separate product/service offerings. As discussed in the data requirement section above, respondents are now required to trade off through ranking the various product bundles in terms of the preferred alternative. Conjoint adopts the bundling of attributes approach because of the belief that consumers evaluate complete products, not individual attributes in isolation, when making purchase decisions.

The trade-off values provided by consumers are translated by the conjoint methodology into numeric measures for each factor level, called *utilities (or part-worths)*. The majority of conjoint computer packages use the MONANOVA (monotonic analysis of variance) statistical method to derive these part-worth measures (although regression analysis with categorical predictor variables can also be used).

A utility measure indicates the *relative value* that consumers assign to a particular attribute option. The conjoint algorithm will assign weights (utilities) to each factor level such that the sum of the factor level weights of a given bundle equals that bundle's ranking given by respondents during the data collection. Thus the conjoint process attempts to re-create the rank order of the product bundles (that is called the *derived* rank order) to coincide with the *actual* (*observed*) rank order of the product bundle assigned by the respondents. The success of the conjoint process depends upon how well the derived rank order of product bundles approximates the actual (or observed) rank order of product bundles given by the respondents.

Once derived, the attribute level utilities (part-worths) can now be used in two ways. Firstly, these utilities can be used to identify the relative importance of individual attributes among all other attributes and secondly to investigate the perceived attractiveness of alternative product offerings (made up of alternative attribute level combinations). To find the relative importance of individual attributes, we would find the utility range within each attribute and then express each attribute's utility range as a percentage of the sum of utility ranges across all attributes. These percentages will provide a researcher with a measure of the importance of various attributes to the consumers of the product/service.

With respect to identifying an alternative desirable product/service offering, the attribute level utilities can be summed for different attribute options. The most desirable product/service bundle is that combination of attribute levels with the 'highest' combined utility.

10.3 An illustrative example: planning a motel chain

A company is planning to establish a chain of motels on the main routes through South Africa. It is therefore seeking information on the mix of motel facilities it should be offering to appeal to the motoring tourist market. Four major attributes (factors) were identified as important by a panel of leisure consultants. They were room facilities, service level, leisure facilities and cost. For each attribute, various levels were identified, as shown in table 17.11 below.

Table 17.11 Attributes and their levels for the motel chain study

Attributes	Levels
Room facilities	Basic (shared bath) Economy (room with bath) Superior (bath and kitchen)
Service level	None Limited Full 24-hour service
Leisure facilities	None Restaurant only Include leisure room
Cost	R75 pp night R95 pp night R140 pp night

To evaluate all possible combinations of attribute levels, a total of 81 product bundles (a full factorial design) would have to be ranked. A fractional factorial design (as described in the data requirement section) requires only nine product bundles to capture sufficient trade-off data to identify part-worths for all attribute levels. The nine product bundles are shown in table 17.12 below together with an illustrative consumer ranking.

Table 17.12 Fractional factorial design — nine product bundles and consumer ranking of bundles

Room facilities	Service level	Leisure facilities	Cost per person per night	Rank
			(R)	
Basic	None	None	75	6
Basic	Limited	Restaurant only	140	9
Basic	Complete	Include leisure facilities	95	4
Economy	None	Restaurant only	95	3
Economy	Limited	Include leisure facilities	75	1
Economy	Complete	None	140	8
Superior	None	Include leisure facilities	140	7
Superior	Limited	None	95	5
Superior	Complete	Restaurant only	75	2

(Rank = 1 most preferred; Rank = 9 least preferred bundle)

The conjoint-derived *utilities* (part-worths) for each attribute level are given in table 17.13. The RxCON Version 1.1 PC statistical package was used to generate these utility values.

Table 17.13 Conjoint-derived utilities (part-worths) for each attribute level

Attributes	Levels	Utilities (part-worths)
Room facilities	Basic (shared bath)	− 1 033
	Economy (room with bath)	775
	Superior (bath, kitchen)	258
Service levels	None	− 258
	Limited	0
	Full 24-hour service	258
Leisure facilities	None	− 1 033
	Restaurant only	258
	Include leisure room	775
Price offerings	R75 pp night	1 549
	R95 pp night	775
	R140 pp night	− 2 324

Interpretation:

These attribute utilities (or part-worths) are meaningful only when compared to each other. A negative utility means that the associated attribute level is less preferred than an attribute level with a positive utility. For the room facilities attribute, for example, the respondents indicated that they most prefer an economy-type room with bed and own bathroom (utility = 775) and least prefer a basic room with a shared bathroom (utility = −1 033). There is also less preference for luxury-type accommodation (utility = 258) than economy-type accommodation. The other attribute level utilities are interpreted in a similar way.

The range of utilities within each attribute is used to determine the relative importance of attributes, as shown in table 17.14.

Table 17.14 Relative importance of each attribute

Attribute	Range	Percentage
Room facilities	1 808 (−1 033 to 775)	22,6
Room service	516 (−258 to 258)	6,4
Leisure facilities	1 808 (−1 303 to 775)	22,6
Cost	3 873 (−2 324 to 1 549)	48,4
Total		**100,0**

Clearly, the cost (48,4 %) of the motel accommodation offered is the most important consideration to respondents, followed by the type of room facilities (22,6 %) and availability of leisure facilities (also 22,6 %). Room service (6,4 %) is of no real importance to the respondents.

The value of conjoint analysis lies in the opportunity it offers to evaluate new product offerings. Although only nine product bundles were evaluated by respondents, it is possible to identify consumer preferences for all 81 product bundles by determining the total utility for each combination of attribute levels. The most preferred product bundle would be that mix of attribute level utilities which gives the largest total utility. Table 17.15 shows a sample of new product offerings and their derived consumer preference (as shown by its product bundle utility) including the three most preferred combinations.

The most preferred motel accommodation is indicated by the product bundle with the largest total utility. Respondents would most prefer an economy-type room, with 24-hour room service, full leisure facilities, and to pay only R75 per person per night. The motel decision makers must balance these consumer preferences against other business considerations.

Table 17.15 Sample of new product offerings and their derived consumer preferences

Room facilities	Service level	Leisure facilities	Cost per person per night	Total utility
Basic	Limited	Include leisure facilities	R95	517*
Economy	Complete	Restaurant only	R140	−1 033
Basic	None	Include leisure facilities	R95	259
Three most preferred combinations				
Economy	Complete	Include leisure facilities	R75	3 357
Economy	Limited	Include leisure facilities	R75	3 099
Economy	None	Include leisure facilities	R75	2 841

*(−1 033 + 0 + 775 + 775 = 517)

Finally, by using the derived attribute level utilities to reconstruct the rank order of the nine product bundles used for data collection, it is possible to validate the conjoint approach. The conjoint approach would be validated if the derived rank order from the utilities equalled the actual rank order of the original nine product bundles. The results of the comparison, as shown in table 17.16, indicate that the conjoint approach accurately reflects the relative importance of consumer preferences.

Table 17.16 Comparison of the actual rank order with the derived rank order

Product bundle	Actual rank order (by respondents)	Total utility	Derived rank order (from utilities)
1	6	−775	6
2	9	−3 099	9
3	4	775	4
4	3	1 550	3
5	1	3 099	1
6	8	−2 324	8
7	7	−1 549	7
8	5	0	5
9	2	2 323	2

10.4 Concluding comments

Conjoint analysis is a valuable marketing tool for uncovering consumer preferences for product offerings by identifying the relative value they attach to the different attributes which characterise the products. To ensure the proper application of conjoint analysis, two issues need to be carefully considered by a researcher. The first refers to the design of the data-collection procedure. While data collection is cognitively straightforward for respondents (they merely have to rank product bundles), some expertise is required to set up an appropriate fractional factorial design model in place of the full factorial design model which generally has extensive data-collection demands.

Secondly, a researcher must be assured that all the significant attributes with relevant levels have been identified. If the identified attributes are incomplete, the conjoint approach will provide only partial (and possibly) misleading information.

11 SUMMARY

Multivariate analysis offers a market researcher insights into marketing issues which cannot be gained by the mere analysis of marketing variables either individually or in pairwise comparisons. The power of these techniques lies in their ability to systematically uncover complex relationships which may exist between several variables simultaneously. However, to use these techniques effectively, a researcher needs to understand the purpose, rationale, data requirements and limitations of each technique. A proper understanding of these issues, and the matching of an appropriate technique to a study's objectives, will ensure that legitimate statistical analysis on multivariate data is performed. This chapter has sought to provide a non-technical understanding of the types of multivariate statistical techniques commonly encountered in marketing literature to help a researcher in the appropriate selection of a multivariate technique to match a study's purpose. Additionally, by making researchers aware of the availability of statistical methods for analysing several variables simultaneously, this may encourage the greater use of these techniques in practice and by so doing enhance the quality of information used in marketing decision making.

SUPPLEMENTARY READING

Hair, Joseph F, Anderson, Ralph E, Tatham, Ronald L, & Black, William C 1987. *Multivariate data analysis*. Third edition. New York: Maxwell Macmillan.

Manly, Bryan F J 1994. *Multivariate statistical methods – a primer*. Second edition. London: Chapman & Hall.

Interpretation and presentation of results

Chapter 18: H de J van Wyk

(This chapter is partly based on chapter 19 'Interpretation of results and report writing' by F E Rädel in Nel *et al* 1988)

Interpretation and presentation of results

1 INTRODUCTION

Data collection and analysis have been dealt with in detail in the preceding chapters. But the results of a research project will have little impact on decision making, however thorough and scientific the researcher's approach, unless the interpretation and reporting are of a high standard. In the first part of the chapter we shall explain how the intermediate results of the analysis are interpreted and integrated to arrive at findings and conclusions. In the second part we move to the preparation of the written report and then conclude with a discussion of oral and visual reporting. Written and oral/visual reporting are not necessarily mutually exclusive; very often the written report is illuminated by an oral/visual presentation.

2 INTERPRETATION OF RESULTS

2.1 Relation between interpretation, analysis and research objectives

In theory it is possible to make a clear distinction between analysis and interpretation. In *analysis* the collected data are broken up into groups or elements which the researcher examines separately and then translates into intermediate results; in *interpretation* the intermediate results are translated into integrated and meaningful general inferences and findings. (Interpretation begins where analysis ends and analysis is the basis of interpretation.) Meaningful means that the findings must be relevant to the objectives of the research.

From your reading of chapter 5 you will remember that we distinguished between management problems and research objectives. The final findings must therefore be relevant not only to the research objectives but also and above all to the management problems which the research has to address in the final instance. For example, the management problem is that product X's market share is declining (chapter 5). It is hypothesised that buyers prefer rival product A. The research objective is 'to determine the extent and reasons why product A is preferred to own product X'. The final findings of the research exercise must be relevant to these objectives and, by either rejecting or confirming the hypothesis, must answer the management problem. If the findings, however interesting, do not provide these answers, the researcher has lost sight of the objectives during the research process by inappropriate data collection, sampling procedures or analyses.

Here again we see that the research process forms an integrated whole, starting with the formulation of the research objectives and ending with the inference of final findings. Now you will understand, with hindsight as it were, how important it is to define the research goals precisely, for they run like a golden thread through the entire process. The research goals have also been linked to a magnet which orients the whole research process, especially the final findings. This holistic view of the research process explains why a clear distinction between analysis and interpretation is more difficult to make in practice than in theory. Since with each analysis the researcher hopes to uncover facts that will help him draw conclusions, analysis contains a certain interpretative element. No wonder there are so many confusing and diverse definitions of analysis and interpretation in the literature.

2.2 Some pitfalls of interpretation

Several pitfalls await the researcher in the interpretation of results. To interpret the results correctly he must be familiar with the method of the research and the limitations of the results. While it is sometimes said that interpretation lets the analysed data 'speak', the researcher should not allow them to say more than is warranted by the research method. One of the greatest pitfalls is that of *overgeneralisation*. The urge to generalise is understandably great since it increases the scope and value of findings. For instance, the findings of a survey on the income and expenditure patterns of households in a certain urban area may only be valid for that particular area and for the survey period. They may not be applicable to other areas and even less to the country as a whole, or to different time periods.

The researcher should also beware of generalising too far *beyond* the range of the observations. If, for instance, the survey mentioned above reveals a linear correlation between savings and income in the income range R1 500 to R2 500 per month, it would be unjustified to conclude that there is a general linear correlation between savings and income since the correlation in the income range below R1 500 and above R2 500 may be non-linear.

A further pitfall is that of *confusing correlation with causation*. Close correlation can be purely accidental. If, for instance, there is a strong correlation between the stork population of a country and the number of births, only those who believe in fairy-tales would conclude that the first variable is the cause of the second. It is when there is a plausible relation between two variables, like the one between income and car ownership, that the researcher is justified in basing his argument on the principles of correlation analysis. The researcher should therefore bear in mind that the absence of correlation invariably proves the absence of causation: the presence of correlation by itself does not prove causation (Ferber, Blankerts & Hollander 1964:427).

For the same reason that correlation does not necessarily prove causation, the confirmation of a hypothesis by statistical tests does not necessarily prove the validity of the hypothesis. Unless the validity of the hypothesis can be proved by other arguments it is advisable to formulate the conclusion more cautiously, for example 'the tests do not disprove the hypothesis' or 'the results of the tests are in accordance with the hypothesis' rather than 'the tests confirm the hypothesis'.

While the researcher should avoid reading more into the data than is warranted, he should also guard against erring in the opposite direction. Very often there may be more information hidden in the data than the researcher cares to or is able to bring to light. It requires experience, disciplined thinking and familiarity with the research method to let the results say what they are able to say.

2.3 Recommendations: part of research?

The question of whether and to what extent marketing research should confine itself to presenting results and findings, or should go as far as recommending alternative or specific actions, is indeed a moot one. It is not merely a technicality; it concerns the essence of research and decision making. Marketing research is a *staff function*, no more and no less, and decision making is an *executive function*. Research has to provide information and it is the task of executive management to translate this information into decisions and action. From this point of view it is logical that research should confine itself to the presentation of findings only.

Yet views on this issue differ in theory as well as in practice. Those who are in favour of policy recommendations by researchers argue that an experienced researcher, who is often more familiar with the problem area under discussion, should not withhold his opinion on the most appropriate action to be taken. This of course applies more to internal researchers than to outside consultants who seldom have the intimate knowledge of the internal situation and climate of the organisation to make meaningful recommendations. And when research is confined to findings the executive seldom has the time and insight into the research to develop courses of action, so the chances are that a potentially valuable report may lie unused on a bookshelf. An executive may therefore appreciate the researcher's recommendations.

Those holding the opposite view argue that recommendations are not part of research; recommendations follow and therefore fall outside the scope of research. They also argue that research only covers one aspect of a management problem and that many other inputs, of which the researcher has no knowledge, influence management decisions. The researcher's recommendation(s) will tend to be one-sided and he should therefore refrain from making them. Moreover the researcher who trespasses into the realm of the executive may arouse jealousy, resistance and even hostility, especially since the executive's company status is usually higher than the researcher's. Last but not least, it is held that the researcher's characteristics and mental attributes, which are akin to the academic's, render him unsuited to decision making where vision, leadership, intuition and risk taking are required.

Both schools of thought may be right in particular situations, depending upon the relationship between research and management, the complexity of the research, the status of the researcher within the organisation, etc. Crisp (1957:475) concludes: 'As in so many controversial areas in marketing research, the question of whether or not recommendations should be included must be answered by "it all depends...".'

In practice, conflict between research and management can be avoided by specifying in the research assignment whether recommendations are required in the final report.

3 PREPARATION AND WRITING OF THE REPORT

3.1 Importance and principles of report writing

After the researcher has spent weeks or even months collecting, analysing and interpreting the data, the writing of the report may seem a mere formality or even an anticlimax. The real work has been done, and what remains is to put it on paper. This is an illusion which may have serious consequences, for several reasons. The report is the culmination of the whole research project. Churchill (1992:766) sums it up as follows: 'Regardless of the sophistication displayed in the other portions of the research process the project is a failure if the research report fails.'

Management generally only takes note of the report and not of the preceding steps of the research process, judging the quality of the research by the quality of the report. A report has therefore also been likened to a lifeline between research and management. Formal communication between management and research is generally limited to the beginning and end stages of a project, that is the research proposal and the final report, and management is unaware of what happens in between. The report is more than just a record of the methodology and the findings of the research. The way it is arranged and written often decides whether management acts on a report.

The logical sequence of facts and arguments should run like a golden thread throughout the report. As the dissertations of graduate students prove, this seems to be so difficult that it may be seen as the greatest shortcoming in report writing. The best way of improving proficiency is to construct a detailed outline or scheme before writing the report. A useful starting point is the general format of the report, to be discussed in section 3.4 of this chapter. This outline or scheme can be elaborated by further breakdowns and subdivisions. The division of the report into chapters which follow one another logically is of especial importance. Once a logical scheme has been constructed it is necessary to ascertain whether each statement or argument is discussed under the right heading.

A concise writing style is required in a scientific report. Churchill (1992:772) defines concise writing as 'maximum use of every word; no word in the concise discussion can be removed without impairing or destroying the function of the whole composition ... to be concise is to express a thought completely and clearly in the fewest possible words'. The report writer should also be selective in his choice of material for the report. There is always the temptation to use all the information and to impress the reader with a wealth of findings. Whatever is not needed to support a conclusion or finding should be omitted.

A report should not, however, be concise to the point of excluding essential information. While it is not easy to strike a balance between conciseness and completeness, the report should contain all the information required by the decision maker, no more and no less, and address every question of the original assignment and every objective of the project.

Finally the report should be correct in every respect (Churchill 1992:767). Loss of credibility sets in when the reader begins to notice spelling and printing errors. Doubts about its contents are strengthened by the presence of further errors, which at best frustrate the reader and at worst give rise to erroneous conclusions and inferences on the part of the reader and the researcher alike. There are several common errors which should be avoided in report writing. A few of them are mentioned below.

☐ Figures in tables do not tally with totals (see section 3.5.2 for the construction of tables).

☐ Figures that should be in agreement differ. The same magnitude appearing in more than one table or quoted more than once in the text should have the same value throughout.

☐ The text is not in agreement with the tables or graphs. The researcher may make erroneous inferences from a table or graph while he is writing by merely copying or transposing figures incorrectly or by attaching the wrong interpretation to a figure.

☐ Statements made in the report do not tally with the facts. For instance, 'Soweto has five million inhabitants' is not in agreement with the official statistics or the results of scientific studies in which the population of Soweto is set at just over one million. A statement of this kind, which runs counter to accepted facts, should be accompanied with the necessary supporting arguments.

☐ Statements and figures are not explained. The above statement about the population of Soweto has a further shortcoming in that a date is not mentioned. Was the figure of five million inhabitants supposed to be correct at the time of writing of the report, or at the time of a survey conducted in the recent or distant past?

In summary, the importance of good report writing cannot be overemphasised. At the same time experience has shown that often researchers, even good ones, are poor report writers. Ferber *et al* (1964:428) summarise the proficiency of researchers for the various steps of the research process as follows:

☐ Researchers are strongest in methodology and techniques.

☐ They are less strong in pinpointing problems and translating them into appropriate methodology.

☐ They are even less strong in the full interpretation of the data gathered.

☐ They are least strong in presenting results in simple, persuasive, business language.

Report writing is often the weakest link in the research process. The material is generally quite acceptable but its arrangement and logical presentation leave much to be desired, mainly because report writing and the preceding steps in the research process draw on different sets of talents, the average marketing researcher's training and interest are geared more to research methodology than to report writing and, last but not least, researchers do not always realise the fundamental truth that a research project succeeds or fails by the quality of the report.

The general guidelines for report writing discussed so far are by no means the only ones for writing a scientific report. There are several formal requirements as well.

3.2 Formal requirements for report writing

A reader of a report needs to be given certain cues in order to assess the results of a research project. He is therefore entitled to expect the writer to conform to certain requirements. Such prescriptions of requirements for the contents of a research report are exemplified in the code of conduct of the Southern African Market Research Association (SAMRA):

☐ The person reading a marketing research report should be able to form a clear picture of the whole survey, its validity, reliability and how it was done. There should be no deliberate misrepresentation of methods or results by the research practitioner.

☐ The following information should be included in the report on a research project:

   – The name of the client for whom the survey was undertaken.

   – The name of the research organisation conducting the survey, including the name(s) of any sub-contractor(s) and whether the whole survey or only a specific part was subcontracted.

   – The objective(s) or terms of reference of the survey.

   – A full description of the method by which the information was collected, that is whether by face-to-face interview, focus group discussion, mail or telephone interview, observation, mechanical recording device or some other method. If the same respondents were used on behalf or more than one client/sponsor then this will also be noted.

- A full and detailed description of the universe covered (actual, not just intended). This should detail population group and geographical coverage and any particular characteristic(s) (such as gender, age, SIC (Standard Industrial Classification) group, employment group, store turnover, etc) which qualify informants for inclusion in the sample.
- The sample and sampling technique. The size, sampling method (probability, non-probability, panel, etc) planned and achieved sample, substitution, weighting procedures, and any limitations or factors affecting representativeness.
- The period when fieldwork was done.
- Relevant information on the field staff employed and any quality control methods and check-back procedures used, with an indication of the number of checks done. In the case of focus group discussions, information on the qualifications of the moderators used.
- Any 'Acts of God' or special events occurring during the course of the investigation which affected the original research technique or results, or which should be borne in mind when interpreting the results.
- A copy of the questionnaire discussion guide, or interviewing schedule as well as copies or descriptions of any other relevant documents and/or exhibits and show cards used during the conduct of the research. Alternatively, if these are not included in the report for a specific reason, this should be stated and documents should be available for inspection by the client/sponsor or a person authorised by the client/sponsor.
- The attention of the reader should be drawn to the degree of reliability, if measurable, and any possible bias of the findings based on samples or subsamples. If the reliability is not statistically measurable it should be stated. Where appropriate a statement is required of response, refusal, non-contactability and substitution rates, and a discussion of possible bias due to non-response or other factors.
- The tables of results should include the base upon which each percentage is calculated and, if weighted, then the weighted base should be shown as well as the number of informants. Any statistical methods or tests should be fully described.

☐ In the case of desk research on secondary information the source(s) should be given.

3.3 Audience for whom the report is written

As we have seen, there are various principles and requirements in report writing that govern the format and scientific presentation of a research report. This does not mean, however, that the language of the report should not be tailored to the report's audience. The writer of the report can do this only if he knows who the readers will be. The most important person obviously is the client, who very often is also the manager of the marketing department or top management. The readers of the report may of course include people outside the organisation. Tull and Hawkins (1990:694) enumerate several points in connection with the readers of research reports:

> First, managers are extremely busy. Second, they are much less interested in the technical and logical aspects of a research problem than the researcher is. Third, they are seldom well versed in research techniques and terminology. Fourth, if there is more than one reader, and there usually is, they are likely to differ in terms of interests, training, and reasons for reading the report. Finally, managers, like everyone else, prefer interesting reports over dull ones.

We shall return to some of these points in the context of the format and structure of the report (section 3.4) and the components of a report (section 3.5). Here we shall conclude with the following quotation from Tull and Hawkins (1990:695):

> Terms such as *skewed distribution, correlation coefficient,* or even *significance level* are not necessarily familiar to all marketing managers. In many research reports, it is often necessary to utilize the concepts that underlie these terms. Three strategies are available for dealing with this problem. The term can be used, followed by a brief description or explanation; the explanation can be provided first followed by the term; or the technical terms can be omitted altogether. Which approach, or combination of approaches, is best depends upon the nature of the audience and the message.

Besides these considerations there are certain psychological aspects of report writing which merit attention. In-company politics and the idiosyncrasies of top executives should be considered when writing the report. This does not mean that the researcher should come forward with findings which top management would like to see. Weiers (1984:536–537) lists a few hints to ensure that the research is taken seriously and put to constructive use:

☐ Identify the persons who might be affected, like executives, 'gatekeepers', etc, without whose support the research findings or recommendations can be expected to be diluted on their way to the top.

☐ Test tentative findings conversationally in order to identify potential objections and resistance so that they can be addressed in the report with particularly waterproof and convincing arguments.

☐ Be cautious if findings point to abrupt policy changes which management may be hesitant to introduce. Either make a strong case of such findings supported by irrefutable arguments or suggest further research which gives management a chance to get accustomed to a major policy change.

3.4 Format and structure of the report

Neither in the literature nor in research practice does one find uniformity in the format and structure of a research report. The format of research reports is influenced mainly by the instructions from executive or client, the nature and complexity of the problem, and the nature and variety of readers for whom the report is intended.

Nevertheless, over the years a certain degree of uniformity has emerged in the contents and arrangement of the report. The overriding consideration, regardless of style and sequence, however, is that of the logical flow of the discussion. A format typically contains the following:

1 Title page

2 Table of contents

3 List of tables

4 List of figures

5 Proposal and letter of authorisation

6 Executive summary

7 Introduction (objectives and arrangement of report)

8 Method followed

9 Interpretation, conclusion and findings (discussion of results)

10 Limitations and shortcomings of the results and findings

11 Recommendations (if required)

12 Annexures

13 Bibliography

Items may be combined in short reports and broken up into a number of subitems in longer reports. The sequence of items may also be changed. Very often the interpretation, conclusion and findings, for example, are discussed before the method followed (8 above), the reason being that persons who read the executive summary (6) may want to know more about the results. For the convenience of such persons the executive summary and detailed discussion of the results are not separated by pages and pages of methodological descriptions in which they may have little interest. Limitations and shortcomings of the report may also be mentioned in the introduction because the writer of the report wishes to draw attention to them at an early stage.

Before discussing each of these items in brief we should note that every report should be accompanied by a covering letter from the researcher to the person(s) to whom the report is to be presented. It may be formal or informal depending upon the relationship between the parties concerned. It serves to announce the completion of the research and the release of the report and to establish rapport between the writer and reader(s). Some writers like to refer to a few findings in the letter in order to arouse interest and encourage the recipient to read the report.

3.4.1 Title page

One of the functions of the title page is to display the title of the report. The title identifies the main theme of the report in the briefest possible way. At the same time it should arouse the reader's interest in the report. Besides the title of the report, the title page also displays the name of the researcher(s) and the research organisation (in the case of an outside consultant), the name of the organisation and/or the person(s) for whom the research was undertaken, and the place and date of release of the report. If the report is for limited distribution, this should be noted on the title page. Some title pages list the names or designations of the persons who may see the report.

3.4.2 Table of contents

The table of contents lists the main and subdivisions of the report, with page references to help the reader find the divisions which are of particular interest. Although it reflects the outline of the report before writing, the table of contents should not be finalised until the report has been completed. The headings of the divisions and subdivisions in the table of contents must correspond exactly to those in the report, a requirement which seems obvious but is often not strictly observed in practice. In addition to the divisions the table of contents also lists the preface, annexures, bibliography and so on with page references – in short, all the sections of the report are listed in the table of contents.

3.4.3 List of tables and figures

After the table of contents it is customary to insert a list of tables and list of figures with page references. The tables and figures in the text and in the annexure(s) are generally listed separately. Again the report writer should make sure that the titles of tables and figures in the list are the same as those in the text and annexure(s).

3.4.4 Proposal and letter of authorisation

The proposal sets out the research objectives, the research plan, the cost estimate and the duration of the project (chapter 5). Many weeks or even months may have elapsed since the proposal was submitted and its execution authorised. Management may therefore not remember exactly what the project was all about. The insertion of both the proposal and the letter of authorisation in the report serves to refresh management's memory; it also serves as a yardstick or benchmark for assessing the report. In the event of a dispute between management and the researcher about whether the required information is contained in the report, the proposal and letter of authorisation may become decisive documents. If the proposal is too lengthy and detailed it is advisable to give only the essence under this heading and the full text in an annexure.

3.4.5 Executive summary

The summary is the core – the most important part – of the report. As many executives read only the summary it represents the researcher's sole chance of reaching them. It is therefore fitting that the summary is generally called the executive summary. To induce executives to read more than the summary the researcher should specify in footnotes or brackets the chapters/sections in which more detailed discussions of findings or statements are to be found.

A summary is not just an abstract of the whole report in which everything is restated in condensed form; it is a coherent combination of the most salient findings of the report, especially those which are of importance to management. Management is of course mainly interested in the interpretation of results and findings. But to avoid overgeneralising or overrating the research findings on the part of management it should contain a brief description of the method followed and the limitations and shortcomings of the research results. Neglecting to draw management's attention to the limitations of results on which far-reaching policy decisions may be based can lead to serious dispute between management and research if the expected results do not materialise.

A summary should also contain a brief statement of the objectives of the study. Whether or not recommendations should form part of the summary depends on whether such recommendations are contained in the full report, a problem which has been addressed in section 2.3 and which will again be referred to in section 3.4.10 below.

A test for a good summary is its self-sufficiency. Sometimes a summary is even detached from the full report and circulated separately. To sum up, a good summary should contain the following items:

☐ Instruction (objectives and methods)
☐ Results of the various elements of the study
☐ Interpretation of results and major findings
☐ Recommendations (if required).

Although the executive summary generally precedes the body of the report, it is obviously not written until the draft of the full report has been completed.

3.4.6 Introduction (objectives and arrangement of report)

The introduction of the research report announces the subject, purpose, scope and plan of the research. Above all, it should describe the research objectives which are the basis for the assessment of the results and findings of the whole exercise. Churchill (1992:775) sums up the functions of the introduction as follows:

> The introduction should state the specific objectives of the research. If the project was part of a larger, overall project, this should be mentioned. Each of the sub-problems or hypotheses should be explicitly stated. After reading the introduction, readers should know just what the report covers and what it omits. They should appreciate the overall problem and how the subproblems relate to it. They should be aware of the relationship between this study and other related work. And they should appreciate the need for the study and its importance. Through all this, the introduction should serve to win the readers' confidence and dispel any prejudices they may have.

3.4.7 Method followed

If the proper research plan is designed before the project begins, the description of the method should not be difficult even if it is adapted during the course of the research. What makes the description of the method difficult is the need to use such non-technical language and terms as management will understand. However difficult it may be, the researcher must explain to management the essentials of the research method followed and the reasons for selecting it. Such essentials include questionnaires, sample size and technique, types and sources of secondary data, and methods of analysis. Dates of the beginning and the completion of major steps in the research process (especially inter-viewing) should also be given. The purpose of this section of the report is to provide the reader with sufficient technical background to appraise the quality of the data obtained and the findings of the research. If the researcher thinks it is necessary to explain a highly sophisticated formula or method in detail, it is best done in an annexure.

3.4.8 Interpretation, findings and conclusions

This may normally be the most important and probably the longest section of the report since management is interested mainly in the conclusion and major findings. Statistics, tables and figures form part of this section in so far as they are necessary as a foundation for the conclusions and findings. The findings should be geared to the objectives of the study. If the objective was the testing of a hypothesis, then the findings must ultimately either prove or disprove the hypothesis. (The interrelation between research objectives, conclusions and findings was discussed in section 2.1 of this chapter.)

3.4.9 Limitations and shortcomings of the results and findings

Research can never be one hundred per cent perfect. It is the essence of marketing research methods that the results achieved are only approximations of the truth with varying degrees of probability. This is why the method followed and the limitations of the results and findings must be set out in the report. Quite apart from the limitations inherent in the method, the fact that no research plan works out perfectly in practice also affects the validity of the findings. The response rate may be much lower than expected or – worse still – a particular section of the sample may not respond at all. If the response rate is lower than expected, the statistical basis of some tables or breakdowns may be too small to arrive at meaningful conclusions. Therefore the shortcomings affecting the validity of the results and final conclusions must be mentioned in the report; the researcher should, however, avoid over-emphasising them and so risk loss of confidence in the whole report.

3.4.10 Recommendations

The problem of whether the researcher should formulate recommendations for executive action was discussed in section 2.3. If the researcher decides or is requested to formulate recommendations, these should obviously follow logically from the conclusions and findings and be presented with reasons and in greater detail than in the executive summary.

3.4.11 Annexure(s)

To a certain extent the decision on what should be incorporated in the text or be attached as annexures is an arbitrary one. As a general guideline anything which would unnecessarily interrupt the logical flow of argument in the text should be attached as an annexure. Such material would include detailed explanations of complicated formulae, copies of questionnaires, maps or a number of essentially similar tables. If, for instance, several tables on consumption patterns of different sizes of household have to be presented, they should be assembled in the annexure and only one table showing the consumption pattern of the average-sized household should be incorporated in the text. At the same time it is inconvenient and frustrating for the reader to refer to the tables in the annexures while reading the discussion in the text.

3.4.12 Bibliography

The bibliography, which typically appears at the end of the report, lists the full particulars of all the works quoted in the report. Bibliographies follow a particular style of reference such as the Harvard method.

3.4.13 Further comments

The logical flow of argument required in the report applies to the contents as well as the sequence of the chapters. Such logical flow can best be achieved by grouping the contents of the chapters into sections and subsections. The decimal classification applied in this book is among the most popular and appropriate methods. There are two variations. In the first the number of the chapter is part of the decimal notation, that is a section numbered 2.1 would be the first section in chapter 2. The second variation, which is the one used in this book, requires that the first section in each chapter be numbered 1.1.

The numbering of tables and figures is discussed in sections 3.5.2 and 3.5.3 respectively, but it is also fitting to refer to their location here. Both of these visual aids are located on the page of the text where they are referred to for the first time, or, if that is not possible, then on the page immediately following. Tables and figures are numbered separately by decimal notation, starting with the number of the chapter containing the figure. The term 'figure' is applied to maps, diagrams and graphs/charts (Churchill 1992:773). In reports containing only one table, one graph and one diagram, the term 'exhibit' may be used for all of them and the notation may be confined to one series.

3.5 The components of a report and their requirements

In our discussion of the format and structure of the report in section 3.4 we saw that a written report consists of the text, tables and figures. The requirements set for these three components of the report are discussed below.

3.5.1 Text

The text is the backbone of the report, with tables and figures serving mostly as aids to illustrate specific aspects of the results. However, important aspects of the report can only be conveyed in words. For this reason clarity is of the utmost importance. The researcher should make sure that each word and sentence conveys a clear message and above all that it conveys the message exactly. He should check each sentence of the draft or, better still, ask a colleague or friend for assistance. The best way is to have the draft checked by a committee before the report is finalised and released. Ambiguous and obscure formulation is probably the greatest shortcoming in report writing and is often a matter not just of wording but of woolly and undisciplined thinking. Churchill (1992:768) is under no illusions when he says, 'if the reader is offered the slightest opportunity to misunderstand, he probably will'. It is safest to call in the assistance of a professional editor.

The arrangement of the text is also of importance. Besides grouping the text into sections, as discussed above, it should also be divided into paragraphs which should be kept short and deal with only one point. The use of various fonts and type sizes is also helpful in emphasising certain facts. Luck, Wales, Taylor and Ruben (1982:476) state:

> Variations in type sizes and skilful use of white space may attract attention to major and minor parts of ideas in the report, as well as facilitating reading. Use capitalisation or 'false' caps (capitalising the initial letter in each word) to emphasise central ideas. Use quotation marks, italics, or underlining to further fortify key words or ideas. Dots, exclamation marks, and lead lines will direct attention to significant parts of a page. Overuse of such devices, however, may cheapen the appearance of a report or delude the reader into superficial consideration of it. Contrasting colours may be used but tend to be distracting and are not worth the effort.

Discussions of tables and figures should not be cluttered with too many facts. Very often directing the reader's attention to the highest and second highest and lowest and second lowest figures will suffice, leaving the reader to consult the table or figure for any further figures required. References in the text to tables and figures are accompanied with the number of the tables; references to the 'foregoing' or 'following' are not acceptable because the table/graph may be moved to a different location for technical reasons. As regards language usage in the report, the researcher should avoid slang, jargon and high-sounding wording as far as possible. For instance, the term OTS is commonly used in media research, but in a report which may be read by the uninitiated first references to such terms should be written out and followed by the abbreviation: ... opportunity to see (OTS) ... The abbreviation may be freely used in subsequent references.

Finally we turn our attention to the treatment of footnotes in the text. There are two types of footnotes. First there is the explanatory footnote, which elaborates on a statement in the text but is not located in the text because it would interrupt the flow. In this textbook such footnotes are located at the foot of the page. The second type of footnote* encompasses references to secondary sources. The function of a footnote referring to a secondary source cited in the text is to give the reader the opportunity to trace the relevant work. Thus the author, year of publication, title, place of publication and publisher are specified at the end of the report (or chapter) and specific page references to quotations are given in the text.

To summarise: writing well is an art which may take years to develop. The researcher should therefore have no qualms about submitting draft reports to experts for critical appraisal.

---

* The term 'footnote' is an anachronism in this context. The Harvard method of referencing, which is the one used in this book, requires the location of references in the text itself.

3.5.2 Tables

In chapter 15 we discussed univariate and bivariate analysis which are fundamental to the construction of most tables. This section will deal with the rules for constructing tables. Like report writing, the compilation of tables is an art which has to be developed.

Before putting pen to paper the researcher should ask himself: 'What is the table intended to show?' The answer to this question will be the key to the construction of the table. It will also serve to exclude unnecessary figures. Like the text, the tables in a report should be simple and easy to understand.

The rules for constructing tables are best illustrated by an example of a table from one of the research reports of the Bureau of Market Research (BMR). The table is reproduced below as table 18.1.

Table 18.1 Distribution of personal disposable income by population group and province, 1994

Province	Asians		Blacks		Coloureds		Whites		Total	
	R million	%	R million	%	R million	%	R million	%	R million	%
Western Cape	358,0	0,8	4 178,0	9,3	16 007,0	35,5	24 486,6	54,4	45 029,6	100,0
Northern Cape	22,0	0,4	1 263,6	22,8	1 459,0	26,3	2 799,1	50,5	5 543,7	100,0
Eastern Cape	289,0	1,2	12 321,8	52,4	2 584,0	11,0	8 319,0	35,4	23 513,8	100,0
Free State	20,0	0,1	9 486,1	50,7	440,2	2,4	8 782,2	46,9	18 728,5	100,0
KwaZulu-Natal	7 694,0	17,1	19 493,3	43,4	1 362,0	3,0	16 395,4	36,5	44 944,7	100,0
Mpumalanga	179,0	1,1	9 178,6	55,4	227,0	1,4	6 978,7	42,1	16 563,3	100,0
Northern Province	82,0	0,8	7 503,2	70,9	63,0	0,6	2 939,1	27,8	10 587,3	100,0
Gauteng	2 795,0	2,4	40 851,5	35,5	3 908,8	3,4	67 664,4	58,7	115 219,7	100,0
North-West	116,0	0,8	8 852,4	58,3	289,0	1,9	5 922,8	39,0	15 180,2	100,0
South Africa	**11 555,0**	**3,9**	**113 128,5**	**38,3**	**26 340,0**	**8,9**	**144 287,3**	**48,9**	**295 310,8**	**100,0**

Source: Martins *et al* (1994:34).

The principles and rules governing the construction of tables are discussed below.

(a) Number of table

As we have said, the decimal system of notation is preferable in numbering sections in the text and in numbering tables. The table number in table 18.1 tells the reader the following:

1st digit: chapter containing the table
2nd digit: first table in the eighteenth chapter

The numbers of tables in annexures are given the prefix A, one of the reasons being that very often an abridged version of the same table is located in the text. If both tables are given the same number, with the prefix A distinguishing the table in the annexure, the reader who is consulting the table in the text has little difficulty in locating the relevant table in the annexure should he wish to do so. In reports containing more than one annexure with tables, the first digit of the table number indicates whether the table is located in annexure A1, A2, etc.

(b) Heading of table

Luck *et al* (1982:477) have the following to say about table headings:

> This should be written after the table is finished so that it may be a proper description. It should be brief – verbs and articles omitted – yet self-explanatory, clearly stating the nature, classification, and time reference of the information given.

Tables may also be given subtitles. Once the list of tables has been compiled the researcher should go through it and without looking at the tables themselves decide whether the titles are indeed descriptive of the contents of the tables.

(c) Arrangement of table

Figures are arranged in columns (vertical) and in rows (horizontal). The number of columns and rows in the table is governed by the size of the page, which may be A3, A4 or A5. Generally the smaller arrangement is vertical in columns and the larger arrangement is horizontal in rows. Long horizontal arrangements (a large number of rows) are carried over to the following page with the word 'continued' printed at the top of the page. (Tables may also be reduced in size to fit a standard page, provided the legibility of the table is not compromised.) Tables which run over two pages are easier to read if they are located on two facing pages. In theory there is no limit to the number of pages a table may comprise, but in practice a limit is imposed to avoid overly long interruptions of the text. Generally a table in the text of the report should not exceed two pages in length. Tables exceeding two pages in length should be abridged when located in the text and printed in full in an annexure. Abridging a table involves adding together groups of figures in rows to form one row (for example districts to regions or individual expenditure items to main expenditure items). The researcher should use the arrangement that brings out the most significant aspects of the data – a geographical arrangement for data relating to political divisions and locations, or arrangement by years, months, etc, for data relating to time, and so forth. When order of magnitude is most important, data are arranged in that order, and this arrangement is most general. Alphabetical arrangement simplifies locating an item on a list. There are other bases as well. One of these is numerical designation, such as sales territories 1, 2, etc. Another is categories such as class expenditures (Luck *et al* 1982:477).

(d) Captions and stubs

Captions are the designations placed over the vertical columns; stubs are those at the left, opposite the horizontal lines of figures. They should be brief and descriptive. A heading over the stubs should describe them as a whole. Where subclasses are shown with their subtotals, the stubs for the subclasses are indented opposite the subtotal. If more than one line is required for a stub, place the figures opposite the first line. If one of the captions is 'miscellaneous', it should be at the right-hand side. Chronological columns may read from the latest time toward the more remote, or vice versa, but the arrangement should be followed consistently. The chronology should be in definite order. A *master caption* can be placed above two or more adjacent columnar captions when it describes something these columns have in common (Luck *et al* 1982:479).

Every column, including the 'stub column', must have a caption and every row must have a stub. In our example of a table (table 18.1) the stubs are listed under the designation of 'Province'. The last row is generally termed the total or average. This figure may also be printed in the first row, but whatever method is used, it should be used consistently in all the tables in a particular report.

(e) Unit of measurement

The unit of measurement is rarely left unspecified in a table. It is up to the researcher to check for the presence and correctness of the unit of measurement in the table. Common errors include failure to specify units of one thousand ('000) and erroneous specification of units of one thousand for units of one million (R'000 000 or R million). The unit of measurement is located just under the heading of the table or, if there is more than one unit of measurement, at the top of the relevant column just under the caption.

(f) Totals

In most tables column totals are advisable. And in tables with the same units in all the columns, cross totals are also advisable. Individual figures must add up to subtotals and to the grand total. Slight discrepancies due to rounding are, however, inevitable.

(g) Ruling, spaces, leaders and emphasis

Here we turn again to Luck *et al* (1982:480) for guidance:

Ruling, spaces, and leaders. Rather than ruling the tables across or vertically, white spaces are often used to set figures apart. Skipping lines between different sections of the data or between every three to five lines also aids the eye. Vertical ruling is needed when complicated captions are used. Horizontal rulings are used after the captions and below the figures. Frequently a helpful procedure is to draw a line under the total (when at the top) or above the total line when it is at the bottom. Using leaders ... in a stub assists the eye and helps smooth over uneven entries.

Emphasis. Emphasis is obtained by contrasting typefaces among the figures, stubs, and possibly captions. Use of light and heavy lines or of double lines also gives emphasis or directs the eye.

(h) Footnotes

There are two types of footnotes: explanatory footnotes and source footnotes. Explanatory footnotes are useful in tables whose captions/stubs need further elucidation or whose figures need to be qualified. Such explanatory footnotes precede source footnotes specifying secondary sources from which the information was obtained.

As in the case of the text, the researcher constructing the table would be well advised to ask for assistance in checking the table for errors and ambiguities.

3.5.3 Figures

As we said in section 3.4, figures encompass diagrams, maps, graphs and charts.

3.5.3.1 Diagrams

There is an example of a diagram at the beginning of chapter 6. Diagrams are commonly used to illustrate flow with the aid of arrows pointing in the direction of the flow. Sometimes figures are added to specify the magnitude of the flow. Diagrams are useful aids to illustrating the interdependence of a series.

3.5.3.2 Maps

Maps are inserted in research reports to show the location of geographic areas or points. A report on personal income per district, for example, should contain a map of the relevant districts, and a report on a shopping centre in, say, Benoni should contain a map of Benoni showing access routes, etc and the location of the shopping centre. Some maps make use of statistics to illustrate population density with various colours, dots, etc. Others contain figures and are related to graphic presentations. Maps of this kind have a major advantage – they present a bird's-eye view – but the serious researcher might find them lacking in detail or accuracy.

3.5.3.3 Graphs and charts*

Graphs and charts are handy aids to reporting because they are effective ways of depicting relations and trends. In the past they were used less often in research reports on

---

* The term 'graph' generally refers to a figure with lines or dots depicting the relation between corresponding values of two quantities; a chart generally depicts quantities with the aid of surface areas. In the USA the term 'chart' denotes both graphs and charts.

account of the lengthy and tedious process of constructing them. Today advanced computer programs facilitate the use of charts and graphs which are seldom drawn by hand in their final form. And even the use of colour in charts and graphs is possible with state-of-the-art printers. In the present situation the researcher should avoid including too many, overly complicated graphs and charts in the report. Being visual aids to understanding tabular and expository materials, graphs should be used sparingly. Whatever the graphic devices selected, the researcher should make sure that they present a complete picture of one central point or idea. In some instances tabular presentations are superior to graphs and charts, especially when masses of data are involved. In others, graphic presentations are undoubtedly more interesting and more illuminating in a report. Indeed a few well-thought-out graphs depicting the key facts in the report may be all the busy executive needs for decision making.

As regards the numbering, title and heading (or subheading) of the graph or chart, the same rules apply as in the case of tables (section 3.5.2). Several aspects of graphs, however, merit the researcher's attention. A graph and some charts have the independent variable on an X-axis – usually on the horizontal scale – and the dependent variable on the Y-axis. The relation between the scales determines the shape of the graph. The horizontal and vertical scales should carry figures along with an explanation of what they represent.

There are many different types of graphs and charts, and each of these types has several variations. Indeed, it is virtually impossible to discuss all of them within the space of a section of a chapter. However, we propose to look at the principal types and their uses.

(a) Line graphs

Figure 18.1 is an example of a line graph. Luck *et al* (1982:481–482) have the following to say about line graphs: 'Ideally these diagrams are used to show continuous functions such as growth or rate of change... It allows several series of data to be shown in one chart and their changes to be compared relative to one another.' The component parts line graph is a variation of the line graph. Luck *et al* (1982:482) describe it as follows: 'The components of each item are added successively to the total of the preceding components; that is, they are stacked up on top of one another. The chart is useful in indicating how the shares of the various components change over a period of time.' Figure 18.2 (page 416) is an example of this type of graph. Line graphs lend themselves to the use of two quite different scales on the vertical axis. For instance, prices and quantities sold of a specific product can be placed on the same axis in order to illustrate the relationship, if there is one, between changes in price and quantities sold. This type of graph is illustrated in figure 18.3 (page 416). Tull and Hawkins (1990:698) believe line charts are generally superior under the following conditions:

> When the data involve a long time period, when several series are compared on the same chart, when the emphasis is on the movement rather than the actual amount, when trends rather than a frequency distribution are presented, when a multiple-amount scale is used and when estimates, forecasts, interpretations or explanations are to be shown.

Figure 18.1 Population, total retail and item sales indices at constant prices, 1977–1993

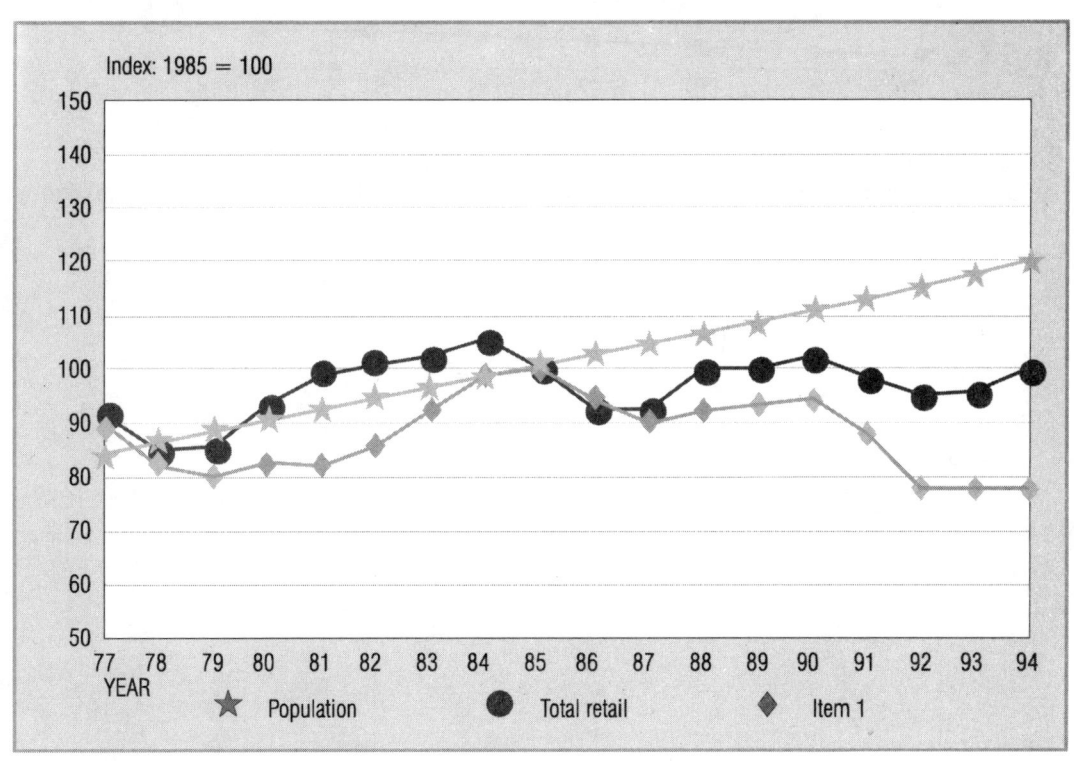

Source: Loubser (1994:47).

Figure 18.2 Personal consumption expenditure by major category, 1980–1988

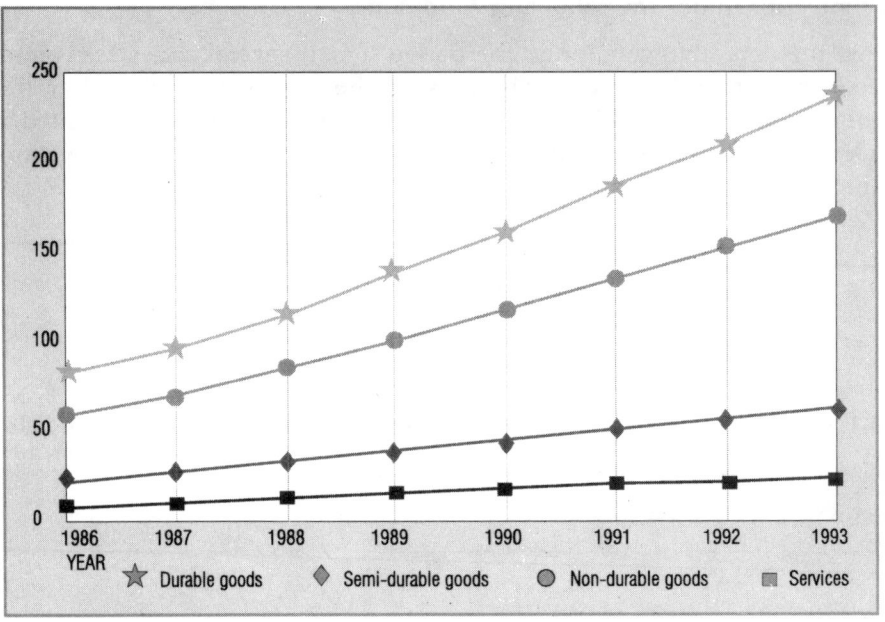

Figure 18.3 Tonnage and average price per tonne of potatoes sold on the fresh produce market in Durban, 1993

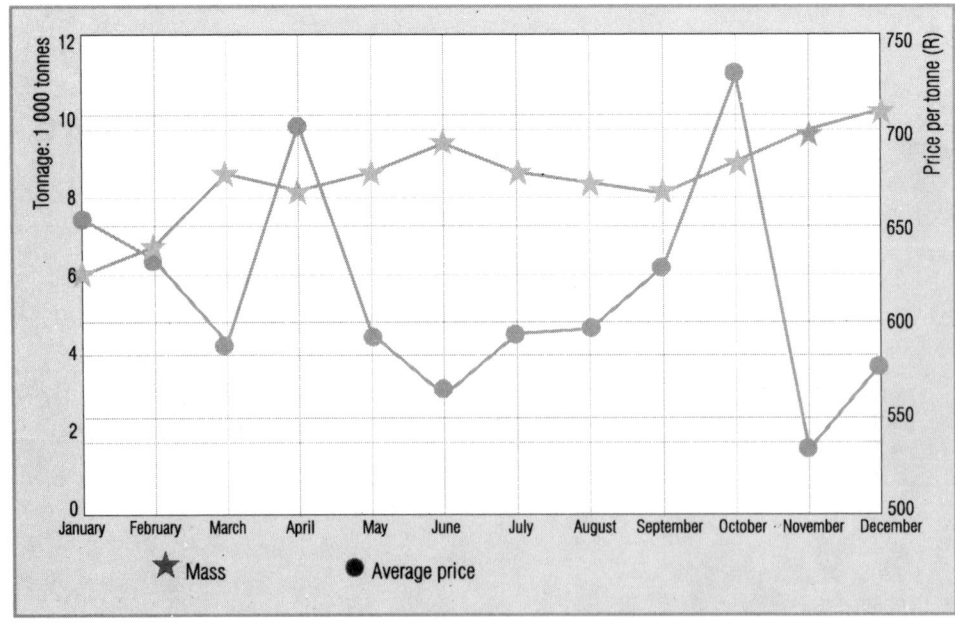

(b) Bar charts

Kinnear and Taylor (1991:674) describe bar charts as depicting magnitudes of the data by the length of the various bars that have been laid out with reference to a horizontal or vertical scale. Figure 18.4 is an example of a horizontal bar chart and figure 18.5, of a vertical bar chart. Luck *et al* (1982:452) say the vertical bars are more appropriate for data that are classified quantitatively or chronologically. Where the classification is quantitative or geographic the horizontal chart is preferable. The chart illustrated in figure 18.5 is a clustered chart and a group chart at the same time because the two years are grouped together throughout. The divided bar chart illustrated in figure 18.6 is also popular. There are many other types of charts besides these such as the connected bar chart and deviation bar charts.

Figure 18.4 Household expenditure in South Africa by province, 1994

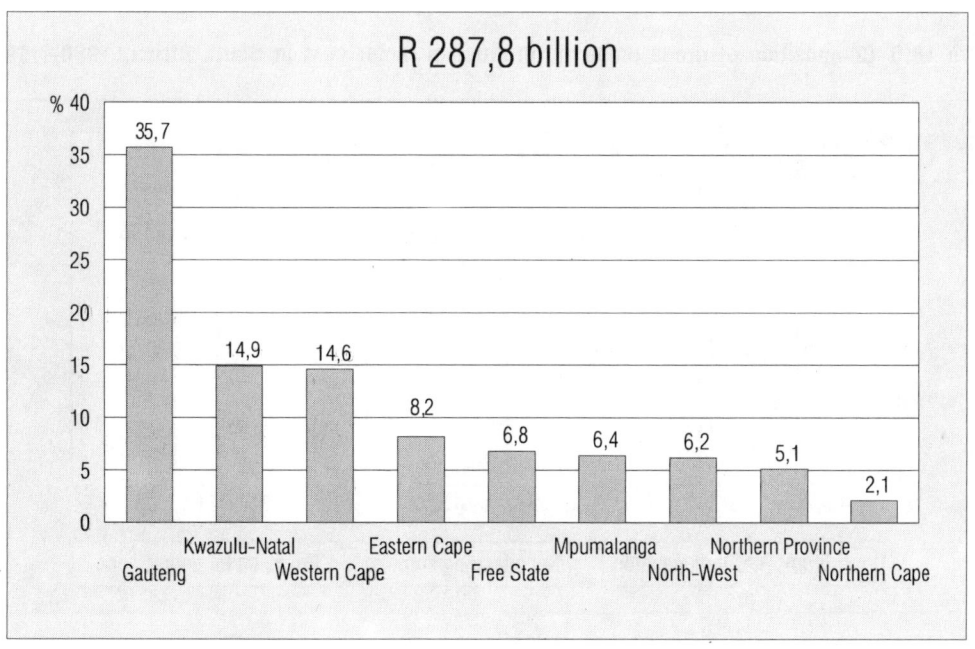

Source: Martins *et al* (1994:43).

Figure 18.5 Urbanisation in South Africa by population group, 1985–1991

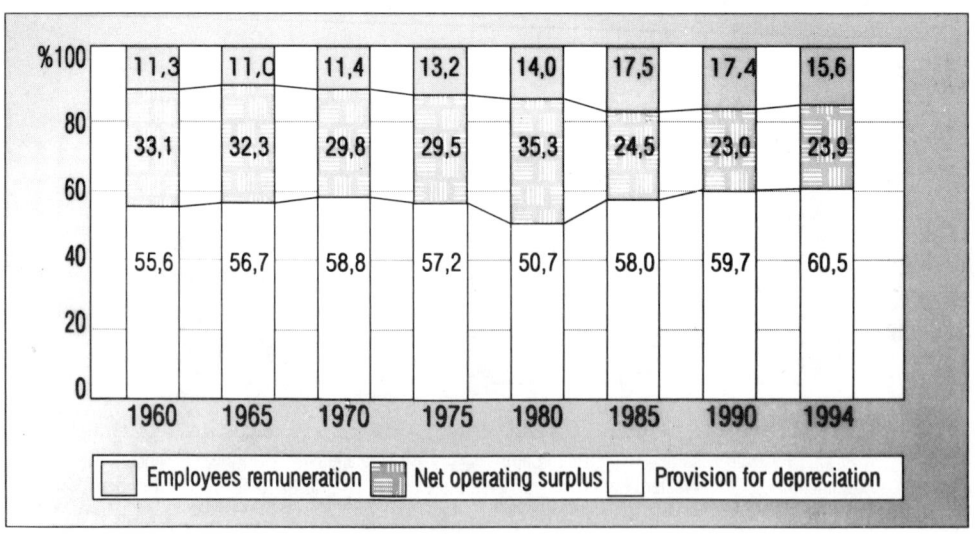

Source: Van der Reis (1994:52).

Figure 18.6 Composition of gross domestic product at factor cost in South Africa, 1960–1994

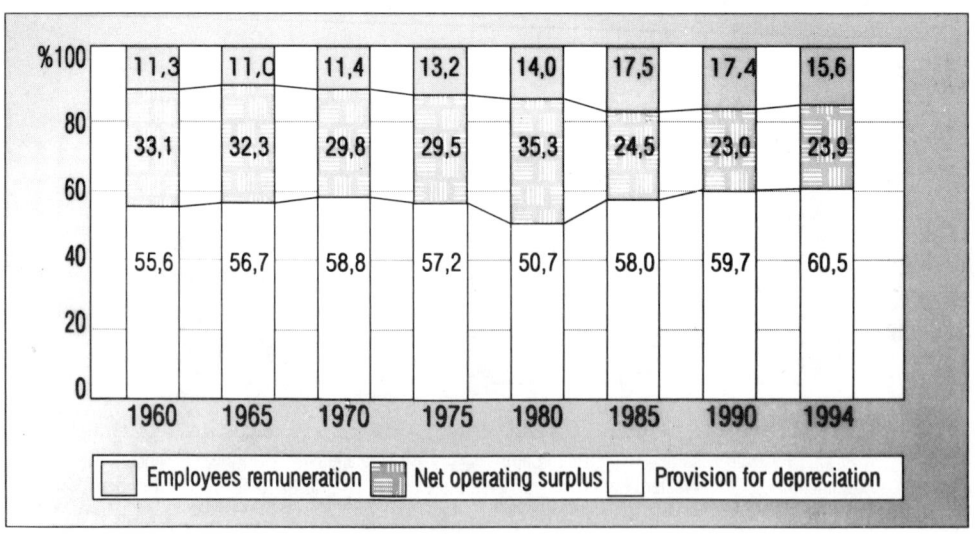

(c) Pie charts

A pie chart consists of a circle divided up into slices, each of which represents a portion of the total. Churchill (1992:792) believes the pie chart is particularly effective for depicting relative size or emphasising static comparisons since the sections are presented as part of the whole or total. Figure 18.7 depicts a pie graph. The exploded pie graph highlights the important parts of the chart. It is illustrated in figure 18.8. A pie chart has the disadvantage that the number of slices which can be used is limited. Kinnear and Taylor (1991:674) state that:

> Pie charts do not lend themselves to illustrating the passage of time nor do they allow you to compare more than one group of data within a single chart. Comparing multiple entities requires multiple pie charts. If you find yourself using more than four pies, you may want to consider a bar chart instead.

Figure 18.7 Household expenditure in metropolitan areas by province, 1993

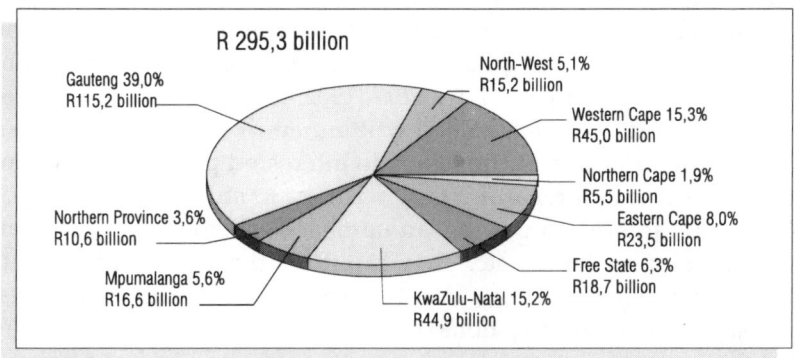

Source: Martins (1994:9).

Figure 18.8 Household expenditure in metropolitan areas by population group, 1993

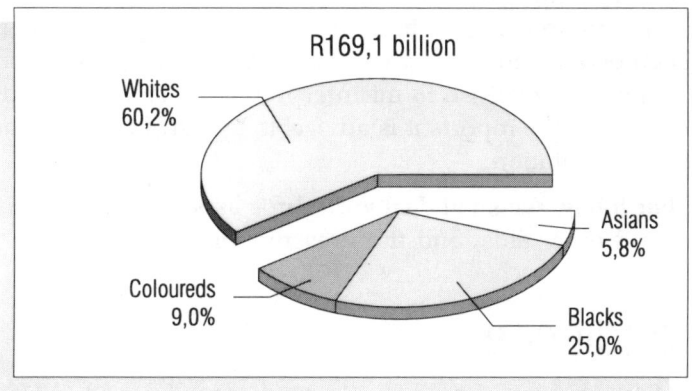

Source: Martins (1994:9).

4 ORAL AND VISUAL REPORTING

Reporting can be accomplished in three ways: orally/visually; in writing; and orally/visually and in writing. Rarely is reporting accomplished only by oral/visual reporting, except perhaps in public presentations on an internal project when the main aim is to publicise a few of the research findings and the presentation becomes more of a public relations exercise. Written reporting on its own occurs when the report is distributed to a large number of users who are spread over a large geographical area, or when the report is short and simple and does not require explanations. Very often the written report is supplemented with one or more oral/visual reporting sessions to assure the maximum exposure of the results to interested parties.

When the written report is supplemented with oral/visual reporting sessions, the question is whether the audience should be exposed first to the written report or to the oral/visual report. The only advantage to be gained from not distributing the report beforehand lies in the prevention of group formation, especially in reporting on unpopular conclusions and recommendations. Luck *et al* (1982:489) also mention the risk of misinterpretation of the report. A well-reasoned written report should not lend itself to misinterpretations. Prior distribution of the report to interested parties gives them the opportunity to skim the report beforehand if they wish, or to study it intensively. If the topic is a complicated one, interested parties can familiarise themselves beforehand with the most important results, methods, etc. They can think through and formulate questions which are not answered in the report, in order to ask them during the oral/visual presentation. It is possible that all the questions of interested parties are answered in the report, in which case the oral/visual presentation may be very short or need not even be held, saving valuable time and money. People who read the report beforehand may also inform the presenter in advance of aspects of the results which they would like to know more about and in this way give the presenter helpful hints in the preparation of the presentation. In any case there is nothing more disturbing to the presenter or to other members of the audience than people paging back and forth in a report while the presentation is in progress. Such people tend to pay scant attention to the presentation itself and this very lack of attention can give rise to misinterpretation. Thus it would seem that with the exception of very simple reports it is advisable to distribute the report to interested parties before the presentation.

In the sections that follow we shall deal with three aspects of oral/visual reporting: the audience, visual and other aids, and the presentation.

4.1 The audience

The presenter's first concern should be the audience. Luck *et al* (1982:489) give the presenter the following advice:

The first step in developing an effective presentation is to know your audience. You must know who plans to attend, and what information they already know and do not know about the subject to be presented. You must know what they are capable of understanding without elaborate explanations and definitions. You must know what areas you will have to stress, and anticipate what questions they may raise. This audience analysis requires much forethought, but it is necessary for effective communication.

It is as well to bear in mind that in any organisation the audience may be influenced by vested interests and internal politics. Kinnear and Taylor (1991:677) tell the presenter to analyse the audience:

> How will they react to the research findings? Will they be in agreement? Hostile? Indifferent? Gauge your opening statements accordingly. It's usually wise to begin a presentation with ideas about which there is agreement.

The presenter's second concern should be his relationship with the audience. If the audience consists of colleagues at more or less the same level of seniority as the presenter, the presentation may be far more informal than when the audience is made up of executives or outsiders. The scientific nature of the presentation should, however, be preserved at all times.

Thirdly the presenter should take the size of the audience into account. The larger the audience, the greater the diversity of its members in interests, background and technical expertise, the more difficult interaction between the audience and the presenter becomes, and the more difficult it is to hold their interest. Far more preparation is required for a presentation before a large audience.

4.2 Visual and other aids

As we saw in the section 4.1, the audience largely determines the aids used by the presenter. There are two key requirements, however: the audience must be able to hear the presenter, and the audience must be able to see the presenter and his visual aids. The presenter should inspect the venue before the presentation to ascertain whether a sound system will be necessary and, if the venue is a large one, whether it has a podium that will allow him to be seen by all the members of the audience. Along with these requirements, the visual aids should be of such a nature and in such a place that all the members of the audience are able to see all the details without effort. Before discussing each of the respective visual aids in turn, we shall focus our attention on a requirement that holds for all visual material, irrespective of whether a table or graphic presentation is involved, and that is the avoidance of too much detail. The presenter should bear in mind that the results of his research may be old news as far as he is concerned, but to his audience they are brand new. This is why all presentations should be as simple as possible. Churchill (1992:789) has the following advice:

Build complexity. If you have a complicated concept to communicate, start with the ground level and use three or four slides to complete the picture ... Make visuals easy to read. Use large, legible typefaces. You can use up to three sizes of type, but use only one or two typefaces. Bold and italics can be used freely for emphasis. With slides, use light type against a dark background.

We shall return to these aspects in section 4.2.3.

4.2.1 Handouts

Handouts contain some or all of the critical results of the research and are handed out to all members of the audience before the presentation begins. Handing out the whole report to the audience is generally inadvisable, for reasons discussed above. In most instances only excerpts from the report (for example selected tables and graphs), or material which has been specially prepared, are handed out to the audience. Handouts have the potential disadvantage that the audience looks at the papers and not the presenter, and the rustling of paper may be distracting. A further disadvantage may be that members of the audience may become so interested in a specific table or graph that they do not listen to the rest of the presentation. In the absence of other visual aids, or in venues that preclude large parts of the audience from seeing visual images on a screen, handouts may be the only aid available and at any rate are far better than nothing at all.

4.2.2 Boards and charts

The best-known type of board is the one on which the presenter writes while he is speaking. Such boards range from the simple to the sophisticated models which roll on at the touch of a button and can even be linked to a copier. Among the charts the flip chart is best known. Luck *et al* (1982:491) describe the uses of the flip chart as follows:

> A flip chart with individual pages bound together at the top may be used effectively. Information written on the pages can be covered with a strip and revealed as the speaker makes a point. With this piece of delivery equipment one can also start with blank pages and write information on the pages as the talk progresses. A third effective presentation method using the flip chart is the use of a pointer to attract attention. One problem associated with the flip chart is that it is difficult to return to earlier exhibits.

Boards and flip charts are most effective in presentations to small audiences.

4.2.3 Projection equipment

The overhead projector is surely one of the best known and most versatile items of projection equipment. Tull and Hawkins (1990:710) comment that:

Overhead projectors are widely used to show previously prepared images against a screen or wall. The materials presented in this manner can range from simple charts to complex overlays. An overlay is produced by the successive additions of new images to the screen without removing the previous images. In addition, the speaker can write on the transparency (the acetate sheet on which the image is carried) and the writing will appear on the screen. Overhead transparency masters can be prepared from the printouts generated by the graphics software described earlier. In addition, coloured transparencies can be produced by colour plotters that work in conjunction with personal computers or independently.

Ease of operation is a prime advantage of the overhead projector. The presenter switches it on or off as required and by positioning it next to the speaker's desk is able to place transparencies on it for as long as necessary. By using a pointer (even a simple pencil will do) the presenter is able to draw the audience's attention to specific aspects. Standing with his back to the screen he may place the transparency badly, however, and prevent the projection of certain parts of it. There are three other types of projection equipment: slide projectors, videotape equipment (VCRs) and projectors coupled to personal computers.

Slides of any subject can be photographed and projected onto a screen. Although these slides are not as flexible as those used on overhead projectors (that is they cannot be written on while in use), remote-control, magazine-loaded projectors allow a smooth, evenly paced presentation using this technique. The ability to make colour slides direct from computer monitors is a significant advantage of this approach.

Videotape equipment (VCR) coupled with large-screen projectors is gaining use in research presentations. It is particularly useful for presenting parts of focus group interviews, showing how product tests were conducted, and presenting other material that does not lend itself to a static presentation.

Finally, *projectors* similar to VCR projectors can be attached to personal computers to project the monitor image onto a wall or screen. This is particularly useful when mathematical or accounting models or formulas have been developed. Executives can then ask 'what if' questions that can be answered immediately.

4.3 Presentation

Certain prior preparations have to be made for a presentation. As we have said, the presenter should inspect the venue beforehand, if possible, to check on the presence or absence of features and items that can make or break the presentation. The presenter should also make a point of checking all the audio-visual equipment to make sure it is in working order and learn how to operate it. In the event of equipment failure, what is to be done? Will it be possible to proceed without equipment and, if so, how should the presentation be adapted? Kinnear and Taylor (1991:677) suggest that a presenter should have one or more practice sessions, preferably in the venue and with the equipment to be used in the presentation. This is a sure way of boosting self-confidence and is the only way to determine the duration of the presentation with any degree of accuracy. It is essential to keep to the allotted time because executives are busy people who may start leaving the venue to attend other meetings before a tardy presenter gets to the critical part of the presentation. Time should be left for questions at the end of the presentation.

The structure of the presentation is a further aspect which requires the presenter's attention. Churchill (1992:788–789) distinguishes two structures:

> Both begin by starting the general purpose of the study and the specific objectives that were addressed. They differ, however, with respect to when the conclusions are introduced. In the most popular structure, the conclusions are introduced after all of the evidence supporting a particular course of action is presented. This allows the presenter to build a logical case in sequential fashion. By progressively disclosing the facts, the presenter has the opportunity to deal with audience concerns and biases as they arise, and thus lead them to the conclusion that the case builds.

> In the alternative structure, conclusions are presented immediately after the purpose and main objectives. This structure tends to involve managers immediately in the findings. It not only gets them to think about what actions the results suggest, but also alerts them to pay close attention to the evidence supporting the conclusions. This format allows managers to evaluate the strength of the evidence supporting an action, since they know beforehand the conclusions that have been drawn from it.

Both structures have advantages and disadvantages, and the presenter has to choose the one best suited to his own purposes.

When the time comes to deliver the presentation, the presenter should exude confidence (without being overconfident) and self-assurance. The presenter should wait until he has the audience's attention before beginning the presentation. He should speak clearly and at a normal pace. (Many presenters tend to talk too fast because they want to fit a long presentation into a limited space of time.) When referring to tables and graphs on a screen, he should leave sufficient time for the audience to absorb what he is showing them. The presenter should remember that he is familiar with the facts, but to the audience they are largely new. He should try to 'read' the audience while he is speaking. If the audience is restless, he may be too long-winded. No one expects the presenter to deliver a scientific presentation without referring to notes, but he should look up from time to time and make eye contact with the audience. Provided that the presenter is self-confident, he may deviate from the written text from time to time to elaborate on a particular point. Question time is one of the presenter's most stringent tests. As we have said, he should anticipate and prepare for certain questions. Still, he may have to field difficult questions from what may sometimes be a critical audience. Kinnear and Taylor (1991:677) advise presenters as follows:

☐ Concentrate on the question. Don't think about the answer until the speaker has completed his question.

☐ Repeat the question. If it's a tough one, rephrase it. This assures that everyone in the audience has heard the question, and gives you the time to formulate an answer.

☐ Don't fake an answer. Admit that you don't know the answer, then tell the speaker that you will try to find it. After the presentation, find out where that person can be reached when you do get the answer to the question. (Make sure you follow through on your promise!)

☐ Answer questions briefly and support your answers with evidence whenever possible.

5 SUMMARY

There are certain requirements for the interpretation of results. The logical flow of argument in a report and completeness are emphasised, and SAMRA's requirements for report writing are enumerated. The audience for whom the report is written should also be taken into account: what are their requirements? Then there is a discussion of the typical arrangement and sequence of the various parts of the report and its components: the text, tables and figures and the requirements set for them. The discussion of figures is dominated by graphs and charts, which are made up mainly of line graphs and bar and pie charts. The various uses of these graphs and charts are briefly reviewed. The next sections deal with the pros and cons and the various forms of oral and visual reporting. The presenter is urged to assess the audience, and various types of visual aids to oral reporting are discussed. The chapter concludes with hints on preparing and delivering a presentation and the pitfalls that await the presenter, such as reeling off the presentation.

REFERENCES

Churchill, Gilbert A (Jr) 1992. *Basic marketing research*. Second edition. Fort Worth: The Dryden Press. (The Dryden Press Series in Marketing.)

Crisp, R T 1957. *Marketing research*. New York: McGraw-Hill.

Ferber, R, Blankerts, D F & Hollander, S 1964. *Marketing research*. New York: Ronald Press.

Kinnear, Thomas C & Taylor, James R 1991. *Marketing research: an applied approach*. Fourth edition. New York: McGraw-Hill. (McGraw-Hill Series in Marketing.)

Loubser, M 1994. *Retail sales forecast for 1994*. Pretoria: Unisa, Bureau of Market Research. (Research Report no 210.)

Luck, David J, Wales, Hugh G, Taylor, Donald A & Ruben S 1982. *Marketing research*. Sixth edition. Englewood Cliffs, NJ: Prentice Hall.

Martins, J H 1994. *Household expenditure in South Africa by area, population group and product, 1993.* Pretoria: Unisa, Bureau of Market Research. (Research Report no 205.)

Martins, J H, Ligthelm, A A, Loubser, M & Van Wyk, H de J 1994. *Socio-economic profile of the nine provinces in South Africa, 1994.* Pretoria: Unisa, Bureau of Market Research. (Research Report no 207.)

Tull, Donald S & Hawkins, Del I 1990. *Marketing research: measurement and method: a test with cases.* Fifth edition. New York: Macmillan. (The Macmillan Series in Marketing.)

Van der Reis, A P 1994. *The advertising and marketing environment in the new South Africa.* Pretoria: Unisa, Bureau of Market Research. (Research Report no 213.)

Weiers, R M 1984. *Marketing research.* Englewood Cliffs, NJ: Prentice Hall.

Part 4

Areas of marketing research

The last part of this book explores special areas of marketing research. It begins with chapter 19 which discusses research in industrial markets in the light of the difference in character between the industrial and consumer markets, which influences research activities and the application of research methods in the two markets. Market forecasting supplies data on the future market situation. Its techniques are discussed in chapter 20. Chapter 21 deals with regional marketing research with special reference to South Africa. Chapter 22 is concerned with international marketing research. Advertising is the subject of chapter 23. The book concludes with a discussion of media research in chapter 24.

Researching the industrial market

Chapter 19: A A Ligthelm

Researching the industrial market

1 INTRODUCTION

The South African market may be divided into two broad segments: the consumer market and the industrial market. Although the industrial segment of the market is far larger than the consumer segment in terms of number of products, volume and value (see chapter 4), the field of industrial marketing research is often overlooked in the literature. This is because industrial marketing research is less widely practised than consumer marketing research, and the principles and methodology applicable to consumer marketing research ought to hold for industrial marketing research. However, the differences in character between the consumer market and the industrial market are so fundamental as to influence the approach to sampling, interviewing and other methods of data collection, and demand skills quite different from those of consumer research. It is important, therefore, that the characteristics of industrial markets are fully understood (Hague 1987:17).

The rest of this chapter will be devoted to the specific characteristics of industrial markets, and above all to their effect on the research activities undertaken and the research methodology used by manufacturers and marketers of industrial products.

2 CONSUMER VERSUS INDUSTRIAL MARKETS

The consumer market is the market for products and services consumed by final consumers such as individuals and households for their personal satisfaction. In contrast, the industrial market is the market for products and services used for the creation of socio-economic welfare. More specifically, industrial products and services are destined for use in producing other products or services as opposed to products destined to be sold to the ultimate consumer. The industrial market consists of a variety of sectors active in value added or production activities, such as farmers, mines, manufacturing firms, construction companies, merchants, government institutions, non-profit organisations, non-governmental organisations (NGOs) and service industries. Some products are both consumer and industrial products in that they are used by private households and in the process of manufacturing other products and services (Nel *et al* 1988:462). For example, wheat flour is a consumer product because it is consumed by private households.

However, it is also an industrial product because it serves as a raw material in the manufacture of many other products such as bread and confectionery.

Industrial marketing is also termed business-to-business marketing or organisation or institutional marketing because even non-profit organisations today are increasingly being run on business principles and have to market their services to their clients (Van Veijeren 1994:2).

The essential difference between industrial products and consumer products therefore lies in their use. Industrial products and services are either processed further or used in producing the final consumer product. Hence, the buyer acquires industrial products and services for use in his undertaking, whereas the buyer and the user of consumer goods is usually one and the same person, who generally wishes to satisfy his needs as an individual. Industrial marketing may therefore be described as the marketing of goods and/or services in industrial markets essentially for use in the production process or the provision of services, as well as marketing between organisational buyers and organisational users (Van Veijeren 1994:2).

3 DISTINCTIVE CHARACTERISTICS OF INDUSTRIAL MARKETS

In some ways the characteristics of industrial markets are very different from those of consumer markets. However, industrial marketing researchers can learn from consumer marketing researchers because consumer product marketing, as explained earlier, has had the benefit of the routine application of sophisticated techniques. In applying consumer research methods in industrial or organisational markets the researcher should bear in mind that purchases in the industrial market are motivated primarily by organisational rather than personal reasons. Many of the differences between consumer and organisational marketing research therefore stem ultimately from differences in consumer and organisational market behaviour.

Because industrial buyers act on behalf of organisations or businesses, organisational buyers are generally more rational and better informed buyers than private consumers. Organisational buyers therefore tend to take objective factors such as quality, delivery, service and especially price into account in evaluating potential suppliers. Although their purchase motives are the primary distinction between private consumers and organisational buyers, other differences between them have implications for marketing research. These differences are discussed below.

3.1 Number of people involved in industrial purchase decisions

Unlike consumer purchase decisions, which typically involve from one individual to possibly the household and close friends or relatives, the buying decision in industry is seldom simple. The larger the establishment and the more sophisticated the product, the greater the likelihood that many people may be involved.

The buying process in industrial markets tends to be a lengthy, complicated one and very often the precise influence exerted by each individual involved in the decision-making process remains unclear (Chisnall 1991:63). The group of individuals responsible for the decision to buy an industrial product is known as the decision-making unit (DMU), purchasing unit or buying centre. The size and composition of the DMU is governed largely by the type of industrial product and the sum involved and by the organisational structure of the establishment. The DMU may differ in size and structure from one establishment to another and within establishments from one purchasing decision to another. Industrial buying behaviour is therefore far too complicated to be ignored in industrial marketing research.

3.2 Derived demand

The demand for a particular industrial product is known as derived demand in that the demand for industrial products is dependent on the demand for related consumer products. A whole chain of derived demand exists because the demand for any industrial product is dependent on the demand for a whole range of other industrial products and ultimately on the demand for a particular consumer product. This can lead to a 'pendulum effect', that is one buyer may decide on a modest cutback on a particular product, creating a knock-on effect back through the chain of production and marketing, resulting in progressively larger cutbacks (Moutinho & Evans 1992:231). The longer the chain of derived demand, the more the industrial market differs from the consumer market and the more necessary it is to identify and research the linkages in an analysis of the market.

3.3 Product life cycle

The demand for some products and services waxes and wanes as fashion and technology change. It passes through specific stages, that is youth, maturity and old age. After a period of relatively slow sales the product or service gains acceptance, demand builds, levels off and eventually falls away as it is replaced by a new product. In consumer markets the life cycle of a product is shorter and more easily recognised. Industrial products have a long gestation period before achieving commercial success (Hague 1987:18–19). Industrial marketing researchers should therefore stay abreast of technological changes and changes in fashions expected in the market.

3.4 Technical knowledge

Usually industrial products and services will be purchased by trained professionals. Organisational buyers are likely to be far more knowledgeable than the typical purchaser of consumer products. Criteria such as quality, after-sales service, availability of supply and price tend to dominate in industrial purchases. This situation requires a very different approach to marketing and selling to organisational buyers.

3.5 Industry structure

The consumer market consists literally of millions of individuals or households. In contrast, industrial customers are generally fewer in number, and losing or gaining one customer can have a significant effect on the sales volume of a particular establishment. In consumer marketing research the target or survey population usually comprises all types of private households, whereas in industrial marketing research surveys often only a small element of the total number of industrial establishments is involved.

The size of the target or survey population influences the choice and use of research methodology: some research methodology is more suitable for surveys of a population comprising a small number of units than for surveys of populations consisting of millions of units (Nel *et al* 1988:464).

3.6 Spatial concentration of industrial demand

A feature of industrial markets is their high degree of geographical concentration. Industry generally tends to locate in close proximity to large markets and interrelated industries also tend to cluster because of forward and backward linkages: one industry supplies the components or intermediate products needed by another industry for the manufacture of a different product. Indeed, as we shall see in section 5.3.4, it is this greater geographical concentration of demand for industrial products that largely determines the choice and use of sampling methodology.

3.7 Purchase concentrations

The difference in size between the various establishments of a particular branch of industry is considerable. Very often one or a few companies in a particular branch of industry are responsible for a large part of total demand in that branch. This phenomenon, which illustrates what is generally known as the concentration of demand or 80:20 principle (see section 5.3.4), operates in most industrial marketing situations. The purchasing power of large companies is so great that their views must be consulted in any survey.

3.8 Contact with buyers

Because of the geographical and purchase concentrations of establishments in industry and the smaller numbers of buyers in industrial markets, marketers of industrial products tend to have closer direct and personal contact with their buyers or potential buyers. Moreover, channels of distribution are much shorter in industrial than in consumer markets. And because marketers make contact with buyers much more easily, direct marketing by sales representatives is of far greater importance than in consumer markets. The fact that industrial sales representatives are in closer touch with their customers facilitates feedback of information to manufacturers and reduces the industrial product manufacturer's need for marketing research.

3.9 Heterogeneity of industrial markets

Despite differences in class, income, race or gender, consumers still wear clothes, eat food and travel by car. Naturally there are differences between consumer groups, but they are less marked than the differences between industrial establishments. Industrial products and services, the channels of distribution created for them and their buying motivations are vastly different. There are few similarities between manufacturers of basic chemicals, electronic component producers, bankers and plumbers' merchants. Each occupies a segment of the market which must be studied separately (Hague 1987:20).

3.10 Reciprocal trading

Reciprocal agreements on buying and internal directives also influence buying decisions. This, in effect, means that two companies can be both buyer and seller at the same time.

3.11 High-tech capital products

In the industrial market the purchase of costly, highly sophisticated capital equipment is a common occurrence. It has given rise to a distinctive behaviour pattern which is absent from the consumer market. This buying pattern has several characteristics:

☐ Previous experience often has a strong influence on industrial buying motivations. It does not follow, therefore, that a revolutionary new product at a lower price will automatically win acceptance.

☐ The process of buying expensive industrial goods may extend over a long period. Van Veijeren (1994:12) puts it at about 1,5 years on average, from the realisation of a need to the final decision to purchase.

☐ The technological complexity of many industrial products makes specialised after-sales service a requirement. The availability of such a service may be a determining factor in the decision to purchase capital goods.

☐ Because of the limited nature of some industrial markets, such as the market for textile machinery, there are strong indications that word-of-mouth advertising which emphasises the credibility of the seller is a determining factor in the marketing process.

☐ Lastly, some of the required functions of the capital equipment which is to be purchased may be completely unspecified. In such instances the seller is expected to develop a product which will meet the potential buyer's requirements. The technical innovation content of such products is generally high and is a measure of the seller's ability to develop a product that will meet the customer's needs.

3.12 Industrial promotion

Industrial promotion budgets are as nothing compared with expenditure on consumer promotions. The industrial company, however, has often a very limited number of buyers and relies heavily on personal selling to reach existing and potential buyers. It is also aware of the top buyers in its market segment and is able to direct its representatives to them. The remaining potential cannot be ignored, but it generally does not justify spending vast sums on additional promotion. Because most of the potential buyers are identifiable, they are readily reached by direct mail, specialised directories, trade journals or exhibitions.

3.13 Captive markets

Another feature of some industrial markets that is not present in consumer markets is the existence of captive markets. Captive markets exist where an institution has no hope of selling the product concerned to another institution because that institution buys it from some other institution only. This is likely to happen where big industrial groups have affiliates in various production fields and one affiliate buys the products from another affiliate only; or where long-term purchase agreements have been closed between institutions (Nel *et al* 1988:473).

All these characteristics influence the research activities and research methodology of the manufacturers of industrial products. Before examining the differences between research activities in the industrial and consumer markets, we turn our attention to the classification of industrial products in the section below.

4 NATURE AND CLASSIFICATION OF INDUSTRIAL PRODUCTS

There are many different industrial products and services on the market, ranging from turbo generators and earth-moving machinery, which are used mostly in industry, to word processors and stationery, which are also purchased by consumers. Compared with consumer products, industrial or organisational products are far more complex and sophisticated and therefore more expensive, for example mainframe computer installations and robot production lines. Besides these capital goods, industrial goods also include new materials, spare parts, intermediate products such as building materials, and a whole range of professional services such as financial, legal, engineering and other services. All these products and services are essential to the profitable operation and the effective management of organisations.

There are several classifications of industrial products and services in the literature. One of the most versatile was developed by Hague (1987:39). His classification, set out in table 19.1, facilitates the development of marketing methods for specific types of product.

Table 19.1 Classification of industrial goods

Classification type	Examples of type of product
1 Capital goods	Plant and machinery, vehicles, office machinery, buildings and tools
2 Raw materials	Fuel, chemicals, cement, aggregates, ore, sugar, timber, steel and aluminium
3 Components	Metal and plastic parts, cable, instruments, electrical and mechanical parts and filters
4 Industrial services	Finance, marketing, plumbing, electrical, transport and local authority services

Source: Adapted from Hague (1987:39).

4.1 Capital goods

Capital goods is the term for the buildings and plant and machinery that are used in the production process. Such installations are purchased by a small number of major buyers. They may be custom made to the manufacturer's specification and are generally marketed through direct and personal contact. Standard capital goods, however, are purchased by large numbers of industrial concerns and by private consumers. It is not uncommon to employ agents or indirect methods in marketing these products.

4.2 Raw materials

The raw materials that are used in the manufacturing process are not always recognisable in the final product. There are many buyers for raw materials such as sugar, but industrial buyers are fewer in number and marketing to them generally takes the form of direct and personal contact. The rest of the market is serviced by indirect marketing methods or by agents.

4.3 Industrial components

Industrial components do not form part of the final product but serve as an aid in the production process. Simple components purchased in bulk by manufacturers are generally marketed direct, whereas replacement items are sold through distributors. High-tech assembled items manufactured to the buyer's specification likewise require direct marketing.

4.4 Industrial services

Industrial services are an essential requirement for effective management. There is generally no scarcity of buyers and suppliers of these services in the market.

There are many industrial products that are clearly similar in nature to consumer products. To a large extent the techniques and procedures developed for the consumer market would be effective in solving the marketing and marketing research problems presented by such industrial products. However, the characteristics of certain industrial products, such as the degree of custom engineering and the sophistication of products such as mainframe computers, do influence the choice of research methods applied by manufacturers of industrial products.

5 INDUSTRIAL MARKETING RESEARCH

The distinguishing characteristics of industrial markets and products discussed above make it necessary to apply some of the techniques developed from consumer marketing research differently in industrial marketing research. This section deals with the application of marketing research in the industrial market.

5.1 Defining industrial marketing research

> The Industrial Marketing Research Association (IMRA) in Britain defines **industrial marketing research** as 'the systematic, objective and exhaustive search for and study of facts relevant to any problem in the field of industrial marketing' (Chisnall 1991:61).

Industrial markets are composed of many establishments whose products and services are required not for the need satisfaction of individuals but for the production of products and services that are ultimately purchased by individuals and households.

The maximisation of a company's profits or the effective management of public bodies is an important variable in purchase decisions. An industrial marketing researcher is therefore concerned with the ultimate need satisfaction of consumers and, above all, with the efficiency of the business. An industrial marketing researcher's raison d'être is to remove, within the constraints of time and funds, the guesswork from business decisions and to contribute in this way to reducing business risks.

The growing internationalisation of markets and rapid technological innovations are fuelling competition in industrial markets. It is becoming essential to collect and interpret the best information for specific marketing problems, and there is increasing pressure on marketing departments to increase sales in a competitive market. Knowledge of the market, customers' needs and new opportunities are prerequisites for survival. It is not surprising that industrial marketing research is gaining in importance and is developing into an acceptable tool for acquiring the necessary information and insight. The use of scientific marketing research techniques in industrial markets may therefore be expected to gain in importance.

5.2 Features of industrial marketing research

Although marketing research techniques and approaches are essentially the same in consumer and industrial research, the distinguishing characteristics of industrial markets and products (discussed above) give rise to differences in emphasis on certain aspects of marketing research. These differences are the following:

5.2.1 Internal and external spending on marketing research

Generally speaking, industrial establishments tend to allocate a far greater percentage of their spending to internal than to external marketing research. The reasons are mainly: commercial marketing research consultants know little about the technical nature of industrial products; the number of respondents in industrial surveys tend to be much smaller than in consumer surveys; a relatively large part of expenditure on marketing research by industrial concerns is earmarked for desk research; and the nature of many surveys in the industrial market requires that all the phases of the research process, such as planning, interviewing, data processing and compiling the report should be handled by one person.

5.2.2 End-use analysis

Certain raw materials such as steel products and 'china clay' or final products such as sugar can be used for different purposes. China clay, for instance, serves as a raw material in the pottery industry and is also used in the manufacture of pharmaceutical, paper and plastic products. Because of these alternative end uses of industrial products, far more detailed research is required in the industrial market. The researcher has to acquaint himself with the various market segments in which specific industrial products are used. Many of these market segments have special characteristics arising from the array of technologies applied in the various market segments and from the differences in purchase behaviour in the various segments. A comparative analysis of the various market segments and the opportunities they offer may, for example, encourage a company to concentrate on only a few market segments and to strengthen its competitive advantage in this way.

5.2.3 Manufacturing cycle

Unlike consumer products, which have a short manufacturing cycle, industrial products may take months and even years to produce and have long lifespans. Industrial marketing researchers are therefore frequently requested to prepare long-term market forecasts. Van Veijeren (1994:17) cites the example of aeroplane engines which have a lifespan of 30 years or more and would feature prominently in the calculations of a researcher faced with the prospect of predicting demand for business and recreational air travel far into the future.

5.2.4 Type of marketing research

The manufacturers of industrial and consumer products in South Africa undertake essentially the same type of research in terms of the three broad functions of research, namely research on products and services, markets, and methods and policies. However, the type of research done by these manufacturers differs widely within the three functions (Nel *et al* 1988:467):

☐ Manufacturers of consumer products undertake comparatively more research on brand and product preference; manufacturers of industrial products do comparatively more research on new product acceptance, product design and product usage.

☐ Manufacturers of industrial products undertake relatively more research on current market potentials and relatively less on market share. Further, market forecasts are far more important for manufacturers in industrial products than for manufacturers of consumer products, the reason being that the demand for industrial products is subject to bigger fluctuations and this can have a tremendous effect on the profitability and survival of a business. The derived nature of industrial markets also makes market forecasts more complicated and more necessary.

☐ Manufacturers of industrial products undertake relatively fewer studies of advertising effectiveness and pre-testing than do manufacturers of consumer products who see advertising as a key marketing instrument. Manufacturers of industrial products allocate higher priority to price as a marketing instrument, as evidenced by the prominence of pricing and price policy in industrial research.

5.2.5 Research methodology

Nel *et al* (1988:469) contend that the three main communication methods of collecting primary data – face-to-face interviews, mail surveys and telephone surveys – are more commonly used by manufacturers of industrial products. Manufacturers of consumer products make relatively more use of panels, store audits and pantry checks.

Although an appreciably higher percentage of the manufacturers of industrial products use the three basic communication methods, a much smaller percentage make use of both probability and non-probability sampling techniques. One of the chief reasons for this is that the survey population in the industrial market is often small (and heterogeneous), which makes it desirable and feasible to undertake a census of all institutions. A further reason is that scientific sampling may not be possible because sample frames are sometimes not available or are far from complete.

5.3 Methodology of industrial marketing research

The industrial and the consumer market have several requirements in common: formulation of a marketing plan, calculation of the size and structure of the market, estimation of future market potential, and allocation of resources to the various elements of the marketing programme. Marketing research plays a vital part in placing the marketing function on a sound footing. The general research process and methodology applied in consumer marketing research hold for industrial marketing research as well. (See part 2 for a discussion of the different elements of the marketing research process.) However, the distinguishing characteristics of industrial markets and products make it necessary to apply some of the techniques developed from consumer marketing research differently in industrial marketing research.

In this section the primary adjustments of marketing research methodology for the industrial market will be highlighted. This particularly holds true for the classification and identification of the survey population, type of secondary sources available, and aspects of primary data collection such as sampling, observation and test marketing.

5.3.1 Classification of industrial activities

As pointed out, the industrial market is far more heterogeneous than the consumer market, where every household or individual is a potential consumer of most consumer products. Even a list of the various components of the industrial market – farmers, mines, manufacturing establishments, financial institutions, construction companies, merchants, government institutions, non-profit organisations, non-governmental organisations – foreshadows the diversity of demand for industrial products. In the manufacturing sector demand may even vary from one industrial branch or from one establishment to another. Whereas the survey population is more or less obvious in consumer surveys, the heterogeneity of industrial markets presents the researcher with the problem of identifying homogeneous groups.

The basic framework for classifying industrial activities in homogeneous groups worldwide is the Standard Industrial Classification of All Economic Activities (SIC). The SIC was developed by the United Nations Organisation as a basis for the uniform classification of economic activities in a country. Almost every country in the world bases the classification of its economic activities on the SIC and publishes its statistical information according to this system.

In South Africa the Central Statistical Service (CSS) has adapted the SIC to local conditions. The classification in the SIC is by type of economic activity and not by ownership, type of enterprise, organisational structure, degree of mechanisation, or size of production unit in respect of turnover, capital or labour. The products produced or services rendered determine the economic activity. The SIC has a numerical structure comprising:

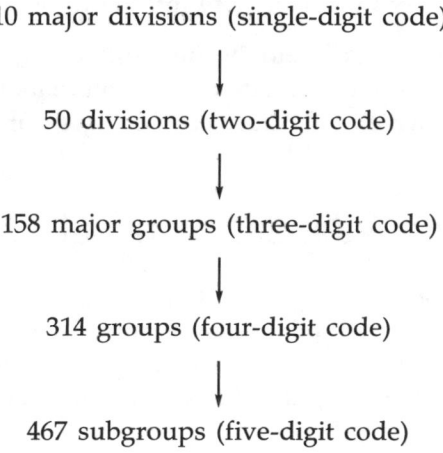

10 major divisions (single-digit code)

↓

50 divisions (two-digit code)

↓

158 major groups (three-digit code)

↓

314 groups (four-digit code)

↓

467 subgroups (five-digit code)

The ten major divisions, which encompass the entire field of economic activity, distinguish the following sectors of production:

SIC code	Sector
1	Agriculture, hunting, forestry and fishing
2	Mining and quarrying
3	Manufacturing
4	Electricity, gas and water supply
5	Construction
6	Wholesale and retail trade; repair of motor vehicles, motor cycles and personal and household goods; hotels and restaurants
7	Transport, storage and communication
8	Financial intermediation, insurance, real estate and business services
9	Community, social and personal services
0	Private households, ex-territorial organisations, representatives of foreign governments and other activities not adequately defined

The first nine of these major divisions or sectors of production are subdivided into divisions and the divisions, in turn, into major groups, groups and subgroups. Manufacturing, for instance, has been subdivided into ten divisions, 60 major groups, 131 groups and 189 subgroups. Table 19.2 shows the subdivision of division 30 (food, beverages and tobacco) of the manufacturing sector into its major groups (301 to 306), groups (3011 to 3053) and subgroups (30111 to 30530). The table on the next page clearly shows that the further breakdown divides economic activity into more homogeneous units.

There are several advantages attached to the subgrouping of establishments and institutions according to the SIC. The classification is an international one, and there is little doubt about the activities which fall under each category or code.

5.3.2 Identification of the survey population

The first task of a researcher initiating a study in the industrial market is to determine the survey population. The survey population encompasses the segments of the industrial market which, as potential users of a specific product, qualify for inclusion as elements in a marketing research project. The survey population is identified by various means.

Table 19.2 Detailed classification of division 30: manufacturing of food, beverages and tobacco

Division	Major group	Group	Sub-group	Description
30				**FOOD, BEVERAGES AND TOBACCO**
	301			**Meat, fish, fruit, vegetables, oils and fat**
		3011		Meat and meat products
			30111	Slaughtering of livestock
			30112	Prepared and preserved meat
			30113	Lard and edible fats
		3012		Fish and fish products
			30120	Canned, preserved and processed fish
		3013		Fruit and vegetables
			30130	Canned, preserved, processed and dehydrated fruit and vegetables
		3014		Vegetable and animal oils and fats
			30141	Crude oil and oil seed cake
			30142	Cooking fats, margarine and edible oils
	302	3020		**Dairy products**
			30201	Fresh milk
			30202	Butter and cheese
			30203	Ice cream
			30204	Milk powder
	303			**Grain mill products, starches and prepared animal feeds**
		3031		Grain mill products
			30311	Flour and grain mill products
			30312	Breakfast foods
		3032	30320	Starches and starch products
		3033	30330	Prepared animal feeds
	304			**Other food products**
		3041	30410	Bakery products
		3042	30420	Sugar, golden syrup and castor sugar
		3043	30430	Cocoa, chocolate and sugar confectionery
		3044	30440	Macaroni, noodles and couscous
		3049		Other food not classified elsewhere
			30491	Coffee and tea
			30492	Nut foods
			30499	Spices, condiments, vinegar, etc.
	305			**Beverages**
		3051	30511	Distilling, rectifying and blending of spirits
		3052		Beer and other malt liquors
			30521	Breweries except sorghum beer breweries
			30522	Sorghum beer breweries
			30523	Malt
		3053	30530	Soft drinks
		306		**Tobacco products**

(a) Computerised registers of names and addresses

A valuable tool for identifying target or survey populations in various sectors of the economy is available in the form of thirteen registers of establishments, compiled and maintained by the Bureau of Market Research (BMR). The following registers are maintained: Mines, Industrial, Construction, Trade, Hotels and Off-sales, Financial and Insurance Institutions, Business Services, Public Sector, Dry-cleaners, Importers, Exporters, Associations and Trade Unions and Commercial Farmers.

The registers list the names and addresses and other particulars of mines, manufacturers, wholesalers and retailers, construction firms, etc, in South Africa. Some of the registers cover neighbouring countries as well. All the information is stored on computer and is sorted and printed as required. The following selection of variables is available:

☐ name, postal and street addresses and telephone numbers of establishments

☐ SIC of establishments according to primary and secondary activities

☐ geographical location according to provinces, magisterial districts, etc

☐ status of establishment, that is head office, branch, affiliated company or independent unit

☐ size codes according to number of employees.

Useful abstracts can be made from the BMR registers, for marketing or research purposes, for example the number of names of leather manufacturers in Gauteng with 100+ employees. A publication is available on the use of BMR registers (Van Zyl & Steenkamp 1992).

The BMR registers are updated continuously but are not necessarily a complete census of all establishments at any given stage. Missing elements do occur, for example in the Trade Register, in which it is difficult to keep track of all the micro and small retailers who annually start and stop trading operations.

(b) Directories, buyers' guides and yearbooks

In South Africa names and addresses are listed in a large number of directories, buyers' guides and yearbooks published by commercial undertakings such as Avonwald Publications, Braby's Directories, Buyers' Guide (Pty) Ltd, EZEE-Dex, FACTS Investors' Guide, Texinform and Intratex. A BMR publication, *A guide to directories, yearbooks and buyers' guides in the Republic of South Africa*, may be consulted for target populations contained in these publications.

Businesses and other organisations are commonly listed by activity in such sources. Nel *et al* (1988:283) believe the coverage in these publications may be incomplete because institutions pay for listing in most of them. Missing elements can be a major problem if such sources are consulted to determine the survey population.

(c) Specialised lists

Many organisations in South Africa maintain lists of the names and addresses of their members. Many of these lists are published in some form or other, or are obtainable on request. For the members of some professions registration is a statutory requirement. Such lists are very comprehensive and serve as excellent sources of determining the survey population. A problem that may occur is that lists indicate the names of individuals and not necessarily partnerships or companies.

The following are some of the organisations with lists of the names and addresses of their members: Institute of SA Architects, National Occupational Safety Association, Association of Consulting Engineers, Association of Consulting Town and Regional Planners, Association of South Africa Quantity Surveyors, Clay Brick Association, Constructional Engineering Association, Electrical Contractor's Association, Federation of Professional Land Surveyors, Institute of Landscape Architects, South African Veterinary Association, South African Market Research Association, South African Medical and Dental Council, South African Institute of Chartered Accountants, Association of Law Societies of South Africa, Pharmaceutical Society of South Africa, South African Chamber of Business, South African Agricultural Union and the South African Institute of Building.

Two BMR reports may be consulted for organisations with membership lists. Before consulting these lists for survey populations, a researcher or marketer should ascertain who or what the lists cover and the proportions assumed by missing elements, duplicate listings and foreign elements.

(d) Telephone directories

Telephone directories and Yellow Pages are comprehensive sources of company listings. Listing in the Yellow Pages is by activity or service. Since payment for listing is required, the listing is incomplete and missing elements are fairly common. Major disadvantages include listing under more than one subheading and overrepresentation of groups through the inclusion of numerous wholesalers and fringe suppliers. Also listing is possible in either the English or the Afrikaans section or both. Without careful cross-checking, a sample frame compiled from a national set of Yellow Pages would contain many duplicate listings. The problem of sampling is further complicated in practice by listings in small print, large print or bigger advertisements, since all listings have to be counted before systematic sampling is applied.

(e) Lists available from local authorities

Like private households, businesses and other undertakings generally buy water and electricity from local authorities and pay property rates. Such lists are an excellent indication of the number of businesses in the areas where local authorities allocate codes to different categories of water and electricity users. Local authorities tend, however, to regard their computerised lists of clients as confidential and are reluctant to release them.

(g) Customer lists

Industrial market researchers have access to lists of their company's customers. Over the years, customer lists tend to expand to encompass most large buyers. Customers may have moved some or all of their purchases to the competition, but their names are still likely to feature on the list and prove useful to the researcher.

5.3.3 Secondary data sources

Like other marketing research methods, industrial survey methods collect data from secondary sources. Industrial marketing researchers tend to lean heavily towards published data (secondary sources).

Secondary data sources exist both within an organisation (product sales records, territory performance, customer profiles, etc) and externally. External data sources include statistics and reports published by government, trade associations, academic and technical institutions and the like. (See chapter 6, section 3, for a detailed description of secondary data sources.)

In South Africa, the Central Statistical Service (CSS) is responsible for publishing official statistics. A valuable guide to its data sources is the user's guide which is updated quarterly in March, June, September and December. Some of the reports applicable to industrial marketing research published by the CSS are:

- ☐ Census of agriculture
- ☐ Census of mining
- ☐ Census of manufacturing
- ☐ Census of electricity, gas and steam
- ☐ Census of construction
- ☐ Census of retail trade
- ☐ Census of motor trade and repair services
- ☐ Census of wholesale trade, commercial agents and allied services
- ☐ Census of catering and accommodation
- ☐ Census of transport and allied services
- ☐ Census of business services: Accounting, auditing and bookkeeping services
- ☐ Census of architects and quantity surveyors
- ☐ Census of medical, dental and other health services.

Secondary data should be gathered first and, after evaluation of its coverage and contribution to the desired state of knowledge, it may be necessary to engage in primary data collection.

5.3.4 Primary data collection

In this section emphasis is placed on some of the methods of primary data-collection and sampling methods in the industrial market.

5.3.4.1 Primary data-collection methods

Of the methods available for collecting primary data, face-to-face interviews and telephone interviews and, to a lesser extent, mail surveys are the most common in industrial marketing research. The complexity of the industrial purchasing process largely excludes the use of other methods such as observation and experimentation.

The choice of a data-collection method or combination of methods is governed mainly by the nature of the particular product, the purpose of the research, the size and heterogeneity of the survey population, and considerations of cost and time. For example, if the product is a very technical one and much information is required, there is little choice but to use face-to-face interviewing. When information about an industrial product in general use (such as a hand-drill) is required, virtually the only practical method of collecting data is the mail survey. In the sections that follow we shall deal with the application of the main methods of data collection in industrial marketing research.

(a) Face-to-face interviews

Personal interviews are face-to-face meetings between researcher and respondent for the purpose of collecting in-depth information. The detail and the accuracy of the information collected in face-to-face interviews more than compensate for their high cost in time and money.

Three types of interviews – depending on the freedom of the interviewer to stray from the sequence and wording in the questionnaire – are used in industrial marketing research, namely structured, semi-structured and unstructured interviews. (See chapter 7 for a detailed discussion of primary data collection.)

Structured questions are generally used in surveys involving large numbers of institutions and are suitable for standard industrial products with a large number of users. Semi-structured interviews are probably the most common type in industrial marketing research because they are flexible enough to accommodate the varied circumstances that exist between companies in different sectors and of different sizes (Hague 1987:245). Unstructured interviews are more like discussions and the interviewer is at liberty to choose any means of obtaining the required information. Very often expert opinions which are highly appreciated in industrial marketing research are elicited in this manner.

Interviewers in industrial marketing surveys should be competent and experienced. Some industrial surveys are of such a nature that interviewers might be expected to have technical or related training or experience. However, thorough briefing of the interviewer(s) is of the utmost importance because it can spell the difference between the success and failure of the survey.

(b) Telephone interviewing

The use of the telephone is rapidly gaining ground in industrial market surveys. Unlike consumers, all industrial establishments are linked to the telephone network. There is no reason that industrial undertakings should ask for unlisted numbers. Duplicate listings, however, are a major problem when telephone directories or Yellow Pages serve as sample frames because many businesses and government institutions have more than one number. In this situation some form of weighting is essential.

Telephone interviewing is ideal for industrial surveys with simple information requirements such as compiling sample frames and market size assessments. Complex studies such as new product research and qualitative surveys should rather be undertaken by face-to-face interviews. (See chapter 7, section 3.2, for a detailed description of telephone interviewing.)

(c) Postal surveys

Postal surveys are a specialised tool with an important role to play in industrial marketing research, provided that they are carried out with the necessary controls. The postal survey is the only practical method of collecting information on a product that is used by a large number of establishments or sectors of the industrial market. The same applies to surveys of certain industrial populations such as farmers, with whom it is difficult and expensive to establish contact.

Postal surveys are most appropriate when questions are simple, factual and can be answered without extensive consultation of company records. Postal surveys should be avoided when many open-ended questions are asked, an industry comprises only a few major companies because the failure of just one of them to respond may affect the findings, and when buying decisions in a company involve more than one department and there is the risk of missing opinions or buying data.

The 80:20 principle can be applied in industrial samples. The researcher can divide the list of companies to be interviewed by size groups, for example:

☐ all the large companies can be surveyed through a personal interview programme

☐ the medium-sized companies can be either visited or telephoned

☐ information from the small companies can be collected by postal questionnaires or telephone.

(d) Observation

Although observation is little used, many circumstances exist in industrial marketing research in which data can be collected by observation. Hague (1987:274) cites several examples. Observation can help the researcher to compile lists for many products. For example, glass packaging manufacturers can be identified by examining products on supermarket shelves and car component suppliers can be established simply by peering under the bonnet. Observation could also be used for recording and analysing respondent reactions, buying and operating procedures, displays, prices, quality checks and new product launches. (See chapter 9 for a detailed description of observation.)

(e) Test marketing

It is a distinguishing characteristic of industrial marketing that test marketing is specialised or even totally absent. The reason is the high cost of developing and manufacturing prototypes. The emphasis in industrial marketing tends to be on calculating market potential rather than on test marketing. Industrial establishments that do use test marketing programmes generally stick to the following methods:

☐ *Product-use test:* A limited number of potential customers who are prepared to try the product for a limited period are selected.

☐ *Trade shows:* Exhibits at trade shows have the advantage that large numbers of potential customers are exposed to new products within a short space of time.

☐ *Dealer display show:* This is a very popular method which has the added advantage of keeping potential customers continuously informed of price and other details.

☐ *Controlled marketing:* A limited number of new products are produced for marketing through sales staff. Promotion offerings and the distribution of catalogues are included here.

5.3.4.2 Sampling methods

There are occasions in industrial sampling when circumstances resemble consumer markets. Mostly, however, they are very different. *It is in the sphere of sampling that the principal differences occur between industrial and consumer marketing research.*

The differences lie in the nature of industrial and consumer buying. In the consumer market each individual is unique, but as individuals they are such a small part of the total market that their impact as buyers is minimal. By randomly selecting a relatively small number of consumers it is possible to construct a picture which describes the whole. (See chapter 13 for a description of sample theory.)

More often than not in industrial markets the various companies are very different in size. Unlike the single consumer, being infinitely small within the whole, the greater concentration of industrial demand implies that a single buyer may be extremely large and account for a high proportion of the purchases in the market. Random sampling techniques might fail to select some of the large buyers and then yield a distorted picture of the whole. If the sample does, however, include the large buyers, it may similarly distort results. This characteristic of industrial markets complicates the application of random sampling techniques and renders sampling on the concentration principle more desirable.

The following are the two sampling approaches which are applied in the industrial market.

(a) A target population where a few large companies dominate

For industrial companies which differ widely in size, a random sample would not work. Imagine a random sample with 95 % coverage of the 200+ manufacturers of iron and steel basic metals in South Africa, which does not include large companies such as Iscor, Union Steel, and Highveld Steel and Vanadium Corporation. The omission of such giants would seriously distort the results. In such instances the 80:20 principle (concentration of demand) in particular is central to the method of sampling. Owing to the concentration of demand or the differences in size between establishments in many industrial markets, a relatively large segment of the market can be represented by a relatively small sample. For instance, the BMR Industrial Register contains almost 14 000 manufacturing establishments. Manufacturers with an employment figure of 20 and fewer represent 47 % of the establishments in the manufacturing sector but only 3 % of its employment. In contrast, manufacturers with an employment figure of 500 and more represent 4,5 % of the establishments but 46,6 % of its employment.

In these markets it is vital to stratify the sample according to the size of the establishments, for instance by purchasing power or number of employees, so that all the large establishments can be interviewed. A sample is taken of the rest. After eliminating the atypical (that is large) establishments the rest of the population is further stratified by size and sub-sampling or disproportionate stratified random sampling is applied (table 19.4). In the example 100 % of the major establishments and 75 % of the large, 50 % of the medium-sized and 25 % of the small establishments have been included. A disproportionate sample of 48,1 % of the establishments drawn in this manner resulted in a coverage of 80,9 % of the employees. The next step is to raise the data on each size group to the universe. For example, the 1 226 establishments in the 'small' category have 13 738 employees, representing 25 % of all employees in the group. Its sample results should therefore be raised by a factor of 4. (See chapter 15 for determining the weighting factor in disproportionate stratified random sampling.)

(b) A target population with no companies dominating purchases

Typical of such target populations are buyers of fertilizers, commercial vehicles, bricks and typewriters. This does not imply that all companies buying these products are small;

Table 19.4 Disproportionate stratified sample of establishments by employment size

Size of establishment by employment group	Establishments		Employees		Establishments in sample		Employees in in sample	
	Number	%	Number	%	Number	%	Number	%
Small 1–20 employees	4 905	37,5	54 950	3,5	1 226	25,0	13 738	25,0
Medium 21–100 employees	4 926	37,7	235 889	14,9	2 463	50,0	117 945	50,0
Large 101–500 employees	2 610	19,9	567 803	36,0	1 957	75,0	425 852	75,0
Major 501+ employees	639	4,9	719 476	45,6	639	100,0	719 476	100,0
TOTAL	13 080	100,0	1 578 118	100,0	6 285	48,1	1 277 011	80,9

on the contrary, many may be large concerns. However, none is so large that it dominates purchases. Where industrial populations are homogeneous in this way they are very similar to consumer markets and consumer sampling methods can be applied. This has the advantage that samples can be selected randomly and the error in the results can be calculated mathematically (see chapter 13).

6 GROWING IMPORTANCE OF INDUSTRIAL MARKETING RESEARCH

The degree of competition experienced in South African markets will probably intensify in the future as domestic competition becomes keener and international exposure increases. Technology is aiding companies to manufacture products to common standards, which makes it more difficult for customers to differentiate between rival products in terms of design, quality and performance. A case in point is the motorcar market. And with the prices of raw materials on much the same level, even the price of a product has lost some of its impact in the process of selecting one product rather than another. Consequently knowledge of the market has become essential. Companies which have this vital information will be able to market products tailored to the customer's needs. Such companies will recognise opportunities for expansion and will have the ability to adjust rapidly to changes in the market. Clearly there will be greater demand for industrial marketing research which can provide the required information in a competitive environment.

7 SUMMARY

Whereas previous chapters focused attention on the research activities and application of research methodology in the consumer market, this chapter is concerned with these aspects of the industrial market. In industrial marketing research the principal methods of marketing research are adjusted for the special characteristics of industrial markets.

There are fundamental differences in character between industrial markets and consumer markets. Industrial markets are distinguished mainly by the large number of persons involved in purchase decisions, derived demand, the product life cycle of industrial products, the degree of technical knowledge needed in the purchasing process, the structure of the manufacturing sector, the concentration of industrial demand, the heterogeneity of the industrial market, reciprocal trading, and the technological nature of capital products. Industrial products, which differ widely from consumer products, are divided into capital goods, raw materials, industrial components and industrial services.

The industrial marketing process is shaped by the specific characteristics of industrial markets and industrial products. The process is guided by a purchasing agent, the decision-making unit (DMU), which makes joint decisions based on criteria such as price, performance, after-sales service and delivery time. Industrial marketing is further characterised by the prominence of direct or personal sales, contact with a limited number of key clients, and custom engineering of industrial products.

Compared with the manufacturers of consumer products, the manufacturers of industrial products spend relatively less on marketing research; more of their marketing research budget is spent on internal research; they do more detailed research on the various market segments for products; and their market forecasting covers much longer periods. The manufacturers of industrial products do comparatively more research on new product acceptance, product design and product usage, whereas the opposite applies to research on brand and product preference. They also undertake relatively more research on market potentials and market forecasting and relatively less research on market share, advertising effectiveness and advertising pre-testing.

The Standard Industrial Classification (SIC) can be used to classify the industrial market into homogeneous groups. The identification of the target or survey population in industrial marketing research is much more difficult than in consumer marketing research, where every household or individual is a potential consumer of most consumer products. The target or sample population is determined with the aid of computerised registers, directories and buyers' guides, specialised membership lists, telephone directories, lists obtained from local authorities and customer lists.

Secondary sources serve as an important data source for industrial marketing research. Of the methods available for collecting primary data personal visits and telephone interviews and, to a lesser extent, mail surveys are most commonly used in industrial marketing research. The complexity of the industrial purchasing process limits the use of other data-collection methods such as observation and test marketing. Data collection by personal interviews in industrial marketing research mostly takes the form of semi-structured interviews.

The principal difference in the application of research techniques between industrial and consumer marketing research is in the sphere of sampling. Firstly, sampling is applied less often in the industrial market and, secondly, the greater concentration of industrial demand with market differences in company size renders sampling on the 80:20 or concentration principle more desirable. In industrial market surveys it is usually advisable to take a census of atypical (large) establishments and then to stratify the rest of the population by size for purposes of subsampling or disproportionate stratified random sampling.

REFERENCES

Chisnall, P M 1991. *The essence of marketing research*. New York: Prentice Hall.

Crimp, Margaret 1990. *The marketing research process*. Third edition. New York: Prentice Hall.

Els, J 1983. *A guide to directories, yearbooks and buyers' guides in the Republic of South Africa*. Pretoria: Unisa, Bureau of Market Research. (Research Report no 104.)

Haque, Paul N 1987. *The industrial market research handbook*. Second edition. London: Kogan Page.

Moutinho, L & Evans, M 1992. *Applied marketing research*. Workingham, England: Addison-Wesley.

Nel, P A, Rädel, F E & Loubser, M 1988. *Researching the South African market*. Pretoria: University of South Africa. (Manualia Didactica 3.)

South Africa. Central Statistical Service 1993. *SIC: Standard Industrial Classification of all economic activities*. Fifth edition. Pretoria.

South Africa. Central Statistical Service 1994. *Users guide: March 1994: we serve you with facts*. Pretoria.

Van Veijeren, C F 1994. *Industrial marketing*. Kenwyn: Juta.

Van Wyk, H de J, Potgieter, L J du P & Julyan A C M, J 1992. *Guide to associations, employee/employer organisations, industrial councils, co-operatives and agricultural boards in the RSA*. Pretoria: Unisa, Bureau of Market Research. (Research Report no 186.)

Van Zyl, S J J, Martins, J H & Steenkamp, H A 1981. *A guide to the standard industrial classification of all economic activities*. Pretoria: Unisa, Bureau of Market Research. (Research Report no 91.)

Van Zyl, S J J & Steenkamp, H A 1992. *A guide to the BMR registers*. Pretoria: Unisa, Bureau of Market Research. (Research Report no 190.)

Market forecasting

Chapter 20: M Loubser

(This chapter was taken from chaper 23 'Market forecasting' by F E Rädel and P A Nel in Nel *et al* 1988. The tables were updated by M Loubser)

Market forecasting

1 INTRODUCTION

Management constantly makes decisions whose consequences will be evident only in the near or distant future. Such decisions are based on the analysis and assessment of the current and *future* market situation. The methods and techniques whereby management obtains the information for assessing the market's probable development we call *market forecasting* in contrast to *market analysis* which has the current market situation in view.

But even market analysis contains a certain element of the future, for the current market situation is certainly not investigated for historical reasons but with a view to policy decisions whose outcome will be apparent only in the near or distant future. By implication the assumption here is that the prevailing market situation underlying policy decisions will remain essentially unchanged for some (unspecified) time. If, for example, management's advertising and new product development decisions are based on market analysis revealing certain consumer preferences, it assumes that consumer preferences will remain essentially unaltered until the results of the policy decisions are evident on the market. Thus we repeat: every market analysis contains a certain forecasting element, and every decision on policy has a future dimension.

Therefore, though market analysis always contains a forecasting element for the near future, management has also to plan for the future further ahead. For this, the researcher will find the methods of market analysis inadequate, and will have to look for other methods and techniques for evaluating the future.

The future dimension in planning and decision making has increased considerably in the past few decades, and for essentially the same reasons that caused the development of marketing-oriented managerial thought (discussed in chapter 1: in particular the origin of the large capital-intensive undertaking characterised by somewhat inelastic production and the extension of roundabout production).

> Sixty years ago few business decisions had a futurity of more than a few years but today it is the exceptional business decision that does not have a futurity of ten years or more ... Technical progress is converting the businessman from short-range trader of classical economics to long-range planner of today who has to take a 20 years' view (Drucker 1955:121).

This structural change has caused a considerable increase in the importance of medium- and long-term planning, and so of forecasting. From the viewpoint that market analysis and market forecasting are equally important for decision making it is amazing that in the literature on marketing research, market forecasting is discussed either very briefly or not at all. This gives the impression that market forecasting is of secondary importance in marketing management. Market forecasting is usually discussed in the context of general economic forecasting, on which a considerable body of literature is certainly available. Probably one reason for this state of affairs is that a detailed discussion of market forecasting methods, and above all of its more sophisticated techniques, would be too long to fit into the framework of textbooks on marketing research. But we consider it essential to devote at least one chapter of this book to market forecasting methods. In the following sections we shall try to explain the dimensions of market forecasting, and then we intend to discuss the various techniques, which will occupy the best part of this chapter.

2 DIMENSIONS OF MARKET FORECASTING

Forecasts may have a bearing on various levels of economic activities: on the national or even the world economy, on a branch of industry, or on a firm. Thus we have different levels of forecasts and shall try to get some clarity about the time base or time dimensions of such forecasts.

2.1 Levels of forecasts

The lot of any capitalistic firm is closely interwoven with the particular sector, with the country's economy as a whole and, in the face of the world's growing international interdependence, even with the world economy. Each of these levels of economic activity is subject to a large number of endogenous and exogenous variables which, being difficult to quantify, make market forecasting a very difficult task. In the light of the interdependence of a firm and its branch of industry, and indeed of the economy (national and international), a firm's market forecasts have also to take into account these two environmental factors. In practice therefore we distinguish three levels or steps in market forecasting:

☐ general economic forecasting
☐ sectoral forecasting (for example the motor industry)
☐ a firm's forecasting or company forecasting (a certain motor manufacturer).

2.1.1 General economic forecasting

In general economic forecasting we are dealing with the forecasting of the general economic situation. In South Africa these general forecasts are available at universities, the large commercial banks, insurance companies, building societies and government departments, all of which publish their forecasts from time to time. As far as the economic series are concerned, the most comprehensive is of course the gross domestic product (GDP), but because this concept is so general, it is not always the most suitable indicator for some branches of industry. A more specific series such as personal income or private consumption expenditure may be a better indicator. Thus data on private consumption expenditure will be a better indicator for consumer-goods industries than the GDP and building firms will find data on approved building plans an extremely good indicator. Population figures and forecasts of them – always readily available – play a special role for industries such as undertakers and producers of baby clothes, where population trends are of paramount importance.

2.1.2 Sectoral forecasting

Sectoral forecasting may entail many different variables, such as employment, consumption of materials, profitability and sales of a given branch of industry, the last being the most important. The first problem is to find factors with significant influence on the sales of the particular sector. So, for example, the following factors determine the sales of motor cars: income, availability and cost of credit, population trends, consumer preferences, traffic conditions and taxation on motor cars. It is practically impossible and uneconomic to work with all these different determinants, so we must select a few of the main ones, being guided by the following criteria:

☐ *Importance:* This is the extent of its influence on the demand for a given product. For example, income is certainly a more important determinant in the demand for motor cars than for medicines.

☐ *Variability:* If during the forecasting period a determinant is not likely to change appreciably (for example population during a short period) it can be eliminated.

☐ *Measurability:* The determinant must be quantifiable. In the demand for religious publications, loyalty to the church would certainly be a very important determining factor although it is hardly quantifiable.

2.1.3 Company forecasting

Companies make forecasts of a variety of variables, such as employment, consumption of material and power, financial requirements, profit, cash flow, production and sales. Of course sales forecasting is the most important because to a large extent the other variables are dependent on it. In this chapter we propose to concentrate mainly on sales forecasting.

Where reliable industrial forecasts exist, company forecasting depends mainly on the problem of determining the market share. Due consideration is given to expected possible changes not only in the company's own product, price, distribution and sales-promotion policies, but also, and above all, in rival companies' policies. A sales forecast is very much the same as what the literature often refers to as sales potential, in contrast to market potential which corresponds to industry forecasting. Thus Nel defines market potential as 'the real or potential consumption or purchases of a specific product by specific consumers within a specific geographical area within a given period of time taking a particular market effort as given' and sales forecast as 'the share of the market potential an enterprise can expect to secure for its product or service' (Nel 1983:2–3).

2.2 Time dimensions of forecasting

In general we distinguish short- and long-term forecasts, sometimes with medium-term forecasts in between. However, in the literature and in practice we find many different definitions of these time horizons. Some companies regard weekly forecasts as short term and yearly forecasts as long term; others regard forecasts of up to two years as short-term forecasts. In sales forecasting a period of one year is the most common. The timespan of the various forecasts is dependent mainly on the *product* and its speed of *innovation* and the speed of changes in the relevant *market*. So, for instance, a long-range time horizon can be as short as several months for a highly innovative product.

The *purpose* of a forecast is, however, a better indicator of whether the forecast should be regarded as a short-term, medium-term or long-term forecast. Thus short-term forecasts are used mainly in technical planning of quotas, expenses, production inventories, and purchasing. Here the trend factor, unlike the cyclical and especially the seasonal factor, is not important.*

Medium-term forecasts are used mainly in decisions on the detailed allocation of resources, which is normally expressed and coordinated in the annual budget. Seasonal influences are generally less important than the cyclical factor, and the trend factor can play a role in fast-changing product lines.

Long-term forecasts are used primarily in strategic or long-term planning for capital equipment and manpower. Although they generally extend over a period of from two to ten years, or even more, long-term forecasts are normally reviewed annually. In such forecasts the long-term trend is the most important variable.

3 FORECASTING TECHNIQUES

There are so many different forecasting techniques and variations that they cannot be discussed exhaustively in the context of one chapter. We therefore confine ourselves to

---

* These concepts are defined in section 3.2.

the more commonly used techniques, and only a few of these can be discussed in any kind of detail.

In the literature the various techniques are normally grouped in three categories: *qualitative techniques, time-series techniques*, and *causal techniques*. Sometimes the last two are combined as quantitative techniques in contrast to qualitative techniques.

3.1 Qualitative techniques

As the name implies, these techniques rely mainly on judgement and subjective evaluation (and therefore are often called subjective methods). The aim of these techniques is to combine all available information and judgement about the variable being forecast (for instance sales). The most important characteristic of these techniques is that they are dependent mainly on experience, talent, intuition and the feel of the market, and the analysis of past performance may or may not be taken into account.

3.1.1 Jury of Executive Opinion

In this method a group of key executives sit round a table and discuss the probable development of the market or sales potential, hoping to arrive at one or other consensus. To help them to arrive at a more reliable forecast, executives are sometimes supplied with relevant background data on the firm, the industry and the general economy before the meeting, so that each participant can evaluate the data at leisure and independently. This technique has the advantage of bringing together the expert opinion of those who are supposed to have the widest experience of the market in which the firm operates, but its main disadvantage is that it is somewhat informal and, above all, it is doubtful whether the 'average' opinion of all the participants is likely to emerge. Executives with high organisational status, and vociferous and strong individuals tend to dominate the discussion while the possibly more significant opinions of others are either not heard or ignored.

In an effort to eliminate these negative side effects the so-called Delphi technique was developed.

3.1.2 Delphi technique

This technique was developed by the Rand Corporation in the 1950s for long-range forecasting. It replaces direct debate with a carefully designed sequence of indirect individual interrogations via a series of questionnaires.

The procedure consists of a number of rounds of questionnaires to be filled in by all participants until a satisfactory measure of consensus has been reached. The results of each questionnaire are tabulated and distributed to the participants. Items requiring additional information are identified, creating the material for the next questionnaire. So each subsequent questionnaire contains the composite responses to the previous one and further questions to be answered. Each participant is asked to reconcile his opinion with the new data and the combined responses of the other participants. The purpose of information feedback is to produce more precise predictions and to encourage opinion convergence. The number of rounds varies but a minimum of three rounds are usually necessary to achieve a reasonable consensus of opinion. The experts or the participants are not identified to each other in any way, which elicits a greater flow of ideas and fuller participation of all. A participant finds it easier to change his mind if he has no ego involvement in defending his initial estimates. The two basic premises upon which the Delphi technique are founded are that

☐ with repeated measurement the range of responses will decrease and converge towards the mid-value, and

☐ the total group response or consensus will successively move towards the correct or true answer.

The chart on the next page (fig 20.1) is a schematic representation of the process.

The Delphi technique is eminently suited to long-term forecasting and should not be used for routine decision making. The choice of the most suitable participants and their motivation are decisive for the technique's success.

3.1.3 Market or consumer surveys

In the literature, market or consumer surveys are often presented as forecasting techniques. This, of course, is unacceptable because traditional consumer surveys concern current, and not future consumer behaviour and preferences, except that every market investigation entails a certain forecasting element, as we have explained before. A special form of consumer survey – which can in fact be regarded as a genuine forecasting method – is the buying intentions and purchasing probability discussed in the following chapter.

3.1.4 Composite sales force opinion

The idea of using the sales force as a body to evaluate future sales prospects rests on the opinion that salesmen, being closest to the marketplace, should have reliable knowledge of prospects and trends, and the responsibility for forecasts is in the hands of those who will have to produce the corresponding sales. Projected sales by this method can easily be broken down by product, customer and geographical area. The procedure is basically the same as that followed in the Jury of Executive Opinion.

Figure 20.1 Schematic presentation of steps in the Delphi technique

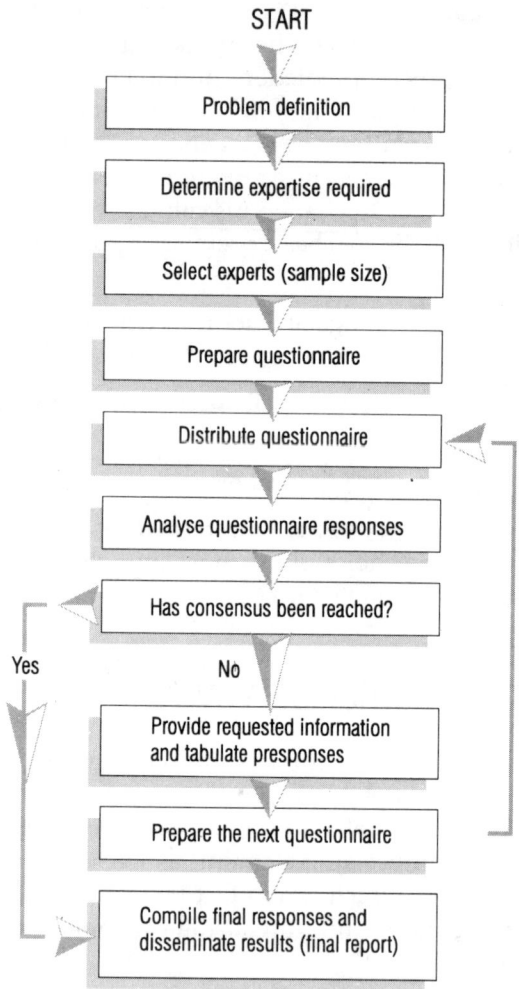

START

Problem definition

Determine expertise required

Select experts (sample size)

Prepare questionnaire

Distribute questionnaire

Analyse questionnaire responses

Has consensus been reached?

Yes   No

Provide requested information and tabulate presponses

Prepare the next questionnaire

Compile final responses and disseminate results (final report)

Source: Tersine & Riggs (1976:53).

The disadvantages of this technique lie in the fact that, however knowledgeable sales representatives may be about their own sales and possibly of those of competitors in their areas, they are seldom abreast of general economic trends and the long-term marketing plans of their own firm. And it is only human for sales representatives to tend to underestimate future sales in the hope that low sales quotas will be set.

3.2 Time-series techniques

Time-series techniques rest on the commonsense premise that if I can establish trends for past performance, I can project the trend into the future and make an evaluation of future events. The chief prerequisite is of course the availability of a reliable historical time series, that is a set of ordered quantitative values over a period of time. Obviously the more historical data I can gather, the more reliable the projected trend will be. Generally about 24 data points are considered the minimum. Thus time-series techniques rest entirely on past recordings and therefore on the implicit assumption that the factors that determined the variable in the past will remain unchanged in the future. Normally, of course, they do not, so that this assumption is the most serious disadvantage of time-series techniques.

Generally, raw time series have to be adjusted or smoothed before they can be used for forecasting. An economic time series normally consists of four components:

☐ the *long-term* trend, which is the underlying tendency of a variable (decrease or increase in a population)

☐ the *cyclical component*, which concerns the wave-like movements of prosperity and depression which normally cover a couple of years

☐ the *seasonal component*, which concerns the up and down movements that occur regularly at a particular time of the year

☐ *random or erratic fluctuations caused by* accidental happenings such as strikes, droughts, etc.

Of the time-series techniques we shall discuss only two in some detail: the moving average technique and exponential smoothing, which are by far the most widely used.

3.2.1 The moving average technique

The moving average technique has the effect of *smoothing* an original time series by moving the arithmetic mean of several consecutive points of the series. The number of data points is chosen with a view to eliminating seasonality and irregularity but bringing out the trend. It is therefore always advisable to plot the raw data of a time series graphically so as to study the series carefully before deciding on the number of data points from which to calculate the average. For example, a three- or a five-point moving average can be calculated from the sales data in table 20.1.

Table 20.1 Moving average of sales showing no trend

Sales periods	Sales (1 000 barrels)	Three-point moving average	Five-point moving average
1	19		
2	25	21,7	
3	21	21,3	21,8
4	18	21,7	23,6
5	26	24,0	23,0
6	28	25,3	22,4
7	22	22,7	22,8
8	18	20,0	
9	20		
10	?		

If no noticeable pattern or trend emerges from the smoothed series, the best forecast for the next period is simply the last moving average available. In our example the forecast for the 10th sales period is 20 000 barrels on a three-point moving average and 22 800 barrels on a five-point moving average.

If a definite trend emerges after the data have been smoothed, a forecast can be calculated by updating the difference between the last two moving averages. The smoothing effect on the data becomes stronger as the number of data points in the moving average increases, as can be seen in table 20.2. On the other hand, the more data points included in the calculation, the greater the loss at the tail-end of the series.

Table 20.2 Moving average of sales showing a trend

Sales periods	Sales (1 000 barrels)	Three-point moving average	Five-point moving average
1	50		
2	53	51,7	
3	52	53,0	52,0
4	54	52,3	52,6
5	51	52,7	53,0
6	53	53,0	53,4
7	55	54,0	53,8
8	54	55,0	
9	56		
10	?		

The sales data in table 20.2 show an upward trend after smoothing but the last value obtained from the five-point moving average is for period 7. We forecast sales for period 10 by multiplying the difference between the last two moving averages by the number of periods between the last moving average and the period for which the forecast is to be made (the lead time T). On the five-point moving average, the forecast for period 10 is 53 800 + (3 × 400) = 55 000 barrels.

3.2.2 Exponential smoothing

Exponential smoothing is another smoothing technique which is very similar to the moving average except that in the moving average technique the same weight is assigned to all data points. In exponential smoothing, however, there is an exponentially decreasing set of weights (seen from the tail-end of the series backwards) or an exponentially increasing set of weights (seen from the beginning of the time series), which gives the more recent data more weight than the older data. This arrangement has a strong common-sense appeal because the more recent data are more akin to the marketing environment of the forecast period than of the earlier period. Also, this technique does not need as many data points as the moving average; in fact it only requires a weight (smoothing constant), the most recent smoothed value and the most recent actual value. Finally, no values are 'lost' at the tail-end of the time series as they are in the moving average technique. The next smoothed value in the series is calculated by multiplying the most recent actual value by the smoothing constant α and the most recent smoothed value by $1 - \alpha$. The formula for exponential smoothing is

$$S_t = \alpha y_t + (1 - \alpha) S_{t-1}$$

where S_t = the smoothed value at time t

α = the smoothing constant

y_t = the most recent actual value

If 0,4 is chosen as the smoothing constant, the following smoothed values can be calculated from the sales data in table 20.2:

$S_1 = 50$

$S_2 = (0,4)\ (53) + (0,6)\ (50) = 51,2$

$S_3 = (0,4)\ (52) + (0,6)\ (51,2) = 51,5$

$S_4 = (0,4)\ (54) + (0,6)\ (51,5) = 52,5$

The smoothed values with 0,4 as smoothing constant are shown in column 4 of table 20.3. The smoothing constant is a value greater than 0 but smaller than 1. The larger the value of the smoothing constant, the greater is the effect of the most recent observation (sales period 9), or the more 'volatile' is the smoothed series. This means that it is closer to the series of actual values than the smoothed values when the smoothing constant is small, as demonstrated by a comparison of the third and the fourth columns of table 20.3 with column 2.

Table 20.3 Exponential smoothing with two different smoothing constants

Sales period	Sales (1 000 barrels)	$S_t(1)$		$S_t(2)$
		$\alpha = 0{,}1$	$\alpha = 0{,}4$	$\alpha = 0{,}4$
1	50	50,0	50,0	50,0
2	53	50,3	51,2	50,5
3	52	50,5	51,5	50,9
4	54	50,9	52,5	51,5
5	51	50,9	51,9	51,7
6	53	51,1	52,3	51,9
7	55	51,5	53,4	52,5
8	54	51,8	53,6	52,9
9	56	52,2	54,6	53,6
10	?			

If no trend emerges in the data, the simple exponential smoothing forecast is equal to the last smoothed value, but if there is a linear trend, a forecast can be calculated from the second order or double exponential smoothing forecast by the formula:

$$\hat{y}_t + T = \left[2 + \frac{\alpha T}{1 - \alpha}\right] S_t - \left[1 + \frac{\alpha T}{1 - \alpha}\right] S_t(2)$$

where $\hat{y}_t + T$ = forecast at time t for a forecast lead time of T

       S_t = the smoothed value at time t

     $S_t(2)$ = second order exponential smoothing

       α = the smoothing constant

Thus the smoothed values are smoothed a second time by the same smoothing constant, as in the fifth column of table 20.3. Using 0,4 as the smoothing constant, we calculate the second order exponential smoothing forecast for period 10 as follows:

$$\hat{y}_{9+1} = \left[2 + \frac{0{,}4 \times 1}{0{,}6}\right] 54{,}6 - \left[1 + \frac{0{,}4 \times 1}{0{,}6}\right] 53{,}6$$

$$= (2{,}667 \times 54{,}6) - (1{,}667 \times 53{,}6)$$

$$= 56{,}3$$

3.3 Causal techniques

Causal techniques rest on the assumption that the variable to be forecast (the dependent variable) is causally related to one or more independent variables. If a causal relation of this kind can be established, and information is available on the future development of the independent variable(s), it is obviously possible to forecast the dependent variable. It is not sufficient, however, merely to establish that a relation exists, because it could be a purely coincidental one. We must therefore make sure that there is a logical explanation for such a relation, otherwise past coincidence will be extrapolated into future disaster. Furthermore we may establish a close relation between two variables that is not causal, but is caused by a third variable which is not included in the equation. So, for instance, the ownership of telephones and TV sets may show a close relation which is not causal but is the effect of a common third variable, household income. It is therefore advisable to use household income as the independent variable to predict ownership of television sets and telephones (dependent variables).

The main advantage of causal techniques over time-series techniques is that causal models search for underlying factors affecting the value of a variable, whereas time-series models ignore them. If any of these influential variables changes significantly, time-series models will be hopelessly inaccurate, although on the other hand causal models are generally more time consuming and more expensive to apply than time-series models. The most widely used technique in the causal category is correlation and regression analysis. In addition, the techniques of leading series, income elasticity coefficients and input-output analysis will be discussed in the following sections.

3.3.1 Correlation and regression analysis

The correlation and regression method of market forecasting may be defined as a technique for measuring the statistical relation between a dependent variable, say, sales of a given product and an independent variable or combination of variables. It provides statistical measures of the degree of correlation between sales and significant market factors. Measurement of the degree of relation between variables is known as correlation analysis. The statistical method of measuring the relation requires an analysis of two or more series to determine the extent to which they move together. The derivation of such a numerical relation is termed regression analysis. When the value of one variable is estimated with the aid of another variable or variables, the estimated variable is the dependent variable and the other(s) are independent variable(s).

The type of correlation analysis applied depends on the number of variables and the nature and degree of their influence. Basically, there are three types of correlation analyses:

□ *simple correlation*, which measures the relation between two variables

□ *multiple correlation*, which measures the relation between a dependent variable and several independent variables

□ *partial correlation*, which measures the relation between one variable and another, while keeping the influence of other variables constant.

Determining independent variables and the nature of the correlation, the application of simple and multiple linear correlation analysis in market forecasting, and the accuracy of such calculations, are discussed in the sections that follow.

3.3.1.1 Determining independent variables

The first step in market forecasting by correlation and regression analysis is to find the independent variables closely related to the dependent variable. Simple methods are sufficiently accurate for this purpose, such as the one involving averages, illustrated in table 20.4.

Table 20.4 Relation between advertising expenditure and sales

Advertising expenditure	Average sales for each rand spent on advertising
R'000	R
5	24
10	26
15	30
20	30
25	25
30	21
35	18

The table clearly shows that sales for each advertising rand spent peak at a certain volume of advertising and then decrease. Thus there can be no doubt about the existence of a relation between the amount spent on advertising and sales.

Scatter diagrams are a common method of testing the relation between variables, as illustrated in figure 20.2. Figure 20.2A correlates sales with the level of education of salesmen. It is evident that there is no relation between the two variables. Figures 20.2B, C, and D show that there is a relation between the independent variables and sales.

Figure 20.2 Examples of the use of scatter diagrams in determining the nature of the relation between variables

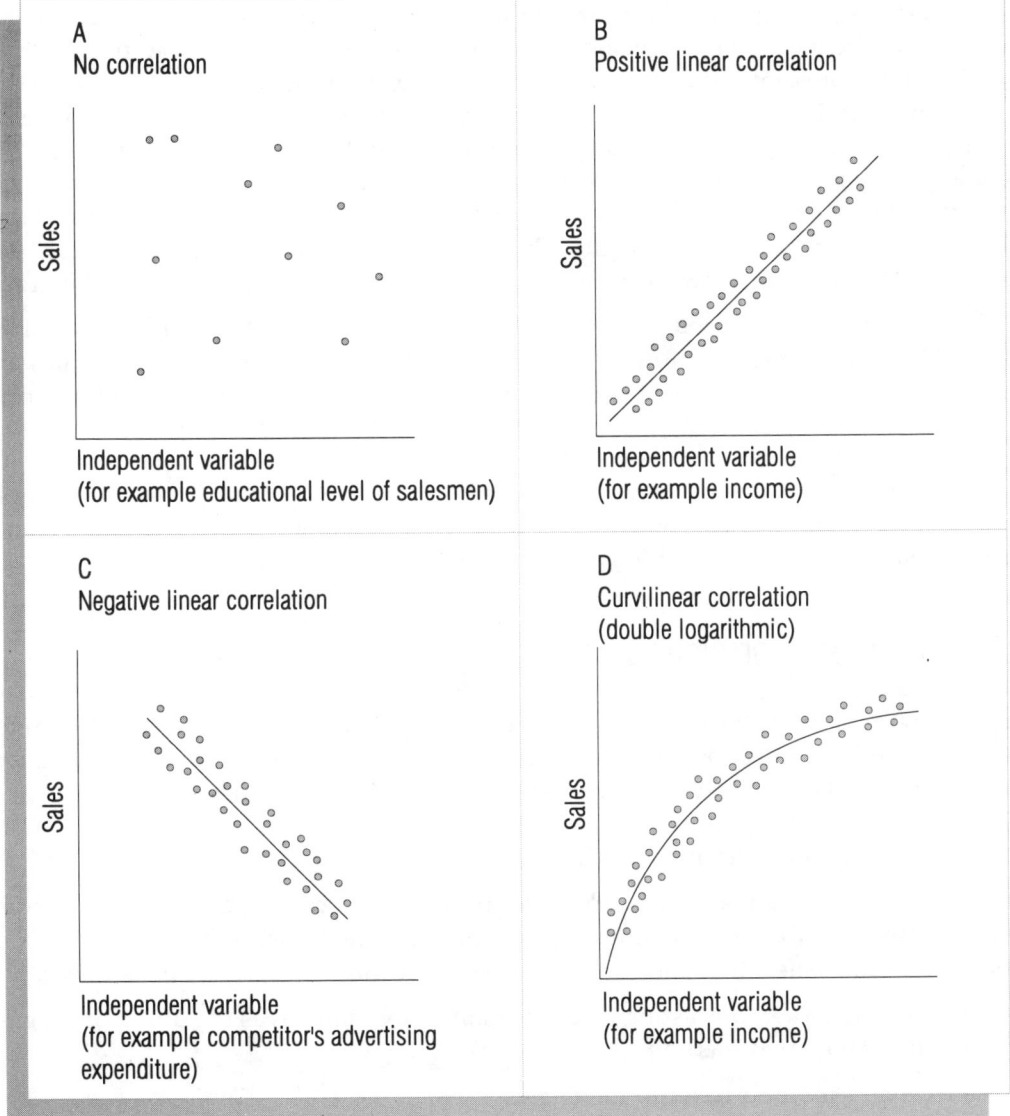

3.3.1.2 Determining the nature of correlation

Once it has been established that there is a relation between the independent variable(s) and the dependent variable, the next step is to determine the nature and the extent of the relation. The nature of the relation between variables determines the function most suited to the expression of the interrelation. A correlation may be positive or negative. In a positive correlation, one variable becomes larger if the other becomes larger, whereas in a negative correlation, one variable becomes smaller if the other becomes larger. The relation between variables may also be linear or curvilinear. There is a linear relation when a change in one variable involves a constant change in another variable. Illustrated graphically, the line is more or less straight. There is a curvilinear relation when there is no constant relation between two variables; instead there is a smooth curve in the graph.

Scatter diagrams are also used to determine the nature of the relation between variables. Figure 20.2B, for example, shows a positive (direct) linear relation between sales and income. In figure 20.2C sales have a negative (inverse) linear correlation with the competitor's volume of advertising. Figure 20.2D illustrates a kind of curvilinear relation (double logarithmic). There are several other well-known curvilinear relations, such as logarithmic inverse, semilogarithmic and hyperbolic. Ezekiel and Fox (1959), for example, illustrate eleven kinds of curvilinear relations and at the same time provide an equation for the best description of each of the curvilinear functions.

3.3.1.3 Linear correlation analysis

Market forecasting by simple linear correlation analysis is discussed below. Brief reference is also made to multiple linear correlation analysis. The use of curvilinear relations and partial correlation analysis in market forecasting is not discussed.

(a) Simple linear correlation analysis

Simple linear correlation analysis is applied in market forecasting once an independent variable with a fairly close relation to the dependent variable (sales) has been found and it has been established that the correlation between these two variables is linear.

The first step in market forecasting by correlation analysis involves the fitting of a regression line by one of two methods:

☐ the freehand method based on averages

☐ the method of least squares.

The 'best fitting' line in a scatter diagram is obtained by applying the method of least squares. A regression line calculated according to the method of least squares represents a line minimising the sum of the squares of the deviations.

(i) Fitting a straight line by the least squares method

A straight line may be described by the equation

$$Y = a + bX,$$

where Y = dependent variable (say, sales)
  a = constant quantity
  b = coefficient of regression
  X = independent variable (say, income)
  N = number of observations

By determining the values of a and b, one can establish what line they represent and their values can be determined mathematically by solving so-called normal equations:

$$Na + b \Sigma X = \Sigma Y \text{ and}$$
$$a \Sigma X + b \Sigma X^2 = \Sigma X Y$$

The values of a and b calculated from these two equations represent a straight line, the sum of the squares of the deviations of which is smaller than in any other line.

The calculation of the values of a and b by the equations above can best be explained by the example in table 20.5 (page 472). The table shows how to estimate sales from the relation between sales and personal income.

The following values are evident from the table:

$$N = 20, \Sigma X = 46\ 500, \Sigma Y = 4\ 678, \Sigma XY = 11\ 121\ 900, \Sigma X^2 = 109\ 775\ 000$$

Substituting the values in the two equations,

$20a + \quad 46\ 500b = \quad 4\ 678$		(1)
$46\ 500a + 109\ 775\ 000b = 11\ 121\ 900$		(2)

By solving the two equations simultaneously a and b are obtained and the equation of the regression line is:

$$Y = -109{,}503 + 0{,}1477X$$

$$\text{Average X series} = \frac{46\ 500}{20} = 2\ 325$$

$$\text{Average Y series} = \frac{4\ 678}{20} = 233{,}9$$

The regression equation above may now be used to fit a regression line to the scatter diagram of income and sales. The regression line is obtained by substituting any two values of X in the formula and determining corresponding sales. Figure 20.3 (page 473) shows the regression line fitted to the example under discussion on the scatter diagram by means of the least squares method.

Table 20.5 Developing a regression line from sales and personal income data

Year	X Personal income (independent variable) R million	Y Sales (dependent variable) R'000	XY	X²
1975	1 850	140	259 000	3 422 500
1976	1 900	180	342 000	3 610 000
1977	1 950	185	360 750	3 802 500
1978	2 000	170	340 000	4 000 000
1979	2 050	190	389 500	4 202 500
1980	2 100	180	378 000	4 410 000
1981	2 150	200	430 000	4 622 500
1982	2 200	220	484 000	4 840 000
1983	2 250	250	562 500	5 062 500
1984	2 300	268	616 400	5 290 000
1985	2 350	260	611 000	5 522 500
1986	2 400	240	576 000	5 760 000
1987	2 450	250	612 500	6 002 500
1988	2 500	270	675 000	6 250 000
1989	2 550	270	688 500	6 502 500
1990	2 600	260	676 000	6 760 000
1991	2 650	280	742 000	7 022 500
1992	2 700	290	783 000	7 290 000
1993	2 750	285	783 750	7 562 500
1994	2 800	290	812 000	7 840 000
Total	**46 500**	**4 678**	**11 121 900**	**109 775 000**

Sales for the relevant year are calculated from the figure by estimating present and future personal income. Let us suppose that personal income for the year 1995 is estimated at R2 900 million and for the year 2000 at R3 400 million. According to this method, the sales potential of the product concerned will be R319 thousand in 1995 and R397 thousand in 2000.

(ii) Accuracy of the calculations

The accuracy of market forecasting by means of the regression line depends on the degree of correlation between the two variables. This degree of correlation is determined mathematically by a correlation coefficient. The correlation coefficient may have any value between +1 (perfect direct correlation) and −1 (complete inverse correlation). A complete absence of correlation is expressed as 0, while plus and minus signs indicate positive and negative correlations respectively.

Figure 20.3 Graphic representation of a regression line fitted by the least squares method

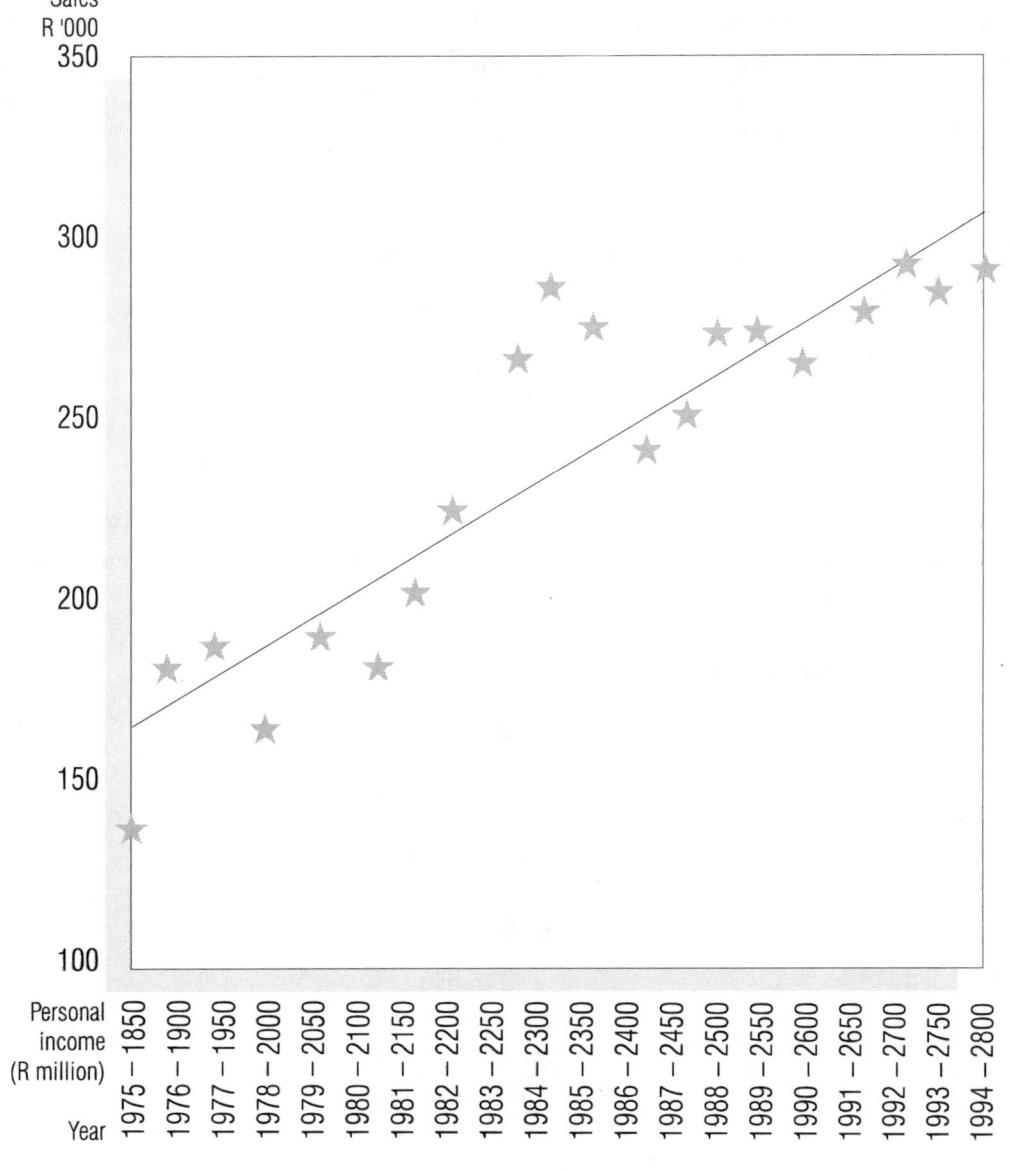

A correlation coefficient of 0,95 or greater represents a high degree of linear correlation between two variables and the value of one variable may be estimated fairly accurately from the value of the other. When a correlation coefficient is lower than 0,75, market forecasting from such information is best avoided. The significance of a correlation coefficient depends on the number of observations on which it is based. Statistical tests and tables do exist for verifying correlation coefficients, but they will not be discussed here.

Karl Pearson's sum product method is one of the most widely used techniques for measuring the relation between two or more variables by applying the following formula to calculate their linear correlation:

$$r = \frac{\Sigma xy}{NS_x S_y}$$

where x = deviations from the average of the X series

y = deviations from the average of the Y series

S_x = standard deviation of the X series

S_y = standard deviation of the Y series

$\dfrac{\Sigma xy}{N}$ = covariance of X and Y

This formula is applied in our example (table 20.6) to arrive at a correlation coefficient of 0,94 between income and sales, which indicates that sales may be fairly accurately estimated from the value of personal income.

$$\text{Average X series} = 2\ 325$$
$$\text{Average Y series} = 234$$

$$\text{Standard deviation of the X series} = \sqrt{\frac{1\ 662\ 500}{20}} = \sqrt{83\ 125} = 288,3$$

$$\text{Standard deviation of the Y series} = \sqrt{\frac{41\ 089,8}{20}} = \sqrt{2\ 054,5} = 45,33$$

$$r = \frac{\Sigma xy}{N\ S_x\ S_y}$$

$$= \frac{245\ 550}{20 \times 288,3 \times 45,33}$$

$$= \frac{245\ 550}{261\ 372,78}$$

$$= 0,94$$

(b) Multiple linear correlation analysis

The preceding section dealt with market forecasting by simple linear correlation, that is from the relation between two variables with a fairly straight regression line in a graphic

Table 20.6 Calculation of the correlation coefficient

Year	X Personal income R million	Y Sales R'000	x Deviation from the average of the X series	y Deviation from the average of the Y series	xy	x²	y²
1975	1 850	140	−475	−93,9	44 602,5	225 625	8 817,21
1976	1 900	180	−425	−53,9	22 907,5	180 625	2 905,21
1977	1 950	185	−375	−48,9	18 337,5	140 625	2 391,21
1978	2 000	170	−325	−63,9	20 767,5	105 625	4 083,21
1979	2 050	190	−275	−43,9	12 072,5	75 625	1 927,21
1980	2 100	180	−225	−53,9	12 127,5	50 625	2 905,21
1981	2 150	200	−175	−33,9	5 932,5	30 625	1 149,21
1982	2 200	220	−125	−13,9	1 737,5	15 625	193,21
1983	2 250	250	−75	16,1	−1 207,5	5 625	259,21
1984	2 300	268	−25	34,1	−852,5	625	1 162,81
1985	2 350	260	25	26,1	652,5	625	681,21
1986	2 400	240	75	6,1	457,5	5 625	37,21
1987	2 450	250	125	16,1	2 012,5	15 628	259,21
1988	2 500	270	175	36,1	6 317,5	30 625	1 303,21
1989	2 550	270	225	36,1	8 122,5	50 625	1 303,21
1990	2 600	260	275	26,1	7 177,5	75 625	681,21
1991	2 650	280	325	46,1	14 982,5	105 625	2 125,21
1992	2 700	290	375	56,1	21 037,5	140 625	3 147,21
1993	2 750	285	425	51,1	21 717,5	180 625	2 611,21
1994	2 800	290	475	56,1	26 647,5	225 625	3 147,21
Total	**46 500**	**4 678**	−	−	**245 550**	**1 662 500**	**41 089,8**

representation. This section deals briefly with multiple linear correlations. As stated, multiple correlations reveal the relation between one variable (the dependent variable) and several other variables. In practice, multiple correlations occur more frequently than simple correlations because product sales are usually affected by a number of variables. For example, sales in an area are a function of population, income and willingness to spend rather than a function of only one variable, say, population.

In the calculation of simple linear correlations in the preceding section, the regression line for calculating market potential was determined by applying the equation:

$Y = a + bX$

In multiple linear correlation analysis the relation between the dependent variable and two or more other variables is symbolically described by the following equation:

$$Y = a + b_1X_1 + b_2X_2 + \ldots + b_nX_n$$

where Y = the dependent variable (sales)

X_1, X_2, X_n = the dependent variables

a = constant quantity

b_1, b_2, b_n = regression coefficients showing the average change in the dependent variable in relation to unit changes in the independent variable

By determining the constant a, and the regression coefficient b, the equation can be solved and the market potential determined with the aid of the regression equation or regression line.

3.3.2 Leading series

The leading series technique can be considered a subtechnique of correlation analysis in that it establishes the relation between variables but does so from the viewpoint of leads or lags. A leading series changes in the same direction but ahead of the variable to be forecast. For instance, the Institute of Economic Research in Germany established that building plans approved for private residential buildings lead the sale of electric stoves by three to five months. By monitoring the movement of building plans approved, a fairly accurate forecast of the sales of electric stoves could be made. To find such a series is the dream of every forecaster and the simplest way to find them is to plot a number of series graphically and to compare their trends, and especially their turning points. Although reservations have been expressed on the validity of the leading series technique as a forecasting tool, especially for long-range forecasting, the technique is generally accepted as being very useful for forecasting turning points, especially in business cycle analysis.

3.3.3 Income elasticity coefficients

The use of income elasticity coefficients in forecasting rests on the assumption that income is the only, or at least the most important factor in the purchase of a particular product or service.

> **Income elasticities** may be defined as the relative (or proportional) change in the quantity consumed or real amount spent, expressed as a proportion of a relative (or proportional) change in real income.

Income elasticities are therefore a measure of the influence of a given change in income on the demand for a specific product. An income elasticity of 1 indicates that the demand for a product will rise by the same percentage as income. For instance, a 10 % increase in real income will cause a 10 % increase in the demand for that product. An income elasticity of less than 1 will give rise to a less than proportionate increase in the demand for the product. If, for example, food has an income elasticity of 0,73 among coloureds and their real income rises by 10 %, their demand for food will only rise by 7,3 %. The opposite applies if an income elasticity is greater than 1. A negative income elasticity indicates a decrease in the absolute sum of money spent on the product when real income rises. Table 20.7 shows the income elasticity coefficients of the four population groups in metropolitan areas by main expenditure item in 1990.

Table 20.7 Income elasticities of the demand of the four population groups in metropolitan areas for the main expenditure groups, 1990

Main expenditure group	Asians	Blacks	Coloureds	Whites	Weighted average
Food	0,71	0,75	0,73	0,42	0,63
Clothing and footwear	1,03	1,04	0,97	0,97	1,12
Housing and electricity	0,84	0,66	0,81	0,90	0,85
Fuel and light	0,51	0,12	0,44	1,09	0,15
Furniture and equipment	1,46	1,24	1,53	1,31	1,29
Transport	1,49	1,25	1,37	1,26	1,27
Medical and dental	1,09	0,98	1,20	0,65	0,78
Insurance and funds	1,79	2,10	1,73	1,24	1,44
Education	1,63	1,16	1,33	1,47	1,35
Washing and cleaning materials, etc	0,64	0,53	0,37	0,46	0,55
Dry-cleaning and laundry	1,69	1,50	1,17	1,54	1,47
Communication	1,19	1,98	1,39	0,58	1,17
Alcoholic beverages	0,46	1,22	0,92	1,03	1,12
Cigarettes and tobacco	−0,02	0,68	0,91	0,06	0,51
Personal care	1,69	1,50	1,17	0,61	1,07
Reading-matter and stationery	1,29	1,16	1,10	0,88	1,01
Recreation and entertainment	1,33	1,64	1,24	1,25	1,30
Holidays	1,81	2,47	1,23	1,32	1,45
Miscellaneous items	1,17	1,22	1,18	1,90	1,64

Source: Loubser (1990:37).

Income elasticities can be calculated in two ways: by time series, or by cross-section analyses of income and expenditure data. The time-series method of calculating income elasticities involves correlation and regression analysis of income and consumption data over time. The chief disadvantage of the method is usually the small number of observations. A further disadvantage is due to technological development in that the products of yesteryear are no longer comparable with their modern counterparts, and whole series of new products are being manufactured which were previously unknown. In South Africa the calculation of income elasticities for the respective population groups by the time-series method is precluded by the lack of annual income and consumption expenditure data on the population groups over time.

The second method of calculating income elasticities involves cross-section analyses by income group, of consumer expenditures gathered in sample surveys. 'Cross-section analyses provide substantially greater flexibility than time series in that they contain an almost complete spectrum of possible differences in household circumstances as well as a potentially unlimited number of observations' (Juster 1966:3). The cross-section analysis method is preferable, especially in South Africa, because it permits the calculation of income elasticities for individual population groups.

The trend of the demand curve, or the nature of the relation between income and consumption, is of vital importance, determining as it does the function most suited to expressing the interrelation. Income elasticities can, however, only be calculated for products whose demand curve is linear, semi-logarithmic, double logarithmic, loginverse or hyperbolic.

Once the constant and the regression coefficients of the chosen function have been determined by regression analysis,* market potentials are calculated by introducing the constant, the regression coefficient(s) and income in the regression comparison concerned. If, for example, the trend of the demand curve of a product is described by the double logarithmic function the equation is $\log V = A + B \log I$ where:

V = consumption
A = a constant showing the position of the demand curve
B = the coefficient of income elasticity
I = income

Provided that present or future income is known, the sales of the product are calculated by assigning values to the constant A, the income elasticity B, and income in the equation.

It may also be necessary to include other variables in the equation – such as family size and prices – when these factors have a significant bearing on the consumption of the product and are subject to considerable change.

Market forecasting by means of income elasticities, however, is confined to the short and medium term. Continuous changes in the major determinants of consumption such as income levels, income distribution, family size, number of earners per family, level of education, occupation structure, age structure, and exogenous factors such as non-

---

* See section 3.3.1.3.

proportionate price increases and advertising, permit the calculation of income elasticities for the shorter term only.

3.3.4 Input-output analysis

Input-output tables reflect the flow of products and services through an economic system. It is customary in these tables to divide the total economy into intermediate demand and final demand categories, as explained in chapter 4. The number of these categories depends on the information available and the purpose of the tables. In the RSA the tables published by the Central Statistical Service have 90 intermediate and 7 final demand categories.

The latest tables relate to 1989. At present more recent tables are being compiled, but the 1989 tables are quite acceptable to illustrate the significance of input-output tables as tools of market analysis and forecasting. Since the breakdowns of such tables are normally on an industry basis they are useful for industry forecasts only, except in monopolies where one firm covers a whole industry.

Nevertheless, since market shares are normally known to individual firms and do not change significantly over the short and medium term, input-output tables are useful instruments even for sales forecasting. The three types of tables are briefly explained below. The examples are abbreviated for technical reasons.

3.3.4.1 Basic input-output tables*

Table 20.8 illustrates inputs/outputs at basic rand values in an abbreviated form. The horizontal rows record an industry's output/deliveries/sales to other industries. For instance, the agriculture, forestry and fishing sector delivered goods to the value of R1 542,0 million to itself and R10,5 million to coal mining. Conversely, coal mines purchased goods from agriculture, forestry and fishing to the value of R10,5 million. All sales and purchases add up to intermediate outputs or inputs totalling R219 631,81 million. The values are given at basic prices which in fact are cost of material, excluding the trade margin and transport costs. Remuneration of employees, gross operating surplus and net indirect taxes are added in each vertical column so that subtotals represent production prices. The table further shows (horizontal rows) that various industries deliver not only to other intermediate industries, but also to final demand, namely private and public consumption expen-diture, gross fixed investment, change in inventories and exports plus re-exports. The question now arises whether a particular product is a delivery to another industry or an investment. Generally speaking, supplies which are used up within one year are treated as deliveries to other intermediate industries, whereas deliveries of capital equipment for more than one year's use are regarded as fixed investment.

---

* See chapter 21, section 7.1.2, for more information on the basic layout of input-output tables.

Table 20.8 Abbreviated input-output table at basic rand values, 1989 (R million)

Sector		Agriculture 1	Coal mining 2	Gold mining 3	Other mining 4	Slaughtering 5	Dairy products 6		Other 90
Agriculture	1	1 542,0	10,5	23,0	2,1	6 476,5	534,7		—
Coal mining	2	0,4	0,3	10,4	42,6	1,6	2,5		—
Gold mining	3	—	—	—	—	—	—		—
Other mining	4	53,1	9,4	27,9	4,1	0,1	0,1		—
Slaughtering	5	—	—	⁄ —	—	821,8	4,4		—
Dairy products	6	—	—	—	—	90,5	341,1		—
Canning of fruit and vegetables	7	—	—	—	—	34,0	23,7		—
Canning of fish	8	—	—	—	—	0,1	0,1		—
Vegetable and animal oils and fats	9	—	1,2	1,0	0,7	2,9	20,0		—
Grain mill products	10	—	—	—	—	6,3	9,3		—
Bakery products	11	—	—	—	—	0,3	0,9		—
Sugar factories	12	—	—	—	—	0,4	19,4		—
Cocoa	13	—	—	—	—	—	4,6		—
Other food products	14	—	—	—	—	33,6	18,1		—
Prepared animal feeds	15	2 128,9	1,6	3,5	0,4	0,6	—		—
Distilleries and wineries	16	—	1,0	2,2	0,2	—	0,1		—
Malt liquors and malt	17	—	—	—	—	—	—		—
Soft drinks	18	—	—	—	—	—	4,0		—
Tobacco products	19	—	1,3	2,9	0,3	—	—		—
Spinning, weaving of textiles	20	—	2,6	15,9	6,7	—	0,2		2,9
Made-up textile goods	21	107,2	2,4	19,5	6,3	1,1	1,3		—
Garment and hosiery knitting mills	22	—	—	—	—	—	—		—
Other knitting mills	23	—	—	—	—	—	—		—
Carpets and rugs	24	—	0,2	0,7	0,5	—	—		—
Other	90	117,6	424,1	1 072,7	989,6	62,6	144,1		140,2
Total intermediate input		9 036,8	2 503,8	7 448,1	4 239,7	8 270,6	1 674,1		9 949,4
Remuneration of employees		2 293,0	1 446,4	6 682,3	2 929,9	353,6	315,2		826,1
Gross operating surplus		10 142,4	1 572,2	6 370,4	4 436,4	257,4	267,7		483,1
Net indirect taxes		409,4	85,8	583,7	138,4	− 23,6	10,1		192,8
Sub-total		21 881,5	5 608,1	21 084,5	11 744,5	8 858,0	2 267,0		11 451,3
Add: Products transferred from other industries		43,1	—	—	1 395,6	80,3	4,3		—
Less: Products transferred to other industries		—	—	− 874,3	—	− 23,4	− 55,3		—
Total input		**21 924,6**	**5 608,1**	**20 210,2**	**13 140,0**	**8 914,9**	**2 216,0**		**11 451,3**

Source: CSS (1989:5–28).

a	b	c	d	e	f	g	h	i	j
Total intermediate output	Private consumption expenditure	Consumption expenditure by the general government	Gross domestic fixed capital formation	Change in inventories	Exports	Re-exports	Imports	Final demand	Total production (a + i)
15 477,3	5 130,0	224,1	—	479,0	1 238,4	11,9	−636,3	6 447,0	21 924,6
2 779,4	158,6	6,2	—	3,5	2 678,6	—	−18,0	2 828,9	5 608,1
45,3	—	—	—	−39,0	20 203,9	—	—	20 164,9	20 210,2
10 269,8	—	68,9	—	91,0	9 239,2	41,3	−6 569,7	2 870,4	13 140,0
2 253,2	6 108,5	190,1	—	144,6	488,1	5,0	−274,5	6 661,7	8 914,9
1 019,3	1 188,1	31,8	—	46,0	34,7	1,2	−105,1	1 196,7	2 216,0
289,9	871,7	17,2	—	85,1	731,3	1,8	−57,8	1 649,3	1 939,2
265,8	933,4	11,7	—	30,3	100,2	5,3	−312,9	768,0	1 033,8
1 270,6	774,0	16,1	—	14,1	184,7	3,5	−472,9	519,5	1 790,1
1 457,1	1 896,1	23,9	—	49,1	215,7	2,6	−310,9	1 876,6	3 333,8
103,4	1 949,7	32,6	—	25,3	12,4	0,5	−9,4	2 011,1	2 114,5
465,1	628,0	12,4	—	1,8	761,3	0,6	−73,2	1 330,8	1 796,0
215,7	777,8	—	—	40,5	36,3	1,1	−49,1	806,6	1 002,4
845,2	1 242,0	30,8	—	47,4	123,7	1,0	−218,7	1 226,1	2 071,2
2 235,0	28,3	13,6	—	10,6	25,1	1,1	−29,5	49,3	2 284,3
1 040,6	965,4	13,4	—	151,9	191,4	13,4	−242,6	1 093,0	2 133,6
501,8	2 229,6	0,4	—	91,2	89,4	0,1	−119,7	2 291,0	2 792,8
240,0	1 173,7	0,0	—	42,1	92,4	0,1	—	1 308,4	1 548,4
13,1	843,6	0,8	—	36,0	103,2	2,0	−13,6	971,9	985,0
3 082,5	535,8	11,8	—	52,1	1 019,5	6,7	−1 037,3	588,0	3 671,2
591,5	380,5	29,0	—	27,6	132,5	6,8	−153,1	423,3	1 014,5
10,7	533,7	—	—	4,0	174,1	1,8	−106,1	607,5	618,2
374,0	263,2	—	—	2,1	125,1	0,0	−96,3	294,1	668,2
284,3	157,0	1,1	—	−4,1	12,0	0,3	−41,3	125,2	409,4
12 904,6	1,455,5	−2 195,1	—	—	—	—	−714,3	−1 453,8	11 451,3
219 631,8	118 288,4	12 783,3	45 438,3	4 147,6	66 161,7	866,7	−53 449,1	194 237,0	413 866,8
90 970,8	2 369,3	26 622,0	—	—	—	—	—	28 991,3	119 962,1
—	—	1 384,0	—	—	—	—	—	1 384,0	94 040,7
10 607,5	11 281,6	797,6	3 136,7	599,5	−1 008,1	2,7	—	14 810,0	25 417,5
413 866,8	131 939,4	41 586,9	48 575,0	4 747,2	65 153,6	869,4	−53 449,1	239 422,4	653 287,1
17 537,1	—	—	—	—	—	—	—	—	17 537,1
−17 537,1	—	—	—	—	—	—	—	—	−17 537,1
413 866,8	**131 939,4**	**41 586,9**	**48 575,0**	**4 747,2**	**65 153,6**	**869,4**	**−53 449,1**	**239 422,4**	**653 287,1**

Table 20.8 reveals the importance of each industry to the various intermediate and/or final purchasers or, expressed differently, the importance of an industry to other industries. Agriculture, forestry and fishing, for instance, delivers about 71 % of its output to other intermediate industries, 23 % to private consumption expenditure, and 6 % to exports and re-exports, whereas gold and uranium mining delivers almost 100 % to exports. From a marketing point of view these figures are therefore a valuable – albeit broad – indication of an industry's main markets.

3.3.4.2 Tables of input-coefficients

In the second type of input-output table, the interdependence of the various sectors becomes even more obvious if the inputs are expressed as coefficients of the output. In other words, these coefficients indicate an industry's requirements or purchases from its supply markets.

The vertical columns in table 20.9 show the input coefficients of the various sectors. For each rand of output of the canning of fruit and vegetables industries, for instance, R0,12349 is required from agriculture, forestry and fishing, R0,0220 from sugar factories and R0,03860 from other food product industries to produce one hundred rand's worth of canned fruit and vegetables.

Experience has shown that these coefficients are relatively stable over short and medium periods, varying only as a result of disproportionate price changes and technological advances. For this reason input coefficients are useful instruments for market forecasting over short and medium terms. If, for instance, the beverage industry is expected to grow by R1 million over a given period, the additional demand for the products of each industry which delivers to the beverage industry is readily calculated by multiplying the coefficients by one million.

3.3.4.3 Tables of inverse coefficients

Input coefficients only denote the primary effect. As a secondary effect, the additional deliveries of the various industries to the beverage industry increase the inputs or market shares of the industries supplying these inputs. The further effects of these output requirements throughout the economic system are calculated to arrive at the total impact of an increase in the output of the beverage industry. The total output required of each industry can best be calculated by using inverse coefficients whereby the relationships, expressed in table 20.9, are traced, as it were, throughout the economic system. Since an increase in the output of the beverage industry can, after all, be generated only by an increase in one or more of the final demand categories, the inverse coefficients indicate the direct and indirect effects of a change in final demand on the various intermediate industries.

Table 20.9 Coefficients per rand of gross output, 1989 (direct requirements per rand of gross output)

Sector	Agriculture 1	Coal mining 2	Gold mining 3	Other mining 4	Slaughtering 5	Dairy products 6	Canning of fruit and vegetables 7	Canning of fish 8	Vegetable and animal oils 9		Other 90
Agriculture 1	0,07033	0,00187	0,00114	0,00016	0,72649	0,24128	0,12349	0,31688	0,18855		–
Coal mining 2	0,00002	0,00006	0,00051	0,00324	0,00018	0,00113	0,00284	0,00308	0,00202		–
Gold mining 3	–	–	–	–	–	–	–	–	–		–
Other mining 4	0,00242	0,00167	0,00138	0,00031	0,00002	0,00050	0,00110	0,00120	0,00002		–
Slaughtering 5	–	–	–	–	0,09218	0,00198	0,00300	0,00007	0,00271		–
Dairy products 6	–	–	–	–	0,01015	0,15394	0,00153	0,00151	0,00088		–
Canning of fruit and vegetables 7	–	–	–	–	0,00381	0,01067	0,07414	0,01503	0,00463		–
Canning of fish 8	–	–	–	–	0,00010	0,00020	0,00030	0,04410	0,02399		–
Vegetable and animal oils 9	–	0,00021	0,00005	0,00005	0,00032	0,00904	0,00491	0,00598	0,30008		–
Grain mill products 10	–	–	–	–	0,00071	0,00418	0,00046	0,00308	0,03024		–
Bakery products 11	–	–	–	–	0,00004	0,00042	0,00045	0,00615	–		–
Sugar factories 12	–	–	–	–	0,00005	0,00876	0,02220	0,00019	0,00065		–
Cocoa 13	–	–	–	–	–	0,00207	0,03007	–	0,01824		–
Other food products 14	–	–	–	–	0,00377	0,00816	0,03860	0,00655	0,01111		–
Prepared animal feeds 15	0,09710	0,00029	0,00017	0,00003	0,00007	–	–	–	–		–
Distilleries and wineries	–	0,00018	0,00011	0,00001	–	0,00003	0,00003	–	–		–
Malt liquors and malt 17	–	–	–	–	–	–	–	–	0,01207		–
Soft drinks 18	–	–	–	–	–	0,00181	0,00225	–	–		–
Tobacco products 19	–	0,00023	0,00014	0,00002	–	–	–	–	–		–
Spinning, weaving of textiles 20	–	0,00046	0,00079	0,00051	–	0,00003	–	–	0,00703		–
Made-up textile goods 21	0,00489	0,00043	0,00097	0,00048	0,00012	0,00058	0,00026	0,00072	0,00046		–
Garment and hosiery knitting mills 22	–	–	–	–	–	–	–	–	–		–
Other knitting mills 23	–	–	–	–	–	–	–	–	–		–
Carpets and rugs 24	–	0,00004	0,00004	0,00004	–	–	0,00012	–	–		–
Other 90	0,00536	0,07562	0,05308	0,07531	0,00702	0,06505	0,08703	0,02123	0,03510		0,01224
Total intermediate input	0,41217	0,44643	0,36853	0,32262	0,92775	0,75547	0,71559	0,68140	0,83150		0,86882
Remuneration of employees	0,10458	0,25792	0,33064	0,22297	0,03967	0,14222	0,14194	0,13016	0,09755		0,07214
Gross operating surplus	0,46260	0,28034	0,31521	0,33763	0,02887	0,12078	0,12355	0,18431	0,10640		0,04219
Net indirect taxes	0,01867	0,01529	0,02888	0,01053	−0,00265	0,00454	0,01235	0,01162	0,00315		0,01683
Sub-total	0,99820	1,00000	1,04326	0,93759	0,99364	1,02301	0,99343	1,00749	1,03860		1,00000
Add: Products transferred from other industries	0,00196	–	–	0,10621	0,00901	0,00195	0,06047	0,00007	0,01249		–
Less: Products transferred to other industries	–	–	−0,04326	–	−0,00262	−0,02496	−0,05392	−0,00754	−0,05108		–
Total input	1,00000	1,00000	1,00000	1,00000	1,00000	1,00000	1,00000	1,00000	1,00000		1,00000

Source: CSS (1989:33–52).

Table 20.10 is an example of a table of inverse coefficients. The reader is referred to its vertical columns. If, for instance, an upswing in private consumption is expected to increase the final demand for products of the canning of fruit and vegetables industry, that industry has to step up its production. This, in turn, requires deliveries from other industries. If the final demand for canned fruit and vegetables is expected to increase by, say R1, agriculture, forestry and fishing likewise has to step up deliveries by R0,19526, the sector of coal mining by R0,01314, and so on. Again, these coefficients are valuable tools for market forecasting over short and medium periods. In fact, since all economic activities are ultimately generated by final demand, forecasts of these demand changes are more readily available than forecasts of changes in intermediate industries. Inverse coefficients are therefore particularly useful in practical marketing forecasting operations.

Table 20.10 Inverse coefficients, 1989 (total requirements (direct and indirect) per rand of delivery to final demand)

Sector		Agriculture	Coal mining	Gold mining	Other mining	Slaughtering	Dairy products	Canning of fruit and vegetables	Canning of fish		Other
		1	2	3	4	5	6	7	8		90
Agriculture	1	1,11551	0,00932	0,01264	0,00559	0,90064	0,34880	0,19526	0,37212		0,02134
Coal mining	2	0,00716	0,01060	0,01387	0,01187	0,00776	0,00954	0,01314	0,01306		0,00850
Gold mining	3	0,00001	0,00003	1,00002	0,00003	0,00002	0,00004	0,00005	0,00002		0,00033
Other mining	4	0,04951	0,03594	0,02013	1,02450	0,04562	0,03611	0,04085	0,04987		0,03423
Slaughtering	5	0,00234	0,00134	0,00118	0,00106	1,10391	0,00500	0,00657	0,00215		0,00610
Dairy products	6	0,00052	0,00051	0,00038	0,00040	0,01384	1,18309	0,00612	0,00264		0,00280
Canning of fruit and vegetables	7	0,00040	0,00006	0,00005	0,00004	0,00510	0,01409	1,08113	0,01669		0,00024
Canning of fish	8	0,00795	0,00016	0,00016	0,00010	0,00649	0,00302	0,00187	1,00740		0,00045
Vegetable and animal oils and fats	9	0,02249	0,00113	0,00099	0,00071	0,01946	0,02468	0,01836	0,01763		0,00140
Grain mill products	10	0,00968	0,00031	0,00029	0,00020	0,00897	0,00962	0,00487	0,00983		0,00086
Bakery products	11	0,00011	0,00008	0,00008	0,00007	0,00017	0,00065	0,00083	0,00634		0,00043
Sugar factories	12	0,00108	0,00031	0,00033	0,00027	0,00136	0,01248	0,02876	0,00149		0,00082
Cocoa	13	0,00054	0,00004	0,00003	0,00003	0,00073	0,00381	0,03614	0,00109		0,00012
Other food products	14	0,00202	0,00047	0,00036	0,00033	0,00687	0,01363	0,05118	0,00996		0,00165
Prepared animal feeds	15	0,11035	0,00123	0,00144	0,00060	0,08919	0,03463	0,01939	0,03694		0,00217
Distilleries and wineries	16	0,00021	0,00064	0,00041	0,00030	0,00031	0,00049	0,00060	0,00034		0,00216
Malt liquors and malt	17	0,00041	0,00019	0,00012	0,00014	0,00041	0,00055	0,00052	0,00040		0,00105
Soft drinks	18	0,00005	0,00007	0,00004	0,00005	0,00012	0,00253	0,00286	0,00012		0,00029
Tobacco products	19	0,00002	0,00025	0,00015	0,00003	0,00002	0,00002	0,00002	0,00002		0,00003
Spinning, weaving of textiles	20	0,00419	0,00613	0,00481	0,00460	0,00461	0,00604	0,00566	0,00449		0,01221
Made-up textile goods	21	0,00638	0,00132	0,00166	0,00109	0,00556	0,00347	0,00226	0,00345		0,00182
Garment and hosiery knitting mills	22	–	–	–	–	–	–	–	–		–
Other knitting mills	23	0,00035	0,00052	0,00041	0,00035	0,00044	0,00060	0,00054	0,00045		0,00106
Carpets and rugs	24	0,00019	0,00013	0,00025	0,00014	0,00018	0,00014	0,00026	0,00014		0,00036

Source: CSS (1989:57–76).

3.4 The use of various techniques

We have confined ourselves to the techniques discussed above because they seem to be the most widely used in practice according to surveys available.

There are, of course, other techniques such as econometric and marketing models and the Box-Jenkins technique, but these are rather more sophisticated and are used in exceptional cases only.

From the discussion of the various techniques, it is obvious that each has its pros and cons and the forecaster makes his choice in the light of the data available, the type of product, the time horizon, the accuracy required and the stability of the market environment. Apart from general guidelines, there is as yet very little scientific information on the relative superiority of one technique over another in a particular situation.

> Over the past decade most research in market forecasting has focused on the development of new, usually more complex, forecasting models on the assumption that these models provide more accurate forecasts than simple existing models... Still rare, however, are comparable studies that attempt to discover those situations in which one type of model might be expected consistently to outperform another (Armstrong 1978).

In a comparative study of forecasting accuracy over a wide range of data series, Schnaars came to the conclusion that simple models are at least as accurate as complex ones. It is therefore advisable to choose the simplest technique that will do the job, even if more complicated models may appear more scientific to management. Better still, it is advisable to combine two or more techniques as a cross-check of the results. In practice, statistical (objective) forecasts are normally evaluated and adjusted by subjective or qualitative techniques, which will allow for the evaluation of the influence of environmental factors not sufficiently taken care of in the statistical models.

4 SUMMARY

Since every manager has to plan, he has to forecast. The question therefore is not whether, but how to forecast. Forecasting is partly a science and partly an art that requires experience and intuition. Forecasting normally comprises three steps: general economic forecasting, sector forecasting and company forecasting.

There is no unanimity on the length of time horizons in forecasting, or on the difference between short-, medium- and long-term forecasting, since it depends on the speed of product innovation and change in the market environment. There is a wide variety of forecasting techniques and they are usually grouped as qualitative techniques, time-series and causal techniques, the last two often being combined as quantitative techniques in contrast to qualitative techniques (table 20.11).

Table 20.11 Summary and properties of techniques*

Technique	Description	Accuracy Short term: 0–3 months	Accuracy Medium term: 3 months to 2 years	Accuracy Long term: 2 years and up	Identification of turning points	Typical applications	Data required
1 Theory of expert opinion	A method that uses expert opinion based on experience, insight, judgement about different scenarios of the future	Fair	Fair	Fair	Fair	Forecasts of long-range and new product sales forecast	A set of possible scenarios about the future prepared by experts in the light of past events
2 Delphi	A panel of experts is interrogated by a sequence of questionnaires in which the responses to one questionnaire are used to produce the next questionnaire. Any set of information available to some experts and not others is thus passed on to the others, giving all the experts access to all the information for forecasting. This technique eliminates the bandwagon effect of majority opinion and dominant personalities.	Usually not applicable	Fair to very good	Fair to very good	Fair to good	Forecasts of long-range and new products sales and technological forecasts	A coordinator issues a sequence of questionnaires, edits and coordinates responses
3 Composite sales force opinion	Sales representatives come together (normally under the chairmanship of the marketing manager) and prepare forecasts like a jury of experts	Fair	Poor	Poor	Poor	Sales forecast	No data required, but other sales statistics on regional basis supplied
4 Survey of buying intentions	Determine intentions to buy (normally restricted to durables)	Poor to good	Poor to good	Very poor	Fair	Forecast of sales by product class	Several years' data required to relate indices to company sales

qualitative techniques

	Technique	Description					Typical application	Data required
time-series techniques	5 Moving averages	Each point of a moving average of a time series is the arithmetic mean of several consecutive points of series. Number of data points chosen to eliminate effects of seasonal or irregular influences	Fair	Poor	Very poor	Poor	Inventory control of low volume items sales forecast	At least 20 to 24 data points required. The more data, the better
	6 Exponential smoothing	This technique is a weighted moving average, except that more recent data points are given more weight. Descriptively, the new forecast is equal to the old one plus some proportion of the past forecasting error. There are many variations of exponential smoothing; some are more versatile than others, some are computationally more complex, and some require more computer time	Fair to very good	Poor to good	Very poor	Poor	Forecasts of production and inventory control, financial data and sales	Less data required than for moving average
causal techniques	7 Regression and correlation analysis	This functionally relates sales to other economic, competitive, or internal variables, and estimates an equation using the least-squares technique. Relations are primarily analysed statistically, although any relations should be selected for testing on rational grounds.	Good to very good	Good to very good	Fair to good	Very good	Sales forecast by product classes	Several years' monthly or quarterly data to obtain meaningful relationships
	8 Leading series	A time series of an economic activity whose movement in a given direction precedes the movement of some other time series in the same direction is a leading indicator	Fair	Fair	Poor	Very good	Sales forecast by product classes	As for correlation and regression analysis
	9 Income elasticity coefficients	Forecast of variables which are entirely or mainly dependent on income	Fair	Fair	Poor	Poor	Forecast of product or service sales	Up to date coefficients and reliable data of personal disposable income
	10 Input-output analysis	A method of analysis concerned with the industry or interdepartmental flow of goods or services in the economy of a company and its markets. It shows what flows of inputs must occur to obtain certain outputs. Considerable effort must be expended to use these models properly, and additional detail not normally available must be obtained if they are to be applied to specific businesses	Fair	Good to very good	Very poor	Fair	Forecast of industry sales	Much data required on product or service flows which are normally outdated when available

Source: Based on Chambers *et al* (1974:63).

Of the many techniques available, we have discussed in this chapter only those that, according to practical surveys, seem to be most widely used. Table 20.11 gives a résumé of the techniques discussed above, indicating their accuracy, usefulness in identifying turning points, typical applications and the data required.

REFERENCES

Armstrong, J C 1978. *Long-range forecasting*. New York: Wiley.

Chambers, T C *et al* 1974. *An executive's guide to forecasting*. New York: Wiley.

Dalrymple, D J 1975. Sales forecasting methods and accuracy. *Business Horizons*, 18(6):71.

Drucker, P F 1955. Management science and the manager. *Management Science*, 1:121.

Ezekiel, M & Fox, R A 1959. *Methods of correlation analysis*. Third edition. New York: Wiley.

Juster, F T 1964. *Anticipations and purchases: an analysis of consumer behaviour*. Princetown: National Bureau of Economic Research.

Loubser, M 1990. *Income elasticities of the demand for consumer goods and services*. Pretoria: Unisa, Bureau of Market Research. (Research Report no 175.)

Nel, P A 1983. *Market potentials of consumer goods: methods of calculation and development of indices*. Pretoria: Unisa, Bureau of Market Research. (Research Report no 108.)

Schnaars, S P 1984. Situational factors affecting forecasting accuracy. *Journal of Marketing Research*, 21(3), August:290–297.

Tersine, R J & Riggs, W E 1976. The Delphi technique: a long range planning tool. *Business Horizons*, 19(2):53.

Researching regional markets

Chapter 21: Prof H de J van Wyk

Researching regional markets

1 INTRODUCTION

The spatial location of current and potential customers is important to most organisations.* Thus small organisations will want to know whether the customer base in the area where they propose to locate is sufficiently large to ensure profitability, while large organisations with countrywide markets have to determine the regional distribution of their existing and potential customers and suppliers. Large organisations find that the need becomes greater as the physical distance between them and their customers increases, as in South Africa, yet regional marketing research is a much neglected topic in local and international literature.

2 THE MEANING OF REGIONAL MARKETING RESEARCH

> **Regional marketing research** is defined as establishing the characteristics of a geographical area or areas smaller than the whole in order to establish its/their absolute and relative historic, current and future importance in relation to the marketing plan.

According to this definition, regional marketing research can be conducted across national and international boundaries. Because of rapid advances in transport and communication and the promotion of free trade, the world is increasingly becoming one large international market. In this context regional marketing research may be seen, for example, as the study of the market and other characteristics of a country or group of countries in relation to the total world market, or of South Africa as part of sub-Saharan Africa. There is also a growing need to study the South African market in conjunction with the markets of neighbouring countries, particularly those which belong to the Southern African Customs Union. (The question of regions will be considered in section 4.2.)

---

* Gold mines are a typical exception, since they are location-bound and their products are not distributed regionally.

The definition also indicates that regional marketing research can have different dimensions. It may concentrate on a single geographical area or on several geographical areas encompassing part of the overall area, or the whole of it. Measurement of characteristics may be either absolute or relative: the absolute sizes of characteristics may be established, or one can determine their importance relative to those of other regions or of all the regions combined. In addition the time dimension can be historical, present or future.

All these aspects will be examined in the sections that follow. In the regional dimension the accent will be mainly on regional research in the national context of South Africa. This means that we shall concentrate on the problems of researching 'open' areas, that is areas where there is a free flow of people and goods across borders.

3 THE NEED FOR REGIONAL RESEARCH AND ITS PLACE IN THE ORGANISATION

From what we have said it is evident that regional marketing research plays an important role in an organisation striving for maximum profit. Before a market-oriented organisation decides to locate in an area, it needs to determine, for instance, whether the demand for its product or service is great enough to justify locating there. The same applies when a market-oriented organisation has to decide whether to withdraw from a particular region: is the reason for its poor performance that the market is too small, or is the existing market not being fully exploited? The only way to determine the reason for an enterprise's poor performance in a particular region is to conduct marketing research.

This applies to an even greater extent to foot-loose organisations (a characteristic possessed to a greater or lesser degree by most types of manufacturing enterprises) and even to raw material-oriented organisations that have a choice of sources of raw material.

Most organisations, however, are already established in a particular locality and will use regional marketing research to optimise their spatial marketing effort. To such organisations it is a matter of exploiting regional markets effectively and of establishing whether market penetration in certain geographical areas is satisfactory. If it is not, they need to determine what management decisions should be taken to reach a satisfactory level.

Clearly, then, regional marketing research provides essential information for management decisions in virtually all organisations. This raises the question of where to locate the regional marketing research function of the organisation. Since it obviously has to be integral to the overall marketing function, the same considerations apply as in the discussion of the place of the marketing research function in the organisation. (Readers are referred to chapter 2, section 2.)

4 DEMARCATION OF REGIONS

In this section we deal first with general considerations in the demarcation of regions and then turn to the regional system used in South Africa. Finally we discuss the requirements that an organisation's own regional system has to meet.

4.1 General considerations in the demarcation of regions

A region, as defined in this book, denotes a geographical unit smaller than the country (national unit) in which it is situated. A region may consist of several subregions or areas* and/or it may be part of a larger region. Both smaller and larger regions and areas have advantages and disadvantages. In smaller regions or areas it may be easier to identify certain tendencies that would not be observed in larger regions. Marketers may need smaller areas when their marketing areas are small, as in the case of a greengrocer. If necessary, smaller areas are easily combined to form a larger region whose boundaries are readily adjusted to meet the needs of the information-seeker. One of the disadvantages of smaller areas is the tendency to lose sight of their connection with the larger whole, especially when coverage is restricted to selected areas. A further disadvantage of small areas is that the number of observations may be so small as to make it impossible to publish statistics without revealing information about individual respondents. This is, in fact, forbidden by law in official census data (SA 1976). The Central Statistical Service (CSS) makes it a rule not to publish data about areas with fewer than four respondents or about areas where the activities of only one or two respondents represent the larger share of the activity. Likewise, non-official bodies conducting surveys usually give assurances about the confidentiality of the data gathered from respondents to ensure their participation in the survey. The CSS publishes hardly any information, except population census data, about areas smaller than magisterial districts. Population census data are usually published for towns and rural areas within magisterial districts, although unpublished population statistics are also available for the so-called enumerators' areas (EAs).

Despite all the disadvantages of magisterial districts, their boundaries should be taken into account when demarcating regions because they are the cornerstones of official statistics in South Africa. Magisterial districts can be subdivided into smaller areas or combined to form larger ones. The way in which this is done is discussed in section 4.2.

4.2 Regions in South Africa

According to the regional system of the CSS, every magisterial district comprises the towns or cities within its area of jurisdiction, plus a non-urban area (where applicable). A number

---

* The units into which a region is divided are sometimes termed 'areas'.

of districts (usually five or six) together constitute a statistical region, while statistical regions in their turn are combined to form larger regions. Formerly these larger regions – altogether nine of them – were called developmental regions, which were the basis of development planning. With some noteworthy exceptions the boundaries of these developmental regions are also those of the nine provinces of the country. Because of certain federal features of the constitution, various functions were devolved to provincial level. The provinces, however, are political entities that do not always take account of economic realities. Where necessary, however, researchers can demarcate regions that deviate from the provinces. Apart from the problem raised above, the CSS regional system does not include neighbouring countries such as Lesotho. Marketing researchers, on the other hand, might prefer to combine Lesotho and the Free State in a single region since they are interdependent, both economically and from a marketing point of view.

4.3 Demarcation of regions for use in the organisation

To conduct regional marketing research it is necessary to develop a regional system for the organisation. The first requirement is that such a system should fit in with the organisation's activities. The regions identified should not be so large that certain trends and ratios are lost; neither should they be so small as to clutter the organisation's marketing information system (MIS), of which they must be an integral part. By and large one could say that the smallest component of the regional system should be too small rather than too big, since it is easy to combine small areas into a larger whole. The question is: to what extent should the regional system used in marketing research conform to regions used by other sections of the organisation? The two types of regions must obviously be comparable. But the demarcation of such regions as sales regions is often based on historical considerations that do not necessarily apply today. Determining what regions are most appropriate for an organisation is a research project in its own right, to which end the marketing researcher would use external and internal secondary data (for example total market sales and sales by the organisation in particular regions). A new regional system for use by all sections of an organisation can be instituted only after intra-organisational consultation in which the needs (and prejudices) of all sections are discussed.

A second requirement that an organisation's regional system has to meet is that it should be reconcilable with other regional systems, notably those of official bodies such as the CSS. This means that the areas demarcated should be reconcilable with magisterial districts and/or statistical regions. Smaller areas should therefore serve as components to constitute districts. Large regions, in their turn, should be composed of districts. As mentioned above, it is sometimes advisable to ignore international boundaries and include neighbouring countries in the regional system.

5 REGIONAL INFORMATION

No decision on spatial settlement or spatial marketing will be meaningful unless it is based on regional information. This section deals with the sources and collection of such information, with the accent on statistical data.

5.1 Secondary regional information

All the characteristics of secondary information discussed in chapter 6 apply equally to regional secondary information. We now deal with specific aspects of internal and external regional information.

5.1.1 Internal secondary information

Any organisation that has some kind of spatial marketing effort must ensure that its internal information has a spatial dimension. In section 4.3 the need for a regional system was emphasised, while chapter 6, section 3.1 dealt with the assignment of regional codes to internal information. Such codes facilitate the integration of internal regional information with the organisation's MIS. The best way of regionalising internal information is to assign regional codes to all trade documents and then feed these into the database along with other data. This makes it possible to analyse sales, purchases, debtors and the like on a regional basis. In this way the regional distribution of the organisation's activities can be analysed. Comparison of this information with external secondary statistics (see section 5.1.2) makes it possible to determine the organisation's regional strengths and weaknesses.

5.1.2 External secondary information

External secondary information and its sources were discussed in chapter 6. The main sources of secondary statistics, namely population and sectoral censuses, are also a major source of regional information. We have mentioned lack of recency as a drawback of census data. Thus population censuses are conducted every five years and it takes at least a year before the data are released, with the result that available population data may be more than six years old. In sectoral censuses whose data are collected by postal surveys, the time lag before the results are released is even longer. The release of data, especially in a regional context, is moreover restricted by the Statistics Act. In practice this means that if there is only one or very few organisations of a particular kind in an area or region, the data are combined with those of other areas or regions. This also applies when one organisation is exceptionally big pro rata to other organisations of the same kind. That is why no district-based data on the mining industry are published; nor are data on the steel industry in Newcastle, because of the dominance of Iscor in that district.

When one looks for alternatives to censuses as data sources, one finds that in South Africa there is very little information suitable for interregional comparison. Such data as are available include the results of ad hoc surveys by urban and regional planners and data collected by city councils in the course of their activities. These data vary from one area to the next in terms of recency, comprehensiveness and quality, which complicates regional comparison. Some data, however, are exact and permit regional comparisons, for instance the water and electricity prices charged by local authorities. If the research department is investigating only one area and there is no need for interregional comparisons, it can conduct a search for secondary information in the particular area. In such a search local authorities will play a major role, although these data, like all secondary data, have to be evaluated. City councils in particular tend to depict their area in unrealistically rosy colours, often unwittingly but sometimes intentionally.

5.2 Primary surveys

The dearth of recent regional secondary statistics compels researchers to consider undertaking primary surveys. As a rule primary surveys of the population are not problematic and are made according to the same principles as countrywide surveys in sampling, etc. When economic activities need to be measured from the point of view of an enterprise, however, the number of actors is frequently so small that sampling can give rise to major errors, particularly when the 80:20 principle is applied (see chapter 13). Often, therefore, censuses have to be conducted, which pushes up costs. In censuses, refusals and defective address lists can lead to serious errors, particularly in refusals or the omission of one or more large organisations. As a result great care should be taken when compiling address lists and conducting the survey, which again pushes up costs. These problems account for the scarcity of quality regional secondary data: often funds for surveys are simply not available.

6 MEASUREMENT OF THE SIZE OF AND CHANGES IN REGIONAL MARKETS

This section deals with the measurement of historical and current sizes and correlations; the problems of forecasting are considered in section 7. Although the principles are the same, differences between the consumer market and the industrial market (see chapter 19) demand different approaches when it comes to regional research. It should be remembered, however, that (as explained in chapter 19) products such as sugar are marketed on both the consumer and the industrial markets. In practice, organisations marketing such products will study both markets in the regional context.

6.1 Regional market potentials for the consumer market

> **Regional market potentials** are defined as the absolute or relative ability of a region or regions to offer a market for products and services generally, or for a particular product or service.

There are two types of regional market potentials, the one absolute, the other relative.

6.1.1 Absolute market potentials for one or more areas

> An **absolute regional market potential** is the size of the market in a particular region or regions, expressed in value for all products or a group of products, or in units or value for a particular product.

The size of the market can be expressed in units only if the product is homogeneous. One can use the example of the motor vehicle market. There is no point in comparing the total motor vehicle market in terms of units, since there are major differences between light cars and heavy trucks, both in terms of unit price and the purposes for which they are used. An enterprise which wanted to establish a garage in an area to sell cars and commercial vehicles would do better to determine the *value* of the total market. But if it planned to sell only twin-cab pickups with six-cylinder engines, it would be interested in the number of twin-cab pickups sold (that is the number of units). Note that the product need not be absolutely homogeneous: the enterprise in the example cited above would be interested not just in twin-cab pickups with six-cylinder engines but in all twin-cab pickups, since four-cylinder and six-cylinder twin-cab pickups can be used as substitutes. When calculating the total market for all products, one would use a unit that measures total buying power, such as total personal disposable income, total expenditure, or in some instances, the total population or the total number of households.

From the discussion so far it would seem that there is little difference in the method used and problems encountered in the calculation of national and regional absolute market potentials. There are, however, two major complications in the calculation of regional absolute market potentials. In the first place, regional data on sales/consumption are much more scarce than national data (this problem was mentioned earlier in section 5.1.2). Of course, the problem can be overcome by conducting primary surveys, but if funding and time do not permit this, one often has to make do with national data or data on other areas, which are then applied to the region on which information is required. For example, in 1993 Martins (1994:18) measured the market potential of some 550 products according to population group for various types of areas, such as metropolitan areas.* He writes:

> Marketers who need figures for smaller areas than the country as a whole or the study areas can make their own calculations of market potentials for magisterial districts or cities or towns from the figures in this report. As a starting point they would have to ascertain the ratio of the respective population groups in the area concerned to the total population of the region in which the area concerned is located. Next expenditure in the area concerned would be calculated in total, and/or for a main expenditure group(s) and/or for an expenditure item(s) by using population as an indicator in the ratio of the population groups represented in the larger region. Adjustments might be necessary for differences in income levels and/or specific circumstances between the area concerned and the region as a whole.

The last sentence implies that information such as differences in income levels has to be available. Such data, however, are frequently either completely unavailable or not available in the required format, in which case assumptions have to be made. As a result, the calculation of absolute market potentials for regions on which no data are available is often subject to major errors.

Secondly, subnational regions are 'open' regions in which people and goods flow freely across regional borders. The smaller the region, the greater the possibility that this flow of people and goods may be significant. Where this flow is controlled, as in flow across national boundaries, inhabitants within the national boundaries on the whole are a captive market and the number of people from across the border who undertake expenditure in the country is relatively insignificant. Total expenditure is therefore much easier to calculate than for 'open' regions. There are three main types of areas that experience heavy flow of people and goods across their boundaries:

☐ Areas in which the number of people within their boundaries varies in the course of one day. This phenomenon occurs mainly in metropolitan areas which contain areas known as dormitory towns and in predominantly industrial and business areas. Examples are Soweto and the Johannesburg CBD, since a large proportion of Sowetans commute to work in the Johannesburg CBD every day. This commuting has certain implications for marketers. Should sales outlets be established at place of work or place of abode? Do people prefer to have their bank accounts near their workplaces or near their homes? Surveys to determine this type of consumer behaviour and data on the

---

* These calculations were based on income and expenditure surveys.

origin and destination of commuters can be used to estimate 'day' and 'night' population.* It must be remembered that in South Africa population census data are based on the place where people slept on the night of the census. Outward commuting weakens the market in an area, while inward commuting has the opposite effect.

☐ Areas in which the number of people within their boundaries varies seasonally. Here one can distinguish between two types of people:

– seasonal workers from outside the area, mainly in agriculture and fishing, but also workers who are employed at holiday resorts

– holidaymakers: any area which contains holiday resorts has considerable seasonal variation in population, although there is always a minimum number of holiday-makers.

☐ In areas which are crossed by major roads there are villages with large filling stations. Only a small proportion of their fuel sales will be sourced from local motor vehicle owners and they would be wiser to use traffic counts to determine market potential.

We mentioned above that the smaller the area (in terms of surface and/or economic activity), the more 'open' it is. In a study of the Johannesburg district as a whole, the effect of commuting is substantially less than in separate studies of the Johannesburg CBD and Soweto, since both these areas are situated in the Johannesburg district. If one studies the effect of commuting on the entire metropolitan area, the commuter effect is usually negligibly small.** Usually very small areas are impractical for purposes of analysis because of their 'open' boundaries. Thus few of the inhabitants of an enumerator's area (EA), that is the smallest area for which population data are available (in urban areas comprising a number of street blocks), work in that EA and most of the establishments settled in that EA draw their clients from a much larger area.

6.1.2 Relative market potentials

> A **relative regional market potential** is the size, quality or growth of the market expressed in relation to those of other areas.

From the definition it follows that at least two regions have to be involved, since the aim of relative market potential calculations is to compare two or more markets. We now consider the various methods of calculating relative market potentials and the different types of relative market potentials.

---

* In South Africa this type of data is hard to come by.

** Of course, this depends on how the metropolitan area is defined. The PWV area as defined by Developmental Region was economically better integrated than Gauteng. In Gauteng there is large-scale commuting to and from surrounding districts such as Sasolburg, Brits and Moretele, which are located in other provinces.

6.1.2.1 Direct method

The direct method of calculating relative market potentials merely entails proportionate representation of the results of absolute market potential calculations.

6.1.2.2 Indirect method

The **indirect method of relative market** potential calculation entails searching for, selecting and combining indicators of the relative size and quality of regional markets, as well as changes in these markets.

The indirect method is used mainly when absolute market potentials cannot be calculated for lack of data. The search for, choice and combination of indicators will now be discussed under the various types of indirect indices.

6.1.2.2.1 General market potential indices

A **general market potential index** is a relative index compiled in order to measure the general ability of a region or area to absorb goods and services.

General market potential indices, also known as purchasing power indices, are used in several countries.* As the definition indicates, this is a general index to measure buying power and spending in a region or an area. Consequently these two components – buying power and spending – have to be covered by the choice of indicators. The nature and number of indicators required and their combination will now be discussed.

(a) Search for and choice of indicators

We have mentioned that recent regional data are scarce. This applies particularly when one wants to calculate indices for small geographical areas such as districts. The only two statistical series that are readily available on a district basis are population figures and personal disposable income.** In population figures, population censuses are the best-known source of district statistics. They not only give population numbers but also provide information on attributes of that population, such as age, type of economic activity, occupation and income. However, as pointed out previously, the most recent population census statistics can be up to six years old. To alleviate the problem, the Bureau

---

  * These indices are in fact simply the percentage share of a region in the national total.
 ** Nel (1968:95) defines personal income as: 'current income earned or received from all sources by the inhabitants of an area, including transfers from government bodies, businesses and persons living in other areas, but excluding transfers between persons living in the same area. Personal disposable income = personal income less direct taxes (chiefly income tax).'

of Market Research (BMR) uses indicators to adapt the number of people per population group in the population census in order to estimate population figures for post-census years. The BMR also calculates personal disposable income by district (that is personal income minus direct taxes – mainly income tax) on a five-year basis. Both population and personal disposable income are measured at the population's place of abode and indicators have to be found that measure activities at the point of purchase. Retail sales have the advantages that they are measured at the point of purchase and that they measure actual expenditure (also called willingness to spend), whether financed from personal disposable income, loans or savings. Unfortunately recent retail sales statistics per district in South Africa are not yet available. In addition, retail sales statistics do not include sales in the informal sector, which vary in importance from one area to another. The CSS does publish regional retail sales statistics obtained from sample surveys. All a researcher can do is assume that districts in the region have changed by the same percentage since the last regional census – an assumption that does not necessarily hold water. Another series that offers possibilities is the Regional Services Councils' (RSC)* levy statistics on turnover per district, which is published by the CSS. Unfortunately these are not strictly district statistics, since organisations with branches in several districts within the same RSC area have to submit only one return. Thus all statistics are allocated to the district in which the head office or regional office is situated.

From this discussion it would seem that personal disposable income data occupy an important place in an area's market potential indices. Retail sales, adjusted for recent years as explained above, and RSC levy statistics on turnover can also be considered. Before we proceed to discuss the combination of indices below, we might mention that the age of statistics has an adverse effect only in as much as disproportionate changes have occurred since the compilation of the statistics, for only then would the relative index (or percentage share) of regions change.

(b) Combination of indices in a single index

Indices can be combined simply by adding them together.** In actual fact this means assigning the same weight to all indices. In most instances, however, the indices are not considered equally important for the compilation of the regional market potential indices and consequently different weights are assigned. These weights can be determined by correlation and regression analyses (Nel 1983:43) or by reasoning. Normally personal disposable income will be assigned a heavier weight than population, since buying power is the principal determinant of a market's absorption capacity. It should also be borne in mind that the size of the population already influences the amount of personal disposable income: usually one finds that the larger the population, the greater the economic activity and the transfer payments.

---

* At the time of writing, other bodies were taking over the function of the RSC.
** Another method, the product method, entails multiplying indices by one another. It is rarely used for general market potential indices, being reserved for exceptional instances of specific indices.

For reasons already given, retail sales should also be assigned a large weight, although in South Africa the usefulness of this series is restricted by the lack of reliable recent statistics and it is therefore not given a large weight.

The following equation is used to calculate market potential indices by weighting the respective statistical series according to their relative influence on consumption:

$$M = \frac{PG_p + IG_i + SG_s}{\Sigma G}$$

where

M = market potential index of a region

P = statistical series representing consumer units expressed as a percentage of the national total

I = statistical series representing ability to spend expressed as a percentage of the national total

S = statistical series representing willingness to spend expressed as a percentage of the national total

G = weights reflecting the relative importance of each series in the consumption of the product concerned.

The application of this formula is indicated in the hypothesised example (table 21.1).

In this example the indices of the population were multiplied by a weight of 1, personal disposable income by 6 and retail sales by 4. The total of the results obtained was divided by 11 (the total of the weights) to determine the general market potential index for each region.

6.1.2.2.2 Specific market potential indices

A **specific market potential index** is a relative index designed to measure the regional market's capacity to absorb a specific product or service.

Like general market potential indices, specific indices for a district or region are also expressed as a percentage of the national or, in some instances, the regional total.

Obviously one can calculate literally thousands of specific market potential indices. To calculate a specific market potential index effectively, the researcher needs to be intimately acquainted with the consumer patterns of the population relating to the particular product or service.

Table 21.1 General market potential indices by region, 19xx

District	Population		Personal disposable income			Retail sales			Total	General index
	Number	Index × Weight = Weighted index (a)	Income (Rm)	Index × Weight = Weighted index (b)		Value	Index × Weight = Weighted index (c)		(a) + (b) + (c)	
A	10 000	21,73 × 1 = 21,73	20 000	20,00 × 6 = 120,00		15 000	16,67 × 4 = 66,68		208,41	18,95
B	20 000	43,49 × 1 = 43,49	50 000	50,00 × 6 = 300,00		50 000	55,56 × 4 = 222,24		565,73	51,43
C	15 000	32,61 × 1 = 32,61	24 000	24,00 × 6 = 144,00		22 000	24,44 × 4 = 97,76		274,37	24,94
D	1 000	2,17 × 1 = 2,17	6 000	6,00 × 6 = 36,00		3 000	3,33 × 4 = 13,32		51,49	4,68
Total	46 000	100,00 × 1 = 100,00	100 000	100,00 × 6 = 600,00		90 000	100,00 × 4 = 400,00		1 100,00	100,00

Two questions have to be asked: who consumes the product or service, and how much do they consume? If these questions can be answered on a regional basis, the researcher would preferably calculate absolute market potentials. However, such data are usually available only at a national level and the researcher has to assume that they apply regionally as well. The calculation of specific market potential indices is best illustrated by an example.

Suppose a manufacturer of luxury cars wants to compile a specific regional market potential index. A national survey conducted in 1994 established that only people with an income of R150 000+ buy luxury cars. It was also found that in the income group R150 000–R209 999, two out of every 10 (20 %) had bought luxury cars during the past five years; the percentage for the income group R210 000+ was 40 %. Regional data on the population according to income group are available from the 1991 population census. From the change in the consumer price index it is determined that R100 000 had the same buying power in 1991 as R150 000 in 1994. Hence the equivalent of R209 999 in 1994 was R139 999 in 1991. By multiplying the number of people in the income group R100 000–R139 999 in each district, according to the population census, by a weight of 1, and those in the income group R140 000+ by 2 (the latter group has a consumption tendency of 40 %, as opposed to the first group's 20 %), and repeating the process with the national totals, a specific index can be compiled (table 21.2).

Table 21.2 Specific regional market potential indices for luxury cars by region, according to place of residence of owner, 19xx

District	Income group R150 000–R209 999				Income group R210 000 +				Total	Index
	No* × weight = product (a)				No* × weight = product (b)				(a) + (b)	%
A	100 ×	1	=	100	120 ×	2	=	240	340	13,38
B	200 ×	1	=	200	50 ×	2	=	100	300	11,81
C	700 ×	1	=	700	400 ×	2	=	800	1 500	59,06
D	300 ×	1	=	300	50 ×	2	=	100	400	15,75
Total	1 300 ×	1	= 1 300		620 ×	2	= 1 240		2 540	100,00

*Number of consumer units.

It would also be advisable to compile an index of regional retail sales of luxury cars and compare the two indices. Deviations can occur because people in metropolitan areas may not buy cars in their residential areas (remember, population censuses are taken according to place of abode) but prefer to buy them in the district in which they are economically active. According to the survey cited above, 75 % bought their cars in their residential district and 25 % in the district where they worked. This gives us weights of 3 and 1 respectively for the two indices.* The calculation is illustrated in table 21.3.

In the example above, the specific index obtained in table 21.2 has been multiplied by a weight of 3 as 75 % of the owners of luxury cars prefer to buy the cars at their places of residence. The index of retail sales has been multiplied by a weight of 1 as 25 % of owners prefer to buy their cars in districts where they are economically active. The indices should be weighted when the series to be combined are different. In Table 21.2 'No.' refers in both cases to the number of people and may be combined direct. This has the advantage of taking into account the relative size of the two populations.

Table 21.3 Specific regional marketing potential indices for luxury cars by region, according to regional purchasing preferences of buyers, 19xx

District	Specific index* × weight = product	Retail sales of luxury cars					Total	Combined index
		Number	index	× weight	=	product/index		
A	13,38 × 3 = 40,14	200	20,00	× 1	=	20,00	60,14	15,04
B	11,81 × 3 = 35,43	200	20,00	× 1	=	20,00	55,43	13,86
C	59,06 × 3 = 177,18	500	50,00	× 1	=	50,00	227,18	56,80
D	15,75 × 3 = 47,25	100	10,00	× 1	=	10,00	57,25	14,30
Total	100,00 × 3 = 300,00	1 000	100,00	× 1	=	100,00	400,00	100,00

* Specific index according to place of residence carried over from table 21.2.

6.1.2.2.3 Quality and growth indices

Quality and growth indices differ from the previous indices in the sense that they cannot be added together to arrive at a total. These indices are ratios which are expressed pro rata to the national index, the latter always equalling 100.

(1) *Growth indices* are measures of relative growth. The following formula is applied:

$$n = \frac{[xt \div x(t-1)]}{[yt \div y(t-1)]} \times \frac{100}{1}$$

where n = index

x = sales per district/region per period

y = national sales in the corresponding period.

The national growth index = 100. Thus an index figure above the average (>100) indicates better than average and a figure below the average (<100) indicates below the average growth in sales.

---

* Of course, purchases outside residential and work districts could also occur, but it is usually assumed that these cancel out between areas.

The application of growth indices is illustrated in table 21.4.

Table 21.4 Growth indices of retail sales by region and product group

Region	Value 1993 R million	% Share in total 1993	Growth indices				
			Average index	1992–1993	1991–1992	1990–1991	1989–1990
Total RSA	35 211,8	100,0	100,0	100,0	100,0	100,0	100,0
Total Cape Province	11 670,7	33,1	102,9	99,6	105,7	102,7	103,4
Peninsula	4 145,2	11,8	100,8	96,6	102,3	101,9	102,4
Boland	1 108,3	3,1	94,5	94,6	96,6	87,0	99,6
PE-Uitenhage	1 227,9	3,5	104,5	95,7	102,2	114,1	105,8
EL-KWT	847,4	2,4	104,9	93,7	123,9	83,5	118,5
Kimberley	330,8	0,9	100,6	104,5	92,5	135,9	69,5
Rest of Cape	4 011,1	11,4	108,6	106,8	111,9	109,4	106,1

According to the table, the Cape Peninsula had an index of 102,3 in 1991–92, which is 2,3 % above the average. The index for the Boland region, 96,6, was 3,4 % below the average.

(2) *Quality indices*, as the name implies, indicate market quality in terms, for instance, of average buying power. An example is disposable income per capita indices, obtained by dividing total regional personal disposable income by the regional population and comparing it with the result of a similar calculation for the country as a whole.* High per capita income (hence a high index) in a region or district indicates that inhabitants on average have incomes higher than those of the inhabitants of the country as a whole and therefore should be better able to afford luxury goods. Table 21.5 gives an example of quality indices.

According to the table, coloureds in the Western Cape had an income per capita of 3 % above the average in 1990 and in the Northern Province their income per capita was 43 % below the average (index of 57).

---

* The formula is $n = \dfrac{[yt \div xt]}{[Yt \div Xt]} \times \dfrac{100}{1}$ where

n = index
y = total income in region for period
x = total population in region for period
Y = national income for period
X = national population for period

Table 21.5 Indices of personal disposable income per head of the population by population group and province, 1985, 1990 and 1994

Province	Asians			Blacks			Coloureds			Whites			Total		
	1985	1990	1994	1985	1990	1994	1985	1990	1994	1985	1990	1994	1985	1990	1994
Total South Africa	100	100	100	100	100	100	100	100	100	100	100	100	100	100	100
Western Cape	150	123	109	167	162	179	102	103	100	100	102	100	164	167	168
Northern Cape	160	121	115	133	133	138	62	57	53	96	95	84	111	109	103
Eastern Cape	165	164	170	58	64	60	92	89	82	100	91	82	53	55	51
Free State	1 652	227	179	107	109	112	70	76	78	96	94	90	95	96	96
KwaZulu-Natal	91	89	87	81	78	76	127	133	153	99	99	97	77	73	72
Mpumalanga	127	137	145	93	96	97	128	142	172	92	92	89	78	80	81
Northern Province	155	165	171	47	48	44	126	128	127	89	88	79	31	33	30
Gauteng	136	145	153	239	235	254	152	150	175	104	106	112	208	209	225
North-West	126	127	128	91	88	79	69	75	89	91	88	82	69	68	62

It should be noted, however, that such averages can be misleading: a district or region may have a low quality index because of a large low income group even though there is a significant group of high income residents. Consequently quality indices should not be used in isolation; the distribution of the population according to income groups (obtained from the population census) must also be checked.

These two indices have two general drawbacks. First, they always have to be discussed in conjunction with importance indices such as specific market potential indices, since relative importance puts them in perspective. An area with a quality index of 200 but with only a 0,001 % share in the total personal disposable income is still unimportant. In addition it is easier to maintain a high growth rate from a small base than from a large one. For example, 10 houses added to 100 existing houses in a village represent 10 % growth, whereas in a town with 10 000 existing houses they represent only 0,1 % growth. Second, because of the nature of their composition these indices tend to be unstable on a regional basis (consider the example of the houses cited above; in the case of quality indices for instance errors in both personal disposable income and the population may make the indices unstable).*

6.2 Regional market potentials for the industrial market

As mentioned already, the principles here are the same as for the consumer market. In this section we merely refer briefly to some aspects of the industrial market that influence the calculation of regional market potentials.

---

* It is advisable, therefore, to measure growth and quality on the basis of three-year weighted averages. These weighted averages are discussed in chapter 4 on the South African market.

6.2.1 Absolute market potentials for one or more areas

The various sectoral censuses are a major source of information when calculating absolute market potentials, since they frequently indicate the source of inputs and destination of outputs (in terms of type of organisation). These data may be used in the compilation of regional input-output tables.* If the geographical origin of inputs and the geographical destination of outputs are known, one can compile interregional input-output tables** as well. Regional and interregional input-output tables indicate the structure of a region or regions and thus contain illuminating information for determining absolute market potentials.

Absolute market potentials can also be calculated by using an indirect method, as illustrated by the following hypothetical example. Suppose a distributor of alternators wants to appoint 10 wholesalers to distribute his products to car and spares dealers and fleet owners (that is the replacement market). From experience he knows the following: on average a car alternator lasts 10 years; in a commercial vehicle it lasts five years; and in tractors two years. The distributor's wholesale prices are as follows: car alternators cost R500 and those for commercial vehicles and tractors cost R1 000. The distributor wants to offer all of the ten wholesalers equally sized markets, indicating to each what the absolute size of that market will be. He proceeds as follows. From secondary sources (CSS) he can obtain the number of cars, commercial vehicles and tractors per district and according to age. Cars aged 10 and 20 years, trucks aged 5, 10, 15 and 20 years, and tractors aged 2, 4, 6, 8, 10, 12, 14, 16, 18 and 20 years will need alternators. Thus it is easy to determine how many vehicles from each category are involved. By multiplying the number of cars by R500 and the number of commercial vehicles and tractors by R1 000 the total absolute market potential can be calculated for each district. By combining districts into regions ten markets of equal value can be created.

6.2.2 Relative market potentials

6.2.2.1 Direct method

The calculation of equal shares for the wholesalers in 6.2.1 above implies calculation of relative market potential indices for each district. Since the market potentials were used as they stood, a direct method was used.

---

* A regional input-output table is usually of the same format as national input-output tables. For a discussion of national input-output tables see chapter 20.

** The use of these tables is outlined in section 7.

6.2.2.2 Indirect method

Here the principles are much the same as for the consumer market. However, enterprises are much more heterogeneous than the members of the consumer market. This heterogeneity has to be allowed for by classifying enterprises according to the Standard Industrial Classification (SIC) and weighting them accordingly (see chapter 19).

7 REGIONAL FORECASTS

Forecasting is dealt with in chapter 20. The question is: how do regional forecasts differ from national ones? There are two main differences. First, because of their 'open' boundaries, areas in the same vicinity influence each other greatly. Second, because of the relatively small number of role players in an area compared with the country as a whole, changes in the activity of one role player can have a considerable impact on general activity in the area. There are examples in South Africa where the closure of a mine or a power station turned towns in the vicinity into virtual ghost towns overnight. But there are also instances, such as Sasolburg, Welkom and Virginia, where new towns mushroomed because of activities that settled in an area. These two differences mean that regional forecasts are subject to far greater errors than national forecasts.

Bearing in mind what has been said so far, we now turn to the various methods that can be used in regional forecasting. Although they are general methods to forecast economic progress, they can also be used to determine the size of the future market, since market changes and economic change go hand in hand. Thus the methods explained below can be used to forecast future job opportunities, population, gross geographical product and personal available income – all entities that can be used to measure the size of the market. Market researchers also need to be acquainted with these methods in order to evaluate any external secondary research that results in forecasts.

Starting with input-output tables, the discussion moves on to economic base and multiplier studies, interregional linear programming, comparative cost studies, industrial complex analyses and the so-called shift-share analyses.

7.1 Input-output tables

The first input-output tables were drawn up by Leontief in 1951 for the USA (Leontief 1951). The first attempt at compiling input-output tables for regions was made shortly afterwards (Moses 1955).

Two types of subnational input-output tables are distinguished: regional and interregional input-output tables. The regional tables were developed first, mainly because their compilation required less data.

7.1.1 Regional input-output tables

Figure 21.1 is an example of a regional input-output table. Regional and national tables are compiled in similar fashion, with inputs and outputs referring to industries within the boundaries of the area and final demand referring to consumption expenditure and general government in the area. Imports and exports cross the boundaries of the area. Further, the sum of each row is equal to the sum of the corresponding column.

Regional input-output tables are compiled in most of the developed countries of the world. However, their main use is in *ad hoc* studies, some of which are continued over long periods (Catterji 1964:93). The size of the study areas varies from one study to the next.

The following information is required to compile a regional input-output table:

(a) *Inverse and direct input quotients**

Inverse quotients may be defined as the outputs required by a specific industry for each increase of R1 in final demand. Because the various industries are interdependent, a change in final demand has a multiplier effect which is reflected in the inverse quotient. Inverse quotients are calculated with direct input quotients as a base. Direct input quotients may be defined as the inputs required by each industry for each R1 output of the industry mentioned at the top of the column. All the direct input quotients in a column add up to 1.

Direct input and inverse quotients for a specific area are usually calculated in surveys which gather information on the geographic origin of the inputs for each sector of production. Information on outputs and their geographic destination is collected in the same manner.

(b) *Value of final demand*

The value of the components of final demand is not set forth in the input-output table and is determined exogenously (Isard 1967:218).

An input-output table can be compiled for a specific period if the outputs of the respective production sectors, the value of the components of final demand and the direct input quotients of an area are known. However, several assumptions have to be made when input-output tables are applied in forecasting. First, the future value of the components of final demand has to be estimated. Second, it is usually assumed that the inverse quotient remains constant: in other words, no changes are made for substitution and relative price changes. This also implies that import quotients will remain constant.

7.1.2 Interregional input-output tables

The second type of subnational input-output table, the interregional table, is characterised by the combination of information on various regions in one table. The framework of a table of this kind for three regions is illustrated in figure 21.2 on page 512.

---

* Quotient – the result obtained when one amount is divided by another.

Figure 21.1 A condensed schematic presentation of a regional input-output table

Serial number	Industry number	The distribution of the output of an industry appears in the row for that industry / The composition of the inputs of an industry appears in the column for that industry	Intermediate demand from industries in region								Final demand in region						Total
			Agriculture, forestry and fishing	Mining and quarrying	Manufacturing	Electricity, gas and water	Construction	Wholesale and retail trade	Transport, storage and communication	Other services	Private consumption expenditure	Consumption expenditure by the general government	Gross domestic fixed capital formation	Changes in inventories	Exports of goods and non-factor services to other regions/countries	Less imports of goods and non-factor services from other regions/countries	
			1	2	3	4	5	6	7	8	9	10	11	12	13	14	15
1	1	Agriculture, forestry and fishing															
2	2	Mining and quarrying															
3	3	Manufacturing				Quadrant I							Quadrant II				
4	4	Electricity, gas and water															
5	5	Construction															
6	6	Wholesale and retail trade															
7	7	Transport, storage and communication															
8	8	Other services															
9		Remuneration of employees employed in region				Quadrant III							Quadrant IV				
10		Gross operating surplus of industries in region															
11		Net indirect taxes collected in region															
12		Total															

Inter-mediate inputs by industries in region

Primary inputs

Expenditure on gross geographic product*

Gross geographic product

*At market prices.

Source: Adapted from CSS, *Input-output tables 1978*, Report no 09–16–05.

Figure 21.2 Interregional input-output flow table 19xx*

		East			South			West		
	Industry purchasing									
Industry producing										
East	1 Agriculture and extraction									
	2 Food processing									
	9 Chemicals									
	21 Government									
South	1 Agriculture									
	2 Extraction									
	3 Food processing									
	9 Iron and steel									
	23 Government									
West	1 Agriculture and food processing									
	2 Extraction									
	9 Chemicals									
	21 Government									
	Total inputs									

Source: Adapted from CSS, *Input-output tables,* Report no 09–16–05.

Compared with the regional input-output table, this table has two advantages: first, it clearly indicates regional interdependence and the flow of goods and therefore reveals the effect of changes in one area on other areas. Constant interregional input quotients are assumed in interregional input-output tables used in forecasting. This means that changes in the value of the final demand sectors of any area are reflected in industries in that area and other areas in the same proportion as in the base year.

Regional and interregional input-output tables have the advantage that the economic interdependence within the area, and in the case of interregional tables, between areas, is represented in an orderly and logical fashion. Certain special characteristics of the economy are clearly evident and some of the missing information can be deduced from the table. In projections, the input-output tables have the advantage that the interdependence referred to earlier is constantly taken into account. However, as a forecasting instrument, the input-output table also has serious disadvantages. In the first instance, the large amount of information required is rarely available from secondary sources because it is not gathered or is not published in the required form (usually for reasons of secrecy). Such data therefore have to be gathered in surveys that are costly and time consuming because of the mass of information requested and the consequent low rate of response. Major problem areas are the origin of inputs and the destination of exports.

In the second instance, the projection of the components of final demand, which are determined exogenously, may present certain difficulties. Consumption expenditure, for example, depends on the size and composition of the population and its expenditure patterns, which in turn are determined mainly by income per head. Thus, the value of the components that are determined exogenously is determined to a greater or lesser extent by components whose value has to be determined from final demand and inverse quotients.

In the third instance, constant input quotients do not make for reliable forecasts. There are several reasons that input quotients may be expected to change over time. First, relative price changes occur over time, and technological changes cause substitution of inputs. Second, there may be changes in the so-called product mix. Only a limited number of sectors of production can be represented in an input-output table compared with the thousands of different goods produced in a modern economy. Thus, changes over time in the mix of a sector will affect the input quotients. Third, it is highly unlikely that both interregional quotients and import quotients will remain constant over time. Particularly in the case of smaller areas, it is also extremely difficult to determine future exports exogenously. The smaller the area and the stronger the links with other areas, the more easily changes occur because such factors as shorter distances, specialisation, and imperfections in the economic structure come into play. Input-output tables are therefore compiled for regions rather than for smaller areas (for example counties in the USA).

A further development of the input-output table is the social account matrix (SAM) (SA 1988:iii–vi).

> This development is of particular significance since the SAM provides a framework within the context of the national accounts in which the activities of households are accentuated and distinguished prominently. The household is indeed the basic unit where significant decisions are taken on important economic variables such as, *inter alia*, expenditure and saving. By combining households into meaningful groups the SAM makes it possible to clearly distinguish between, and study the effect, interaction and the economic welfare of each group.
>
> The development of the SAM, with the household as focus point, must also be seen in the light of the fact that conventional national accounts often do not provide sufficient information, and also no framework to properly investigate and address important policy issues regarding aspects such as income distribution, personal saving, employment, etc.
>
> In order to eliminate the above-mentioned shortcomings, provision is made for the SAM to show the activities of households in far greater detail than was the case in the past. Specific criteria are used to attain this level of detail, *inter alia*, population group, occupation and income group. By distinguishing and presenting those national accounts components that relate to the household sector, such as remuneration of employees (employment), private consumption expenditure and personal savings, according to the aforementioned criteria, a large variety of important information becomes available.

By estimating and forecasting certain attributes of households such as income and expenditure regionally, the impact of these on other entities such as employment can be determined and vice versa.

7.2 Economic base and multiplier studies

Although input-output tables largely took over, the economic base study is still applied in forecasting economic activity when input-output tables cannot be constructed for want of information.

> This method of analysis is based on the premise that the reason for existence and growth of a region, regardless of whether it is a small resource-dependent area or a large metropolitan city, lies in the goods and services it produces and sells beyond its borders. These 'basic' activities provide the means of payment for raw materials, food and manufactured products which the region does not produce itself. The basic activities also support the 'service' activities which are local in productive scope (Mahoney 1967:40).

It is evident from this that three requirements must be met by researchers who use this type of study for forecasting purposes. First, the economic base of the area must be identified. One of the best-known methods of doing this involves location quotients. Isard describes location quotients as follows:

> It is a device for comparing a region's percentage share of a particular activity with its percentage share of some basic aggregate. The location quotient for industry i in the given state is
>
> $$\frac{Si/Ni}{S/N} \text{ or } \frac{Si/S}{Ni/N}$$
>
> where Si = number of wage earners in manufacturing industry i in a general state
>
> S = number of wage earners in all manufacturing industry in the same state
>
> Ni = number of wage earners in all manufacturing industry i in the nation
>
> N = number of wage earners in all manufacturing industry in the nation (Isard 1967:330).

Second, the economic activity of basic industries must be projected into the future. Such projections may be based on extrapolation, shift-share techniques, or surveys of development potential.

Third, the researcher must determine the ratio between basic and all other activities. The ratio between total economic activities and basic activities is called the regional multiplier, which may be determined by several methods. In one of these methods, the ratio is determined by employment or input-output surveys. A second method calls for the calculation of the volume of basic activities by location quotients or input-output frameworks, deducting the result from the volume of total activities and regarding the balance as non-basic activities. In this instance, it is assumed either that the ratio between basic and total activities remains constant if the proportions of basic activities changes, or that the ratio between the changes in basic and total activities remains constant.

The economic base method of forecasting has the advantages of being fairly simple (although refinements are possible) and of requiring considerably less data than the input-output table. Among its major shortcomings is the fact that basic industries are not easily identifiable. Location quotients, for example, are a very rough method of identifying basic activities in which local factors are ignored. Surveys to determine basic components on the other hand present practical problems, including non-availability of data in business records and poor response to lengthy questionnaires.

The unit of measurement also presents problems. Labour statistics generally are readily available or easily gathered. Most establishments are wary of revealing financial data, but readily provide researchers with employment figures. Unfortunately, employment statistics do not reflect different wage levels, productivity per worker and many other important factors.

Thirdly, it is extremely difficult to estimate the future ratio between basic and service activities. It is thought that this ratio rarely remains constant over time within an area owing to changes in the size and composition of the population, changes in productivity, improved transport facilities and many other factors.

7.3 Comparative cost studies and industrial complex analyses

In studies of this kind, it is assumed that an establishment will be located at a site offering the highest possible profit.

> Comparative cost analysis, whether of a single industry or an industrial complex, involves simply estimating the profitability or cost advantage of an industry or group of industries in a region, based on the assumption in general that input and output can be purchased or disposed of at known prices. It is a partial analysis and, like most partial analyses, can be extraordinarily misleading in the analysis of regional growth (James & Hughes 1972:23).

This type of study aids decision making on the location of an establishment and is used by researchers to indicate the possible location of certain establishments in the future. As such establishments generally have the choice of several locations, the method is of little use.

7.4 Shift-share analyses

This method may be described as a refined method of extrapolation.

> The shift and share technique decomposes economic growth in a region into two principal components. The first is the growth anticipated in the market for the output of the region. If the region maintains its share of the markets in which its output is sold, the rate of growth of regional output will be identical to that anticipated in the total market. If this share is not maintained (if there is a shift in the share of the market satisfied by the region), then the region's growth is asserted to respond to a so-called 'competitive component' which can, of course, be positive or negative, depending on whether the region is growing more or less rapidly than its markets (James & Hughes 1972:18).

Perloff, one of the pioneers in analyses of this type, puts it as follows:

> It is based upon the fact that the shifts in total employment (or in other important eco-nomic growth components) observed among the states and regions in relation to the national average are generated by two distinct types of phenomena. We call

the resultant employment shifts 'proportionality employment shifts' and 'differential employment shifts'. The net differential shift in employment arises out of the fact that some regions are expanding in some employment section more rapidly than other regions. Proportionality shifts … arise out of the fact that nationwide some of the employment sections or industries expand more rapidly than others (Perloff 1961:71).

Briefly, this forecasting method involves the use of historical differential and proportional shifts in each area for forecasting purposes and the comparison of the results of all the areas with forecasts of the total number of wage earners in the country as a whole (Mahoney 1967:40). This method has the advantage of being simple and cheap and the statistics involved in the calculations are mostly secondary. It is preferable to extrapolation because the components of growth, that is the proportional and differential effect, are forecast separately, which makes for greater reliability.

On the negative side, the method relies on historical trends, especially in the differential effect. As far as larger areas are concerned, the differential effect may be forecast from historical data on the medium term, but the method is less than satisfactory in smaller, rapidly developing areas. Nonetheless, the method is a useful one in terms of its analytical capabilities.

8 SUMMARY

Although in most instances the principles observed in national and regional research are the same, regional research is much more complicated because of certain factors, mainly the open boundaries of subnational areas. As a result, changes in areas in the same vicinity exert considerable mutual influence. Because of conceptual problems and deficient regional statistics in South Africa, it is extremely difficult to quantify these influences. Nonetheless regional research is essential for virtually all organisations, particularly in a country where distances are as great as they are in South Africa.

REFERENCES

Catterji, M K 1964. An input-output study of the Calcutta industrial region. *The Regional Science Association Papers*, 13:93.

Isard, W 1967. *Methods of regional analysis: an introduction to regional science*. Massachusetts: The MIT Press.

James, F J & Hughes, J W 1972. *Economic growth and residential patterns: a methodological investigation*. New Jersey: Rutgers University.

Leontief, W W 1951. *The structure of the American economy, 1919–1939*. New York: Oxford University Press.

Mahoney, P S 1967. *A regional economic study: projections of employment and population in the Denver SMSA by a shift-share analysis.* PhD thesis, University of Colorado.

Martins, J H 1994. *Household expenditure in South Africa by area, population group and product, 1993.* Pretoria: Unisa, Bureau of Market Research. (Research Report no 205.)

Moses, L N 1955. The stability of interregional trading patterns and input-output analysis. *American Economic Review,* 45.

Nel, P A 1968. *Metodes vir die berekening van markpotensiale vir verbruiksgoedere en die ontwikkeling van regionale markpotensiaalindekse. Volume 1.* DCom thesis, University of South Africa, Pretoria.

Nel, P A 1983. *Market potentials of consumer goods: methods of calculation and development of indices.* Pretoria: Unisa, Bureau of Market Research. (Research Report no 108.)

Perloff, Harvey S 1961. *Regions, resources and economic growth.* Baltimore: Johns Hopkins Press.

South Africa 1976. Statistics Act, no 66 of 1976. Pretoria: Government Printer.

South Africa. Central Statistical Service 1988. *Final social accounting matrix for South Africa, 1988.* Pretoria. (CSS Report no 04–03–02 (1988).)

Researching international markets

Chapter 22: M Leibold

Researching international markets

1 IMPORTANCE OF INTERNATIONAL MARKETING RESEARCH

Rapid changes characterise global business activities and global markets. The impacts of a new world trading order under the World Trade Organisation from 1995 and the increasing formation of regional, multilateral and bilateral trading blocs and partners are giving a new dimension to the task of researching international markets.

As marketing horizons widen internationally for many countries and organisations, there are also new complexities and risks emerging. Marketing research fulfils a crucial role in international business decisions, with the single most important cause for failure in international business being insufficient preparation and information (Czinkota, Ronkainen & Moffett 1994: 387). Firms wanting to do sustainable business internationally must

☐ be aware of the differences between international and domestic marketing

☐ have a clear framework for international marketing research

☐ know the categories of information requirements

☐ be aware of secondary data and primary data-collection approaches

☐ have a well-designed international marketing information system

☐ be appropriately organised for international marketing research.

2 DIFFERENCES BETWEEN INTERNATIONAL AND DOMESTIC MARKETING RESEARCH

International marketing research differs from domestic marketing in three major ways (Jain 1990:318):

☐ The effects of the international environment on the whole company as a profit-oriented enterprise are considered. For example, the marketing research project concerned with the ramifications of a substantial price hike in a particular foreign country must consider questions that do not apply to the domestic market; for instance, will the company's subsidiary be nationalised if prices are increased beyond a certain level?

☐ Many concepts and frameworks (that is marketing segmentation) which constitute the core of marketing decision making in the domestic arena may be unusable in international marketing, not because the concept cannot be transferred, but because the information necessary to make such a transfer is not available. For example, if there is a lack of current income distribution data on a country, any analysis of the demand for a product will assume incorrect income categories and therefore have little significance in practice.

☐ Finally, the ethnocentric nature of marketing makes cultural differences among nations a significant factor. Thus, culture in a domestic market can be considered to be naturally understood, but in international marketing the culture must be fully investigated.

Although the procedures, methods and techniques of conducting marketing research are basically the same for both domestic marketing and international marketing, the complexities of international marketing result in a number of additional considerations such as:

☐ additional parameters, including changes in currencies, duties, modes of transportation and international documentation

☐ new environmental factors such as cultural impacts on market demand and carrying on business, political systems and their stability, and differences in societal structures, language, legal interpretations and industry-governmental regulations

☐ a broader definition of competition because of a much wider variety of competition than is found in the home market. As a result, a firm must determine the breadth of competition, track competitive activities, and evaluate potential competitive impacts to a much greater degree than in the domestic market.

The above differences and additional considerations raise a variety of conceptual, methodological and organisational issues in international marketing research relating to

☐ the complexity of research design, caused by operation in multicountry, multicultural, and multilinguistic environments

☐ the lack of secondary data available for many countries and product markets

☐ the high cost of collecting primary data, particularly in developing countries

☐ the problems associated with coordinating research and data collection in different countries

☐ the difficulties of establishing the comparability and equivalence of data and research conducted in different contexts

☐ the intrafunctional character of many international marketing decisions

☐ the economics of many international investment and marketing decisions.

International marketing research is therefore an important activity for any firm wishing to do or currently doing international business, and it needs to be approached in a different manner from domestic marketing research.

3 FRAMEWORK FOR INTERNATIONAL MARKETING RESEARCH

When operating internationally, or intending to start international operations, a firm needs a clear framework to guide its international marketing research activities. It is useful to think of this as a common series of major tasks (Jain 1990:320):

☐ Define the problem and the information needed for support of management's decision-making process.

☐ Identify alternative sources of information.

☐ Plan and execute data collection.

☐ Analyse the data and prepare an appropriate report.

The above framework can be applied in two broad contexts, either with an *exporting/selling* focus or with an *importing/buying* focus.

3.1 The framework of tasks to be performed

3.1.1 Defining the problem

This first task, which sounds deceptively simple, may be the pivotal task in the entire study. In defining the problem, two important considerations are market structure and product concept. *Market structure* refers to the size of the market, its stage of development, the number of competitors and their market shares, and the channels through which the market is approached.

In addition a product may be viewed differently in different cultures. Thus even before attempting to define the marketing research problem for study, exploratory research may be necessary to understand the *product concept*, that is the meaning of the product in a particular environment. In this way problem definition will be appropriate to the concept of the product held in the particular country of interest.

Let us assume a multinational marketer is interested in finding out the potential market for a brand of yogurt in England and Thailand. The problem definition in the two countries will have to be stated differently. In the United Kingdom the yogurt might be primarily perceived by the consumers as a healthful and relaxing product to be used before retiring at night. In Thailand the research problem would determine if yogurt would be considered mainly an energy food used to start the day.

3.1.2 Identifying alternative information sources

After the problem has been defined, one must determine where the necessary information may be found and how to obtain it. In some cases the study may be confined to *secondary data*, that is published information that has been collected elsewhere. It may be available free (for example government statistics), for a price (for example syndicated research supplies), or through restricted distribution sources (for example trade association statistics).

Let us assume that Ford Motor Company is interested in assembling its new world car in India in collaboration with an Indian company. Before committing itself to the joint venture, Ford would like to study the car's marketing potential in India over a ten-year period. Fortunately the Indian government regularly collects a variety of socio-economic-demographic information. This information is readily available. Ford, therefore, can confidently use such secondary information as population projections, income data, consumer expenditure patterns, and rural–urban population shifts to assess the market potential.

Sometimes internal data are also useful. Existing files may often provide important insights into the question at hand. In the above example, Ford might have found that it had already gathered sufficient information on population trends in India when the company negotiated earlier to assemble tractors there. Thus there would be no need for another source of information.

When no amount of investigation of secondary sources or of internal data provides the required information, *primary data* will have to be compiled from scratch through interviews and other direct methods of data collection. Primary data may be gathered in various ways (to be discussed later) from trade association representatives, governmental experts, managerial personnel, and/or the buying public.

For example, a company may be interested in introducing its prefabricated houses in Latin America. The company would have to study house-buying behaviour in the target countries. Since this type of information may not be readily available from secondary sources, primary data collection may be necessary.

3.1.3 Data collection

The actual collection of data must be planned and executed carefully. Although international data collection will be discussed at length in later sections of this chapter, it should be noted here that obtaining reliable, usable data sources can be time consuming. This is particularly so when a variety of sources are pursued concurrently. In fact, the search can go on with decreasing returns unless personnel with knowledge of the country appraise the progress that is being made.

Interview questions must be tested for their appropriateness so that they produce the desired results. A sound approach is to conduct professional level interviews in two phases: collect basic data, and explore interview questions not anticipated at the start of the project.

Once basic data have been collected, the process of cross-checking can begin. This step requires that all information should be examined critically for its relevance. Cross-checking establishes the reliability of data by comparison of one source with another. It is important to document the criteria used by the project team to determine the reliability of collected data.

3.1.4 Analysis, interpretation, and report preparation

For the final step – the preparation of the report – the data must be analysed and interpreted. Here, also, attention should be paid to a country's cultural traits. For example, in an examination of the beer market it was found that beer was perceived as an alcoholic drink in northern European countries but was considered a soft drink in Mediterranean countries. Thus, other products listed with beer as alternative drinks would influence the research findings. Similarly, in Japan non-carbonated fruit juices often replace bottled soft drinks (Mayer 1978:9). In brief, the significance of different concepts of the product in various countries must be taken into account.

Reports must be complete, factual and objective. It is particularly important to communicate the reliability and the limitations of the facts presented. Particular attention should be given to the following aspects of a report:

☐ Data sources must be identified. Different sources of data warrant varying degrees of confidence. For example, information on a Third World country which is obtained from the United States Agency for International Development is probably more reliable than information available from the government of that country.

☐ Data projection must be explained. As a matter of fact, statistical computations should be simplified as much as possible. Detailed description of the statistical/mathematical procedures followed can be included in an appendix at the end of the report.

□ The identity of all those interviewed and their titles or qualifications should be included. (This rule does not apply to consumer research.) The requirement may have to be relaxed when anonymity has been guaranteed.

□ The alternative courses of action developed from analysis and interpretation of the data must be labelled as such, clearly reserving to management the responsibility for selecting the appropriate course of action.

3.2 The contexts of exporting and importing

3.2.1 Going international – exporting

A frequent objective of international research is foreign market opportunity analysis. When a firm launches its international activities, it will usually find that the world is uncharted territory. Fortunately information can be accumulated to provide basic guidelines. The aim is not to conduct a painstaking and detailed analysis of the world on a market-by-market basis, but to utilise a broadbrush approach. Accomplished quickly and at low cost, this approach will narrow the possibilities for international business activities.

Figure 22.1 illustrates the sequential process of researching foreign market potentials.

Such an approach should begin with a *cursory analysis* of the general variables of a country, including total and per capita GNP, mortality rates, and population figures. Although these factors in themselves will not provide any detailed information, they will enable the researcher to determine whether corporate objectives might be met in the market. For example, high-priced consumer products are unlikely to be successful in the People's Republic of China because their price may be equal to a significant proportion of the annual salary of the customer, the benefit to the customer may be minimal, and the government is likely to prohibit their importation. Similarly, the offering of computer-software services may be of little value in a country where there is very limited use of computers. Such a cursory evaluation will help to reduce the number of markets to be considered to a more manageable number – for example from 50 to 5.

As the next step the researcher will require information on each individual country for a *preliminary evaluation*. Information typically desired will highlight the fastest-growing markets, the largest markets for a particular product or service, demand trends, and business restrictions. Although precise and detailed information may not be obtainable, information is available for general product categories or service industries. Again, this overview will be cursory but will serve to quickly evaluate markets and further reduce their number.

At this stage the researcher must select appropriate markets for in-depth evaluation. The focus will now be on *opportunities for a specific type of service, product, or brand*, and will include an assessment of whether demand already exists or can be stimulated. Even

Figure 22.1 A sequential process of researching foreign market potentials

Stage One
Preliminary screening for attractive country markets
Key question to be answered: Which foreign markets warrant detailed investigation?

↓

Stage Two
Assessment of industry market potential
Key question to be answered: What is the aggregate demand in each of the selected markets?

↓

Stage Three
Company sales potential analysis
Key question to be answered: How attractive is the potential demand for company products and services?

Source: Adapted from Czinkota *et al* (1994:391).

though aggregate industry data have been obtained beforehand, this general information is insufficient to make company-specific decisions. For example, the demand for medical equipment should not be confused with the potential demand for a specific brand. Now, the research should identify demand and supply patterns and evaluate any regulation and standards. Finally, a *competitive assessment* needs to be made, matching markets to corporate strengths and providing an analysis of the best potential for specific offerings.

3.2.2 Going international – importing

When importing, the major focus shifts from supplying to sourcing (Jain 1990:320). Management must identify markets that produce the supplies or materials which are desired or have the potential to do so. Foreign firms must be evaluated in terms of their capabilities and competitive standing.

Just as management would wish to have some details on a domestic supplier, the importer needs to know, for example, about the reliability of a foreign supplier, the consistency of its product or service quality, and the length of delivery time. Information obtained through the subsidiary office of a bank or an embassy can prove very helpful.

In addition foreign regulations must be scrutinised to determine whether exportation is possible. As examples, India may set limits on the cobra handbags it allows to be exported, and laws protecting a nation's cultural heritage may prevent the exportation of pre-Columbian artifacts from Latin American countries.

The international manager must also analyse domestic restrictions and legislation that may prohibit the importation of certain goods into the home country. Even though a market may exist in South Africa for foreign umbrella handles, for example, quotas may restrict their importation in order to protect domestic industries. Similarly, even though domestic demand may exist for ivory products, its importation may be illegal because of legislation enacted to protect wildlife worldwide.

4 INFORMATION REQUIREMENTS OF INTERNATIONAL MARKETING RESEARCH

The nature of marketing decisions does not vary from country to country, although the environment does. For this reason the sort of information required to complete a marketing study may vary from one country to another. For example, in a situation in which a marketer is free to set prices based on competition, a detailed analysis of competition should be made. But in a country where the price is set by government, information on governmental cost analysis would be of greater importance. Because the environment determines what kind of information is needed, international marketing research efforts are quite different from domestic marketing research work (Cavusgil 1984:21).

Figure 22.2 shows the types of marketing studies a company may want to conduct in different areas such as promotion, distribution, price, products, or markets. Each of these types of studies takes a different form of information, as the following discussion makes clear (based on Jain 1990).

4.1 Market information

Market research is required for testing, entering, or leaving a market and deals with market performance, market shares, and sales analysis and forecasting. Marketing performance research involves market measurements, either to compare a company's performance against specified standards or to project a possible future outcome. *Market potential* refers to the total market demand under optimal conditions; *market forecast* shows the expected

Figure 22.2 Major types of marketing research studies required for doing business abroad

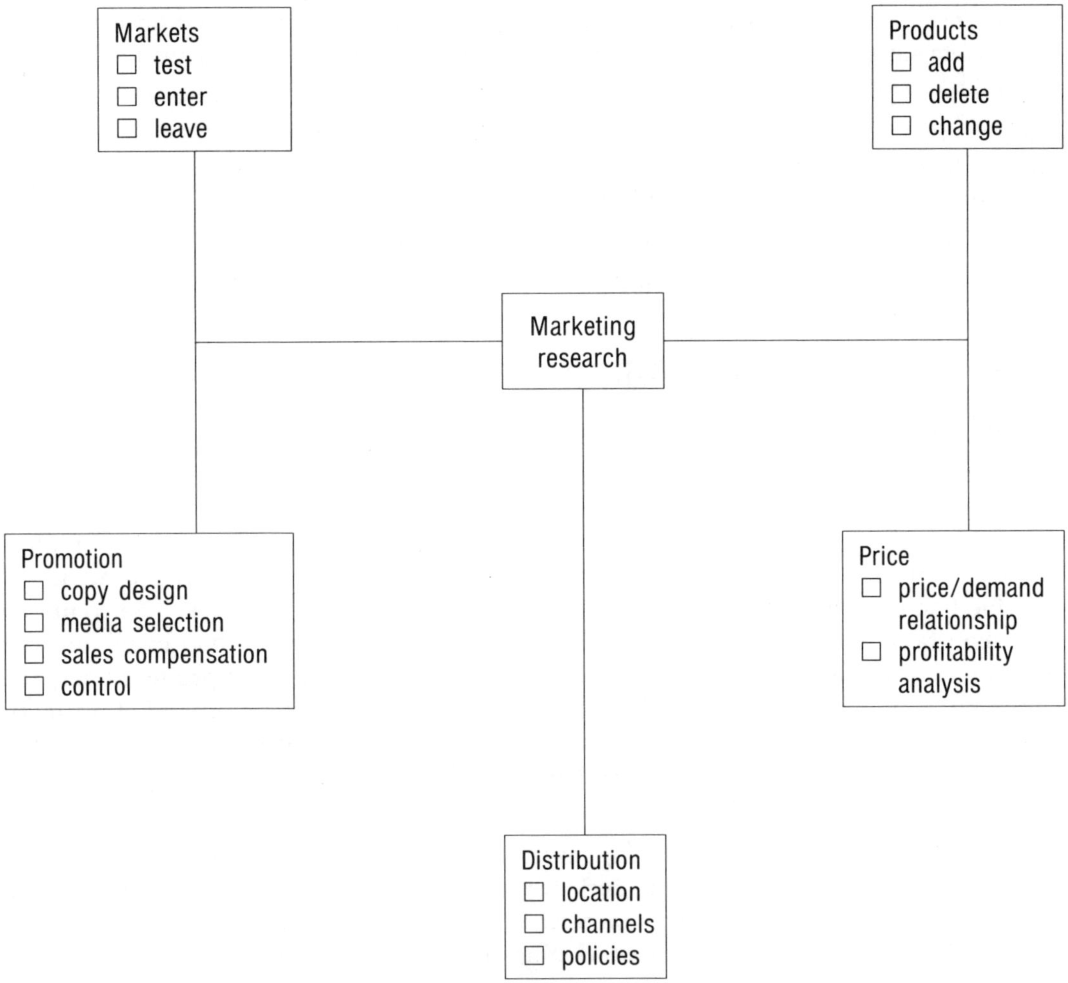

Markets
- ☐ test
- ☐ enter
- ☐ leave

Products
- ☐ add
- ☐ delete
- ☐ change

Marketing research

Promotion
- ☐ copy design
- ☐ media selection
- ☐ sales compensation
- ☐ control

Price
- ☐ price/demand relationship
- ☐ profitability analysis

Distribution
- ☐ location
- ☐ channels
- ☐ policies

Source: Adapted from Jain (1990:323).

level of market demand under the given conditions. To illustrate: when Pepsico decided to expand its Pizza Hut business into certain Middle Eastern countries such as Saudi Arabia it conducted market potential research beforehand with a horizon of five years in each country.

Market share refers to a company's proportion of total sales in an industry during a set time, usually a year. The market shares held by competitors shape marketing strategy for a company. The competitor with a respectable market share will have a cost advantage over its rivals. This cost advantage can be passed on to the customers through lower prices, which in turn strengthens the company's hold on the market. Because of the strategic importance of market share, business corporations keep constant watch on its fluctuations. Data supplied by industry associations, if properly analysed, usually show respective market shares, or enable their calculation.

Past sales information can be analysed in different ways: by amount of profit from different products, by productivity of sales territory (for example Latin America or Western Europe) or by customer type. Sales analysis can pinpoint problems.

Sales forecasts refer to estimates of future sales of a product during a specific period. The sales forecast is the single most important basis for preparing budgets.

4.2 Product information

Product research means both product line research and individual product research. This kind of research investigates when to add, delete, or change the product.

A company operating overseas must often decide which product line it should add, which it should drop, and which needs rejuvenation. These decisions require a variety of information. Consider this example. A large paper products company manufactured an expensive line of writing paper, as well as other kinds of paper products. The company had about a 30 % market share in Latin America, and the demand had been constant for a number of years. As part of a programme for simplification of product lines, the company wondered if there had been changes in the office environment in Latin American countries that made the use of expensive paper obsolete. In other words, should the product line be abandoned? The company undertook marketing research to find an answer to this question.

A manager may also require marketing research information on each individual product. As a product passes through its life cycle, different marketing programmes must be developed for every stage. Thus it is important to place a product on its life cycle curve in order to choose the appropriate marketing programme, and marketing research can be of real value in plotting a product's life cycle in different countries.

4.3 Promotion information

Promotion research indicates research for advertising and personal selling. Companies consult the findings of objective research before spending money on advertising campaigns in order to select appropriate copy and appeals and make the best media selection. A trading stamp company operating in Europe, for example, redeemed stamps saved by consumers in two ways: in merchandise and in travel. Over the years it was found that more and more customers preferred overseas travel to merchandise. For the company, however, merchandise was more profitable; so the company considered starting an ad campaign to entice consumers to redeem their stamps in merchandise. The company wondered if a merchandise catalogue which emphasised the virtue of material acquisitions as status symbols would be persuasive in Europe. The production of the catalogue would cost about two million dollars, and the catalogue's market effectiveness had to be tested beforehand.

Personal selling, like advertising, must produce profits. Consider the complaint of the sales manager of a US pharmaceutical company: 'My salespeople in Italy are not productive enough even though we pay them a lot more than the industry average there.' Marketing research can provide insights into problems related to *personal selling*, which involves questions about how many salespeople to hire and how much to pay them, how to form sales territories, and how much time to spend on retaining old customers and how much on developing new accounts.

4.4 Distribution information

Distribution research consists of channel research and location research. *Channel research* can help a company decide on the channels to use for distribution of its products. Marketing research can provide information on the availability of channels and their relative desirability.

A water systems manufacturer, for instance, traditionally used manufacturer's representatives for the distribution of its water pumps in the Canadian market. The company, however, was becoming dissatisfied with the manufacturer's representatives and wanted to use its own sales force. A marketing research firm was asked for a study of the effect on sales of making such a change.

Location research concerns decisions about warehousing, inventory, and transportation. For example, the decision to own a warehouse in Germany or to use a public warehouse, or to enter into a strategic alliance with a warehousing firm there requires marketing research.

4.5 Price information

A company sets the prices of its products to meet both short-term and long-term objectives. To set prices, information about the ability of consumers to pay, about dealer reaction, and about the effect of price on demand is necessary. Studies that measure the public perception of a product's quality in relation to price also help in making pricing decisions.

4.6 Environment information

No matter which sort of international marketing study is planned, the researchers must take into account the foreign country's environment in all its aspects: legal, political, social, cultural and attitudinal, as shown by both the buying habits of its consumers and the business practices of its enterprises. Naturally, familiarity with the environment is equally important in domestic marketing, but knowledge of domestic environment can come more easily from personal experience. For example, if a South African company is interested in doing business in China, it must learn about a political system that is different in ways that are taken for granted in the South African political structure.

4.7 General research information

All marketing research requires three general groups of overall information in addition to the more specific categories already discussed:

☐ General information about:

- community-type conditions (for example political happenings − campaigns, elections; cultural events − county fairs, special annual ethnic or religious celebrations; national events − sports, championships, holidays)

- business conditions (for example business ethics and traditional associations)

- lifestyles and living conditions, that is social and cultural customs and taboos (for example marriageable age for men and women and the role of women in society)

- general economic conditions (for example the standards of living of various groups of people and the economic infrastructure − transportation, power supply, and communication).

☐ Industry information about government decisions affecting the industry; resource availability (for example labour and land); current or potential competitors (that is general information about their markets and their problems); competition from South African companies, local companies, and/or third country companies; industry policy, concerted actions in the industry, and so forth.

☐ Study-related information: collateral data generated to complete a specific market research study. For example, a study concerned with market potential needs information on supply and demand in market areas of current and potential interest (for example capacity, consumption, imports, exports). But a study concerned with the introduction of a new product requires information about existing products, the technical know-how available in the country, sources of raw material, and leads for joint ventures.

The amount of information to be gathered in a given case depends on the cost-benefit relationship of such information.

Finally, the nature of the information required will vary according to the objective of research. Figure 22.3 on page 534 illustrates this point of listing the type of information a firm needs to determine export potential.

5 SECONDARY DATA COLLECTION

Secondary data can be gathered at home (home country) and/or abroad.

5.1 Collecting secondary data at home

There are six major sources of information in a home country: international agencies, the government, consulting firms, foreign government offices, financial institutions (especially banks) and specialised foreign trade organisations (for example SAFTO).

5.1.1 International agencies

The United Nations, the World Bank and the International Monetary Fund gather a variety of economic and social information on different countries of the world. This information is available to the public. For example, the United Nations Yearbook provides information on worldwide demographics. Also *The World Bank atlas* summarises information on living patterns via such indicators as daily calorie supply, life expectancy at birth and school enrolment. The International Monetary Fund (IMF) provides historical information on the national economic indicators (GNP, industrial production, inflation rate, money supply) of its member countries. This information is available on computer tapes.

The information available from these international organisations, however, has two drawbacks. First, the information is based on data supplied by each member country. It is difficult to determine the criteria and means which have been used. In some cases the reliability of the data may be suspect because the information compiled has been passed along by various bureaucrats who may have slanted the data for their own purposes. Second, the information is dated. It takes time for an international organisation to gather information from all over the world, analyse it, and make it available to the public in summary form.

Figure 22.3 Information needs for determining export potential

---

Phase One: Preliminary screening

Preliminary screening involves defining the physical, political, economic and cultural environment

Demographic/physical environment
- Population size, growth, density
- Urban and rural distribution
- Climate and weather variations
- Shipping distance
- Product-significant demographics
- Physical distribution and communication network
- Natural resources

Economic environment
- Overall level of development
- Economic growth; GNP, industrial sector
- Role of foreign trade in the economy
- Currency, inflation rate, availability, controls, stability of exchange rate
- Balance of payments
- Per capita income and distribution
- Disposable income and expenditure patterns

Political environment
- System of government
- Political stability and continuity
- Ideological orientation
- Government involvement in business
- Government involvement in communications
- Attitudes toward foreign business (trade restrictions, tariffs, non-tariff barriers, bilateral trade agreements)
- National economic and developmental priorities

Social/cultural environment
- Literacy rate, educational level
- Existence of middle class
- Similarities and differences in relation to home market
- Language and other cultural considerations

The export marketer will eliminate some foreign markets from further consideration on the basis of this preliminary screening. An example would be the absence of comparable or linking products and services, a deficiency that would hinder the potential for marketing company products.

Phase Two: Analysis of industry market potential

Market access
- Limitations on trade: tariff levels, quotas
- Documentation and import regulations
- Local standards, practices, and other non-tariff barriers
- Patents and trademarks
- Preferential treaties
- Legal considerations: investment, taxation, repatriation, employment, code of laws

Product potential
- Customer needs and desires
- Local production, imports, consumption
- Exposure to and acceptance of product
- Availability of linking products
- Industry-specific key indicators of demand
- Attitudes toward products of foreign origin
- Competitive offerings
- Availability of intermediaries
- Regional and local transportation facilities
- Availability of manpower
- Conditions for local manufacture

Phase Three: Analysis of company sales potential

The third stage of the screening process involves assessing company sales potential in those countries that prove promising based upon the earlier analyses.

Sales volume forecasting
- Size and concentration of customer segments
- Projected consumption statistics
- Competitive pressures
- Expectations of local distributors/agents

Cost of internal distribution
- Tariffs and duties
- Value-added tax
- Local packaging and assembly
- Margins/commission allowed for the trade
- Local distribution and inventory costs
- Promotional expenditures

Landed cost
- Costing method for exports
- Domestic distribution costs
- International freight and insurance
- Cost of product modification

Other determinants of profitability
- Current price levels
- Competitive strengths and weaknesses
- Credit practices
- Current and projected exchange rates

Source: Adapted from Cavusgil (1985:30–31).

5.1.2 The government

The South African Department of Trade and Industry has an Export Trade Division which publishes a wide range of general and specific information. Its publication *Global Trade* is produced every two months. The department has various regional offices, situated in Pretoria, Durban, Cape Town and Port Elizabeth. Each office can give information about major issues such as

- ☐ trade and investment opportunities abroad
- ☐ foreign markets for South African products and services
- ☐ services to locate and evaluate overseas buyers and representatives
- ☐ financing aid for exporters
- ☐ international trade exhibitions
- ☐ export documentation requirements
- ☐ foreign economic statistics
- ☐ South African export licensing and foreign national import requirements
- ☐ export seminars and conferences.

In January 1995 the Department of Trade and Industry also had some 44 offices in 37 countries.

5.1.3 Consulting firms

Many management consulting firms specialise in services for South Africa business abroad. Some of these firms conduct original research. One such firm is Deloitte & Touche, who provide services in market studies (for example tourism), and another is Price Waterhouse, who publish booklets on select countries, providing perspectives on doing business there.

5.1.4 Foreign government offices

Almost all major countries of the world maintain embassies or consulates in Pretoria and other major cities of South Africa. An embassy usually has a commercial attaché who may be a good source of information on the country. For example, let us assume research is being done to prepare a market-potential study in order to decide whether a company should assemble television sets in Nigeria. Import data on television sets in Nigeria for the past five years are needed. The Nigerian consulate in Johannesburg might have a government publication that quickly and easily provides such information.

5.1.5 Financial institutions, trade associations and chambers of business

Financial institutions with worldwide connections such as Old Mutual and Absa Bank, and local trade associations and chambers of business, are additional sources of secondary information. Many of these institutions maintain libraries with regulated access for customers, be they present or prospective customers.

5.1.6 Specialised foreign trade organisations

The South African Foreign Trade Organisation (SAFTO) is well known for its information services in terms of country, markets, products and other foreign trade information, and its training courses. These services are provided to its members, who pay annual and other fees to the organisation.

5.2 Advantages and disadvantages of secondary research at home

5.2.1 Advantages of secondary research at home

Secondary research conducted in the home country is less expensive and less time consuming than research abroad. The research at home keeps commitment to future projects at a low level: no contacts have to be made overseas, and no high-level decisions have to be made on exploring markets outside South Africa. Research in the home environment affords easy communication with sources of information. In addition, requests for certain kinds of information are often received more favourably by foreign sources located in South Africa where political pressure and business customers do not inhibit response. Research undertaken in South Africa about a foreign environment also gains in objectivity. The researcher is not constrained by overseas customs or mores and can apply the same standards of quality and analysis that would be used for a project related to domestic business.

5.2.2 Disadvantages of secondary research in the home country

Secondary research undertaken in the home country has various limitations (Jain 1990:324). First, current information may be scarce in the home country. After all, there is a time lag between data gathering in a foreign country and its transmission to South Africa. Further, certain things may be uncovered in the foreign environment that will ultimately bear on the project. For example, a company may be exploring the feasibility of establishing a plant in Saudi Arabia to manufacture air conditioners. Research done in South Africa is likely to reveal good potential there for air conditioners based on secondary data such as high per capita income, hot climate, low rate of air conditioners per hundred house-holds, and encouragement by the Saudi government. However, these data omit an important fact about Saudi living: a large proportion of the people live in mud houses. Additionally, there are regions without electricity. Such facts would become immediately obvious to a researcher on the spot.

5.3 Secondary research abroad

An addition or alternative to doing secondary research in South Africa is undertaking secondary research abroad. The availability of reliable secondary data is directly related to the level of economic development of a country. Even among Third World countries, data-collection activity has greatly improved since the 1970s. This may be attributed partly to United Nations' efforts at impressing upon countries the desirability of keeping national statistical information accurate and current.

5.3.1 Foreign sources of information

The following are the major sources of secondary information for an international marketer (Samli, Still & Hill 1993:387–388):

(a) Government sources

The single most important source of secondary information in a country is the national government. The quality and quantity of information will vary from country to country, but in most cases information on population statistics, consumption standards, industrial production, imports and exports, price levels, employment, and more is readily available. On the other hand, data on retail and wholesale trade may be found only in certain countries. Government data are usually available through a government agency or major publishers in the country. In many countries marketing-related information gathered by the government is not separated from other sorts of information. Thus the researcher must go through a plethora of information to choose what is relevant.

(b) Private sources

In many countries there are private consulting firms (such as Business International Cor-poration, New York City, and Predicasts, Cleveland, Ohio) which collect and sell com-mercial information. Information from private sources may in fact have been collected by the government originally. But consulting firms analyse and organise it in such a manner that business executives can more easily make sense of it. The commercial attaché at the South African embassy should be able to provide the names and addresses of local consulting firms. For example, International Information Services Ltd (IIS), a global product pick-up service located in Sussex, United Kingdom, provides answers to such specific issues as the most popular pizza flavours in France and retail pricing structure for shampoos in Venezuela compared with that of its neighbours in Colombia and Brazil. Each day over 400 IIS shoppers visit supermarkets in 120 countries searching for information requested by clients such as Coca-Cola, General Foods, Procter & Gamble, Nestlé and Unilever. The information gathered by IIS shoppers is stored, along with data from the company's comprehensive library of foreign trade publications, in a computerised database, enabling IIS to offer clients continuous updates on new food, household and pharmaceutical products introduced worldwide. IIS uses these data to compile bimonthly indexes of new products.

(c) Research institutes, trade associations, universities, and similar sources

Although not every country in the world has trade associations or research institutes, in both developed and developing countries (such as India, Brazil, South Korea and Egypt) such sources could be important sources of secondary data. In some countries they are set up with the help of international agencies and/or the government. Information on these sources should be sought from the appropriate South African embassy or the Department of Trade and Industry.

(d) Local businesses

A South African company may be in contact with one or more businesses in a foreign country. These contacts can serve as important sources of secondary data. Even if these businesses have collected no data on their own, they could gather and communicate data available through other local sources such as those mentioned earlier.

(e) South African embassies and trade consulates

The South African embassy in a country may have gathered information on a particular industry in a country in order to understand its impact on South African business at home (for example the impact of the Japanese auto industry on South African automobile companies might be better understood with information from the South African embassy in Japan). Embassy appointees may be requested to be mindful of South African trade prospects for particular raw materials (for example the South African embassy in Colombia would be aware of the Colombian coffee bean trade). In addition, the embassy could lead the marketing researcher to offer sources of secondary data in the country, such as trade associations or research institutes.

5.3.2 Problems with foreign secondary data

Secondary data available in a foreign country suffer in comparison with similar information available from South African sources at home. The researcher must be aware of problems and shortcomings when interpreting information. The following brief summaries deal with some of the difficulties with the reliability of foreign secondary data.

(a) The underlying purpose of data collection

As mentioned earlier, the single most important source of marketing-related secondary data in a country is the government. The government as a political institution may not approach data collection with the same objectivity as a business researcher. This problem is particularly severe in developing countries, where governments may enhance the information content in order to paint a rosy picture of economic life in the country. In this way, political considerations overshadow the reliability of the data.

It is worth noting that South Africa as a society is more open than many other countries. No matter how embarrassing data may appear to be for the government or the nation, the free flow of information is considered desirable. This, however, is not true elsewhere. It is not surprising therefore that the plight of the poor in the United States seems exaggerated when measured by standards of poverty in developing countries. The researcher must ascertain that the data available are accurate within the limits of their source and that there are no hidden assumptions that might distort the information from the researcher's point of view.

(b) Currency of information

Information gathering is an expensive activity. When the government has limited resources, data gathering becomes a lower priority. Thus, information may not be gathered as frequently as desirable. The researcher needs to be very careful that information available overseas has not become outdated.

(c) Reliability of data

It was mentioned above that political considerations may affect reliability of data. In addition, the reliability of data may be affected by data-collection procedures. For example, the sample may not be random, so that the results cannot be assumed to reflect the behaviour of the total population. Even when a good sampling plan has been laid out, it may not be properly adhered to (that is the interviewers might substitute other subjects when those required by the sampling plan cannot be reached).

It may be difficult for researchers to judge the reliability of secondary data available in a country, and it would be impossible to try to test that reliability. If the researchers are very much concerned with reliability, they would be better off undertaking primary data gathering. Researchers should judge for themselves how far to accept the data on the basis of inputs from different contacts in the country about their own experiences with secondary data there.

(d) Data classification

Another problem has to do with the classification scheme of the available data. In many countries data reported are too broadly classified for use at the micro level. For example, in Malaysia the category 'construction equipment, machinery, and tools' includes large bulldozers as well as hand-operated drills. Thus, a company interested in manufacturing heavy construction machinery in Malaysia cannot get a clear idea of the current availability of such equipment in the country from the information given under such a category.

However, the problem of data classification may be solved in the future (Jain 1990:336). For years the international trading community has had to contend with the lack of a standardised goods classification system for products being traded in the international marketplace. The use of diverse systems has complicated the preparation of documents, hampered the analysis of trade data, created uncertainty in the negotiation and interpretation of trade agreements, and slowed the movement of traded goods. But, as countries adopt the Harmonized Commodity Description and Coding System, information across countries will be similarly classified, eliminating many of the problems that arise from the use of a non-standardised system.

The Harmonized Commodity Description and Coding System (HS) is an international goods classification system designed to standardise commodity classification for all major trading nations. The system assigns all products a six-digit code, which would be used by all countries for both imported and exported goods. The HS was developed under the auspices of the Customs Cooperation Council (CCC) in Brussels, Belgium, and is based on the Customs Cooperation Council Nomenclature (CCCN), formerly known as the Brussels Tariff Nomenclature (BTN). It is more detailed and contains many new subdivisions to reflect changes in technological and trade patterns, and user requirements.

Use of a common system would accelerate the movement of goods and their associated paperwork. International traders would no longer have to re-describe and re-code goods as they move through the international marketplace. The elimination of the these obstacles would save time and money.

The Harmonized System consists of 5 019 four-digit headings and subheadings. Under certain circumstances developing countries will be able to adopt the system at the four-digit level; developed countries, however, must use all six digits. The first two digits represent the place in the chapter where the goods are described, and the next two digits represent international subdivisions within the heading.

(c) Comparability of data

Multinational corporate executives often like to compare information on their host countries about such matters as review of market performance and strategy effectiveness in different environments. Unfortunately the secondary data obtainable from different countries are not readily comparable. Keegan (1989:224) reports, for example, that in Germany purchases of televisions are classed as expenditure on recreation and entertainment, whereas in the US such purchases are included in the category of furniture, furnishing, and household equipment. These discrepancies make brand-share comparison nearly impossible.

(d) Availability of data

Finally, in many developing nations, secondary data are very scarce. Information on retail and wholesale trade is especially difficult to obtain. In such cases primary data collection becomes vital (Malhotra 1988:70).

6 PRIMARY DATA COLLECTION

An addition or alternative to secondary data is primary data collection. Primary data presumably provide more relevant information because they are collected specifically for the purpose in mind. However, the collection of primary data is an expensive proposition in terms of money and time. Thus, the underlying purpose must justify the effort. For example, when a company has to make a decision about appointing a dealer for the occasional sale of its product in a developing country, it is not necessary to have primary data on the long-term market potential. On the other hand, if the company is considering the establishment of a manufacturing plant in the country, it may be important to undertake a market-potential study.

6.1 Problems of primary data collection

Primary data collection in a foreign environment poses a variety of problems not encountered in South Africa. These problems are related to social and cultural factors and the level of economic development and can be grouped under three headings (Jain 1990:338): sampling problems, questionnaire problems and the problem of non-response.

6.1.1 Sampling problems

A good piece of research should reflect the perspectives of the entire population. This is feasible, however, only when the sample is randomly drawn. Unfortunately in many countries it is difficult to get completely representative information on the socio-economic characteristics of the population because such information is lacking or, at best, is inadequate. Most samples in the end are likely to be biased. Cateora (1983:270) adds:

> In many countries, telephone directories, cross-index street directories, census tract and block data, and detailed social and economic characteristics of the universe are not available on a current basis, if at all. The researcher then has to estimate characteristics and population parameters, sometimes with little basic data on which to build an accurate estimate. To add to the confusion, in some cities in South America, Mexico, and Asia, street maps are unavailable; and in some large metropolitan areas of the Near East and Asia, streets are not identified nor houses numbered.

Limitations aside, directories are available to help the international marketing researcher to draw an adequate sample, especially in the industrial marketing area. *Boltin International*, for example, provides names and addresses of more than 300 000 firms in 100 countries, under 1 000 product classifications, by trade and by country. Another source is *Kelly's Manufacturers and Merchants Directory*, which lists firms in the United States and other major trading countries in the world.

Even if a workable random sample is drawn, inadequate means of transportation may prevent the interviewing of people as planned. For example, in developing countries many areas, especially rural ones, are quite inaccessible. Thus data gathering may have to be confined to urban areas. Further, only a small percentage of the population may have telephones. The World Bank statistics indicate, for example, that there are only four telephones per thousand population in Egypt, six in Turkey, and thirty-two in Argentina (Jain 1990:337). In many countries the postal system is so inefficient that letters may not be delivered at all or may reach the addressee only after a long delay. A study in Brazil in 1983 revealed, for example, that an estimated 30 % of the domestic mail is never delivered (Douglas & Craig 1983:224). In brief, it may be extremely difficult to obtain a proper random sample, especially in developing countries.

6.1.2 Questionnaire problems

In many countries different languages are spoken in different areas. Thus the questionnaire has to be in different languages for use within the same country. In India, for example, fourteen official languages are spoken in different parts of the country, while most government and business affairs are conducted in English. Similarly, in Switzerland German is used in some areas, Italian in others and French in still others. In the Republic of Congo the official language is French, but only a small part of the population is fluent in French. Unfortunately, translating a questionnaire from one language into another is far from easy. In the translating process many points are entirely eclipsed because many idioms, phrases and statements mean different things in different cultures.

6.1.3 Problem of non-response

Even if the sample element is successfully reached, there is no guarantee that he or she will cooperate and furnish the desired information. There are many reasons for non-response (Jain 1990:337):

☐ Cultural habits in many countries virtually prohibit communication with a stranger, particularly for women. For example, a researcher simply may not be able to speak on the telephone with a housewife in an Islamic country to find out what she thinks of a particular brand.

☐ In many societies such matters as preferences for hygienic products and food products are too personal to be shared with an outsider. In many Latin American countries a woman may feel ashamed to talk with a researcher about her choice of a brand of sanitary pad, hair shampoo, or perfume.

☐ In many cases respondents may be unwilling to share their true feelings with interviewers because they suspect the interviewers may be agents of the government seeking, for example, information to impose additional taxes.

☐ Middle-class people, in developing countries in particular, are reluctant to accept their status and may make false claims in order to reflect the lifestyle of wealthier people. For example, in a study on the consumption of tea in India, over 70 % of the respondents from middle-income families claimed they used one of the several national brands of tea. This finding could not be substantiated since over 60 % of the tea sold nationally in India is unbranded, generic tea which is sold unpackaged.

☐ Many respondents may be willing to cooperate but are illiterate, so that even oral communication may be difficult. In other words, their lack of exposure to the modern world makes it extremely difficult to elicit adequate responses from them.

☐ In many countries privacy is becoming a big issue. In Japan, for example, the middle class is showing increasing concern about the protection of personal information. Information that people are most anxious to protect includes income, assets, tax payments, family life, and political and religious affiliation.

☐ The lack of established marketing research firms in many countries may force the researcher to rely on ad hoc help for gathering data. How far such temporary help may be counted on to complete a job systematically can only be guessed.

6.2 Resolving the problems

There are no foolproof methods for taking care of all the problems discussed above. The following suggestions, however, may help to eliminate some of the problems (Jain 1990:338).

The international marketing research effort should be undertaken in conjunction with a reputable local firm. Such a firm may be a foreign office of a South African advertising firm such as Ogilvy & Mather or a locally owned firm which belongs to a third country such as a Japanese advertising agency in Italy. The resources of the cooperating firm will be invaluable; for example, its knowledge of local customs, including aspects such as the feasibility of interviewing housewives while husbands are at work; its familiarity with local environment, including modes of transportation available for personal interviews in smaller towns; and its contact in different parts of the country as sources for drawing a sample.

From the beginning, a person who is fully conversant with sound marketing research procedures and the local culture should be involved in all phases of the research design. Such a person can recommend the number of languages in which the questionnaire should be printed and the types of cultural traits, habits, customs and rituals to keep in mind in different phases of the research.

The questionnaire may first be written in English, and then a native fluent in English can translate it into the local language(s). A third person should retranslate it into English. The retranslated version can then be compared with the original English version. The three people involved should work together to eliminate differences in the three versions of the questionnaire by changing phrases, idioms and words. Ultimately, the questionnaire in the local language should accurately reflect the questions in the original English questionnaire.

If feasible, the persons hired to conduct the interviews should have prior experience. The local cooperating firm discussed earlier may be helpful here. In any event, complete instructions and training should be given before work starts. As a matter of fact, the conducting of interviews should be practised. Ways to ensure that the interviewers follow the instructions must be found for proper sampling control. For example, the researcher might accompany the interviewer sporadically.

Finally, the researcher should draw the best possible sample. If the sample is not random, the researcher should employ appropriate statistical techniques in analysing the collected information so that the results reflect the reality of the situation.

7 ORGANISATION FOR INTERNATIONAL MARKETING RESEARCH

International marketing research can be carried out both at the headquarters in South Africa and in the host country.

Marketing research studies in host countries are concerned mainly with day-to-day operations, tactics to achieve designated goals, and short-term marketing planning (Jain 1990:340). For example, a study may examine the factors responsible for poor sales performance in the previous quarter. Similarly, marketing research may be undertaken to decide if a concentrated six- or ten-week advertising campaign is preferable to spreading advertising over the whole year. Naturally, sales forecasting will be done to develop budgets. As mentioned above, the headquarters may also make sales forecasts. Thus for discussion of annual plans and budgets the host country manager would use his or her forecasts as the basis for resource allocation, while the headquarters' people use their forecasts to negotiate and approve the country budgets.

Marketing research is unquestionably an important function that must be conducted both at the headquarters and in the host countries. The persons to take charge at these two locations would vary from company to company. For example, at National Cash Registers (NCR) a staff assistant who reports to the vice-president of international marketing is responsible for marketing research at the corporate headquarters (Jain 1990:340). The marketing research function for NCR in host countries is performed at different levels according to the importance of each country to the parent company. In Japan, in the United Kingdom, and in Germany, NCR has a large marketing research department simply because the company is extremely active in these markets. On the other hand, in a country such as Pakistan where NCR commitment is meagre, marketing research study might be assigned to an outside consultant.

In addition to undertaking marketing research at the corporate level and in the host countries, in many companies marketing research may also be conducted at the regional level. A company may divide its international operations into regions, for example Western Europe, Far East, Latin America, Middle East, Africa and South East Asia. Each country manager for a region will report to the regional executive. Under such arrangements the regional executive may seek marketing research information to formulate regional marketing strategy or to develop the marketing perspective of a country in the region. There may be a specific person responsible for marketing research in the region, or one of the staff may bear this responsibility.

It is important to recognise that marketing information is important at all levels. However, the process of gathering, analysing and reporting marketing-related information may not necessarily be called marketing research. Further, marketing research responsibility may not necessarily be assigned to a marketing person. Of course, the extent of marketing research that a company undertakes would vary according to the style of management and the importance of a particular foreign country for a given product.

8 INTERNATIONAL MARKETING INFORMATION SYSTEM

Earlier in this book (see chapter 1) the concept, nature and components of a marketing information system (MIS) were introduced and explained.

Most large multimarket, multiproduct companies have some sort of multinational marketing information system in operation. It is difficult to say, however, how many of these systems can be labelled 'sophisticated' or 'advanced'. But the increasing popularity of the international data networks made available by such companies as Control Data Corporation, Data Research Inc and General Electric Company indicates that companies are moving toward the establishment of computerised information systems (Douglas & Craig 1983:279). These systems may serve the information needs of marketing and other functional areas of the business in the following manner:

☐ By providing aid decisions about international market expansion, for example whether new countries are potential candidates for market entry or existing products may be carried into new markets.

☐ By monitoring performance in different countries and product markets based on criteria such as return on investment and market share, so as to diagnose where existing or potential future problems appear to be emerging and, hence, where there is a need to adapt current marketing tactics or strategies.

☐ By scanning the international environment to assess future world and country scenarios and to monitor emerging and changing environmental trends.

☐ By assessing strategies for the allocation of corporate resources and effort across different countries, product markets, target segments, and modes of entry to determine whether changes in this allocation would maximise long-run profitability.

9 SUMMARY

The methods, tools and techniques of international marketing research do not vary according to whether research is done in South Africa or abroad. An international marketing research project essentially follows domestic procedures: problem definition, research design, data collection, analysis and report preparation. However, several factors make international marketing research more challenging and more difficult.

The two sources of data are secondary data and primary data. Secondary data may be gathered either in South Africa or abroad. There are a variety of sources of information from which secondary information may be gathered at home; foremost among them is the South African Department of Trade and Industry. Secondary information available in host countries may be plagued by problems of timeliness, reliability and comparability. But the collection of primary data abroad also poses difficulties, such as inability to draw a random sample, unwillingness of the sample population to cooperate, and inability to develop an adequate questionnaire.

Despite the inherent problems, a researcher can adopt measures to solve some, if not all, of the difficulties involved. Two helpful measures are the involvement of South African talent in data collection and cooperation with respectable foreign marketing information sources.

The international research activity may be formally organised at home, in the host country, or at both locations. Further, the marketing research organisation may be just a one-person department or a large entity in accordance with the scope of marketing activity in a country. A company deeply involved in business around the globe should establish an international marketing information system with formal structuring to determine information needs, to identify information sources, and to gather, analyse and disseminate information.

REFERENCES

Cateora, P 1983. *International marketing*. Fifth edition. Homewood, Ill: Irwin.

Cavusgil, S T 1984. International marketing research: insights into company practices. *Research in Marketing*, 7:30–31.

Cavusgil, S T 1985. Guidelines for export marketing research. *Business Horizons*, November–December.

Czinkota, M R, Ronkainen, I A & Moffett, M H 1994. *International business*. Third edition. Orlando: The Dryden Press.

Douglas, S P & Craig, C S 1983. *International marketing research*. Englewood Cliffs, NJ: Prentice Hall.

Jain, Sumati Chad 1990. *International marketing management*. Third edition. Boston: PWS-Kent.

Johansson, J K & Nonakeo, I 1987. Market research the Japanese way. *Harvard Business Review*, May-June.

Kaynak, E 1978. Difficulties of undertaking marketing research in developing countries. *European Research*, November.

Keegan, W J 1989. *Global marketing management*. Fourth edition. Englewood Cliffs, NJ: Prentice Hall.

Kinnear, T C & Taylor, J R 1991. *Marketing research: an applied approach*. Fourth edition. New York: McGraw-Hill.

Malhotra, N K 1988. A method for modelling consumer perceptions of country of origin. *International Marketing Review*, Autumn: 70.

Mayer, C S 1978. The lessons of multinational marketing research. *Business Horizons*, December:9.

Samli, A C 1986. International strategic information systems. *Proceedings of Second World Marketing Congress*, Stirling, Scotland.

Samli, A C, Still, R & Hill, J S 1993. *International marketing – planning and practice*. New York: Macmillan.

Advertising research

Chapter 23: J H Martins

Advertising research

1 INTRODUCTION

Marketing management applies four policy instruments in its marketing mix: product, price, marketing communication and distribution. Marketing communication, in turn, comprises media advertising, personal selling, supplementary marketing communication methods (such as exhibitions, trade fairs, competitions and couponing) and publicity. The consumer is the focal point of marketing and is therefore the object of advertising.

The importance of advertising in South Africa is reflected in the enormous sums advertisers spend on promoting their products and services. The South African Research Foundation (SAARF) set the sum spent on advertising in 1993 at R5 508,8 million. Some idea of the sums paid to the media and the cost of producing advertisements can be gained from Market Research Africa's estimates of advertising expenditure from 1989 to 1993 (table 23.1). Of total advertising expenditure in 1993 print media advertising made up R1 842,1 million or 33,4 % and expenditure on television advertising ran to R1 222,8 million for television time and R270,1 million for producing the commercials. The R1 492,9 million spent in total on television advertising represented 27,0 % of total expenditure on advertising in 1993.

In terms of marketing management's communication task **advertising** may be defined as the controlled, non-personal, outward communication through various media pertaining to a product, service or idea directed at a specific target audience or market with the object of informing and/or reminding and/or persuading it to take a particular course of action.

Table 23.1 Summary of estimated advertising expenditure in the RSA, 1989–1993

Media category	1989 Rm	1990 Rm	1991 Rm	1992 Rm	1993 Rm
i(a) PRINT — BRANDED					
Newspapers (daily, w/end, country)	493,1	553,4	659,2	727,8	731,0
Magazines and black publications	248,0	266,2	282,3	367,4	388,3
Trade and technical	104,5	127,3	150,1	144,1	146,9
Production costs	114,2	123,1	141,9	185,9	188,9
PRINT — 'BRANDED'	959,8	1 070,0	1 233,5	1 425,2	1 433,1
i(b) PRINT — OTHER					
Financial & mining					
Hotels & restaurants					
Property & auctions	323,3	371,8	331,9	358,4	409,0
Selling & classifieds					
Theatre & entertainment					
Recruitment advertising	97,5	77,8	58,9	54,6	55,0
TOTAL PRINT	**1 283,1**	**1 441,8**	**1 565,4**	**1 838,2**	**1 842,1**
ii RADIO					
Time	172,1	211,8	262,4	351,2	424,7
Production	12,9	15,9	21,0	28,1	29,7
TOTAL	**185,0**	**227,7**	**283,4**	**379,3**	**454,4**
iii OUTDOOR					
'Space'	35,0	51,1	66,3	85,2	111,0
Production	7,2	10,2	13,4	16,2	22,0
TOTAL	**42,2**	**61,3**	**79,7**	**101,4**	**133,0**
iv CINEMA					
Screening	17,6	23,1	29,1	31,0	31,1
Production	3,5	4,4	5,4	6,2	6,2
TOTAL	**21,1**	**27,5**	**34,5**	**37,2**	**37,3**
v TELEVISION					
Time	478,6	611,5	857,6	1 030,1	1 222,8
Production (includes Bop TV)	124,3	142,6	199,4	206,0	270,1
TOTAL	**602,9**	**754,1**	**1 057,0**	**1 236,1**	**1 492,9**
vi DIRECT MAIL					
Total estimate only	187,2	217,2	279,4	335,2	402,2
vii EXHIBITIONS & SHOWS					
Total estimate only	29,2	35,6	*134,0	160,8	180,1
viii WINDOW DISPLAYS & POINT OF SALE					
Total estimate only	111,5	128,2	155,5	178,8	205,6
ix PUBLIC RELATIONS					
Total estimate only	55,8	64,2	73,8	88,6	104,5
x OTHER					
Miscellaneous	34,5	39,7	45,3	50,7	57,0
General sport sponsorship	145,0	189,0	225,0	270,0	337,5
Yellow Pages	138,0	170,0	200,0	230,0	262,2
GRAND TOTAL	**2 835,5**	**3 356,3**	**4 133,0**	**4 851,7**	**5 508,8**
PERCENTAGE CHANGE	**+ 21,1 %**	**+ 18,4 %**	**+ 23,1 %**	**+ 17,4 %**	**+ 13,5 %**

NOTE: Figures for media *i* to *v* are based on fairly factual analyses, but media *vi* to *x* can best be described as 'qualified guestimates'.

* The marked increase is as a result of 'new' data that has become available on exhibitions and shows.

Source: Adapted from SAARF (1994:30–31).

Two aspects of advertising call for closer inspection: the advertising message and the media. Advertising research is research into advertising or the advertising message.

> **Advertising research** is the systematic, objective collection, analysis and interpretation of information for decision making on advertising strategy which comprises the planning, creative development, pre-testing and post-testing of advertising and the evaluation of advertising campaigns.

Media research is concerned mainly with the media audience. Sometimes advertising and media research are collectively termed advertising research.

Advertising and media research activities can be classified under six broad headings:

- ☐ WHO are the potential customers?
- ☐ WHAT should they be told about the product?
- ☐ HOW should the 'story' be presented?
- ☐ WHERE should it be told?
- ☐ WHEN should it be told?
- ☐ HOW SUCCESSFUL was the telling of the story?

Before proceeding with our discussion of advertising and media research it should be noted that general marketing research is used in formulating marketing communication policy and strategy which, as we have said, is only one of the four elements of the marketing mix. Therefore research is necessary on all these elements for the best possible decision making on each of them, separately or in combination. This chapter deals with advertising research, and chapter 24 with media research. Although advertising and media research cover two different fields and will therefore be discussed separately, one should never lose sight of the close connection between them. The message and the vehicle of the message cannot be separated physically and so the vehicle can impose limitations on or enhance the message.

Advertising research can be an aid to producing good advertisements but can never supplant the creative function. Advertisements are not created by advertising researchers. This function is performed by a creative team which needs information about the product or service, rival products, the market situation and an intimate knowledge of the Living Standards Measure (LSM), spending habits, level of education and other aspects of the target audience.

Research may be undertaken at various stages in the development of the advertisement. Basically there are four stages:

- ☐ *Strategic or planning research:* This research precedes development of the advertisement. Its aim is to gather information about the product or service and its users for the development and evaluation of advertising ideas.

☐ *Creative development research:* Research on creative strategy alternatives is intended to help formulate the most suitable wording, etc for the advertising message and reveals trends and attitudes in the target market.

☐ *Evaluative research or pre-testing:* After the creative strategy alternative has been chosen, the creative people set about translating the strategy into advertisements. Many alternative approaches may be developed and the final selection is based on research. The research goal is to determine which execution of the copy concept is most productive. This step saves unnecessary expense since placement in the media is the largest single cost item.

☐ *Advertisement and campaign evaluation research:* Post-testing is undertaken to evaluate the effectiveness of an advertisement or campaign after it has run and has had time to have an effect. The results supply information that is crucial to future advertising activities.

There are methods of testing advertising copy before, during and after the appearance of an advertisement. They measure qualitative or quantitative aspects. Qualitative and quantitative research into advertising campaigns should be regarded as complementary operations. Each can be applied to examine different aspects of an advertising campaign. The information required from each of them is different but linked: the qualitative study develops constructs or hypotheses for quantification and the quantified study checks and verifies the hypotheses developed via the qualitative work.

Advertising is aimed mainly at stimulating sales. If a change in sales following a promotion campaign is measurable, then the effectiveness of the promotion campaign is measurable. Researchers, however, are not able to develop a cut-and-dried method of measuring advertising effectiveness, because the effect of advertising is extremely difficult to isolate from the effects of other communication elements and marketing instruments. Ideally, the choice of any particular research technique or measurement for evaluating the effect or effectiveness of an advertisement or a campaign should rest on at least a judgemental model of 'how advertising works'. A discussion of these models is beyond the scope of this book, however.

There are several methods of data collection in copy testing. The depth interview, focus group discussion and the use of structured questionnaires are all involved in advertising research, and the basic principles are the same as in marketing research in general. Panels should be avoided because periodic questioning of the same consumers about advertising or advertisements renders panel members atypical in the sense that they develop a heightened awareness of advertisements and begin to study, look at and listen to them more attentively than before they joined the panel.

In this chapter we shall concentrate on basic methods and techniques for testing advertising effectiveness.

2 STRATEGIC OR PLANNING RESEARCH

A company engaging the services of an advertising agency has certain objectives in mind. These objectives must be brought into line with the company's general marketing objectives. Together the company's marketing department and the advertising agency take the first step towards defining advertising objectives within the overall marketing plan by devising an advertising strategy.

Advertising strategy is devised by applying various research techniques. Typically, large-scale quantitative studies are conducted that monitor the overall performance of the product or brand or service to be advertised and identify areas of competitive strengths and weaknesses. These studies generally include retail audits, consumer panels and questionnaires to ask about product performance, attitudes and usage behaviour. Focus group discussions and in-depth interviews are supplementary techniques but may also be the only alternatives, as in campaigns against drug abuse. Internal and even external secondary sources can be most helpful during this phase. The method of collecting the information will depend on the target group and the variety and nature of the information. Part 2 of this book deals with the collection of primary and secondary data.

3 CREATIVE DEVELOPMENT RESEARCH

Strategic planning research is very helpful in isolating areas where effort might usefully be directed but less helpful in suggesting how the desired results might be achieved. The purpose of creative development research is to help the creative team develop a piece of advertising which not only incorporates the message that best meets the strategy but also conveys that message in an interesting, stimulating and persuasive manner that is appealing to the target group and in keeping with the values of the product or brand or service.

By far the most common technique in creative development research is focus group discussions, but individual depth interviews or even small-scale quantified studies are also conducted.

3.1 Focus group discussions

Focus group discussions are organised in the usual way with groups of target consumers invited to an interviewer's home, a research viewing facility, a local hotel or the home of one of the respondents. It can be a traditional (classical) group of 7–9 respondents, a mini group of 4–6 respondents, a creativity group in which screened respondents are interviewed for at least two hours, or an accelerated development group in which there are at least two repeat group sessions with the same respondents.

The creative work is invariably at a rough, unfinished stage and commenting on such material is an unfamiliar task. The moderator must be an experienced convenor to encourage respondents to use their imagination and to respond on emotional and rational levels to the stimulus material. A large part of the value of creative development research lies in its diagnostic information. Essentially it is part of a learning process; testing or evaluation will be carried out when the advertising ideas have reached a far more advanced stage.

3.2 Individual depth interviews

Individual depth interviews are discussed in chapter 7. The aims in planning and conducting depth interviews are largely similar to those discussed in the previous section. Besides the usual individual depth interviews there are also conflictual dialogues. Conflictual dialogues are simultaneous in-depth interviews of two people who generally speaking have the socio-economic features but are different in that they have diametrically opposed consumer attitudes. These face-to-face interviews by a psychologist make it possible to collect significant information relating to the sometimes unconscious thought processes of the respondent.

3.3 Quantitative studies

Quantitative studies can be useful in narrowing product concept options and can be seen as an extension of the strategic planning stage. Face-to-face interviews using a structured questionnaire are not suitable for checking rough advertisements but can be used to rate alternatives. The key questions usually are: likely interest in trial or purchase, or a rating scale. Diagnostic information about, say, reasons for interest, or lack of interest, believability and uniqueness of the concept is also collected.

4 EVALUATIVE RESEARCH OR PRE-TESTING

Generally only finished or nearly finished material is evaluated or pre-tested since the primary objective is to test the performance of the actual advertisement, and not the strategic thought or the creative idea behind the advertisement, by making a diagnostic evaluation of the effectiveness of the advertising communication. A holistic approach in which the advertisement in its entirety is tested or a Clucas approach in which the advertisement is broken down into sections and the sections are tested can be followed. The Clucas technique attempts to look at a commercial in a bit-by-bit, atomistic way. The underlying theory is that any commercial is a series of separate (but linked) devices, each with its own particular purpose in terms of attracting attention, generating involvement, gaining sympathy or communicating a message.

The first step is to predefine exactly what each small section of the commercial is trying to achieve. In the research, the respondents are shown the commercial and then asked to underline on a copy of the script what they remember having seen and heard and what they liked and disliked, and to indicate what each section communicated to them about the product.

Opinions differ on the purpose of evaluating or pre-testing advertisements. There are those who hold that the only thing that can be measured with any validity is whether the advertisement said what it set out to say – where 'said' is extended beyond the transmission of rational, verbal messages to include successfully conveying a mood, emotion or association. Some think the only thing really worth measuring is whether the advertisement will influence sales. And still others see this stage of advertising research as a source of information leading to more efficient use of the advertising budget.

The choice between the research techniques available is governed by the advertiser's personal or corporate model of how advertising itself works.

4.1 Opinion and attitude ratings

The opinion method is one of the simplest techniques for *pre-testing* in the broad sense. Usually people are only too eager to give their opinions of advertisements.

The test advertisement presented to respondents for their opinion should look and/or sound as much as it will look and/or sound in the media. Because of the expense involved in producing and then testing TV commercials cheaper methods of pre-testing have been developed. TV commercial material is pre-tested as raw storyboards, filmed storyboards, animatics (a sequence of drawings), photomatics (a sequence of photographs) or commercials where inexpensive actors (stunt men) substitute for celebrities. A combination of these materials can be filmed. Incorporating photographs may be important when the presenters are celebrities or when illustrations, say of cooked food, would not be realistic.

Next the test material is put onto cassette for use in a video cassette recorder (VCR). The final arbiters on the state of the rough TV commercial material should include the creative director whose responsibility it is to make sure the basic ideas of his commercial are communicated by the chosen means.

Once the question of the equipment is solved, the place needs to be chosen. The alternatives are:

☐ a theatre or large hall where large audiences can be exposed to the commercial

☐ a focus group discussion facility with built-in equipment for showing TV material

☐ a room in a house or hotel specially equipped for a particular test to run there

☐ a mobile unit

☐ respondents' own homes using easily portable equipment.

One of the considerations in deciding on a venue is that testing TV commercials on large screens can be misleading. Most consumers have (relatively) small television screens in their homes. A further consideration is that quite a large proportion of the sample invited to a theatre test do not come. Those who do arrive may not be representative of the sample because they tend to be people who ordinarily have little social life.

Private homes are preferable as venues for television commercial tests because a representative sample can be drawn and the viewing conditions are closer to normal. However, the method can be expensive unless it is limited to small-scale qualitative work. The major shortcoming in all these test situations is that exposure is forced on the test subjects, whereas in real life the commercial has to capture its audience. In the section that follows we shall deal with direct and indirect opinion measurement in advertising research.

4.1.1 Direct opinion measurement

In direct opinion measurement respondents are asked direct questions about a particular advertisement. They are usually approached individually. If the sample is large enough, it is generally known as a consumer jury.

4.1.2 Indirect opinion measurement

As the term implies, this is an indirect method of ascertaining the respondent's opinion of a particular advertisement. The respondent is not asked for a opinion of the advertisement; the opinion is inferred from actions. If, say, changes in brand preference are to be determined, audiences are exposed to films or simulated television or radio programmes in an auditorium, studio or cinema theatre hired for the purpose. Among other things these films or programmes contain the test advertisement(s). Before the test commences the audience are invited to select particular brands of products on a shopping list. After the test, which contains one or more advertisements of the brands concerned, participants are required to complete a second shopping list. Changes in brand preference are evident from comparison of the two lists.

An alternative objective measure is to test on a large scale near a supermarket. The advertisement is shown in an auditorium or mobile unit near the supermarket and the participants receive money-off coupons which are redeemable at the supermarket for a particular product (not brand). Their brand choice is compared with the choice of another group who have made their purchases at a similar supermarket without being exposed to test advertisements.

A third method of assessing an advertisement involves questioning a group of respondents after showing them the advertisement. On the strength of previous surveys certain values are assigned to questions, bearing in mind the purpose of the test. Then the interviewer assigns values to the answers respondents have given to questions asked after the showing of the advertisement. A comparison is made between the values obtained in this survey and the standard values. Values higher than standard values point to favourable responses to certain aspects of an advertisement, and the opposite applies to lower values.

A fourth alternative is the Dodge technique. An advertiser prepares various test advertisements for an advertising campaign. To each of these advertisements he adds the same coupon offer. The test advertisements are mailed to matched samples of potential users and the response levels to the various advertisements are established. The effectiveness of the various test advertisements is determined by comparing their respective response rates. A prerequisite on receipt of the coupon is that the advertiser is able to distinguish the advertisement from which it originated.

Lotteries represent a fifth method of testing advertisements without the respondents knowing what the experiment is about. Expensive products lend themselves to the use of this method. Respondents are asked which brand they would choose if they were to win. Two lots are drawn – one before and one after the commercials have been flighted.

4.2 Focus group discussions

For the purpose of pre-testing a commercial, each member of the group is issued with an electronic evaluator which allows that person to evaluate any aspect of the commercial at a given moment. With the exception of group evaluations of certain parts of the commercial, each member of the group assigns individual and confidential values to the parts of the commercial which are illustrated graphically on a screen in the room. These are discussed later. Chapter 7 of this book gives a detailed explanation of focus group discussions as a research method.

4.3 Non-verbal interviewing

More recently researchers have turned to non-verbal communication by means of photographs, colour cards and even music in their efforts to make a closer study of human emotions. The respondent is given a set of photographs or cards or listens to music which he is required to link with various concepts. The photographs depict different personality types (visual image profiles) or different scenic situations (image configurations). Once the respondent has linked the photographs and/or music with the concepts, the researcher is able to determine which emotion is associated with which concept.

4.4 Readability tests

In readability analysis the reading level of the copy is established by analysing the content of advertising copy. One of the methods of assessing reading level involves an expert or team of experts who analyse interviewers' verbal reports on the reaction of respondents.

In another method the respondent is required to guess the words which have been left out of a piece of copy. This test rests on the principle that the predictability of the advertising message supports the learning process. An extract is prepared from an advertisement in which for example every sixth word has been omitted. This is shown to a respondent who is required to supply the missing words. Besides the correlation between predictability and recall there is also a relation between the predictability and the likeability of the message.

The chief advantage of readability tests is their greater degree of objectivity. Mechanical testing (which is discussed in the section below) also offers a greater degree of objectivity.

4.5 Mechanical testing

In most advertising tests it is impossible to measure the reaction of the respondents at the moment of seeing or hearing the advertisement. Mechanical pre- or post-testing, however, can be conducted in theatres, studios or auditoriums, and in most instances testing apparatus can also be set up in the respondent's home, which has the advantage that the relaxed domestic atmosphere is largely retained.

There are several fairly sophisticated devices for testing audience reactions. A few of them are discussed below:

☐ The *communiscope* consists of a slide projector and a shutter device which is fitted over the lens of the projector, permitting brief exposures on the screen. Slides which represent advertisements are projected on to the screen and the respondent is asked whether he recognises the advertisement in question.

☐ In a *psycho-galvanic test* a modified lie-detector reveals the emotional reactions of the person viewing a number of selected advertisements by measuring skin response on the person's fingertips. Some emotions induce sweating which is detected by the device.

☐ A *polygraph* is an instrument developed to account for emotional reaction by taking a range of physiological measures, including galvanic skin response and pupil dilation.

Whereas the apparatus used in the psycho-galvanic test only measures skin response the polygraph is a more sophisticated device which measures a greater number of physiological responses such as perspiration, heart beat and breathing.

☐ The *eye camera*, which records the eye path of the observer, is another instrument for testing reaction to advertisements. In this way the eye camera reveals the words or parts of the advertisement that interest the observer first, the most or very little. If it is found that the most important aspect arouses the least interest the advertisement's layout and/or copy should be revised.

More recent experiments concentrate on measuring tension in the eyebrows, analysing voice pitch and examining hemispheric activity. These physiological measures are very costly and are likely to remain a matter for experiment.

5 ADVERTISEMENT AND CAMPAIGN EVALUATION RESEARCH

Advertising is only one aspect of the marketing mix that leads to sales, with product characteristics, availability, price, packaging, sales promotion, merchandising and point-of-purchase displays all making a major contribution. In post-testing it is the aspect (or aspects) of the marketing mix or advertising campaign to be tested that governs the choice of method.

5.1 Inquiries and sales measures

Most advertisements aim at ultimate response in the form of purchases, or some intermediate step such as inquiries about the advertised product or service. Even the inquiries and similar intermediate steps are intended to stimulate sales.

Besides being a direct means of promoting sales, advertising inquiries can also be helpful in testing advertising effectiveness.

5.1.1 Inquiries

Printed advertisements and radio, television and cinema commercials can be tested for effectiveness by the *inquiry method*. For instance, the audience may be invited to ask for more information, a booklet, or a free sample of the advertised product. In press advertising such invitations to inquiry may be clearly visible (for example a coupon may have to be filled in) or they may be hidden in the copy. Hidden or buried invitations mean that the advertisement has to be read before the invitation is observed, whereas coupons can be filled in without the advertisement having been read. In radio commercials the invitation to inquire may be direct or indirect. Conspicuous invitations usually elicit more reaction than 'buried' ones but the advertiser at least has the assurance that respondents who react to the 'buried' invitation have heard or read part of the advertising message.

Very often the *split-run technique* is combined with the inquiry method of testing advertising effectiveness and other advertising research methods. In the split-run technique an identical publication is printed and distributed in two or more separate production runs and deliveries to facilitate the insertion of different advertisements in each. This arrangement makes it easier to compare the measured effects of alternative pieces of advertising copy.

5.1.2 Sales measures

There are various sales measures of advertising effectiveness, that is, measures of the direct impact of a particular advertisement or advertising campaign on sales. One way of measuring advertising effectiveness is to ask the consumer whether the advertisement persuaded him to buy the advertised brand, product, or service.

Econometric modelling tries to isolate the influence of advertising on sales. In essence econometric modelling involves the use of a mathematical formula for assigning a value to each of the marketing variables whereby variations in the key dependent variable, that of sales, are best explained. Developing a model of this kind requires not only a rigorous process of statistical testing, but also a reliable series of prior data on all the key variables before the formula can be derived. It follows that the technique is available only to those companies who routinely and consistently collect all the necessary input data. The use of econometrics in this context is explained more fully in *How to plan advertising* (Cowley 1987, chapter 8).

The correlation between sales and exposure to advertisements during test marketing is another measure of advertising effectiveness. In this method two identical consumer samples are constituted, the only difference being that the members of the first sample have either seen or heard the advertisement and the members of the second sample have not been exposed to it at all. The effectiveness of the advertisement is measured by correlating sales with the two samples during test marketing.

5.2 Memory tests

The memory test is one of the techniques for measuring the effectiveness of an advertisement. All memory tests measure two distinct audience reactions: how much attention the advertisement was given, and how well it was remembered by the respondent.

Of the various kinds of memory tests two of the most popular are recognition tests and recall and association tests. Yet recognition and recall as such are only indirectly related to advertising success, so that these methods have to be refined to attain optimum results. Respondents can, for instance, be asked to note down their main thoughts while they are watching the different parts of a commercial. Subsequent analysis will show whether the thought processes which the creative team imagined would be set in motion were in fact evoked. The rest of this section will deal with recognition and recall tests.

5.2.1 Recognition tests

Recognition testing is one of the best-known and most popular techniques for *post-testing* advertising effectiveness. Its purpose is to establish whether a particular advertisement is recognised and has therefore been seen or heard by the respondent. Respondents are usually divided into two groups: those who merely noted the relevant advertisement and those who read or heard most of the advertising message. Because only those who have read or heard the advertisement are questioned, the results of the studies are not applicable to the population as a whole and should be related only to the audience.

5.2.1.1 Simple recognition test

This is a very elementary method which usually involves particular issue of a paper, a magazine or a specific radio or TV channel. Representative samples are drawn and interviewers call on potential respondents who are asked whether they read the magazine or tuned in to the radio or TV channel concerned. If not, they do not qualify for interviews. Those who read the magazine or usually tune in to the radio or TV channel qualify for interviews and are noted as respondents. The interviewer then pages through the magazine or plays/shows the commercial and requests the respondent to say which advertisements he recognises. Usually all that is wanted is comment on particular advertisements, such as advertisements taking up half a page or more.

To make the test as objective as possible the interviewer pages through the magazine with the respondent, thus ensuring that every page is given proper attention. He avoids drawing the respondent's attention to particular advertisements and begins each interview on a different (random) page. This method was developed by Daniel Starch and Staff. This test is criticised on the grounds that respondents are not selected carefully enough, recognition claims may be false; factors such as fatigue and boredom of interviewers or respondents can interfere with correct procedure; representative sampling is costly; and suitable interviewers are hard to find.

5.2.1.2 Controlled recognition method

The controlled recognition method is designed to measure the degree of inflation which results from false recognition claims by respondents. It rests on the principle that all variables except one are kept more or less constant.

The procedure is to present an unreleased test advertisement which the public has not yet seen or heard to a sample of respondents who are asked whether they recognise the advertisement. Then the advertisement is placed or flighted in a single medium and a parallel sample drawn from the universe is tested for recognition of the advertisement.

The first test or pre-examination counts the number of people who falsely claim to recognise the advertisement which had not yet been released to the public. The second or post-examination in turn quantifies the number of persons who erroneously claim to recognise that particular advertisement plus those who actually 'read' the advertisement in the medium concerned. The difference between these two figures represents the number of respondents who actually recognise the advertisement.

Despite its frequent use the method has practical disadvantages, such as the increased cost of dual surveys, but the most serious criticism is that the percentage of respondents who make false claims is assumed to be the same in both surveys.

5.2.2 Recall and association tests

Recall tests go slightly further than recognition tests. Recognition tests are concerned with the respondent's ability to recognise a particular advertisement, whereas recall tests measure the advertisement's impact in terms of the respondent's ability to recall and describe parts of it. The difference is one of degree; being less superficial, recall tests measure an advertisement's impact at a deeper level. Recognition tests are typically used in the printed media and recall tests in the electronic media.

Variations of the recall test are applied in *pre-testing* (in the broad sense) but the majority are used as *post-tests*.

5.2.2.1 Unaided recall test

In the unaided recall test the respondents are not given any help; they are asked to describe advertisements they have seen or heard recently. If more prompting is required, the test becomes an aided recall test.

5.2.2.2 Aided recall and association test

In the electronic media the respondents in an aided recall test are required to describe the commercial for a certain brand.

A respondent in an *aided recall test* for print media is given a list of the advertisers or brands of products which are advertised in the test publication. As a control measure the list includes several names and brands which are not represented in the test publication. If a respondent who claims to recall an advertisement describes it accurately without consulting the test publication, the advertisement is regarded as 'recalled'. This is termed Proved Name Registration (PNR) in Gallup & Robinson's impact test which is one of the best-known aided recall tests.

There are several *tests of association*. The best known are sponsor identification (see sponsorship under media research), masked identification, association of advertising themes with brands, and uncontrolled brand associations. All these methods test the respondent's ability to associate various aspects of advertisements, such as their sponsors. For instance, radio listeners or television viewers are telephoned and asked to identify the company (or brand) which sponsors a programme they listened to or viewed at a particular time.

Another example is the *triple association test* which measures ability to associate products, brand and advertising themes. A respondent may be asked: 'Which bank is advertised as follows: "Who do we have to thank?"' If the person answers 'Boland ... Boland Bank', the desired association has been made. These methods have the advantage of revealing the associations made with advertisements.

5.3 Newcomer noting

In essence, noting is a measure of recall. After the release of a new advertisement a sample of respondents is asked whether the advertisement has been observed. The spontaneous noting method merely requires that respondents be asked whether they have noted any new advertisements in, say, the past two weeks. In prompted noting a list of products, services or companies with new advertisements is read aloud and respondents are required to say whether they have noted any of them. Respondents who claim to have noted the relevant advertisements (in spontaneous or prompted noting) are asked to mention the main features of the advertisement.

In this way a newcomer noting index is compiled that allows comparison of the notings of new advertisements. The comparisons are quantitative rather than qualitative. Additional questions that require the respondent to, say, rate the advertisement being recalled on a likeability scale, can furnish limited qualitative information.

5.4 Advertising tracking

Advertising tracking measures advertising wearout over time and monitors advertisement placings in the media. Various methods of advertising tracking have been devised, depending on the purpose of the required information. These methods include personal interviews with respondents, analysis of the viewing patterns of TV programmes, and analysis of the number of commercials flighted.

In personal interviews respondents are required to recall advertisements, as described in section 5.2.2. Such information provides a measure of advertising wearout over time, which has financial implications in that it helps the advertiser schedule his advertisements effectively. Overexposure places an unnecessary strain on the advertising budget by repeating the advertisement far too frequently, whereas with too little exposure the advertising message is forgotten because of insufficient repetition.

Advertisers are interested in their competitors' volume of advertising and media choice. They also need to track their advertisements if they are to verify media placings. Advertisements in the printed media are easily read and recorded. TV and radio commercials are more difficult to track, especially without the help of TV and radio station logbooks which detail advertisers and flightings. Electronic verification of TV and radio commercials is a new development. TV commercials are recorded by monitoring signals from the vertical blanking interval – that is the lines contained in the black bar usually seen only when a TV screen is 'flipping'. It verifies whether commercials run at the correct time, in full, in colour and with the desired audio and video quality. Commercials can also be tracked by using inaudible signals on sound tracks that are picked up by decoding units. It can identify the source and time of a commercial play on TV and radio.

The peoplemeter used in TV media research (see next chapter) measures viewer profiles, usually for 15-minute periods. But advertisers also want to know how many viewers have seen their commercials. An electronic metering system has now been developed for measuring the use of TV sets over much shorter periods. The Information Resources Inc electronic metering programme in America records set status (whether the TV set is on or off and, if on, to which channel it is tuned) by five-second intervals. This extremely fine time detail makes it possible to study channel-switching in a precise manner.

5.5 Content analysis

In the preceding sections we saw that advertising effectiveness is testable among a sample of respondents by such techniques as memory tests, opinion and attitude ratings, mechanical and readability tests, and inquiries. In content analysis, which also is a form of *post-testing*, the advertisement and not the respondent is the sample unit. A distinction is made between pure content analysis and content analysis linked with some performance measure or other. A pure content analysis study may for instance be aimed at identifying differentiation opportunities in advertising by tabulating the frequency of occurrence of various creative factors by product group. On the other hand a content analysis study linked with a performance measure may be aimed at identifying the creative factors with the most impact on the performance of advertisements. For example, multiple regression analysis may single out colour and advertising appeal as the most significant predictors of recall. Rademeyer (1988:25) defines content analysis as a research technique for the objective, systematic and quantitative description of the manifest content of communication.

The requirement of objectivity in content analysis calls for the application of a set of rules or definitions that will leave no doubt about the classification of the unit of analysis into a specific category. Systematic means that all possible categories are represented and the results of the content analysis have practical applications and can be analysed quantitatively. Only the manifest or overt content can be analysed by this method; analysis of the latent or hidden content calls for the application of one of the other methods discussed above.

In content analysis the researcher begins by drawing a representative sample of the advertisements to be analysed from the universe which encompasses the titles (magazines, newspapers or channels), the dates of the titles, and the content to be covered. Next the unit of analysis is selected. It can be a word, theme, character, item, space or time unit. These units of analysis are then divided into categories which are compartments for the classification of the content being analysed.

6 ADVERTISING RESEARCH IN SOUTH AFRICA

There are a number of marketing research organisations in South Africa that do advertising research on an ad hoc basis. Their activities and techniques include focus group discussions, depth, semi-depth and structured interviews, pre- and post-testing of television advertisements with mobile testing units, and psychological techniques. Some firms specialise in fields such as mining, food, construction, plastics, beverages and pharmaceutical, veterinary, agricultural, industrial and consumer areas. Admonitor, undertaken by Research International, helps establishments to make the most effective use of their advertising expenditure by monitoring measures relating to advertising effectiveness.

At the beginning of this chapter we examined the close relation between media and advertising research. Adtrack and Magtrak are discussed in section 9 of chapter 24. Depending on whether the information collected by Adtrack and Magtrak is used for media planning or post-testing of advertisements, it is classified as media research or advertising research.

7 SUMMARY

Research for decision making on advertising copy is termed advertising research. It is undertaken at four stages in the development of the advertisement: before the development of the advertisement (strategic or planning research), during the development (creative development research), after the development (pre-testing individual advertisements) and post-testing individual advertisements or evaluation of advertising campaigns.

Strategic or planning research defines advertising objectives within the overall marketing plan by devising an advertising strategy. Typically, large-scale quantitative studies are conducted that monitor the overall performance of the product or brand or service to be advertised and identify areas of competitive strengths and weaknesses.

Creative development research helps the creative team develop a piece of advertising which not only incorporates the message that best meets the strategy but also conveys that message in an interesting, stimulating and persuasive manner. By far the most common technique in creative development research is group discussions, but individual depth interviews or even small-scale quantified studies are also conducted.

Generally, only finished or near-finished material is evaluated or pre-tested since the objective is to test the performance of the actual advertisement. A holistic approach in which the advertisement in its entirety is tested or a Clucas approach in which the advertisement is broken down into sections and tested can be followed. The choice between the research techniques available is governed by the advertiser's personal or corporate model of how advertising itself works. The options are opinion and attitude ratings, group discussions, non-verbal interviewing, readability tests and mechanical testing methods.

In advertisement and campaign evaluation research it is the aspect (or aspects) of the marketing mix or advertising campaign to be tested that governs the choice of method. Besides a wide variety of inquiries and sales measures and memory tests, the newcomer rating, advertising tracking and content analysis methods are also used as post-testing methods.

REFERENCES

Churchill, Gilbert A (Jr) 1992. *Basic marketing research*. Second edition. Orlando: The Dryden Press.

Cowley, Don (ed) 1987. *How to plan advertising*. London: Cassell in association with the Account Planning Group.

Haskins, J & Kendrick, A 1991. *Successful advertising research methods*. Ill: NTC.

Rademeyer, A P 1988. *The influence of creative factors on the performance of TV commercials directed at white audiences*. Pretoria: Unisa, Bureau of Market Research. (Research Report no 147.)

South African Advertising Research Foundation (SAARF). *AMPS 94 and trends 1991/1994*. Condensed pocket edition:30–31.

Media research

Chapter 24: J H Martins

Media research

1 INTRODUCTION

Media research is the systematic and objective collection, analysis and interpretation of information for purposes of decision making for optimal media selection.

Media selection is the art and science of putting advertising money to work where it does the most good. It involves identifying the prime prospects for a product or service and selecting the vehicles that will reach them often enough to foster awareness of the copy claim. The overall requirement in implementing any advertising brief is optimum cost effectiveness. This goal is attained by selecting advertising vehicles in such a way that the size and nature of the audience and the pattern of their opportunities for contact with the advertisement are optimal according to some agreed set of criteria. The question is how many people who are in the current or potential market for a product or service are likely to see and/or hear an advertisement in the various media available.

Media research measures the size of the audience, the composition of the audience by all socio-economic factors, the cumulative audience, duplication with other media, repetition or frequency of exposure, the cost of audience provided, product usage by audience, and distribution of audience. Various yardsticks are applied but media research, like other social sciences, does not have precise measures. There is no such thing as the absolute truth in media measurement.

In the rest of this chapter we shall deal separately with the various types of media research. The chapter closes with an assessment of media research in South Africa.

2 PRINT MEDIA RESEARCH

Publishers, advertisers and advertising practitioners have need of printed media research for reasons that vary with the party who commissions it: a publisher's research will be publication oriented whereas advertisers and their agencies seek to maximise the efficiency of media selection. However, some fields of research do overlap. Our concern in this chapter is only with media research in so far as it relates to advertising.

The circulation figures of leading newspapers and magazines are published in most countries. In South Africa the *Audit Bureau of Circulations (ABC)* of South Africa performs this function for its members. Circulation figures supply the quantitative data which advertisers or their agents need for further research, but the amount of further research that is required is determined by the nature of the product or service to be advertised.

Besides interviewing respondents personally and by telephone, readership can also be measured via self-administered questionnaires. In publications with narrow or specialised audiences it is not uncommon to obtain self-completed questionnaires from a sample of a magazine's subscribers or to insert a questionnaire in all copies of a particular issue. The response rate for these questionnaires is usually very low and the characteristics of readers who choose to return a questionnaire inserted in the actual publication can be markedly different from those of its total audience. A further shortcoming is that pass-on readership is not directly measurable.

Expectations are that the electronic industry will come up with a Universal Paging Watch in the second half of the 1990s that does print, radio and television media measurement. Worn on the arm like a watch it will attempt to link media exposure to its wearer's purchase patterns of package goods over the counter, pharmaceutical products, and alcoholic beverages and tobacco products on a purchase-by-purchase basis. The watch will be capable of being altered to measure magazine readership by means of chips that will tell the watch when it is removed from the wrist, sense the absence of motion for five minutes and sound a warning, store the data obtained from a chip placed inside the pages of the magazine and will store the programme codes transmitted from television and radio frequencies. The watch will also signal the cash register of its presence and will be required to download each week.

The watch will eventually look like an ordinary timepiece, but will be equipped with a recorder and will receive the signal from a transmitter chip embedded in magazines. Research is already under way to make such a chip for inclusion in every copy of every issue of every magazine for an extended period. The watch will start recording when it comes within seven inches of an opened magazine. It will stop recording when the reader puts the magazine down and moves the watch hand further than seven inches from the magazine.

2.1 Issue audience

The **issue audience** of a newspaper or magazine may be defined as the number and types of people that come into contact with either a specific issue of a given newspaper or magazine or the average issue.

Often such persons are termed readers and they are the ones with an opportunity to see (OTS) an advertisement carried by the issue. The statistic that has achieved almost universal acceptance as the main measure of a newspaper or magazine's audience is its average issue readership (AIR). This is the number of different people who will have contact with the average issue, usually on a relatively broad definition of 'read or looked at', over its life. The issue audience may be further subdivided into the page audience comprising the number of people who look at anything on a page or spread, and the advertisement audience comprising those who have contact with the advertisement itself.

Before discussing research techniques we turn to operational definitions of an issue audience or issue readership, which set out the criteria for qualifying as a reader. The All Media and Products Survey (AMPS) in the RSA takes respondents to be all those who have personally read or paged through all or part of a publication, their own or someone else's, anywhere, in the past six months. Claimed readership over the past six months is determined by a system of displaying masthead cards, and only titles which pass this filter are subjected to the remaining questions of the section. To qualify as a reader a respondent must have read a copy – any copy – of the title under consideration within a period before the interview which is no longer than the issue period of that title (in the case of a weekly magazine, therefore, within seven days of the interview); furthermore, the respondent must have read that issue for the first time within that period.

Two points in this definition serve to illustrate the contention that readership is not an absolute concept. First, a respondent qualifies as a reader irrespective of the proportion of an issue seen and whether that proportion has been read intently or merely skimmed. Second, the definitions allow readership of current and outdated issues to count equally.

There are two basic approaches to measuring issue audience: a person's recall of a previous reading occasion(s), and a person's recognition of a specific issue of a newspaper or magazine as one read before. The selection of elements for inclusion in a one-time readership survey can be made from a single sample whereas different samples or panels are used for regular surveys. We turn briefly to these two methods below.

2.1.1 Recall

The recall approach can be subdivided into two alternative routes:

- [ ] the *recency or recall reading* approach where people are asked when they last read any issue of a given newspaper or magazine
- [ ] the *frequency approach* where people are asked how often they read or page through different issues of a newspaper or magazine.

There are at least three distinct approaches to *reading frequency measurement*. First, consistent questions on issue readership can be repeated twice or more to the same individuals in a panel context. As a second method the recall of two or more different issues of the same publication (as having been read before) can be measured on the same sample at successive interviews. Third, a reader is asked to make a subjective estimate of his reading frequency on a numerical or purely verbal scale. Generally the difference between a numerical and a verbal scale is not great. Ratings on such scales which are thought to be too high are adjusted by a factor termed issue probability.

The *use of prompt aids* during interviewing reduces the risk of underclaiming of issue contact, especially with titles which the respondent sees infrequently or irregularly. Methods of questioning include reading out the names of the newspapers or magazines, showing the names, logos or mastheads, or showing the covers of the latest issue of newspapers or magazines.

2.1.2 Recognition

Formerly the recognition approach required that the interviewer page through the complete copy of the magazine while questioning the respondent. Known as the Through-the-Book (TTB) method, it was later renamed the editorial interest method after the introduction of certain refinements. These included replacing the complete issue of a magazine with an abridged version (skeletonised issue) containing only key pages, which reduces interviewing time and the physical load the interviewer has to carry. Respondents are first taken through an abridged issue and asked, in relation to the items of its contents, whether they would find them of interest. As a final question, which is intended to appear incidental and unloaded, they are asked whether they think they have seen the test issue before.

2.2 Page audience

Continuous issue audience research is undertaken in most of the developed countries, mostly by the recall method, whereas page audience research is less common. Advertisers are especially interested in establishing whether particular pages in an issue are read more than others and whether particular page positions for advertisements are more effective than others. Only respondents who qualify as readers of a specific issue of a newspaper or magazine are interviewed in an in-depth interview on advertisements in that newspaper or magazine. The page audience poses the same two basic problems as the issue audience: selecting a workable operational definition that encompasses the basic concept, and devising the best technique for measuring an audience against this definition.

> The **page audience** comprises persons whose perceptual field at some time encompassed the page.

Methods of establishing the page audience vary from recall and recognition to far more complex observational techniques.

2.2.1 Glue-spot technique

In the glue-spot technique facing pages of magazines are sealed with a thin layer of glue. To open pages the readers must open the magazine far enough to see the advertisement(s) on these pages. The requirements of the test are that the layer of glue is thin enough to escape the notice of the reader, pages do not again adhere to each other once they have been opened, the opening of the pages concerned is not interfered with, the pages do not become unstuck until they have been opened, the respondent will receive the copy in a normal way, and there is a check that the issue has been handled only by the respondent between placement and recall interviews.

2.2.2 Direct eye movement observation technique

This technique makes it possible to take a continuous record on film of a respondent in a reading situation. Equipment for this purpose can show not only which pages were opened and for how long but also the direction of the gaze in relation to the page.

2.2.3 Recall and recognition

The two methods discussed above do not lend themselves to general use, and information can be collected only from a limited number of elements. Recall and especially recognition methods are far more popular. In the Gallup Field Readership Index respondents who claim to have seen a particular issue at all are taken through it page by page and asked to indicate each item that they have previously looked at. Page traffic is then defined as the proportion of the issue audience claiming to have seen one or more items on the page in question. The disadvantages of bias in this method of questioning – respondents tend to claim to have read status articles or reports and not to have read socially less acceptable articles or reports – led to respondents being asked instead to indicate their thoroughness of reading on some scale or other. A third alternative is to question respondents about their reading habits without the help of aids.

Observational, recall and recognition research techniques are also applied in establishing the double-page or double-spread audience. In the case of magazines especially it seems almost unthinkable that the reader would fail to notice what is printed on the opposite page, even if only subconsciously.

2.3 Advertisement audience

The advertisement audience is studied in media research because the audience can be influenced by media variables. We discussed research on the advertising message under advertising research. Some of the media variables which influence the reader are the advertisement's size in absolute terms and in proportion to the page and other advertisements, its position on the page, the page's position in the newspaper or magazine, and whether it is printed in colour or black and white. In a study (Rademeyer 1990) of media factors that affect advertising effectiveness a large number of advertisements (and consequently the number of pages) were found to have a negative influence on readership. The position in the issue of consumer magazines does not seem to affect the performance of advertisements on inside pages, but advertisements on inside and outside cover pages do attract more readers. In industrial magazines enquiry generation does not vary with issue position of the advertisement. There is no conclusive proof that advertisements on right-hand pages, which are seen first when a magazine is paged through from front to back, perform better than advertisements on left-hand pages. Readers of newspapers and magazines seem to single out items of interest to them, so that page position of advertisements is of little significance. The proximity and type of editorial environment seem to have very little if any effect on the performance of magazine and newspaper advertisements. Most effective is the repetition of the advertisement in a different medium or publication because the appearance of a familiar advertisement in a new environment arouses the audience's curiosity.

In terms of OTS, the advertisement audience is virtually equivalent to the page audience of the page carrying it. The ideal is to count only within the advertisement audience those who have actually noticed the advertisement. Recognition and recall techniques similar to those discussed under advertising research can be used in this research.

3 TELEVISION MEDIA RESEARCH

The choice of research methods is governed by the way commercials are screened and the advertiser's degree of control over the placing of commercials. Commercials may be screened as part of a sponsored programme, as isolated commercials, as part of a short break of several commercials as used by both the South African Broadcasting Corporation and M-Net in South Africa between and in programmes, as part of a larger block of commercials, and within short pieces of entertainment material. The degree of control over the placing of commercials determines how far detailed audience measurement data are actionable. Control over the placing of commercials can be to the nearest minute, including position in a break, a break within a programme, as part of a sponsored programme, within broad time segments, day of transmission, week or longer period of transmission, or as part of blocks with time roughly specified or unspecified.

Until recently television viewing was based upon regular habits of time and place and was more often set in a family context. A higher proportion of all contacts with the medium was planned and a smaller proportion happenstantial. Viewing occurred most often in a particular room in the home and the time-sequential presentation of the material demanded attention. Further, television itself is an attention-arousing medium. These characteristics made the audience measurement research task theoretically easier for television than for other media. Accurate recall-based measurement of viewing sessions could be ascertained reasonably well by prompting on time and content of viewing. The simplicity of the television measurement task was only relative rather than absolute. The reconstruction of time and programmes was a lengthy process and the respondent could easily confuse regular, usual or intended behaviour with actual behaviour when making claims.

Modern developments in the electronic media are changing these characteristics of television and have complicated TV media research considerably. The proliferation of viewing channels through closed circuit or cable television and satellite transmissions is one of the important developments influencing the degree of difficulty of media research. Growth in video cassette recorders (VCRs) and increasing ownership of television sets per dwelling are weakening the factors that facilitate recall: viewing is no longer tied to one location; it no longer has to be contemporaneous with transmissions. Other inventions such as remote control devices make it easier to switch from one channel to another. Zapping, that is skipping over the commercials in prerecorded programmes, is also possible when playing back a programme recorded on a VCR. However, electronics have also contributed to TV media research through advances such as the peoplemeter.

3.1 Peoplemeter

A **peoplemeter** is a small computer connected to the television set which automatically registers when a television set is on, what channel it is tuned to and who in the household is watching. This information is stored until it is called up by the central computer.

Ideally a peoplemeter reports:

☐ 'on', 'off', channel change and other set tunings

☐ the channel to which a set was tuned

☐ the use of a VCR for recording and the channel tuned to

☐ the use of a VCR for playback

☐ the use of the set for teletex or viewdata reception

☐ the use of the set as a display for a microcomputer

- [ ] the timings of the patronage of the set by individuals in the household and guest viewers

- [ ] the above information for more than one television set

- [ ] audience appreciation (rating of programmes and commercials by viewers)

Peoplemeters in South Africa are installed by SAARF in the homes of TV owners to make up panels of viewers. Ideally the peoplemeter should automatically record the first six functions above while one or more of the family members registers the viewing pattern of individuals on the peoplemeter. A screen on the peoplemeter flashes the words 'who's watching'? when the TV set is turned on. If no one registers, a buzzer sounds to encourage response. Once the first viewer registers (each member of the family has a number) the following questions appear on the screen: 'Who else is watching? Any guests? and, if so, are they male/female? and what age group are they?' Questions are flashed to check whether the viewers are still being registered correctly. If a respondent has a telephone, the stored information is called up via the telephone line by the central computer during a quiet period, normally between midnight and 04h00. If the respondent happens to use the telephone during this time the transfer of the stored information is continued after the call. In total the transfer will take 20 to 25 seconds. Respondents without telephones are called on once a week by other respondents living close by who have agreed to transfer the week's stored information via their telephone lines to the central computer. Thanks to recent developments in electronics the viewing pattern data of a respondent without a telephone who lives fairly close to a respondent with one can be transmitted by radio signal to the peoplemeter of the respondent with a telephone. Both sets of data are then transferred to the central computer via the telephone line of the respondent with a telephone. The transfer takes about three to four minutes. The central computer is able to provide a daily profile of viewers with adjustments for viewers without telephones with daily transfer facilities whose information is processed weekly.

Besides profiling viewers at different times and for different programmes the peoplemeter's facilities now include the rating of programmes and commercials and the daily registration of non-durable product purchases by family members. Programmes and commercials are evaluated by a question flashed on the peoplemeter's screen, asking viewers to rate the programme, usually on a ten-point scale. Individual members assign their own rating scores. Daily purchases are recorded with a bar-code scanner pen attached to the peoplemeter. The daily purchases of respondents and their ratings of programmes and commercials are transferred during the night together with the viewing pattern data to the central computer.

3.2 Observation methods

Observation studies are conducted by recruiting and training a member of the household, such as a student, to act as an observer in the family context. Another possibility is to persuade the family to allow an interviewer to sit in while they are watching television. A third alternative is to install a closed-circuit television camera for observing the viewing pattern in a household.

The disadvantages of unrepresentativeness arising from the absence of suitable members to undertake the observation in some families and the disruption of the normal family viewing pattern by a strange interviewer or a camera disqualify the method for general application in TV media research. In certain circumstances it is suitable for exploratory research on viewing behaviour over a relatively short period such as during a commercial.

3.3 Coincidental interviews

In a coincidental interview the respondent is asked as soon as personal or telephone contact is made to say which programme, if any, he is watching. The advantage of the method is that it presents the truest picture of the respondent's viewing pattern. The respondent does not have to rely on memory and there can be no doubts about the actual situation, the respondent's intentions and the normal viewing pattern.

This method is very expensive because so little information is obtained at one time from the respondent. Large numbers of elements have to be approached to ensure a representative number of responses per time period. When face-to-face interviews are conducted it is usually necessary to limit the number of areas covered by the survey and to apply clustering. There is also a possibility that for some reason, like not wanting to interrupt a popular programme, the interviewer's knock goes unanswered. Telephone interviews can be conducted more cheaply over a larger geographic area. People without telephones or with unlisted numbers, busy lines and telephones left to ring can affect the reliability of the coincidental telephone interview. Nonetheless the method is a useful one for evaluating the reliability of other findings, especially relating to peak time, because the contact rate is very low early in the evening and interviewers refrain from making late evening calls.

3.4 Semi-coincidental interviews

This method is an extension of the coincidental interview in that the semi-coincidental interview begins with a question about the programme the respondent is viewing at the moment and then information is requested about the viewing pattern preceding the contact period. Personal face-to-face or telephone surveys can be conducted.

This method of interviewing has cost advantages over the coincidental interview because it covers a longer timespan. However, the respondents may recall fewer details about their viewing behaviour the further back they are questioned before the contact period.

It may be necessary to probe, and this is more easily done in personal face-to-face interviews than in telephone interviews because aids can be used in personal interviews.

A further disadvantage of semi-coincidental interviews is that some of the respondents will be reluctant to give relatively long interviews, especially when popular programmes are being televised.

3.5 Recall interviews

As the term suggests, recall interviews require that respondents rely on their memory in order to recall their viewing pattern. Personal home interviews are preferable because recall can be aided, but telephone interviews are also conducted in recall surveys.

The most common technique is to question people about the previous day's viewing. The researcher draws a sufficient number of observations for each day of the week and then calculates an average per programme or time of day, making the necessary adjustments for programmes that vary from week to week.

Respondents are prompted to varying degrees in recall interviews. At one extreme they are asked only what programmes or at what time they watched television yesterday without the benefit of aids to refresh their memories. This method usually gives rise to overreporting of prime viewing time and underreporting of other times. Respondents are prompted in four ways during interviews: a list of programme titles may be shown with a question 'Which, if any, of these did you view yesterday?' Alternatively a full schedule of programmes may be shown in chronological order. The third possibility is to reconstruct the respondent's behaviour throughout the previous day, establishing the starting and ending times of viewing sessions. Fourthly the activities reconstruction approach introduces programme schedules as an additional recall aid.

In these survey methods comparability is assured by following the same method of questioning and prompting from one channel to another. The reconstructive approach to establishing the previous day's viewing behaviour may well prove the most accurate. Much depends on motivating the interviewer to be thorough and making it easy to administer the interview by careful layout of the questionnaire and prompt aids. An operational definition will also help the interviewer decide whether a person is an attentive viewer. For example, a person must see at least half of a programme to qualify.

Just as it is more economical to extend purely coincidental interviews to semi-coincidental interviews, the extension of the time period in recall surveys also has cost advantages. However, the further in the past the recall period was, the less reliable the information becomes. If the recall period is seven days, more or less the same number of interviews should be conducted on each day of the week, thus making provision for poorer recall as the recall period lengthens. Each programme will also be subject to the same recall error.

3.6 Diaries

The diary method of TV media research requires that the respondent completes an unsupervised record of viewing, ideally at the actual time of viewing but not necessarily so in practice. Besides the usual considerations such as sampling, the method of recruiting respondents, replacement of dropouts, timespan and layout of the diary, collection or return of the diary and conditioning, the researcher also has to decide whether one person in the household or more are to keep diaries, or whether one respondent is to record the behaviour of all the viewers.

3.7 Detectors

Detection devices are capable of registering whether a television set is on from outside the house. They help interviewers establish whether refusals and non-contacts in a coincidental survey had their television sets switched on.

Some devices also operate inside the home. It is technologically possible to operate some kind of electronic counter in the television room which would either count and record numbers present and even identify individuals who are willing to carry some identifiable object. Detectors have not yet been applied to any great extent in practice since it is considered immoral to invade people's privacy without their consent.

3.8 Concluding remarks

In most of the developed countries peoplemeters are commonly used to gather information about television audiences. The method is, however, a costly one and is unlikely to replace diaries and personal interviews as methods of data collection, despite the decline in diary use where peoplemeters have been installed.

4 RADIO MEDIA RESEARCH

Like other media research, radio media research sets out to estimate the opportunity to hear (OTH) a commercial or series of commercials with the object of establishing the cost efficiency of the medium, a particular station, or a specific schedule of commercials or spots. Before proceeding to a discussion of the measurement techniques we shall enumerate some of the characteristics of radio listeners that are of importance in this context.

Listeners do not always know the name of the station and/or programme to which they are tuned in. It is generally believed that much radio listening, especially to 'pop' stations, happens by chance and that radio does not demand the same degree of undivided attention as press or television. Radio, it is said, supplements people's ongoing lives rather than requiring everything else to come to a halt. These views do not apply to a large section of the black population in South Africa where, in addition to English and Afrikaans, nine other ethnic languages are broadcast from their own radio stations. Tuning in to these stations is a deliberate action.

With portable transistor radios it is possible to listen to the radio just about anywhere inside and outside the house. Car radios, radios at work and at shopping centres make it possible to listen to broadcasts quite by chance away from home. All these factors often detract from the 'memorableness' of radio broadcasts and so hamper radio media research.

The research techniques for measuring radio audiences are recall-based measurements, coincidental and semi-coincidental interviews, usually for the past 24 hours, and diaries. The methodology of these techniques is largely similar to the methods discussed under television media research.

From an electronic engineering point of view there would be no difficulty in designing a meter which would accurately record whether a radio set was on or off and to what frequency it was tuned. Such meters, however, would be disproportionately large and heavy compared with most portable radios and for this reason are very seldom used in radio media research.

5 OUTDOOR MEDIA RESEARCH

Posters, hoardings, signs and bus advertisements are classified as outdoor advertising. A special characteristic of an outdoor advertisement is that its only purpose is to display an advertisement. The opportunity to see (OTS) an outdoor advertisement is not definable in terms of the media audience as it is in other media because here the medium and advertisement are the same. The main reasons that the public watch or listen to the other media are for entertainment and news. The events which qualify an individual as a member of a cinema, radio, television, newspaper or magazine audience may be memorable to a greater or lesser degree, but in so far as they are memorable they are measurable. In outdoor media research a person qualifies by chance as a member of the audience by passing the outdoor advertisement. It is quite possible for a person to have passed any number of these advertisements in the course of the day but there is no particular reason for making the event memorable. As a result the outdoor media audience researcher has generally approached the concept of OTS from the point of view of exposure to the environment of the advertisement.

The seven basic techniques for outdoor advertising media research are discussed in the sections that follow.

5.1 The Copland method

This method allows the outdoor media audience of one town or area to be compared with another town or area. Media research is not undertaken for specific sites; it is undertaken for towns or for areas as a whole. The Copland method involves the following steps:

(a) Take the universe of sites in each of the test towns and then draw a representative sample of sites from the total.

(b) Take a photograph and then draw a tiny map of the immediate vicinity of each of the poster sites drawn in step (a) of the procedure.

(c) Draw a random sample of adults in each test town and question them about

□ their awareness of each site

□ whether they have ever been to the site area

□ whether they have passed it in the 'past 7 days'

□ and if so, how many times they have passed it in the 'past 7 days'.

(d) By linking the data collected in the above steps with the Copland formula, the population of the test town and the number of sites in the campaign, a fair estimate can be made of the audience size, the coverage and the frequency of exposure of a campaign of average sites.

Brian Copland called the average number of passages past an average poster site by an individual in a week the 'A-value' and a firm relationship has been found to exist in many countries between the A-value and the population of the town or area in which the sites are situated. The useful fact is that once there seems to be a consistent relationship between two sets of numbers, a mathematical formula can be devised to forecast it.

The Copland formula, which was modified after poster media research in Belgium and Spain (Hofmans 1982:21–36), now takes double audience accumulation into account and yields a more reliable average audience figure per day for the average site. Being a method of average measurement it is not suited to calculating the OTS of a specific site, which varies quite considerably from one site to another.

5.2 Traditional traffic count

This method simply consists of having either counters or meters counting the number of vehicles or pedestrians passing the test sites. The strength of this approach lies in the restriction of counts to passages where there is a genuine OTS, such counts being independent of any visual restriction on the people making these passages. On the other hand, data do not provide information on frequency of passage and in campaign terms do not provide coverage information reflecting normal audience demographics.

5.3 Photographic methods

By mounting movie or intervalometer cameras on top of or behind sites people have been photographed with their eyes turned in the direction of the hoarding and a fairly realistic estimate of the actual audience of the test site has been made. Demographic information is limited to what can be inferred from the photographs.

5.4 Personal activity method

This method requires the respondents to describe in detail where they went yesterday. It is a modified version of the traditional origin and destination surveys undertaken by traffic consultants or planners and, by marrying the routes travelled to site locations, the researcher can check on the OTS occasions that the respondents had yesterday.

This method requires less initial preparation than the Copland method but the analysis of the results is more complex and costly. It requires plotting all the cities and towns where interviewing takes place.

5.5 Travel diary

In this method a cross-section of motorists keep a detailed log book of their travelling activities. The routes followed are fed into town maps on computer and subsequently linked to site locations and the travelling routes of buses which carry advertisements. The effect of changes in bus routes and site locations of outdoor advertisements on the OTS can be calculated immediately.

5.6 The recognition method

This method consists in showing a random sample of respondents photographs of a cross-section of actual posters and asking them whether they recognise the posters. If the posters have been 'debranded' beforehand, the respondents are required to say which brand is being advertised, whether they like or dislike it and whether they think it will promote sales of the product or service. This method is similar to the through-the-book method, which is generally accepted as the most reliable readership measure. It has met with criticism because fictitious posters which were included with the real posters obtained substantial recognition scores. A researcher may apply a controlled recognition method, similar to the one discussed in chapter 23, section 5.2.1.2, to reduce the effects of false claims.

5.7 The Politz approach

Instead of asking where the respondent had been the day before, the American researcher Alfred Politz experimented with a camera mounted in the car. By taking a frame every five seconds while the car was in motion the camera recorded the actual route(s) followed by the car. The results were very difficult to analyse, however.

5.8 Concluding remarks

The number of persons passing a particular point is a measure of the OTS the advertisement. But passage is not the only factor influencing OTS. In February 1992, at a presentation before the Outdoor Advertising Association of South Africa, Neil Shepard-Smith of the Telmar Outdoor Planning System stated that poster sites in the same area sometimes vary in terms of two main dimensions: visibility and the amount of traffic passing. It is therefore theoretically possible (and indeed desirable, although it may be difficult) to classify sites by measuring visibility and audience potential. An 'impact factor' is associated with each grade code, which may be thought of as the probability of those members of the target market passing the site and receiving an impact from the advertisement. The precise definition of each grade may be a matter for discussion, but each site may be categorised into one of three visibility classifications ('Good', 'Average' and 'Poor') and one of three classifications of potential audience ('High', 'Medium' and 'Low'). These two dimensions, of three cells each, would give a possible nine combined categories or grades. The combined impact factor calculated from the intersection of the two dimensions may then be associated with all sites of the particular grade and may be incorporated in any application of a reach and frequency formula.

6 CINEMA MEDIA RESEARCH

The cinema audience is easy to define because qualification depends on the purchase of a ticket. As a medium, film advertising incorporates vision, sound, colour and movement.

The total audiences with an OTS must be close to sales of tickets in absolute terms because a cinema-goer can hardly avoid seeing the advertisement. In practice, however, the attendance figures based on ticket sales overstate the commercial's audience because some cinema-goers leave the cinema during the interval or enter it after part or all of the commercial reel preceding the feature film has been shown.

Every six months the Audit Bureau of Circulations of South Africa publishes the average theatre attendance per week of Ster/Kinekor (Pty) Ltd and Nu Metro theatres, the two main cinema proprietors in South Africa. In themselves these figures are inadequate for campaign planning because they do not reveal total admission for a given period for a given selection of cinemas. Nor do the reports contain socio-economic information about the audiences. A further shortcoming is that admissions data reveal nothing about the net coverage of a cinema campaign or the OTS frequency distribution.

Because a visit to the cinema is a planned action, a frequent cinema-goer will recall it fairly easily. Reliable results will be obtained with a recall questionnaire which requires information for the past seven days. In England the *Cinema and Video Industry Audience Research (AVIAR)* has started compiling audience profiles for specific films or types of film from personal interview data. The profiles can also be related to the theatres where the films are shown.

7 BELOW-THE-LINE ADVERTISING

Below-the-line advertising includes the following, whether or not it is supported by media advertising:

- [ ] in-store consumer promotions such as premium offers, reduced price offers, stamps and coupons, competitions and banded packs
- [ ] trade incentives or discounts to the retailer
- [ ] display material whether in support of specific promotions or not
- [ ] point-of-sale aids such as leaflets, brochures, store demonstrations
- [ ] direct mail to the consumer such as couponing or free samples
- [ ] sports and art sponsoring.

Three trends in retailing enhance the importance of below-the-line advertising. The first is the shift towards self-service, hence the manufacturer's concern with displaying his product among rivals in such a way that the consumer will notice and purchase it. The second is the growing concentration of trade in the hands of a few major undertakings. This trend also has the effect of intensifying competition among manufacturers at point of sale. The third trend is the ever-increasing range of brands available to the consumer. As brand names proliferate so does the need to spend more on below-the-line advertising. Very little research is done on below-the-line advertising as an advertising medium. In the following we examine a few below-the-line media.

7.1 Direct mail

Direct mail is the mailing of informative literature or any other promotional material to selected prospects. The purpose of the mailing may be direct mail selling, and may be solely for the sake of its promotional and image-building functions. As an advertising medium, direct mail has very definite advantages for marketers who are targeting a specific audience. Mailing houses are equipped to inform advertisers of the characteristics of people or businesses on a particular mailing list. All the advertiser has to do is find out whether there is a mailing list that will meet his needs. Advertising goes directly to his target audience.

Direct mail marketing is researched before and after launches in many different ways, using a variety of methodologies. The most common methods are the following:

☐ *Qualitative*, both in-depth interviews and group discussions. Conducted before or even during a direct mail shot, depth interviews and/or group discussions will help the direct marketer decide on the form the marketing should take (for example a magazine or newsletter), its colour, and the type of envelope and reply envelope.

☐ *Quantitative*, usually telephone or postal self-completion. Recall of and response to a mail shot can be researched telephonically while postal research can be done by means of a separate mail shot or can be part of the original mail shot to see whether addressees have read the mail.

The effectiveness of direct mail selling can also be measured by sales, and the effectiveness of direct mail for promotion and image building, and by inquiries from the target audience. When other types of advertising accompany direct mail, respondents are required to specify the type of advertising to which they responded.

7.2 Sponsoring

Sponsored events in marketing are part of a public relations programme to gain favourable publicity for an organisation or product by paying all or some of the costs of a public sport or spectacle such as cricket or motor-racing. The technique can be applied to any event which is likely to be patronised or otherwise come to the attention of the target audience.

Opportunity to see (OTS) and association testing are the most common research techniques. The audiences of different sports and cultural events differ not only in size but also in terms of their composition. A further consideration is the degree of variation in television exposure from one area to another, which can be very great. The OTS method of evaluating advertising through sponsored events measures the amount of exposure received by area in terms of patronage and the number of viewers with the opportunity to see the sponsor's name (see television media research).

An association test involves simply asking the respondent who sponsored a particular sports or other event, such as an art exhibition. A personal survey can be conducted to identify people who have attended a sponsored event but the attendance data are inflatable only to the attendance figures of the particular event. Many more people gain access to an event through the media (for example TV, radio and press) than actually attend it. This is especially true of major events such as rugby matches, and the research should therefore encompass the whole population. Because the question is a simple one, surveys about sponsorship are readily conducted by telephone, provided that telephone penetration is adequate.

7.3 In-store promotional activity

There are three methods of gathering information about the effectiveness of in-store promotional activity. The first method requires personal face-to-face interviews with respondents before and after a shopping trip. The respondents are asked when they intend to go shopping and are questioned about their intended purchases. After the shopping trip they are again questioned about what they have bought and why their actual purchases deviate from their intended purchases. If there were any special promotional activities in the store to which they did not respond, they are asked whether they noticed the promotional activity and why they did not respond.

The second method is a combination of observation and personal interviews. With the respondent's permission the interviewer (who is also the observer) follows the respondent through the store. When specific purchasing actions are performed by the respondent, the interviewer asks why certain choices were made and, if promotional activities are noticed and ignored, the respondent is also questioned about such actions.

The third method involves conducting depth interviews and/or group discussions with store employees and executives who, once a good relationship has been established, are quite willing to share their market knowledge.

7.4 Other below-the-line advertising

Existing techniques, like those discussed in this chapter, are modified for other below-the-line advertising. For exhibitions, trade fairs and the like, an audience survey of a representative sample of attendees is the most comprehensive way of assessing an exhibit's performance and the value of a show. A survey of this kind measures basic demographics and characteristics of the audience, the potential audience for products, and an exhibit's effectiveness in reaching a potential audience. It can also measure buying intentions and buying influence levels.

8 MEDIA SYNERGY RESEARCH

As we said in the introductory section of this chapter, media selection involves identifying the prime prospects for a product or service and selecting the vehicles that will reach them often enough to foster awareness of the copy claim. Media synergy research is not concerned with the effect of one medium in isolation but with the effect certain combinations of media have on the audience.

> **Media synergy research** is the study of multimedia effects.

Synergism refers to the synchronisation or joint application (implementation) of individual media in such a way that the result of their simultaneous application is greater than the sum total of the individual efforts. In essence it is the extent to which, and the manner in which, communication becomes more effective when more than one medium is employed in support of a particular campaign.

The method of research differs from the methods we discussed in previous sections. Conclusions are drawn from specific advertising campaigns that synchronise more than one medium. The data generated by and the impact of the various combinations of media are captured on computer for future selection within a specific budget.

There are various methods of measuring the effect of media combinations. Some of them are applied in the studies described below.

In 1986, at the start of an investigation in South Africa, the initial questions posed were: How effective is press advertising in its own right? And what happens when a person is exposed to both press and TV advertising compared with only one medium, or to no advertising at all?

The first study was based on nine actual multimedia campaigns. It measured the reach and effectiveness of press and TV advertising by dividing respondents into nine groups or cells according to their press exposure (high, low or nil) and their TV exposure (high, low or nil) and the combinations of these (for example high TV, low press). The idea was to assess each of these nine cells against a measure of response to advertising that would highlight differences, if any, in the key reactions of the different exposure groups. MRA's *Adexpose*, a recognition technique, was applied. Respondents were shown black and white reproductions of press advertisements and TV storyboards for the nine campaigns and asked to sort them into one of three categories: 'I have not seen this ad before', 'I have seen it once or twice' and 'I have seen it several times'. Before being shown the recognition card respondents were also questioned about spontaneous awareness, current usage and the degree of interest in use for the different products or services in the nine campaigns. In addition, after exposure to the Adexpose cards, diagnostic questions were asked about respondents' reactions to the advertisements themselves. MRA concluded that press and TV are complementary media. Used in combination, they not only increase reach, but also raise spontaneous brand awareness and interest in use to levels which would not be achieved with either medium on its own.

In 1988 the second study in South Africa applied stepwise regression in a statistical analysis of a variety of campaigns which had run their full life according to their media schedules to discover the likely effects of different media, on their own and in combination.

In Britain, Research Business and Communication Research Ltd interviewed 14 000 consumers in 1989, asking them to describe their response to the TV commercial before and after being shown a print advertisement for the same product. Their separate responses to both media were recorded, and a control group was shown only the TV commercial (with a 'filler' print ad of an unrelated product). This allowed the research teams to identify the effects of TV alone, of print alone, and of both media together.

Through the technology of The PreTesting Company in America in 1988 it was possible to set up 'opportunity for exposure' in a controlled test. To accomplish the objective of providing the opportunity for exposure and not artificial forced exposure, the PreTesting Company's patented *PeopleReader* and *Simulated Network* techniques were used. The PeopleReader is a lamp with two TV cameras in the pedestal, one focused on the reader's eyes and the other on the page of the magazine to determine proof of exposure. The Simulated Network is an ordinary television set with a remote control connected to three synchronised VCRs. The respondents can switch to any one of the three channels at any time and their exposure is recorded electronically. The interview questions elicited first and second brand choice for each product category (pre- and post-exposure), unaided and aided brand recall of all the ads in the magazine and TV programme, and a competitive imagery score. For the latter the respondents were asked to compare the test brand against its major competitor on an agree or disagree strongly basis (on a scale of 1 to 9) on each of the attributes the advertiser wanted to stress in the campaign.

In 1988 a West German study called Media Mix and Advertising Effectiveness researched the effectiveness of advertising communication via two media versus a single-medium approach, using a large number of individual campaigns from different product fields. It measured the long-term advertising effectiveness levels among readers of the print media, TV viewers, and users of both by analysing the answers to three questions: What media are being used by what persons and with what frequency? What brands actually advertised in what media and with what frequency? What advertising effectiveness level can be established for the brands under observation? The effectiveness level for all brands was established by measuring awareness and intent to purchase the individual brands. Linking the three datasets (media consumption, schedules and effectiveness criteria) demonstrated the effect of advertising on people exposed at differing levels to different media and media combinations.

9 MEDIA RESEARCH IN SOUTH AFRICA

The first media survey in South Africa was undertaken in 1948. It was followed by other surveys and then by regular readership and radio listening surveys. The first television viewing survey was conducted in 1976. The early surveys were sponsored by the Society of Advertisers (now the Association of Marketers (ASOM)), the Newspaper Press Union (NPU) and the South African Broadcasting Corporation (SABC). Since the formation of the South African Advertising Research Foundation (SAARF) in the mid-seventies, media research in South Africa has been largely controlled by this body.

The formation of SAARF caused quite a stir in the advertising world and even featured in the editorial of the American *Journal of Advertising Research* :

> But as a model for the rest of the world the most interesting approach is that of South Africa. There, anticipating the introduction of television in 1976, the major advertisers have agreed to pay the whole cost of a multimedia, multiproduct survey administered by a body the advertisers intend will represent all sides of the industry – clients, agencies, press, and the powerful South African Broadcasting Company. On October 24, 1973, a date which may prove a milestone in worldwide media research, Francis Meyer, executive director of the Society of Marketers (the South African counterpart of our Association of National Advertisers) announced: 'The Society of Marketers has established an Advertising Research Foundation, recognizing the importance of creating a system whereby objective and sophisticated media audience measurement research will be undertaken' (Ramond 1974:55).

In February 1992 Neil Shepard-Smith of the Telmar Outdoor Planning System had the following to say about the development of media research:

> Let me start by making the general point that you are probably more advanced in South Africa than any other country in the world in your use of computers in media planning. My personal view is that this stems from the very open-minded and positive way in which the South African advertising industry has always listened to new suggestions and developments. You were the first country in the world to have a suite of media planning programs available on micro-computers and today you have systems on IBM-compatible micro-computers to handle Press, TV, Radio, Cinema and mixed multi-media schedules. All these systems are widely-used, based on industry-accepted research and the Cinema and the new TRANSMIT TV system in particular are the most comprehensive systems in their field available anywhere and are far more sophisticated than those used in other countries.

9.1 *The media book*

The media book 1991/1992 is written and edited by Mike Leathy and Paul Voice and printed by WTH Publications CC. This book, the third in the series, is an authoritative work of 217 pages on the South African media industry.

The book is in six sections. Section one, 'Introduction to Media', gives an overview of the industry, its place in society, its structure, history and how its various parts integrate

(10 chapters). 'Media Information Sources' tells readers where to get information and how to use and assess it (17 chapters). 'The Media' reviews the various types of media, how to use them and the problems and opportunities associated with them (19 chapters). 'How to Plan Media' explains some of the principles and techniques of planning (16 chapters). 'Implementing Media Plans' completes the cycle (10 chapters). Section six (the yellow pages) contains various appendices for reference, including a Mini-AMPS, a list of print media and contacts and an updated Dictionary of Media Terms.

9.2 All Media and Products Survey (AMPS)

The *All Media and Products Survey (AMPS)* is undertaken under the jurisdiction of SAARF.

AMPS is a detailed study and analysis of people, the duplication of media exposure, and the duplication of media groups. People are analysed in terms of who they are, their reading habits (newspapers and magazines), listening habits (radio), viewing habits (television), cinema-going habits, plus some of the things they do, financial services and type of institutions used, durable items in their homes, some of the products used and bought, and their shopping habits.

The AMPS analysis of duplication of media exposure involves newspaper readers of other newspapers, magazine readers of other magazines, newspaper readers of magazines, and magazine readers of newspapers. The duplication of media groups is analysed by newspaper, magazine, radio, television and cinema. AMPS compiles profiles of each of the magazines and newspapers by main demographics. It also prepares profiles of radio and television services by channel and, in the separate self-contained volumes based upon the radio and television diary panel surveys, there are analyses by quarter-hour by day of the week.

The print media measured in AMPS include newspapers (daily, Sunday and weekly) and magazines (weekly, fortnightly and monthly). Besides frequency of publication, the language in which these newspapers and magazines are printed and the sociocultural groups at which they are aimed are categorised. Print media are measured in the AMPS to find out how many people have the opportunity to see an advertisement in an average issue of a publication. Questions are asked inter alia about recency, frequency, thoroughness of reading and source of copy.

The electronic media measured in AMPS are *radio and television*. AMPS provides measures of an individual's OTS a commercial on television and OTH a commercial on the radio. A peoplemeter system (called AMPS Meter) with a panel of about 880 households of all population groups monitors TV audiences. AMPS Meter data are published weekly in the form of a printed report and a computer tape. Users also have on-line access to the data via a computer bureau which subscribes to the tapes. The report covers the seven-day period to 02h00 on Monday and is available on the Friday of the same week.

AMPS Meter monitors viewing of TV1, CCV, NNTV and M-Net. Data for each television station for one day are published on a two-page spread as follows:

- □ AMPS ratings (ARs) for the total audience by quarter-hour, by programme and by channel, as well as for each commercial break
- □ audience share for each quarter-hour
- □ comparative ARs and audience sizes per quarter-hour for the preceding week
- □ the exact commencement times of programmes and commercial breaks, and the duration of commercial breaks
- □ the top ten programmes for each station, station patronage and average viewing minutes.

The third medium covered by AMPS is the *cinema*. Drive-in and indoor cinemas are treated separately. The objective is to find out how many people have the opportunity to see an advertisement on the cinema screen and what sort of people they are. In AMPS outdoor-advertisement measurement respondents are shown a set of cards and asked if they know a sample of outdoor sites and, if they do, whether they have been there in the past seven days and, if so, how many times.

A composite demographic, the *AMPS Living Standard Measure (LSM)*, has been developed by using a combination of variables from AMPS. Information on eight LSM groups and three LSM super-groups can be obtained from the printed reports and computer tapes.

9.3 Audit Bureau of Circulations of South Africa

The primary function of the *Audit Bureau of Circulations of South Africa (ABC)* is the certification of circulation and cinema attendance figures by independent professional auditors using standard audit procedures for each category of publication and for cinemas. Established in 1947, its 1994 membership includes 44 advertisers, 47 advertising agencies, 366 publisher members (including cinemas) and 9 associate members.

The ABC issues all publisher members with sets of audit forms specifying the method of ascertaining the figures on a standard and uniform basis. Different audit forms are used for newspapers; consumer magazines; trade, technical, professional and specialised publications; free distribution publications; and for cinemas. The ABC also issues Media Data with the ABC certificate for each trade, technical and professional publication. This circulation breakdown by geographical area, standard industrial classification and job title also includes information on the availability of readership research.

In the ABC Report audited circulation data are given for 42 urban daily and weekly newspapers, 28 country newspapers, 55 periodicals, 133 specialist publications and 2 cinema proprietors. The ABC's Verified Free Distribution Report gives information on 68 free distribution publications.

9.4 Retail Data Library (RDL)

AMPS does not monitor the community newspapers and does not allow for data to be analysed on tight enough regional bases to permit meaningful marketing and readership assessments necessary to some retailers and marketers. Thus a new survey, called *Retail Data Library (RDL)*, has been undertaken to redress these problems.

The RDL survey provides advertisers and their agencies with a large scale micro-marketing database on all adults aged 16 plus in selected major metropolitan areas.

The following are the specific objectives:

☐ to gather detailed demographic information on adults aged 16 plus in the areas defined

☐ to gather information on selected shopping patterns, including shopping behaviour, use of financial institutions, motor vehicles and advertising leaflets

☐ to gather readership information on daily, weekly and community newspapers and selected newspaper supplements circulating within the coverage areas

☐ to interrelate the marketing and media information at city, town and suburban levels that advertisers need to reach target audiences effectively.

Personal interviews over the telephone are conducted using a structured questionnaire. All interviewing is undertaken in the evenings between 17:00 and 21:00 to ensure the inclusion of working people and students in the sample. Similarly, interviewing is conducted over four evenings from Monday to Thursday in each area to ensure the inclusion of people who work or go out on specific nights and to get an accurate reflection of readership patterns over different days of the week as far as possible. Fifty-three sample areas are drawn from the distribution areas of the local newspapers. These areas are situated in Gauteng, the Cape Peninsula, the Durban Complex including the nearby coastal areas, Newcastle and Port Elizabeth. The RDL research results are released as they become available, in a form that allows incorporation in an RDL file.

9.5 Sociomonitor

It is generally accepted that demographically similar people may have different attitudes, motivations and beliefs which influence their consumer behaviour in terms of the products and media they use and would like to use. *Sociomonitor*, a Market Research Africa (MRA) study, segments markets according to the psychographic differences which exist among people and provides conceptual models for explaining and interpreting market behaviour. Sociomonitor is probably the most widely used psychographic segmentation study in this country.

Work on the South African Sociomonitor began in 1975. Sociomonitor has been developed for both the white and the black market, and each study is conducted biennially. The area stratified probability sample for both studies is drawn from adults living in urban areas (including towns and villages). Approximately 2 000 whites and 2 000 blacks are interviewed in each survey. Among whites, the first half of the questionnaire is conducted face to face by the interviewer and the second half is self-completion. The questionnaire for blacks is filled in entirely face to face in the vernacular.

Media planners make use of the data when selecting media most appropriate for the users of a product. The matching is carried out by a specially developed computer program called Media Match which compares the pattern of trend scores displayed by the target group of consumers with those exhibited by the users of each medium in turn. The output is a listing of all the media, ranked in order of compatibility with the target group. *Media Match* is useful as a media planning tool to be used in conjunction with other considerations such as reach and cost efficiency. Media Match is available from MRA or the subscribing media owners.

9.6 Media involvement studies

The latest media involvement study, *Media Wise*, is intended primarily to research the qualitative aspects of media, that is the relationship between the audience and the medium and its impact on advertising effectiveness. Released in September 1990, the Media Wise media involvement study was underwritten by five members of the Magazine Publishers Association and conducted by MRA.

A total of 2 006 interviews among whites were conducted between June and mid-August 1990, the sample being drawn on an area stratified probability basis from MRA's computerised household census. The objectives of the study were: to determine which major media type was most effective in providing useful ideas about various subjects; to investigate attitudes to various media types; to establish attitudes to advertising carried in the various media types; to establish readership of various categories of newspapers and magazines as well as key readership issues such as number and frequency of readership, origin of copy, pick-up times, time spent reading, thoroughness of reading, importance of publications and where they are 'disposed of'; to establish yesterday's radio listenership and TV viewership; and to establish a means of segmenting TV viewers and magazine readers on the basis of how heavily they use these media – termed media franchise.

Media types included consumer magazines, news and business magazines, Sunday newspaper colour supplements, daily and Sunday newspapers, radio and television.

9.7 SA Business Research Evaluation (SABRE)

The marketers' and media data provided by the AMPS and Sociomonitor tend to concentrate on general consumer markets. They provide only a limited amount of information on the decision-making and media consumption habits of executives in business. Yet those responsible for controlling company budgets, who also rank among the country's most wealthy people, are exposed to many media vehicles and advertising money. To help correct this lack of data the first *South African Business Research Evaluation (SABRE)* was released in 1986.

A total of 2 000 interviews were conducted in 1990 among males and females of all population groups aged 25 years and older who had a household income of R5 000 and over and were currently employed in top or middle management, professional or technical occupations. Face-to-face interviews were conducted. The sample was stratified by area and the selection of respondents quota-controlled according to AMPS, with area disproportionate sampling in some instances to obtain viable sub-samples. However, in the final analysis they were all weighted back to correct proportions.

9.8 Adtrack

The AMPS Meter measures audiences and is the basic tool for media planning and buying. It does not take into account the characteristics of different commercials. Marketed by Impact Information, *Adtrack* is an advertising tracking system which measures the recall of commercials on a weekly basis and helps media planners to take the penetrative abilities of a commercial into account in their media planning.

The sample comprises 200 whites interviewed by telephone on the Witwatersrand each week. Two hundred personal interviews per week are also conducted among blacks in Soweto. The sample is quota controlled by age, income, sex and language and is selected at random each week. Each respondent is taken through a standard questionnaire. The Adtrack system has measured the Verified Noting of more than 6 000 commercials, each tested within two to three weeks after its first appearance. Thus the results of a commercial are compared with the averages formed by these 6 000 commercials for similar lengths and similar flightings.

9.9 Magtrak

Magtrak is a magazine-tracking study conducted by MRA. It is commissioned by Nasionale Tydskrifte whose management sees three major shortcomings in existing research: the circulation data in the form of ABC Certificates are valuable but faceless and do not reveal reader characteristics; AMPS is a massive and comprehensive work but too slow a vehicle for strategic planning in a dynamic and rapidly changing magazine market; and there is a lack of ongoing up-to-date data for reviewing markets and competitors regularly.

The study makes use of the established monthly Omnijet surveys and in each Magtrak 'month' 2 000 white adults over the age of 16 are interviewed (50/50 male/female resident in major metropolitan areas, cities, towns and villages).

Magtrak confirms the reader profiles of the magazines covered in the study, shows duplication of readership and provides further data on such key indicators as spontaneous awareness of titles, never/sometimes and regular readers, and given-up reading.

9.10 Other media research

MRA compiles *Adindex* which is the most authoritative source of media expenditure data in South Africa. Adindex is a means of comparing the media expenditure of competitors and is often cited in advertising journals as proof, for instance, of the expansion of the TV medium at the expense of print.

In a study, *Reaching critical mass*, radio, and in particular ethnic radio, almost stands on its own. It is virtually universally rated in the black market as the most credible medium, and so is its advertising. This is partly because of its high listenership, but even blacks who regularly watch television, or read magazines or newspapers, rate ethnic radio differently to other media.

South African Rates and Data (SARAD) is an alternate monthly directory listing virtually all media which carry advertising in South Africa and major media in neighbouring countries. Each medium, be it a newspaper or a television station, is listed separately under its own title and within its appropriate section and subsection. A listing will contain the title, language, frequency (if appropriate), the name, address, telephone, telex and fax numbers of the publisher or media owner. It may also contain details of commission and discounts.

The *Delphi Lifestyle Segmentation System* combines demographic, attitudinal and psychographic variables as an aid to creative development. Media preferences are analysed in the *Delphi Lifestyle* framework and also by the usual demographic categories. Thus a complete demographic/lifestyle cross-tabulation is developed. The information is presented not only in aggregation but also by segment, that is the favourite television programmes, regular radio station, etc, for each of the Delphi groups. This information can be used in formulating a marketing strategy with the appropriate media mix for a specific market segment.

Sponsortrack has been conducted by Impact Information since mid-1990. Two hundred telephone interviews per week are conducted with whites living on the Witwatersrand

and 200 personal interviews per week with blacks in Soweto. The respondents are simply asked: 'Who sponsors ...?' (the name of the event).

10 SUMMARY

Media research is concerned with audience size, audience composition by demographic characteristics, cumulative audience, media duplication, repetition or frequency of exposure, cost of audience provided, product usage by audience, and audience distribution. Print media research starts with circulation figures, the basis for determining the issue audience of a newspaper or magazine, the page and spread audiences, and the advertising audience. Various techniques are applied in print media research, such as recall and recognition methods, and the glue-spot technique. In television media research a profile of the audience is developed by applying observation methods, coincidental, semi-coincidental and recall interviews, diaries, and through the use of devices such as peoplemeters and detectors.

In radio media research the opportunities to hear (OTH) a commercial or series of commercials are estimated by recall-based measurements, coincidental and semi-coincidental interviews, and diaries. There are seven basic techniques for outdoor advertising media research: the Copland method, the traditional traffic count, photographic methods, the personal activity method, the travel diary, the recognition method and the Politz approach. The use of a recall questionnaire is recommended in cinema media research. The section on below-the-line advertising as an advertising medium deals briefly with direct mail, sponsoring, in-store promotional activities, and exhibits and trade fairs.

The effect of various combinations of media is discussed under the heading of media synergy research. The chapter concludes with an overview of media research in South Africa.

REFERENCES

Hofmans, P 1982. Coverage and frequency in urban outdoor advertising. *European Research*, 10(1):21–36.

Rademeyer, A P 1990. *Factors in advertising effectiveness and advertising testing*. Pretoria: Unisa, Bureau of Market Research. (Research Report no 172.)

Ramond, C 1974. Editorial: the South African solution. *Journal of Advertising Research*, 14(4):55.

Appendix
Statistical tables and symbols

Table A-1 The standard normal distribution

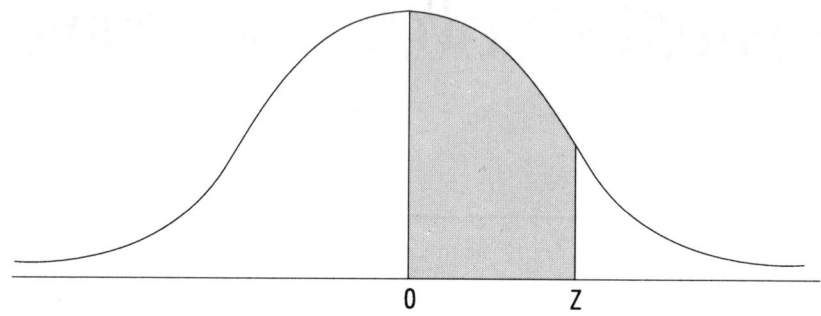

z	,00	,01	,02	,03	,04	,05	,06	,07	,08	,09
0,0	,0000	,0040	,0080	,0120	,0160	,0199	,0239	,0279	,0319	,0359
0,1	,0398	,0438	,0478	,0517	,0557	,0596	,0636	,0675	,0714	,0753
0,2	,0793	,0832	,0871	,0910	,0948	,0987	,1026	,1064	,1103	,1141
0,3	,1179	,1217	,1255	,1293	,1331	,1368	,1406	,1443	,1480	,1517
0,4	,1554	,1591	,1628	,1664	,1700	,1736	,1772	,1808	,1844	,1879
0,5	,1915	,1950	,1985	,2019	,2054	,2088	,2123	,2157	,2190	,2224
0,6	,2257	,2291	,2324	,2357	,2389	,2422	,2454	,2486	,2517	,2549
0,7	,2580	,2611	,2642	,2673	,2704	,2734	,2764	,2794	,2823	,2852
0,8	,2881	,2910	,2939	,2967	,2995	,3023	,3051	,3078	,3106	,3133
0,9	,3159	,3186	,3212	,3238	,3264	,3289	,3315	,3340	,3365	,3389
1,0	,3413	,3438	,3461	,3485	,3508	,3531	,3554	,3577	,3599	,3621
1,1	,3643	,3665	,3686	,3708	,3729	,3749	,3770	,3790	,3810	,3830
1,2	,3849	,3869	,3888	,3907	,3925	,3944	,3962	,3980	,3997	,4015
1,3	,4032	,4049	,4066	,4082	,4099	,4115	,4131	,4147	,4162	,4177
1,4	,4192	,4207	,4222	,4236	,4251	,4265	,4279	,4292	,4306	,4319
1,5	,4332	,4345	,4357	,4370	,4382	,4394	,4406	,4418	,4429	,4441
1,6	,4452	,4463	,4474	,4484	,4495	,4505	,4515	,4525	,4535	,4545
1,7	,4554	,4564	,4573	,4582	,4591	,4599	,4608	,4616	,4625	,4633
1,8	,4641	,4649	,4656	,4664	,4671	,4678	,4686	,4693	,4699	,4706
1,9	,4713	,4719	,4726	,4732	,4738	,4744	,4750	,4756	,4761	,4767
2,0	,4772	,4778	,4783	,4788	,4793	,4798	,4803	,4808	,4812	,4817
2,1	,4821	,4826	,4830	,4834	,4838	,4842	,4846	,4850	,4854	,4857
2,2	,4861	,4864	,4868	,4871	,4875	,4878	,4881	,4884	,4887	,4890
2,3	,4893	,4896	,4898	,4901	,4904	,4906	,4909	,4911	,4913	,4916
2,4	,4918	,4920	,4922	,4925	,4927	,4929	,4931	,4932	,4934	,4936
2,5	,4938	,4940	,4941	,4943	,4945	,4946	,4948	,4949	,4951	,4952
2,6	,4953	,4955	,4956	,4957	,4959	,4960	,4961	,4962	,4963	,4964
2,7	,4965	,4966	,4967	,4968	,4969	,4970	,4971	,4972	,4973	,4974
2,8	,4974	,4975	,4976	,4977	,4977	,4978	,4979	,4979	,4980	,4981
2,9	,4981	,4982	,4982	,4983	,4984	,4984	,4985	,4985	,4986	,4986
3,0	,4987	,4987	,4987	,4988	,4988	,4989	,4989	,4989	,4990	,4990

Table A-2 The t-distribution

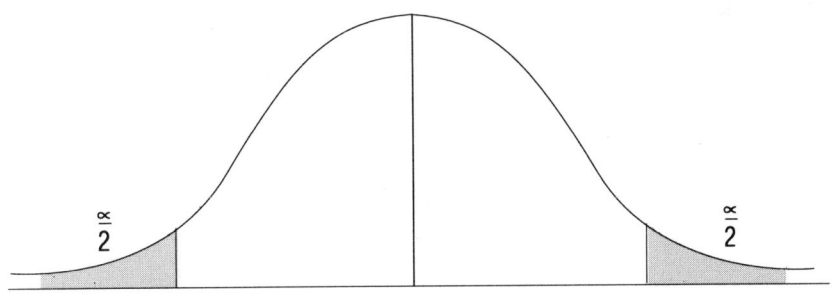

Two-tail area (α)	,20	,10	,05	,02	,01
Degrees of freedom					
1	3,078	6,314	12,706	31,821	63,657
2	1,886	2,920	4,303	6,965	9,925
3	1,638	2,353	3,182	4,541	5,841
4	1,533	2,132	2,776	3,747	4,604
5	1,476	2,015	2,571	3,365	4,032
6	1,440	1,943	2,447	3,143	3,707
7	1,415	1,895	2,365	2,998	3,499
8	1,397	1,860	2,306	2,896	3,355
9	1,383	1,833	2,262	2,821	3,250
10	1,372	1,812	2,228	2,764	3,169
11	1,363	1,796	2,201	2,718	3,106
12	1,356	1,782	2,179	2,681	3,055
13	1,350	1,771	2,160	2,650	3,012
14	1,345	1,761	2,145	2,624	2,977
15	1,341	1,753	2,131	2,602	2,947
16	1,337	1,746	2,120	2,583	2,921
17	1,333	1,740	2,110	2,567	2,898
18	1,330	1,734	2,101	2,552	2,878
19	1,328	1,729	2,093	2,539	2,861
20	1,325	1,725	2,086	2,528	2,845
21	1,323	1,721	2,080	2,518	2,831
22	1,321	1,717	2,074	2,508	2,819
23	1,319	1,714	2,069	2,500	2,807
24	1,318	1,711	2,064	2,492	2,797
25	1,316	1,708	2,060	2,485	2,787
26	1,315	1,706	2,056	2,479	2,779
27	1,314	1,703	2,052	2,473	2,771
28	1,313	1,701	2,048	2,467	2,763
29	1,311	1,699	2,045	2,462	2,756
30	1,310	1,697	2,042	2,457	2,750
40	1,303	1,684	2,021	2,423	2,704
60	1,296	1,671	2,000	2,390	2,660
120	1,289	1,658	1,980	2,358	2,617
α	1,282	1,645	1,960	2,326	2,576

Table A-3 . The χ^2-distribution

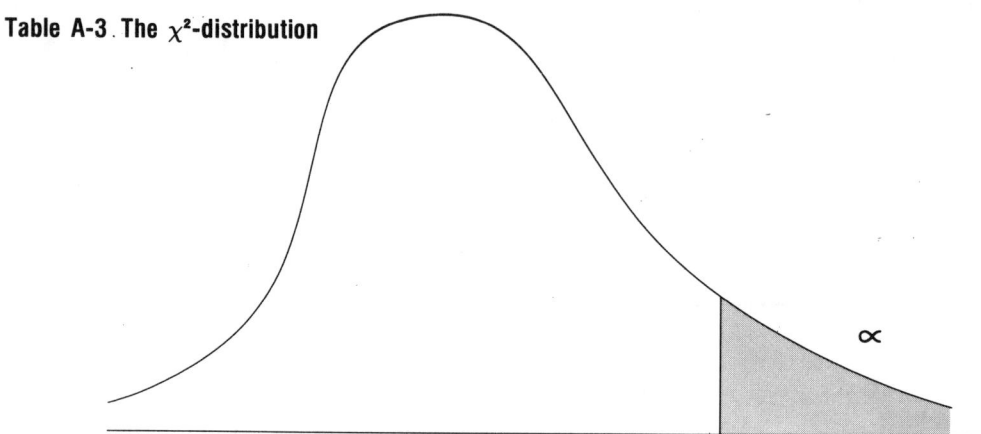

d.f.*	α ,10	,05	,025	,010	,005
1	2,71	3,84	5,02	6,63	7,88
2	4,61	5,99	7,38	9,21	10,6
3	6,25	7,81	9,35	11,3	12,8
4	7,78	9,49	11,1	13,3	14,9
5	9,24	11,1	12,8	15,1	16,7
6	10,6	12,6	14,4	16,8	18,5
7	12,0	14,1	16,0	18,5	20,3
8	13,4	15,5	17,5	20,1	22,0
9	14,7	16,9	19,0	21,7	23,6
10	16,0	18,3	20,5	23,2	25,2
11	17,3	19,7	21,9	24,7	26,8
12	18,5	21,0	23,3	26,2	28,3
13	19,8	22,4	24,7	27,7	29,8
14	21,1	23,7	26,1	29,1	31,3
15	22,3	25,0	27,5	30,6	32,8
16	23,5	26,3	28,8	32,0	34,3
17	24,8	27,6	30,2	33,4	35,7
18	26,0	28,9	31,5	34,8	37,2
19	27,2	30,1	32,9	36,2	38,6
20	28,4	31,4	34,2	37,6	40,0
21	29,6	32,7	35,5	38,9	41,4
22	30,8	33,9	36,8	40,3	42,8
23	32,0	35,2	38,1	41,6	44,2
24	33,2	36,4	39,4	43,0	45,6
25	34,4	37,7	40,6	44,3	46,9
26	35,6	38,9	41,9	45,6	48,3
27	36,7	40,1	43,2	47,0	49,6
28	37,9	41,3	44,5	48,3	51,0
29	39,1	42,6	45,7	49,6	52,3
30	40,3	43,8	47,0	50,9	53,7

*Degrees of freedom.

Table A-4 The F-distribution

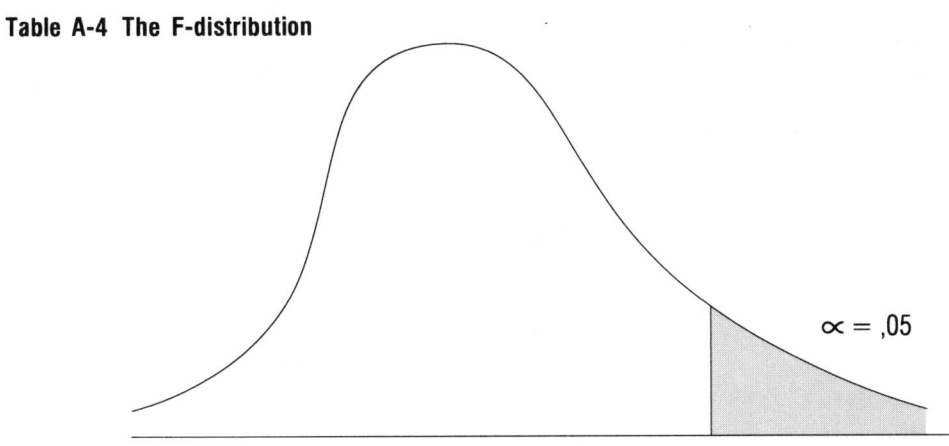

$\propto = ,05$

V_1 = Degrees of freedom between groups

	1	2	3	4	5	6	7	8	9	10	12	15
1	161,4	199,5	215,7	224,6	230,2	234,0	236,8	238,9	240,5	241,9	243,9	245,9
2	18,51	19,00	19,16	19,25	19,30	19,33	19,35	19,37	19,38	19,40	19,41	19,43
3	10,13	9,55	9,28	9,12	9,01	8,94	8,89	8,85	8,81	8,79	8,74	8,70
4	7,71	6,94	6,59	6,39	6,26	6,16	6,09	6,04	6,00	5,96	5,91	5,86
5	5,61	5,79	5,41	5,19	5,05	4,95	4,88	4,82	4,77	4,74	4,68	4,62
6	5,99	5,14	4,76	4,53	4,39	4,28	4,21	4,15	4,10	4,06	4,00	3,94
7	5,59	4,74	4,35	4,12	3,97	3,87	3,79	3,73	3,68	3,64	3,57	3,51
8	5,32	4,46	4,07	3,84	3,69	3,58	3,50	3,44	3,39	3,35	3,28	3,22
9	5,12	4,26	3,86	3,63	3,48	3,37	3,29	3,23	3,18	3,14	3,07	3,01
10	4,96	4,10	3,71	3,48	3,33	3,22	3,14	3,07	3,02	2,98	2,91	2,85
11	4,84	3,98	3,59	3,36	3,20	3,09	3,01	2,95	2,90	2,85	2,79	2,72
12	4,75	3,89	3,49	3,26	3,11	3,00	2,91	2,85	2,80	2,75	2,69	2,62
13	4,67	3,81	3,41	3,18	3,03	2,92	2,83	2,77	2,71	2,67	2,60	2,53
14	4,60	3,74	3,34	3,11	2,96	2,85	2,76	2,70	2,65	2,60	2,53	2,46
15	4,54	3,68	3,29	3,06	2,90	2,79	2,71	2,64	2,59	2,54	2,48	2,40
16	4,49	3,63	3,24	3,01	2,85	2,74	2,66	2,59	2,54	2,49	2,42	2,35
17	4,45	3,59	3,20	2,96	2,81	2,70	2,61	2,55	2,49	2,45	2,38	2,31
18	4,41	3,55	3,16	2,93	2,77	2,66	2,58	2,51	2,46	2,41	2,34	2,27
19	4,38	3,52	3,13	2,90	2,74	2,63	2,54	2,48	2,42	2,38	2,31	2,23
20	4,35	3,49	3,10	2,87	2,71	2,60	2,51	2,45	2,39	2,35	2,28	2,20
21	4,32	3,47	3,07	2,84	2,68	2,57	2,49	2,42	2,37	2,32	2,25	2,18
22	4,30	3,44	3,05	2,82	2,66	2,55	2,46	2,40	2,34	2,30	2,23	2,15
23	4,28	3,42	3,03	2,80	2,64	2,53	2,44	2,37	2,32	2,27	2,20	2,13
24	4,26	3,40	3,01	2,78	2,62	2,51	2,42	2,36	2,30	2,25	2,18	2,11
25	4,24	3,39	2,99	2,76	2,60	2,49	2,40	2,34	2,28	2,24	2,16	2,09
26	4,23	3,37	2,98	2,74	2,59	2,47	2,39	2,32	2,27	2,22	2,15	2,07
27	4,21	3,35	2,96	2,73	2,57	2,46	2,37	2,31	2,25	2,20	2,13	2,06
28	4,20	3,34	2,95	2,71	2,56	2,45	2,36	2,29	2,24	2,19	2,12	2,04
29	4,18	3,33	2,93	2,70	2,55	2,43	2,35	2,28	2,22	2,18	2,10	2,03
30	4,17	3,32	2,92	2,69	2,53	2,42	2,33	2,27	2,21	2,16	2,09	2,01
40	4,08	3,23	2,84	2,61	2,45	2,34	2,25	2,18	2,12	2,08	2,00	1,92
60	4,00	3,15	2,76	2,53	2,37	2,25	2,17	2,10	2,04	1,99	1,92	1,84
120	3,92	3,07	2,68	2,45	2,29	2,17	2,09	2,02	1,96	1,91	1,83	1,75
α	3,84	3,00	2,60	2,37	2,21	2,10	2,01	1,94	1,88	1,83	1,75	1,67

V_2 = Degrees of freedom within groups

Table A-4 The F-distribution (continued)

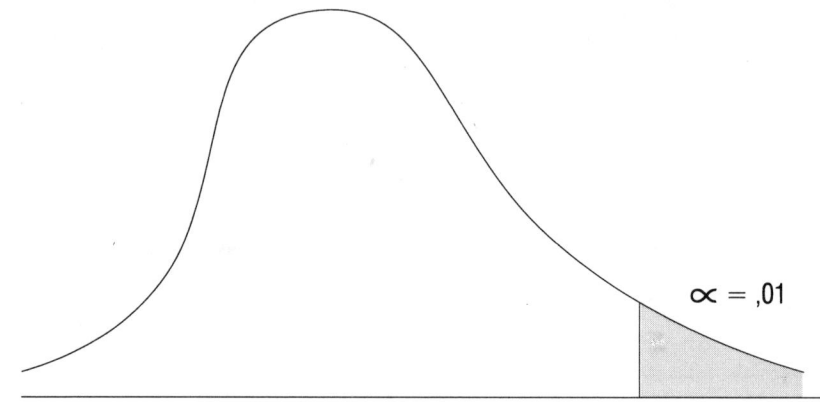

$\alpha = ,01$

V_1 = Degrees of freedom between groups

	1	2	3	4	5	6	7	8	9	10	12	15
1	4 052	4 999	5 403	5 625	5 764	5 859	5 928	5 982	6 022	6 056	6 106	6 157
2	98,50	99,00	99,17	99,25	99,30	99,33	99,36	99,37	99,39	99,40	99,42	99,43
3	34,12	30,82	29,46	28,71	28,24	27,91	27,67	27,49	27,35	27,23	27,05	26,87
4	21,20	18,00	16,69	15,98	15,52	15,21	14,98	14,80	14,66	14,55	14,37	14,20
5	16,26	13,27	12,06	11,39	10,97	10,67	10,46	10,29	10,16	10,05	9,89	9,72
6	13,75	10,92	9,78	9,15	8,75	8,47	8,26	8,10	7,98	7,87	7,72	7,56
7	12,25	9,55	8,45	7,85	7,46	7,19	6,99	6,84	6,72	6,62	6,47	6,31
8	11,26	8,65	7,59	7,01	6,63	6,37	6,18	6,03	5,91	5,81	5,67	5,52
9	10,56	8,02	6,99	6,42	6,06	5,80	5,61	5,47	5,35	5,26	5,11	4,96
10	10,04	7,56	6,55	5,99	5,64	5,39	5,20	5,06	4,94	4,85	4,71	4,56
11	9,65	7,21	6,22	5,67	5,32	5,07	4,89	4,74	4,63	4,54	4,40	4,25
12	9,33	6,93	5,95	5,41	5,06	4,82	4,64	4,50	4,39	4,30	4,61	4,01
13	9,07	6,70	5,74	5,21	4,86	4,62	4,44	4,30	4,19	4,10	3,96	3,82
14	8,86	6,51	5,56	5,04	4,69	4,46	4,28	4,14	4,03	3,94	3,80	3,66
15	8,68	6,36	5,42	4,89	4,56	4,32	4,14	4,00	3,89	3,80	3,67	3,52
16	8,53	6,23	5,29	4,77	4,44	4,20	4,03	3,89	3,78	3,69	3,55	3,41
17	8,40	6,11	5,18	4,67	4,34	4,10	3,93	3,79	3,68	3,59	3,46	3,31
18	8,29	6,01	5,09	4,58	4,25	4,01	3,84	3,71	3,60	3,51	3,37	3,23
19	8,18	5,93	5,01	4,50	4,17	3,94	3,77	3,63	3,52	3,43	3,30	3,15
20	8,10	5,85	4,94	4,43	4,10	3,87	3,70	3,56	3,46	3,37	3,23	3,09
21	8,02	5,78	4,87	4,37	4,04	3,81	3,64	3,51	3,40	3,31	3,17	3,03
22	7,95	5,72	4,82	4,31	3,99	3,76	3,59	3,45	3,35	3,26	3,12	2,98
23	7,88	5,66	4,76	4,26	3,94	3,71	3,54	3,41	3,30	3,21	3,07	2,93
24	7,82	5,61	4,72	4,22	3,90	3,67	3,50	3,36	3,26	3,17	3,03	2,89
25	7,77	5,57	4,68	4,18	3,85	3,63	3,46	3,32	3,22	3,13	2,99	2,85
26	7,72	5,53	4,64	4,14	3,82	3,59	3,42	3,29	3,18	3,09	2,96	2,81
27	7,68	5,49	4,60	4,11	3,78	3,56	3,39	3,26	3,15	3,06	2,93	2,78
28	7,64	5,45	4,57	4,07	3,75	3,53	3,36	3,23	3,12	3,03	2,90	2,75
29	7,60	5,42	4,54	4,04	3,73	3,50	3,33	3,20	3,09	3,00	2,87	2,73
30	7,56	5,39	4,51	4,02	3,70	3,47	3,30	3,17	3,07	2,98	2,84	2,70
40	7,31	5,18	4,31	3,83	3,51	3,29	3,12	2,99	2,89	2,80	2,66	2,52
60	7,08	4,98	4,13	3,65	3,34	3,12	2,95	2,82	2,72	2,63	2,50	2,35
120	6,85	4,79	3,95	3,48	3,17	2,96	2,79	2,66	2,56	2,47	2,34	2,19
α	6,63	4,61	3,78	3,32	3,02	2,80	2,64	2,51	2,41	2,32	2,18	2,04

V_2 = Degrees of freedom within groups

Table A-5 Synopsis of statistical symbols

Symbol	Description
$\bar{x}$	arithmetic mean
μ	population mean
σ	standard deviation
$\sigma_{\bar{x}}$	standard deviation of the sampling distribution
n	sample size
E	allowable error
Z	normal value that will yield the desired level of confidence — obtained from the normal distribution table
M	population mean
Σ	summation sign e g $\sum\limits_{i=1}^{n} = x_1 + x_2 + \ldots + x_n$
W_i	weight assigned to stratum i
i	used to indicate specific elements, e g σ_i = standard deviation of stratum i x_i = i^e element in a row of x's
v	variance (more generally σ^2)
P	proportion of the population who posessess the characteristic of interest
t	critical t-value for a given level of significance (α) obtained from the t-distribution table
H_0	null hypothesis, e g H_0: $\mu = 0$
MST	mean sum of squares between groups
MSE	mean sum of squares within groups/mean square error
df	degrees of freedom
F	critical value obtained from the F distribution table
U	statistic computed for use in U-test
R_j	sum of ranks in the jth sample
H	statistic for use in the Kruskal-Wallis test
χ^2	statistic computed for use in the chi-square test
0_i	observed number in i^{th} category

Table A-5 (continued)

Symbol	Description
E_i	expected number in i^{th} category
k	number of categories
ANOVA	analysis of variance
MANOVA	multivariate analysis of variance
MONANOVA	monotonic analysis of variance
$\hat{Y}$	predicted value of Y
R	multiple correlation coefficient
R^2	measure of the proportion of variation in the dependent variable explained by the best linear combination of independent variables
AID	Automatic interaction detection

Subject index